From FAUSTIANA To THE FALL OF ATHENS

Ten Plays by Ruth Wolff

BROADWAY PLAY PUBLISHING INC
New York
www.broadwayplaypublishing.com
info@broadwayplaypublishing.com

FROM FAUSTIANA TO THE FALL OF ATHENS

Plays - Copyright © 1964-2012 by Ruth Wolff

Theatrical Relations - Unpublished Work Copyright ©2012 by Ruth Wolff

No part of this publication may be photocopied, reproduced, stored in a retrieval system or transmitted, in any form or by any means, electronic, mechanical, recording, or otherwise, without the prior permission of the publisher. All rights, including but not limited to the professional, motion picture, radio, television, videotape, videodisc, foreign language, tabloid, recitation, lecturing, publication and readings, are reserved. Additional copies of this book are available from the publisher.

The amateur and stock acting rights to the plays included in this volume are controlled exclusively by Broadway Play Publishing. Without permission of the publishers in writing no performance of the plays may be given. Royalty must be paid every time a play is performed whether or not it is presented for profit and whether or not admission is charged. A play is performed any time it is acted before an audience, whether by professionals or amateurs. For professional and all other rights please contact the author's agent, Dennis Aspland, Aspland Management, 245 West 55th Street, Suite 1004, New York, NY 10019, 212 245-9111, dennisaspland@aol.com.

First printing: September 2012
I S B N: 978-0-88145-532-8

Book design: Marie Donovan
Page make-up: Adobe InDesign
Typeface: Palatino Linotype

CONTENTS

About the Author .... *v*
Theatrical Relations—The Art of Collaborating in This Collaborative Art 1
FAUSTIANA 43
ARABIC TWO 101
AVIATORS 155
THE SHAKESPEARE ROAD 205
HOTEL VICTORY 265
BUFFALOES 319
THE SKY POOL 385
THE ARDENT PHILANTHROPIST 443
STILL LIFE WITH APPLES 511
THE FALL OF ATHENS 541

Broadway Play Publishing Inc has published nine of Ruth Wolff's biographical plays in the volume:

NOTABLE WOMEN
AND A FEW EQUALLY NOTABLE MEN

The volume begins with the essay, *Dramatizing Lives—The Art of Writing the Biographical Play* and concludes with the reprint of Wolff's New York Times Magazine article *We Open in Florence.*

The plays include:

THE ABDICATION

THE PERFECT MARRIAGE

HALLIE

EMPRESS OF CHINA

SARAH IN AMERICA

ELEANOR OF AQUITAINE

GEORGE AND FREDERIC

JOSHUA SLOCUM SAILING ALONE AROUND THE WORLD

THE SECOND MRS. WILSON

ABOUT THE AUTHOR

Ruth Wolff's play THE ABDICATION premiered at the Bristol Old Vic starring Gemma Jones as Christina of Sweden and David Neal as Cardinal Azzolino. The Eureka Theatre of San Francisco presented its American Premiere. Produced throughout the United States and around the world, it has been performed in many languages with notable prize-winning productions in Canada (in French), in Italy (in Italian) and in the Hague and Belgium (in Dutch). It was produced in London in 2005. The Warner Bros film of THE ABDICATION, with screenplay by Wolff, and starring Liv Ullmann and Peter Finch, is available on DVD through Warner Bros Classics.

Produced by Roger L. Stevens, the Kennedy Center premiered Wolff's play SARAH IN AMERICA starring Lilli Palmer as Sarah Bernhardt, directed by Sir Robert Helpmann. The play was also produced at the Pasadena Playhouse starring Katherine Helmond and at Hofstra University featuring Tovah Feldshuh. Ms. Wolff's film about the early life of Sarah Bernhardt, THE INCREDIBLE SARAH, starred Glenda Jackson and Daniel Massey.

Her play EMPRESS OF CHINA premiered in New York at the Pan Asian Repertory Theatre directed by Tisa Chang and starring Tina Chen. Other productions include those at the Cincinnati Playhouse, the Tinfish Theatre in Chicago, the East Coast Theatre Company in Sydney, Australia and (in Italian) at the Todi Festival in Italy.

The acclaimed premiere of her play THE SECOND MRS. WILSON, about the critical last year of the Wilson Administration, took place at the Barter Theatre, the State Theatre of Virginia, in September 2001. Her highly-praised play AVIATORS premiered at the New Jersey Repertory Theatre and was subsequently produced at the Barter Theater.

The Rhode Island Shakespeare Theatre presented the premiere of her one-man play JOSHUA SLOCUM SAILING ALONE AROUND THE WORLD. GEORGE AND FREDERIC, Wolff's play with music about the love affair between George Sand and Frederic Chopin, premiered at the University of Utah. Wolff's adaptation of THE GOLEM appeared Off-Broadway.

ARABIC TWO premiered Off-Broadway at the New Theatre Workshop. Other productions include those at Smith College and at Greenwich, Conn., produced by the Greenwich Players. STILL LIFE WITH APPLES was presented at the O'Neill Theatre Center. It was also broadcast on radio starring George Gaines.

Wolff's play THE PERFECT MARRIAGE, in which Mary and Percy Bysshe Shelley battle out their relationship at the gates of Heaven and Hell, was seen in staged readings at the East Hampton Playwrights Theatre and at the Roundabout Theatre, in New York. Her contemporary comedy BUFFALOES was given staged readings in Newport, RI (director, Bob Colonna), East Hampton, NY (director Robert Kalfin) and in Los Angeles (director John Frankenheimer). Staged readings of HALLIE were given at Smith College, Vassar College and the Writer's Theatre. ELEANOR OF AQUITAINE was read at the O'Neill Theatre Center and Playwrights Horizons.

Other staged readings include: THE ARDENT PHILANTHROPIST (HB Studio starring Rochelle Oliver) and THE FALL OF ATHENS (Coffee House Club starring Simon Jones). The New Jersey Repertory Theatre presented staged readings of four of her plays: HOTEL VICTORY, THE SKY POOL, THE SHAKESPEARE ROAD (starring Robert Cuccioli) and FAUSTIANA (directed by Robert Kalfin). THE SHAKESPEARE ROAD was also presented by the East Hampton Playwrights Theatre in East Hampton (starring Lisa Harrow and Harris Yulin) and at the National Arts Club (starring Lisa Harrow and Brian Murray).

A native of Massachusetts who now lives in New York, Ms. Wolff was educated at Smith College and Yale University. Her essays have appeared in The New York Times and other publications. She is the recipient of a Rockefeller Foundation Playwrighting Fellowship, is a Fellow of the MacDowell Colony and a member of the Dramatists Guild, the League of Professional Theatre Women, and the Writers Guild of America, West.

For all those with whom I have had happy relations—
theatrical and otherwise.

Theatrical Relations
The Art of Collaborating in This Collaborative Art

THEATRICAL RELATIONS

"Theatre is a collaborative art" is a truism. But let me amend that statement.

"Theatre is a collaborative art—but it all begins with the text. The play."

I know there are groups of players who get together without any scribbles on paper, who throw lines at each other invented out of their own heads, then the lines are written down (or not) and performed. But that's not my kind of theatre. My kind of theatre begins in the head of (usually) a sole creator, someone who sits alone and imagines an entire construct, someone who gives birth to the thing on which everything else is based. That someone is called a playwright. And what that playwright creates is called a play.

So it's the playwright's baby. But the paradox is: That baby doesn't truly come alive until a host of other folk get involved with it. There's the producer, the director, the actors, the designers, the stage hands, the agents, the investors, the critics, the relatives, the guy who brings the coffee, the gal who hands out the programs and a host of others. Oh, yes, and there's the audience. The list, in fact, gets to be endless. Everybody becomes a part of this enterprise which one person originated. Everybody has something to say and something to contribute. And as this crowd surges in, with everyone intent on Bringing up the Baby, the Baby either comes gloriously to mature life or gets smothered and ignominiously dies.

It's nicer, of course, if the baby gets to live, in fact, to thrive. This is why it's so important that the various collaborators understand each other. We each spend time, sometimes a lifetime, honing the skills of our separate departments. But we spend much less time trying to understand the aims of our collaborators. Having spent a lifetime giving birth to these babies—and working with all the talents involved in giving them further life—I want to say something about Theatrical Relations, how we get along with each other, and how, if we only understand what each contributor's aims are, we can, with the least amount of friction, bring the piece of theatre to successful life.

For a moment, let's probe the fantasy life of theatre's collaborators:

What do playwrights want? They want to write the perfect play. They get the stars of their dreams to play it. They get the director of their dreams to direct it. They get a production which perfectly captures every stage effect they ever conceived of. Opening night they sit cloaked in darkness, hiding anonymously in the audience. At the end of the play there are waves and waves of applause. The cry goes up, "Author! Author!" The playwright is wafted magically onto the stage to receive the plaudits of the crowd—

which realizes that everything they've witnessed on this triumphal evening began in the head of the author. In the midst of this adulation the playwright is handed a little something. "What's this? A Pulitzer Prize? For Little Me? I'm speechless!" The play runs for years, selling out nightly, it's translated into 137 languages and, eventually, the sun never sets on a day when, somewhere in this world, someone is doing this play.

What do directors want? Directors want to be King. Only they know the real meanings in the play. Only they see the whole—while all the others only see fragments. Directors want to tell the actors, do this, do that. They want to tell the playwright, do this, do that. They want to tell the designers, do this, do that. They are masters of all they survey. If anything good happens with this at all, it is due solely to their efforts. When the curtain goes up, no one sees them—but they are the master puppeteers behind everything. The play was splendid? Without me, it would have no substance, no shape. The performances were great? I molded that. The set stunned everybody? That was my concept. The next morning the sign in front of the theatre is changed—the pinnacle is reached—possessory credit. The director's name above the title, the playwright's under. New assignments come thick and fast. The director has, at last, all the credit deserved—plus the house in the country he always coveted.

What do actors want? They want to be given the role of their lives. They are never off stage. Their character owns the scenery. They look out at an audience and make them laugh. They make them cry. They make them sit transfixed at the wonder of their performance. They tear all passions to tatters. At the curtain, there are endless curtain calls, waves and waves of applause from the crowd which realizes that everything they've witnessed on this triumphal evening is due to the actors' performances. The actors are called out again and again. Roses are thrown. Orchids. Hollywood contracts! Thousands line up at the stage door to get their autographs. They can hardly beat their way to their limosines. The next day sandwiches are named after them at Sardi's. What's that at my door? A Tony? I'm overwhelmed! They are named UN Cultural Ambassador. Their picture is on the cover of Time.

What do designers want? The curtain goes up, no one is on stage, the audience breaks into overwhelming applause. The start of the play is held up for five minutes, people will not stop applauding the scenery. Every now and then, throughout the evening, the designers can hear little gasps, even clapping, for stage effects they created. They have given more to the play in atmosphere than anyone thought the play had in it. When the play and the performances begin to bore people, the designer knows the audience can always be kept interested by letting their eyes wander over the intricacies of the setting. They become classics. It is said everywhere, "The set designs made this play what it was." One day, those original drawings will hang at the Met and a one-person show of the designer's drawings and models will be on display permanently at the Library of the Performing Arts. After this triumph, every producer in the business wants to hire them—they open a larger atelier and, miracle of miracles, sometimes they actually have to refuse more work!

What do producers want? They want to put all this together. No one is more important *than they are because, without them, this production would not exist. They own the playwright, the actors, the directors, the designers. They bring in the stash. They sign the checks which keep this engine going. Without them, all these people would be suppliants, wandering the streets empty-handed with their supposed talents. All that applause on the opening? That's all for the producer. When they stand in the lobby as people leave the theatre, and they hear "Wasn't that wonderful! I must tell my friends to see it!" they know the main person responsible was them. The next morning, there's a line at the box office which goes around the block. The producer pays off the investors, pays off the mortgage on his country home and buys a bigger vacation retreat in the Greater Antilles.*

Of course this is all illusion. Theatre looks like a fine romance but actually it's just like real life—only more so. Most of the time—I hate to break this to you—nobody gets everything they want. The playwright says, "It was a wonderful play ruined by the actors and director." The director says, "The script was weak, the actors phoned in their roles and didn't understand the characters they were supposed to be playing." The actors say, "I did my best—but the role wasn't there for me to perform." The designers say, "I had a wonderful concept. Unfortunately the producers didn't want to spend more than a nickel." The producers say, "Everybody let me down. When I first read the script I thought I saw something in it, but after that everything went haywire." In other words, everybody thinks, "Everybody screwed up but me."

And so another theatrical venture bites the dust. More often than one would like to think, the aims of the various participants conflict with one another. While everyone concerned thinks they're acting "for the good of the show", what one thinks is good and what another thinks is good may be diametric opposites. I've been through enough of these adventures, good and bad, to have a few things I want to say about them. Sometimes what comes out good seems like a miracle. Sometimes what fails, never should. Most often, productions exist somewhere in the middle. They exist at "Okay". But okay isn't enough in the theatre.

The process of putting on a play is a very complex one. Sometimes problems arise simply because each talent is so focussed on their own concerns that they don't understand what's going on in the minds of their collaborators. As a playwright, I realize I have sometimes not understood the actor's or director's process as they moved to try to realize what I'd written. And I've often felt that others had no idea what I'd gone through to get these pages to where they would be a living whole—something able to be produced.

I have been pondering this subject of theatrical relationships. And I thought it would be useful, in the interests of mutual understanding, to record some of those thoughts from a playwright's point of view. The various creative participants go through quite different processes as they try to bring to life a theatrical production. As in diplomacy, if we understand, as the jargon says, "where each is coming from", in other words the others' points of view, the creative process for each of us could be smoother and the final result might reflect that, along the way, there had been a meeting of the minds.

Naturally, in theatre as in life, anecdotes about difficulties, blow-ups, rivalries, back-biting, colossal cock-ups are more delicious than accounts of harmonious happy people working together toward the same end, so I hope you won't mind if I pepper some of this advice with hells gone through, either by me or by others.

While everybody else in the theatre often hates to admit it—everything begins with the playwright. Without some poor benighted fool sitting alone in an empty room with a blank piece of paper (yes, I know it's a computer screen, but allow me the literary fancy)—without that fool sitting alone with that blank paper—and a full imaginative mind—there's nothing to make theatre, nothing to perform.

As a playwright, the kind of relationship I've never had, and the kind I envy, is the kind of relationship which Shakespeare had with Burbage and his men—a longtime relationship with a theatrical producing company. In this collaboration, the playwright knows the actors he or she is writing for, the company knows what the playwright is writing and likes the idea of it, and the playwright knows, while writing, that the company is going to perform it. The playwright writes the play, the company performs it and the playwright goes on to write another play for the same company.

This could be an immensely rewarding theatrical collaboration—as long as it doesn't become confining and as long as everybody around you doesn't feel they can have a hand in what you write. I'm afraid I'm not a fan of the kind of theatre where actors ad lib and improvise and the playwright sits there writing it down. On the other hand, having a ready-made theatrical troupe at hand could mean a writer could get them to try out a few scenes to see what's working and what's not working. Or they could be immensely useful in honing and shaping. I envy the playwrights who have had long successful relationships with theatre companies. As for me, I've written all of my plays in what feels like Joyce's "silence, exile and cunning" (although I don't think I've managed much in the way of "cunning"). I mean to say, for good or ill, I've written the plays in solitude—and then have begun the long hard slog to get them produced.

It's when others get involved that the path gets tricky. I can't wait for the manuscript to be finished and for others to come on board in the enterprise. But that is where all the fun—and all the problems—begin.

THE AGENT

After one's mate, significant other and/or "kitchen cabinet", the first one to see one's play is the playwright's agent. I was lucky. Supremely lucky. As a young wife and mother in Cambridge, Mass., the only agent I'd ever heard of was the most exalted one: Audrey Wood, the legendary representative of Tennessee Willia ms, William Inge, Robert Anderson and a fine small stable of other noted names. So I looked up her address and sent her the play. I got back a brief letter—and the play—almost instantly, saying she wasn't, at that moment, reading plays "from the outside".

A year later, I sent her another play and this time she responded, quite promptly, that, since it was my second submission, she would read it. (This was a stroke of luck because, if she had read that first effort she would never, later, have given me the time of day.) I still remember receiving her next letter, the one written after she'd read this play. She said she had read the work, could see that I had talent, that this particular play was not strong enough for the theatre, that she would like to submit it for television production and that, while she was doing so, I should go on and write my next play. I remember holding that precious letter in my hand and crying out in joy. This famous agent thought I had "talent"! She would take my work on! It was one of the most joyous moments I ever had in theatre—and, indeed, in life.

This was the beginning of a relationship which lasted for 18 years—until Audrey Wood lapsed into the coma which ended her conscious existence though not, for another five years, her life. I can say, outside of my immediate family, it was the most meaningful relationship I ever had in my entire existence. While she was not responsible in any way for what I was writing in my study, she was largely responsible for everything which happened to the work outside it. Audrey wasn't "easy". She was small of stature but patrician in manner, commanding in demeanour, and had a solid confidence in her own judgement.

She had a very rare quality: she understood writers. She knew what our lives were like when we were writing. She knew never to call me during my working hours. She also knew how much a call from her meant. In the times which were fruitful in the study but "dry" in the world outside, with no promise of any production and no interest from anyone in any play I'd written, she knew that a call from her out of the blue, usually every week, saying, "How are you?" or "I mentioned your play to so-and-so" could give me the courage to continue.

She would read and comment only slightly on a new manuscript. I don't ever recall her saying anything "wasn't ready to be sent out", although I know other writers got this comment from her. I heard, once, that one reason Tennessee Williams split from her after decades was that she said, of a new play, "It needs work". (It probably did.) She was direct and swift, with good news and with bad—and in her life with me she often had to break the news of one as often as the other. She was tough. She taught me to be tough. And she was generous. I felt any connection she had was a connection of mine. She would send things out without my asking and without telling me—only telling me if something good came of it. And a lot of good came of a lot of things because, when a script arrived with Audrey's name as representative of it, that play got read. Quickly. Few agents today have that kind of sterling reputation. Her name vetted a play as worthy.

One of the major things one discovers in this theatre world is that few have complete confidence in their own judgements. They have to know that someone else—someone whose taste they trust—likes something before they decide they can like it, too.

Unlike most agents, who will desert a ship as soon as it shows the slightest sign of leaking, she was with me in bad times as well as good. At the opening of THE ABDICATION, at the Bristol Old Vic, she gave me a Victorian miniature brooch and enclosed a note, which I keep always before me. It says: "Dear Ruth—Whatever happens tonight or tomorrow—or tomorrow—remember you are a gifted writer and, in my belief, will continue to flourish. Admiringly, Audrey Wood."

The part I treasure most about that note is not the "gifted writer" (which is praise indeed from so eminent a judge of plays and playwrights), but the words "whatever happens". There are very few agents—or anyone else in the theatre for that matter—who will remain steadfastly beside you "whatever happens", very few who will continue to have faith in you—and urge you to have continued faith in yourself whatever storms you may have to face.

An agent's ten percent increases in exact proportion to your ability to succeed. Most agents show astonishing alacrity in their ability to desert a sinking ship. It is the measure of Audrey's magnificence that, if she believed in you and your particular project, her resolve on your behalf would only strengthen when the hurricanes began to blow. The moments when you were most down were the moments she showed the most strength and inventiveness. Her faith was that, for you and for your work, there was always going to be a "tomorrow". Whatever had happened had happened; now we would, together, move on.

As I've said, this spirit is exceedingly rare and is not to be expected in the usual run of representatives. What can and should one expect? I don't expect my agent to be my best friend or my severest critic, but I do want my agent to read a new script within a reasonable amount of time and respond positively and constructively. Some don't realize how much the playwright is waiting to hear that response (cogent or not); before that response, all time seems to be frozen.

But, in general, an agent's job is not literary criticism. Their first job is encouragement. They should see what you were trying to do in a particular play and say whether or not they think you have succeeded. After all, their primary interest is in having an instinct about whether or not what you have presented them with can sell. On the crassest level, they are merchants—and you are providing them with the goods they feel they can or cannot hawk. Put it this way: our job may be art, theirs is always commerce. You have every right to expect that they like the sort of thing you write and have every wish for your—and its—welfare. An agent who takes you on for reasons other than liking your work should not be your agent. Sooner or later a relationship based on anything else, even including friendship, will come to grief.

I would expect, if I am not too demanding, that an agent answer my phone calls as promptly as possible. In between Audrey and long representation by the Last of the Great Gentlemen Agents, Robert Lantz, I spent some years represented by a variety of others. One neophyte, who took over on the death of a man I liked but who was known for never returning calls, seemed to be out to beat his mentor's record. He could not be reached, ever. I would call, then send a FAX, (it was before emails), then send a letter. No return contact. Finally, I wrote a letter complimenting him on his talents as an agent and saying, but for this flaw of not answering phone calls or letters, he had a great future in the field. Do get back to me, I wrote. He never did. And that was the end of our relationship.

No matter what the fact or fiction surrounding this cultivated hard-to-reachness, I insist—and you have a right to insist—on a certain amount of human politeness and courtesy. There is no use having an agent who treats you like the scum of the earth. Whatever your rank in the world of theatre, you are not their inferior. You are doing the creating. They may know the best spot for your goods in the bazaar, but all the goods they are hawking were created by you.

An agent is there, first and foremost, to handle the business aspects of your life, leaving you free to handle the creative aspects. An agent should be able to make connections for you, connections you can't make on your own. They should send scripts out as requested. An agent's name says someone outside of you likes your work and believes in it. It says you are a professional. Few and far between are the producers or theatres who will read scripts sent in by the playwright personally. A good agent should have a strong enough reputation to get your script closer to the top in the producer's or theatre's pile. A good agent spends years making contacts which will be useful to his or her clients—and is generous in using those contacts—although some hold those contacts close to the chest and refuse to liberally share.

An agent can be a buffer between the playwright and other collaborators.

He or she deals with contracts—what rights will and won't be agreed to between you and your collaborators. They deal with the knotty thing known as "money". In certain cases, when ticklish or downright nasty problems raise their ugly heads, the agent can say things the client would be a cur to ever utter.

An agent should be my staunch ally and be able to speak to others in a tone compatible with mine and, when necessary, to be as tough as I need them to be, while still representing my wishes. They are a go-between, not a principal. But it's quite legitimate for the two of you to play good cop/bad cop so you can say "My agent forbids me to do such and such" and they can display muscle when you need it but when too much muscle displayed by you could sour a relationship.

An agent should be knowledgeable on contracts and should execute them promptly. You don't get paid—and they don't get their ten percent—until that contract is executed. It behooves them to read and respond to contracts in a timely fashion, to know from experience what's reasonable and what isn't, to hold firm when necessary and to compromise when it's better for your career to sign off on a disagreeable contract in order to get the project realized rather than, through confrontation, have the whole opportunity go down the drain.

An agent can be protective, but sometimes an agent can be too protective, saying No when you are desperate enough for a production to happen to want to say Yes. Sometimes an agent will not give permissions you would give gladly. Sometimes an agent seems to be living your life and keeping you at a distance from it. (This is good in some cases, unfortunate in others.) They can, for example, be lax in not forwarding rejection letters to you, leaving you in a limbo of doubt or hope when you could be accepting of rejection and figuring out other ways of moving onward.

The best agent should have ideas—knowing what company, what director, what actors should be best for your enterprise. Ideally, they should be able to contact that perfect collaborator and get him or her to read your script. What an agent is not is a spiritual adviser, a tear-drier, or a miracle worker. Audrey Wood, who, remember, plucked me out of nowhere, a babe-in-the-woods neophyte, wanted to make all contacts for me. Once I did the writing, she wanted everything to be put into her hands.

Because of this, I was spoiled and didn't realize what other playwrights knew—that we have to, ourselves, be out there beating the bushes, making contacts, making things happen. It was a lesson I had to learn very late, when I found myself with other, less protective agents. An agent gives a playwright credibility and professional protection. But an agent is not the one primarily responsible for a writer's career. That responsibility belongs to the writer him or her self.

What does an agent want from a playwright client? That the playwright write a great play, obviously. But, beyond that, that they not be under the illusion that they are the agent's only client and that the agent should devote to them 100% of their time, that the writer not pester them constantly asking for the moon, for impossible feats the agent can't possibly manage, that the writer not expect the agent to sell the unsellable, that the writer not expect the agent to listen to all their problems, in the study, in production or in their lives, that the agent not be expected to go up and down the writer's many high and low moods.

There are very few one-client agents, but playwrights are expected to have only one agent. Playwrights have only their own work, agents are representing the works of many. Fidelity, in this relationship, is an imbalanced thing. A playwright has to understand the agent's busy thousand-phone-call and thousand-email-a-day life, so different from the writer's usual isolation. There are times when the playwright's crisis must be dealt with immediately, and other times when another client's crisis takes up most of the agent's attention. An agent is not a hand-holder, nose-wiper or sweeper up after a client's messes, although sometimes they are forced to function in all three capacities.

In the best playwright-agent relationships, each understands and respects the other's life and function. In fact, this can be said about all others the playwright comes in contact with in the work along the way.

THE PRODUCER

If Theatre were a logical business, which it seldom is, the next person to get involved in moving a play from page to stage is the Producer. In the Olden Days, the days before endless readings, workshops, out-of-town productions, etc., there was a time-honored way in which theatre worked. The producer read the play, said they'd like to produce it, on Broadway, off Broadway or someplace else, and took an option on the play for a limited time, with the possibility of extension. At this point, a certain amount of money passed from the producer's bank account to that of the playwright. Some of these agreements are set by the Dramatists Guild, some are not. Of course there are many times when producers say, "I'd like to show this around"—and there's no contract and no exchange of lucre but the playwright, hungry for production, gives permission based on that hunger or the goodness of the playwright's heart.

I was fortunate, in my life, to have, as my first and foremost producer for many years, the eminent producer Roger L. Stevens. Audrey Wood made the connection when I was still wet behind the ears. Roger liked to encourage young playwrights. With and without his partner, Robert Whitehead, he had produced many plays whose names are deathlessly inscribed in the annals of theatre, like WEST SIDE STORY, BUS STOP, CAT ON A HOT TIN ROOF, A MAN FOR ALL SEASONS, etc.. Roger was tall, balding, and enigmatic. Sometimes he mumbled so you wouldn't know what he was saying. Coming out of the Midwest, he had made his fortune in real estate (he once owned the Empire State building), although where his monies were coming from when I knew him, I never knew.

Soon after I met him, he became Chairman of the Board of the Kennedy Center. He was a man with money and power who wore those mantles lightly. I remember one of my earliest meetings with him. My husband and I had come to Washington and were staying at a hotel not far from the site of the future Kennedy Center. Roger said he'd like to show me the center, which was then under construction, and would come to pick me up. To my husband, I wondered, aloud, what would he pick me up in? My husband thought he would be driving a car, possibly a Cadillac. I thought he'd come in a limo, being driven by a chauffeur.

We both lost. Roger arrived on foot. Together, he and I walked over to the building site. We walked past piles of concrete into unfinished halls, only recently roofed over. At one point, walking along a wooden plank which stood in for flooring, Roger slipped and one of his feet sank ankle-deep into thick mud. Roger looked down in surprise, said calmly, "Oh, bother", pulled his soggy foot out of the mud—and we continued the tour.

That was Roger. Always understated. Always unexpected. Sometimes convivial, sometimes completely opaque. He optioned play after play of mine—which was one of the things which kept me writing. While he didn't get some of them into production, knowing a play was under option gave me the spirit and impetus to go on to write the next one. That was Audrey's and Roger's prime philosophy—that's what you were doing this time 'round, you were writing plays, and no matter what happened your function was to keep on writing.

Roger would read a play, respond quite quickly with only a phrase or two to summarize its qualities, option it, then send it on. His name and connections would get things read and responded to quite quickly. Under his aegis two of my plays were produced, THE ABDICATION at the Bristol Old Vic in Bath, England and SARAH IN AMERICA at the Kennedy Center. But his presence enlivened my life and his encouragement dignified my labors as worthy, no matter how tough the road. And make no mistake about it, if there's one thing the theatre road is, it's a rough road. One needs allies on the journey. He and Audrey were the best I could have had.

What does one want in a producer? First and foremost, a producer has to have—or be able to lay their hands on—money. Does this sound crass? No. That's the producer's job. They'll be signing all the checks, so if there's no bank account to back it up, the playwright and the production are in very iffy territory. The producer should have taste. They've picked your play, that certainly shows good taste, but there will be lots of choices of collaborators, artistic decisions on script, set, costumes, etc., on which the producer will have some say and their sense of what the play is should jibe with the playwright's or the result will be catastrophic.

The best producer is one who trusts the play and the collaborators they've chosen to bring it to life then stands back and lets the artists do their work, only popping in now and then to see what's happening with their investment, but not interfering. A producer who thinks his or her judgement on artistic matters is greater than the artists' is a pest and a destroyer. It's a delicate balance, to produce with a free but firm hand. But this approach will get the best work out of those involved in the presentation.

The producer should provide the space—literal and figurative—for the artists to do their work. They should wisely arbitrate when there are artistic conflicts and should soothe the waters rather than taking sides. They should be solicitous of the artists' comfort so the work can proceed smoothly. Producers should have the courage of their convictions. They liked this play to start and their faith should outlast the first reviews of a fledgling project. They should have enough reserve in the kitty to be able to advertise when things are slow and only ads will bring the public in.

With so much at risk, producers often first want to test a play by having readings. Readings are a good thing. They allow the playwright to get an idea of what the play will be in production, help in giving a playwright an objective view of the work when it begins to stand on its own, and help in identifying necessary cuts or revisions. There are many levels of readings: off-the-cuff, rehearsed in the morning and read in the afternoon or readings with days of rehearsal then one or two "performances." Readings can happen at many levels: with the actors one wants, with any actors available, a reading just for the intimate "family"—playwright, producer (if one is attached), a few trusted others, up to a reading for a public, even a paying public.

In my view, the best kinds of readings are either off-the-cuff or rehearsed for days. The kind of reading which has a read-through in the morning and a performance in the afternoon tires the actors and clouds the playwright's judgement. The playwright needs to have a fresh eye and the actors have to either have spontaneity or be far enough along in the process to "act" it. The playwright has a right to be careful where the reading takes place and who is invited. The very same script can sound wonderful in one situation and awful in another. Readings carry the same risks as performances: how the work is perceived is influenced by every element which went into the performance and the reception of it. The absolutely worst audience for a reading is a roomful of potential backers. Their judgmental attitude casts a pall over the most lively proceedings; their reactions never equal the reactions of a regular crowd.

Readings are good things but a writer can fall into several kinds of "Reading Hell." One is that one gets so many suggestions, and acts on them, that the play becomes a jumble of others' ideas; then the process, instead of being helpful, is actually deadening. Another is that one gets trapped in readings—has reading after reading and never gets the play on. Another is when someone who sponsors a reading gets possessive and thinks they have a right to be thanked in all future programs or who even expects a percentage because they've contributed to the play's development. Quite a few regional theatres manage to raise money for readings, so give a series of them, the promise being the possibility of full production—most of which never happen. This kind of reading serves the theatre more than it serves the playwright.

Caution is advised. Readings can be deceptive. An ill-conceived reading can scare a producer off as much as a well-presented reading can convince the producer or theatre to continue. Because of readings' unpredictable nature, they can prove something or nothing about the work. At best they are a simulacrum. Readings are of value—but take the reaction to them, whether it be good or ill, with a grain of salt.

In today's economy, productions are so expensive that it is more than likely that a production will need more than one producer. In fact, sometimes the number of producers is greater than the number of people in the cast. In such a situation, each producer having his or her say on artistic matters is not only ridiculous, it's unhealthy. The idea that rich gentlemen and ladies who think it will be fun to invest in a theatrical production for the thrill of it should have any say at all in what theatre artists should do is beyond absurd, it's criminal. If there are dozens of producers, the artists should insist they speak in one voice where artistic decisions are concerned.

In the present world, where Money is God, it may sound shocking to say this, but, in a production, the money is not the most important thing—the work is. Producers think, "But I'm the one who's putting up the money!" The artists think, "Yes, but I'm putting up my reputation and my life." Producers may be risking a lot of pelf, but they will seldom be begging on the street if the production loses its investment. Artists may end up in quite dire circumstances. It's not only the artist's livelihood, it's also their soul and their blood. The producer can be the one who made the specific production happen, but the producer is not the one who gave it life.

There is another kind of producer with which playwrights have relationships: Institutional theatre—a theatre company which runs a season of plays year after year (rather than a producer who puts together a group for a specific production). Many plays begin their lives in this kind of theatre. In fact, a single-project producer may try to get a play produced first at this sort of venue—to work out kinks and see the result.

In this situation, the playwright's relationship to the producing organization is quite different. An institutional theatre's first loyalty is not to the individual play, but to the survival of the institution. Those who work in this kind of theatre have more-or-less permanent jobs. They will produce your play, and then someone else's, and then another someone else's, and then the works of still other playwrights. Their choosing to present your play happens when their aims and yours coincide.

I have had plays produced under these circumstances and almost always have had very happy experiences. For one thing, the pressure to succeed is not as great when the burden for the entire producing structure is not on the shoulders of this one production. While the producing and artistic directors of regional theatres may rule with firm hands over their fiefdoms, they usually do not have as much riding on each production—which is good in that there is not as much pressure to "succeed" as in other situations, and bad in that there is less incentive—and sometimes even less ability—to bring things to a perfected shine.

If the producing and artistic functions (Producing-Artistic Director) at such a theatre are incorporated in one being, that's a lot of power concentrated in one person. But, in my experience, these producer/directors know that working for the good of the specific play is also working for the general health of their theatre and they want your work to be shown to its best advantage as much as you do. Some theatres ask for a percentage of the play's future profits. If their production gives the play its first life and helps you to hone it to its best state before it moves onward, this is a fair request.

I have to say I believe I always hold these theatres in a bit more affection and nostalgia than they hold me. My experience with them is exceptional while, to them, my script is just another play in a long long list of plays they've done before and will do after. But, if I've never found the company which would be "mine", one I could have a permanent relationship with, as Shakespeare had with the King's Men, the regional theatre experience comes closest to it. I treasure each experience I've had in my however-brief connections with regional or repertory theatres. Such collaborations can be less stressful and more healthy than those collaborations at higher levels, where too much, in money and in reputation, is on the line.

A word of caution: There are those who want to play producer without actually being a producer. I mean the sort who flirt with scripts and actors and directors, leading them on with the promise of a production which never comes off. No money has been invested, but lots of time on everybody's part has been wasted. In the meantime, the fake producer has had a lot of distraction, a lot of fun, and, at dinner parties, has names to drop and something to talk about. Often times theatre folk are so hungry for something to happen in their careers they'll play along with the fake producer's illusion, hoping against hope that the person who says they want to promote and present your marvelous work, but don't at the moment want to hand over any $$$ for the privilege, will somehow perform miracles. To this, all I can say is: Dream on.

The worst part of dealing with producers of all sorts, particularly those in institutional theatres, is that they don't respond to submissions—either in timely fashion and sometimes ever. They receive scripts—the submitter receives No Answer. You can wait years, sometimes, for a yes or a no and sometimes never receive either. You remain in limbo. They don't even send the courtesy of a printed post card saying "We have lots of scripts to read before yours, but we thank you for thinking of us and we'll get to consider your work eventually." I sometimes feel I could throw the scripts off the balcony and let the pages fall where they may—they'd get a better chance of being read by somebody. I put considerable thought into deciding where a script should be submitted—I would like the simple courtesy of a reply.

The main thing to understand about producers is that they are in Power—but they are, essentially, Powerless. They need to have the work come out well—but they can't do the work. They have to have enough ego to build and hold a production together, but enough humility to know the borders of their abilities and where the creative team must take over. In other words, they have to trust their own decisions in their choices—and then provide the most fertile field possible so those talents can flower. That sometimes means spending money on good rehearsal space, clean dressing rooms, perhaps providing a car for an exhausted actor. A producer's task is not just to raise and save money, their task is to know when to spend it wisely to help all the others in the production do their best work.

THE DIRECTOR

A director is many things but, contrary to the belief of many, god isn't one of them. "In the beginning" there is a script. A playwright. A director comes into the mix later. If a playwright makes the acquaintance of a director, it's possible to bring the script to him or her before there's any plan for a production. The director then becomes "attached" to the script—and that attachment will have to be approved by others later, when and if a production occurs. Usually, however, a director comes on board after a producer is found and the play is optioned. In that case, the director to be hired is agreed upon between the producer and writer.

Bringing a director or actor into the mix at an early stage can sometimes be an advantage, sometimes a hindrance. If the name and reputation are big enough, and if this person's attachment can make the production happen, it's an advantage. However, if others, like potential producers, do not approve of the playwright's choice, such an attachment can work to the production's detriment. The attached soul then has to be unattached, the playwright ends up feeling guilty, the star or director ends up feeling used and there's bad feeling all around.

According to the Dramatists Guild contract, the playwright has approval of the director. Once the director comes on board, what should the playwright expect? First and foremost, in my view, is that, beyond a talent for directing, the director should have a healthy respect for the script, for the writer and for all who join this collaboration. In a first meeting, the playwright should sense that respect in a director and also feel that the director's comments and concepts jibe with those of the playwright. The director is the captain of the ship. The best director has an instinctive understanding of the author's intentions in the script and can bring the pages to life in the best possible way.

Before rehearsals begin, the director should work with the playwright in a mutual give and take, each listening as much as speaking. In this period, ideally a mutual trust grows between these two and each can judge whether their aims in the production coincide. If not, if the playwright feels the director is going to take the play off into unintended directions, these doubts should be voiced—and early, before a course is set from which there is no return. Once rehearsals begin the playwright and director should have one vision of the result they're after, one unified sense of the "perfection" they want to achieve through the talents of everyone else.

It's extremely necessary to keep one's objectivity. Most directors become directors because they like to manage things, like to shape things, and they bring all sorts of personality tricks into the service of one aim: taking total command. One of the worst things that can happen is when the playwright gets seduced into feeling the collaboration is going so well, and trusts the director so much, that the playwright allows the director to take the play in directions the playwright didn't intend—then it has to be taken back and reshaped later.

The director should have enough connections and enough experience in the field to be able to have appropriate ideas about casting and the design team. On all these the playwright has acceptance or veto power—and should use it. There's no use acceding to a choice one doesn't agree with out of sheer comity and then have to suffer the consequences of that choice down the line.

Let us say that, with the director's input, the script has been honed and the production elements agreed upon. Then the rehearsals begin. As the playwright, I feel my position is to hand them the script and retreat to the back of the room. It may not be every playwright's way, but that's where I feel most comfortable. I want to be able to see the work as a whole, from a bit of a distance. I don't want the actors to feel they're being judged by the person who wrote the lines they're speaking. And I feel the director is in charge of the room. I prefer to let what happens in rehearsal happen.

But at the end of each rehearsal, I expect the director to make time for me so that we can speak privately, I can say what I think of what's happening, and let the director interpret those thoughts to the actors—without prefacing his remarks with "The author thinks". At that point, what the director thinks and what I think should be coinciding. I can be the director's other eyes—not possessive of my precious words, but thinking only of the living thing we're trying to create together. I can see things which don't fully convey my intention. I can see things the director, while concentrating elsewhere, has overlooked.

Most directors have a certain way of dealing with actors—a vocabulary—a method of conveying, usually without giving line readings, what they're trying to achieve in a line or in a scene. When the playwright is uneasy about what it seems actors aren't achieving, the director should know which actors develop their parts slowly, which come quickly to what will be the final result and which will never achieve what the writer and the scene are after.

The best directors make me feel I'm part of the director's process by listening to my thoughts and, where appropriate, conveying them to the actors (or, if we're discussing design or music, to those participants as well). I never challenge the director's authority by attempting to deal with these things directly. I feel there can only be one person in command of this galleon. I built the ship and I plotted the course, but it's the director who gives the command, "Steady as she goes."

Directors, like all playwrights, like all humans, have flaws, and I've come across lots of them in my travels. Some, with immense egos, like to take credit for the writing. Without their shaping it, they believe, the script would be an incomprehensible mess of trash, a nothing. This kind of director is always making odious comparisons to various masterworks and will refer to your highly-honed work of art as "the piece"—as if, without them, this thing you've written would be only a fragment. In speaking to others, this kind of director comes very close to making it seem as if they wrote the play.

There's the kind of director who spends so much time around the table with actors, analyzing every word and discussing every sentence, that staging goes out the window. Each actor goes on such an interior journey that the play never holds together as a whole. This director indulges in and lets the actors indulge in endless psychological analysis of the characters, the play, and all its subtle meanings. The pursuit of the play's inner life—that's what they seek. Some of this is helpful; depth and resonance can be the result of these explorations. It becomes distinctly unhelpful if what's forgotten is that audiences will see—not all these esoteric theories—but the result. There's a time, early in the rehearsals, when such analysis is enriching. After a while, however, it's time to get down to the presentation and begin to work on what others will see as the play. This kind of director will not have read-throughs or run-throughs early enough so that the playwright can judge the length of the evening and can make cuts if necessary. In other words, in concentrating on the minutiae, what's forgotten is the eventual effect of the whole.

There is the kind of director who cares more about the technical aspects—the set, costumes, lighting, sound and special effects—than the meanings in the words and, in the interest of enhancing the words, will actually do everything to drown them. These directors tend to be the ones who consistently go over-budget, causing panic in the producers. These will always complain that, if the producers had only sprung for such and such a stage effect, the thing would have worked, but without it—well, they're not to blame. These directors are more interested in the looks of things than in the inner emotional life of the characters. A playwright would do well to either avoid such a director or to do one's best to keep him or her on track to the play's inner life.

Some directors are martinets, dictators, very hard on everybody. Some directors are pussycats, so gentle and considerate they forget an enterprise of this complexity needs to be kept on a tight rein. Then there's the director who considers himself above it all. I worked with one whose reputation was so elevated he didn't think it his job to talk to the playwright. I was instructed to communicate anything I wanted to say to his side-kick assistant. Needless to say I was young and inexperienced when this occurred and there's no way I would tolerate such treatment nowadays. I should have voiced my objections either personally to the director or should have talked to the producer. Producers are around to deal with problems such as this.

There's the kind of director who quits working just before the end of the rehearsal period, feeling it's "fine" when you feel that it requires a bit more effort, that there are a few things that aren't quite perfected yet. There's the kind of director who's good at the emotional aspects and the pacing, but who has no visual imagination. Gower Champion once told me that if a set isn't good, it's the director's fault—the fault of the concept. In a similar way, if the set is excellent, some of the credit belongs to the director, the one who had a visual concept for the entire production and knew what would be needed along the way.

The director cannot change a sentence, a word or a comma without the writer's approval. Once, in the midst of the rehearsal period for a play, I came into the rehearsal room and the stage manager handed me a list of "Script Changes"—changes, mostly brief cuts, which the actors already had in hand. I was stunned, furious, but said nothing. Rehearsal began and the director asked me, what did I think of the changes. I said, calmly, "I'll talk to you at the break." At the break, I spoke to her, quietly and privately. I told her that she couldn't hand out cuts before I'd seen them, that changes could not be made without my approval, that this had never happened before in my professional life. She said "But they were just suggestions." I said that it hadn't been put to me that way. She apologized and asked, since the actors already had their cuts, what were they to do? I said I'd listen to the play and would see what worked and what didn't.

I did listen. I did approve most of the trimming. Where I didn't approve, I told her and the lines were restored as originally written. We hadn't had a confrontation, but I'd been quietly firm and, since the director knew she was completely in the wrong, she and I were able to handle a ticklish situation like diplomats and come to a satisfactory conclusion.

I don't like confrontations. I never have. I think nothing gets solved that way and, even if things are smoothed over, ruffled feelings remain. So I do my very best to support the director, to let him or her be the ultimate authority, but to have them quietly know that I'm both their greatest ally in the room and their critical eye.

If we disagree, the last thing I want to hear as a reason to do it the director's way is "trust me". When someone says "trust me", I never do. "Trust me" is a phrase used to get you to shut up about something you know is a problem. I need more of an explanation or I need a demonstration which will be a more convincing proof.

I should drop in an observation here, to say that, in the close cauldron of creativity, theatrical relationships can border on personal relationships, between actors, and also between playwrights and directors. Playwright/director conferences can become quite intimate sessions. My advice is that it is best not to become emotionally entangled with one's director—or other collaborators. Judgement and objectivity, those valuable twins, fly out the window. And if things explode on a personal level the entire creative collaboration can completely disintegrate.

Women may be more vulnerable to this kind of magnetic entrapment, but my advice is avoid it at all costs—if you can. It may not, at times, feel like it, but theatre is a career, a business. One gets very personal very quickly, dealing with feelings and emotions. But always know you are dealing with these for the purpose of getting a play on; private life should be kept at a distance. Share every ounce of your creative energy—but, lest you risk disaster, do not share your whole self.

The director should have a positive spirit. But there are those who like to divide in order to conquer, to shore up their own power. I once worked with a director who was very pleasant to me, but, to me, bad-mouthed the actors. Then I found out that he was being pleasant to the actors while bad-mouthing me and the script. Allowing anyone like this anywhere near your work is poison. Avoid it if at all possible. If you ever find out it's happening, let the director know in no uncertain terms that you know what's going on and insist that it stop. If they've chosen to direct this script they should show loyalty to it.

Of course these character traits are things none of us know about in advance. With some collaborators, respect and fondness grow the more you come to know them, the more you see them under stress and under fire. With others, it's just the opposite. Their flaws only begin to show when you know them better, when the chips are down. If you begin to feel there's something seriously wrong with how things are going under the director's guidance the only one who can be appealed to or complained to is a higher authority—the producer. But don't be surprised if the producer is already in the director's pocket and that complaints have already been filed in the highest court against the script—and you.

Does working in the theatre begin to sound like being in a conspiracy? It is. It's a worthy conspiracy if all are conspiring toward one goal: the best realization of your play. If the atmosphere begins to feel more like plots and counterplots, it's good to get it all out in the open and try to resolve misunderstandings calmly and quietly. Putting on a play involves endless interdependencies. Each contributor has to realize how much they need the others. The only way for the work to be realized is if people work toward that one goal.

What a director wants from a playwright is that the playwright not challenge the director's authority, that the playwright understand that the director has many aspects of the production to deal with and many concerns which go beyond dealing with the script—sound, lights, costumes, etc.. The director wants the playwright to have enough faith to allow him or her to guide the play into production via their particular rhythm and personal process. What the playwright wants from the director is, quite simply, to create the best possible realization of the play.

THE ACTORS

No one is more appreciative of what actors do than I am. The physical, mental and emotional drain on these professionals is immense. They have to abase themselves to audition for roles while being told again and again "you're not right for the part". Once cast, they can often be working for very little money, have to slog through rehearsals tolerating everyone else's indecisions, memorize pages upon pages, go out and perform the same stuff, night after night. No wonder they want to be coddled. What they do is physically, mentally and emotionally incredibly difficult. Their instrument is themselves; they can never escape from it. When the time comes for the curtain to go up, it's all in their hands. They're the front line—the only ones out there—while all their collaborators disappear into the shadows.

They suffer in crowded sweaty dressing rooms, they have to squeeze themselves into tight costumes, slather on (and later take off) pounds of make-up, rev up their minds and emotions to full power night after night till their brains are reeling and their emotions are raw. They have to tolerate inattentive audiences, vicious critics and poisonous backstage rivalries. They suffer as many brickbats as plaudits. And when the run of the play is over, they wander once more in the wilderness feeling, no matter how famous they are or how high their star has risen, "I'll never work again".

In short, the actors are the heroes of the enterprise. And yet, and yet—if they didn't have the fine lines some playwright (Shakespeare, you, somebody) wrote, they would be silent inanimate dolls, waiting to be wound up and given voices. I am speechless with admiration for the work they do, but I sometimes wonder, do actors have any idea what playwrights go through to give them those marks on paper they then call their "roles"?

Right after actors have said, at the first read-through, "I love your play", they are apt to admit to being puzzled by a lot of it and some feel they can't truly get into the role unless they make the lines really theirs, in other words, not speaking what's written but their own reworking of them. They sometimes ask the meaning of sentences whose meaning I consider perfectly obvious. And some few, hoping to throw the writer off-balance and pretending their inquiry is crucial to their understanding of their role, will ask obscure background questions like, "Is this a character who cuts his toe nails?" or "Did this character do well in third grade?" The answer should not be "How the heck should I know?" or even "Ask the director". The answer should be, "Make your own decision."

Actors seem to be an odd combination of extremely insecure and immensely self-confident—these two opposing qualities held in suspension, in a delicate balance. "Emotionally immature" is the label some put on actors. But I think these complexities come because their instrument is their mind and soul and emotions. All these have to be available to be used and displayed to the public. For that reason, actors often seem like creatures without skin, people of extreme sensitivity, easily wounded, always on the alert for any possible criticism or attack.

And they have this other quality—a thing which many of us were born without—they want to show themselves in front of other people. They want to get up there and display all these emotions in front of crowds. In my view, that's an extraordinary desire. I have none of it Their fears (even as they're forcing themselves—with less or more eagerness—to do what none of us want to do), their stage fright, their pride, their necessity, in fact their demand, to be pampered and praised and taken care of, their feeling they are the center of the world—all this makes them volatile yet invaluable creatures. As playwrights, we need them. I say again, they need us, too.

A playwright's first contact with actors on a production is usually during casting. The playwright sits beside the director at a table. Actor after actor comes into the room. They hand over their head shots and résumés and proceed to read, alone or with another, a bit of the part they're trying out for. One can tell quite quickly those who are completely unsuitable and these must be dismissed as kindly as possible.

It's in the call-backs, when a few who might possibly fit the roles, and one hears them a second or third time, that the choice becomes difficult. Some actors give excellent readings—but their performances will never develop. Some give rocky readings, but the director knows (personally or from recommendation) that this actor has a great deal more to give and their performance will grow and grow. It's wonderful when all agree—oh, this actor is perfect! But sometimes the actor who seems right to the director doesn't seem right to the playwright—and vice versa. In this case there's a lot of discussion and soul searching. Sometimes I've been right in my original instinct, sometimes I've been wrong. I have at times been dissatisfied with all the choices for a part but have then been told that this is all that's available and we have to settle on somebody. Then I just have to grit my teeth and hope for the best. Casting is supremely important. A wrong choice now can doom the enterprise.

Other considerations come into play—do we want or need a star? A star is a whole different animal. Some are human, some are super human, some are some lesser kind of beast. A star is usually a tangled mass of great ego, great vulnerability and great insecurity. Theater has a pecking order and when a star becomes involved in a project that order becomes immediately apparent. They consider themselves the top of the chain. Some people in theatre are "famous"—others are not. Some carry that fame lightly, knowing how fleeting it is, others carry it heavily and expect you to genuflect every time they come into the room.

For these, no one is as important as they are—and they are aware of that constantly. They may pretend they want you to treat them like just another human being, but when you do that they somehow let you know that that is not acceptable. They are special. In a play of mine I once had an actress—a "star"—but one whose star had somewhat faded. She expected everyone on the production to have read her autobiography. If you did not know the facts of her life and happened to indicate that lack in some conversational slip, she would refer you haughtily to the book, assuring that we would never again be unaware of any episode of her past existence. I was pleased that she was lending her starry self to this enterprise, but I was dealing not with her Then, but with her Now. And her Now was very tricky to handle. She sometimes seemed like just another human being, sometimes like a grande dame, and still other times like a wounded child. But, whatever she was, she required extremely sensitive handling. "Actor's temperament" is not a term I would use lightly, but she had it—in spades and at all times had to be treated gingerly.

A star who is not right for the role, who takes the part for a variety of personal reasons (wanting to work, wanting the income), can ruin a play even as their name brings people into the theatre. A star who wants you to rewrite the play to fit their persona or their politics or their theories of life or their skewed view of the character you've written can be seductive as they pull you along into writing what will become, for them, a vehicle, and, for you, perhaps a disaster. It may be worth it if their presence ensures a hit, giving you enough money to go on to write the next play. Whether one has sold out for a morally legitimate purpose is a moot point. Look to your conscience. And, when casting, realize that a star can also raise the weekly operating nut beyond what the budget can bear.

In casting, many other considerations come into the picture. There's the matter of balance in the look or feel of the combinations of actors. There's the matter of the availability of the actors one really wants. Would it be worth it to change the production's dates? There's even a director's knowledge that so-and-so is "trouble"; they may have given a great reading but, in rehearsal and during a run, they tend to cause problems—whether it's plain cussedness or, more seriously, have a tendency to indulge in drugs or drink.

During early days of rehearsal in the rehearsal room I usually sit beside the director. When we have an instinct for each other's reactions to actors' readings, I can point to a line in the script or we can exchange a glance at an especially good or an incorrect interpretation and the director knows exactly what I'm thinking. This is a good time for me to hear any redundant verbiage, to sense where an idea or emotion can be covered by "acting" rather than needing explanation in a line. It's a good time to make cuts or changes as it's unfair to actors to still be making those late in the game.

In early days, actors are feeling their way into the roles and a playwright must not expect a finished performance too soon. As the performance is being molded, outside of the actors' hearing I'll indicate to the director where I think an interpretation is going in the right direction and where it's off. Some actors are able to adjust. Others are not good at accepting the director's criticisms. They want to do it their way. I feel there is a difference between being sensitive and being self-indulgent. We are all working toward a whole which only the playwright and director have in mind and actors must be able to shape themselves into what is expected of them.

Some actors are expert in "emotional blackmail". Disagreeing with a line or the interpretation desired by the director and/or playwright, they'll say, "I can do it your way—but I won't feel it and it won't come out well." Then, by purposely not giving themselves to your line or the director's instructions, they proceed to show you how only their way will work. This does not help the enterprise.

Sometimes an actor will balk against some line, giving some reason, but the real reason is quite other. In an early production of mine, one actor in a minor role kept insisting he needed something additional in a scene. Since the scene was working as the director and I meant it to, we felt he needed nothing. At last, the director understood what the actor really wanted. He wanted an exit line. Since this was the actor's final exit in the play he wanted a line which would bring him applause. I felt that since the point of the scene was not him, but the other roles, working to get him applause would only be a distraction. I changed nothing. Faced with the same problem now, I might be more malleable. But this illustration demonstrates how some actors, many, in fact, see the play only from their own part and never escape from the prison of it, never see what's happening in the play as a whole.

Once rehearsals begin on stage I tend to sit in the back of the theatre, in the shadows, partly to get some perspective on the whole, partly so the actors can't see my face. What I want to project is love and strength and the fact that I am with them in their quest for the realization of their roles. But I think that they sometimes feel I'm looking on with disapproval, that I'm impatient and dissatisfied as they struggle to bring out their parts' full potentials. Quite simply, they don't want to be constantly observed by the one who wrote these lines, they want to be making the part their own.

Outside of rehearsals, I don't fraternize very much with actors, fearing that they'll ask me a question about their part and my answer will be too detailed, too "thinky". The playwright's aims in a scene sometimes do not coincide completely with the aims of each individual actor. That is—I may need a climax somewhere, or need some information to be given, and while I try to build this into the character logically, sometimes the answer to an actor's question is, quite simply, that this scene has to be this way because of the development of the play's main idea, for the play's structure. Over-intellectualized explanations can sometimes confuse an actor, who has to interpret the part emotionally. If there are questions of interpretation, I prefer to convey my thoughts privately to the director and to have the director translate those ideas into words the actor will natively understand.

It almost never fails, in the emotionally charged atmosphere of the rehearsal sessions, that somebody sometime will explode with an emotional outburst. Since it's the actors who are trading in raw emotion, in my experience it's usually one of them. Suddenly there's a meltdown. There's shouting. There are tears or cursing or even a screaming fit followed by someone's slamming out of the space. Theatre is a tough business and one of these outbursts per person can be countenanced—but only one. This sort of behavior can be tolerated if it clears the air, breaks a bubble, and if, on the other side of it, there's smooth sailing. If people don't get over it and it ruins the atmosphere for the rest of the rehearsals and the run, such an explosion is a tragic mistake.

My favorite scene of this sort occurs in THE BAND WAGON, when Fred Astaire, playing, as he usually did, the most debonair, controlled and civilized of characters, suddenly explodes in a rehearsal after his co-star (played by

Cyd Charisse) and director have, with extravagant politeness, been constantly diminishing his role. He suddenly stops the rehearsal, stands center stage, makes an impassioned farewell declaration, then walks out. In the next scene, Cyd Charisse comes to his hotel room to apologize for her behavior. They reconcile very civilly, each admitting to their personal uncertainties. After a buggy ride, one of the loveliest numbers in all the Astaire canon follows: *Dancing in the Dark*. In this extremely insightful Comden and Green sequence, an explosion is followed by mutual understanding and, eventually, by love. The problem is, in life rather than in the movies, a happy result is not predictable. By and large, when it comes to emotions, it's preferable that the only ones on display be those called for in the script.

What actors want from a living playwright is that they be supportive, that they understand the actors' methods of preparation no matter how slow and stumbling, that the writer stay out of the actors' ways as they try to memorize their lines and develop their interpretation of a role, that the playwright tolerate idiosyncrasies and individualities rather than insisting on a preconceived vision of a character, that the playwright listen to reason when an actor says "I can't say that line" and rewrite if necessary, that the writer not come up with endless changes, particularly close to opening when memorization is a problem, that the playwright refrain from giving acting notes and be suitably congratulatory once the play opens and the performance is honed. I try to do all this, but I sense that there will always be some actors who remain uncomfortable in the presence of flesh and blood living playwrights. They'd rather be doing something by Shakespeare, Aeschylus or Ibsen—somebody who will not be constantly looking on and getting in their way.

I don't feel comfortable in actors' dressing rooms. It's their private world, the world in which they're physically and emotionally undressed and I feel it's not my place to be there. I don't even feel comfortable going back after a performance—when one is expected to make an appearance, when one has to smile, air-kiss, hug and cry, "You were wonderful!" Nothing cogent is ever said. A lie sounds the same as a truth in these situations. It's awkward for everybody. But I've learned to accept it as part of life in the theatre. Actors, especially, need affirmation and approval. (I do wish people understood that a playwright needs affirmation and approval, too. I am always surprised and, in fact overwhelmed, if anyone thinks of sending me—the author—a bouquet at an opening! It's nice to feel that you've been responsible for some of what happened on the stage that night—not only when the whole thing tanks, but when it succeeds.)

From the beginning, one of my aims has been to write strong roles for women. At the time there had been endless outcries from actresses, bemoaning "Where are the roles for women?" I thought—I can write for them. I did. And then I discovered—it's producers who choose what plays will be put on, not actresses. Very few actresses in this day and age can say "I want to do such and such a play"—and get it on.

I hate to say it but some female actors aren't as wholly committed to their careers as most male actors. Women take time out for lovers, husbands, child-bearing, child-rearing—domestic concerns which male actors think of as peripheral. There were a couple of years in my writing life when it seemed that all we had to do was send a script to an actress and she'd get pregnant. Some actresses prefer not to travel far from family or to get signed up for long runs. It's just a fact of the business—the limited availability of some actresses. I've almost never heard of a "domestic concerns" excuse from an actor; from actresses I hear them all the time.

One can write with a certain actress in mind and then not be able to get her either because she doesn't see herself in the role or she has other commitments. So I write what I wish, usually without anyone specific in mind, writing strong roles for men as well as for women. Can women write roles for men? Of course they can—as well as men can write roles for women. The entire process of writing is slipping into someone else's skin; whether that skin is masculine or feminine makes no difference to the creative mind.

What about getting a script to an actor or actress before there's a producer? Actors are wary about this because they like to feel there's an "offer", that if they spend time reading the thing there's the real possibility of a job. Before there's a producer attached, one can get a script to an actor or actress, they can say "I love it, I'd love to do it"—then you find that, in spite of their name, you can't get a producer to produce it. The actor feels at the least used, at the most insulted. The situation is even worse if the producer looks at it, wants to do it—but with someone else. It's embarrassing for all concerned.

In general, what actors want from a playwright—aside from their providing a great role—is that the playwright stay out of the actors' way and let them do their work. What playwrights want from actors is that that work be splendid.

THE DESIGNERS

When a production begins to get physically real, designers of sets, lighting, music and costume enter the picture. The playwright contractually has approval of sets and costumes—but it's usually the director who has concepts for both. The director can bring the writer into the process early, but sometimes the director meets with the designers separately and then all the playwright can do is voice approval or disapproval of designs already in a sketch or, sometimes, even executed.

The best place for the playwright to have their say on these aspects is in the set and character descriptions in the script. These can be elaborated on in conversations with the director. Some directors read the playwright's descriptions carefully and come up with an approximation of the writer's desires. Others like to show their creativity and, out of nothing more than perversity, will, for example, have an entrance you saw on stage left put on stage right, reversing everything, making the production a mirror image of the production you had in your head. Some directors will invite the playwright to participate in early discussions with designers, most feel these conversations are their province, that they will then show the designs to the writer and interpret the writer's comments to the designers. Such a director wants to control the process and never have the playwright meet with designers face to face.

My approach is to try to look at designs with an open mind, accepting others' ideas no matter how unlike my original imaginings, protesting only when I feel something works against the idea of the play, and being very clear when I feel a design element is distracting or makes the staging of some scenes impossible. A director should have thought out the play scene by scene and should know if the set works for every moment. I try to go through the play in my head moment by moment, imagining it on the set in this drawing or model, asking the director how or where such and such a scene will happen. Sometimes some dramatic moment called for in the script will prove to be impossible in this stage design. It's best to realize this now, rather than when the set is built.

The limitations of each specific theatre, plus budget limitations, will often dictate what the design will be. Plays of mine have had designs which were quite different from what I imagined, yet they worked very well and I enjoyed seeing them. At other times, the physical realizations were quite contrary to what I've wanted and have, in my opinion, worked to the detriment of the play.

I've never been a fan of the realistic stage set and, for most of my plays, have specified something quite simple and abstract. I only rarely get it. It takes an immense amount of talent to do less rather than more, to provide an atmosphere of defined space rather than detail (much of it borrowed from copy books). With plays which have had many different productions, I always prefer the designs which were the simplest.

I feel the same about costumes. Like the set, they should never distract from the substance of the play. They should be correct for the character, but not take attention away from what the character is saying. As in stage design, costumes can be "over-designed"—particularly in the professional theatre. Costumes have to be made to last through many (it is hoped) performances, so they should be sturdy. But they should allow the actors to move freely and not be so heavy that the actors get over-heated and can hardly breathe.

Lighting is a mysterious art and, with today's technical achievements, can be magical. Here, the script can describe an effect, a sense of light or dark or time of day. As a playwright I've never been involved in any part of the lighting process and only have some say when it's all completed and I either gaze with wonder or nudge the director to quietly say, "You can't see the actor in that corner" or "This scene happens in winter. Can the lighting make the atmosphere a little more cold?"

The playwright's objectivity, coming in at the end and seeing the result rather than being involved in the process, can be valuable to a director and lighting designer. Sometimes the effect one imagined is possible, sometimes, with limitations of instruments, it isn't. But one thing I think is primary—that the audience be able to see. More than one realizes, the audience's ability to hear is partly based on their ability to see the faces of the actors. Murky light can be marvelously atmospheric. But if the audience can't grasp what's going on, it doesn't serve the play.

Sound design is an art to itself. Sound should be supportive and appropriate. As should the music. Whether the music is chosen or composed especially for the work, I'm always in awe of musicians' skills. A sensitive and responsive musician can bring wonderful colors to the theatrical experience.

Sound and light are very close relations. What must it have been like before body mikes and spotlights, when all those iambic pentameter lines floated upward through the opening in the roof of Shakespeare's Globe Theatre? It's a wonder that any of the Bard's lines were heard by anybody! Yet they were, weren't they. What I'm saying is: sound and lighting effects are all wonderful enhancements to contemporary theatre, but perhaps we've come to depend on them too much. Perhaps we should remember that the center of theatre is still the actor and the script.

As noted before, on design, the playwright has a say—"approval"—but should remain open to others' concepts. Sometimes they enhance, sometimes the opposite. What I want from the designers, including the choosers or composers of music, is that the designs support my original concepts. What the designers want, I believe, is that I remain open-minded to concepts which are different from what I had in mind. If I disagree with a design, they want me to respect their attempts to realize in physical terms that which can be described simply but which may be difficult to achieve in reality on a stage. When we disagree, I try to make my comments straightforwardly and gently. Sometimes I manage to get what I think is best for the play, sometimes I don't. The bottom line is: Can the actors work in the space which has been provided for them—and does that space enhance and support the ideas and emotions embodied in the play.

THE REST OF THE TEAM

Every time I have a play produced I'm astounded at the number of people who work to make that production happen. Beyond the collaborators mentioned above, there are stage managers, prop people, carpenters, electricians, casting directors, vocal coaches, hair and wig designers, wardrobe supervisors, business managers, box office attendants, photographers, advertising and public relations people—the list goes on and on. And every one of these people probably has an assistant or two—except for the playwright. The playwright usually works alone.

The playwright's personal relationship with any of the above is only peripheral. The stage manager can be a rock or a dictator, but what they usually have is a great love of being at the theatre night after night and making sure that everything goes smoothly. A good stage manager is the mainstay of a production. During rehearsals they keep the script up to date, call time out for the actors, make sure there's a table with water, aspirin and sometimes sandwiches and generally cater to the well-being of everyone, all this time taking notes and becoming the director's other arm. Some stage managers can be martinets who consider their only loyalty is to the director and feel the playwright is an annoyance to be tolerated or worse. But a solicitous stage manager can be a boon to a playwright and somewhere along the line I like to let them know their devotion to the night after night functioning of the work is valued.

Many of the decisions some of these people make will have nothing to do with the playwright. We will not be consulted on the prices of tickets, the number of comps, the look or frequency of the advertising, the placement of publicity (unless we're asked to contribute our presence to it). We will not be consulted about how many performances a play will give a week. We will not be consulted when the producers decide a play will close. Clearly much of what these people do will have a direct effect on the success or failure of the production. We may not know their names, know who they are or what they're doing, but what they're doing will have a direct impact on us just the same.

All these contributors are very far from being the "little people". Their contributions make things happen. As playwrights, we can treat them well, even if all they do is bring us a cup of coffee or offer moral support. On the morning of September 11, 2001 I was in Abingdon, Virginia at the final tech for the next day's opening of THE SECOND MRS WILSON at the Barter Theatre. Having watched the Trade Towers collapse to rubble on TV earlier that day, I stood at the back of the theatre numb and in a daze. I will never forget the production assistant who came all the way over from the production office to the theatre to give me a hug and murmur her condolences, sensitive to what was happening in the town where I live when I was so far from home.

These people who surround a production, all of them, are invaluable. We should let them know they are appreciated. They're the ones who grease the wheels and keep the production running smoothly long after the playwright and director have moved on to other pastures. As with everyone connected with a production, they should be treated with respect.

THE CRITICS

The play opens—and then what happens? People come see it and let you know in no uncertain tones what they think of it. I hate to admit it, but the critics are important to the theatre. They are important to the playwright's play. Wise or stupid, their words are read by more people than will ever read the playscript. One can't work to please them—partly because they're unpredictable—but one can't ignore what's being said on TV, on the radio, in print or on the web.

I would like to say I'm impervious to criticism—good or bad—but it isn't true. Actors will say they "don't read reviews"—but then they somehow divine the content of them. I usually have someone else read them. Only when it's safe, when my nerves are no longer raw from the production process do I eye them myself. Being only human, of course I like it when people like my work and hate it when they dislike it. Unfortunately, I never forget the insults, but I find I can't remember the words of praise. So reading reviews is a dangerous enterprise—particularly if it's going to discourage one from going on.

The thing about criticism that I hate is their sarcastic tone, the tone that says "I could do better" combined with "you couldn't possibly have done worse". Reviewers love to be smart and witty. It's hard to be witty while saying good things about anything. But one can be devastatingly clever if one is tearing something to shreds. Reviewers exercising their wit at my expense hurts. I admit it. I also admit we all read other people's negative reviews with a measure of delight. There is a perverse pleasure in readng a negative review of someone else's work. *Schadenfreude* is a very human reaction, especially in theatre. It just doesn't feel good if the daggers are aimed at one's self.

What the critics say is serious business. They have the power to close a production and the power to keep it running. There's a certain kind of theatre, either a musical or a play featuring a star, which, with enough advertising can get bad reviews yet run forever. This seldom happens with a straight play. In such a situation what one can salvage is the future. Everyone walks away with nothing, but the playwright walks away with the play. It might live to shine another day. Another life in another venue. The play still exists no matter what the critics think of it. If this embodiment didn't work, another might. This can be cold comfort, but it's comfort nevertheless.

I only wish critics had some quality of compassion. As soon as a play exposes itself in any way in any place it is fair game. When critics sense there are changes while the play is on the road they swoop in like barracudas smelling blood in the water. You can think you're working way out of town, in a protected situation, that you have the freedom to experiment, but, if critics sense you're trying this and that, they think you don't know your own mind—when actually what you're trying to do is see what works best with an audience and what doesn't. You can't tell that until you expose your goods to the viewing public. Part of that public will be the Media Judges. They will hand down their verdicts. It matters not how many years you've worked or how many obstacles you've had to overcome in the climb to do this little thing—get the play on. The Great Voices will pronounce your sentence. The quality of mercy comes into the picture not at all.

Some reviewers are "soft," summarizing the plot and handing out a few compliments. Some reviewers are "tough," seeming offended that they were even forced to sit though your evening of unadulterated trash. There are sometimes quite even-handed reviewers. These seem to understand what they're seeing, to appreciate the efforts of all involved in the enterprise, and to wish the participants well no matter how much the presentation isn't working at the moment. Seeing plays in an out-of-town situation, these few can be quite insightful about what direction a rewrite or reworking should take.

A problem today—or perhaps it's an advantage—is that there are so many outlets for reviews that all of them are slightly devalued. A producer can always find a word or two from somebody, even from some remote corner of the web, to praise the effort. With the advent of the internet, articles which in the past would fade into oblivion now can be Googled. Someone can always find out what was printed after the opening in that remote village in Iowa—and can reprint and publicize it, negative or positive, till the end of time. Today, certain kinds of "entertainment" can be kept alive by advertising in spite of bad reviews and live, not to suddenly become works of quality, but to, at least, provide their participants income for many many more days, even years.

From the writer's point of view, it's best, I think, to take all reviews with a grain of salt, merely squinting at them, not memorizing either the slams or the compliments. If your work did not exist that review would not exist. It feeds off of you. You need not make a meal of it in return. And then remember this: The creator is always superior to the critic—no matter how much power the critic may seem to have for the moment. This may be cold comfort as you suffer the retreat of a cowardly producer and the closing of a show based on critical reception of it. But on Judgement Day this knowledge leaves you serenely above all of them all the same.

The true test is: Did I, in this play, in this production, achieve what I was trying for? If so, no matter what its reception, I've succeeded. If not, on to another battle another day.

THE AUDIENCE

It's all for them, the audience. The Great Unknown. That's who you're doing all this for. Those nameless (certainly not faceless) people who will sit out front and witness what you and your collaborators have put together.

Audiences have their quirks. No two are alike. There are quiet audiences who may seem bored but actually are very much moved by the performance. There are loud audiences—audiences with a couple of boisterous laughers—who seem to be appreciating everything but actually are only drunk or out to have a good time. There are those who get the jokes, and those who don't. There are those who are super-critical, intellectually challenging, wanting to show they know more about a subject than you do. There are audiences which are hard to please and easy to please and it's hard to tell which of these you value more. You want them to like what you've set out before them, that's the main thing. What are my aims with an audience? First to entertain, second to move people, third to make them think.

Audiences gravitate to the kind of theatre they think they'll like. Tourists want to come to the big city to see a hit musical. (At those prices they don't want to risk a bad investment.) Some go to well-reviewed plays and pat themselves on the back because they've been intellectually challenged—whether or not they've understood a word or even been monumentally bored. There are sometimes obtusely written plays which have to be seen only because they're this season's fashion. They've gotten the imprimatur of the critics and even if the viewer doesn't enjoy, or even understand, them, the member of the audience has to go because they have to say they've seen it in order to discuss it at their next soirée. In my humble opinion, this is Emperor's New Clothes time. Audience members should form their own opinions. Yet perhaps, because of the money they're paying for tickets, they have to feel they haven't wasted their money and time.

Like any one, I appreciate appreciation. Quite simply, I like it when I feel the audience likes the play. I usually can feel it from the back of the house. One can sense whether their silence is that they're bored or that they're spellbound. There's great satisfaction when they murmur together when something surprising happens, or they laugh together when something tickles their fancy. That's the kind of audience you'd like to ask back night after night. I don't appreciate an audience member who comes up at intermission or after the performance and tells me how to fix the play. A litany of the play's flaws is unnecessary. Quite sufficient would be "It's not my cup of tea" and move on.

Of course I know I have to please the audience, but I don't have to pander to it. Some imagined perfect audience is not in my mind when I choose a subject or when I write the play. (Perhaps they should be, but they're so unpredictable that trying to predict what "audiences will like" is a foolish undertaking.) I think my job is to lead, not to follow. I'm human, they're human, we ought to like more or less the same things—know good from evil, have a sense of what's tragic or what's comic, what will arouse laughter and what will not.

Speaking of audiences, I must speak a little about the savage ritual of opening night. For those outside of you—your friends, relatives and strangers—it may seem like a celebration. All those telegrams! "Congratulations!" "Break a leg!" Or, in Italy, a phrase others think most appropriate to be sent to me: *"In Boca al Lupo"*—"In the mouth of the wolf." Every phrase may be thrown at you except "Good Luck", which, the superstitious say, will only bring bad luck. As I say, for all those folk outside of the playwright it seems like a celebration, for the playwright it may feel more as if you're about to offer yourself up publicly as the sacrificial lamb.

At such times, it is not necessary to climb up on the altar voluntarily and personally light the match which will immolate you. What I mean is—let's face it—there are very few of your relatives and acquaintances who are as supportive as you wish them to be, very few who whole-heartedly wish you well without one single twinge of jealousy. There are, in fact, those whose smiles barely disguise their hopes for your imminent disaster. No matter what your conscience may dictate, you do not need to personally invite these negative spirits. There'll be plenty such spirits around without your inviting in those you personally know.

As the playwright, one is extremely exposed at openings. There's no place to put oneself, except with the public, no place to hide. Why should you have to subject yourself to observing others quiver with delight as they watch you being burned at the stake? If the night turns into a triumph, a peek at their sour faces will spoil your sense of victory. In moments of success, there will always be one close acquaintance who can find just the right remark to prick your happy balloon. If you must, invite just a chosen few, those who know just what to say, when to say it, how to be graciously reassuring in your hour of defeat and generously congratulatory in sharing with you the glow of your success.

THE PLAYWRIGHT

When one speaks of theatrical relationships, the most important relationship for a playwright is with him or her self. Your relationship with your brain, your emotions and your creative juices. Your relationship with the pages you write.

You can only write in your own voice. You can no more change that than you could change your blood type or fingerprints. Any particular play may work well or less well, but it is *your* play. You do your best in the writing of it because you know, when it is completed it will be competing with every play ever written since the dawn of time. Theatres need plays and playwrights—but they do not need those playwrights to be living. Yet you are. And before all the theatrical relationships with whom you will get involved if you should be so fortunate as to be seeing a play of yours into production, you will have weeks, months, years of a relationship which is primary—your relationship with your self.

Novelists often say, "I envy you playwrights. Writing novels is such a lonely business. At least you're in a field where you have people around you." An interesting concept. I've never found it to be true. There were a few lucky dramatists, like Shakespeare, who were attached to a company, who wandered in and out of a theatre daily, a denizen of front stage, back stage and dressing rooms, a compatriot of actors, directors, producers, costumers, set designers and stagehands. There are even, in this day and age, a few playwrights attached to theatre companies, playwrights whose pages are instantly snatched up and given stage life in a form close to what they created or embellished by fellow artists in the fray. Playwrights, in short, who live a life in the theatre.

Not me. I write. That's what I do. I do it alone. I do it at my desk, the way a novelist does it. Except when a play is in production, in my work I live a life of solitude, a life peopled daily only by my characters. A life in which, even as I yearn for "connection", I am trying to push the world away. It is the only way I know how to work—in that bell jar of my brain. Maybe Henry James was able to steal a noonday hour from work for an omelette, Chablis and brilliant conversation with companions. I can't do it.

Gentle of nature as I believe I am, I am also fiercely independent of spirit. I couldn't endure office life or having anybody tell me what to do daily. Similarly, I recoil from having to tell anyone else what to do. Some people get their jollies from giving orders. I view everyone outside me as an equal. I do my thing, they do theirs. I have my area of expertise, they have theirs. We consult, we collaborate, but I neither give nor take orders. In the world outside the study there is always a hierarchy I want no part of. I don't want to know what rung of the ladder I'm on at the moment. I want to be walking through a field, no matter how treacherous, on my own.

Why do I need this isolation? There is something about the writing of a play which requires that one have the whole of it in one's head at the same time. In the early phases, when it's only a developing outline, one needs to view it all of a piece, as the base of the work entire. The structure needs to be a coherent whole—the building of which can't be interrupted. Then comes the writing. The writing, I have always felt, ideally should be done in the time it takes to play the play. In under three hours. If not, in three days. If not that, in three weeks for one draft. Of course many drafts follow. But for each draft I would like three weeks of absolutely uninterrupted flow. Any interruption, any break in the work process is like a crack in a vase. It may only be a small crack, but all the contents will spill out nevertheless.

This driving necessity—to get it all down as a whole before it flows away—exists for several reasons. One is that the characters to whom I'm giving life are jealous. They want my whole attention. They've just started to live their lives and resent it when I don't breathe life into them consistently. Daily. Hourly. If I don't give them my full and undivided attention, they start to rebel. They go off in directions of their own, then I have to race after them and pull them into line again.

Furthermore, the greatest reality of a play doesn't reside in the plot, in the words or in the descriptions of the action. The truth of the play, its highest existence, is in something that exists outside of all these—it is a construct which exists only in the audience's mind. It is the invisible thing they build out of the air which wafts above and between what is spoken and what is acted. It is the ineffable, the puzzle, the wonder, a fragile thing which playwrights do not write, but intend.

The true play exists on a level of what the viewer is thinking about what's happening. This mystical airy creation, this unwritten thing—as invisible as air but as sturdy and ever-present as an asteroid—is what one is creating in the creating of a play script. One has to be constantly and uninterruptedly in tune with it, on its magic wave length, as one writes. Or it does not exist.

And so I have this habit of withdrawal. During a work phase, in the writing of a draft, I have no lunches out, no nights at the opera, no escape weekends to the country. I have total and complete concentration. I see no one. Talk to no one. Visit no one. Accept no phone calls during working hours. (Husband, son and agent always excepted.) Friends know not to invite me to dinner on weeknights. They know not to call during the day. They know to ask, "Are you 'in' or are you 'out'?" When I'm "out" I love to see people. When I'm "in" I am slave to the creation of the work, I live in a social vacuum which I simultaneously revel in and rail against mightily.

If I know there's some social event I must attend of an evening I can't work the day before or the day of it. And I certainly can't work the day after. Having had all my mental pixels rearranged in talk and food and drink, the day after such an entertainment my concentration is completely shot. And while I like to be accommodating and seem normal, ordinary, not a snob and not a misanthrope, the truth is, after all these years before the mast, I know my nature. It drives me to the brink of madness to break the onrushing demand of the writing, to lose days of work when all anyone asks is my presence at their function for a couple of hours. So I refuse invitations. And then, of course, they stop asking. And I wonder where my people are and why they've stopped calling.

But I have been fortunate that there have been a few in my life who understand that when I'm "out" I do, truly, want to see them. They are not insulted when, released from labors, I suddenly call and ask: "Shall we have coffee?" They are artists, generally. Non-artists—civilians—do not understand the joyous desperate prison which is a life within the making of the art. For to be alone within one's art is not to be lonely. It is to keep company with the best, the highest which is within oneself.

Most people live a daily real life, but artists live in the area of potential. In the real world, what *is* is only what *is*. But what *could be*—what we could create—that's what drives the artist onward, that is the center of our existence. No one else can see it until it's there. So we stick with it, lashed to it, until it's no longer mere potential, until, having wrested it out of molten magma, it is there.

Aye, but there's the rub. When the thing is finished it is a *play*. Unless I play the parts myself—and I am no player—the work I've created alone needs other people. It needs actors, director, producer. It needs a stage. And so, at the end of a length of solitude, when I finish the work I must reach out to the world I pushed away from me. Having worked so hard to keep the phone from ringing, I now enter a phase of needing to hear it ring. I enter a phase of unanswered phone calls, of scripts sent to theatres which might as well be thrown into the sea, they are never responded to. Silence.

The "mating game" phase, in which my work and I and my agent search the world for that right connection, can be long and frustrating but supremely necessary. For, of course, only when a written play is produced—is embodied by others—does it really live. When the search succeeds, when a play finds the person or persons who promise it life, it is only the beginning of the battle.

As writer, stepping from my aloneness into the world of production, I now must make a transition from the self I was in the study to the self I must be in this unit, this unit which is making my play come alive. I gave it birth and I give it over to be born again. Other hands carry it onward. Who am I in all this—sitting in the darkness, once more alone, in the back of a rehearsal hall or empty theatre while at some distance in front of me others have their way with the thing I worked so hard to create?

Playwriting is often a matter of rewriting and when rehearsals begin I am now the rewriter. I am the one who had a vision which is now being adapted to another's vision, to several others' visions. It is fortunate if we have the same vision. But during this rehearsal process, I am still alone. I am not like any of them. None of them do what I do. They can look at me in awe, in anger, in love, in misunderstanding, in a whole range of feelings. But they all look at me as the "other"—someone some of them admire and some resent.

Surrounded by my cast, by my whole production unit, accompanied by my director, even the ones with whom I have the most rapport, I am still, somehow, separate. Different. Yet I yearn for them to know how thankful I am for their efforts, for their embodying when I could only posit. I am eternally grateful to the actors—to the fact that there are creatures in this world who actually want to memorize and say someone else's lines, to stand boldly in the light before hundreds or thousands of observers, who will give themselves to the immense physical, mental and soul-wrenching thing it is to get out there to impersonate, to act.

These folk who enter my life through giving life to my play never seem to sense my love and support enough. In the theatre, love terms are legion. "Love you!" "You're terrific!" "It was great!" The words sound hollow for we all know how often, when they're said, they are empty and insincere. So I don't effuse. I support. I watch their efforts. I want to be part of the process of the company's creation, a member of the wedding, but I remain outside it.

When the play opens and I go to see it, then I am more alone than ever. I do not feel comfortable seated with the audience. The person you happen to sit beside will say exactly what you don't want to hear. I want to be unseen, anonymous, but there, bearing witness, beyond congratulation and beyond criticism. There should be a Playwright's Room in all theatres—somewhere high up with an overlook like the one Ziegfeld had from his office—where the writer could retreat during rehearsals, could witness without being witnessed, and where one could have a bird's eye view without being seen during the show.

Yet, paradoxically, alone in the theatre, wherever I am, I am not alone. I am everywhere. When a production exists, when it exists well, when the characters are embodied vibrantly, when it all flows, when the audience breathes as one, floating on the air of that construct I built in seclusion, that is my satisfaction. That is my companion and my joy. That is when, silent and invisible, I wish to say, "This is my gift to you—the gift I created in my solitude, the gift meant to be experienced when people are gathered together."

If they, together, can experience what, alone, I first experienced, then it has all been worth it. Unheard by them, I am saying: Accept what I have made for you—the thing I live for, the thing which I could only create—alone.

WOMEN IN THEATRE

Is it harder for women playwrights? Yes, I believe it is. Not as hard as it was, but still, for women, a rockier road. There are a lot of female playwrights being produced now. Yet the percentage is nowhere near their percentage in the population, even in the playwriting population. I believe the reasons have to do not so much with prejudice against women as against their subject matter. Today's theatre requires that a play break through the glass. Women's subjects, women's problems, are derided the way women's maladies are derided or marginalized. Women's rage at their condition can be viewed as distasteful—unless blunted by humor. On the other hand, sometimes women's works can be rejected for the opposite reason: They can be more gentle than the current fashion, less "in your face". In my opinion, women playwrights whose plays are brutal, shocking and violent—qualities I would call "masculine"—have a greater possibility of getting productions. I regret this. There are voices of compassion, grace and intelligence which might be labeled "feminine" which I believe also should be heard.

It's also true, I think, that some directors and producers don't want to work with women, believing them to be more unreasonable and emotional and temperamental. If each actor is allowed one blow-up per production, female playwrights are allowed none. I have wept alone in foreign hotel rooms and in theatre ladies rooms but, on a production, I've never allowed myself the grand explosion which others feel it is their right to indulge in. Good behavior is what all concerned want of women. Women can't show temper no matter what the provocation. There's always someone out there ready to call her "that bitch". But in my experience women's negotiating skills are actually quite solid, rational and effective. Contrary to popular belief, when all around you people are losing their heads, it's the woman who usually remains sensible and calm.

But fear of women's temperament is not the only thing that keeps women's plays from happening. Some producers, I believe, see a female name on the cover of the script and feel repulsed about it instantly. The female voice is not something they want to hear. Except in narrow circles, feminist plays feel out of date now, as if others feel the fight has been won so shut up about it. I also find that being a woman playwright is not necessarily a recommendation to female artistic directors. Some women view all other women as rivals. Some women prefer to work with men.

Does a woman have to be tough to survive in this field? I think so. I also think, with my tendency to compromise, that I may have been less tough than I could have been along the way. A couple of times I've agreed to producers' or directors' demands, even when I thought them unreasonable, because I wanted the production to happen. Sometimes I was right to do this, sometimes not. In the long run, I guess I believe getting the play on is such a difficult and dicey thing, and one hungers so for production, that any sacrifice one can stomach—and survive—is worth the gamble. If all fails, everyone but the playwright comes away with nothing. The playwright, at least, comes away with the script. It might live to fight another day.

THE AMELIORATING LIE

A great deal of dissembling goes on in theatre—not all of it on the stage. We lie about why we want to be part of some enterprise, lie about how much we've always enjoyed so-and-so's work, lie about why so-and-so's script or audition has been rejected. It's lies which keep the wheels—if not going—then certainly lubricated.

I have to say that, in most cases, it seems to me that sparing others the whole hideous truth about themselves is a charitable, indeed a creditable, act. There's no need to tell a playwright their beloved script is the greatest piece of ____ you've ever laid eyes on. No need to tell an actor you don't want him or her in the role because their audition stank. Living with self-illusion—even *delusion*—is a way of life in the theatre. And it's to no one's credit to destroy another's ego or dreams of triumph. They'll get the idea soon enough, when the no's become too numerous and the yes's all too rare.

Who knows, one's negative opinion may turn out to be wrong. Some actors, seen before they're fully baked, can seem talentless but go on to great success when their talents hit their stride. The same can be said of playwrights and all other contributors to the theatrical enterprise.

While the totally talentless don't necessarily need to be encouraged, no one has the right to destroy another with the bayonet of personal opinion. When one soul is in position to reject another, the ameliorating lie—the gracious fib—is not only allowable, it's in everyone's best interests. It is not your job to administer the *coup de grace* to the hopeful—no matter how merciful you feel the sword of brutal honesty's incision may be. The rejectee's faith and hope deserve your charity. It's possible that, with wings not too badly clipped, the rejected pigeon may soar in the future.

CONCLUSION

So what, after all, are the keys to good theatrical relations? Respect for each other's ideas and talents. Steady cooperation. Understanding of each other's points of view, each other's challenges and difficulties. Withholding judgment until each talent shows the best they can contribute.

In the hurly-burly of theatrical collaboration it may take all of one's negotiating skills to achieve a result which is satisfactory to everybody. Infinite tact may be required and an ability to calmly and lucidly explain your point of view while listening to others with an open mind. Using quiet reason and trying to understand other people's concerns is paramount. If there's still conflict about a line or a scene it's a good idea to ask that it be looked at both ways, and perhaps, if there's time, to show both ways in front of an audience, to see which way gets the better response.

I like to be pleasant and non-confrontational, agreeing with others' visions when I can, when not, firmly but quietly holding my ground. I like to avoid conflict when possible—but always with the hope that I'm not compromising the art. Sometimes deciding what's "right"—in a line, a scene, an interpretation, a set design, a lighting effect or even a costume—is quite difficult. That's when all one's diplomatic skills come into play. It's a blessing (sometimes a miracle) if the talents working on the production feel secure enough to say "I don't know"—and work together to find a solution. Holding rigidly to an idea out of pride or just plain cussedness is, to say the least, unhelpful. In an atmosphere of mutual trust, criticism among collaborators should be seriously listened to and considered. Everyone is working toward one goal: the success of the production. If the destination is clear, there will have to be some compromises, some changing of minds along the way.

Sometimes the creation process and the result seem to have little to do with one another. One can have a wonderfully smooth collaboration, a marvelously happy rehearsal period, a great relationship with all involved in the enterprise—and the whole thing can fail miserably when it's exposed to an audience. Conversely, the whole experience of building the show can be fraught with conflict—no one got along, the director was a tyrant, others rewrote the script, the producers asked for cuts, the actors weren't talking to each other, the entire process was full of fury and horror—and the show opens and it's a hit. Having a good time while the show is a-building is no guarantee that the outcome will be a success.

If all fails, if critics hate the thing and audiences stay away, who's at fault? There are plenty around on whom to pin the blame. With a new play, one without a previous reputation for being a masterpiece, it's the playwright who bears a lot of the burden. But, of course, the playwright has many excuses: We had the wrong star, the wrong director, the set didn't support the action, the weather was frightful, the play is a tragedy and everyone in the audience was looking for riotous comedic escape. It may be months, even years, before one can assess what happened and make sense of it.

When you're involved in a production it seems like a matter of life and death—it isn't. It's only theatre. This too shall pass. The show must go on? Why? It's because stopping it feels like a death. When a play opens and is not well received you discover what you're made of and whether or not you can take it. Eventually you may find you are impervious, made entirely of scar tissue. Nothing can wound you. Like Sarah Bernhardt in SARAH IN AMERICA, you say *"Quand même"*. "In spite of everything." Like the Dowager Empress in EMPRESS OF CHINA, as everything around you is shattering to pieces, you stand above the wreckage saying, "I survive".

At least, as a playwright, you can always write. The others are always waiting for jobs, for an assignment, for the right script to come along. You need wait for no one to sit down at the work. Your job is creating, not waiting. You will do a heck of a lot of waiting for others. But you win, or at least you're ahead of the game, if, while you're waiting, you also continue to create. Actors can go on to other roles. Directors can go on to other plays. All you have is what you've written and will be writing.

Those who enter upon this career should be under no illusions. It takes a great deal of courage to navigate in this business and to survive in it. No matter how successful one gets, it will always be a struggle. That struggle will never be over. It takes courage to do what all in theatre do—courage for the playwright to sit down before an empty page or screen and create something out of nothing, courage on the part of all those who come together to bring those pages to life, courage to face all those who come to see the work (every one a critic), courage to stand head high in the town square subject to the all the world's slings and arrows. As Thomas Mann said, "You cannot pluck a leaf from the laurel tree of art without paying for it with your life." The only consolation is to know that you did your best—and damn the consequences.

There are fine moments, too, of course. Times when you'll be treated with honor and respect, when the work seems to shine in the way you always hoped it would—and when others can see it. Treasure those moments. In the roller-coaster life which is life in the theatre they are memorable and can be all too rare.

When involved in production, and it's going well, it feels like family, it's a love fest. You feel you will love these people forever, and they will forever love you. But by and large it's only passing affection. The affection can remain, but it's never as once it was—when you all had one common concern, the production of the play. Conversely, when the going's been rough and one thinks "I'll never talk to so-and-so again," often the rough feelings fade.

I'll never forget what Ingrid Bergman told me. Her rule for survival in show business. It sums up almost everything one needs to know in order to survive. She said, "In this business, it's important to have a sense of humor—and a short memory." She meant that what may seem like a matter of life and death—isn't. One can get over the most awful disaster by looking at it with detachment, with a sense of humor. And the short memory? Forget all the slights and barbs. Don't burn your bridges. Tables turn and even the worst relationships can heal eventually.

What's most important is that what you contribute to the theatrical enterprise be as good as you know how to make it. And, whatever happens—tomorrow or tomorrow or tomorrow—you go on to work another day.

FAUSTIANA

CHARACTERS & SETTING

Bo
Faust
Sly
Greta
The Fisherman

Time & Place: This story is timeless, happening in an indeterminate time and place.

Setting: Two settings are indicated: A mountain top and Faust's study. The study, an enclosed space, represents the Past, the repository of all human knowledge. The mountain top, open to the sky, represents the Future. It overlooks all which could be.

In keeping with the style of the play, realism in the physical surround is not expected.

ACT ONE

Scene One — Mountain Top

(At rise:)

(BO, a cocky young servant, takes the last steps up to the mountain top from stage right carrying a picnic basket. He is jaunty and full of energy. FAUST, a serious man, past fifty, enters from the climb totally winded. BO breathes the air and revels in the height. FAUST looks around for a rock to sit on.)

FAUST: I can't go one more step.

BO: You don't have to.

FAUST: I'm exhausted. I can't go on.

BO: There is no on. We're here.

FAUST: I don't know why I let you talk me into this climb. I refuse to go any farther.

BO: I tell you—there is no farther. This is it! The top!

FAUST: *(Bored, sitting on a rock, exhausted)* So?

BO: For heaven's sake, Master Faust. Look around you!

FAUST: *(Bored, looking down the mountain off left)* Swamp. And at the end of that, endless water.

BO: Look the other way.

FAUST: *(Looking down from where they came)* City. Tangled mess.

BO: Look up.

FAUST: *(Looking up briefly)* Sky. So what? I could see that from below. What did you drag me up here for?

BO: For lunch. I have all sorts of delicious—

FAUST: Even more pertinent—why did I allow myself to be dragged?

BO: *(Opening the picnic basket)* Salami, cheese. I couldn't get any strudel—

FAUST: I hate strudel! What am I doing here?

Bo: This mood you're in—have been in for months. It's up to me to cure you of it.

Faust: I like my misery. Leave me to it.

Bo: I don't like it. It upsets me.

Faust: Too bad, Bo.

Bo: Do you think I like waking up every morning having to do for a Master who can't smile, can't say thank you—

Faust: *(Dully)* Thank you.

Bo: It's dragging me down, I tell you! You're a great man! Why do you moan and pout?

Faust: It has nothing to do with you.

Bo: It has everything to do with me. You're making me miserable!

Faust: You're not as miserable as I am.

Bo: I'm twice as miserable as you are. A proper servant shares the feelings of his master. I'm miserable for you and I'm miserable for me.

Faust: You don't have to be miserable for me. I'm miserable enough for the both of us.

Bo: You used to be full of life, full of ideas. Now you're as limp as a noodle.

Faust: A noodle. Splendid.

Bo: In the old days, when the black mood got you, you used to pull yourself out by mixing potions, conjuring up things out of thin air. Now you just sit there. Staring. What's wrong?

Faust: I can't tell you.

Bo: You can.

Faust: You don't want to know.

Bo: I do.

Faust: You couldn't take it.

Bo: I could.

Faust: A good master doesn't ask his servant to share his burdens.

Bo: In the name of all that's holy—SHARE!

Faust: You could guess if you had half the brains you pretend to.

Bo: It can't be because of the girl you bonked and got preggers and she and the little bugger died.

Faust: *(With an ironic grin at* Bo's *coarseness)* The girl I "bonked" and got "preggers" and she and the "little bugger" died. You put it so succinctly!

BO: That was years ago!

FAUST: In your universe you have no conception of what guilt is! To you, guilt is something you feel for a moment and the next moment—zip!—it's gone.

BO: Exactly! It's a waste of time!

FAUST: It doesn't matter to you that when I walk down the street people spit at me.

BO: They don't!

FAUST: With their eyes, Bo. They spit at me with their eyes! They hate me!

BO: They don't, Master!

FAUST: It's a marvelous thing to be hated by everyone. ...It's even worse to be hated by yourself.

BO: So stop.

FAUST: I walk down the street—I can see what people are thinking: "There goes Faust, vile seducer! Defiled an innocent virgin! Got her with child! They died, you know. Both virgin and child. And look—he still walks the streets! Assassin! Murderer!" ...It's a wonder they don't hang me!

BO: Lover. That's what you were. Lover.

FAUST: Yes... Lover... Worshipper of perfection. And by wanting to—possess—that perfection—I soiled it—destroyed it and its glorious future—Marguerite—her son—my son. *Our* son.

BO: You're not the first man that ever happened to.

FAUST: I am the first to have a conscience of such an enormous size.

BO: Oh. Size. Every man thinks his is bigger than anybody's.

FAUST: What can I do to cleanse myself of my sins—short of making a quick end by falling on my sword. If I had a sword.

BO: I could get you one but that won't solve anything.

FAUST: Are the spitters down there so much better than I? Look at them. They live in squalor. Their streets are clogged with refuse, their buildings crumble and decay around them as they toil, the air they breath is toxic from their garlic breath and their industry. In that foul place year after year they cough and choke and struggle and suffer and rot. It repels and horrifies me!

(SLY *suddenly appears—as if from no place.*)

SLY: Why don't you do something about it?

FAUST: You!

SLY: Yes. Me.

BO: He? Who? Where did he come from? How did he—?

FAUST: *(To* BO:*)* Quiet! *(To* SLY:*)* Go away!

BO: Master, that's rude!

FAUST: *(To* BO:*)* Shut up!

BO: *(Insulted)* Even more rude! *(To* SLY:*)* Excuse him, Stranger.

SLY: Oh, I have infinite patience with your master. He and I are old friends.

BO: Are you? *(To* FAUST: *)* Who is this fellow?

FAUST: I call him—Sly.

BO: Pardon my boss, Mr. Sly. He's been very out of sorts lately.

SLY: I know. That's why I'm here.

FAUST: *(To* SLY:*)* Go away! I swore I never wanted to see you again!

SLY: Don't be ridiculous. You summoned me.

FAUST: I did not.

SLY: You uttered thoughts which were driven by desire. That is my summons.

FAUST: I am beyond desire!

SLY: Don't be absurd, Faust. You burn with it! You are being consumed by it!

FAUST: Don't overdramatize.

SLY: You're dying of it. Dying of desire.

FAUST: If ever I get caught panting for another woman, shoot me!

SLY: Not desire for a woman.

FAUST: For what, then? Fame? A hollow fantasy. Gold? It doesn't last. Love? A ridiculous illusion.

SLY: No. For none of those.

FAUST: For what, then?

SLY: For action. For the ability to change your world.

FAUST: You think I want that?

SLY: You are suffering from the nagging discontent of one whose life has no purpose.

FAUST: Succinctly put.

SLY: You want to reclaim your reputation—to show people that you were—how can I put it?—that you were, that you are, "good".

FAUST: Oh, "virtue". I've given up on virtue.

SLY: The hell with virtue. You're starved for something else.

FAUST: What else?

SLY: Redemption. Expiation.

FAUST: There is no way—

SLY: There is.

FAUST: How?

SLY: You thought of it yourself when you described your city.

FAUST: I despise it! It's rank! It festers! It stinks!

SLY: Yes.

FAUST: The people live within it like pigs in a sty.

SLY: True.

FAUST: Twisted streets, rotting buildings, twisted, rotting minds...

SLY: And so?

FAUST: So what?

SLY: You want to change all that.

FAUST: I never said so.

SLY: You cannot mention negatives without having their opposites in mind.

FAUST: Their opposites...

SLY: You have it in your head, Faust, don't you...

FAUST: Do I?

SLY: You'd like to give it to them—as your gift—

FAUST: To give—

SLY: To be remembered—not as the destroyer, but as the creator.

FAUST: The creator...

SLY: Of the Ideal City.

FAUST: The Ideal City! *(He thinks. Then)* Yes! Instead of twisted streets, great thoroughfares. Instead of rotting structures, fine edifices which reach up to the sky. Instead of stinking alleyways, broad avenues, great green open spaces...

SLY: You see? It all is in your mind already.

FAUST: But where? Where could I build it?

SLY: *(He points down off left.)* There!

FAUST: In the swamp?

SLY: In land reclaimed from swamp. It's possible, you know, to drain the swamp, to fill in land, to build on that land a splendid city by the sea—

FAUST: A splendid city by the sea! Oh, if only I could do it!

SLY: Why couldn't you?

FAUST: I don't have the power.

SLY: I do.

(SLY *strides upstage left and gazes down at the swamp.*)

BO: *(Aside to* FAUST:*)* What's he talking about? Who is he?

FAUST: He is—the fulfiller of dreams!

BO: Not the dev—!

FAUST: Come on, Bo—! (FAUST *starts to exit, right, down the mountain.*)

BO: Wait! You haven't eaten your salami!

FAUST: The hell with salami! I'm going to sink my teeth into something that satisfies far, far more!

(FAUST *exits.* BO *grabs the lunch and runs after him.* SLY *watches them go then comes downstage and says to us:*)

SLY: Faust! ...My most worthy subject. Faust. ...Does it surprise you that I should want to encourage him in such an enterprise? You have the wrong idea about me. You assume that I, the ruler of the dark place, only want what's bad for human beings. Nothing could be further from the truth. I am—have always been and always will be—man's enabler, the fulfiller of his dearest dreams.

I am the supporter of action, not of inaction—of moving forward, accomplishing things, not of stasis, frustration and defeat. I am man's—and woman's—nowadays we have to add that—greatest ally. I help them realize their fondest hopes, achieve their deepest wishes, fulfill their heart's desires.

If they fail and end up stumbling blindly down to my abode to keep me company, that's no fault of mine. It's because they all have fatal flaws—for which I am not responsible. I don't judge them. And when they fail, which they inevitably do, they all find an extremely warm welcome with me. *(He smiles.)*

(Blackout)

Scene Two—Faust's Study

(*It is a large space with bookshelves which reach to the ceiling. In it are Faust's enormous desk, several chairs, an oak table on which sit towers of large books, and a ladder for reaching the tallest shelves.*)

(FAUST *is sitting at his desk. On it are strewn many huge volumes. He is poring over one avidly. As he finishes and closes the book, he rings a bell. Nothing happens. He rings again. Still no response. He rings again, more insistently.* BO *appears, munching a chicken leg.)*

FAUST: You're going deaf!

BO: I was in the kitchen, Master.

FAUST: The kitchen is still in the house, isn't it?

BO: Yes, Master.

FAUST: Well, leave the door open! Then you can hear.

BO: Yes. I will. *(He won't.)*

FAUST: Get me Athens.

(BO *shoves the chicken leg into his pocket, goes to the table and peers at the titles of the large books. He starts to get a volume near the top of one of the piles.* FAUST *cries.)*

FAUST: Wipe your hands!

(BO *does so, on his trousers. Then he extracts the book and brings it to* FAUST.)

FAUST: Thank you.

(BO *starts to go.* FAUST *stops him.)*

FAUST: Wait! ...Stay here. ...I may want other volumes.

(Grudgingly, BO *perches toward the side of the room, surreptitiously grabbing a bite of his chicken now and then.)*

FAUST: It was glorious, you know. Athens in the fifth century before our era. The agora.

(Then, explaining, as BO *shrugs ignorance)*

FAUST: The city square... The Parthenon.

(Again, BO *evinces ignorance.)*

FAUST: The Temple on the hill. What a place that was! A magnificent civilization rising amid a universe of barbarism! ... Splendid Athens! ... Bring me Rome!

(BO *confronts the tower of books on the table. He finally locates it three or four books down from the top of a pile. After removing the other books, he extracts the right volume and brings it to* FAUST.)

FAUST: Good... Rome... With its feats of engineering. The Colosseum. The Baths of Caracalla. ...Great roads! ...Did you know the Romans built highways stretching all the way north through Britain to the border of Scotland?

BO: *(Who doesn't care)* No, Master.

FAUST: And they built miles and miles of aqueducts. The ancient Romans had running water!

Bo: *(Flatly)* Wonderful. Can I go finish my lunch now?

Faust: They had sanitation! Water to clean their streets! To keep their privies clean!

(Bo *shrugs.*)

Faust: Don't you care that the Romans had working toilets?

Bo: *(Couldn't care less)* I'm thrilled.

Faust: Their sanitation was better than that which you see in the city right outside your window.

Bo: Then let's go to Rome.

Faust: That was in the past.

Bo: Then why are we talking about it?

Faust: *(Furious at him)* The past is the template for the future! ...Get me Constantinople!

(Bo *looks through all of the volumes on the table. He can't find it.*)

Bo: Not here.

Faust: It is. I put it there myself.

Bo: It's gone.

Faust: Look again.

Bo: *(Looking)* It's vanished!

(*Exasperated,* Faust *comes over, looks, then points to one next to the bottom of a tall tower of books.*)

Faust: There!

Bo: Of course. It would be there.

(*Removing the books by two's and three's,* Bo *finally extracts the volume and hands it to* Faust.)

Faust: Thank you, Bo. I appreciate your labors. *(He smells the book.)* I'm sure the chicken smell will disappear—eventually. *(He opens the pages.)* Constantinople. ...The fabled city rising from the sea—as my city will rise from the sea.... Cities which feature water are special cities! ...Get me Venice!

Bo: *(Not looking)* It isn't there.

Faust: I know it isn't there. *(He points to the very top of one of the bookshelves.)* It's there.

(Bo *gets the ladder, moves it to the correct bay and starts to climb. Meanwhile,* Faust *says, more to himself than anybody:*)

FAUST: There could be nothing more glorious than creating a city! It may not stand forever, but the memory of it will. And I, instead of being remembered as the seducer and murderer, will be remembered as the creator—the creator of one of the most perfect cities ever to exist on this imperfect planet.

(SLY *suddenly appears.*)

SLY: So you want to do it!

(*At the top of the ladder,* BO *is shocked by* SLY'S *sudden appearance.*)

FAUST: Of course I want to do it!

SLY: You don't think it's just one of my vile temptations which you'll fall for hungrily and later live to regret?

FAUST: If you say you can achieve it—

SLY: I know I can.

FAUST: Then let's begin—

SLY: There's just one thing—

FAUST: With you there's always "just one thing". What is it?

SLY: Once it's achieved—once you say you're satisfied—that there's nothing more you want in life—you and your soul will belong to me.

FAUST: I'll die and go to Hell.

SLY: You put it so baldly. But yes. You'll die and go to Hell.

(*Up on the ladder* BO *displays terror.* FAUST *is perfectly sanguine.*)

FAUST: I thought you had my soul already.

SLY: Ah, yes. But the punishments for creating an entire city are rather more delicious than the punishments for seducing one innocent maiden. Do we have a bargain?

FAUST: We do. ...Do you need to seal it in blood?

(BO *reacts.*)

SLY: No. A witness will be enough.

FAUST: Come here, Bo.

(*Fearfully,* BO *descends the ladder.*)

SLY: Oh. There's just one subsidiary clause.

FAUST: (*He knew there'd be one.*) How surprising... Go on....

SLY: You may build your city—but you will not be able to enter.

FAUST: Like Moses.

SLY: If you choose to see it biblically. (*He shudders.*) Yes. Like Moses.

FAUST: I can see it from a distance, but never walk its streets, never stroll in its gardens...

SLY: Correct.

FAUST: This is harder to accept.

SLY: Why? All cities seem better when contemplated from a distance than in their physical reality. Isn't that what you've found in your travels?

FAUST: Not necessarily.

SLY: But sometimes.

FAUST: Yes. Sometimes...

SLY: Then let this city always be for you—distantly contemplated perfection.

FAUST: As long as it truly exists. That it won't be an illusion.

SLY: Oh, it won't be an illusion.

FAUST: Then, yes. I agree. See my city and die. I'm tired of this existence anyway.

SLY: You may not be tired when you see what you've achieved. You may see it as the promised land and yearn to enter.

FAUST: No. It's not for me. It's for them. And for Marguerite. To cleanse me of my guilt. It is my penance.

SLY: You understand the terms of our bargain?

FAUST: I understand them. ...I accept.

SLY: So when you say—"I'm satisfied. It's complete! It is my ideal city!"—you will join me in my nether kingdom?

FAUST: With pleasure.

(SLY *produces a document and holds it out to* FAUST *for his signature.*)

FAUST: You always were a stickler for formalities.

SLY: Things are more pleasant that way. No arguments later.

(FAUST *signs then says:*)

FAUST: Now you, Bo.

(BO *pulls back fearfully.*)

FAUST: You're just a witness. Nothing bad will happen to you.

(BO *grabs the pen, scribbles his name and fearfully retreats.* SLY *takes the contract, folds it and puts it in his pocket.*)

FAUST: Good. That's settled. Now I can begin to design my city.

SLY: *You* design it!

FAUST: Of course. I see it in my mind's eye.

SLY: What's in your mind's eye may not be so easy to translate into bricks and mortar.

FAUST: *(After a moment, realizing)* No... That's true...

SLY : So you need—

FAUST : You know what I need!

SLY: Do I?

FAUST: You are infuriating!

SLY: Am I? Forgive me. Every now and then it amuses me.

FAUST: Goddam you—!

SLY: Really, Faust. You know that word means nothing to me.

FAUST: In the name of—! ...How are you and I going to manage to work together?

SLY: We haven't done so badly thus far.

FAUST: I wonder...

SLY: I want to hear you tell me what you need.

FAUST: All right! I'll say it! ...I need a Master Designer. An Architect.

SLY: There now, that wasn't so difficult to say, was it?

FAUST: How am I going to find one?

SLY: How, indeed.

FAUST: You have one in mind already, don't you!

SLY: Of course, my good man. If I didn't, the concept wouldn't have come to you.

FAUST: So?

SLY: So...?

FAUST: Stop teasing! The tortures are supposed to come later!

SLY: So they are. I got carried away. It's my nature. ... Rest easy, Dr. Faustus, I will bring you your Architect.

FAUST: Thank you, Sly. I hope you've chosen wisely.

SLY: I'll tell you nothing about the architect I have in mind except for one thing: I'm sure you'll like her.

(Blackout)

Scene Three—Faust's Study

(FAUST *and* BO *are working to straighten up the room for the arrival of visitors.*)

FAUST: A woman! For architect, he's trying to saddle me with a Female! He deals in curves, that Sly! Always one more trick up his sleeve.

BO: I don't trust him.

FAUST: Can a woman handle a commission this complex, this enormous? It'd be hard enough for a man, never mind the complications of the female brain! I won't let him thrust on me someone I can't work with!

BO: Should I serve beer and pretzels or tea and cakes?

FAUST: Beer and cakes, tea and pretzels! Does it matter?

BO: When it comes to food, everything matters.

FAUST: Then serve everything!

BO: Can we have strudel?

FAUST: No strudel.

BO: I like it.

FAUST: I don't. ...I insist, whoever she is, that I approve of her.

BO: And she'll have to approve of you.

FAUST: Why wouldn't she?

BO: Don't ask me, Master.

FAUST: It's the commission of a lifetime!

BO: Maybe she'll find a way of getting along with you. I have.

(*The doorbell rings.*)

FAUST: What do you mean by that?

BO: Nothing—only—

(*The bell rings again.*)

FAUST: What—?

BO: Knowing you, it won't be easy.

(*The bell rings a third time.*)

FAUST: Damn it! Answer the door, Bo, and none of your insolence!

BO: (*Bowing insolently*) Yes, Master.

(BO *exits.* FAUST *says to us:*)

FAUST: Who does he think he is? Impudent peasant! ...That's who I'm building the city for? Him and his like? ...I only hope the beauty of it will rub off on people somehow. Elevate them. Help them live on a higher plane. I have always believed—put savages into a civilized atmosphere—and you can change their lives. ... But would it work with the likes of Bo, his relatives and his descendants—if, God help us, there are any?

(BO *enters followed by* SLY *and* GRETA. *She is a handsome woman in her 40s, poised, intelligent, self-possessed, clearly any man's equal.* BO *exchanges a glance with* FAUST, *who, annoyed, makes a gesture dismissing him.* BO *dips his head slightly, mockingly, and leaves.*)

SLY: Doctor Faustus, may I present Greta Baumann.

FAUST: How do you do?

GRETA: I'm pleased to meet you Doctor Faustus. I've heard a great deal about your work.

FAUST: Good things, I hope.

GRETA: It depended on who was speaking.

(*That was a slight jab.* FAUST *counters:*)

FAUST: I must say, I haven't heard a great deal about yours.

SLY: We can go into that later. We're here to talk about your project.

GRETA: I understand you want to build a city.

FAUST: Is that too big a challenge for you?

GRETA: Why do you ask that?

FAUST: I just thought—

GRETA: Because I'm a woman?

FAUST: Well, I—

GRETA: Doctor Faustus—

SLY: Oh, please—just call him "Faust". This "doctor" business is beginning to annoy me.

GRETA: Very well,—Faust. You have to know that I'm up to this project. That's fair. And, as for me, I'd have to know if I want to accept.

FAUST: Why wouldn't you? It's the commission of a lifetime!

GRETA: If the commission of a lifetime turns out to be the headache of a lifetime, it's not worth it. I'll have to know that your ideas and mine agree. Tell me what it is you want, Faust.

FAUST: (*A bit put off balance by her*) Well, I—

(*At that moment,* BO *enters, with difficulty balancing drinks and edibles on a huge tray. He puts it down and reels off:*)

BO: Beer, wine, tea, coffee, pretzels, scones, tarts, cucumber sandwiches, custard tarts, mocha eclairs, chocolate-covered cherries, marzipan elves, mushrooms, turnips—

FAUST: Thank you.

BO: —and no strudel!

FAUST: All right, Bo!

(FAUST *gives him a dismissive wave, but* BO *refuses to acknowledge it. He retreats to a corner, taking the pose of a waiter ready to wait on people—but actually wanting to be present when* FAUST *tells his ideas.* FAUST *says to* GRETA:)

FAUST: What will you have?

GRETA: Nothing, thank you. I'm anxious to hear you tell me what you're thinking—

SLY: We're all anxious—

GRETA: Where do you want to build your city?

FAUST: Between the mountains and the sea.

GRETA: What's there at present?

FAUST: Swamp. Nothing but swamp as far as I could see.

GRETA: No one living on it?

FAUST: Of course not. It's swamp! ...As I stood on the mountain and looked west I saw a desperate city, full of crumbling buildings, crumbling souls, crumbling minds. When I looked to the east, I saw waving watery grasses extending all the way to the sea. I want to reclaim that space, fill it in, push back the waters—

GRETA: Like Moses—

FAUST: What?

GRETA: Nothing.

FAUST: Can it be done?

GRETA: I believe so.

SLY: It can be done. I guarantee it.

GRETA: All right. Suppose swamp becomes buildable-upon land. What then?

FAUST: Then—(*He goes over to his desk. On it is a tall pile of the books he has been reading. He puts his hand on them and says:*) I want to build—from scratch, a city which will surpass the beauties of Alexandria, Athens, Rome, Constantinople, the lost cities of the Incas! ...They all tried to achieve splendor—and did, for a moment, till they perished. But I want a city which will not perish. I want a city which will live forever—and longer than forever in the minds of future generations. *(He pauses. He reaches for a large stack of drawings and says:)* I've sketched out a few of my ideas...

(GRETA looks appalled. SLY raises an eyebrow. BO rolls his eyes and shakes his head.)

BO: Marzipan, anyone? Pretzel—?

(All glare at him. BO retreats.)

FAUST: I want—wide boulevards, green parks, splashing fountains, magnificent places for shelter and habitation. Spaces for speed and spaces for strolling. A place which bustles by day and glitters by night. A place which offers excitement for those who wish excitement—and peace and quiet for those who seek that. A place where people are free to live their lives in health, safety and comfort.

GRETA: No one can disagree with that.

(To GRETA's increasing discomfort, FAUST displays a drawing. He gestures for GRETA and SLY to come over and shows them what he has drawn.)

FAUST: We will take as our template the plan of China's ancient capital—Changan. The logic of streets on a grid—everything at right angles. A broad central avenue leading to the city's most important structure—the Emperor's palace. We will have places for assemblage—like the Coliseum of Rome.

GRETA: You're planning to have chariot races?

FAUST: Of course not! Other entertainments! Whatever people want to do there!

GRETA: I see...

(As FAUST shows his drawings, GRETA studies them with her palms together—like "The Praying Hands of the Apostle"—the index fingers pressed against her lips.)

FAUST: We will have a central gathering place like the agora of Athens in the Age of Pericles—where democracy can flourish. We will have a shining temple on a hill—like the Parthenon—

GRETA: May I point out that in your swamp there is no hill?

FAUST: We'll build one. We will have the waterways of Venice and the promenades of Isfahan. The courtyards of Cordoba, the piazzas of Florence, the palaces of Delhi, the temples of Pompeii. We will have colonnades like those at the Temple of Luxor—

GRETA: Why not a few pyramids?

FAUST: Those are for the dead.

GRETA: I assume there'll be some.

FAUST: My concern is for the living!

GRETA: Go on.

FAUST: We will have greenery and flowers everywhere, like the hanging gardens of Babylon.

GRETA: Why not recreate the gardens of Versailles and insist all the women dress like Marie Antoinette?

FAUST: You're mocking me!

GRETA: Have you anything else to add?

FAUST: I do! At the edge of the sea I want to build a tower, like the ancient Pharos of Alexandria, the Pharos which was both a fortress and a beacon, one of the seven wonders of the ancient world. My tower must be a great beacon of light, the structure toward which all the highways of the city will lead. My tower will be the tallest building in the world. An illuminated tower whose light will be able to be seen from beyond the mountains, beyond the horizon of the sea, from the moon—

SLY: A lighthouse—

FAUST: Not just a lighthouse. A column of light. A shape which will announce: "Here is the capital of civilization. Here is the place where men and women live in happiness and peace."

GRETA: A tall order. And I don't mean it as a pun.

FAUST: Can you design it?

GRETA: If you can conceive it, I can design it.

FAUST: My tower will stand—as the symbol of the new city—the image forever emblazoned on the minds of future centuries. The enduring symbol of Faustiana—

GRETA: "Faustiana"—!

SLY: I was wondering what you were going to name it!

GRETA: No modesty about you, is there.

FAUST: It is my legacy and it must bear my name. Faustiana. With its tower of light at the entrance to the harbor.

GRETA: A monument to you!

FAUST: No! A monument to reason, beauty and splendor. Long after I am gone, the image of this tower will remain forever embedded in the consciousness of the world.

(FAUST *finishes with a flourish—turning the page to show a rough sketch of his tower. There is silence.* SLY *and* BO *exchange glances—but* GRETA *is still looking at the drawings. She is silent for a long time—while* FAUST *waits proudly in suspense to be congratulated for his concepts. At long last she picks up the drawings, tears them in half—and drops the pieces into the wastebasket.*)

FAUST: How dare you—! *(He is in shock. Speechless. Furious!)*

GRETA: You are clearly a voracious reader, Dr. Faustus. How much has gone into that rapacious brain of yours! ...Let me outline what it is you want: Quiet streets and major highways, bustling thoroughfares interspersed with gently flowing canals. You want temples for people who have little or no religion, one major road which leads to the palace of the Emperor when there is no Emperor. Are you building for slaves or kings, farmers or dukes, peasants or bankers? Are you building for classical Greeks, Mandarin Chinese or people alive at this moment? Your city is a chaotic jumble of plagiarized ineptitudes!

FAUST: It is based on the finest of achievements of the past!

GRETA: But we don't live in the past. We live in the present. In attempting to include everything, your plan achieves nothing.

FAUST: I refute that!

GRETA: Faustiana—*(She has trouble saying the name.)*—isn't Rome or Athens or Alexandria! It's a city for this time and this place. You can't take fluted columns and marble pediments and glue them onto a present-day city! Architecture isn't stolen elements from past civilizations, it's structure, it's function, it's what works for this place, this time and these people!

SLY: A woman of principle!

GRETA: Have you asked the people in the old city what they want in the new?

FAUST: Of course not. They wouldn't know what's best for them.

GRETA: Patrician snob! Are you building this city for your use or theirs!

FAUST: Theirs!

GRETA: Then for heaven's sake find out what they want before you impose it on them! ...Have you explored the area on which you wish to build?

FAUST: I saw it from the mountain top.

GRETA: Have you measured it? Walked it?

FAUST: Strange as it may seem, I cannot walk on water.

GRETA: Have you swum or boated across it? Do you know how deep is the swamp and what's beneath it? Do you know if you'd be building on rock or on sand? In short, Doctor Faustus, do you have any idea what you're doing?

FAUST: I am building something which will last for ages!

GRETA: Not if you build it on silt and impose amenities on people who do not want, do not need them.

FAUST: They would only ask to recreate their present squalor without the stench!

GRETA: You have a dim view of human nature, Doctor. They might surprise you. But you will not be able to improve their lot if you give them things they don't want, and for which they have no use.

FAUST: What are you proposing?

GRETA: I am proposing that you give me time to speak to the people of the city, discover what they want, and from that draw conclusions on what they need. I am proposing that I explore the area on which you wish to build—so I can understand what is possible and what is impossible to achieve there. I am proposing that the design not come from books!

FAUST: From where, then?

GRETA: Why—from the mind of the architect.

FAUST: From *your* mind...

GRETA: If you wish me to design your city—yes, Faust.

FAUST: *(Uncertain)* I—*(Then, forcefully)* I will have my tower! You can change everything else—but I will have my tower!

GRETA: *(After a moment, like someone placating a child)* You may have your tower.

FAUST: Then fine. Go do whatever it is you have to do. Let's get this started.

GRETA: *(Bowing her head briefly)* Excellent. You will hear from me again when I have something to show you. *(She exits.)*

SLY: I must say, you were a paragon of charm, Faust.

FAUST: Greta tore up all my work and threw it into the wastebasket!

SLY: The most appropriate place for it.

FAUST: She could have had more tact!

SLY: I would say her tact about matches yours. Would you like to be working with someone less straightforward? Less honest?

FAUST: Is she capable of handling this big a job?

SLY: Would you ask that if she were a man?

FAUST: Oh, don't start that man/woman thing. She's an infuriating person!

SLY: That's what you need, isn't it? Someone to be a challenge?

FAUST: She's damn annoying!

SLY: Oh, I do like to see you when somebody's got your goat. You're so delightfully unattractive!

(SLY *exits.* FAUST *goes to the wastebasket, pulls out a few torn fragments of his drawings, looks at them and throws them in again.)*

BO: Nobody ate anything! If there'd been strudel, they'd—

FAUST: Wastebasket!

(BO *takes the food toward the wastebasket. Just as he's about to throw everything in, he snatches something, takes a bite. He chews, considers, shrugs, throws it all in and exits.*)

(*Blackout*)

Scene Four—Faust's Study

(BO *enters and says to us:*)

BO: You think there were enough books in here before? You won't believe it—but in these past weeks the Master has brought in more. (*He points to new piles of books all around the room.*) Books! Books! Books! This is a man who never learns his lesson. Today she's coming to show him what she proposes for the city. And you know what he's been doing all this time? He's been—GETTING IDEAS!!!

(FAUST *enters, absorbed in looking at an illustration in a book.*)

FAUST: We could have something like this—

BO: I thought she was coming over today to show you her finished designs.

FAUST: Her *preliminary* designs. If I don't like them—(*He waves the book.*)

(SLY *suddenly appears*)

SLY: Why wouldn't you like them?

FAUST: You! I should have known you'd arrive for the great unveiling!

SLY: Wouldn't miss it!

FAUST: Have you seen her plans?

SLY: No. This will be a revelation for both of us.

FAUST: I hope it'll be a positive experience.

SLY: Do you have doubts?

FAUST: She said the designs will be what the people want, that may not be what *I* want.

SLY: Isn't it possible the two might coincide?

FAUST: What do *you* want?

SLY: I want what *you* want. That's the way it's always been between us.

FAUST: It always seems so. Yet somehow when I get what I want, there's always some distortion—and it isn't what I wanted at all.

SLY: This time, it will be. Trust me.

BO: (*In a whispered aside to* FAUST:) Never trust anyone who says "trust me".

(The doorbell rings.)

FAUST: Get the door, Bo!

(BO exits.)

FAUST: I hope we'll like what we see.

SLY: You'd be a happier man if you'd do as we do in my domain—abandon hoping.

FAUST: Impossible. In our domain, hoping is how we get through the days.

SLY: Expect nothing and you'll never be disappointed.

FAUST: On this, I tell you frankly, I expect everything. I will not accept anything less.

(Ushered in by BO, GRETA enters, carrying a roll of plans.)

GRETA: Good day, gentlemen.

FAUST: *(Aside to BO)* You may leave—

BO: But I want to see—

FAUST: Later!

(Unwillingly, BO exits. FAUST says to GRETA:)

FAUST: You must be nervous—showing your plans for the first time.

GRETA: Not at all. These are the best plans for the site. I'm certain of it.

FAUST: Such humility!

GRETA: I'd say my humility about equals yours.

SLY: May we see the plans—or would you two prefer to continue jousting?

(GRETA unrolls the plans. FAUST and SLY look at them. SLY understands them immediately and moves away. It takes FAUST longer to absorb them. He stares at them as GRETA explains:)

GRETA: First we drain the water from the swamp and channel it to create a river—the water feature you are so intent on having. The shore curves here—and therefore so do the streets. The city center will be here, with satellite centers here, here and here, so all major amenities will always be within walking distance.

FAUST: What are these rectangles?

GRETA: Those are buildings. You'll get a better idea when you see the elevations. All functions—work, home, pleasure—are integrated. No sunless urban centers which die at night while everyone deserts them for their isolated homes. Major and minor roadways. Fast public transportation systems. Busy and contemplative areas. Areas for sun and areas for shade.

FAUST: I don't see my—

GRETA: Here—this circle at the edge of the sea—your tower of light, crowning all.

FAUST: But how does it look? How does it all look?

GRETA: Of course. You need to see pretty pictures.

FAUST: I'd like to be able to visualize—

GRETA: The elevations. *(She takes up another roll of drawings)* Faustiana—will look like this.

(With flair, GRETA unrolls the final sheet and stands back waiting for FAUST's and SLY's comments. For many beats they study them intently, saying nothing.)

SLY: Ahh...

FAUST: Mmm...

(The silence lasts a beat too long.)

GRETA: Well—?

FAUST: Everything's so plain!

GRETA: You want pilasters, dadoes, fancy fretwork?

FAUST: I understand not recreating Rome or Athens—but why not forms that dip and bend—like these. *(He opens the illustrated book.)*

GRETA: More scribbles from the past!

FAUST: Not from the past. From your contemporaries!

GRETA: Ah, my unprincipled contemporaries—who would bastardize anything to pander to bourgeois taste.

FAUST: Why is everything straight edges? Why, for example, couldn't this building curve?

GRETA: Because that's a museum and paintings don't enjoy being hung on convex or concave surfaces.

FAUST: Why can't these walls lean inward?

GRETA: They could—if only pygmies were going to use the spaces at the edges of the rooms.

FAUST: Why can't we undulate this path?

GRETA: Because that's not a path, it's a rail line and trains don't undulate.

FAUST: In short, anything I say, you're against.

GRETA: You've yet to say something sensible.

FAUST: You say you want to listen to the people, well, I'm people! Or perhaps the only person you refuse to listen to is me!

GRETA: That isn't true—

FAUST: You claim you're completely adaptable, but you won't take any of my suggestions!

GRETA: I'll take to your suggestions when they have value!

FAUST: I want something more—spectacular!

GRETA: You want curves and convolutions for no reason! Doctor Faust, buildings are not sculpture! They are habitable forms meant for use!

FAUST: Of course they're meant for use but—

GRETA: The kind of building you have in mind is more a monument to the architect who designed it than a tribute to those who will live within it. Architecture is not meant to glorify its creator; it is meant to shelter and inspire those who will live in the spaces enclosed by its walls.

FAUST: That may be so, and yet—

GRETA: Everything you see in my concept is based on space—on people moving in space. Walls rise vertically because people do. The shapes of the buildings are not imposed from the outside, they are the result of understanding the uses of the buildings from within.

FAUST: They're not—sensational!

GRETA: No thing, no person, can be sensational without very soon becoming obsolete and boring. Fantastical creations can amuse for a day, perhaps a year. But you want your city to last for decades, even centuries.

FAUST: I want its image to be indelible. So when people see that image they will instantly know—that's "Faustiana"!

GRETA: Is Faustiana to be a monument to yourself—or a gift to those people whose welfare you claim to care about so deeply?

FAUST: It's for the people but I want—

GRETA: I know what you want, Doctor Faust! Perhaps I'm not the architect to give it to you! *(She begins to roll up her drawings, about to leave.)*

FAUST: No, wait! Wait! ...I didn't see my tower.

(GRETA *unrolls the drawings again.*)

GRETA: Here. Here is your tower.

FAUST: ...It is—more beautiful—than ever I could have imagined.

GRETA: I can give you beauty and splendor. I can't give you the non-functioning architecture of the absurd.

(GRETA *waits. At last* FAUST *says:*)

FAUST: You're right. Never let it be said that when a new idea has merit I refuse to embrace it.

GRETA: Splendid. Then you agree we can build Faustiana exactly as I've envisioned it?

FAUST: Exactly.

SLY: *Mirabile dictu*!

FAUST: Let's begin construction at once.

GRETA: I wish we could!

FAUST: Why can't we?

GRETA: There are two problems.

FAUST: Problems?

GRETA: The first is—We don't have permission to build on this land.

FAUST: So get it.

GRETA: I've tried. The answer's always No.

SLY: I can get it changed to Yes.

GRETA: Excellent.

FAUST: The other problem?

GRETA: There's a family of Fishermen living on the land—exactly where you want your tower.

FAUST: Get them to move.

GRETA: They won't.

SLY: They will. I'll take care of that, too.

FAUST: Thank you, Sly.

SLY: Not at all, Faust. For your grand plans am I not always your Great Facilitator?

(Blackout)

SCENE FIVE—MOUNTAIN TOP

(Several weeks later. The mountain top has now become the on-site work space. There is a plank table set under a protective canvas. Working drawings are spread out on the table. BO arrives, panting and sweating, lugging more drawings and design paraphernalia. He says to us:)

BO: She had to set up her work space on the top of the mountain. The master insisted on it—and she agreed. And who's the one who has to cart things up to the summit? Me! I'm sorry I brought him up here in the first place! Now his every thought, night and day, is the city, the city, the city! And there's nothing to be seen yet!

(FAUST *enters from the right with* GRETA *who says to* BO:)

GRETA: Thank you, Bo.

BO: *(The martyr)* Don't mention it. Is there anything else you need?

GRETA: Not at the moment. Thank you.

(BO *beats a hasty retreat before anyone can request another service of him.* FAUST *has been peering down left through binoculars.*)

FAUST: When are we going to get permission to start?!

GRETA: Patience! Our friend is working on it—as you very well know.

FAUST: I hope it gets done sometime during my lifetime! This city is all I'm going to leave behind. My legacy.

GRETA: And mine.

FAUST: Yours! It was my idea. My concept.

GRETA: Yes, but it is my design.

FAUST: So you want to take credit for creating Faustiana!

GRETA: A considerable portion of the credit. Yes.

FAUST: You're vain, my dear Greta. Do you know that?

GRETA: When it comes to vanity, my dear Faust, mine doesn't come anywhere near matching yours.

(*Annoyed with* FAUST, GRETA *goes to the work table, unrolls a drawing and starts studying it in her usual pose—palms together at her lips. Noticing that,* FAUST *says:*)

FAUST: I knew someone—long ago—who used to think that way.

GRETA: What way?

FAUST: In an attitude of prayer.

(GRETA *instantly separates her hands.*)

FAUST: You remind me of her in other ways, too. For some reason, she made me feel—as you do—both better and worse about myself at the same time. In fact, you both have the same way of looking at me when I—

GRETA: Let's drop the subject, shall we? No woman wants to be told she's like some other woman.

FAUST: She was very special in my life, that woman.

GRETA: Still. If you don't mind, I prefer to be just me.

FAUST: You haven't told me anything about you. Where you came from, where you studied, where you practiced.

GRETA: You haven't told me anything about you, either.

FAUST: I don't have to. Everyone knows who I am. You know, don't you?

GRETA: I'm very much afraid I do.

FAUST: So, let's drop the subject.

GRETA: Pretty soon the only thing we'll be able to talk about is the things we can't talk about!

FAUST: We can talk about the delays! ...When, in the name of all that's holy, can things begin!

GRETA: How many times do I have to repeat! We have to get permission—

FAUST: Well, get your friend to get it! He's supposed to be all-powerful, isn't he? Why can't he achieve this?

GRETA: I tell you, he's working on it!

FAUST: Yes, but—

GRETA: Excuse me. I have to go down and supervise the surveying. Why don't you come with me?

FAUST: I prefer to observe from up here.

GRETA: You've never once come down to the site.

FAUST: I want to retain my perspective.

GRETA: But if you see it close to—

FAUST: I can see it all from up here, I tell you!

GRETA: Fine! Do as you wish! I would have thought you'd have more interest! For someone who seems so eager to have his great plans realized, you certainly keep yourself detached and aloof! *(She goes.)*

FAUST: *(To himself)* Who is that woman? There's something about her—. A manner—, a spirit—. What is it? ...Has Sly brought her here to help me or to destroy me? I must stay on my guard. Be ever vigilant. I've already pledged Sly my soul. What more does he want? To amuse himself by seeing me tortured in whatever is left of my wretched earthly life?

(Blackout)

SCENE SIX—MOUNTAIN TOP

(A rainy day. Protected from the rain by the canvas, SLY is inspecting the drawings as GRETA paces up and down.)

SLY: You're really making progress.

GRETA: *(Distracted)* Am I?

SLY: These are definitely coming along.

GRETA: Guess they are.

SLY: Some interesting solutions.

GRETA: Think so?

SLY: Light somewhere, will you? All this pacing. It isn't like you! What is it? What's wrong?

GRETA: *(After a moment)* ...I think Faust is beginning to suspect it's me.

SLY: What makes you think so?

GRETA: He's not an idiot.

SLY: You must have given a hint—

GRETA: Not consciously. But it seems—when I was young and foolish—I had the habit of brooding like this—*(The attitude of prayer)* And—older and wiser—apparently I still do it.

SLY: You should be more careful!

GRETA: I can age—but I can't erase who I am.

SLY: You remember our bargain?

GRETA: One tends not to forget a bargain with you.

SLY: I—borrowed—you, from that disgustingly angelic upper place, so you could help Faust build his city. You'll go back up there again only if you do not reveal to him who you are. But if you tell him who you are those pearly gates will be barred to you forever. You will come and live in my region—and your eternal soul will be mine for all time.

GRETA: I have no intention of adding my soul to your collection. ...Why have you brought me back and put us together again anyway?

SLY: A little experiment.

GRETA: An experiment!

SLY: It is my belief that Time Kills Love. I'm sure I'm right, but—you and he—that's my great chance to prove it!

GRETA: Faust and I—?

SLY: It was a great love, wasn't it?

GRETA: I once thought so.

SLY: Irresistible attraction! Passions flaming beyond all ways of quenching save one.

GRETA: Something I'm happy to forget.

SLY: All great love dies! Turns to ashes! I want to prove it!

GRETA: You can prove it by me! My first incarnation cleansed me of all sentimentality.

SLY: I was talking about love.

GRETA: I am immune.

(FAUST *enters from the right with* BO. *He is out of breath, wet and angry.*)

FAUST: *(To* SLY:*)* So there you are! We've been looking for you! All you had to do was get a piece of paper—!

SLY: I have it... Somewhere... Now let's see—(*He takes an official document from his pocket and waves it in the air.*) Ah, yes. Permission to build.

GRETA: *(To* FAUST:*)* I told you to have faith in—

FAUST: How did you manage it?

SLY: Simple. By knowing which palms to cross with silver.

FAUST: You bribed someone?

SLY: Several someones.

FAUST: Was that necessary?

SLY: Only if you want to move ahead.

FAUST: I didn't think you'd have to resort to bribery.

SLY: For a man your age, your innocence astounds me.

FAUST: But to begin to build my city based on—

SLY: Do you want to move forward or do you not?

FAUST: *(Retreating, disturbed)* I do... I do...

BO: *(Comforting him)* It's the way things are done. Why fuss about it?

FAUST: *(Gives* BO *a look. Then, to* SLY:*)* Look here. I don't want you to use illegal methods ever again! This city is to be my legacy and everything about its creation must be clean and above board! *(To* GRETA:*)* Don't you agree?

GRETA: I agree. But knowing our facilitator's character, I'm not sure that's the way things will happen.

FAUST: You're in his pocket!

GRETA: No. But I know the workings of his mind. And I know the only way to get along with him is to accept him, flaws and all.

SLY: Thank you.

GRETA: *(To* FAUST:*)* Look at it this way—now that we have official permission, there's nothing to stop us from beginning construction.

SLY: There is one thing.

FAUST: What is it?

SLY: The Fisherman and his family. They refuse to move.

FAUST: Didn't you offer them enough silver?

SLY: I didn't offer them silver.

FAUST: Enough gold, then.

SLY: Gold didn't work either. ... I offered them Heaven!

FAUST: Heaven!

SLY: Eternal salvation. I choked on the words, but that's what I proposed.

FAUST: And they wouldn't take it?

SLY: They said they believe they can get there on their own.

FAUST: Directly from their private Eden at the edge of the sea. Obstinate peasants!

GRETA: We can change the plan, Faust. Leave them there and build around them.

FAUST: No! That's the best location—the entrance to the harbor. My tower has to go there! Why should this insignificant Fisherman and his family have their way? I want my city to be perfect! We can't start out with compromise! *(To* BO:*)* Go down. Bring them here to me. I'm positive I can talk them into moving. They're simple folk, I'm sure. I won't try bribery. I'll appeal to their better natures.

(BO *exits.*)

SLY: I wish you luck, Faust. Let's see if, in this battle, you have more power than I.

(Blackout)

SCENE SEVEN—MOUNTAIN TOP

(*Coming from the left,* BO *arrives at the mountain top with the* FISHERMAN—*a strong older weathered man who seems like a quiet force of nature.* BO *ushers him into the canvas-protected work area.*)

BO: You want to sit?

FISHERMAN: Why?

BO: The climb—

FISHERMAN: Why should I be bothered by the climb?

BO: Because you're—*(He breaks off, can't end the sentence.)*

FISHERMAN: Because I'm old, you think. You young 'uns see grey hair and think the rest of us must be withering. That climb was nothing. Try fighting to land a giant fish in a gale!

BO: There's no chairs anyway. Just rocks.

FISHERMAN: Rocks make fine chairs. No one needs better. ... Where's him I came to see?

BO: He'll be here in a minute.

(From outside the work area, FAUST *approaches from the right with* GRETA *and* SLY. *He gestures them to stay outside the canvas, instructing them to overhear. He goes in, making a gesture of dismissal to* BO, *who leaves and, uninvited, stays outside to overhear at the opposite side from* GRETA *and* SLY.*)*

FAUST: I apologize for asking you to meet me on this mountain top.

FISHERMAN: I like it here. It brings back memories. In my youth, before my wife and I were wed, we used to climb up to this very spot—and gaze out, picturing our future.

FAUST: And has your life become what you envisioned?

FISHERMAN: Oh, yes. It's even better... It was from this very place that we chose the bit of land on which we live today.

FAUST: You are attached to it.

FISHERMAN: As if it were my very own limb.

FAUST: And yet you know I've asked you here to see if we can entice you to sell us your little plot so we can complete the new city's master plan.

FISHERMAN: I do know.

FAUST: I wanted you to come up here so I could show the plan to you. *(He gestures toward the drawings on the table.)*

FISHERMAN: I see it.

FAUST: You see the streets, the green spaces, the buildings—

FISHERMAN: Yes. I see them.

FAUST: You see that, instead of all that marshland, is going to rise something memorable and superb.

FISHERMAN: Yes. I know.

FAUST: And you understand—right where you and your wife and sons have your little shack—is the very spot on which we plan to build the glory of the city—this tower.

FISHERMAN: It is a handsome tower.

FAUST: A beacon to be seen for miles around—from land and from sea.

FISHERMAN: A most impressive thing.

FAUST: So you'll sell us your land.

FISHERMAN: No.

FAUST: Money's no object.

FISHERMAN: It's no object to me either. My land is not for sale at any price.

FAUST: We'll give you any other land you want. Twice the acreage you have now. Three times. Four times.

FISHERMAN: Sorry.

FAUST: We'll build you a palace ten times the splendor of your shack—

(FAUST *sees the* FISHERMAN *looking at him.*)

FAUST:—or, if you prefer, we'll move every precious timber of your present residence and reconstruct it perfectly.

FISHERMAN: No, no.

FAUST: What do you want?!

FISHERMAN: To stay where we are.

FAUST: But, Old Man—

FISHERMAN: You wonder why I refuse.

FAUST: I do.

FISHERMAN: You wonder why I—one insignificant being—and his family—why can't we little folk cooperate, let ourselves be uprooted and transplanted to some new place, to what seems to you some better place—for the greater good.

FAUST: I couldn't have put the matter better myself.

FISHERMAN: It's not because my sons and I reclaimed our plot of land from the sea and made it yield after years of overwhelmingly hard labor. It's not even because I know the waters around that spot so well and have such an affinity for its creatures that they now swim into my nets with a sense of joy—as if they were volunteering to help us survive. It's because—after this long in this spot—we're part of it. We don't own the land and sea—we *are* it. We can't sell it to you—we can't move from there—because it is us. ...In the many years in which we cultivated the land and farmed the sea from that spot, we made a pact with Nature. We have that space in trust—to inhabit and to care for as long as we and our sons and daughters and their sons and daughters and their sons and daughters exist. To let it go would be to betray a sacred trust, an oath we made to earth and sea and sky—to preserve and cherish them. I will be glad to see you build your tower—just not here—not on this sacred spot.

FAUST: I see that nothing I can say, nothing I can give, can sway you.

FISHERMAN: You are a wise man, Dr. Faust. You know when to give up on a fish which refuses to be reeled in.

FAUST: I do.

FISHERMAN: Then I wish you good day. I hope having your city at last makes you happy. *(He goes.)*

FAUST: *(To no one:)* What does he mean by that? What makes him feel that I'm not happy?!

(FAUST *frowns, shakes it off, then gestures* GRETA *and* SLY *to come into the work area.)*

FAUST: You heard?

SLY: Yes.

FAUST: The man's impossible!

SLY: He's even more of an idealist than you are.

FAUST: He's a mule! A selfish beast!

GRETA: I said it before and I say it again: We can relocate the tower.

FAUST: No! ...My fine new city with their abominable wooden shack right at the entrance to the harbor? That ramshackle hut the symbol of the city? Absolutely not! ...Do you realize, if we let them keep that hovel—when the tale of Faustiana is told—the focus of the world's attention will be, not on our splendid city, but on that little hut! The symbol of one peasant's defiance! And all the rest—all you and I and we have done—will be ignored, or will stand to mock us!

SLY: You give up too easily.

FAUST: You gave up before.

SLY: I'll try again.

FAUST: You think there's something you can do?

SLY: There's always something.

FAUST: Well, then, go do it! Promise them anything! But get them out!

SLY: I'll try. *(He goes.)*

FAUST: It's incredible how one stubborn mule can ruin an entire project.

GRETA: He's not the only one who's stubborn.

FAUST: You think I should bend?

GRETA: I think there's always compromise.

FAUST: I am not compromising with my city!

GRETA: Ah... so now it's "your" city. It's my city, too. And if I would be willing to compromise, so should you!

(GRETA *returns to her table to work on the drawings. Needing air to cure his frustration,* FAUST *leaves the work area and goes outside.* BO *says to him:*)

BO: You were rough on the Fisherman.

FAUST: I don't need a lecture on manners from you, you're as much of a peasant as he is!

BO: You didn't recognize him?

FAUST: Why should I?

BO: He and his wife were very good to you, you know. Back then.

FAUST: Back when?

BO: When you had all that trouble. When they died. The girl and the baby. When you collapsed and nearly went out of your mind. I was afraid you were going to kill yourself.

FAUST: I nearly did.

BO: I didn't know what to do. I heard about this couple who could heal people I got you to their hut, only half alive. They took you in. You stayed with them for months. The Fisherman and his wife nursed you.

FAUST: They were the ones! I didn't recognize him.

BO: I thought you didn't.

FAUST: Is his wife still alive?

BO : She is. I'd have brought her along but she couldn't have made it up the mountain.

FAUST: I didn't know it was there—to that place—that I'd been taken to recover. I was in such a fever of despair I didn't know where I was.

BO: It was there.

FAUST: That must be why I so much want my tower to be there. It's a magical place. I must have felt it.

BO: Yes. Magical. A very special place. And, as you saw, very special people...

(*A beat. Then—something occurs to* FAUST. *Suddenly he runs toward where* SLY *exited and shouts down the mountain:*)

FAUST: Sly! Don't hurt them! Do you hear me? Get them out! But—whatever you do—don't hurt them! ...Sly, can you hear me? (*No answer*) ...SLY—!

(*Blackout*)

END ACT ONE

ACT TWO

Scene One — Mountain Top

(At rise:)

(Several months later. In the mountain top field office, things have changed. In addition to drawings and models there are now samples of materials—brick, marble, etc. FAUST *is far upstage left standing on a rock and looking down on the city through binoculars.* BO *enters from down left laden with very heavy sacks and bundles of more materials. Exhausted, he puts them down and, out of Faust's earshot, says to us:)*

BO: I'm not a servant any more, I'm a pack horse! *(He shows some of the contents of the sacks.)* Samples of marble. Samples of brick. Samples of tile... You'd think they were going to build the city at the top of the mountain! But no. He wants me to lug these up here so he can look at them, hold them up while he stands on the mountain top, imagines how they'll look down there, chooses what he likes—which won't be what *she* likes—and then the words fly! It's a wonder they haven't come to blows!... *(He starts going through the sacks.)* Where's my ham sandwich—

(FAUST comes down to him and says:)

FAUST: At last! Real progress!

BO: Progress.

FAUST: It's a wondrous time!

BO: If you say so.

FAUST: Once Sly managed to convince the Fisherman and his family to relocate, everything began to move!

BO : It certainly did.

FAUST: It's miraculous! It's beginning to be real! One can start to see, not just in the mind's eye, but in reality, how everything will look when it is finished. Come see, Bo.

BO: I've seen.

FAUST: They've driven pilings for the major structures. The framings have begun to rise! You can actually begin to see what the buildings are going to look like!

BO: Unless they look like a ham sandwich, I'm not interested.

FAUST: You've walked around in it. Tell me what you've felt—

BO: It's a mess! I've slogged through mud and tripped over tons of brick and wood and nails. I've stepped in wet concrete up to my ankles.

FAUST: The primordial ooze out of which a great civilization will rise! Describe exactly what it's like to walk through—

BO: Wish you could walk through it yourself—

FAUST: I don't mind. As I've said before, it's like life, Bo. One has to stay at a certain remove to retain perspective.

BO: *(Suddenly finding it)* My sandwich! *(Bites in ravenously then feels guilty)* Want some?

FAUST: *(Shakes his head)* No. It must be marvelous to be someone who can satisfy his appetites so easily! All you need is a little ham, a little beer, a little strudel—

(Suddenly GRETA enters from the city, furious.)

GRETA: He's ruined it!

FAUST: I beg your pardon?

GRETA: Sly. He's ruined it!

FAUST: What has he done?

GRETA: He moved the road!

FAUST: What road?

GRETA: The main road! The road I planned so carefully! The road which is the main street of the city. The road whose every curve and angle is intricately designed to make this city work! How could he do it?!

(SLY suddenly appears.)

SLY: It's better that way.

GRETA: *(Wordlessly crying out in frustration:)* Ahhhh!

SLY: *(To FAUST:)* It occurred to me that, although your tower is visible from the sea, from the land we haven't taken advantage of its beauty. I simply told the builders to add a long reflecting pool—to catch the tower's reflection and enhance everyone's appreciation of it.

GRETA: You've cut off the major circulation routes of the city! You've choked the heart out of the center! Now nothing works!

SLY: Nonsense. It's just a small change.

GRETA: You've displaced not just everything around it—but everything farther out and farther out—in concentric rings. Look—(*She shows them on the plan:*) If you put a pool here, this building has to be moved to here, and this to here, and this to here and the circulation I worked so hard to achieve so everything will work together is ruined!

FAUST: I like it.

GRETA: What—?

SLY: I knew you would. It reinforces the iconic effect of your major image.

FAUST: It's perfect.

GRETA: It's totally destructive of the master plan!

FAUST: You have to learn to compromise.

GRETA: I don't notice *you* compromising. When the Fisherman wanted to stay in his place, you insisted—

FAUST: (*To* SLY:) And you persuaded them to go—

SLY: I did.

FAUST: So, on that, I didn't have to compromise.

GRETA: You both approved what I drew. Every structure, every road, every path, every tree is planned to work with every other element! Change on a whim and you destroy the perfection you both are so intent on having!

FAUST: It's just one small change! There's no reason why you can't—

GRETA: If either of you dares to give commands for changes at the site one more time without my consent—I will resign!

(GRETA *goes to her corner and starts angrily working revising the plans.* FAUST, *feeling comfortable with* SLY, *says to him:*)

FAUST: A reflecting pool. That was an inspiration! To see my tower not only as it is, but reflected, day and night. It will reinforce the symbol of the city, make it indelible.

SLY: I knew you'd like it.

FAUST: (*Aside, beyond* GRETA's *hearing*) She's so protective of her design! Unable to accept the smallest adjustment. I can't believe this little change would "ruin everything". One has to adapt.

SLY: You are so right.

FAUST: The Fisherman and his family adapted.

SLY: They did.

FAUST: You never told me how you got them to move.

(SLY *puts a finger to his lips. His secret.*)

FAUST: I suppose even they had their price.

SLY: Doesn't everybody?

FAUST: I'd like to thank them. Invite them to my house for dinner.

SLY: Not necessary.

FAUST: I'll get Bo to take a message. Where have they moved to?

(*From the corner where he is just finishing his sandwich,* BO *murmurs:*)

BO : I suggest you not ask. (BO *hastens to exit stage right.*)

FAUST: (*To* SLY:) Where are they!

SLY: In a place where they can't be reached.

FAUST: ...You had them killed—?!

SLY: Let's say—your perfect city could only be achieved by their elimination.

FAUST: You had them slaughtered!

SLY: They were removed. Why the fuss?

FAUST: It never occurred to me that—

SLY: Come now, Faust. You're not an innocent. You're aware of how little in your world can be achieved merely by diplomacy and reason.

FAUST: I never thought—

SLY: Stop whining! You're going to have your tower exactly where you want it.

FAUST: I didn't want it at such a cost!

SLY: Why, Doctor—surely you know that, for your dearest dreams, you must dearly pay.

(SLY *swiftly exits.* FAUST *turns to* GRETA *and asks:*)

FAUST: Did you know?

GRETA: I didn't know—but, knowing him, I suspected.

FAUST: And you don't care—?!

GRETA: I know him. And I know whatever he does can't be undone. ...Did they mean that much to you?

FAUST: As if they were my own flesh and blood. I was brought to them—half dead—after the tragedy.

GRETA: What tragedy?

FAUST: Why—the death of Marguerite.

GRETA: Marguerite...

FAUST: And the baby.

GRETA: The baby...

FAUST: *He* was my future. Not this—*(He gestures toward the city.)* Not concrete and stone. My flesh and blood son.

GRETA: And you mourn him?

FAUST: Wouldn't you? *(He looks at her intently. Who is she?)*

GRETA: *(Suppressing her immense emotions)* ...I am an architect. I build buildings. Not children.

FAUST: I mourn him. I still mourn them both. I loved her.

GRETA: So they tell me.

FAUST: When she and the baby died, I fell into a despond so deep I nearly died myself. ...I went mad. Tried to kill myself—but our "friend" had made that impossible. I was fated to suffer on earth—as humans suffer. I destroyed everything I could lay my hands on, including what I could reach of my wretched flesh. When I was naked and bleeding, I mercifully lost consciousness. When I woke up I was in the Fisherman's hut and his wife was tending to my wounds. She's the reason I'm still here. I owe them my life! And now—

GRETA: Now?

FAUST: They're dead! That isn't what I wanted! I didn't realize my desire to build this city would have such consequences! ... Sly paid bribes to get the permit to build where we wanted. Once I got used to the idea I thought—"That's all right. It's expected." ... But to kill! To spill the blood of the Fisherman, his wife, their three sons—

GRETA: And no doubt the son's wives and their children—

FAUST: Yes, yes. I didn't think of that. There'd be wives and children. I was thinking of the sons as the little tykes who played around my bed while I was living with them.

GRETA: Little tykes grow, Faust. That is, if they're not snuffed out before they really have existence...

FAUST: Dear God! Is there no way to achieve what we want on this earth without compromise and murder? Is there no clean path—?

GRETA: Not with this Facilitator.

FAUST: "Facilitator"! All he's facilitating is my soul's entrance into Hell!

GRETA: He's making Faustiana possible.

FAUST: At such a price!

GRETA: Don't be naive. You knew you'd have to pay.

FAUST: I didn't know I'd have so much blood on my hands! Marguerite's, my son's, now the Fisherman and his family. I wanted to give the people this city to atone—. If only I could bring them back. *(In memory)* ...Marguerite! Marguerite! *(Directly to* GRETA, *a pleading question—)* Marguerite—?

GRETA: *(Turning away and parrying his query)* What's one more added to the pile of bodies, Doctor Faustus? Marguerite's death weighs no more than the death of one of the Fisherman's youngest sons.

FAUST: *(Directly to her)* She was—she still is—everything.

GRETA: Don't say that. She wouldn't want you to say that...

FAUST: But how am I going to make amends for all these crimes?

GRETA: I don't know. ...All I know is what I must do. To compensate for what our friend has changed—and what you approved of—I must get to work. *(She goes back to her work table.)*

(Blackout)

SCENE TWO—FAUST'S STUDY

*(*FAUST *is sitting, listless, in a chair, doing nothing, looking at nothing. A tray of food sits, untouched, beside him.* BO *enters, sees the untouched tray and says:)*

BO: You have to eat!

FAUST: Why?

BO: People need food.

FAUST: Why?

BO: To live!

FAUST: But what if you don't care whether you live or not?

BO: Somebody else might care.

FAUST: Who, for instance.

BO: Me, for instance.

FAUST: I appreciate your loyalty.

BO: Just tell me what I can do for you—

FAUST: Do you know, in ancient Egypt, servants were entombed with their dead masters. You can accompany me to the afterlife.

BO: I don't think I'd like that.

FAUST: Why?

BO: They don't have strudel there.

FAUST: I wish I had your hungers. Something which can be satisfied with strudel.

BO: How about an apple? A pomegranate? I'll go out and get—

FAUST: You can't save a soul with fruit.

BO : Then save your stomach!

FAUST: I don't care about my stomach! Don't you understand? I don't care about my life!

BO: What's wrong with you? You're smart. At least you used to be. These past years, no matter what befell, you could always think of something to make it better.

FAUST: Not this time.

BO: But, Master—

FAUST: Let me be, I tell you!.

BO: There was a time, when you were low, when you'd raise your spirits by doing your magic.

FAUST: My magic...

BO: You haven't gone in for it for longer than I can remember.

FAUST: What could my magic do for me at present?

BO: ...It could bring him back.

FAUST: Who?

BO: The Fisherman. You could bring him to life again!

FAUST: Oh, you're driving me out of my mind! He's dead! They're all dead! Get out of here! Leave me alone and don't let anyone disturb me!

(BO *beats a hasty exit. Alone,* FAUST *slowly rouses himself and begins to think.*)

FAUST: Magic. ...I haven't practiced it in years. ...There was a time... Do I still remember—? (*He closes the curtains and lights a candle. He takes some beakers out of a cupboard and blows the dust off them. He takes some vials out of the back of his desk drawer. He mixes some potions. They froth and send up smoke. He makes magic gestures and recites an incantation:*) Spirits of the other world—hear me. I know I've been neglectful—but that's given you a rest. Bestir yourselves. Remember our fine friendship—and all that, once upon a time, we did together. The visions of the past you let me see. Grant one more request. I beg you. Just this one. Restore to me the Fisherman whom I have wronged so greatly. He wanders where I can no longer reach him. I have apologies to make, things to ask him, things to tell him. In the name of darkness, in the name of light— restore the Fisherman to me.

(There is a puff of smoke. FAUST *stands back—expecting the* FISHERMAN *to appear. But nothing happens.)*

FAUST: I plead with you—!

(Another puff of smoke. Again, nothing appears. FAUST *gives up. Dejected, he sits in his chair, exhausted from his efforts. He murmurs to himself:)*

FAUST: You can't neglect the spirits and then expect them to be there for you when you want them. I deserted them. Why shouldn't they desert me now? ...I'll never again lay eyes upon the Fisherman...

*(*FAUST *closes his eyes. After some moments, the* FISHERMAN *appears from the shadows. He seems to have come from nowhere. Not seeing him,* FAUST *says:)*

FAUST: If I could only see him, I would say—

FISHERMAN: What would you say?

*(*FAUST *is startled.)*

FAUST: You're here!

FISHERMAN: You called. I came.

FAUST: How glad I am to see you!

FISHERMAN: Why have you brought me here?

FAUST: I want to say—I'm sorry. Just that. I'm sorry!

FISHERMAN: I don't know why you apologize.

FAUST: I took so much from you!

FISHERMAN: Nothing of value.

FAUST: Your land—

FISHERMAN: It turned out not to be so precious after all.

FAUST: Your life...

FISHERMAN: Life on earth turned out to be just an interlude.

FAUST: An interlude...

FISHERMAN: Between before and after.

FAUST: Before and after what?

FISHERMAN: Existence.

FAUST: Then there *is* existence after—?

FISHERMAN: It's the time when, at last, we see.

FAUST: What do you see?

FISHERMAN: For one thing, that "I'm sorry" has no meaning. You can't undo the past, so don't expect credit for giving it a try.

FAUST: I live in torture that I cannot make things up to you!

FISHERMAN: I have no wish that you should make things up to me.

FAUST: But—your wife. Your sons. Their wives. Their children—! I destroyed them!

FISHERMAN: As to that, you would have to speak with them yourself. But, for myself, I enjoy understanding—so much more than I did—the wind, the waves, the stars. ... To have reached—Enlightenment.

FAUST: About what are you enlightened?

FISHERMAN: The nature of Nature.

FAUST: And how about the nature of Man?

FISHERMAN: I'm enlightened about that, too.

FAUST: Including this poor example?

FISHERMAN: Yes, Faust.

FAUST: I came to you once when my life was torture. You cured me. I repaid you by taking your land and having you and all your family slaughtered. How can I rid myself of this unquenchable guilt?

FISHERMAN: Simple. Forget it.

FAUST: "Forget it." So easily said.

FISHERMAN: Forgetfulness achieved, your mind is relieved of all its darkness.

FAUST: It isn't! I still have this unbearable feeling of regret.

FISHERMAN: For what?

FAUST: ...For the difference between what might have been—and what is. Are those happier who only want what they can have? When they have it, they must be content. But I am never content—something is always missing.

FISHERMAN: You're about to have your city—

FAUST: It is not sufficient!

FISHERMAN: What more could any human want?

FAUST: What too few people have—I want to be remembered.

FISHERMAN: You lie.

FAUST: I'm telling you the truth!

FISHERMAN: Then you're lying to yourself. ...It's true you want to be remembered—but not as you are, only as you see yourself. Or, since you see your flaws so distinctly, as you wish that others might see you—as society's benefactor, the ultimate compassionate magnanimous man.

FAUST: Is it too much to ask?

FISHERMAN: Who you are, who you seem to be, who you wish you were—all these are not only beyond your power to change, they're an illusion.

FAUST: Then tell me the answer to contentment!

FISHERMAN: Wisdom isn't something you can get from others, it's something you must stumble upon yourself.

FAUST: You can share—!

FISHERMAN: Find your way on your own!

FAUST: I am lost—!

FISHERMAN: Be at peace, Faust—if you can. Though I fear it's beyond your capabilities.

FAUST: Tell me the secret—!

FISHERMAN: Are you sure you want to know?

FAUST: I do!

FISHERMAN: The secret is: ...Nothing matters.

FAUST: Success matters!

FISHERMAN: ...Nothing.

FAUST: Achievement matters!

FISHERMAN: ...Nothing.

FAUST: Forgiveness matters!

FISHERMAN: ...Nothing.

FAUST: Tell me you forgive me!

FISHERMAN: How can I forgive you? I am dead.

(The FISHERMAN *disappears as quickly as he came.* FAUST *calls out:)*

FAUST: Fisherman! Come back! Come back! There's so much more I need to know—! *(Silence)* ...So that's what my life has amounted to. Nothing. ...Vanity. ...Nothing more... *(Then, suddenly)* No! It isn't so! The secret of life is striving! The secret of death is—you don't have to do that any more. But I'm still alive! And while I'm alive I still have something to accomplish. Faustiana! *(Then his mood darkens again.)* ...But none of the creation of it is in my hands. ...Could the reality of it ever equal my ideal? ...I don't dare to look at it until it's completed.

*(*FAUST *retreats into his shell, then suddenly becomes aware of a commotion outside his door.* GRETA *breaks in, followed by* BO:*)*

GRETA: I have to talk to you!

BO: She broke in! I couldn't stop her!

GRETA: There's trouble!

FAUST: What's the problem?

GRETA: It's stopped.

FAUST: What's stopped?

GRETA: Everything. The workmen have laid down their hammers and trowels and are just sitting.

FAUST: They're on strike?

GRETA: If you want to put it that way. Yes.

FAUST: Why? What do they want?

GRETA: Money! Seems they haven't been paid!

FAUST: Since when?

GRETA: For three months.

FAUST: They haven't been paid in three months?!

GRETA: Not one penny.

FAUST: Who is in charge of paying them?

GRETA: Who do you think?

FAUST: Bo! Get Sly!

BO: From where? Where could I find him—?

FAUST: *(Calling out into the air:)* Damn you, Sly! Come here! Immediately! *(Nothing happens. He calls out again:)* I know you hear me. I realize you have other clients, but Greta and I demand your attention! Now! *(Again, no response)* Get here at once—or else!

BO: Or else what—?

FAUST: *(To Bo:)* Ssh—! *(Shouting, threatening)* ...Sly!!! Goddam it! Get your ass in here!

(Slowly, for him, SLY materializes. He is very much changed from his earlier appearances. He is disheveled, his collar unbuttoned, his hair in disarray.)

FAUST: What's happened to you?

SLY: *(In a weak, dispirited voice)* Could someone lend me a comb?

(No one has one. SLY tries to slick his hair back with his fingers.)

FAUST: What's going on?

SLY: *(Weakly)* May I sit?

(On FAUST's gesture BO *brings over a chair.* SLY *sits.)*

FAUST: Is this you or some counterfeit apparition?

SLY: It's me. Or it isn't.

FAUST: You're a mess!

SLY: I know..., I know...

GRETA: What happened?

SLY: ...Something...

GRETA: What?

SLY: *(After a long pause)* ...I walked through the city.

FAUST: You were attacked?

SLY: No.

BO: Something fell on you?

SLY: No.

GRETA: You decided you hate it.

SLY: No. ... That's just it—*(A very long pause, then, tortured:)*—I love it!

GRETA: You love it—?!

SLY: *(Tortured)* It's too beautiful! I can't stand it!

FAUST: Can't stand that it's beautiful?

SLY: That you've created it! The two of you! And it's—wonderful!

FAUST: So—?

SLY: *(A wrenching admission)* I'm—jealous!

GRETA: Of us?

SLY: Of what you've managed to accomplish.

FAUST: But you were arranging for it, financing it—

SLY: I know. But I didn't think it was going to be—this GOOD!

GRETA: *(Smiling)* Oh, my God...

FAUST: But you knew what we were doing from the start. You were facilitating it!

SLY: I knew it—but I didn't *know* it! Now that I see it—really becoming real—it's more than I can take!

GRETA: So you stop it all by refusing to pay the workers?

SLY: *(Pitifully)* That's the only thing I could think of! *(He seems near collapse.)*

BO: Would you like a drink of water?

SLY: *(Weakly)* Whiskey...

FAUST: Whiskey.

(FAUST gestures for BO to get it, which BO does, and hands the glass to SLY who takes a strong draught.)

FAUST: Are you strong enough now to explain—?

SLY: *(Getting up and pacing)* All right—it's envy! I admit it! You two can create, I can't. All I can do is destroy. There was this force unleashed—the relentless growing of the city—the beautiful city—the too beautiful city. Then I realized—I could stop it—without lifting a finger. I could stop it—just by withholding the cash!

GRETA: Sly, that's cruel.

SLY: *(Savoring it)* Yes.

FAUST: You know how much the city means to us.

SLY: *(With perverse pleasure)* I certainly do, I do, I do..

FAUST: *(Becoming furious)* Then why the hell would you—!

GRETA: Wait, Faust—! *(Stopping FAUST with a gesture she takes another tack:)* But Sly, you *are* contributing something.

SLY: What am I contributing?

GRETA: The financing.

SLY: That's not creative.

GRETA: It's indispensable.

SLY: But it's not creative.

GRETA: *(Turning to FAUST, aside:)* Think of something—!

FAUST: *(Thinks, then gets an idea:)* Sly—, you're contributing something else.

SLY: What else?

FAUST: ...The pitchfork in the behind.

SLY: The pitchfork in the behind?

FAUST: That's what keeps us going.

SLY: *(Beginning to perk up)* Is it?

FAUST: Of course it is. In the creation of every work of art there's as much pushing one from behind as pulling one forward, something we're trying to flee from as much as something we're running toward. Do you think what urges us on is only the splendid vision of the grand and glorious Faustiana? That's part of it. But the greater part is—the utter wreckage our lives will have been if we fail.

GRETA: *(To* FAUST:*)* Hold on a minute, I'm not—

FAUST: *(To her, aside:)* Quiet! *(He turns to* SLY:*)* What if we'd been alive and our lives added up to nothing? What if we'd been on this earth and left no mark? We were given life and wallowed doing nothing till you jabbed us with your threat of hell and forced us to keep moving—racing to escape your triple prongs of poverty, obscurity, the horror of failing while, around us, others are surging forward! You're our motivating force, our goad, our fuel. Without the threat of being stabbed in the rear by you we couldn't create at all!

SLY: Truly?

FAUST: You're indispensable! It's your threatening us with the purgatory of a wasted life that forces us to keep going. By powering our motor, you're superior in creativity to us all!

SLY : *(Hopefully)* Am I?

FAUST: Never doubt it.

SLY: Then—everything in the ideal city is inspired by me!

FAUST: Without the terror of being jabbed in the backside by you—none of our best thoughts would exist!

SLY: *(Almost his old self at last)* Thank you, Faust. It's good to be appreciated.

GRETA: Then you'll go and pay the workers?

SLY: Immediately. After all, after it's completed, how many more opportunities to be creative I'll have in store! *(He makes a few "pitchfork in the behind" gestures, then slicks back his hair, buttons his shirt, and, once more his old self, swiftly exits.)*

GRETA: You see? I told you it was good. Come and see it.

FAUST: No.

GRETA: Why not?

FAUST: I prefer to appreciate it in my mind's eye.

GRETA: You think it won't come up to your expectations.

FAUST: I didn't say that.

GRETA: You can't bear to see what can be achieved by a mere woman—by me.

FAUST: That's not it—

GRETA: If it's bad, you'll be depressed. If it's good you'll be even more depressed.

FAUST: Think what you like. I'm not going to enter it—ever!

GRETA: Stay here and rot, then! You are the most infuriating man I've ever met! *(She slams out.)*

BO: I'm glad *she* said it.

(Blackout)

SCENE THREE — MOUNTAIN TOP

(Months later. The protective canvas and all signs of the field office are gone. GRETA *is alone on the mountain top looking down on the city. She says to us:)*

GRETA: It's finished! At last! Finished! It's almost frightening — to conceive of something — and then see it achieved. And achieved well, I think. If I achieve nothing more than this, I will have achieved all I could ever want in this incarnation. ... I don't care what Faust says! I was not creating this city because I was being jabbed in the backside by Sly's pitchfork! And I don't think Faust was either. ... All these months together and I hardly seem to know him! How they change — men. How crusty, stiff and cold they get when age begins to rust them. He has none of the passions he once had — for me or for his namesake city. He is definitely not the same man who, so long ago, I loved.

*(*SLY *enters, his old self again.)*

SLY: I must say — it's a wonder to behold! I congratulate myself for pitchforking you into it.

GRETA: It is — as close as I could make it — exactly what I planned. It lacks only one thing —

SLY: It lacks nothing!

GRETA: It lacks people.

SLY: Ah, yes. A small detail. People.

GRETA: Now we can invite them in. And then the city will live.

SLY: Is there nothing else you want?

GRETA: Nothing.

SLY: You have no nagging dissatisfaction?

GRETA: No.

SLY: It doesn't bother you that Faust won't come up here to see it?

GRETA: Why should I care?

SLY: I thought his ignoring your great achievement might bother you.

GRETA: I am beyond anything he might do or not do bothering me.

SLY: Then you have no lingering affection for him?

GRETA: Quite the opposite!

SLY: A remnant of the old flame doesn't flare up now and then?

GRETA: Not even a spark.

SLY: Excellent! My point is proven!

GRETA: What point?

SLY: That what you people call "eternal love" does not survive!

GRETA: Not in me, at any rate.

SLY: Superb! My experiment has succeeded!

GRETA: I will be perfectly happy if I never see him again.

SLY: Too bad—because here he is!

(FAUST, *in an impenetrable mood, enters from the right, accompanied by* BO.)

GRETA: So the great "I am" has condescended to pay us a visit.

FAUST: I decided it was time to view it all myself. See what I think.

GRETA: Who cares what you think?

SLY: *(To* GRETA:*)* Come, now. You know accomplishments have no meaning unless the right eyes see them.

GRETA: I see none of those present.

BO: *(Aside to* FAUST:*)* Why do you let her insult you? Let's go back!

FAUST: *(To* BO:*)* Did you bring the glasses?

BO: Yes.

(BO *hands* FAUST *binoculars.*)

GRETA: Oh, for heaven's sake! You don't need glasses! Look! It's there! You can't miss it!

(FAUST *looks at the completed city. He is silent for a long time.*)

GRETA: Well...?

SLY: Well...?

FAUST: Well...

BO: Well, what???

FAUST: I thought my opinion didn't matter...

(*From each of the others, an impatient breath. He continues:*)

FAUST: ...As you well know—nothing in life lives up to one's expectations—

GRETA: I thought so! Why did you come up here! Go back down! I refuse to subject my work to your snobbish, pretentious, supercilious hyper-ventilations!

FAUST: As I said—nothing in life lives up to one's expectations—except for this.

This city surpasses my every dream. It is more than I ever thought it could be. It is a wonder.

GRETA: Stop teasing.

FAUST: I'm not teasing. It's a miracle. ...Tell me—is it real?

SLY: It's real.

GRETA: There—at the edge of the sea—is your tower.

FAUST: My tower...

GRETA: Soon it will be evening—and you'll see it. Illuminated. You will see how it lights the city and the ocean.

SLY: You'll see how it lights the reflecting pool.

GRETA: Even that compromise no longer disturbs.

FAUST: I must say—seeing the city whole is overwhelming. (*He keeps looking at it, looking away, then looking back, amazed.*) And on the seventh day He looked at it—and saw that it was good.

SLY: Ah, when people start quoting a certain book, it's time for me to busy myself elsewhere. I think I'll go down into the old town and round up some prospective inhabitants for the new one. They can start moving in tomorrow.

(SLY *exits right.* FAUST *says to* BO:)

FAUST: Follow him.

BO: Must I?

FAUST: He doesn't have to see you. Follow him! And let me know who he invites.

(BO *exits.* FAUST *and* GRETA *are alone. For some moments, there is awkward silence. Then:*)

FAUST: I wonder what the population will be—if they all come at *his* invitation.

GRETA: Whether it's he who invites them or others, I'm afraid, once they come live here, he'll make his presence known in the town.

FAUST: I'm sure he will.

GRETA: So—before the human element arrives—and our friend begins his work—come walk with me in the city.

FAUST: No. Sorry.

GRETA: I asked you many times before. I ask you again. Come down.

FAUST: ...No.

GRETA: (*With growing fury*) Reality is too much for you, is that it? You can only appreciate your ideal from afar!

FAUST: That's not it—

GRETA: You see yourself as a utopian visionary! I see you as an arrogant condescending bore!

FAUST: Many thanks.

GRETA: I thought, once it was built, you couldn't wait to touch its stones as I do!

FAUST: I beg you—

GRETA: I thought it was something you and I would give the world together. Our child.

FAUST: Our child—

GRETA: But I see all you cared about was your idea, not my execution of it.

FAUST: Not true!

GRETA: If you cared about the town you would walk its streets!

FAUST: *(At last, bursting out)* It is not allowed!

GRETA: My God! So that's your agreement with Sly! You may see Faustiana from a distance—you may never enter.

FAUST: Exactly.

GRETA: I should have guessed.

FAUST: I can view the city from afar—but I can never walk its streets.

GRETA: If you do, you will die.

FAUST: Brave as one likes to suppose one is, when it comes to the point, one is never ready for voluntary dying.

GRETA: I understand that.

FAUST: So, here I am—

GRETA: —viewing the promised land from a distance.

FAUST: I admire your work more than you can imagine. Seeing what you've achieved, I begin to feel the stirrings of an emotion I only half remember. I hesitate to call it love, because love comes so rarely—

GRETA: So rarely...

FAUST: I've only truly loved once in my life—and the girl I loved, I ruined.

GRETA: *(Quietly, after a moment)* ...No. Not ruined. Saved.

FAUST: Saved?

GRETA: *(After a pause)* ...So we could create—our child. *(She gestures toward the city.)*

FAUST: *(Looking at her intently)* Marguerite—?

GRETA: ...Yes.

FAUST: But why didn't you say—?

GRETA: He and I—we, too, have our bargain.

FAUST: Which is—?

GRETA: That I never reveal to you who I am.

FAUST: If you did, what would he gain?

GRETA: Why, the only thing I have to give—my soul. In fact, my life.

FAUST: You mean:—Now that you've told—you'll be damned like me?

GRETA: Yes! And gladly!

FAUST: Marguerite! *(Then, suddenly, impulsively)* Let's go for a stroll in Faustiana!

GRETA: But if we do—

FAUST: We'll both be whisked off instantly to Hell.

GRETA: I'm afraid that is our fate.

FAUST: And a magnificent fate it is!

GRETA: He wouldn't dare imprison us in two separate circles!

FAUST: He might. You're purer than I, so you'll burn at a lesser heat. Except for confessing to me who you are you've never sinned.

GRETA: But I have! I'm a greater sinner than you!

FAUST: Not possible!

GRETA: I am! And my greatest sin is this: I loved you—heart, soul and body—when I was a virgin.

FAUST: You loved me—

GRETA: As much as you wanted me—I wanted you.

FAUST: What are you saying?

GRETA: I'm saying—back then—you didn't seduce me, I seduced you.

FAUST: Oh, my love—!

GRETA: You had a vision of the ideal which drew me to you—irresistibly.

FAUST: But the ideal was you—and now, what you've achieved in this city which you planned.

GRETA: *We* planned. That's what we always shared—the belief that there was something perfect out there which was worth a lifetime's seeking—even if we could never reach it.

FAUST: *(To her:)* I've reached it—with you. Marguerite...

GRETA: And I with you. ...Dear Faust. ...I loved you then. I love you now. ...But now it's too late—!

FAUST: Oh, no! For us—not ever!

(FAUST *comes to* GRETA *and they embrace passionately. Climbing up the mountain from the old city,* SLY *appears, dragging* BO, *berating him as they approach:*)

SLY: You were spying on me! How dare you—?

BO: No, no! I thought you might need help going down the mountain, I—

SLY: Liar! One thing I always know is when people lie! I am going to inform your master—

(SLY *suddenly sees* GRETA *and* FAUST—*embracing.*)

SLY: What's this? What's going on here?

GRETA: Exactly what you see! We love each other!

SLY: No, no! That can't be! Love doesn't last!

FAUST: It does. Marguerite and I still love each other.

SLY: *(To* GRETA:*)* You told him who you are?!

GRETA: Yes! And you can have me, soul and body, forever!

FAUST: You can have me, too!

SLY: This is too much!

FAUST: You told me—for you to possess my soul—all I needed to say was "I have all I wish! I'm satisfied." I say it! I am satisfied! Take me!

GRETA: All I needed to say was "I'm Marguerite". I've said it. Take me as well!

SLY: You two are fools! You are both beyond disgusting!

GRETA: We'll be together, he and I, in your dark realm!

(GRETA *reaches out.* FAUST *takes her hand.*)

FAUST: Marguerite and I will take, together, whatever you have planned!

BO: This is Marguerite? The one who caused you so much trouble—?

FAUST: It is. And we're in love again.

(BO *claps his hands to his head, confused and speechless.*)

SLY: This is revolting! I can't have this in my domain! ... Get away from me! Get out, get going, both of you!

FAUST: But we—

SLY: "We"—the world's worst pronoun! "I"—that's the word which is supreme over all!

GRETA: I love—

FAUST: We love—

BO: *(Disgusted)* They love!

SLY: Enough! ... Go down! Have your city! Live there! Breathe there! You deserve your horrendous fate—daily life as ordinary citizens! It's worse than anything I can offer! Watch as it all decays around you! Watch as garbage piles up in the streets, as the pristine walls are slathered with graffiti, the handsome terraces are festooned with laundry, the sidewalks are caked with gum, the flowers are trampled, the highways are clogged with traffic, the dust falls, the fog descends, the stench rises—

GRETA: Who cares! Come, Faust! You do want to see it close up, don't you?

FAUST: Hand-in-hand with you beside me? You know I do. Come, my love—

(They start to go, but pause as SLY stops them with:)

SLY: —the sweetness cloys, the noose tightens, the blood boils, the eyes wander, the screams bellow, the claws sharpen, the mirror cracks, the great dream shatters—

FAUST: Our dream? Never!

GRETA: Never!

FAUST: *(To GRETA:)* On to Faustiana! ... Oh, I do like that name, don't you?!

(With a wry smile, GRETA says, teasing:)

GRETA: It's acceptable.

(FAUST laughs, grabs her hand, and, together, they exit toward the city. Looking after them, SLY says:)

SLY: I give that union three weeks.

BO: Who knows? All I know is: If she's with him, I quit! I don't want to be the servant of two masters!

SLY: Come work for me, Bo. I promise you you'll have whatever your heart desires.

BO: I'm not sure—

SLY: Come on! ... Come visit the new town with me! People will be streaming in tomorrow. You can help me do all the things I want to do there!

BO : *(A pause, then:)* ...Will there be strudel?

SLY: Absolutely!

BO: Mister Sly, I'm your man!

(SLY *exits toward the city. Just as* BO *is about to follow, he turns to us and says:*)

BO: Don't worry. It's only temporary. Till the master and his mistress separate. They will, don't you think? ...Or do you????

(BO *shrugs, puzzling this mystery. As he turns to exit toward the city—*)

(*Blackout*)

END OF PLAY

ARABIC TWO

CHARACTERS & SETTING

PETER
POLLY

Time: The Present

Setting: A wintergarden in a private, somewhat upscale, home. There are lots of trees and glass and, in this particular wintergarden, which is being used as a living space, there are a sofa, some chairs, a table with a telephone on it and an artist's easel.

ACT ONE

(At rise:)

(Midday. Bright sunlight)

(Although there is nothing specific to indicate it, the wintergarden looks like a wedding bower.)

(PETER and POLLY stand downstage center, hand in hand, looking radiant. PETER is about thirty-five, well-bred, attractive. POLLY is about thirty, looks younger. She is lithe, agile, an "original".)

(They smile at us for a moment, then gesture a welcome expansively. POLLY says, all buoyant and happy:)

POLLY: Ladies and gentlemen, welcome to a divorce!

PETER: *(As elated as she)* Glad you could come!

POLLY: Delighted to see you! Peter and I have wanted to get everybody together for a long time.

PETER: We haven't all been together since—well, since our wedding.

POLLY: And since you were all there then, at the beginning, we thought—wouldn't it be wonderful to have you back again—for the end.

PETER: It was Polly's idea.

POLLY: I'm Polly.

PETER: They know that!

POLLY: With your relatives, you can't be sure. *(To the guests:)* The reason I thought of this was—there are so few great events in one's life—birth, marriage, death—that's all there is, really. For the first you're too young to celebrate, for the last, you're too old, and at a marriage you don't know what you're getting into. But at a divorce, you know what you're getting out of—so everyone should get together and rejoice! Rejoice!

PETER: Bang the cymbals!

POLLY: Strike up the music!

PETER: They look a little shocked.

POLLY: *(To the guests:)* You do look a little shocked. You'd better explain, Peter.

PETER: It's very simple. As soon as you hear that some friends are getting divorced, what's the first thing you want to know? Why.

POLLY: So you invite over the spouse with the loosest tongue—and try to get that spouse to open up to you.

PETER: Sometimes you invite both spice—on different evenings.

POLLY: That's very sneaky. Afterwards, you compare their stories.

PETER: We wouldn't want you doing that with us.

POLLY: We'd rather have you all here and tell you right out why we're splitting up.

PETER: It's a very simple reason.

POLLY: *(Very pleasantly)* We hate each other's guts!

PETER: That isn't so!

POLLY: I know. But it sounds delicious.

PETER: We swore to tell the truth, to answer everything you ask us.

POLLY: I'll tell you all. The deep, dark everything. *(Confidentially)* Living with him is utter torture.

PETER: *(Pleasantly)* Living with her is absolute hell.

POLLY: *(Having as much fun as he is)* He's impossible.

PETER: She's ridiculous.

POLLY: He's so perfect, he doesn't even file his fingernails. They don't grow.

PETER: She's air! She's fluff! Just whimsy, whimsy, whimsy!

POLLY: He's solid as a battleship. Total lead. ...What's that, Cousin Jane? How come we got together in the first place? Surely you remember. We were the perfect couple!

PETER: Tell them how we got together.

POLLY: You mean, how I proposed to you?

PETER: You didn't!

POLLY: I did!

PETER: Your memory's going!

POLLY: Your saying "Don't mind if we do" is not what I call proposing!

PETER: I was indulging in understatement.

POLLY: That kind of understatement could put an end to the human race.

PETER: I don't think I'm so darned backward. Tell them about the night we met.

POLLY: No, Peter.

PETER: We said we'd tell all—

POLLY: But it's too soon. ...Have you ever told anyone before?

PETER: No.

POLLY: Neither have I. It was the moment that began our marriage.

PETER: We married three months later. They all were present.

POLLY: We married the night we met. We were alone.

PETER: I talk of legally—

POLLY: I talk of really—

PETER: Legally and really are the exact same moment.

POLLY: They aren't!

PETER: They are! Take a vote! Ask the guests—

POLLY: Don't be silly. I'm sure it's just like our wedding. There are more here from your side than from my side.

PETER: The only reason I had more guests was that I had more family.

POLLY: That's all you ever had was family.

PETER: Funny. You used to say that all I had was looks.

POLLY: I lied.

PETER: Wretch!

POLLY: Show-off!

PETER: Crumb!

POLLY: Miser!

PETER: Spendthrift!

POLLY: If ever again I marry a man in the money business—

PETER: For the last time, I am not in the money business! I give advice!

POLLY: *(To the guests:)* He's in the advice business. He inherited his father's advice business. Why, some of the advice he gives is over fifty years old!

PETER: It's incomprehensible to her that anything could be fifty years old. She has no age at all. She's reborn every minute!

POLLY: You kill me ever minute, but I refuse to die! If I did, you'd be a widower and wouldn't have to go through this horrendous separation ceremony.

PETER: It's not horrendous.

POLLY: You think it won't hurt, but it will. If we had a Roman marriage, it would be easy.

PETER: What are you talking about?

POLLY: Marriage is two becoming one, isn't it?

PETER: Yes.

POLLY: So? The Roman number two is two one's. Poof, they're together, poof, they're apart. It's simple.

PETER: Right!

POLLY: But we have an Arabic marriage.

PETER: Oh, God—!

POLLY: And the Arabic number two is just one number! You have a hell of a time separating that into two pieces! Look, I'll show you— *(She takes PETER's hand and, holding it, tries to pull away from him.)* Now pull! Pull! *(She screams.)* A-a-a-ah—!

PETER: What's the matter?

POLLY: I think we've grown together. I think we're Siamese twins, like Chang and Eng. I think they may have to slice us apart. Get the knife! Get the knife! Oh, Peter!

PETER: *(Pulling his hand away)* I can't stand the noise!

POLLY: I love you for your tender ears.

PETER: Oh, lord—

POLLY: For your aristocratic tongue—

PETER: Holy smoke!

POLLY: For your cleanliness and godliness—

PETER: I can't wait for this whole thing to be over!

POLLY: *(Suddenly serious)* Is she waiting outside?

PETER: No.

POLLY: I thought perhaps I could turn you over to her—with the keys—like a used car.

PETER: That won't be necessary.

POLLY: Ladies and gentlemen, please notice. He's using his superior tone. If you're keeping score, write down his "superior tone." I can't stand it!

PETER: And what about the things I can't stand? What about the litter?

POLLY: Where?

PETER: In your mind.

POLLY: My mind's a mess, I suppose, compared to yours—which is a total vacuum.

PETER: Your admiration bowls me over.

POLLY: I was wondering—

PETER: What?

POLLY: Whether we'll come to blows.

PETER: Don't be silly.

POLLY: *(Quite seriously)* I have a feeling, before the day is out, you'll hit me.

PETER: Come on, Polly—

POLLY: *(To the guests:)* If he hits me, it'll be worth your coming, won't it!

PETER: Polly!

POLLY: Well, why not? They'd like to have a show.

PETER: They don't want a show. They want information.

POLLY: What information?

PETER: The facts. *(To the guests:)* You'll be wondering about our plans, I suppose. Our plans for the future. I am planning to remarry when our divorce is final. And Polly, at long last, is going to be able to devote herself to her art.

POLLY: Yes, dear friends. After years of dabbling, I'm going to jump in, head first.

PETER: Marriage holds an artist down. Especially a woman. Being tied to me held her down. But now she can just zoom ahead.

POLLY: I'm about to become another Rembrandt! The only thing I don't have that he had is a wart on my nose.

PETER: I think you're as good as Rembrandt.

POLLY: Thank you, you're very loyal.

PETER: That portrait that you did of me—

POLLY: Do you want it?

PETER: Of course I do.

POLLY: Very touching. Very loyal

PETER: You didn't want it for anything, did you?

POLLY: A dartboard.

PETER: Polly—!

POLLY: Don't worry. I can find another.

PETER: You really can be very cruel sometimes.

POLLY: You're about to escape! Courage in the final moments!

PETER: I thought we were going to try to get through this thing decently.

POLLY: I don't feel indecent, do you?

PETER: I really wish you'd let me give you something. Money—

POLLY: No, no. I want to suffer. I think it would be good for my art.

PETER: I thought you suffered enough these past ten years with me.

POLLY: I'm planning to descend even further—if possible

PETER: All I mean is, it's customary—

POLLY: But I am not.

PETER: Then let me give you the house.

POLLY: I don't want the house.

PETER: Why not?

POLLY: It faces east.

PETER: Only one side faces east.

POLLY: That's one side too many.

PETER: You always said the light here was perfect!

POLLY: So's the light in a field.

PETER: You can't live in a field.

POLLY: I can't?

PETER: What are you going to do, Polly?

POLLY: I'm going to live in a field in Tasmania and paint, and eat bread and cheese and wine and roasted field mice.

PETER: I want to see that you're taken care of somehow—

POLLY: *(To the guests:)* He wants to "do the right thing".

PETER: Yes, I do want to do the right thing!

POLLY: *(Intensely)* Then come live in a field with me and eat bread and cheese and wine and roasted field mice—

PETER: Polly—!

(Silence. PETER *and* POLLY *look steadily at each other.)*

POLLY: There will be a moment of total silence while Peter Endicott Bradshaw regrets his life...

(Silence.... The phone rings. POLLY *answers.)*

POLLY: Hello. ...Yes. ...Yes, it is. ...Why, how nice of you. ...Thank you. ...No. ...No, I'm sorry. ...It's all right. ...Don't mention it. ...Yes, yes, fine. ...Goodbye. *(She hangs up.)*

PETER: Who was that?

POLLY: Magazine subscriptions.

PETER: Nice there are no telephone directories for cell phones. Speaking of which—where's mine?

POLLY: I recycled it.

PETER: What—?!

POLLY: It was the wrong color. I tried to turn it from blue to puce. In the washing machine. It didn't work.

PETER: So now we only have this—? *(He points to the phone.)*

POLLY: 'fraid so.

(The phone rings again. PETER *runs to pick it up but* POLLY *beats him to it.)*

POLLY: Hello? ...No. ...Oh, no. I'm afraid that's impossible.... Not at the moment.... Oh, I do understand, but— ...No. Quite out of the question. *(She hangs up.)*

PETER: Who was that?

POLLY: Wrong number.

PETER: *(To his guests:)* That's what I married her for! Her airy quality! She's dreams, quicksilver, a complete original! Do you know what it's like to be married to an original? It drives you mad!

POLLY: In your world, if your hankies aren't monogrammed, you're an original

PETER: In your world, you consider it affectation to blow your nose on anything but a sleeve!

POLLY: He's exaggerating for effect, friends.

PETER: I learned it from her.

POLLY: You don't do it as well as I do.

PETER: Give me time.

POLLY: Do you mean you'll become more and more like me after you've remarried? It'll go on and on. A mystic transference. And one day Stephanie will wake up married to me!

PETER: Stephanie! Good lord, what time is it?

(The doorbell rings.)

POLLY: Mail time.

PETER: *(Mumbling to himself)* Stephanie... *(He is supposed to call her. He goes toward the phone, then realizes POLLY hasn't gone out of the room yet.)* Aren't you going to go get the mail?

POLLY: Why?

PETER: To see what's in it.

POLLY: I don't care what's in it.

PETER: I care.

POLLY: Then *you* go get the mail.

PETER: Polly, come on. Pick it up. For me.

POLLY: Can't go to that part of the house. Don't have a passport.

PETER: You could do me a favor—

POLLY: And get attacked by a Hepplewhite settee?

PETER: I'm only asking you to get the mail!

POLLY: I might be kidnapped!

PETER: *(Going to get it himself)* The sooner the better! All I want to know is—if our marriage began the day we met, when is it going to be over! *(He exits angrily into the house.)*

POLLY: *(Seriously)* It will be over—when one of us goes, finally, out the door. *(Suddenly in a panic, she calls out:)* Peter—!

PETER: *(Off)* Yes?

POLLY: Are you still there?

PETER: *(Off)* Do you know how much mail there is here?

POLLY: No idea. *(Silence. ...To the guests:)* What if he goes out of the room and doesn't come back? Or what if he sends me out and slips away forever? The great moment will have happened and I won't even know about it. Peter! Peter!

(PETER re-enters with an armful of mail.)

PETER: What the hell's all this?

POLLY: It looks like mail.

PETER: There's mountains of it out there. Months and months of it, all over the carpet! Don't you ever pick it up?

POLLY: Why? Only bad news comes in envelopes. Good news comes by phone.

PETER: *(Remembering)* Phone... *(Again, he knows he urgently must make a call. He invents.)* Er, Polly—

POLLY: Yes, love?

PETER: Polly, I have a terrible headache. Would you mind getting me an aspirin?

POLLY: That's me in your head. I'm taking up residence.

PETER: To get rid of you, I'll need more than aspirin. I'd really appreciate it if you'd go get me some.

(PETER *waits for* POLLY *to leave the room. Instead, she takes two aspirin out of a vase.*)

POLLY: Here you are, dear. *"Semper paratus"*.

PETER: *(Surprised, but not daunted)* I'll need some water.

POLLY: At your command.

(POLLY *pours some from a watering can into a small vase and hands it to* PETER. *Stymied, he swallows the aspirin. Then he makes another attempt to get her out of the room.*)

PETER: You know what I really need?

POLLY: What?

PETER: A cup of coffee.

POLLY: I'll get some. *(She starts out. He moves toward the phone. She turns back.)* Of course,—it's almost tea time.

PETER: Then let's have tea.

(POLLY *starts out again. He starts toward the phone. Again, she turns back.*)

POLLY: Earl Grey or Oolong?

PETER: Oolong. *(Again, he moves toward the phone.)*

POLLY: Milk in it?

PETER: No!

POLLY: No, *thank you*. Where's your breeding?

(POLLY *starts to exit.* PETER *starts to dial a number. As he does so, he shouts out:*)

PETER: And make sure the water boils!

(POLLY *produces a kettle from under a palm frond.*)

POLLY: I will.

(PETER *puts down the phone.* POLLY *takes a hot plate out from under a chair, puts the kettle on it, fills the kettle with water from the watering can, then sits down and stares at the kettle.*)

PETER: What are you doing?

POLLY: Watching the pot. It's a scientific experiment.

PETER: When did you move in the hot plate?

POLLY: Yesterday.

PETER: *(To the guests:)* I had to marry a girl whose great ambition was to live in a nutshell! Some people want more and more room to live in. My Polly wanted less and less. When we got the house—

POLLY: Inherited the house.

PETER: Inherited the house. From my mother. And moved in—

POLLY: It was a unique sensation. Like living underneath his mother's skirts.

PETER: And is living in the wintergarden any different?

POLLY: Yes. It's like her bustle. She never used it.

PETER: This—waif—began to move us more and more into the wintergarden. Until finally, everything we did, we did here.

POLLY: And beautifully.

PETER: I said to myself, one day she'll start to cook in here. And look! It's happened!

POLLY: I cook beautifully.

PETER: *(Touring the room)* This is where she paints, this is where she sews, this is where she reads...

POLLY: This is where he plays, this is where he hums, this is where he thinks...

PETER: This is where we eat, this is where we lie— *(Correcting himself)* This is where we lay—

POLLY: This is where we lay—together—and where we—

(The tea kettle whistles.)

PETER: I don't want tea.

POLLY: Too late, my love. Like the progress toward divorce, it's irreversible. *(She starts to prepare the tea.)*

PETER: *(Coming out with it)* All I want, all I really want—is to be able to call Stephanie.

POLLY: You're perfectly free—

PETER: I thought, perhaps, you'd prefer not to be in the room!

POLLY: Oh, I don't mind.

PETER: I do!

POLLY: She has a very nice voice on the phone.

PETER: How do you know.

POLLY: She called before, but she had the wrong number.

PETER: Goddam it to hell—!!!

POLLY: *(Triumphantly)* He never swore before me! I corrupted him!

PETER: Are you going to let me make my call or not?!

POLLY: Be my guest.

(PETER *goes to the phone.*)

PETER: I'm supremely grateful. *(He starts to dial.)*

POLLY: Actually, I want you to know I never blamed you for falling for someone else.

PETER: Thank you.

POLLY: It's perfectly natural. It happens all the time.

PETER: Yes, it does.

POLLY: I mean, we're all human aren't we?

PETER: *(His attention on the phone call)* H-m-m-m...

POLLY: You're human. I'm human.

PETER: *(Annoyed at her bothering him)* I know that you're human!

POLLY: You don't mind then?

PETER: No. Go on. Be human.

POLLY: Thank you. I knew you'd understand.

PETER: *(Looking at her)* Understand what?

POLLY: That I'm human.

PETER: Are you trying to tell me—?

POLLY: I *was* trying. Have I gotten through?

PETER: Are you trying to tell me that you have someone—?

POLLY: *(Nodding and smiling)* He's human, too.

(PETER, *astounded, slowly hangs up the phone.*)

POLLY: Darling, what's the matter with your face? I thought you loved surprises!

PETER: I do, I do. I just have to get my wind back, that's all.

POLLY: You're not against it, are you?

PETER: No, no. Of course not.

POLLY: I mean, after all, you—

PETER: I know!

POLLY: Your tea is ready.

PETER: I do not want tea!

POLLY: It's good for shock. *(To the guests:)* Everybody who has ever had an extra-marital affair, hold up your hand!

PETER: Polly. ...Would you sit down?

POLLY: *(Sitting down)* Anything to please you.

PETER: Would you tell me a few things?

POLLY: My mind is yours.

PETER: How long has this been going on?

POLLY: Oh, ever so...

PETER: How did you meet?

POLLY: First?

PETER: Yes.

POLLY: With our eyes.

PETER: Where did you meet?

POLLY: First?

PETER: First, second, third—

POLLY: Mostly, we meet here.

PETER: Right—here—?

POLLY: Well, you wouldn't want me knocking about the town—

PETER: No, no, of course.

POLLY: People might see.

PETER: Yes.

POLLY: And talk.

PETER: Yes.

POLLY: So we meet right here and nobody knows but you, love.

PETER: I can't believe this! I trusted you!

POLLY: I never gave you cause.

PETER: But here—! Right under my nose—!

POLLY: Your nose was with you, at the office. *(To the guests:)* Isn't it strange how little we know each other in our absences? When we're away from each other we fill in—imagine—what the other must be doing. But who's to say it's so? ...I think of him at the office, out to lunch, at the office, and home again. He thinks of me standing at my easel from the moment he walks out of here till the moment he gets back. He probably doesn't even think I go to the bathroom!

PETER: It so happens that I do!

POLLY: Well, six points for your side! ... But what about the rest? What about the picnic lunches in the wood I never happened to mention? What about the days I spent speeding through the countryside—in his car? What about last month, when I met him in St. Louis?

PETER: You met him in St. Louis?

POLLY: Oh, what the jet has done for the modern love affair! In the morning, when you left, I was standing at my easel. By noon, I was in St. Louis, making love. By five, when you got home, I was standing at my easel.

PETER: He must be very rich to pay for all this!

POLLY: Oh, *he* didn't pay. *You* did.

PETER: *I* did?

POLLY: I charged it.

PETER: I will not pay!

POLLY: I'll visit you in debtor's prison!

PETER: I am not responsible for your debts from the minute you leave my bed and board!

POLLY: But I haven't left your board—or your bed—yet.

PETER: *(In a very weak voice)* My bed... Him in the afternoon, me in the evening?

POLLY: *(Nods)* Sometimes in St. Louis, Palm Springs, Denver. Sometimes here.

PETER: *(Weakly) Where* here?

POLLY: Oh, not on our bed. That would be sacrilegious!

PETER: *Where* here?

POLLY: *(Pointing to the wicker couch)* Here...

PETER: But it creaks!

POLLY: Not as much as you do.

PETER: Of all the lying, cheating, outrageous, licentious—

POLLY: And what about Stephanie and you?

PETER: It's all above board and in the open.

POLLY: You mean—you and she never—?

PETER: Never!

POLLY: Certain?

PETER: Certain!

POLLY: Did it ever occur to you you may have trouble with that girl? She's so formal, she probably sleeps standing up.

PETER: It's none of your business—

POLLY: I want you to be happy—

PETER: Then how could you go off, and behind my back, without my knowing—

POLLY: You should have known! Why didn't you know? I thought when we were married that some extrasensory thing would develop between us. I thought I could think things and you'd know them. I thought I could do things away from you and you'd know exactly what I was doing without my saying a word. But no, you never managed it. You didn't! Why can't you read my mind?

PETER: Can you read mine?

POLLY: Yes!

PETER: Well—?

POLLY: You want to make your call.

PETER: My call...

POLLY: You wish I'd go away so you could make it.

PETER: Yes, exactly!

POLLY: There's nothing in the world I want more than your happiness!

PETER: So—?

POLLY: So I think I'll take a shower!

PETER: Allah, be praised!

(PETER *waits for* POLLY *to leave the room. Instead, she goes toward a dense group of tall plants, throws a garden hose over a high branch, and starts taking off her clothes.*)

(PETER *just stares.* POLLY *turns on the water. He turns to the guests.*)

PETER: I've lived with her for ten whole years, and still I can't get used to her!

POLLY: *(Calling from inside the shower)* Wait till I've got it on full force. Then I won't hear you.

PETER: *(To the guests:)* But the one thing in the world I never suspected her of was deception.

POLLY: *(Over the shower)* Not yet!

PETER: *(To the guests:)* When I said I was at the office, I was at the office. When I was supposed to be having lunch, I was having lunch! The relationship with Stephanie began after Polly and I started thinking about breaking up.

POLLY: *(Over the shower, which is at full force)* Okay!

(PETER picks up the phone.)

PETER: And now she tells me—

(The shower goes off. PETER puts down the phone.)

PETER: What's the matter?

POLLY: Too hot.

(The shower goes on. PETER picks up the phone.)

PETER: Now she tells me—

(The shower goes off. PETER puts down the phone.)

PETER: Too cold?

POLLY: I'll get it right in a minute.

(The shower goes on.)

PETER: *(To the guests:)* Now she tells me there's this someone else that I never once, not once, suspected! I had no evidence of his existence in any way! No strange cigarette butts in the ashtrays. No lipstick on her collar—. Well, of course there wouldn't be. But there was absolutely nothing. Nothing. Not even— *(And this pains him terribly)* —not even a cooling off towards me!

POLLY: Okay! Go ahead! I'm in for keeps now!

(The shower noise continues steadily. PETER picks up the phone and dials.)

PETER: To think that she could lie so well—! *(Into the phone)* Hello, Mrs Washburn? ...Peter Bradshaw. ...Fine, thank you. ...Really, very fine. ...Yes ...Yes. ...May I please talk to Stephanie? ...Thank you...

POLLY: *(Singing from the shower to the tune of Swanee)* "Stephanie, How I love you, How I love you, My dear old Stephanie"...*(Etc...)*

PETER: I thought you couldn't hear!

POLLY: What did you say?

PETER: *(Shouting)* I said I thought—! *(Into the phone)* Oh, hello, Stephanie.... Fine, thanks. ...Really, fine. ...And you? ...Good. ...You did? When? ...Oh, you must have had the wrong number. ...No, I meant to call earlier but—

POLLY: *(Singing loudly from the shower:)* "You do something to me —" *(Etc...)*

PETER: *(Into the phone)* You found a house? ...Where is it? ...Yes, that's a nice part of town. ... But Polly hasn't decided about this house yet. ...I see. ...Well, do they have to know today? ...But you can't come over! Polly's here!

POLLY: *(Singing loudly from the shower:)* "It seems we stood and talked like this before—" *(Etc...)*

PETER: Look, Stephanie, I just couldn't take another scene at the moment! ...All right. .. All right. ...Yes. I'll try to get her to go out for a few minutes.

POLLY: *(Singing loudly from the shower)* "Sons of toil and danger, Will you fear a stranger, And bow down to Burgundy. Onward, onward, on against the foe—!" *(Etc...)*

PETER: *(Into the phone)* Yes, yes, as soon as I can. ...Yes, I'll call you. ...Yes. The same to you. ...Goodbye, Stephanie.

(PETER hangs up. The shower goes off.)

PETER: How come the shower went off the exact moment the receiver went down?

POLLY: Coincidence. *(She appears, wrapped in a bath towel.)* How's Stephanie?

PETER: Stephanie's fine.

POLLY: *(To the guests:)* Stephanie's always fine. Stephanie is dark-haired and very stable. Stephanie and Peter never met—they were born knowing each other. Stephanie's top teeth fit inside her bottom ones, like this, so every word she says is— *(In imitation)* —"simply fascinating". Stephanie wears a necklace of impeccably matched pearls and carries impeccably crafted alligator handbags. Stephanie has never been seen in the nude. Stephanie has no nude!

PETER: Don't you have some books that have to go back to the library!

POLLY: I don't read about it any more. I do it.

PETER: With whom?

POLLY: Do you really want to know?

PETER: Yes.

POLLY: The milkman.

PETER: I'm warning you—

POLLY: The grocer.

PETER: Polly—

POLLY: Actually, it's the cleaner. I knew you'd prefer a sanitary triangle.

PETER: In other words, you won't tell me.

POLLY: Do you think those men aren't good enough for me? Do you think, after the privilege of you, I should save myself for the Czar?

PETER: The Czar wouldn't stand for your lip!

POLLY: Ask him!

PETER: Very well. You're not going to tell me who he is. Will you tell me just one thing?

POLLY: If I can.

PETER: Do I know him?

POLLY: *(To the guests:)* Does he know him? The classic question. What does he want me to tell him? Would he rather be cuckolded by a stranger or by a friend? *(To* PETER:*)* Or isn't that what you mean after all? Is it just the same old question, the social question, the snob question: *(In upper class accent:)* "Guess who I bumped into yesterday? Nigel van Rensselaer." "Nigel van Rensselaer. Do I know him?" ... If you don't know him, he doesn't exist. *(To the guests:)* You didn't know me, did you, at the start, all you dearly beloved. And isn't that what you said to each other when Peter announced his engagement? "Polly Garth. Do we know her?" ...You didn't know me. I don't exist. *(To* PETER:*)* I could stab your Aunt Harriet in the ribs, she wouldn't feel a thing, she doesn't acknowledge my existence. *(She pours a cup of tea and proffers it.)* Have a cup of tea, Aunt Harriet. It's me, Aunt Harriet! Have a cup of tea, Aunt Harriet! *(She hands over the cup as if to a person and it smashes on the floor.)* You see? She doesn't see me. I don't exist.

*(*PETER *bends down and starts cleaning up the floor.)*

PETER: You make us out to be monsters.

POLLY: No. *I'm* the monster. I'm the one who was born, like Venus, from the sea. I spent my early life curled in the whorl of a triton shell. I came to you one night, with seaweed in my hair. All wet and dripping seaweed—

PETER: For God's sake, put something on!

POLLY: She was only a fisherman's daughter, but she still was allergic to sharks.

PETER: I'll get your clothes. *(He goes into the fronds to get them.)*

POLLY: *(To the guests:)* I know you think I came to him without a legacy. But the sea is something. My father gave me—the sea. Northern fishermen are crusty. But my father fished in the warmer waters, where the currents are gentle and there is lots of time for dreams. He was the one who told me I was born from the sea. He called me, all his life, his little mermaid. And he said, the legend is, when mermaids love—

*(*PETER *returns with her clothes.)*

PETER: Here. Please put them on.

POLLY: *(Pointing to a guest:)* Give that man a glass of champagne! He asked *the* question!

PETER: What question?

POLLY: Did we swear to answer anything they asked us?

PETER: Yes.

POLLY: Honestly?

PETER: Yes.

POLLY: Then someone wants to know—were we happy in bed?

PETER: I don't see that it's any of their—!

POLLY: Were we happy in bed? Were we sometimes or always? Were we happy in bed? Tell me. I've always wanted to know.

PETER: *(Matter-of-factly)* We were always very happy in bed.

POLLY: *(To the guests:)* You see? He won't answer.

PETER: I just did!

POLLY: Evasions! Evasions!

PETER: What do you want me to say?

POLLY: I don't want you to *say*. I want you to *show*.

PETER: Polly, cut it out!

POLLY: *(Posing provocatively in one part of the room)* Show them the twenty-second of June ten years ago on the Costa Brava—

PETER: Would you consider going out and getting me some cigarettes?

POLLY: *(In another part of the room)* Show them dawn, in May, in the Budapest railway station, with the baggage piled up all around—

PETER: And another thing, we're out of Scotch. If you could just be a good girl and go—

POLLY: *(In another part of the room)* To Chamonix! *Viens, viens, monsieur*—! *(She holds out her arms.)*

PETER: Polly, if you'll go out and get it now, before I change my mind, I'll let you buy a whole new wardrobe.

POLLY: A trousseau for my divorce?

PETER: Yes.

POLLY: I already bought one. A wild extravaganza! *(Holding out her arms again:)* Viens, monsieur! Viens, vite!

PETER: *(To the guests:)* You remember we travelled around the world for a year after we were married.

POLLY: Honeymooned.

PETER: Honeymooned.

POLLY: *Je t'aime, mon amour*—!

PETER: *(To the guests:)* And when we got back, Polly would pretend—

POLLY: *We* would pretend—

PETER: We would pretend—that different parts of the room were places we'd loved especially. And we would play out our happy times again and again.

POLLY: Each time as perfect as the first time. ...What place did you love most?

PETER: ...The garden of the monastery at Vicenza...

POLLY: Come...

PETER: No, Polly, no—

POLLY: Why not?

PETER: The Abbé might see us!

POLLY: He preaches love—

PETER: Not this kind!

POLLY: Come lie with me! Come now! Come quickly!

PETER: Polly— *(Surrendering to love. Holding her)* The grass is cold...

POLLY: You didn't shiver then. Why now?

(PETER *disengages himself from* POLLY *gently.*)

PETER: How terrified we were—because we'd lost our heads—that you'd get pregnant.

POLLY: I did.

PETER: What?

POLLY: I mean—I pretended. Do you know we have children two, four, six and eight years old?

PETER: Boys or girls?

POLLY: Even Steven.

PETER: If we had them now, we'd have to divide them.

POLLY: How lucky they are, then, to be unborn.

PETER: *(To the guests:)* I know you wonder about that. About our not having children. The truth is, we put it off, deliberately. We wanted to wait until Polly got established in her career.

POLLY: Only thing was—I never did get established.

PETER: You will now—if you're not distracted by your lover.

POLLY: Lovers inspire.

PETER: And husbands?

POLLY: That's another matter.

PETER: I guess it is. I wonder why.

(The phone rings. PETER answers)

PETER: Hello? ... Yes, Stephanie... *(He turns away and continues talking into the receiver confidentially. As he does, POLLY says to the guests:)*

POLLY: We sent all of you cards that year. How come you never answered? How come not one of you wrote back?

PETER: *(Into the phone)* I'll see what I can do. ...I'll call you back. *(He hangs up.)*

PETER: Are you sure you don't have books to return to the library?

POLLY: Peter?

PETER: Yes?

POLLY: Why don't you stop beating around the bush? Just tell me what's going on here.

PETER: Well—Stephanie found a house she wants us to buy.

POLLY: Congratulations!

PETER: But I thought, if you didn't want this one, we'd keep this.

POLLY: I don't want it. You keep it.

PETER: But Stephanie hasn't been in it since we were children.

POLLY: Was Stephanie ever children?

PETER: There are buyers for the other house. She has to make a quick decision.

POLLY: So she wants to come and see this one right now?

PETER: Yes.

POLLY: That's wonderful! Tell her to come right over! I'll take her for a tour of Indochina!

PETER: I thought you might like to go out!

POLLY: *(To the guests:)* Ah, good people, he wants to avoid a scene. He's always avoiding scenes. What do you think, Cousin George, should I help him avoid everything?

PETER: I just don't think it's proper to—

POLLY: Darling, have her in. I'll be absolutely open, charming, and straightforward. *(As if to Stephanie:)* Come in, come in, Stephanie. I'm delighted to meet you at last. I know we've passed each other going to and fro on life's highways and byways. But it's so—intoxicating—to meet you at last, face to face. Is this your first marriage? Is there any particular reason you held on to your maidenly treasure for so long? You do still have it, don't you? Your maidenly treasure? Of course. Imagine my asking! Your eyes are the eyes of St. Apollonia at the stake! Tell me, Stephanie, what does your father do? I'm sure it's something very distinguished. Is your daddy planning to take Peteykins into the firm?

PETER: *(Who has been pacing more and more furiously)* Polly—!

POLLY: He'll be a great asset. But do watch out for his sudden rages.

PETER: I'm warning you—!

POLLY: He's quite all right, except for those sudden rages. They've only come on recently. Quite irrational. He can blow up when you least expect it. Just a casual remark—and pow!

PETER: I do not rage!

POLLY: No, of course not.

PETER: And if I do, it's brought on by you!

POLLY: Anything to help a friend.

PETER: I am not going into her father's business!

POLLY: Of course. You're an independent.

PETER: I'll be damned if I'll stand here and let you do this to me!

POLLY: Poor Persecuted Peter.

PETER: I'm going—!

(PETER *strides toward the door.* POLLY *suddenly shouts after him:)*

POLLY: I'll tell you his name!

(PETER *turns.* POLLY *repeats quietly:)*

POLLY: I'll tell you his name.

PETER: The name of your lover?

POLLY: He has—a name. We all—have names. It's what distinguishes us from the animals. We give each other names. And the names take on—all kinds of magic. Auras. Emanations. And at last they mean—something more—than the things they name.

PETER: What is his name?

POLLY: Come in. I'll tell you.

(PETER *comes back into the room.*)

PETER: I'm in. Tell me now.

POLLY: His name—is Adam Hero.

PETER: A likely story!

POLLY: You hoped it would be an ugly name.

PETER: "Adam Hero" isn't a name, it's a slogan!

POLLY: I think his family chose well for him. His father's name is Charles Hero. But I think if you're born into the Hero family, Adam is the only possible name that you should have.

PETER: And does he suit his name?

POLLY: You mean—is he beautiful?

PETER: Yes.

POLLY: He's English.

PETER: Does that answer the question?

POLLY: *(With slight accent)* It most assuredly does, dear man.

PETER: *(Triumphantly)* He's a stuffed shirt!

POLLY: Think so, if it comforts you.

PETER: What does Adam do?

POLLY: Everything! Superbly!

PETER: How often do you meet him?

POLLY: How often do you meet her?

PETER: What do you talk about?

POLLY: What do you talk about with her?

PETER: What do you see in him?

POLLY: What do you see in her? *(To the guests:)* It's a draw!

PETER: Polly, look. As a favor to me—couldn't you possibly go out for a few minutes so Stephanie could come over?

POLLY: Have her come. We'll make it a foursome.

PETER: You don't mean—

POLLY: That's why I can't go out. You see—I'm expecting Adam any minute.

PETER: Here? In this room?

POLLY: In this very room.

PETER: In that case, I'm not budging.

POLLY: Delighted to have you.

PETER: I want to meet this man.

POLLY: I know he's awfully eager to meet you. I've told him all about you.

PETER: I can imagine.

POLLY: I never say anything derogatory.

PETER: Why the sudden onslaught of discretion?

POLLY: I chose you, didn't I? I wouldn't want him to think I have bad taste.

PETER: Then what do you find to tell him?

POLLY: Facts. Like the fact you like pajamas with no buttons. Or the fact you love asparagus and are allergic to eggs.

PETER: Pajamas, asparagus and eggs? That's all you tell him?

POLLY: Oh, no. I tell him all about you. I tell him about your career.

PETER: I'll bet you do!

POLLY: I tell him how—

PETER: You have no right telling him anything! Absolutely no right, do you hear me?

POLLY: All I said was—

PETER: You're trying to drag me down, aren't you! Aren't you! I know what you're doing!

POLLY: Would you like to have a rage while we're waiting? Maybe you could show our friends a sample of a really big one!

PETER: I tell you I won't stand for this!

POLLY: What are you screaming about?

PETER: My God, you always act so innocent!

POLLY: All I said was "I tell him about your career" —and you hit the ceiling!

PETER: Don't start that with me! Telling me what you said and what I said and what you said and what I said and proving how I started everything!

POLLY: We're into it again, aren't we?

PETER: Into what?

POLLY: The Argument.

PETER: What argument?

POLLY: For the nine millionth, nine hundred and ninety-nine thousandth, nine hundred and ninety-ninth time! The Argument! The self-same Argument!

PETER: I don't know what you're talking about—

POLLY: *(To the guests:)* When we first were married, I didn't even know we had one. It was invisible. Oh, it might stick up its head every now and then. Not often. But now, it's always there. ...It isn't even about anything. It just *is*. The Argument. I say "Good morning, darling," and he says "You're doing this to get me!" Or I say "How are you?" and he says "How the hell do you think I am? Can't you see by just looking at me? And who made me this way? You!" ...And then we're shouting back and forth, back and forth, and I don't even know what's happened.

PETER: Oh, you don't, do you?

POLLY: No, I don't. I have no idea!

PETER: You're doing this to get me!

POLLY: *(To the guests:)* See? I told you—

PETER: Where the hell is he?

POLLY: Don't hit him on the mouth! On his beautiful mouth!

PETER: What is this sudden obsession with hitting. Have you ever seen me hit anyone?

POLLY: No.

PETER: Then why, all of a sudden, do you start screaming at me—

POLLY: I'm not screaming at you, *you're* screaming at *me*!

PETER: When will he come!!!

(POLLY *goes to the window and looks out. Then suddenly she says):*

POLLY: Oh, my gosh!

PETER: What is it?

POLLY: There he goes—

PETER: What do you mean?

POLLY: Oh, Peter, you're going to be awfully angry with me.

PETER: Let's have it—

POLLY: I forgot. I truly forgot!

PETER: What?

POLLY: Our signal.

PETER: What signal?

POLLY: He never comes while your car is in the drive.

PETER: That makes sense.

POLLY: And then I cross the tops of these trees to indicate all clear.

PETER: You've got it down to a science, haven't you?

POLLY: It's sort of necessary.

PETER: What will he do now?

POLLY: Cruise around till your car is gone.

PETER: I'll move it.

POLLY: I really forgot. I'm terribly sorry.

PETER: I don't know why, but I believe you.

(He starts out. She calls after him)

POLLY: Peter—!

PETER: Yes?

POLLY: Will you be back?

PETER: *(With rising annoyance)* What kind of a question is that? I said I was going out to move the car, you know why I was going to move it, you know I want to meet this fellow, and then you ask me—

POLLY: Never mind. Nothing. Go on. Go ahead.

(PETER goes, slamming the door behind him. POLLY winces at the sound, then says to the guests:)

POLLY: This time doesn't count—his going out. It isn't permanent. His final time out, there'll be a tremendous pop. Peter will go this way and Polly will go that way. I wonder if we are like Siamese twins—and when we pop apart, one or both of us will die. I wonder which of us has the heart, and which the kidneys. I wonder if I'm pumping blood through him or him through me.

(PETER returns.)

POLLY: We may be sharing just one liver!

PETER: What's that?

POLLY: You're back awfully quickly.

PETER: I seem to have lost my keys.

POLLY: Impossible. It's not in your character.

PETER: Nevertheless, I can't find them anywhere.

POLLY: *(To the guests:)* What if I get all the keys and he the locks?

PETER: Did you see them—?

POLLY: What if I get all the colds and he the Kleenex?

PETER: Help me look. Think back—

POLLY: What if our minds have merged into one, and when we pop apart, one of us becomes a raging maniac! *(Frankenstein's monster imitation)*

PETER: What are you burbling about?

(The phone rings. POLLY *gets it.)*

POLLY: Adam! Where are you! I was worried to death! I thought something had happened to you!

*(*PETER *grabs the phone.)*

PETER: Look here, old man. This is Polly's husband. I know about everything and I want you to get the hell over here so we— *(He stops short.)* —It's Stephanie!

*(*POLLY *shouts into the mouthpiece:)*

POLLY: Stephanie, what does your father do?

PETER: *(Into the phone)* I'm sorry. Things are getting out of hand. ...I don't care about houses today, this one or that one! ...No, you can't come here, I'll come to you. ...I'll get there when I get there! *(He slams down the phone.)*

POLLY: Tsk, tsk. Keep your temper. You wouldn't want her to know the awful truth too soon.

PETER: Why don't you just go stand on the curb and flag him down?

POLLY: It's beneath my dignity.

PETER: Well, we'd better find the keys soon or, Adam or not, I'm going to have to go to Stephanie.

POLLY: Mavis Mandwell wants to know what attracted you to me in the first place.

PETER: *(To the guests:)* It was her total lack of organization!

POLLY: I married him for his big toe. I ran across this lady who reads feet and she said—

PETER: Are you looking for my keys?

POLLY: Yes.

PETER: Where?

POLLY: Borneo.

PETER: I already looked there. Try Minsk.

POLLY: Your best man wants to know if I'm going to keep your name. ...Of course. I'll be known as "The First Mrs. Bradshaw."

PETER: My mother was the first Mrs. Bradshaw.

POLLY: In that case, I'll go back to my own.

PETER: Will you look for the keys?

POLLY: The Talbotts wonder why we didn't invite them over more often.

PETER: He depresses me.

POLLY: How?

PETER: By balding young.

POLLY: Your Great-Aunt Gwendolyn wants to know, if neither of us wants the ottoman, can she have it?

PETER: Great-Aunt Gwendolyn has bad breath!

POLLY: Cousin Jack wants to know why you don't answer the questions.

PETER: Because they're too damned trivial!

POLLY: Cousin Jack wants to know if you really were happy in bed.

PETER: *(Seeking him out)* Where are you, Cousin Jack? Why do you ask me? Why don't you ask Polly?

POLLY: Because Polly would tell the truth.

PETER: Then why doesn't Polly tell?

POLLY: If Peter will tell after.

PETER: Peter will. He swore to.

POLLY: Peter is absolute perfection about sex. He reads all the right books and sticks absolutely to the national average: two and a half times a week. That half time is a real wowzer!

PETER: That's unfair to me!

POLLY: Well, take your turn at bat then.

PETER: Polly pretends to be a passion flower, wanting more and more and more.

POLLY: Go on, you've got them glued—

PETER: But nobody can satisfy her. She's got this vision of the perfect time, that fantastic, overshattering moment—

POLLY: I haven't—!

PETER: I sometimes wonder what would happen if I really came after you as fully and as often as you claim to want it. I think you'd run the other way.

POLLY: Only because it's you.

PETER: And what other beautiful thoughts would you care to share with this congregation? Where are my keys? I want to get out!

POLLY: Now we're really getting down to it, aren't we. So the best thing is to get out!

PETER: I thought we were going to try to stay civilized to the end!

POLLY: Why do that? Why not show ourselves as we really are?

PETER: I was not a savage until I married you.

POLLY: I'm flattered to know I've had so much influence.

PETER: Where are my keys?

POLLY: Your Cousin Alfred wants to know what marriage has done for you—

PETER: Go to hell, Alfred!

POLLY: My father wants to know—

PETER: Your father's been dead for sixteen years!

POLLY: All the more reason why you should be honest with him. My father wants to know what you liked most about me in the beginning.

PETER: *(A pause, then:)* Your eyes.

POLLY: Why?

PETER: Because in them I looked good to me.

POLLY: And what do you hate most about me now?

PETER: Your eyes. Because in them I look—*(He breaks off.)* Oh, the hell with all these questions!

POLLY: Are you now what you thought ten years ago you would be?

PETER: God, you really know how to stick the knife in, don't you!

POLLY: It's them asking! Vanessa wants to know when we first began thinking of escape.

PETER: I can't remember.

POLLY: Why didn't we have any children?

PETER: We answered that!

POLLY: Do we hate each other?

PETER: Tell them to go home!

POLLY: Listen—!

PETER: To what?

POLLY: Listen to what they're whispering...

(PETER *and* POLLY *listen.*)

POLLY: They say you never loved me to begin with.

PETER: No more of this—

POLLY: They say we were never happy, it was all pretense.

PETER: I said, no more—

POLLY: They say by tomorrow we'll have forgotten all about each other. And if we pass in the street, we wouldn't even know we'd met. They say we wasted ten whole years— *(To the guests:)* It's not true! It's not so! What's the matter with you? Why don't you tell them, Peter—!

PETER: Polly, I don't want to play this game any more!

(*Sudden silence. A pause. Then:*)

POLLY: *(Seriously)* They want to know—are you really in love with Stephanie?

PETER: *(Seriously)* Yes. I am really in love with Stephanie.

POLLY: Even though she's the seventh daughter of the seventh daughter? Even though nothing but distilled water runs through her veins?

PETER: Yes. ... And you? ...Are you really in love with Adam Hero?

POLLY: *(After a long pause, deeply:)* I am in love with Adam Hero with every fiber of my soul and body. I am obsessed with him. All day long I say his name over and over like an incantation. "Adam Hero. Adam Hero." It's like the naming of a god. And in saying his name, I call to myself all the wonder, all the beauty, all the grace, that ever there was in any living being. Adam Hero... Adam Hero... Adam Hero...

(*Silence. There's nothing more to be said.*)

PETER: I'm going now.

POLLY: But Adam's about to come—

PETER: I no longer want to meet him.

POLLY: You can't leave our guests—

PETER: You entertain them.

POLLY: But the keys—

PETER: I'll hitchhike!

POLLY: Will you be back?

(A long pause. Then, very slowly, very quietly:)

PETER: Goodbye, Polly...

POLLY: *(Quietly, expressionlessly)* Goodbye...

(Their eyes hold each other's for a long time. Then PETER gives one last look at the room—and goes out. The closing of the door goes through POLLY's body like a physical shock.)

(POLLY stands quite still for a moment. Then she goes to a potted plant and digs into the earth with her fingers. She takes out a set of keys.)

(POLLY holds the keys like a sacred talisman. And she says, in a voice like the naming of a god:)

POLLY: Peter Bradshaw... Peter Bradshaw... Peter Bradshaw... Peter Bradshaw...

(She continues this whispered incantation as the lights slowly fade.)

(Blackout)

END ACT ONE

ACT TWO

(At rise:)

(About an hour later. Twilight.)

(POLLY is asleep, crouched on the floor, her head on the sofa where she had fallen asleep saying PETER's name.)

(There is a noise outside in the underbrush. PETER enters.)

POLLY: *(Stirring)* Who is it? *(Silence)* ...Who is it?

(Still, PETER is silent.)

POLLY: Adam, is that you?

(Anger flashes across PETER's face and he hides in the greenery. POLLY rises to turn on the light.)

POLLY: Adam—?

PETER: *(In an English accent)* Don't turn!

POLLY: Why not?

PETER: *(Continuing in an English accent)* I have a surprise for you.

POLLY: *(Obediently facing forward)* Oh, Adam! What is it?

PETER: *(With English accent)* First—tell me how much you missed me.

POLLY: *(Still facing away from him)* More than I can ever say. You weren't out of my mind, not for one second.

PETER: Not one?

POLLY: Surely you could feel me thinking of you?

PETER: Of course I did. But you haven't said how much you love me, Polly.

POLLY: I love you with a fire that could drive Elizabeth Barrett Browning speechless!

PETER: That much?

POLLY: I love you in all kinds of funny, tiny ways. I love you in big, big ways—so that if someone says, "What does a quasar look like?", I'm sure it looks like you.

PETER: Go on.

POLLY: I love you in foolish ways. I preserve the impress of you in this room. You make me talk to furniture! *(She moves about the room, still not looking at him. She says to a chair)* Adam touched you. *(To a sofa:)* Adam let you feel his full weight. *(To a flower:)* Adam breathed your breath. *(To a glass:)* Adam kissed you. *(She puts her lips to the edge of the glass.)* So when you're gone, you're here. And when I touch these things, I touch you. When you're light years away, and I drink from this glass, don't you feel it?

(PETER comes silently up behind her. He puts his hand gently over her eyes and closes them. He turns her to him. He puts his lips to hers. They kiss, her eyes still closed, and as the kiss goes on, it is obvious that POLLY becomes more and more overwhelmed with passion. At last, drowning in her embrace, PETER thrusts her forcibly away from him, shouting at her:)

PETER: Rat!

(POLLY's eyes fly open. She says nothing.)

PETER: Snake in the grass! Tramp! Traitor! Why don't you ever feel that way with me?!

POLLY: *(Calmly)* Hello, Peter.

PETER: Earthquakes for Adam Hero, but not a tremor for me! If you'd known it was me—!

POLLY: *(Evenly)* I did know.

PETER: Liar!

POLLY: *(To the guests:)* Does he really think a woman can't identify the kiss of her own husband? All lips are different.

PETER: The voice of experience.

POLLY: I knew from the first rustle of the leaves that it was your rustle. I could identify your footfall, in sneakers, on a six inch pile carpet. If a thousand men sneezed in unison, I'd know exactly to which sneeze to address my "God bless". There's not a sound, a smell, a curve of you that's unfamiliar country.

PETER: I must bore you to death!

POLLY: Oh, well. That's marriage.

PETER: But in spite of the fact that you knew it was me, that—quiver of delight—was for Adam, wasn't it?

POLLY: Well, of course it was for Adam! *(She turns to the guests:)* Everybody kiss the nearest stranger! *(She waits a second, then:)* Isn't it beautiful? ...Everyone who ever loved us, get divorced with us now!

PETER: I shouldn't have come back—

POLLY: Why did you?

PETER: To spy on you.

POLLY: Oh, yes? What have I been doing?

PETER: Nothing.

POLLY: Did you see Adam?

PETER: Did he come?

POLLY: Only if you saw him.

PETER: My car's still in the drive. Do you realize I could end your affair forever by abandoning it there?

POLLY: Then how would you transport Stephanie?

PETER: *(Morosely)* Stephanie...

POLLY: I thought you were supposed to go to her.

PETER: She stood me up.

POLLY: No!

PETER: I walked over to her place. She wasn't there. Her maid told me she said to tell me she got fed up with the nonsense and went to the hairdressers.

POLLY: But what about the house?

PETER: God knows.

POLLY: You should have followed her to the hairdressers. You should have burst into the inner sanctum, scattering hairpins and rollers left and right. You should have confronted her beneath her hair dryer. *(Screaming)* Stephanie!

PETER: She's not deaf.

POLLY: Everyone is beneath a dryer. Even Stephanie. *(Shouting)* Stephanie! *(Coolly, imitating Stephanie, a pillow wrapped around her head)* Yes...? *(As* PETER*)* Come out of there at once! *(As Stephanie, imperiously getting a manicure)* Do them superbly, please. They must be smooth and sharp—for my wedding. *(As* PETER*)* Stephanie—! *(As Stephanie)* I'm a virgin, of course. He isn't. But his first wife was a sea urchin, so she doesn't count. *(As* PETER*)* I need to talk to you—! *(As Stephanie)* You're stepping on my alligator shoes! I'll have to get a pedicure! *(She throws off her shoes. As* PETER*)* I wouldn't hurt you for the world, you know that—. Please, Stephanie... *(As Stephanie, her bare feet pointed out to ministering attendants)* I'm listening! I'm listening! ...Gently on the bunions! *(As* PETER*)* I adore you, Stephanie. I adore your feet, your nails, your teeth. Come fly with me across the reaches of the Amazon, let me worship you on the barges of the Nile. Come fly with me now through space and time— *(As Stephanie)* I can't possibly. ...It would muss my hair!

(Proudly POLLY, as Stephanie, begins to march away, arms and feet akimbo, drying nails. PETER is convulsed with laughter.)

PETER: *(Hugging her)* Oh, Polly, Polly, Polly girl! That's why I married you! You're such a hoot!

(PETER and POLLY hug and laugh. He kneels and puts her shoes on her feet.)

POLLY: Do I have her right?

PETER: Too close for comfort.

POLLY: Is she awful?

PETER: She's very correct.

POLLY: That will be a refreshing change from me.

PETER: Don't think that I won't miss you.

POLLY: Thanks. That's nice of you to say.

PETER: Want to know something funny?

POLLY: Sure.

PETER: I don't even know how we got into this whole divorce thing in the first place. One minute we were going along swimmingly in the usual love-hate fashion. The next minute we were calling the whole thing off!

POLLY: It does seem peculiar.

PETER: Why did we get into this anyway?

POLLY: I don't know. To have a party?

PETER: Do you hate me very much?

POLLY: No. Not very.

PETER: Will you ever forgive me for the pain I'm causing you?

POLLY: There's nothing to forgive.

PETER: I sometimes wonder...

POLLY: What?

PETER: I sometimes wonder—whether we'd have thought another dozen times about breaking up if—if we'd had children.

POLLY: I suppose we should have.

PETER: ...Polly?

POLLY: Yes?

PETER: Why don't we—think of it now?

POLLY: Of reconciling?

PETER: Of having children.

POLLY: Which would you like to have? The-eight-year old or the two?

PETER: I'm not joking!

POLLY: Here it comes, folks. The little bundle of joy to save the marriage! Is your marriage floundering? Get a wah-wah. That'll save it every time!

PETER: I'm serious!

POLLY: If marriage vows and double beds and matching rings can't solder a couple together, bind them up with diapers and teething rings.

PETER: Polly!

POLLY: That's the ticket to salvation! Bring on the little human bucket of glue!

PETER: I'm sorry I mentioned it! I'm an ass for bringing it up! I didn't mean to bring on another of your song and dance routines!

POLLY: Peter—

PETER: I only came back here because I couldn't think of a place to go. But, by God, I'd choose a hotel over a fun house! I'll pack and be out of your life forever in ten minutes!

POLLY: Marvelous! I'll paint! You're keeping me from it!

(PETER *angrily goes into the house.* POLLY *thrusts a canvas on her easel and wildly starts to paint.*)

POLLY: Yes, ladies and gentlemen, in the last ten minutes of her marriage, while her world was crashing all around her, she calmly painted, for all eternity to see, the masterpiece of the—

(*The telephone rings.* POLLY *answers.*)

POLLY: Hello? (*She listens. She listens for a long time. Her face exhibits a wide range of tumultuous emotions and finally she shouts into the receiver:*) ...How dare you walk in alligator shoes? Alligators are dying out! They're dying out! You're causing their extinction! Assassin! Murderer! (*She listens for another second and says, more or less straightforwardly:*) I'll tell him—if I see him. (*Then, almost pathetically*) Stephanie? ...What does your father do? (*But Stephanie has hung up.* POLLY *puts down the receiver.*)

(PETER *appears.*)

PETER: Who was that?

POLLY: The weather.

PETER: They call you?

POLLY: When it's going to be stormy, they call me. They've been calling me a heck of a lot lately.

(POLLY *notices* PETER *is carrying his suitcase. She is suddenly seized with a demonic desire to paint. She returns to her easel and starts to work at a tremendous pitch.*)

PETER: Polly, I decided upstairs that our last minutes together are going to be very decent.

POLLY: *(Painting)* Decent.

PETER: There's no use screaming at each other.

POLLY: *(Painting)* No use.

PETER: I, at least, intend to remain calm and absolutely civilized.

POLLY: *(Painting)* Absolutely civilized.

PETER: I'm not going to let you get my goat!

POLLY: I don't want your goat!

PETER: Will you listen to me? There are a few things we have to get settled—

POLLY: You don't mind if I go on painting, do you? I'm having a burst of inspiration and I don't want to break the creative flow.

PETER: Not at all. Go on.

(*Throughout the following,* POLLY *paints. She no sooner finishes one canvas than she puts up another and goes spiritedly on. As she paints, she repeats, like an incantation:*)

POLLY: Adam Hero... Adam Hero...

PETER: *(Absolutely determined to remain calm)* There's the house—

POLLY: Ah, the house – *(Under her breath)* Adam Hero... Adam Hero...

PETER: I insist that it's yours.

POLLY: Adam Hero... Adam Hero...

PETER: My attorney will be in touch with you—

POLLY: Is he the man who will saw us in half?

PETER: I want you to be taken care of. If there's ever anything you need or want don't hesitate to get in touch with—

POLLY: The man with the saw! *(A cry for help)* Adam Hero! Adam Hero!

PETER: *(At his wit's end)* I said we'd be calm—

POLLY: *You'll* be calm. I'll be anything I want to be. *(To the guests:)* It's just hit me. The wonder of being free! Ladies, join the liberation movement! Sally, imagine not having to grin when you don't feel like grinning. Clarissa, imagine having kippers for breakfast even though Albert can't stand bones.

PETER: Polly, could we please end this charade?

POLLY: Vanessa, you can bathe and the bathroom will never be steamed up before you get there.

PETER: Pay attention—!

POLLY: Mavis, if you wake up and want to laugh at midnight, you can laugh your head off, you won't be waking him!

PETER: Polly, please—

POLLY: It's the ideal state! That's why they call it single blessedness! Men, rise up on the road to independence! Follow Peter and—

PETER: Polly, I said I didn't want to play any more!

(Total silence. The spirit goes out of POLLY. After a long time, she moves back to her easel, grasping at the words "Adam hero... Adam Hero... " as if for air.)

PETER: I know you're trying to get a rise out of me, but I won't bite, Polly. If we can't preserve some shred of decency and civility—

(The phone rings. PETER gets it.)

PETER: Hello? ...Yes! ...No, she didn't tell me. ...What? ... You did? ... Yes, yes, of course. ... Well, I'll try—... I don't know if I can—... All right! All right, Stephanie. Goodbye! ... *(He hangs up.)* I thought we were playing fair with each other. Why didn't you tell me she called?

POLLY: She didn't say anything I felt worth repeating.

PETER: She bought the other house.

POLLY: *(Flatly)* Huzzah.

PETER: She wants me at her place in three minutes or else.

POLLY: Or else what?

PETER: Or else she's coming to collect me.

POLLY: I'll protect you, Peter!

PETER: Polly—

POLLY: Adam and I will protect you!

PETER: Could you and I have one straight moment before—

POLLY: And when your great Brunhilde pounds upon the door—

PETER: Good God, will you let us part decently?

POLLY: Is that your last request?

PETER: Yes.

POLLY: Granted.

PETER: I want to make sure your financial affairs are straightened out.

POLLY: My affairs are never financial.

PETER: *(Picking up the mail)* I'll take care of all these things.

POLLY: What do you think of him, Adam? Is he gallant or isn't he?

PETER: And when other bills come through, just send them on.

POLLY: *(To Adam:)* Generous to a fault, wouldn't you say?

PETER: But the one thing I won't finance is your infidelity!

POLLY: Naturally.

PETER: I won't pay for your calls to Adam.

POLLY: Why should you?

PETER: And I won't foot the bill for your trips!

POLLY: Naturally not.

PETER: Let Adam Hero support his own love life!

POLLY: It'll be his pleasure.

PETER: *(Opening the phone bill)* There's no record of long distance calls—

POLLY: I reversed the charges.

PETER: Good girl. *(He opens another bill.)* When did you go?

POLLY: Where?

PETER: To St. Louis.

POLLY: Sometime last month.

PETER: It's not on the bill.

POLLY: I suppose they're behind in their work.

PETER: Denver and Palm Springs aren't on here, either.

POLLY: When they come through, Adam will pay them.

PETER: They should be through by now—

POLLY: Maybe they have a new policy: free rides to people in love. ... You'd better go. You wouldn't want to risk the wrath of the Valkyrie.

PETER: *(After a moment)* Polly... I want to talk to Adam.

POLLY: I'll arrange it sometime.

PETER: I'd like to talk to him right now.

POLLY: While he's riding around in his car?

PETER: He doesn't sound like the kind of man who'd do that for four hours.

POLLY: Then who knows what he's doing?

PETER: Where's home to him?

POLLY: Denver.

(PETER *picks up the phone.*)

POLLY: He's not there now.

PETER: I'll leave a message. What's his number?

(POLLY *is silent.* PETER *says into the phone*)

PETER: Operator. Get me long distance information. Denver, Colorado.

POLLY: It's unlisted.

PETER: Where's his office? I'll talk to anyone who knows him.

POLLY: *I* know him.

PETER: *(Slamming down the receiver)* Show me one shred of evidence that he exists!

POLLY: He called before.

PETER: When you said it was the weather?

POLLY: Yes.

PETER: That was Stephanie.

POLLY: Before that.

PETER: I didn't hear his voice. Give me some evidence that he exists!

POLLY: I love him!

PETER: *Evidence!*

(*For an answer,* POLLY *traces the path she traced before around the room. Slowly, lovingly, she touches the arm of the chair, the sofa, the flower. She puts her lips to the glass.* PETER *watches her. And as she quietly stands with her lips to the glass, he says, softly, deeply:*)

PETER: As far as I know, the only person who ever touched those things—was me.

(*There is a long, long silence.*)

POLLY: *(Softly)* You've used up your three minutes. The Valkyrie must be galloping over to collect you.

PETER: *Is* there an Adam?

POLLY: God made many.

PETER: Do *you* have one?

POLLY: Do you want me to?

PETER: Polly—

POLLY: What do you want me to say? If a tree falls in the desert and no one hears it, does that mean it hasn't fallen? Just because you don't see Adam, does that mean he doesn't exist? It only means I've practiced my deception beautifully! It only means you're asking the wrong questions. What was the tree doing in the desert in the first place? How come one minute it was standing and the next minute it began to fall? What sound could it make on sand? And who could hear it? You're asking the wrong questions! The wrong questions!

PETER: Oh, God, Polly—I wish we had that glue to make it harder to unstick us. Why were we so damned careful—for ten years—so damned careful? We should have thrown caution to the winds—!

(POLLY *laughs and laughs.*)

PETER: Why are you laughing?

POLLY: I did.

PETER: What did you say?

POLLY: I threw "caution" to the winds—many months ago.

PETER: And—?

POLLY: Wouldn't it be funny, Peter—if our sterility were not by choice. And all these years we were going to such lengths—of hygiene and of self-restraint—when it wasn't at all necessary!

(PETER *looks at* POLLY, *unable to speak.*)

POLLY: That would be a cosmic joke of the first dimension! Wouldn't you feel privileged? To be the butt of a cosmic joke? *(She laughs.)* They knew all the time.

PETER: Who?

POLLY: Sally, Harriet, Vanessa, Mavis. All the ladies. They've been clucking at it behind their fans for years! *(To the guests:)* Haven't you? Haven't you! ..."They can't have children. Don't you know they can't have children?" ... *(To* PETER:*)* They knew before we knew. Today's gossip is tomorrow's prophecy. *(To the guests:)* So keep the clichés flowing, ladies! Never believe that two people could be "saving themselves" for something else!

PETER: *(Who has been keeping an eye on the window)* She's out there. Stephanie—

POLLY: They're wrong about you.

PETER: I'd better go to her.

POLLY: *(To the guests:)* You're wrong about Peter!

PETER: I'll be right back!

POLLY: I've always admired that about you.

PETER: What?

POLLY: How easily you come and go.

(PETER exits. POLLY goes to the window and watches.)

POLLY: She's twenty feet high. She's pacing back and forth. With every step, the sidewalk trembles. He's coming to her. She lifts him up in her palm and—a-a-ah!!!

(POLLY screams and makes a gesture of Stephanie crushing PETER in her fist. PETER rushes back in.)

PETER: Why did you scream?

POLLY: I didn't.

PETER: Are you sure?

POLLY: Is Stephanie coming in?

PETER: She says she'll wait outside for me.

POLLY: It's just as well. If she came in, she'd hit her head.

PETER: I'm going to have to go, Polly.

POLLY: Right.

PETER: These things you've been telling me... If it's true—and we didn't—we couldn't—you couldn't—. Well, who's to say you couldn't with somebody else?

POLLY: Adam—

PETER: With Adam or anyone.

POLLY: The world's my oyster!

PETER: You have beauty and talent—

POLLY: I am a very special person!

(A moment)

PETER: You said that I could have your portrait of me. May I?

POLLY: Gladly. Go and take it.

PETER: Thank you. *(He goes toward the rack of paintings.)* Whereabouts?

POLLY: Somewhere there.

(PETER *starts to look.*)

PETER: *(Holding up a solid blue canvas)* Is it anywhere near this?

POLLY: Somewhere.

PETER: *(Holding up a solid red canvas)* Near this?

POLLY: Somewhere near.

PETER: *(Holding up a solid orange canvas)* Near this?

POLLY: That's it.

PETER: What do you mean "That's it"? This is a plain orange canvas.

POLLY: Does it say "Peter" on the back?

PETER: *(Looking)* Yes.

POLLY: Then that's it.

PETER: I don't understand.

POLLY: Don't you like the way it looks?

PETER: *(Feeling the paint, which is still wet)* You painted it over! *(Stunned, he takes out canvas after canvas. They'll all in solid colors, and all still wet.)* You painted them *all* over!

POLLY: So I did.

PETER: But why, Polly? Why?

POLLY: Let's see. I must have had a reason... Oh, yes... They were no good.

PETER: You worked years on these things! They were beautiful!

POLLY: I made you think so.

PETER: I know they were good! I loved them!

POLLY: You were mistaken.

PETER: But Polly, you spent ten whole years—!

POLLY: I was mistaken, too.

PETER: But what will you do now?

POLLY: Marry Adam.

PETER: *Is* there an Adam?

POLLY: The man thinks in circles! ...You'd better go before you start to think in squares.

PETER: I can't go till I know what you'll be doing.

POLLY: Traveling.

PETER: Traveling like you've been traveling.

POLLY: Yes.

PETER: And making extravagant purchases like you've been making extravagant purchases.

POLLY: Extravagantly!

PETER: *(Looking at the bills)* There's nothing here to indicate you've been going anywhere or buying anything! For all I can tell, by the looks of these things, you haven't been out of the house for months!

(POLLY laughs.)

PETER: *Have you?*

(POLLY laughs again.)

PETER: Have you!

POLLY: Look into my eyes.

(PETER does.)

POLLY: What's the answer?

PETER: Polly—

POLLY: You have no instinct for what I say any more, do you?

PETER: No—

POLLY: Then the miracle has happened! Suddenly, painlessly, without either of us knowing it—we're divorced! *(To the guests:)* This is the moment you came to see! Sing! Dance! Celebrate! It's over!

PETER: Polly—

POLLY: Oh, Peter, how do you feel? How does your body feel? Am I exorcized? You are out of me. I feel light as air! *(She dances.)*

PETER: I'd like to know what's true here and what isn't!

POLLY: Go to Stephanie. You're free to marry now. I know you'll make a lovely couple—even though you have to reach up so high to take her hand.

PETER: She's five feet two!

POLLY: What does her father do?

PETER: Why do you keep asking that?

POLLY: They want to know.

PETER: Who?

(POLLY gestures toward the guests.)

POLLY: Them.

(PETER is silent.)

POLLY: They say you're marrying Stephanie for safe harbor. They say you're marrying Stephanie to become her father's son. They say you can't get things on your own, you have to have them handed to you on a silver platter. They say you're no man, just a parcel of inheritance. They say you have no backbone, just family line. They say you're going to go down the drain just like the rest of the sons of fathers whose fathers were fathers whose fathers were fathers whose fathers were fathers—

PETER: *(To* POLLY:*)* You can't say things like that about me!

POLLY: *I'm* not saying it, *they* are!

PETER: Who?

POLLY: The guests!

PETER: Don't you think we've gone far enough with that?

POLLY: *(To the guests:)* But I won't listen to you! You're wrong! Totally wrong!

PETER: Polly, there's nobody here!

POLLY: *(To the guests:)* You have no right to talk about him in that fashion!

PETER *(To* POLLY:*)* We were only pretending! ...You knew we were only pretending—didn't you?

(POLLY *is silent.*)

PETER: Why—we haven't had anybody over here for years.

POLLY: How can you say that? You have your father's eyes and your Uncle Jared's way of talking. I have my grandfather's love of flowers and my great Aunt Jessica's nose. We're made of them. They're always with us.

PETER: Perhaps they are. But still, we are alone.

(An automobile horn blows outside.)

PETER: I'm going to have to go, Polly—

POLLY: *(To the guests:)* I don't care what you say! You're wrong about him!

PETER: Come say goodbye, decently goodbye—

POLLY: *(To the guests:)* He loves the lady, that's why they're marrying! Stop nodding and smiling and chattering, "I told you so! I told you so!"

PETER: Polly, please—

POLLY: See what joy it's giving them—to be right about us! They knew from the beginning this would happen. *(To the guests:)* You're loving it, aren't you? You're cruel! You're cruel! We shouldn't have asked you over—to give you such enormous pleasure!

PETER: Polly, I beg you—

POLLY: Peter, send them home!

PETER: I didn't mean to hurt you—

POLLY: Hurt me? You cannot hurt me. I am invulnerable. I am going to become another Rembrandt and marry Saskia and paint something wonderful and hang in the Louvre!

PETER: I can't bear to see you this way—

POLLY: And when I die and turn all brown and yellow, you will make a fortune. Because I am me, my masterpiece, and I am leaving me to you and you will sell me for a king's ransom—and I will have been able to save you after all.

PETER: Don't talk of dying—

POLLY: Right! Let's not be morbid! The marriage egg has broken and we're out, scot free! So off you go to be devoured by the usual, the expected—

PETER: Polly, you're cracking up—

POLLY: So you noticed.

PETER: Polly, girl, hold on. Please hold on!

POLLY: For my sake, or for yours?

PETER: For us both!

POLLY: *(In sing-song)*
"Pretty Peter Coupon Clipper, Pretty Peter Dandy,
Proper Peter took a wife who fed him dreams and candy.
Proper Peter lost his wife, a Pretty Kitty found him.
Constancy became his life—"

PETER: I asked you to stop it—

POLLY:—"With silver spoons she bound him."—

PETER: You're doing this on purpose, aren't you!

POLLY: Be on guard with her! She will lure you with veneers and graces—

PETER: I know what you are doing, Polly, and it isn't going to work!

POLLY: I ought to give you something magic—to protect you from her—

PETER: You're trying to upset me, aren't you?

POLLY: *(To the guests:)* What shall I give my husband to protect him?

PETER: You're doing this so I won't go!

POLLY: A pebble from the seacoast of Iberia? *(She picks one up.)* No, no. Not strong enough.

PETER: I'm sick of all this pretending, Polly—

POLLY: I must have something— *(She searches the room wildly, picking up and rejecting objects.)*

PETER: I'm tired of a life that's all imaginary! All, all lies!

POLLY: What shall I give him to keep him safe? A book? *(She picks one up.)* No— *(She throws it away from her.)* A leaf— *(She takes one.)* No— *(She tears it up, her actions getting wilder and wilder.)*

PETER: You're lying now! Pretending to go mad so I will stay with you—!

POLLY: A branch—! *(She rips one off.)* No—! *(She throws it across the room. A tree—!* (She lifts one up.)*

(PETER pulls it away from POLLY.)

PETER: I know you're just pretending, so pull out of this!

POLLY: It has to be something that was close to me! *(She starts tearing at her clothing.)* It has to be a part of me! *(She starts tearing at her hair.)*

PETER: *(Trying to restrain her)* I'm telling you to stop it! I won't fall for it!

POLLY: Help me, father! What shall I give him? Father, help me! Help me! Help me! *(She tears wildly at herself and at her clothing.)*

PETER: *(Grabbing her)* Stop it! Stop it! Stop it! Stop it! *(He slaps her violently, knocking her to the floor.)*

(POLLY lies there, motionless.)

(PETER is stunned. For a minute, he stands frozen. Then, like someone in a trance, he moves toward her.)

PETER: Polly?

(No answer)

PETER: Oh, God— *(He bends over her.)* Polly—!

(POLLY opens up one eye and says:)

POLLY: She died.

PETER: Faking! I should have known! *(But he's relieved, nonetheless.)*

(POLLY rises. She cheerily addresses the guests:)

POLLY: I said he'd hit me and he hit me!

PETER: Polly, sincerely, I didn't mean to hurt you—

POLLY: *(To the guests:)* Do I know him or do I know him?

PETER: I don't know what's been going on with me these past few months. Don't understand it—

POLLY: *(To the guests:)* I mean, have I got his number or have I not?

PETER: It's as if the whole civilized world were slipping from its moorings—. And I couldn't hold on! I couldn't hold on!

POLLY: *(To the guests:)* Now, ordinarily I'd say, when a woman knows a man so well she can foretell him—that's a marriage. But—when a woman brings the beast out in a man—well, that is not.

PETER: So please forgive me. I didn't know what I was doing.

POLLY: *(Gently)* You'd better go. Stephanie's waiting.

PETER: What are you going to do?

POLLY: Wait for Adam.

PETER: There is no Adam!

POLLY: ...Then the world is a great deal poorer than I thought.

(Long pause)

PETER: How different everything is now from what it was in the beginning.

POLLY: How very different.

PETER: You found me on a rock by the sea.

POLLY: We didn't know each other's names.

PETER: I sat on one side of the rock, you on the other.

POLLY: Two separate people...

PETER: We fell into the waves—

POLLY: —and we were one.

PETER: And it was my first time.

POLLY: And it was my first time.

PETER: And it promised everything. *(Silence)* What happened to us?

POLLY: Time. Only time.

(PETER goes to get his suitcase, which is by the sofa. But as he bends to get it, he sees something on the pillows.)

POLLY: We'll do better, next incarnation.

(PETER turns to her, holding his keys.)

PETER: Where did you find these?

POLLY: What?

PETER: My keys.

POLLY: I didn't.

PETER: They were here on the couch—

POLLY: Of all places!

PETER: They weren't there before when I looked.

POLLY: You never were a good looker.

PETER: They have mud on them! I think you buried them and dug them up!

POLLY: Don't be absurd!

PETER: You didn't want me to go!

POLLY: That is ridiculous!

PETER: You're lying, Polly girl! You love me!

POLLY: No!

PETER: Another lie!

POLLY: I want you to go to Stephanie—

PETER: Liar!

POLLY: I do want you to go to Stephanie. We mermaids never lie.

PETER: You want me to renounce the Bering Straits?

POLLY: Take Stephanie—

PETER: She would get nauseous.

POLLY: Take her to the Himalayas.

PETER: It would muss her hair.

POLLY: You're right to marry her—

PETER: An alligator handbag?! *(He pulls her by the hand.)* Come with me now to the Costa Brava—

POLLY: No, Peter—

PETER: Come with me to Budapest—

POLLY: Please, no—

PETER: Come with me to the garden of the monastery—

(PETER *wraps* POLLY *in his arms. She cries out:*)

POLLY: Stephanie! Help! Oh, help! He's drowning!—Stephanie!

(PETER *and* POLLY *freeze, expecting Stephanie to enter. They wait a long time, but Stephanie doesn't come.*)

(*At last,* PETER *lets* POLLY *go. He looks out the window.*)

PETER: She's gone... *(He turns.)* She probably ran off with Adam.

POLLY: You know—I think they'd suit each other very well.

PETER: Not half as well as you suit me.

POLLY: You still can go...

PETER: And leave you to handle all these guests alone? Don't be ridiculous! Look! They're pouring in at all the doors!

POLLY: I didn't know we had that many friends—

PETER: Well, what's keeping you? Take their coats and hats, and fill their glasses.

POLLY: *(Coming alive)* Gladly. Oh, yes, gladly! Welcome, everybody! Please come in!

PETER: Come in! Come in! Polly and I are so happy to see you!

POLLY: We missed you very much—

PETER: We did indeed.

POLLY: Stay the night!

PETER: Stay the week!

POLLY: Stay the century!

PETER: *(Tenderly, to* POLLY:*)* It's wonderful to see you...

POLLY: *(Directly to* PETER:*)* We love you all...

(Blackout)

END OF PLAY

AVIATORS

CHARACTERS & SETTING

Jan Hawkesworth
Harry Hawkesworth
Frederica

Time: The present

Place: A room for living in a house poised between land and sea. The sea is off, upstage right. The land is opposite, downstage left, out front beyond the invisible fourth wall.

Upstage right, tall glass doors open onto the sea. Nearby are a small dining table and two chairs. Upstage, near them, is a folding screen. Center stage left is a sofa with a chair beside it. Behind the sofa is a table used as a desk, with a chair behind it. Upstage center is an opening to a dimly-lit hallway. If one exits through it toward stage left, one goes out the front door. If one exits through it toward stage right, one goes into all the other areas of the house. The house, provided by the college, is the home of academics, so the walls are entirely covered with bookshelves on which are books and papers—not in sets but in some measure of disarray. They are books which are used.

There is something about this space which moves away from realism. Is it the colors—all in monotone? Is it the fact the books seem to blend into each other and become almost like wallpaper? Is it the mystery of the dark space of the hallway, into which people seem to disappear when they enter it? Is it the angle of the rafters—which gives a sense of the space being askew? There are no "extras" in the room—no bits of decor which are not used within the action.

The house is neither old nor new. Standing where it stands, alone, between the sea and the land, it has an atmosphere of both enclosure and exposure, of providing shelter but also of being vulnerable to invasion by land and by sea.

ACT ONE

SCENE ONE

(At rise:)

(Late afternoon. Spring.)

(JAN is standing upstage right reading a book. HARRY is seated upstage left at the table, grading some examination booklets. Both academics, they are in their late forties or early to mid-fifties. The room is filled with the loud pulsating sounds of the sea. JAN listens to the waves breaking and receding. They are so loud she closes the book, looks out toward the sea through the glass doors and says:)

JAN: Harry,—let's go for a walk!

HARRY: *(Busy with his papers)* Can't possibly.

JAN: Let's go for a swim!

HARRY: *(Holding up the exam books he has yet to correct)* Sorry. Can't.

JAN: But the sea is calling! Listen!...What is the sea saying? Multiple choice: Swim me?...Sail me?...Clean me?...Drown in me?

HARRY: None of the above.

JAN: What do you mean?

HARRY: I think that sound is not the sea. I think that sound is coming from the other direction.

(JAN stops and listens for a moment.)

JAN: So it is. I always said you had the best ears in the family.

(On the way to downstage left she passes him at the desk and kisses his ears. Then she walks downstage and looks out through the unseen window in the fourth wall.)

JAN: Good Lord! Look at all those people! What are they doing on the lawn? ...They're saying things. I understand them less than I understood the ocean. ...They're waving things.

HARRY: Lengths of rope?

JAN: No, no, no! They're smiling. I think. God, I've never seen so many people!

HARRY: Are you sure that, whatever they're there for, it has something to do with us?

JAN: Who else? There's not another house around for acres.

(At last he puts his exam books down and comes to look out the window.)

HARRY: Well! That *is* a lot of people! Perhaps it's a convention of lemmings making their way to the sea.

JAN: Seems to me they're not so much making their way to the sea as congregating on our lawn.

HARRY: What are they waving?

JAN: Looks like papers. Newspapers.

HARRY: I think I see some kids from my classes... Ah, yes. There's the wag from History 101 who's always trying to trap me with obscure questions about the rise and fall of the Roman Empire.

JAN: You know, I think I see a few of *my* more enthusiastic fledglings out there...Oh, God. Yes! There's the joker from English Composition who keeps showering me with pornographic limericks!

HARRY: Is there any other kind?

JAN: If only his rhymed. Or had meter. Or made sense. They might actually be amusing.

HARRY: You'll have to recite some for me someday.

JAN: I promise you, if ever I recite to you pornographic limericks, they will be my own.

HARRY: Can't wait.

(They lightly kiss. Then:)

JAN: I wonder what they're all doing out there, jumping up and down and waving things—and shouting something. What in the world are they shouting?

(The sound of the sea rises.)

HARRY: I think they're calling "Hawkesworth! Hawkesworth!"

JAN: *Jan* Hawkesworth or *Harry* Hawkesworth?

HARRY: Can't tell.

JAN: Have they come to praise us or to lynch us?

HARRY: Can't tell that either...Only one way to find out... *(He starts upstage to go toward the front door.)*

JAN: Don't! Don't go! I have an awful premonition—

HARRY: If there'd been any truth in any of your premonitions, we'd long ago have been dead.

JAN: There's always a first time—

HARRY: Perhaps. But I have a premonition this isn't it. *(Melodramatically)* If they eat me alive and throw my skeleton into the sea, you finish grading my exams, sweet.

JAN: I promise.

(HARRY *exits.*)

(JAN *turns to us and says:*)

JAN: Harry was always braver than I. Smarter and braver. He has this solid way of looking at life. Clear. Right in the eye. He doesn't go up over hills and down into the valleys, as I do. He steers along, absolutely straight. No pebbles trip him up. No boulders block his road. Neither snow, nor rain, nor heat, nor gloom of night stops him from making his way through existence. He just surges forward, oblivious of all the pitfalls. Steady. Unsuppressible. While I—

(HARRY *returns. He is carrying a newspaper.*)

JAN: Well?

HARRY: It seems that it *is* Hawkesworth they are chanting.

JAN: Yes, and—?

HARRY: And it seems the Hawkesworth they're shouting at the top of their lungs for—is you.

JAN: Me—?!

(HARRY *tantalizes her with silence for some seconds, then:*)

HARRY:...It seems you've won a Pulitzer.

JAN: What?!

HARRY: It's right here in the college newspaper. "Jan Hawkesworth Wins Pulitzer Prize for Poetry."

(*She looks at the paper.*)

JAN: That's crazy. ...Excuse me, but that's crazy. ...I published one volume. One very thin volume. One very thin volume from a university press. One very thin volume from a university press which sold maybe two hundred copies. One very thin volume from a university press which sold maybe two hundred copies all of them at this school. One very thin volume from a university press which—

HARRY: Okay, okay! What you say has truth, beauty, rhythm, granted no rhyme, and is not a limerick, and yet—here it is. And your subjects have come to congratulate you.

JAN: My goodness—!

HARRY: May we quote you, Madame? On receiving news that she had won a Pulitzer, Poet Hawkesworth cried: "My goodness!"

JAN: I'm speechless—

HARRY: That's rather inconvenient as I think your students and mine and the rest of the intellectual rabble out there are expecting a speech.

VOICES: *(From outside)* Hawkesworth! Hawkesworth!

JAN: Can't face the crowd without my hair combed—

HARRY: No, you're not that kind of poet.

JAN: Where's my comb?...Oh, got it. *(She searches for her comb, finds it and combs her hair.)*

HARRY: Lovely. Now get out there—

JAN: Can't face the crowd without some lipstick. *(She searches for and puts on lipstick.)*

HARRY: Jan! How far is this dolling up going to go?

JAN: Can't face the crowd in this blouse—

HARRY: You could—

JAN: No. I couldn't. *(She goes off up right to change her blouse.)*

HARRY: *(To us:)* This is a bit of a shocker. My wife. Jan. A Pulitzer Prize. Don't mean to be disloyal about my beloved's poetic capacities but they are, to put it bluntly, minor. I say so. She'd say so. Anyone who's read her would say "minor". She's dreamy, when the present world of poetry is sharp as a bayonet. She's insubstantial. Given to flights of fancy. I keep telling her: "Be precise. Be specific." She prefers to deal in air. And—I don't mean to knock a major prize, but there's the political aspect. You don't get the glittering prizes unless they know you. They don't know you unless you've blown your horn someplace where they can hear. And outside of this—I can only say "minor" institution—who has heard of Jan Hawkesworth?...For that matter, who has heard of *Harry* Hawkesworth?...Our extreme anonymity mitigates against the major medals—

(Jan reappears, having changed her blouse.)

JAN: Ah, yes. Very handsome, my dear. The perfect costume in which to receive congratulations on a Pulitzer. Not too casual, not too assumptive—

JAN: I had to sew on one of the buttons—

HARRY: Glad you did. Unbuttoned is unacceptable. Particularly on national TV.

JAN: National TV!

HARRY: I glimpsed mikes from all the networks and several cable channels in the crowd. I thought I'd better warn you. You'll find tape recorders. Film and still and television cameras. The works. Watch out, baby, they want to grab your soul.

JAN: *(She checks herself in the mirror.)* One is never prepared for such a thing. Could never be prepared for such a thing. What if they ask me to quote a few of my lines? I don't know any by heart! My brain's total jelly! What if they ask me about our lives?

HARRY: You've lived them. You know what to say. *(A beat)*...What not to say.

JAN: Harry! I'm not ready!

HARRY: Jan, dear Jan—you are. *(He puts both hands on her shoulders.)* You are ready because, no matter what you may think, no matter how much, in bed at night, you've thought of yourself as an "obscure poet and always will be", you knew, in your heart, you deserved recognition. You create, not giant volcanoes, but tiny gems. Insightful, perfect, deep, mysterious, enchanting gems The world is to be congratulated for noticing. ...Go out and receive their congratulations. You already have mine.

(He kisses her lightly on the forehead.)

JAN: But *you're* the star in the family—

HARRY: Dearest Jan, go out and twinkle.

JAN: Come with me—

HARRY: No, sweetheart. The twinkling of this day is thine.

(He bows mockingly, formally. She smiles and exits toward the front door. When she has gone, HARRY goes to the window to observe what's happening and says to us:)

HARRY: She was right to dress for the occasion. Whatever you're wrapped in as they snap you for the front page of *The Times* becomes iconic. If your hair happens to fall across your brow they call you windblown, though your tresses are usually impeccable. Intricacies of character are read into your threads. Diplomats don't want to give any clue to what they're thinking. That's why they all wear the same grey suit! Now Jan, as she appears before the multitudes is—*(Suddenly he looks surprised, puzzled, concerned. He is silent. Then he says to us, finally:)* They're walking away! The whole crowd! Dispersing! Just as she got out there—they turned their backs and started walking away!

(JAN re-enters, carrying a white envelope. She is walking slowly. Stunned)

HARRY: What happened?

JAN: It seems, my pet, there is another me! The prize goes not to a Jan, but to a *Janet* Hawkesworth!

HARRY: I never heard of her—

JAN: Apparently there's another obscure Hawkesworth minor poet! Just as I made my appearance someone in the crowd got the news on their cell phone and they've all departed to shout "Hawkesworth" on the lawn of this unknown but anointed Janet!...Harry, what if I'd gone out there earlier? What if I'd presented myself to the public and the press and blushed and stammered and cast my eyes down modestly—and they'd ululated and cooed and fawned all over me—and then I had to watch them back off!...What an ass I'd have made of myself!

HARRY: *You're* not the ass! *They* are!

JAN: I knew the news of such a triumph should come over the telephone, or in an envelope marked Special Delivery, Priority Mail. It doesn't come with assorted friends and strangers shouting your name on your front lawn. ...My God! How humiliating!...Are they all gone?

(He looks out the window.)

HARRY: All. Every one of them marked absent.

JAN: I have only one regret.

HARRY: Yes?

JAN: That I changed my blouse for nothing.

HARRY: Yes, but you sewed on a button. So you profited something.

JAN: Yes. I profited something.

(A silence. HARRY *looks at the envelope she's carrying.)*

HARRY: What's that?

JAN: Oh. I picked it up from the mailbox... I thought it might be my official notification. *(She looks at it for the first time.)* No. It has your name on it.

(She hands it to him. He opens it. He reads it, then, expressionlessly, says:)

HARRY: It's from President Cadwell. He wants to see me in his office.

JAN: When?

HARRY: Tomorrow morning.

JAN: Why?

HARRY: Doesn't say.

JAN: Perhaps he's ready to cut the size of your classes, as you requested.

HARRY: It doesn't say that.

JAN: Maybe it's about tenure.

HARRY: Doesn't say.

JAN: Perhaps he wants you to teach *Twenty-First Century Thought*—ideas for the future—the course you've been begging them to institute—

HARRY: There's no hint—. Just my name. The time. And the summons.

JAN: What time?

HARRY: Ten o'clock.

JAN: *(After a pause)*...You don't think they've found out, do you?

HARRY: *(After another pause)*...After all this time? I don't think so.

JAN: We've done marvelously so far—

HARRY: *(With concern)* Marvelously...

JAN: Who cares about what he might say? You don't have to be everybody's hero. You only have to be mine!

HARRY: Your hero? What have I done to deserve that appellation?

JAN: You know. My God, but you were splendid!

HARRY: Hero Guy. That's me! Killing the roach who moved into our kitchen. Unstopping the toilet when our plumbing was clogged—

(JAN *brings out a small model of the Spirit of St. Louis and holds it.*)

JAN: Flying solo across the Atlantic! First one to do it—ever!

HARRY: "Flying solo across the Atlantic—!"

JAN: How I wish I could have flown that journey!

HARRY: So do I!

JAN: Do you wish you'd known me then? Do you wish you could have taken me with you?

HARRY: What I wish is that I could have done it!

JAN: But you did! Tell me again how you thought about it, dreamed about it, Lindy!

HARRY: "Lindy—!"

JAN: Tell me again how you made your plans so carefully. Checked the winds, checked the plane, checked the skies—

HARRY: Jan, darling, if you're going to pretend I'm somebody else, why not Beethoven? Why not Julius Caesar? Why not Elvis? *(He does a mock bump and grind.)*

JAN: Tell me again how you suited up—so tall and blond and handsome—

HARRY: Tall and blond and handsome. A combination devoutly to be wished.

JAN: I worshipped you for that. I still do.

HARRY: How about some dinner?

JAN: You never had the hungers that the world had. You were above that. You craved for more. The conquest of the sky—

HARRY: Jan, I don't want to play. I'm tired—

JAN: Not you. You're never tired. You are superhuman!

HARRY: *(Beginning to get annoyed)* Jan, for Chrissake—! Quit it.

JAN: Of course you were careful to a fault—because there's no use killing yourself—

HARRY: At this point I'm not so certain—

JAN: Why are you jettisoning everything, including your pen and your handkerchief?

HARRY: If I play, will I get to eat?

JAN: First you have to run the check list.

HARRY: You run it.

JAN: The pilot has to run it!

HARRY: *(Giving in reluctantly)* It's lucky I was an eagle scout—. Let's see—... Ailerons—Check. Engine—Check. Propeller—Check. Roast chicken—

JAN: Stop it!

HARRY: Franks and beans?

JAN: If you don't run the check list correctly, you will not survive! Fasten your safety belt—

HARRY: *(Still with reluctance)* Fastening my safety belt.

JAN: Rev up your engine!

HARRY: Revving up my engine—*(He makes engine revving up noises.)*

JAN: Taxi down the runway. Take off!

HARRY: Taking off—

JAN: Careful of the wires! Under the wires—then up above the fog!

HARRY: You've got me taking off in fog?

JAN: It'll clear—

HARRY: I certainly hope so.

JAN: Altitude! Altitude!...Isn't it great to be up at last—alone—and secure in your little cockpit?

HARRY: It is delicious to be secure in my little cockpit—

JAN: Isn't it glorious—up near the heavens?

HARRY: Glorious.

JAN: Keep your eye on the compass! Don't go off course! Over the ocean now. Night is falling. Stars are coming out.

HARRY: I am getting bored—

JAN: Don't fall asleep!

HARRY: Jan, I don't want to play any more! I'm tired! I have no idea why Cadwell wants to see me and I—

JAN: Stay awake or you'll crash! How does one feel in the moment between life and death? Does one meet God? Or does black nothingness replace one's being?

HARRY: Nothingness...*(Distracted, worried with his own concerns)* How does one feel on the brink of nothingness...

JAN: Pay attention!

HARRY: How can I pay attention? I'm flying blind! I'm going to crash!

JAN: You're not. You're going to succeed—my hero, my darling—

HARRY: For God's sake, enough! Stop now!

JAN: That you, the idol of the world, should want to marry me! Little mousy me! That you should whisk me above all the world and propose when we were high above the clouds—

HARRY: Jan! In the name of heaven! Come back to earth! Stop pretending to be Lady Lindy and look at me!

(She looks at him. She says, exceedingly normally:)

JAN: Did you say you wanted dinner?

HARRY: No. I've lost my appetite. What happened to you? What was going on with you?

JAN: What are you talking about?

HARRY: Never mind. *(He indicates the airplane.)* Where did you get that?

JAN: This? I've always had it.

HARRY: I never saw it before.

JAN: You don't know everything about me. *(She puts the airplane down on the table)*...Shall I try to think up something for dinner?

HARRY: No. I'm not hungry any more.

JAN: Neither am I. Let's go to bed. *(He puts out the lights and they exit up right toward the bedroom.)*

(Shortly after they exit, a YOUNG WOMAN *appears outside the glass doors stage right. She turns the handle and enters. Attractive and intelligent, she looks slowly around the room, observing everything. Her eye lights on the airplane. She picks it up, turns it in her hand, then puts it down again. She looks carefully around the room. Then she takes out a notebook and starts making notes.)*

(Blackout)

Scene Two

(The next morning)

(The YOUNG WOMAN has fallen asleep on the couch. HARRY crosses the hallway past the upstage opening on his way out to get the paper. He doesn't see her.)

(The YOUNG WOMAN hears the outer door slam. Hearing JAN about to enter from the hall, the YOUNG WOMAN jumps up, straightens her clothes, picks up her notebook and starts toward the glass doors.)

(However, just as JAN enters from the hallway carrying two cups of coffee, HARRY appears outside the glass doors. Seeing no means of escape, the YOUNG WOMAN hides behind the screen just as JAN comes into the room carrying two cups of coffee and HARRY comes in brushing sand off the newspaper)

HARRY: That paper boy is getting better and better at missing the porch completely. Today he managed to throw this halfway down the beach!

JAN: Coffee?

HARRY: Half a cup. I have to leave soon.

(JAN looks out of the downstage left window.)

JAN: No people...

HARRY: No people!

JAN: A blessing.

HARRY: A relief.

(They sit at the upstage right table by the glass doors. HARRY gives JAN a piece of the paper and they start to read.)

JAN: This is how I like us best. Alone together. ...Don't we have fun?

HARRY: *(Singing)* Every morning,
Every evening,
Ain't we got fun?

JAN: *(Singing)* Times are bum
And getting bummer
Still we have fun.

Jan & HARRY: *(Singing together in harmony)*
There's nothing surer
The rich get rich and the poor get poorer
In the meantime, in between time
Ain't we got fun!

(They laugh together.)

JAN: What *is* that?

HARRY: Tin Pan Alley Song. 1921. Lyrics by Gus Kahn and Raymond B Egan, Music by Richard Whiting.

JAN: How much you know! Love that. Love you... And I'm sorry you can't sleep.

HARRY: I sleep.

JAN: You didn't last night.

HARRY: I did.

JAN: You kept twitching.

HARRY: I didn't.

JAN: You did.

HARRY: I must have kept you up.

JAN: Not at all.

HARRY: If you'd been asleep, you wouldn't have been aware of my twitching.

JAN: All right. I was up.

HARRY: Then why didn't you say that?

JAN: What?

HARRY: That you didn't sleep. Instead you say *I* didn't sleep and we go through this whole rigmarole of your pretending to be worried that *I* didn't sleep when actually it's *you* who didn't sleep. Why do you pretend this is about me when it's about you?

JAN: Because it *is* about you. It's about your meeting this morning.

HARRY: You didn't sleep because of my meeting?

JAN: What's it going to be about, Harry?

HARRY: We've been through this—

JAN: You have some idea but you won't tell me—

HARRY: I don't.

JAN: You have suspicions. You're keeping mum.

HARRY: I've never been "mum". I am not "mum" now. If I had any idea I wouldn't be too shy to say!

JAN: I'm not accusing you of shyness, trepidation or timidity, I just want to know—

HARRY: In the name of heaven—!

JAN: Morning explosion number one! Do you notice how little it takes for an argument to ignite between us recently? We have the reputation on campus of being The Ideal Couple. They should see us now! I ask something simple like: "Do you know what today's meeting with President Cadwell is going to be about" and you go ballistic!

HARRY: "Go ballistic" is a cliché unworthy of a poet and an authority on literature and the English Language.

JAN: That's a favorite trick of yours—when you can't criticize my ideas, criticize my vocabulary!

HARRY: Your vocabulary is part Milton, part prepubescent teen!

JAN: I'll say it very clearly, then, eschewing slang and all words you might consider of unworthy provenance: ...Could it be over?

(Silence. Then he notices—the sun is in her face.)

HARRY: I know what the problem is: the sun is melting your brain.

JAN: Harry, I'm asking you: Could it all, today, be *fini*?

HARRY: Do you want me to pull down the blind?

JAN: It's broken.

HARRY: Why don't you tell me these things?

JAN: What things?

HARRY: About the broken blind!

JAN: Oh, for God's sake, it's not about the blind, it's about our survival!

(HARRY starts to pull the screen in front of the glass doors to shade JAN's eyes. The YOUNG WOMAN is revealed. JAN and HARRY are stunned.)

HARRY: What the devil—?

JAN: Who—?

HARRY: Who the hell are you?

JAN: What were you doing behind—?

HARRY: *(To JAN:)* Call the police—

FREDERICA: Wait. Wait! I can explain—

JAN: Is she armed?

FREDERICA: Of course I'm armed.

(She reaches inside her bag. The others recoil. She pulls out a pad of paper and a pencil)

FREDERICA: My weapons. I have a license to carry them. I'm a reporter.

HARRY: For what paper?

FREDERICA: No paper. I'm free lance.

HARRY: Out—!

FREDERICA: When the others left, I stayed.

JAN: I can't imagine why.

FREDERICA: *(To* JAN:*)* I love your work. I want to interview you.

HARRY: If you don't belong to a paper—

FREDERICA: When I've written it, I know I can get it published. *(To* JAN:*)* Just let me talk to you—

JAN: To Jan Hawkesworth who is not Janet Hawkesworth? What would it be: "An Interview with Jan Hawkesworth—The Poet Who Did Not Win the Pulitzer Prize"?

FREDERICA: You should have won. You *could* have won. Your work—

JAN: —is completely unknown.

FREDERICA: That's my point. Why not make a virtue out of *not* being Janet Hawkesworth?

JAN: Portrait of a Loser.

HARRY: Our numbers are legion.

JAN: How did you discover my work?

FREDERICA: It was given to me by a friend.

JAN: But for you to print a story about a mistake—

FREDERICA: *(To* JAN:*)* It'll bring you a public.

JAN: I *would* like the work to have a few more readers. One does want to feel one isn't shouting into the dark—

FREDERICA: Then you'll do it—

HARRY: This is a bad idea—

JAN: Why?

HARRY: We have other things to do today! *(He looks at his watch. His meeting is imminent.)*

JAN: *You* do. *I* don't. *(She turns to the girl)* What's your name?

FREDERICA: Frederica.

JAN: *(Gesturing* FREDERICA *to a seat)* A pretty name. Well, Frederica, what do you want to know?

FREDERICA: You were born—

JAN: Yes. Yes, I was. I was born. In a little town in the East—

(As the interview begins and continues, under, HARRY *turns to us and says:)*

HARRY: Ah, the temptation of making revelations to the press, which has entrée everywhere, and the vanity of each of us, unable to resist reaching out for our fifteen seconds of fame. What my wife wouldn't tell her sister—if she had a sister—she will tell this woman. What she wouldn't tell her best friend— if she had a best friend—she would be happy to see in a six page full-color spread in Keyhole Magazine—or even in one paragraph on the next to last page of the last section of the Daily Wigwag. It's a disease! Our need to show off! Expose! Make every intimate detail of our lives public! *(He interrupts the interview. To* JAN:*)* I have to leave soon and I think this interview should take place only in my presence. So hurry up and get the story over with. Tell it! Birth! Parents! Grandparents! School! College! Work! Hubby! Hobby! Travel! Death! *(To us:)* Is there anything else to a life? Doesn't everybody's always serve itself up in the same predictable courses? *(To* FREDERICA:*)* Tell me, are you after only the meat and potatoes—or are you going to urge her to do a little more creative cooking and spill out to you some of the more intriguing ingredients of her mysterious sauce? If you want to know the secrets of her sauce, ask me.

JAN: This is *my* interview.

HARRY: I know you—

JAN: You don't know me better than I know myself—

HARRY: Don't I? *(To* FREDERICA:*)* Interview *me* about Jan Hawkesworth. I know more about her than she knows herself. More than she knows I know. More than she would ever tell.

JAN: And I know more about you—!

HARRY: A draw!

FREDERICA: I would like to interview you, too, Professor Hawkesworth.

HARRY: Ah, she knows I'm a professor—

JAN: *(To* FREDERICA:*)* A considerably distinguished one—. Protégé of the great historian Jonathan Stone. The only one on earth worthy of inheriting Stone's mantle.

FREDERICA: *(To* HARRY:*)* Impressive... I would like to interview you each separately—. But since you're here together, perhaps I can ask the questions which relate to you both.

JAN: Shoot.

HARRY: "Shoot"?

JAN: Isn't that what everybody says to reporters?

HARRY: I don't know what one says to reporters. But if everybody says it, I wouldn't.

FREDERICA: Have you always worked together? I mean in the same college?

JAN: Ever since we married.

FREDERICA: Which was how many years ago?

(Both answer simultaneously.)

JAN: Twenty-six / HARRY: A century.

FREDERICA: You both taught at a college before this, didn't you.

JAN: At an Ivy League institution whose name is so well known it shall be nameless.

FREDERICA: And left it quite suddenly, so they say. Why?

HARRY: We were offered a splendid opportunity at this establishment—

JAN: And this house by the sea which we couldn't resist.

FREDERICA: How long ago was that?

JAN: Seven years ago.

FREDERICA: As I understand it, there was some pressure for you to leave your former place of employment—

HARRY: Where did you get this information?

FREDERICA: Obscure corners of the web—

HARRY: That shallow sewer of misinformation! We left because they were trying to fence us in—and, for both of us, our interests had expanded.

JAN: My poems were beginning to be published. And Harry's articles were beginning to be published, too.

FREDERICA: I would have thought that would have made your presence at your previous institution even more valuable.

HARRY: I'm sure you're aware of the bitterness of academic jealousies. If you half-succeed, they praise you. But if you succeed too much, the knives come out to slice you to bits.

FREDERICA: That's why you left?

JAN & HARRY: Yes.

FREDERICA: But why in the middle of a semester?

HARRY: *(To* FREDERICA:*)* Excuse me for interrupting the inquisition but are there going to be photos with this feature? Is my wife going to have her face scrutinized, air-brushed, color-toned? When you've done scratch-scratch, are you going to go click-click?

FREDERICA: I would like to. I didn't bring my camera.

JAN: Oh, we have a camera!

HARRY: One of those idiot-proof instruments where you can't fail—except, at the same time, you can never quite succeed.

FREDERICA: I'd be happy to take a picture if you—

JAN: Harry, why don't you get it for her?

HARRY: What?

JAN: I said—why don't you get it for her?

HARRY: I—

JAN: Go on. It's upstairs in the study. Go get it, Harry.

HARRY: *(He starts, reluctantly, to exit.)* Don't go too far in your confession! I will be able to hear—*(He exits into the house up right.)*

(When the women are alone:)

JAN: He can't, you know. Hear. The camera's way off on the other side of the house. I apologize for my husband. He's in a mood. He has an appointment this morning—with the President of the College—

FREDERICA: On something crucial?

JAN: That's just it. We don't know. *(Troubled)* We don't know...

FREDERICA: Talking to me could help you keep your mind off things.

JAN: When you can't know the future, relive the past, is that it?

FREDERICA: Are you happy with your past?

JAN: *(Flatly)* Ecstatic.

FREDERICA: And your present?

JAN: *(Still flatly)* Ecstatic about the present, too.

FREDERICA: One thing I haven't asked—

JAN: What's that?

FREDERICA: About children.

JAN: What about them?

FREDERICA: Do you have any?

JAN: *(After a long pause)* No. No children.

FREDERICA: You didn't want them? Or you couldn't—? You tried and still you—?

(JAN *gets out a worn and battered old-fashioned teddy bear.*)

JAN: *(Holding the teddy bear, she is silent for a long time, then says)*...We had a son... But he was kidnapped.

(HARRY *has entered just in time to hear this last. He thrusts the camera into* FREDERICA's *hands and says*)

HARRY: Take her picture now. Why don't you take her picture? The light is just right. *(Indicating the teddy bear)* But first get rid of that thing—

JAN: No! *(Clutching it to her)* I still can't understand it. We all were in the house! You'd think we would have heard—!

HARRY: *(To* FREDERICA:*)* Don't listen to her—

JAN: He was only two! Such a perfect child—! Asleep in his crib—! And they snatched him!

HARRY: *(To* FREDERICA:*)* We never had a baby.

JAN: Snatched in the night from his second floor bedroom! I went in to gaze at him, to tuck him in again, and he was gone!

HARRY: Jan, this lovely young woman does not have to be treated to your ravings—

JAN: This is what came of my marrying the most famous man in the world!

HARRY: *(To* FREDERICA:*)* She likes to exaggerate, my wife. I'm known in my field, but I definitely am not famous—

JAN: Reporters followed him everywhere. When my father, the Ambassador to Mexico, announced our engagement, it was front page news!

HARRY: *(To* FREDERICA:*)* Her father had a shoe store north of Boston—

JAN: On the weekend when the press suspected we were going to be married, they staked out my parents' country house in New Jersey. Meanwhile, Charles and I—

FREDERICA: *Charles* and you—? I thought he was Harry—

JAN: Charles and I let the reporters catch a glimpse of us lolling about in ratty old clothes. We pretended we'd invited a few friends over for a cook-out. Instead, when everyone arrived, we got hitched!

HARRY: Jan and I were married in a Registrar's Office in Massachusetts—

JAN: What fun we had that day! Outwitting the reporters! Charles made a great show of having his plane ready and serviced at the air field—

HARRY: She totally discounts the fact that I get airsick—

JAN: Instead, we escaped to the sea and honeymooned on a yacht!

FREDERICA: A clever ruse. And when you returned, how did you manage to—

HARRY: *(To* FREDERICA:*)* For heaven's sake, don't indulge her in this fantasy!

FREDERICA: Is it a fantasy?

HARRY: Poetic license. She is a poet, therefore flights of the imagination are required. Jan's flights allow her to escape from mental terra firma. It's a game she plays, sometimes for hours, the game of let's pretend.

FREDERICA: And in that time she cloaks herself in some other persona.

HARRY: Exactly.

FREDERICA: At the moment, she seems to be choosing to be Anne Morrow Lindbergh. *(To* JAN:*)* If you can pretend to be anyone, why do you choose to be her?

JAN: You don't *choose* to be who you are. You *are* it. Inescapably!

FREDERICA: *(To* HARRY:*)* I thought you said—

HARRY: She is pretending that she's not pretending...My wife slips into new identities as easily as she slips into a new blouse.

JAN: You can't escape the glory. You can't escape the pain. I remember it as though it were yesterday. My first sight of the empty crib—

HARRY: Jan, please—

JAN: I went around the house, asking who had picked up the baby. But no one had him. We all hurried to the nursery. The window was open. None of us had opened it. There was a ladder propped up outside against the building. We knew, then, that our precious babe was gone...*(To* HARRY:*)* If only you had been anonymous—! In anonymity is safety!

HARRY: You're right. Forget this interview!

FREDERICA: Was there a ransom note?

HARRY: *(To* FREDERICA:*)* Stop egging her on—

JAN: Of course there was a ransom note. Scrawled. In not good English—

FREDERICA: Whom did you suspect? The servants?

JAN: No matter how hard you check up on them, you can never be sure...

HARRY: Jan, this has gone far enough—. I really must get going—

JAN: *(To* HARRY:*)* You shouldn't have tried to find the kidnappers yourself! You should have left things to the police!

HARRY: They're a bunch of bumbling clods! You do your best to point the way to truth then find that you yourself are under suspicion—...What am I talking about! Now you've got me doing it!

JAN: *(To* FREDERICA:*)* You can not imagine what it's like to love a thing so much—a little thing whose eyes look up at you with such trust, such unquestioning devotion, a little thing who puts his tiny life in your hands, to cherish and keep safe—*(She holds the teddy bear close and begins to keen back and forth.)* —a little thing which you have, and then, which you don't have. A thing you had once and loved with every fibre of your being—and which, in one day, is gone...

(As JAN *rocks to and fro, the baby in her arms,* HARRY *takes* FREDERICA *aside and says to her:)*

HARRY: Whatever you do, you mustn't report this.

FREDERICA: She really seems to think she's Mrs Lindbergh.

HARRY: I told you—she's *pretending* she thinks she's Mrs Lindbergh.

FREDERICA: Is there a difference?

HARRY: Yes, of course. In one you're merely masquerading, in the other you're truly mad.

FREDERICA: And you think she's not mad.

HARRY: Jan mad? Impossible. You'd know if you'd lived with her for a hundred years as I have.

FREDERICA: But why is she doing it?

HARRY: Why do we all do what we do? Entertainment for an hour. Escape.

FREDERICA: But why *this* escape? Why the Lindberghs?

HARRY: Why not the Lindberghs?

FREDERICA: There were happier lives.

HARRY: Do you lead a happy life, Frederica? Do you have all you want? Or think you can one day have all you want? You're attractive. Young. Intelligent. *(Slightly suggestively)* Tell me, do you have all you want?

JAN: *(Observing them together)* Would you like me to leave so you and Frederica can have the living room alone together? Or perhaps the two of you would like to go upstairs—

HARRY: Don't be absurd—

JAN: I could go for a walk on the beach and leave you two to your own devices. I used to do that, did you know it, Harry? I used to pretend I wanted a long walk on the sand, when you were tutoring a student and I knew you wanted to be alone.

HARRY: Jan, quit this—!

JAN: *(To* FREDERICA:*)* You're not so much beyond the age of one of Harry's students—

HARRY: I said stop it!

JAN: Of course the thing that Harry doesn't realize is—*I* had students, too... Did you know that I had students, too, Harry? The great thing about teaching is that you always know each other's schedules. Always know when your mate is imprisoned in a classroom, always know when you can have the house to yourself—to do whatever you want.

HARRY: You don't have to go into—

JAN: Why not? Get out the yearbook. The yearbooks. I'll show you their pictures! *(To* FREDERICA:*)* But there are worse betrayals than betrayals of the body—

HARRY: Enough, Jan! I beg you!

FREDERICA: Mrs Hawkesworth—

JAN: Mrs *Lindbergh*.

FREDERICA: Was it splendid? Flying with him, just you two? In an open cockpit?

JAN: It was splendid! The wind blowing through my hair—

HARRY: I would have thought your hair would be tight inside an aviator's cap—

JAN: It was figurative! The wind blowing through my hair is a figure of speech! It's what I need! What I must have in my life! But you loved that, too, Lindy!

HARRY: *(Sardonically)* Yes. I loved it, Annie. Loved that high flying with you. It's *this* high flying that's trying my patience. I have to go see the President—

JAN: Calvin Coolidge.

HARRY: Ebenezer Cadwell.

JAN: Heads of State begged to have their pictures taken with Lucky Lindy. Before he hurries off, come snap a picture of Lindy and me. Go on. Go ahead. Take a picture of the woman and her hero—

(JAN *takes* HARRY's *arm.* FREDERICA *starts to point the camera at them.)*

HARRY: No! Enough of this nonsense! *(He grabs the camera away before she can shoot.)*

JAN: Forgive my husband. He gets tired of having his picture taken. It steals the soul, you know. And I suspect he feels that now his soul is gone.

HARRY: I have to go to this meeting! I have to be composed! Somehow have my wits about me.

JAN: Isn't it odd how upset my dear husband can get at the thought of a little meeting, when, in the defining moment of our married life, he showed absolutely no emotion?

FREDERICA: And what do you consider the defining moment of your married life?

HARRY: No! Don't tell!

JAN: When they took our baby!

(HARRY, *expecting another response, is almost relieved.*)

JAN: When we didn't know what happened to him for days and days!

HARRY: *(Wearily)* We never had a baby.

JAN: I thought I might die, or go insane, or rip the flesh from my living body—but you went through the days like an uninvolved detective, sifting clues, winnowing possibilities, weighing ideas.

HARRY: Will you, for God's sake, cease and desist from this so I can go to my meeting with a clear head?

JAN: But you had a clear head. A totally clear head, when what was called for was to scream with horror! When they found my baby's body—

HARRY: You never had a baby!

JAN: You went to see it, identified the body from its little teeth and didn't even cry!

HARRY: *(Putting on his jacket)* I have to go—

JAN: And even when I slept with another man, you stood like a rock. Immutable.

FREDERICA: Anne Morrow Lindbergh slept with another man?

HARRY: *(Coldly)* Jan Hawkesworth slept with another man. She thought I didn't know. I knew.

JAN: You could not be moved. Even then. *(To* FREDERICA:*)* He is a rock, my husband. Emotionless. Inhuman. But I understand it. If he allowed me a dalliance, it was because he had deeper guilts of his own.

HARRY: You'll excuse me, Frederica. Jan—or Anne—whoever you are. I have to go. *(To* JAN:*)* But remember this: there are things we have never said that need never be said. About which we swore to each other we'd be silent forever... And further remember: anything you say to this young woman you could find published on the front page of a tabloid newspaper—in bold black type. *(He goes out the front door.)*

(JAN *and* FREDERICA *are alone.*)

FREDERICA: He doesn't trust the press.

JAN: He has every reason.

FREDERICA: People who don't trust the press usually are hiding something. Are you hiding something?

JAN: That's a very direct question.

FREDERICA: I find sometimes one gets further with direct questions.

JAN: I am not hiding any more than most married people hide on their main subject.

FREDERICA: Oh? And what is their main subject?

JAN: Their relationship. The nature of their relationship, of course.

FREDERICA: And yours is not what it seems?

JAN: What does it seem?

FREDERICA: It seems—special.

JAN: Yes. I think it is.

FREDERICA: Able to stay steady through the storms—

JAN: You mean, you think tragedy would bind a special couple like us together.

FREDERICA: I would think so.

JAN: It did just the opposite. It tore us apart.

FREDERICA: What tragedy are you talking about? The kidnapped baby?

JAN: No. Not the kidnapped baby.

FREDERICA: What, then?

JAN: *(Sits and says:)*...There are some tragedies which are too deep for words.

FREDERICA: In spite of the prickly veneer and the bantering discord, you two seem to have an absolutely unseverable bond.

JAN: An illusion. Everything you see before you is an illusion.

FREDERICA: What's the reality?

JAN: The reality is I didn't win the Pulitzer. The reality is the man I married is exactly like a stone. The reality is I have no son.

FREDERICA: Actually, I know you have a son, Mrs Hawkesworth. I'm married to him.

(JAN, *speechless, stares at* FREDERICA.)

(Blackout)

END ACT ONE

ACT TWO

SCENE ONE

(Moments after the preceding scene. JAN *has gotten up, paced excitedly and now asks* FREDERICA:*)*

JAN: How is he? How is Adam? Is he well? Where are you living? Is he fine?

FREDERICA: He's very well. We live—only about an hour away from here.

JAN: Only an hour... Are you really a reporter?

FREDERICA: I am really a reporter. This, I'm afraid, is one assignment to which I wasn't assigned. I hope you don't mind. There won't be a printed interview—

JAN: I'd rather have a daughter-in-law than a thousand lines in any paper.

FREDERICA: I just wanted to know you. I was sorry that Adam wouldn't let me invite you to the wedding.

JAN: When was it?

FREDERICA: Two years ago.

JAN: Was it a big affair?

FREDERICA: Very small. Adam isn't, as you know, much of a crowd person.

JAN: Yes. He liked a pared down life. Parents, it seemed, took up too much room in it.

FREDERICA: Why do you and your husband pretend to have no son?

JAN: It makes things simpler. Adam left us before we came here. Slammed the door and said he never wanted to see us again. Ever.

FREDERICA: Did you never try to contact him—?

JAN: Of course I tried. In the beginning. But he refused to respond. He decided we did not exist so, when we got here, we decided *he* didn't. It was easier than explaining. I'm surprised he let you know we were still on this earth.

FREDERICA: He did at first tell me he was an orphan. But eventually he admitted you were alive.

JAN: So kind.

FREDERICA: What caused the rift?

JAN: He didn't tell you?

FREDERICA: He won't talk about it.

JAN: Discreet. Silent and discreet. Impenetrable. That's Adam.

FREDERICA: I've never found him impenetrable—except, perhaps, about this.

JAN: What's he doing?

FREDERICA: Writing.

JAN: Ah, the family curse.

FREDERICA: He writes well.

JAN: What is it? A novel? Dealing, as all first novels do, with his early life more or less in disguise?

FREDERICA: I don't know. He doesn't want me to read it until it's finished.

JAN: We shall be exposed, his father and I. ...When he talks to you what does he say about us?

FREDERICA: Aside from that time he admitted you were alive, he never mentions you.

JAN: And yet you came... How did you find us?

FREDERICA: There aren't that many Hawkesworths who are both professors. It was easy.

JAN: So you looked us up and came by to check us out.

FREDERICA: I wanted to see—

JAN: What we are. Who we are. If his silence about us hides a house of horrors.

FREDERICA: I never thought that.

JAN: Whatever made you come, I'm glad—so very glad—you did. After a while, one has a yearning for family. To have more family than I suspected pleases me more than I can say.

FREDERICA: Thank you.

JAN: I miss Adam. A lot. But Harry won't let me speak about him. Tell me more. Tell me everything. Tell me how you met and how you came to love each other. Tell me—

(She hears HARRY coming into the house. Even before he enters the room she is calling:)

JAN: Harry! Harry! We have a daughter! Frederica is our daughter!

(HARRY enters. He looks unsettled—like a man who has heard bad news.)

HARRY: We have no son, but suddenly we have a daughter. And fully grown.

What a miraculous event! Did you give birth to her sometime when I wasn't looking? Or did you just adopt her in the past half-hour?

JAN: She's married to Adam.

HARRY: Who's Adam?

JAN: *(To* FREDERICA:*)* You see? He's been erased. Harry refuses to remember. *(To* HARRY:*)* Harry. Frederica knows he exists. She and Adam are married.

HARRY: I'm not going to say I have a son just because he married. He cut out of here. As far as I'm concerned, that was a final goodbye.

JAN: Harry—

HARRY: You don't ask how it went.

JAN: What went?

HARRY: My interview with the President. You don't ask what he wanted.

JAN: For each of us to take on extra classes?

HARRY: No.

JAN: For you to chair the history department again?

HARRY: No.

JAN: What then?

HARRY *(A look at* FREDERICA, *then—)* He wants us out.

JAN: Wants us to leave the faculty?

HARRY: Leave the faculty, leave the school, leave the house.

JAN: *Why*?!

HARRY: Why leave the house? They're demolishing it to put up a gym, he says. As he points out, they own the house, they can do whatever they want with it. And what they really want—on this very spot of land, is a gymnasium. A gymnasium by the sea.

JAN: When does he want us to leave?

HARRY: Immediately.

JAN: *Now*—?!

HARRY: This afternoon. He claims they put a notice in our box some weeks ago. I claim he's lying. However, the wreckers will be here at any moment, so—

JAN: This is impossible—!

HARRY: They're shovelling us out, kiddo. Take what you think you need and let's go.

JAN: This is ridiculous! They can't—!

HARRY: That's life, my pet. Either there are crowds on the lawn waiting to shout your praises and carry you in triumph on their shoulders—or there are bulldozers on the lawn waiting to shovel you out.

FREDERICA: I don't understand. They may want to demolish your house. But why do they want you off the faculty?

HARRY: *(He hesitates a moment, then)*...Something from the past has suddenly reared its ugly head and bit us.

JAN: What are you saying?

HARRY: *(To* JAN:*)* I need to talk to you in private. Something has happened. Something this new daughter of yours—

JAN:—ours—

HARRY—doesn't have to know.

JAN: Frederica can hear everything. She's family. We can be open with our family. Whatever it is, Frederica can know.

HARRY: ...All right. *(A pause, then he says, to both of them:)* It seems—I've killed a man.

JAN: What—!

HARRY: To be more precise—I've killed him again.

JAN: What do you mean you've killed him again?

FREDERICA: I don't understand. How can you kill someone twice?

HARRY: You're young, Frederica. You don't know this yet: the worst murder isn't killing someone outright. The worst murder is if you wound them mortally but then they linger. And then, one day, when you've come to believe they're no longer a threat, they suddenly rear up and, just as they die, kill you.

JAN: What are you saying?

HARRY: I am saying that Jonathan Stone is dead. Killed himself. That's the news that President Cadwell summoned me to his chambers to impart to me. Jonathan Stone killed himself.

JAN: Oh—!

HARRY: Shot himself—

JAN: Where?

HARRY: Where did Jonathan Stone shoot himself? You mean in the heart? In the head? In the foot? He shot himself in the bathtub! He was so fastidious. Wouldn't you know if he had to shoot himself he'd do it in the bathtub—to make it easier for people to clean up after him.

JAN: *(Musing)* So Stone was not a stone after all...

FREDERICA: Is this the Jonathan Stone whose mantle you inherited?

HARRY: Whose mantle I *was* to inherit.

JAN: A man historians worshipped like a god. When Harry was a graduate student Stone was his mentor. He was the one who taught Harry how to look at the past and see what really was. Without Professor Stone—

HARRY: I have always credited him with my success—such as it is, such as it was. Always!

FREDERICA: But what has his demise to do with you?

HARRY: The old professor left behind a farewell epistle.

JAN: A suicide note?

HARRY: Oh, much longer than a note. A six page letter which he e-mailed to President Cadwell yesterday—apparently just before he pulled the trigger. *(Interrupting himself. At the window)* Oh, look! The bulldozers are arriving. How shiny they are! New brooms—to sweep us out clean...

FREDERICA: What happened back then? How long ago are you talking about?

JAN: We're talking about when Stone had just retired and Harry had taken his place on the faculty.

HARRY: *(To* FREDERICA:*)* After he retired, Stone published a book summing up his years of pondering the history of human civilized life. *The Times Literary Supplement* asked me to review it.

JAN: The editors knew Harry had been Stone's disciple. It was clear they expected him to heap his old professor with praise.

FREDERICA: *(To* HARRY:*)* But you wrote a negative review?

JAN: A very negative review.

HARRY: It was a review as honest and straightforward as I could make it. His theories were completely untenable!

FREDERICA: You'd learned from him—

HARRY: Yes. But these ideas he'd kept to himself. In order to publish them for the first time in his great summing-up volume.

JAN: In any case, in words quite unmistakable—Harry skewered Stone's magnum opus.

HARRY: I told the truth! His theory was so bleak it couldn't be borne!...In this book Stone said that humans are and always will be motivated primarily by malice—a deep-seated desire to cause others pain! It grieved me more than I can say to have to hurt the man who had nurtured and encouraged me. But I could not, in all honesty, let his theory stand!

FREDERICA: And this one negative review destroyed Stone's reputation?

JAN: Oh, it wasn't only that. It was that, in his review, Harry felt compelled to point out that several paragraphs of Stone's huge volume had been lifted word-for-word from earlier works.

HARRY: What should I have done? Ignored the fact that—

JAN: You could have exercised a modicum of compassion—I told you—

HARRY: *(To* FREDERICA:*)* She thought I shouldn't have pointed out the plagiarism—

JAN: *(To* FREDERICA:*)* I thought, in the name of mercy, he should have let the paragraphs go—

HARRY: The paper was testing me!

JAN: Nonsense! None of them knew. The passages were too obscure. You told me you'd just happened—by chance—to come upon the old volumes in which these passages appeared a few months before reading his book.

HARRY: Yes. By chance. By total chance.

JAN: It's likely no one else on earth could have made that discovery.

HARRY: No one— *(To* FREDERICA:*)* But once I realized what he'd done, what was I to do?

JAN: *(To* FREDERICA:*)* He could have chosen clemency. I begged him – *(To* HARRY:*)* I begged you to act with leniency and grace and give him a pass—

FREDERICA: Perhaps the professor forgot these were paragraphs he knew by heart rather than invented.

HARRY: It doesn't matter how he came to do it. Once I noticed what was blatant plagiarism I couldn't ignore it! It wasn't just *his* career that was on the line, it was *mine*. If there'd been just *one* double-dome to point out that I'd missed such a thing—I would have become the laughing-stock of my profession.

JAN: *(To* FREDERICA:*)* And so he told on his old professor.

HARRY: It tore me apart—!

JAN: *(Cynically)* Oh, yes—

HARRY: But I had to!

JAN: "You had to!" *(To* FREDERICA:*)* For years Stone had taken Harry under his wing, shared his wisdom with him, encouraged him, groomed him, confided in him, made sure all along the way that Harry was promoted to the next rung of every ladder. And then, when it was Harry's turn to repay all of Stone's trust and friendship, Harry turned on him.

HARRY: I was doing what Stone always taught me to do: I was being honest!

JAN: Your review shattered Stone's reputation! You reduced to nothing the sum and substance of the thinking of the man's entire life!

FREDERICA: What happened?

HARRY: Rather than congratulating me for my intellectual honesty, the faculty saw me as a traitor.

JAN: Harry and I were shunned. Colleagues turned away when we walked across the campus.

FREDERICA: They shunned both of you?

JAN: I stood by him. That's what a wife does, doesn't she? You don't desert the ship just because you hit rough seas.

FREDERICA: When the Professor read Harry's review, how did he respond?

JAN: By withdrawing from the world completely. He retreated into the hills. His young wife left him—this former student with her enviable combination of brains and beauty—left him. Stone went silent. Until yesterday, when, it seems, he blew his brains out.

HARRY: His entire life he had suicidal tendencies! The perfect life or self-annihilation! It was always his position!

JAN: And so the old professor shot himself—. *(She turns to* HARRY:*)* But not, apparently, before sending Cadwell a letter which somehow implicated you.

FREDERICA: But that review—it must have come out years ago. How many years ago was it?

JAN: Seven.

FREDERICA: When Adam left you—

JAN: Yes. When Adam left us. He judged us both—and his judgment was severe.

HARRY: Like our colleagues, Adam saw my honesty as betrayal. Like them, he decided to treat us as if we didn't exist.

JAN: We lost our jobs—and our son—at the same time.

FREDERICA: But why, if this happened so far in the past, did it take seven years for Jonathan Stone to kill himself?

HARRY: *(At the window, trying to distract from the conversation)* The shovels are moving into position—!

JAN: Murderer!

HARRY: It was not my fault!

JAN: So many died. So very many died…

HARRY: I went through hell knowing how hard it would hit the old professor—but the only path was the path of intellectual truth!

JAN: Herded into box cars!

HARRY: Hearing that he exploded his brain with a bullet leaves me suffering the tortures of the damned!

JAN: Marched off into gas chambers—

FREDERICA: *(To* HARRY:*)* But why are they blaming you for his suicide? Had you been in touch with him recently?

HARRY: Since that incident? Never.

JAN: Killer! People were shoved into furnaces and when the flames died all that was left was charred and steaming bones.

HARRY: *(To* FREDERICA:*)* Go to the window. See if more equipment has arrived. *(To* JAN:*)* Jan, listen to me. We have to organize—

(FREDERICA *looks out:*)

FREDERICA: There are two bulldozers, a wrecker's ball and a dump truck. Those machines—they are enormous!

JAN: People burned to bits! And it was my husband's fault—my adored husband—standing on podiums telling everyone that Hitler was a savior!

HARRY: Oh, God, has she slipped back again? Am I suddenly, once again, tall and blond?

JAN: Traitor! Betrayer! Betrayer of our country. Betrayer of me.

HARRY: Jan, don't do this. Please. I beg you—

JAN: Once you had vision. Once you could see. Your flights—higher and faster and farther than anyone—gave you perspective no one else had. And instead of seeing true and using your fame to fight for people to be free to live in dignity and peace, you—

HARRY: *(To* FREDERICA:*)* What am I going to do? She's driving me crazy!

FREDERICA: Perhaps if you humor her—

HARRY: I can't bear to see her this way—

FREDERICA: Why don't you play along. Pretend. It may help her to get over whatever it is that's troubling her.

JAN: You should have had some sympathy for those your actions ended up destroying!

HARRY: All Lindbergh ever said was that Hitler had superior military forces! That was a clear-eyed honest unflinching appraisal! As was my appraisal of Stone's book!

JAN: You should have known the horror that would result from your words—but you were blind! Went everywhere making speeches—tall and blond and beautiful—making speeches—saying we had nothing to fear from the monster. That he had made you promises. That there would be no war—

HARRY: No one can know in advance the consequences of one's actions—

JAN: You liked them, didn't you, those Germans. You thought they were so smart! Those uniforms. Their sense of order. Just like your sense of order. They had what you admired most—precise unsentimental minds!

HARRY: Their planes were better than our planes. They had enough air power to win!

JAN: They were fighting for a bad idea! But you didn't care, did you. You loved them! My hero. Seduced by the glamor of the Luftwaffe.

HARRY: I wanted peace!

JAN: You didn't care that innocents were being slaughtered—

HARRY: I made an objective judgment!

JAN: People died because of you—

HARRY: Lindbergh didn't know about the camps—

JAN: *(To* FREDERICA:*)* You see how vain he is? Referring to himself in the third person? *(To* HARRY:*)* People died because of you. Where was your sense of compassion? Where was the humanity I always believed was behind your cool impassive eyes? Where was your sense of the holiness of each and every life—?

HARRY: I did what I thought was right!

JAN: People died!

HARRY: Jan, in the name of God, I am not Lindbergh! I don't have to defend a man for how he lived his life! You're going mad and somehow I've become the enemy! Come out of this tailspin! I need you to be sane!

FREDERICA: *(At the window)* The bulldozers are moving closer.

HARRY: We're under attack on every side! I need you to hold steady!

JAN: How does it feel to have killed, my hero? How does it feel to have destroyed all those lives?

HARRY: One life. Perhaps one life!

JAN: Every life is connected to all other lives. When you kill one, you kill all the others.

HARRY: I called it as I saw it!

JAN: Jonathan Stone died for the way you saw it! Died in an oven!

HARRY: He shot himself in a bathtub!

JAN: Stone died in an oven because you stood on a platform and said Hitler was superb! You stood on a platform and let him annihilate millions!

HARRY: I wrote a negative review which pointed out that Jonathan Stone had copied several paragraphs —!

JAN: There must have been something more if they're condemning us now. What is it?

HARRY: There's nothing.

JAN: Betrayer! You betrayed your country, you betrayed Stone and you betrayed me!

HARRY: *(To* FREDERICA:*)* Are you taking this down? It's poppycock! Drivel! You are witnessing insanity. A profound slippage of the mind—

JAN: After his betrayal, everything went bad. We were both let go from our jobs. It was hard to find a perch. Only this brain-forsaken place would take us. And our son left home. When he saw what his father was—and what I seemed to condone—he left. Slammed the door and never once looked back. Never called. Never told us he was married. *(To* FREDERICA:*)* What Harry did is tantamount to murder, isn't it?

FREDERICA: I can't judge—

HARRY: You can. You must! You can't stay neutral! Tell her that my hands are clean!

JAN: Assassin!

HARRY: *(To* FREDERICA:*)* Do you think that I should have her put away?

JAN: *(To* FREDERICA:*)* Don't you think that he should be punished—for all he caused to die?

HARRY: *(To* FREDERICA, *at the end of his rope:)* What should I do?

JAN: *(To* FREDERICA:*)* Should I have left him? Should I leave him now? We have five surviving children—

HARRY: We have no children—

FREDERICA: You have a son—

HARRY: If he disowned me, I disown him! Ties of blood come untied if the rift is as wide as ours is.

JAN: How do you go on loving a man who was your hero when he is no longer a hero? How do you go on living, when that love was the center of your life?... What should I do? Should I leave—?

HARRY: My God, go! I can't stand the madness any longer! The bulldozers are moving in. We've been fired. Don't you understand? They've let us go and they're shovelling us out. Me because I'm the man whose standards were so high he caused another's self-destruction. And you because you stuck with me and stayed silent—which showed that you approved.

JAN: I did not approve. I put the sacredness of my marriage above my principles.

HARRY: The more fool you. I'm sorry for you, that in your faith in me you were so self-deceived.

JAN: I can still leave you—

HARRY: Too late. There is a tide in the affairs of men—and women—which, taken at the flood—. But your flood tide has come and gone, my darling. Come and gone and left you beached on this very dry and arid shore. *(To* FREDERICA:*)* You're not taking notes.

FREDERICA: I think—all this—should not be written.

JAN: Should it be told?

FREDERICA: To Adam? I don't know. I didn't tell him I was coming here to see you.

JAN: Why did you come?

FREDERICA: I came to see what Adam was running away from. You can't understand another until you can understand their past.

HARRY: The past can never be totally understood. I'm a historian and I say so.

FREDERICA: Even what can be glimpsed by the light of a match is helpful.

JAN: And have we helped you to see?

(The sound of the motor of a bulldozer)

HARRY: Excuse us. We're about to be scooped up and thrown into a dump truck. We have to pull together our few valuables, such as they are.

JAN: My book of poems. His white silk aviator's scarf—

HARRY: Oh, yes. My white silk aviator's scarf. With which, if the occasion demands, we could both hang ourselves.

FREDERICA: Adam's expecting me. But I could stay—I *should* stay—

JAN: Oh, no. This should not be witnessed.

FREDERICA: I could stay and help you pack—

JAN: It's good of you to suggest. But no. You couldn't tell what few things we value—

FREDERICA: *(Touching the airplane and the teddy bear)* Actually, I think I could.

JAN: Take them.

FREDERICA: No. They're yours.

HARRY: *(Gently)* Please. Go now...

FREDERICA: *(As she starts to go)* I'm glad I came. Even if we never see each other again, I'm glad we saw each other. I hope things will work out well for you.

JAN: Give our regards to—

(On a warning look from HARRY, JAN *stops and is silent.)*

FREDERICA: *(At the exit, turning back, she says:)* Perhaps you'd like to know—...I'm carrying your grandchild.

*(*FREDERICA *exits.)*

JAN: *(Joyously)* She's carrying our grandchild! There'll be another—

(The roar of the bulldozer gets louder.)

HARRY: Another Hawkesworth or another Lindbergh?

(The mechanical roar gets louder and louder.)

(Blackout)

Scene Two

(Later that afternoon.)

(HARRY, alone, is upstage right at the glass door looking out toward the ocean. He doesn't find what he is looking for. He turns to us and says:)

HARRY: Jan went for a walk on the beach two hours ago and hasn't returned. That's not like her. Can't see her. She doesn't usually go out of sight of the house. *(He crosses the room and looks out the downstage left "window".)* Momentary quiet. The wreckers are taking their afternoon break. A small crowd has gathered. To watch the walls come tumbling down. Are they the same ones who yesterday came to praise? Have they returned today to see us reduced to rubble? *Sic transit gloria mundi...(He returns to peer out the upstage glass door.)* Why doesn't Jan come back? I wonder if she's gone forever. Perhaps she walked into the sea. It would be just like her to end it with stones in one pocket and a copy of Virginia Woolf in the other. The coward's way out!...No. Walking into the ocean is the essence of brave. As one walked in deeper and deeper there'd have to be tremendous will to fight the instinct to keep one's head above the water, to not struggle against going under. ...What if the waves refused to take you? What if they screamed "No!" and buoyed you up and cast you onto the beach—humiliatingly alive. ...No. The waves don't care if you want to float or if you want to drown. To them it makes no difference. Live or die, it makes no difference. ...Goddam it, Jan, where are you?! *(He starts to open the door to go out then stops himself.)* Oh, what the hell! If that's what you want to do, do it! I won't stop you. God knows you have every reason. Now that we've come to the end of the line. *(He comes into the room.)* If she's done it, I ought to have the courage to do it, too! One always has it at the edge of one's mind—self-destruction. We all are Hamlets under the skin, wondering whether to be or not to be. It's not whether or not we want to exit—it's how to do it that's the question. By the time you've figured it out—and assembled the instrument that will help you on the road to kingdom come, you feel it's so much bother you may as well live a little longer. ...My God! What if she's actually seen it through! Actually chosen to go by water! What if, even now, she's being tossed up on the shore, bloated and blue—! *(Suddenly panicked, he starts rushing upstage right toward the glass door.)*

(Just as he gets there, JAN *enters, windblown, her jacket pockets bulging. She moves*

slowly, in a contemplative trance)

HARRY: You didn't kill yourself—

JAN: Neither did you.

HARRY: I worried.

JAN: Why not? What better do you have to do?

HARRY: Why were you gone so long? What were you doing?

JAN: *(Taking a handful from her pocket)* I was collecting seashells....And thinking.

(HARRY *looks out the downstage window.*)

HARRY: This is not a good time for thinking. They're coming back from their break—those workers in their jeans with the union labels. The unwelcome mat is being spread out before us. Gather ye mementoes and exit while ye may.

(Through much of the following he goes through the room picking up books and papers and making a pile of them on the table. He is very busy. JAN *is very still.)*

JAN: What are you planning to wear?

HARRY: For what?

JAN: For our exit.

HARRY: I hadn't thought about it.

JAN: I think we should go naked. Give 'em a picture no paper will print.

HARRY: One will.

JAN: True. It's an irresistible story: "Naked Grandma and Grandpa Evicted from Ocean Cottage".

HARRY: "Grandma and Grandpa".

JAN: It's what we're going to be.

HARRY: Two decrepit homeless wandering old relics.

JAN: Two decrepit homeless wandering old relics who will never see their grandchild. I will never see my grandchild and will never see my son.

HARRY: We got over that—

JAN: You did. I didn't.

HARRY: He walked out—

JAN: You could have begged him not to go.

HARRY: That's not my style.

JAN: You could—just once—have begged—

HARRY: Never. If you cared so much, you could have gone off with him.

JAN: No, I couldn't.

HARRY: You could have found out where he was and gotten in touch.

JAN: And gone against you? Contacting Adam would have meant betraying you.

HARRY: You made a choice. Live with it.

JAN: But not contacting Adam meant betraying myself. ...You tear me apart, you two.

HARRY: If he cared about you, he could have let you know how he was. But he didn't.

JAN: Perhaps he did. Perhaps he sent Frederica.

HARRY: I doubt it. She's an independent woman. She came on her own. Came, perhaps, to see if we had two heads, to see what her baby might inherit.

(*The sound of the motor of heavy equipment is heard sporadically.*)

HARRY: They're manning their assault weapons. We'd better pull together anything we want—

JAN: When it comes, I want to see that baby!

HARRY: Go, for God's sake! Go and good riddance!

JAN: You know my first loyalty has always been to you.

HARRY: Except once.

JAN: Yes. Once.

HARRY: When you had those secret meetings with your student.

JAN: With my student.

HARRY: That one time—when you made it so clear you had something on the side.

JAN: Do you want to know the truth of it? God's truth?

HARRY: Oh, we're bringing God into it, are we? Then perhaps I will, after all these years, get a true confession.

JAN: ...I met the young man only once. And talked him into declaring his love for the girl of whom he was so fond.

HARRY: You.

JAN: Not me. More's the pity. He was young and handsome and I suspected you of wandering. I did meet that young boy with the intention of inflicting on him tea and sympathy. He'd have been a pushover. But I couldn't do it. That all-too-brief encounter only proved to me how ridiculously complete was my attachment to you.

HARRY: Then, all these years, these little hinted boasts of your infidelity—?

JAN: Were my best fiction.

(The heavy motor sound increases, stronger, more continuous than before.)

HARRY: Ah, the lies we perpetrate—to burnish our image with our uncommitted sins—

JAN: I know it will disgust you, at this late date, to hear it—but I was always faithful to you, Harry.

HARRY: You shouldn't have been. You should have had adventures!

JAN: Don't say that—

HARRY: You should have kicked up your heels and danced and wallowed with whomever you wanted whenever you liked!

JAN: You wouldn't say that if I had.

HARRY: You don't know—

JAN: *You* don't know. How I feel. What I'm thinking.

HARRY: I know what you were thinking on the beach. You were thinking about losing touch with Adam. That's what hurts you most, isn't it!

JAN: *(A breath, then—)* Yes.

HARRY: You had to choose between us and you chose me. You made a bad choice, old bean!

JAN: I didn't— ...I can't understand why you closed the door so firmly against Adam.

HARRY: *He* closed the door against *me*! Do you know how hard it is to live knowing your child hates you? Sometimes I think the only reason we have children is so there can be someone alive to confront us with our sins. To accuse us of every shortcoming, every deviation from the narrow. They can accuse! They don't know what's down the line! ...It's easy enough to judge others when you're at the beginning of the journey. When you're farther down the road you get some idea of how unexpectedly bumpy the trip can be.

JAN: I never understood—you wrote a negative review—and our son left us. Was his idea of ethical action so elevated—his sense of righteousness so intense—he had to leave?

HARRY: ...It wasn't that.

JAN: What was it?

HARRY: God's truth?

JAN: God's truth.

HARRY: *(After a long pause)*...He saw me with Stone's wife. With Stone's young wife. Adam saw us together.

JAN: Stone's wife—?

HARRY: You didn't know—? About his wife and me?

JAN: No. I suspected there was someone. I had no idea it was her!

HARRY: Oh, yes. My betrayal of my mentor was more than words in a review. It was much more personal.

JAN: Stone's wife... But why—if this all happened back then—is everything exploding *now*?

HARRY: ...It seems, when Stone's wife moved out, she left behind some diaries. And this week, cleaning out a closet he'd never rummaged in before, Stone found them.

JAN: And in them he discovered the affair between the two of you.

HARRY: Yes.

JAN: So he did himself in because of an affair that happened years ago?

HARRY: Oh, no. People no longer kill themselves when they discover that their mate's been sleeping elsewhere. That's old-fashioned. In her diaries he discovered something that, to him, was far worse.

JAN: Go on.

HARRY: Are you sure you want to hear this?

JAN: Certain.

(There is the sound of motors revving up.)

HARRY: I'll tell you later.

JAN: Now. You'll tell me now.

HARRY: *(A long pause. Then, finally:)*...It seems that, in her diary, Stone's wife boasted of how, in the very middle of the act of love, she'd told me about the passages which Stone had copied. She'd typed his manuscript for him. She knew from what obscure texts they had been copied down.

JAN: *(Laughing ironically)* So your identifying those passages wasn't based on esoteric knowledge of your own! It was based on inside information from Stone's wife, the woman with whom you were sleeping!

HARRY: It was her joke! A joke we shared together! Far more satisfying than what we shared between the sheets! We were making a fool of the great man! ...This week, when Stone at last discovered our collusion, it filled him with self-hatred and revulsion. He could bear her giving her body to another. In a sense, since she was much younger than he, that was almost to be expected. But for her to betray him by revealing to me the passages he'd copied, and for me to reveal that copying to the world based on inside information from her, that he could not bear. He wrote out the whole sordid tale in a long incoherent yet brilliant letter, fired it off to Cadwell—then shot himself.

JAN: Harry—

HARRY: He got me—after all these years, the old buzzard. Killed himself—and did me in with the same sword. The perfect drama, no, my love? Hamlet and Laertes rub each other out simultaneously—I do Stone in, he does in me!

JAN: No—Harry—. What you did was cruel, yes. But you felt you were being honest!

HARRY: Jan, wake up! I didn't damn his book out of unflinching intellectual honesty! I did it out of envy!

JAN: That's not true!

HARRY: It is! Let me, finally, at least be honest with *you*. I was trying to destroy him. I knew that no matter how many paragraphs Stone lifted from the works of others he would always be a giant, while I, no matter how many clever revelations of others' failings I managed to uncover, would always be a pygmy.

JAN: His theory was flawed!

HARRY: Don't you understand? I skewered his book out of pure unadulterated malice. By doing that, I proved his theory right!

JAN: Harry—!

HARRY: By damning his book out of malice I put a curse on myself and you and all our family. Since then, I haven't known a minute's peace, not one. *(He pauses. Spent)*

JAN: ...Why didn't you tell me this before?

HARRY: ...Because I was your hero.

JAN: My hero—

HARRY: I wanted to be that for you, but I botched it.

(The sound of heavy equipment being moved closer interrupts them)

HARRY: I'd better look around upstairs —to see if there's anything we might want to take.

(He exits up right.)

(Alone, JAN starts taking more shells out of her pockets. As she does so, she says to us, with growing wildness:)

JAN: There's cockle shell, that's for remembrance. There's nautilus, that's to forget. I've been told something I do not want to know. How can I forget it?...

There's clam, that's to eat. ...Not raw. Unless you want to do yourself in. Why not? Why shouldn't we end it? Why shouldn't we let them scoop up our lifeless bodies with the detritus of our lives? *(She starts to sing:)*
She wheeled a wheelbarrow
Through streets wide and narrow
'Twas there that I met
My sweet Molly Malone...
(Becoming increasingly disturbed) Harry says people no longer kill themselves when they discover that their mate's been sleeping elsewhere. Caring about such a thing—it's so—old-fashioned! *(Confused, upset)* Abalone shell, that's for ashtrays. ...Levels of betrayal, mind and body. Mind *or* body. I pledge to thee the exclusive usage of my skin. I pledge to thee the eternal beauties of my true-blue mind. Blue, so very blue. *(Verging on breakdown)* Oyster shell, that's for finding pearls. ...Pearls of wisdom. "This above all: To thine own self be true." But isn't it selfish to be true only to one's self? Isn't it a higher thing to be true to others? But which other? My husband or my son?...Adam. *(Wildly)* Adam—! *(Attempting to control a growing hysteria)* Snail shell, that's for making yourself go slowly, slowly. ...Why did I stay? Out of love? Or was it vanity and pride? The world observes thou hast a perfect love. Do not shatter their illusions! ...But my husband was brave, was he not?—to speak out honestly in print—in spite of all, in spite of me? And did I not admire him for daring all that honesty? Was it honesty? Or was it malice—as he just now confessed? ...Lies! Thickets of lies! How overgrown the paths get after a while! And how narrow! How small the choice of roads one could still take! *(She moves toward the glass door which leads to the sea.)* Nora walked out and slammed the door. But she was younger! She deserted the field! I always thought the honor was to stay! *(Singing)*
'Twas there that I met
My sweet Molly Malone...
(Keening. On the brink of madness) There's winkle. And there's armadillo. There's turtle shell! Pull in your head! You'll be safe at home! ...Safe. ..."When I am old and gray and nodding by the fire... Remember how love fled..." Yeats. Not Hawkesworth, loser of the Pulitzer. I planned to sit by Harry's fire forever. I planned freedom, him and me together. Not exile! I planned light! Not this dark sky! I planned peace in this time of my life—! *(Crying out in despair)* It was going to be splendid! Not this. ...In place of splendor—what? Nothing. How do you go on loving—living—when your world is over? *(Singing)*
Crying cockles and mussels
Alive Alive-O
Alive Alive-O
Alive Alive-O
Crying cockles and mussels
Alive...
(Spoken)

Alive...
(Flatly)
Oh.
(HARRY *has returned and heard the last verse, watching her, unobserved, with love and pity,* JAN *sees him. Quietly, she says:)* And what am I supposed to do—now that I know all I know?

HARRY: You could leave me.

JAN:...Make my way alone—without my only friend?

(A moment. HARRY *breathes deeply then says, quietly, humbly:)*

HARRY: Jan, dear Jan—forgive? For flowers never sent, and diamonds never given, and beds never made, and lawns never mowed, for muffins never eaten, and jokes never laughed at... For tears never dried, and loveliness never complimented, for brilliance never acknowledged, and praises never sung, for devotion never recognized, and affection never valued... For hungers never satisfied, and joys never appreciated, for desires never gratified, and fidelities not treasured...For depths of soul and heights of spirit and moments of inexpressible beauty not sufficiently cherished... And for my betrayals—of mind and body—mentioned and unmentioned, forgive, pardon, grant absolution. *(He kneels at her feet.)* I am—so very sorry—that I've ditched our plane in the ocean and that you're drowning with me. Forgive. Please forgive me. *(He is weeping.)* I am so sorry...

(She holds him, comforts him for a time. Then, finally:)

JAN: Don't be sorry.

HARRY: We flew higher than anybody, didn't we?

JAN: We did, my darling.

HARRY: Crossed oceans, crossed continents. You as my co-pilot. What a team we were.

JAN: ...What a team we *are.* (JAN *takes a shell out of her pocket.)* Look, Harry....Look what I found out by the jetty. *(She opens her hand.)* A shell. A perfect shell. An ordinary kind, but most unusual. No gull smashed inside it with his beak to extricate his dinner. Yet it's empty. Some sea creature must have just walked out of it to find a new home.

HARRY: Are you saying we could do that, too?

JAN: Listen... The sea. *(She puts the shell to his ear.)* Wherever we go, we can take it with us. Even if we are destroyed, there's comfort in knowing the ocean will never cease. It just renews itself, forever and always.

HARRY: Is that what saved you when you were walking by the water?

JAN: I was thinking about our grandchild, the child whom we will no doubt never see. There's hope in that young life. It makes the destruction of us that much easier to take. There'll be another wave on the beach when our wave is gone.

HARRY: Anne Lindbergh found comfort in shells.

JAN: ...Who's Anne Lindbergh?

(They exchange a smile. The sound of a bulldozer, approaching, becomes louder.)

HARRY: We'd better go.

JAN: Desert this shell and just move on?

HARRY: As quickly as we can.

(He starts picking up things and putting them in a duffel bag.)

(Suddenly, JAN *says:)*

JAN: ...No. I have a better idea. Let's resist!

HARRY: What?

JAN: Barricade ourselves inside our fort and dare them to attack us!

HARRY: Why not? What have we got to lose? Let's do it!

JAN: No one shall say the Hawkesworths gave up without a fight!

HARRY: Come fire, come flood, come earthquake, come tornado! No one shall move us!

(The sound of the bulldozer becomes overwhelming.)

HARRY: They're almost at the porch!

JAN: They'll never dare to touch the house while we're still in it! Never! *(She calls out the window:)* Go on! Attack! You don't dare, do you!

(The bulldozer's giant maw makes contact! There is the sound of wood smashing and crashing down. Debris falls from the hall ceiling. Suddenly brilliant daylight streams in from above left through the upstage opening. HARRY *goes to the entryway and looks, then says in disbelief:)*

HARRY: The front door is gone! The porch! The steps—! A gaping hole—!

*(*JAN *and* HARRY *are taken aback at the reality of it.)*

(We hear the bulldozer pull back and move around to the right of the house, revving up its motor to attack.)

JAN: They're moving around to attack us from the other side!

*(*JAN *and* HARRY *are frozen, paralyzed. Heard clearly above the din,* HARRY *says:)*

HARRY: How do you go on when you can't go on? Where do you go when you have no place to go?

(For a moment they are completely lost.)

(As the sound of the bulldozer grows louder from stage right, FREDERICA suddenly appears from the left in the upstage opening. Bathed in its brilliant light, she says:)

FREDERICA: Adam's here. ...He wants to see you.

JAN: *(Joyously)* Adam—!

(She starts toward the opening then turns back toward HARRY and extends her hand toward him.)

(HARRY says, with apprehension, yet with hope of reconciliation)

HARRY: Adam—

(HARRY takes JAN's hand and they exit through the rubble-filled upstage opening.)

(Illuminated in the opening, FREDERICA extends her hand in the direction of the off-stage reunion—and smiles.)

(Blackout)

END OF PLAY

THE SHAKESPEARE ROAD

CHARACTERS & SETTING

Blane Powers
Samantha Snow
Off-Stage Voice

Time & Place: The Present. A dressing room in a theatre.

Setting: This is not a realistic play—and the setting reflects that. The ceiling soars higher and the space is more generous than any dressing room any actor has ever seen. And yet there is a tremendous sense of being shut in. There are no windows. The walls seem to tilt inward. The colors are grey and monochromatic. It is from another world—and from no world. Still, it being a space for working actors, there are enough indications of "reality" for actors to feel it is the kind of space they have often worked in before.

There are two long dressing tables with chairs before them, one stage right, the other stage left. There is a full-length mirror. There are also a cot for napping, a folding screen and an intercom. Upstage center is a recessed area with a pole on which to hang clothes and costumes. Offstage right of this is the entrance door. Offstage left is the door to the bathroom. A star affixed to the wall proclaims this to be the star's dressing room. At rise, the space is uninhabited, so there are no personal items present—just the bare essential furniture. The place is neither luxurious nor seedy, it is simply serviceable. It is the essence of "dressing room"—with no particularity at all.

ACT ONE

(At rise:)

(No one is on stage. BLANE POWERS *enters carrying a garment bag, a duffel bag and a smaller case. He is an actor of a certain age, tallish, ruggedly still attractive, perhaps a bit heavier than he was in his youth, but still muscular. He has taken a little less care of himself than he should have, but any pleasures or dissipations he has indulged in along the way have only served to make him more interesting.)*

*(*BLANE *looks around, is satisfied with what he sees—the size of the place is acceptable. The star on the wall is definitely acceptable. He puts the smaller case on the stage left dressing table, puts down the duffel bag and hangs up the garment bag on the metal clothes bar. He takes off his jacket and throws it over a chair. He is whistling:)*

BLANE: Whistle while you work,
Tra-la-la-la-la-la-la *(Etc)*

*(*BLANE *takes his stage make-up and his brush and comb out of his small case and puts them on the dressing table stage left. Still whistling, he looks into the mirror, likes what he sees, brushes back his hair in an automatic gesture—checking what he suspects may be a hairline receding at the temples. Then he takes a towel, shaving equipment, toothbrush and toothpaste out of his duffel bag and goes into the bathroom—from which we can hear him, still whistling.)*

(A moment later, SAMANTHA SNOW *enters. She is an actress of a certain age. She is in very good shape. She has taken very good care of herself—and looks it. She would never go anywhere without wearing full make-up and strikingly dramatic clothing. Even though she is entering an empty space, she makes an "entrance". She is carrying several small Louis Vuitton cases.)*

*(*SAMANTHA *gives a cursory look around the room. Yes. It's large enough for her. She touches the star on the wall. This pleases her even more. She smiles. She is putting down her bags when she becomes aware of someone whistling. Instantly, she covers her ears. She can still hear it. She calls out:)*

SAMANTHA: Whoever you are, for God's sake stop whistling!

(The whistling continues.)

SAMANTHA: Don't you know you mustn't whistle in a dressing room! It's bad luck!

(The whistling continues.)

SAMANTHA: Stop it! Stop it!

(BLANE, stripped to the waist, comes out of the bathroom wiping his face with a towel and sputtering)

BLANE: Goddam it! Who the hell do you think—! *(Drying his eyes, he opens them and sees SAMANTHA:)* Oh—! ...Miss Snow—!

SAMANTHA: Mister Powers—!

BLANE: I thought you were the prop girl!s

SAMANTHA: I thought you were the plumber.

BLANE: Sorry for my rudeness. I humbly apologize.

SAMANTHA: As do I. Let's begin again. Shall I retake my entrance?

BLANE: No, no. I'm sure it was a beautiful entrance, but it's not necessary. *(In a courtly way, he comes over and shakes her hand. If it were another era, he'd probably be kissing it.)* I'm very pleased to meet you. Pleased we're going to be working together.

SAMANTHA: Thank you. So am I. At last. At long last.

BLANE: I don't know how it happened that our paths didn't cross—in work or in life—until this moment.

SAMANTHA: I almost did a guest shot on that Australian detective series you did a few years ago.

BLANE: *Holmes of the Range.*

SAMANTHA: That's it. Unfortunately, the director thought I was too—refined—to play a barman's mistress.

BLANE: Speaking of barmen, Miss Snow. May I offer you a drink? *(He takes a bottle of Scotch out of his duffel bag, pours a drink and offers it to her.)*

SAMANTHA: *(Shaking her head, with only the barest hint of disapproval)* No, thank you. And please, call me Samantha. In the theatre, one has to move so quickly to dealing with intimate things—the soul, the emotions—formality has no place here.

BLANE: *(Drinking the drink himself and assenting)* Samantha...Blane.

SAMANTHA: Blane... Is anybody born "Blane"?

BLANE: Actually, I was born "Peter". My parents didn't seem to notice that my initials would be P P. After barely surviving my first first grade recess, I changed it.

SAMANTHA: Very wise.

BLANE: Surely you weren't born Samantha.

SAMANTHA: I was. I was Samantha before everybody was Samantha.

BLANE: And "Snow". Did that come to you at birth?

SAMANTHA: Not quite. I was born Schwendangle. Samantha Schwendangle.

BLANE: Not much marquee value.

SAMANTHA: Not much.

BLANE: I think we remade our names rather nicely, don't you?

SAMANTHA: Very nicely. ...I think this whole enterprise is going to be fun. It's grand that we'll get a chance to hone our performances here on the road—

BLANE: —then move into town trailing clouds of glory!

SAMANTHA: Exactly... You know, a few years ago I suggested you to play Loveborg opposite me in *Hedda Gabler*.

BLANE: But—?

SAMANTHA: What can I say? The producers couldn't see you as a poet with vine leaves in your hair.

BLANE: *Tant pis.*

SAMANTHA: But I'm more delighted than I can say that we're working together now. I've always wanted to do scenes from Shakespeare.

BLANE: So have I.

SAMANTHA: I asked—but no one seemed to be able to answer—have you ever done Shakespeare before?

BLANE: Oh, yes.

SAMANTHA: Where—if you don't mind my asking.

BLANE: In acting school.

SAMANTHA: Ah...

BLANE: You, of course—

SAMANTHA: Of course. Every chance I get.

BLANE: Not that those chances came along too often.

SAMANTHA: True. Not often enough.

BLANE: Well, we'll get our chance now.

SAMANTHA: I look forward to it. I want you to know you are always welcome in my dressing room. (*She opens her bag and starts putting her make-up and other things out onto the dressing table stage right.*)

BLANE: Uhm—actually—this dressing room is mine.

SAMANTHA: Oh? That can't be. I saw no other door with a star. My contract says I have the star's dressing room.

BLANE: So does mine.

(He pours another drink. There's another look, of a little more disapproval, from her. He puts the bottle down on his dressing table. It seems a territorial gesture.)

SAMANTHA: Obviously some misunderstanding. We'd better straighten this little matter out.

BLANE: Yes. We'd better.

(There's an intercom box near the entry. SAMANTHA *presses the button and says into it:)*

SAMANTHA: Hello? ...Hello?...

(There's no response.)

SAMANTHA: I didn't see anybody at the stage door, did you?

BLANE: No. Nobody.

SAMANTHA: There must be someone somewhere. *(Into the intercom)* Hello? Hello? Is anyone there? *(While she waits, she says to him:)* I know we're going to get on famously.

BLANE: I'm sure we will.

SAMANTHA: It's so important to have a good working relationship, don't you think?

BLANE: Couldn't agree more.

SAMANTHA: I think it'll be very interesting working with this new young genius director.

BLANE: Actually, I never heard of him.

SAMANTHA: To tell the truth, before this, neither did I. I never heard of the director. I never heard of the producer. I didn't even know there was a theatre on this block.

BLANE: Neither did I. I've passed this way hundreds of times and never noticed it.

SAMANTHA: Yet—here we are.

BLANE: Yes. Here we are.

SAMANTHA: It's a job.

BLANE: Yes. It's a job.

SAMANTHA: Did anyone greet you when you came in?

BLANE: No one.

SAMANTHA: It doesn't bode well. I'm stunned that there was no one here to greet us. No one to show us to our dressing rooms. No one to say "Welcome Aboard". I hope it's not a harbinger of how we're going to be treated on this production.

BLANE: I must say, it's all very mysterious.

SAMANTHA: Ah, yes. "The Mystery of Theater".

BLANE: It has nothing on the mystery of life.

SAMANTHA: "The Mystery of Life". *(Unwilling to think about that, she once more goes to the intercom.)* Hello? ...Hello? ...Is anybody there?

(No response.)

BLANE: I always thought your work had great—quality.

SAMANTHA: I always thought your work had great—strength.

BLANE: *Merci, Madame.*

SAMANTHA: Do you often speak French?

BLANE: I just played the Count of Monte-Cristo in a little independent film we shot outside of Paris. Haven't yet dropped the habit.

SAMANTHA: *(Aside:) Tant pis.*

BLANE: What?

SAMANTHA: Nothing. *(Into the intercom:)* Hello? Hello?

(At last, a male VOICE—*a straightforward, grounded, workaday male* VOICE—*comes over the loudspeaker.)*

VOICE: *(O S)* Can I help you?

SAMANTHA: This is Samantha Snow. I'm afraid there's been a mix-up. Mister Powers and I seem to find ourselves in the same dressing room.

VOICE: *(O S)* There's no mix-up.

SAMANTHA: What do you mean?

VOICE: *(O S)* We only have one star dressing room. Your contracts say you each must have it. You do.

BLANE: Impossible!

SAMANTHA: We insist you find another dressing room for one of us immediately.

VOICE: *(O S)* There's only one dressing room on stage level. The others are all up three flights.

SAMANTHA: *(To* BLANE:*)* This is absurd—

VOICE: *(O S)* If either of you wants a room above, I'll be happy to arrange it.

(SAMANTHA *turns to* BLANE.)

SAMANTHA: Unbelievable! I'd fire my agent—but I fired him last week.

BLANE: I'd fire mine—but he's in a sanitorium.

SAMANTHA: What shall we do?

BLANE: Well—I don't like to be territorial, but—I got here first. *(He gestures to his things, all set out and homey.)*

SAMANTHA: I can't possibly run up and down some twisty iron staircase!

BLANE: Shall we toss for it?

SAMANTHA: We could... Or you could just be a gentleman and—

BLANE: Under most circumstances, I'd be happy to. But I have several very quick entrances. There's no way I can—

SAMANTHA: Neither can I!

(The Voice interrupts:)

VOICE: *(O S)* Why don't you share?

(SAMANTHA *pulls her finger off the button. She'd forgotten all about it.*)

SAMANTHA: *(To* BLANE:*)* I hadn't realized he was listening... It's an idea.

BLANE: Yes. It's an idea.

SAMANTHA: The room is certainly big enough. We could put up a curtain to divide it if we want to.

BLANE: Ah, modesty, modesty—.

SAMANTHA: There is a screen... What do you think?

BLANE: A little crazy. But—why not? We're grown-ups.

SAMANTHA: And we're going to get along so famously.

BLANE: Contrary to our reputations—famously.

SAMANTHA: *(Into the intercom:)* We'll do it. *(To* BLANE:*)* I'll go get the rest of my luggage. *(She goes out upstage right.)*

BLANE: *(To us:)* Well, this is going to be an adventure. I suppose you think I should have done the gentlemanly thing and given her the star's dressing room. Not on your life! Did you notice that little intimation of superiority? *She* was doing Hedda Gabler, while I, poor benighted ex-film star, was only doing *Holmes of the Range*. Ha! Her Hedda was so far off the main stem they had to issue maps with the tickets! While my series—before it was cancelled—was in the top ten for almost the entire length of its run! *(He peers at himself in the mirror and says:)* Drink up, kiddo. It's going to be a bumpy ride! ... I'd better fortify myself with a breakfast pizza. *(He presses the intercom button.)* Would somebody please bring me a pepperoni pizza? Anchovies, mushrooms, onions. Heavy on the onions. *(He takes a very long, very deep drink.)*

(SAMANTHA enters wheeling in two enormous Louis Vuitton trunks. He stares. She says:)

SAMANTHA: I wouldn't mind a little assistance.

BLANE: Oh. Sorry.

(Suddenly once more the gallant, BLANE helps SAMANTHA wheel them in, then sits down and watches her put out her things. She's very precise about it. Much more precise than he. At first she's self-conscious with his watching. Then she forgets and keeps making her space into the home she always makes it. He starts to whistle. She gives him a look. He stops. He's stunned and appalled by the amount of stuff she has, the amount of space she begins to take up on the clothing rack, the amount of make-up and beauty products which she lays out carefully. Then, as the final flourish to the decor, she begins to take out her collection of miniature elephants.)

BLANE: And those are—?

SAMANTHA: Mascots. For good luck.

BLANE: You think you're going to need that many?

SAMANTHA: I once did a play which had a good luck elephant in it. Since then, people keep giving them to me on opening nights. I don't dare leave one of my little pachyderms behind, lest he get angry and jinx everything.

BLANE: Yes, it would be tragic to cross an elephant, especially on an opening. *(He presses the intercom button.)* Hello? Is somebody going to get my pizza? *(He says to her:)* I do believe I'm going to have to get it myself... Want one?

SAMANTHA: No, thank you.

BLANE: *(Watching her put out an electric tea kettle, a hot plate and her own set of fine china:)* I'll leave you to it, then. A bientôt! *(He goes.)*

(Once SAMANTHA is alone she turns to us and says:)

SAMANTHA: A bientôt! I'm going to be playing Cleopatra opposite Monte-Cristo of the Range! ...Look how he travels. Like a gypsy! ... He thinks that I think I'm a superior talent. I do. I am! He has made his way on looks alone. On "charm"! A debased and all-too-common characteristic of male actors—particularly those who work mainly in film and television. They get away with so much! Their instruments get rusty. You know he was not my first choice for co-star in this enterprise. But what could I do? The actors I wanted—ones with a certain amount of classical background—all seemed to have other commitments. So I was talked into taking him. They say he's a draw. That he'll bring people into the theatre. But what kind of people! I ask you—!

(BLANE *returns, empty-handed.*)

SAMANTHA: No pizza?

BLANE: ...No director.

SAMANTHA: Excuse me?

BLANE: As I was going out the stage door I heard a phone ringing. There seemed no one around to answer it, so I picked it up. It was our esteemed director. It seems he's walked out on us for another job.

SAMANTHA: How could he—?

BLANE: Hollywood beckoned.

SAMANTHA: Ah! The lure of the screen and its filthy lucre! I knew we should have gone with someone tried and true—and mature!

BLANE: The asshole.

SAMANTHA: What are we going to do?

BLANE: I suppose—get another director.

SAMANTHA: At this late date? We open in three weeks! How will we ever find someone who knows the plays, knows our work? I was just waiting for Crisis Number One! I never thought it would come so soon and be so catastrophic! How can we—!

BLANE: I could do it.

SAMANTHA: Do what?

BLANE: Direct this thing.

SAMANTHA: You?!

BLANE: I've directed.

SAMANTHA: What?

BLANE: Some very elaborate, very sensitive—commercials.

SAMANTHA: Commercials! (*She looks at him with barely disguised scorn.*)

BLANE: They had great—quality.

SAMANTHA: (*Doubtful*) Hmmm.

BLANE: Who knows? I may not be the idiot you think I am.

SAMANTHA: (*Under her breath*) I doubt it.

BLANE: Why don't we give it a try?

SAMANTHA: (*Considers, then:*) I suppose we could do worse. (*Aside:*) ...'Though not by much.

BLANE: *(Aside)* ...She probably doesn't take direction anyway.

(BLANE *gets his script.* SAMANTHA *gets her script and starts toward the exit.)*

BLANE: Where are you going?

SAMANTHA: To the stage. Aren't we going to rehearse there?

BLANE: That's another thing. Before we arrived, I was told the stage would not be available. They're still constructing the set.

SAMANTHA: *(Sarcastically)* Perfect! ...What are they building—a reconstruction of the Globe?

BLANE: No, no. They say it's simple. Stuff that can be taken on the road. Just some screens, some levels and a few set pieces.

SAMANTHA: How long can that take?

BLANE: I'm sure it'll be ready shortly. We can rehearse here.

SAMANTHA: Here?!

BLANE: This space is big enough.

SAMANTHA: I suppose, the first few days, we'll be sitting down anyway... Oh, why not?

BLANE: *(A moment. He gets his script. Then:)* ...Why don't we start at the top?

SAMANTHA: With Kate? No. I don't feel shrewish... Let's start with *Antony and Cleopatra*.

BLANE: *(Keeping his temper. Already, she's disagreeing.)* Right. *Antony and Cleopatra*. *(He turns to the page.)* Page seventeen. Antony in Egypt. *(He begins, emoting grandly.)*
Let Rome in Tiber melt and the wide arch
Of the ranged empire fall! Here is my space—
Kingdoms are clay—

SAMANTHA: *(Interrupting)* Wait a minute! Wait a minute!

BLANE: What's the matter?

SAMANTHA: Is that the way you plan to do it?

BLANE: Something like that. Is something wrong?

SAMANTHA: You're playing to the balcony. Antony is alone with Cleopatra. He's telling her private things. Why do you have to project to the fifty-fifth row?

BLANE: He's proud of the size of his—love. He's showing off to her.

SAMANTHA: He doesn't need to show off. He's a hero. He's quietly self-confident.

BLANE: Who's directing this, you or me?

SAMANTHA: You are. But as there's no way for you to be objective about yourself, I think I should have the right to express my opinion.

BLANE: As long as you realize it's just that—opinion. And if I don't agree with your criticism I have the right to reject it.

SAMANTHA: And I have the right to reject yours.

BLANE: There has to be some overall vision—

SAMANTHA: And it has to be the *right* vision! You can't substitute theatrics for an inability to act with subtlety.

BLANE: Antony and Cleopatra are not ordinary street people. They're grand and glorious! There has to be some size—some grandeur and dimension.

SAMANTHA: I agree completely! But what I'm saying to you is this: The grandeur can't be fake!

BLANE: "Fake"!

SAMANTHA: Fake.

BLANE: *(With growing fury)* Say your line.

SAMANTHA: We have to both agree on the concept—

BLANE: *(Shouting)* Say your line, goddam it! *(He pulls completely back and says, starting exceedingly quietly and politely, then building to a shout:)* Oh, excuse me. I beg your pardon, Miss Snow. I wonder if you would be so kind as to say your line so we can GET THIS SHOW ON THE ROAD!!!

(They start to rehearse, reading lines from their scripts. We don't hear them. the lights change. music indicates a passage of time.)

(The rehearsing continues—in half light and in dumb show.)

(As the next scene begins, the lights come up to full. BLANE and SAMANTHA are seated, doing a scene. Suddenly she stops and puts down her script.)

SAMANTHA: Time for a break.

BLANE: We just started—

SAMANTHA: Yes. But it's noon.

BLANE: Equity says—

SAMANTHA: I don't care what Equity says. I have a very strict eating schedule. Breakfast at eight, lunch at noon, tea at four, dinner at seven.

BLANE: God, it's like feeding time at the zoo!

(SAMANTHA goes briefly into the bathroom with her electric kettle and comes out having filled it. She plugs it in, gets out a small packet from her case, tears open

a corner and pours the powdered contents into a mug. BLANE *watches the whole operation with great interest.)*

BLANE: What's that?

SAMANTHA: Lunch.

BLANE: I mean—what *is* it?!

SAMANTHA: Powdered spinach and tofu. I have it every day for lunch.

BLANE: And what do you have for dinner? Powdered rhinoceros horn?

SAMANTHA: Don't you keep to a diet?

BLANE: My diet is "Eat anything anytime."

SAMANTHA: You'll rue the day—

BLANE: That I didn't spend my life dining out of envelopes? Never.

(SAMANTHA *pours boiling water into the mug and stirs.* BLANE *takes a hero sandwich out of his duffel bag and starts to unwrap it. She turns away in disgust and starts to drink her lunch. The sight of the viscous green liquid repels him. He takes a bite of his sandwich and says:)*

BLANE: About your Ophelia. What I feel is—

SAMANTHA: I'm sorry, Blane. It's one of my strictest rules—not to discuss work while I'm eating. It interferes with my digestion.

BLANE: So sorry. *(As he watches her drink the glop:)* Tell me, what does your husband think of this diet?

SAMANTHA: I have no husband.

BLANE: I thought you did.

SAMANTHA: I did. But—at the moment—we're separated.

BLANE: "At the moment"?

SAMANTHA: Just temporarily.

BLANE: All I know is what I see on T V. And I remember all those images of you two billing and cooing—

SAMANTHA: Well, the cooing turned into cawing somehow and it got so we couldn't look at each other without screaming at each other—I don't know why. It just seemed it would be better if we were away from each other for a while. We'll probably—someday—get back together. He's still my best friend. We just need—a little vacation from each other.

BLANE: Which number husband is he, if you don't mind my asking?

SAMANTHA: Only number three. These days, that's not excessive.

BLANE: No. Not excessive.

SAMANTHA: Are you married at the moment?

BLANE: I've never been married.

SAMANTHA: Never?

BLANE: Never.

SAMANTHA: You don't like being faithful?

BLANE: I don't like being yoked.

SAMANTHA: Men!

BLANE: For your information, I've had a series of very fine, very solid relationships.

SAMANTHA: Ha!

BLANE: I was always—well, almost always—faithful.

SAMANTHA: That is the world's biggest "almost!"

BLANE: Were *you* always faithful?

SAMANTHA: Always.

BLANE: Was he? Were they?

SAMANTHA: Who knows?

BLANE: What caused the splits?

SAMANTHA: If you're really interested in the particulars—

BLANE: Oh, I am.

SAMANTHA: My first husband thought he was prettier than I was. He thought it would be nice to be married to a star—until I started getting more attention than he did. For the second, I was a trophy wife. He loved being photographed with me looking glamorous on his arm. But he didn't understand that I couldn't spend my life partying! That I needed my energy, that I had to be devoted to the work! My third, on the other hand— *(She trails off, in regret, and memory of affection. To still the emotions, she opens another packet and mixes up another powdered concoction.)*

BLANE: What's that?

SAMANTHA: Dessert.

BLANE: I mean, what *is* it?

SAMANTHA: Powdered cactus and prunes.

(BLANE *grimaces, takes out a candy bar and begins to munch.* SAMANTHA *looks on in disgust.*)

BLANE: Do you have any children?

SAMANTHA: A daughter. Sired by husband number one. I think that's why he left—she was getting more attention than he was.

BLANE: How old is she?

SAMANTHA: Just out of college.

BLANE: What's she doing?

SAMANTHA: A little of this, a little of that.

BLANE: Do you see her often?

SAMANTHA: What is this—the third degree? How often I see my daughter is my business, it has nothing to do with—

BLANE: Sorry.

SAMANTHA: *(Recovering her composure)* Do you have any children?

BLANE: Not that I know of.

SAMANTHA: Ah, this modern life!

BLANE: The patter of tiny feet has never appealed to me.

SAMANTHA: They might if the feet were related to you.

BLANE: I doubt it. I always make it clear in the beginning I don't want that kind of tie. I tell anyone I get involved with I'll take reasonable care it doesn't happen, but if it does, it'll be none of my concern.

SAMANTHA: And your bedmates go along with that?

BLANE: Most of my women—

SAMANTHA: Good God, do they come by the carload?

BLANE: Men, too, you know, can be something of a trophy. I'm well aware that most of my women go for me because of my fame, my looks.

SAMANTHA: Vanity, thy name is Blane!

BLANE: Just being realistic. I never felt that any of them really knew me, really loved me.

SAMANTHA: Did you love them?

BLANE: Honestly?

SAMANTHA: Honestly.

BLANE: I can't say I ever did. Although the one I'm seeing at present, she's different. She— *(He breaks off. He notices her glass is empty.)* If you've finished your epicurean repast there's something I want to talk with you about.

SAMANTHA: Yes? What is it?

BLANE: *(A hesitant beat, then:)* The scene we're doing from *Hamlet*. I don't think we should do the one with Hamlet and Ophelia, I think we should do one with Hamlet and Gertrude.

SAMANTHA: Why?

BLANE: It's obvious, isn't it?

SAMANTHA: We're doing Romeo and Juliet.

BLANE: I want to talk with you about that, too. I think we ought to cut it.

SAMANTHA: Cut my Ophelia, and now cut my Juliet.

BLANE: Substitute Gertrude for Ophelia, and let Juliet go—

SAMANTHA: We're not doing the plays. We're doing our impression of the roles. It takes maturity to understand what young lovers felt! You can't have them played by teenagers!

BLANE: But still—

SAMANTHA: I know what you're thinking. I'm too long in the tooth to play Juliet, but you'd be perfect as young Romeo!

BLANE: I didn't say that.

SAMANTHA: You can see yourself climbing up a balcony—but not to kiss an old harridan like me!

BLANE: I didn't say that either!

SAMANTHA: You wish you were working opposite a younger—and not to put too fine a point on it—thinner—actress!

BLANE: This is all in your head. I never said a thing about—

SAMANTHA: You don't think I should play someone with whom you could fall in love, you think I should play your mother!

BLANE: You're taking this the wrong way. I'm trying to spare you the embarrassment of—

SAMANTHA: *(With growing heat)* I worked hard to prepare for these roles! I memorized all these parts—Juliet, Ophelia, Portia, Rosalind, Viola, Beatrice, Lady Macbeth, Cleopatra! I worked my butt off and I think I can do justice to every single one of them. Why don't you wait till you see what I can do before you start cutting things!

BLANE: Sorry. Sorry—

SAMANTHA: I'll trade you my Ophelia, but I absolutely will not give up my Juliet!

BLANE: Keep her, for God's sake!

SAMANTHA: Tho' it'll take all the skill I have to play someone who's supposed to be besotted with you!

BLANE: Romeo's feelings are mutual, I'm sure.

SAMANTHA: I'm going out for a breath of fresh air!

BLANE: Be back in twenty minutes.

SAMANTHA: I always take a walk after lunch. You should, too. It keeps one from getting flabby.

BLANE: Thanks for the hint.

(SAMANTHA *heads for the exit.*)

BLANE: Twenty minutes!

(SAMANTHA *goes out.*)

(BLANE *is nonplussed. He presses the key and says into the intercom.*)

BLANE: What's the matter with her?

VOICE: *(O S)* She's very nervous.

BLANE: Does she think I'm not?

VOICE: *(O S)* She hasn't worked in three or four years.

BLANE: I haven't worked in front of a live audience in decades!

VOICE: *(O S)* Try to be patient with her.

BLANE: Did someone get my Scotch?

VOICE: *(O S)* It's in your mailbox.

BLANE: I'll pick it up on my way out. I need a cigarette. ...Do you really think she can play a thirteen-year-old?

VOICE: *(O S)* Your guess is as good as mine.

(BLANE *starts to exit.*)

(*Music. The lights change.*)

(*As* BLANE *goes out,* SAMANTHA *re-enters. They pass each other with only a slight nod of the head. When he has gone, she says to us:*)

SAMANTHA: He's a slave driver! I may be scrupulous about breaking for lunch, tea and dinner on time, but he's scrupulous about ending those breaks exactly on the second! We've only been rehearsing for a week and he has us on our feet already! I've told him time after time we should be working on interpretation first. Being on our feet this early is exhausting. For God's sake, it's only the two of us. How much staging do we need? He has us dancing this way and that like waltzing mice! ...And his drinking! He doesn't think I know, but I know. I know about the bottles he has hidden here and there, and the little flask which he takes a nip from every time I turn my back. He rinses out his mouth with mouthwash afterward, but I can still smell it. Liquor and mouthwash—they're both equally repellent. Thank heaven I don't have to kiss him. At least I think I don't! *(She presses the button on the intercom.)* Do you think we could have a little more air conditioning in here? The air is impossibly close.

VOICE: *(O S)* Happy to oblige.

SAMANTHA: By the way, I've never asked your name.

VOICE: *(O S)* No, you haven't.

SAMANTHA: What is it?

VOICE: *(O S)* Call me anything you like.

SAMANTHA: Anything?

VOICE: *(O S)* Anything.

SAMANTHA: All right. I'll call you Pops. The guardians of our welfare are always called Pops. Is that all right with you?

VOICE: *(O S)* It's fine.

SAMANTHA: I need to talk with you about Blane, Pops. There are certain things that—

(BLANE *bursts in waving a newspaper.*)

BLANE: Have you seen this?

SAMANTHA: What is it?

BLANE: The ad for this presentation.

SAMANTHA: Yes, I've seen it.

BLANE: You approved it?

SAMANTHA: Certainly.

BLANE: Your name is above mine. In the ads. On the marquee. On the posters. Everywhere!

SAMANTHA: Is there something wrong with that?

BLANE: I was distinctly promised that our billing would be equal.

SAMANTHA: It *is* equal.

BLANE: It's the same size type, but our names were supposed to be side by side! *(He demonstrates in the air.)* Samantha Snow and Blane Powers. And sometimes—*(Crossing his hands)* Blane Powers and Samantha Snow. We are supposed to be side by side, in the same size type, on the same line, and sometimes I'm supposed to get first billing!

SAMANTHA: Do you think that's gentlemanly?

BLANE: Gentlemanliness has nothing to do with it.

SAMANTHA: What, then? Conceit? Pride?

BLANE: We're in this together.

SAMANTHA: *(Wryly)* We certainly are.

BLANE: And I hope you don't think it churlish of me to point it out to you but—I'm the main draw.

SAMANTHA: Not on stage, you aren't.

BLANE: My presence in this thing means we can attract a wider audience.

SAMANTHA: If that audience can read, your name will not escape them.

(Suddenly the VOICE interrupts:)

VOICE: *(O S)* Are you going to rehearse or are you going to argue?

(They are both taken aback. SAMANTHA says, in a whisper:)

SAMANTHA: I didn't know he could hear when we don't have our finger on the button.

VOICE: *(O S)* Don't you think you should call a truce? The papers are full of your squabbling. They're taking bets you might kill each other before opening night.

SAMANTHA: Get them to stop!

BLANE: Tell them to keep it up! It's great publicity!

SAMANTHA: How we feel about each other off stage is none of their business!

BLANE: Are you afraid they might find out you're not the gracious grande dame you want them to think you are?

SAMANTHA: Goddam you—!

BLANE: Sock me! Go on and sock me! My black eye will make a great photo for the evening news!

SAMANTHA: I won't give you the satisfaction.

VOICE: *(O S)* Is this a rehearsal or is this a prize fight?

SAMANTHA: It's a rehearsal.

BLANE: All right, all right... Let's do the closet scene again. This time, off book.

SAMANTHA: This is a new scene. I told you I will have it memorized before we open.

BLANE: And I need to see how much you know by heart right now.

SAMANTHA: I suppose you're letter perfect.

BLANE: I know my lines. Yes. I'm a very quick study.

SAMANTHA: Don't worry. I'll have my lines down by the time of the opening.

The audience won't be disappointed.

BLANE: The trouble is, you treat the audience as an enemy. I treat it as a friend.

SAMANTHA: You treat it as something you're trying to seduce. I treat it as something I'm trying to entertain, uplift, move, inspire—

BLANE: Let's get to work, shall we? We've hardly accomplished anything today.

SAMANTHA: Arguing takes the wind out of me.

BLANE: Please stand where I told you to stand yesterday.

SAMANTHA: Why can't we begin to rehearse on the stage?

BLANE: They haven't finished constructing the set.

SAMANTHA: I need space. I need to feel the room!

BLANE: Start, for god's sake! ...You love me.

SAMANTHA: *(Seething)* Oh, yes. I love you. *(She takes a breath. She "prepares.")*

BLANE: But you feel I have betrayed my stepfather. *(He begins:)*
Now, Mother, what's the matter?

SAMANTHA: *(Somewhat by heart but needing frequent glances at the script:)*
Hamlet, thou hast thy father much offended.

BLANE: Mother, you have my father much offended.

SAMANTHA: Come, come, you answer with an idle tongue.

BLANE: Go, go, you question with a wicked tongue.

SAMANTHA: Why, how now, Hamlet?

BLANE: What's the matter now?

SAMANTHA: Have you forgot me?

BLANE: No, by the rood, not so!
You are the Queen, your husband's brother's wife,
And, would it were not so, you are my mother.

SAMANTHA: Nay, then I'll set those to you that can speak.

BLANE: Come, come, and sit you down. You shall not budge.
You go not till I set you up a glass
Where you may see the inmost part of you!

SAMANTHA: What have I done that thou dar'st wag thy tongue
In noise so rude against me?

BLANE: Such an act
That blurs the grace and blush of modesty,
Calls virtue hypocrite, takes off the rose

From the fair forehead of an innocent love,
And sets a blister there.

SAMANTHA: Aye me, what act,
That roars so loud and thunders in the index?

BLANE: *(Angrily)* Look here upon this picture, and on this,
The counterfeit presentment of two brothers.
See what a grace was seated on this brow:
Hyperion's curls, the front of Jove himself,
Where every god did seem to set his seal
To give the world assurance of a man.
This was your husband. Look you now what follows.
Here is your husband, like a mildewed ear
Blasting his wholesome brother. Have you eyes?
Could you on this fair mountain leave to feed,
And batten on this moor?
O shame, where is thy blush? Rebellious hell—

(She breaks from the scene.)

SAMANTHA: Wait a minute.

BLANE: What now?

SAMANTHA: I know you hate it when I say anything. And I don't mean to criticize—

BLANE: Go on.

SAMANTHA: I can't help but notice—and I think the audience will notice, too: Your Hamlet is— surfacey.

BLANE: "Surfacey"?!

SAMANTHA: You're skimming over the surface, not getting inside the man.

BLANE: That's what you think?

SAMANTHA: You're not feeling what he was feeling.

BLANE: How do you know I'm not feeling what he was feeling?

SAMANTHA: You're not showing it. Hamlet's not just angry at his mother—he feels betrayed. But he's conflicted. He also loves her. Loves her very much. It would help if I felt that Hamlet, underneath it all, really loved me.

BLANE: *(Through gritted teeth)* I'm working on it.

SAMANTHA: I need to feel an actor is giving me something.

BLANE: *(Ambiguously)* I'll give you something.

SAMANTHA: I'll bet, when you're doing a film, you don't stick around to support your co-stars when they're doing their close-ups.

BLANE: Could we please get back to work? ...Let me see, Madame Director, if I can do this to your satisfaction. *(He begins again.)*
Rebellious hell,
If thou canst mutine in a matron's bones,
To flaming youth let virtue be as wax
And melt in her own fire.

SAMANTHA: *(Unemotionally)*
O Hamlet, speak no more.
Thou turn'st mine eyes into my very soul,
And there I see such black and grained spots
As will not leave their tinct.

BLANE: Nay, but to live
In the rank sweat of an enseamed bed,
Stewed in corruption, honeying and making love
Over the nasty sty—

SAMANTHA: O, speak to me no more.
These words like daggers enter in my ears.
No more, sweet Hamlet.

BLANE: Now who's being surfacey?

SAMANTHA: I wasn't.

BLANE: You're holding back.

SAMANTHA: Yes. Because Gertrude has farther to go in this scene. I'm not going to give expression to all her emotions this early.

BLANE: There's something in the lines that you're resisting.

SAMANTHA: It's *Gertrude* resisting. That's what, at this point, I think she'd do.

BLANE: As Hamlet, I need more.

SAMANTHA: No, you don't! At this moment, Gertrude still has to be in control. She'd still hold on.

BLANE: She wouldn't.

SAMANTHA: She's his mother! Do you know how hard it is to listen to a child tell you you've hurt them? You didn't mean to. You were just living your own life—which children never seem to realize you have. You were just living your own life, in your own imperfect way, and then the flesh of your flesh confronts you and tells you you're ruining theirs!

BLANE: That would hurt Gertrude to the quick and she would show it.

SAMANTHA: She would not show it! You have no idea what it feels like to have your child attack you. As you listen, you cannot give way. You have to retain your strength, your dignity, the sense that you're the one in authority over her—over him—

BLANE: The mother would show her pain!

SAMANTHA: What do you know! You've never bothered to commit to any woman, any child, any human being whatsoever! You don't know true committed love so you have no idea how to portray it in these roles!

BLANE: How dare you—!

VOICE: (O S) What's the matter with you two?! You open in two weeks! Are you going to be ready?

(BLANE *takes a breath and says:*)

BLANE: I'm going up to check progress on the stage.

SAMANTHA: Are you taking your flask with you?

BLANE: It's my only hope for survival.

SAMANTHA: If you are going to indulge, don't forget to take your toothbrush.

BLANE: I hope there's not a real gun in the prop room. I'd be sorely tempted.

SAMANTHA: Go ahead! Shoot me! It would put me out of my misery.

BLANE: I'll be back in ten minutes. I hope, by then, you'll be in a more cooperative mood.

SAMANTHA: I won't. But I'll pretend. After all, I am an actress.

BLANE: That has yet to be proved. *(He goes out.)*

(*Alone,* SAMANTHA *addresses the air:*)

SAMANTHA: You see what I mean? He's constantly tearing me down! I know his game. I've worked with directors like this before. They tear you down in order to get total control over you.

VOICE: (O S) Perhaps he's tearing you down to goad you into doing your best.

SAMANTHA: At the moment, he's goading me into doing my worst.

VOICE: (O S) Are you afraid? Is that why you're spending so much time in personal battles?

SAMANTHA: He's inciting me!

VOICE: (O S) Is he? Or are you defensive—about the quality of your work.

SAMANTHA: *(Half admitting it)* ...I haven't tackled Shakespeare in a decade. He trips you up. He makes you go inside to places you don't want to go.

VOICE: (O S) Where don't you want to go, Samantha?

SAMANTHA: You, too! Why is everybody trying to crawl inside my head? This is not about me, it's about the women I'm playing!

VOICE: *(O S)* Whatever fears you have, you have to face them.

SAMANTHA: He's driving me over the brink! *(She goes over to* BLANE's *dressing table, grabs a candy bar he has left there and is about to tear it open—)*

VOICE: *(O S)* That won't help, you know.

SAMANTHA: *(Shocked)* Can you not only hear—but see?

VOICE: *(O S)* I see.

SAMANTHA: How?! *(She starts looking around for a camera, finds nothing.)*

VOICE: *(O S)* I see.

*(*SAMANTHA *puts the candy bar back on* BLANE's *table.)*

SAMANTHA: Where are you? When I go out, I never catch a glimpse of you.

VOICE: *(O S)* What are you afraid of, Samantha?

SAMANTHA: ...Of getting out there and drying up. Of making a fool of myself. Of becoming a laughing stock.

VOICE: *(O S)* Is that all?

SAMANTHA: I fear the words—what's in them—I fear I'm not up to the challenge.

VOICE: *(O S)* I think you've really been getting somewhere.

SAMANTHA: Thank you... Why doesn't *he* say that?

VOICE: *(O S)* Has it never occurred to you that he's just as scared as you are?

SAMANTHA: The dress rehearsal is only a few days from now. Will we be ready to go on? ...The words. If I could just feel steady on the words...

(Music. Lights change.)

(In the half-light, SAMANTHA *paces with her script, trying to memorize.)*

(As the lights come up on the next scene, BLANE *enters wearing a raincoat and carrying their costumes in two clothing bags.)*

BLANE: Our costumes were just delivered. *(He looks into the bags.)* This is mine. This must be yours.

*(*SAMANTHA *opens the garment bag and takes out a long black velvet dress.)*

SAMANTHA: This is it? This is what I'm to wear through the entire performance?

BLANE: You'll be able to accessorize—a scarf here, a necklace there. It's a good base.

SAMANTHA: If it fits. Do you realize I haven't had a single session with the costume designer since I sent in my measurements?

BLANE: Why don't you try it on?

SAMANTHA: If it doesn't fit—what then?

BLANE: Try it!

(SAMANTHA *goes behind the screen.*)

(BLANE *takes off his coat. He proceeds to get into his costume. Black tight-fitting pants, black turtleneck. He's self-conscious about his physique. He examines himself in the long mirror and murmurs:*)

BLANE: O that this too, too solid flesh would melt—

SAMANTHA: *(Behind the screen)* What did you say?

BLANE: Nothing. *(He is examining himself in the mirror, testing the rolls of flab at his hips, wondering how he'd look if they were snipped off.)* ...Have you had much—work done?

SAMANTHA: *(Behind the screen)* What do you mean?

BLANE: You know—a nip here, a tuck there.

SAMANTHA: *(Behind the screen)* If I have, it's my business.

BLANE: Every time you look at me I can see you thinking "He should get a tummy tuck."

SAMANTHA: *(Poking her head over the screen)* And every time you look at me I can see you thinking, "What did she do with the tip of her nose?"

BLANE: What *did* you do?

SAMANTHA: *(Behind the screen)* Had it auctioned off!

BLANE: It must have been quite a shock for your first husband when he got a glimpse of your new baby. What did you name her?

SAMANTHA: *(Poking her head above the screen)* Pinocchio!

BLANE: Very funny.

SAMANTHA: *(Behind the screen)* She was the most beautiful child you could ever hope to see.

BLANE: Is she still attractive?

SAMANTHA: *(Behind the screen)* She was when I last saw her.

BLANE: When was that?

SAMANTHA: *(Coming out in her long black form-fitting costume)* Oh, you *do* need a tummy tuck!

BLANE: You'll need a girdle.

(BLANE *and* SAMANTHA *look at themselves in the mirror.*)

SAMANTHA: Maybe we should *both* go in for tummy tucks! ...I knew we should have had these things to work in before tonight's dress. I can play Cleopatra in this, I can play Gertrude. But I can't play Juliet or Rosalind or Viola. I can't play Beatrice. It's too somber.

BLANE: I've told you: You'll have some—things—to lighten it up.

SAMANTHA: What things? When? I can't move in this! The hem's too long. I'll trip all over myself! If I turn quickly, I'll fall flat on my rear!

BLANE: You'll learn to move in it.

SAMANTHA: If I have to worry about my costume, I won't be able to keep my mind on the lines.

BLANE: You'll work in it during tonight's dress rehearsal. You're a professional. You'll manage it.

SAMANTHA: I hope so. All we've got is tonight's dress, tomorrow's preview, then—it's the opening. *(She moves around in the dress, practicing turning, stepping backward, etc.)*

BLANE: Who have you invited to the opening?

SAMANTHA: No one. I never invite anyone to any opening. Even out of town. It's too nerve-wracking. ...And I never want anyone at the previews—except my husband—my almost-ex husband. That was our way. He'd always come, for the first time, the night before I opened. He'd come backstage afterward. He'd tell me how good I was. He knew just what to say. That's what always sustained me through the opening. ...I sent him a ticket for the preview tomorrow night. Things being the way they are, I don't know if he'll come...

BLANE: Didn't you invite your daughter?

SAMANTHA: *(After a pause)* To tell you the truth, I have no idea where she is.

BLANE: What happened between you two?

SAMANTHA: Are you trying to upset me?

BLANE: As your director, I think there's something—something in your mind—that's blocking you from doing your best work.

SAMANTHA: You think arguments I had with my daughter years ago are getting in the way of my work?

BLANE: Yes.

SAMANTHA: My work and my life are totally separate.

BLANE: They aren't.

SAMANTHA: I don't have to subject myself to your amateur psychoanalysis!

BLANE: But you do have to do your best work—

SAMANTHA: Are you never going to let me alone on this?

BLANE: Not until I get to the heart of it.

SAMANTHA: All right, all right! Since you're going to keep picking at the scab, I'll tell you. ...My daughter seemed to be my rival—or my enemy—from the very beginning. ...She liked to boast about her famous mother when she was with other people. When she was with me, she specialized in tearing me down.

BLANE: Did you try to prop her up?

SAMANTHA: I tried. God knows I tried. But she was a torrent of complaints. If I went on tour, I was neglecting her. If I stayed home, I was limiting her freedom. If I brought her presents, I was over-compensating with bribes. In her eyes, I could never do anything right.

BLANE: This is exactly why I don't want to have any children.

SAMANTHA: It all grew and grew until we never had a minute's peace with each other. And one day she screamed at me she couldn't breath. I was sucking up her air! She just packed up and moved out—I have no idea where to. ...Sucking up her air. I probably am. But this is me. This is what I do. The only thing that could give her breath again is my dying and, God forgive me, I don't yet want to do that. ...I still want to reach something in the work I've never reached before. Perhaps with this. I try with the work. I tried with her. If she still hates me, there's nothing I can do about it!

BLANE: I see.

SAMANTHA: And you think I should carry all this on stage with me, tear out my guts, expose them in public and let them feed my performance! You're trying to kill me! *(She runs out in the direction of the bathroom.)*

(BLANE says, to the air:)

BLANE: I told you she's emotionally unstable! All I was trying to do was to get to whatever is blocking her from doing her best work. ...But she doesn't want to go there. Touching on any sensitive spot sends her reeling. How are we going to get through the dress rehearsal, the preview and the opening? Not to mention the run.

VOICE: *(O S)* She's momentarily upset—

BLANE: If you're upset every moment, that's not momentarily!

VOICE: *(O S)* She just needs a few minutes to compose herself.

BLANE: She doesn't know her lines.

VOICE: *(O S)* She thinks you hate her work.

BLANE: She hates mine! She criticizes everything I do. She doesn't take direction.

VOICE: *(O S)* You have to get along, you two. You have to come to some level of mutual understanding.

BLANE: It takes two to have mutual understanding. I could have understanding up the kazoo, she wouldn't have any in return.

VOICE: *(O S)* Try.

BLANE: I'm trying! *(He takes a new bottle out of his coat pocket and starts to unscrew the lid.)*

VOICE: *(O S)* Not that way.

BLANE: *(Only slightly surprised)* I knew you could see us.

VOICE: *(O S)* You're going to need every brain cell you have to keep on top during your performance.

BLANE: Don't worry about me. I'm fine. But I wish we'd planned for more than one preview. At least we have tonight's dress rehearsal—

VOICE: *(O S)* Well, actually—

BLANE: What?

(Wiping her eyes, SAMANTHA reappears from the bathroom in time to hear:)

VOICE: *(O S)* The stage floor isn't dry yet. If you walk on it, you'll stick to it like glue. We have to cancel the dress rehearsal.

SAMANTHA: You can't—!

BLANE: This was going to be our only tech! What'll happen with the lights?

VOICE: *(O S)* The tech people say you'll each have a follow-spot and they'll rig up some general lighting—

SAMANTHA: This is intolerable!

VOICE: *(O S)* You'll have tomorrow's preview.

BLANE: Just one performance before the opening!

SAMANTHA: It's madness!

(SAMANTHA sits down in her chair and puts her head down on the dressing table. BLANE unscrews the cap of his flask and, as if he were boldly displaying it to unknown hidden cameras, takes a long drink.)

(Music. Lights change.)

(In the half-light the two prepare for the preview performance. They adjust their costumes. Then, with a good deal of nervousness, they go about putting on make-up.)

(As the lights come up, SAMANTHA is doing aerobic exercises, bending from the waist in a circular motion. Then she does the same with her neck. Then she starts making strange calls from the depths of her throat.)

BLANE: Are you going to do that before every performance?

SAMANTHA: Absolutely. *(She does the call again.)*

BLANE: You sound like a whooping crane in heat.

SAMANTHA: What do you do to warm up?

(BLANE takes a swig of Scotch.)

SAMANTHA: I should have guessed.

(Suddenly they are interrupted:)

VOICE: *(O S)* Ten minutes to curtain!

BLANE: Jesus!

SAMANTHA: I don't think he can help us.

BLANE: Let's run lines.

SAMANTHA: I don't like to use up energy before a performance.

BLANE: This is not to use up energy. It's to set the lines in our heads. Just a speed-through. To see if we have any weak spots.

SAMANTHA: I tell you—

BLANE: Miss Snow, Miss Snow, MissSnow, MissSnow, Miss NO! Is it necessary that every thing I do or say I have to get an argument from you? Isn't it possible that every once in a while you might find I'm doing things for your benefit and that you—

SAMANTHA: *(Interrupting)* I wonder that you will still be talking, Signior Benedick. Nobody marks you.

(As they continue putting on their make-up and getting into their costumes — SAMANTHA into her dress, BLANE into a flowing-sleeved shirt — they go over their lines, in flat uninflected voices, very swiftly.)

BLANE: What, my dear Lady Disdain! Are you yet living?

SAMANTHA: Is it possible disdain should die while she hath such meet food to feed it as Signior Benedick?

BLANE: It is certain I am loved of all ladies, only you excepted; and I would I could find in my heart that I had not a hard heart, for, truly, I love none.

SAMANTHA: *(Aside:)* That's the truth.

BLANE: What?

SAMANTHA: Nothing. *(Into the air:)* Pops! Is my husband coming tonight?

VOICE: *(O S)* Yes.

SAMANTHA: *(Happily)* So he's still in my corner after all!

BLANE: Could we get back to what we're doing? For, truly, I love none.

SAMANTHA: A dear happiness to women; they would else have been troubled with a pernicious suitor. I had rather hear my dog bark at a crow than a man swear he loves me.

BLANE: God keep your ladyship still in that mind! So some gentleman or other shall scape a predestinate scratch'd face.

SAMANTHA: Scratching could not make it worse, an 'twere such a face as yours were.

BLANE: Well, you are a rare parrot-teacher.

SAMANTHA: *(Forgetting her line)* Ah... Er...

BLANE: *(Prompting)* A bird of my tongue is better than a beast of yours.

SAMANTHA: What?

BLANE: That's your line. A bird of my tongue is better than a beast of yours! ...I thought elephants never forget.

SAMANTHA: Contrary to popular belief, I am not an elephant!

BLANE: I don't know why you've asked your husband tonight. Family gets in the way! They'll jinx you every time.

SAMANTHA: Obviously, you don't have any family. No doubt you were found under a rock—

BLANE: I had an immensely loving father and a loving mother—

SAMANTHA: And your lady friends?

BLANE: *(Sarcastically)* I'm inviting them all to the opening! The theatre will be overflowing with them! There's hardly enough room for all of them to have seats!

SAMANTHA: I hope their cheap perfume doesn't waft up to the stage.

BLANE: In God's name, continue—!

SAMANTHA: *(As angry as he is:)* A bird of my tongue is better than a beast of yours.

BLANE: I would my horse had the speed of your tongue. But keep your way, i' God's name; I have done.

SAMANTHA: You always end with a jade's trick; I know you of old.

(The scene ends.)

BLANE: You went up on your lines.

SAMANTHA: You were upsetting me!

BLANE: I hope you're going to get things right when we're in front of an audience.

SAMANTHA: Don't you worry about me! Think about yourself—with your brain awash in Scotch.

BLANE: Don't you worry about me! I'm known in the trade for always having my lines down letter perfect.

VOICE: *(O S. Interrupting)* Places!

SAMANTHA: Oh, God!

BLANE: This is it.

(They both breathe deeply, close their eyes for a second, trying for some inner calm, then say:)

SAMANTHA: Break a leg.

BLANE: Don't break a leg. Just try to remember your lines.

(Music. Lights change.)

(The dressing room lights go out.)

(Bright stage lights illuminate the downstage. Music rises. As if the fourth wall has disappeared, SAMANTHA and BLANE rush forward into the light and he begins:)

BLANE: O for a Muse of fire, that would ascend
The brightest heaven of invention,
A kingdom for a stage, princes to act,
And monarchs to behold the swelling scene!

(Music rises. They begin their performance, we see it as a montage. A spotlight picks each out of the darkness as they speak. As Juliet, SAMANTHA begins:)

SAMANTHA: Oh, Romeo, Romeo. Wherefore art thou Romeo?
Deny thy father and refuse thy name.
Or, if thou wilt not, be but sworn my love
And I'll no longer be a Capulet.

(SAMANTHA continues speaking, under, but the music rises so we do not hear her. The lights fade out on her and come up on BLANE, at another part of the stage, addressing the Roman Forum as Antony.)

BLANE: Friends, Romans, Countrymen. Lend me your ears.
I come to bury Caesar, not to praise him.

(BLANE's speech fades under, music rises, the spotlight picks out SAMANTHA as Portia.)

SAMANTHA: The quality of mercy is not strained.
It droppeth as the gentle rain from heaven
Upon the place beneath—

(Music. Lights focus on BLANE *as Macbeth.)*

BLANE: Is this a dagger which I see before me
The handle toward my hand? Come, let me clutch thee.

(Music. Lights focus on SAMANTHA *as Desdemona.)*

SAMANTHA: Oh, banish me, my lord, but kill me not!
Kill me tomorrow, let me live tonight!

(Music. Lights focus on BLANE *as Lear.)*

BLANE: Blow, winds, and crack your cheeks! Rage! Blow!
You cataracts and hurricanoes, spout
Till you have drenched our steeples, drown'd the cocks!

(Music. Lights focus on SAMANTHA *as Lady Macbeth.)*

SAMANTHA: Out damned spot! Out, I say! ...What need we fear who knows it, when none can call our pow'r to account? Yet who would have thought the old man to have so much blood in him? ...The thane of Fife had a wife; where is she now? —What, will these hands ne'er be clean? ...Here's the smell of the blood still; all the perfumes of Arabia will not sweeten this little hand.

(Music. Lights focus on BLANE *as Hamlet.)*

BLANE: O, that this too too solid flesh would melt,
Thaw, and resolve itself into a dew!
Or that the Everlasting had not fix'd
His canon 'gainst self-slaughter. O God! God!
God—

*(*BLANE *has gone up on his lines.* SAMANTHA *prompts:)*

SAMANTHA: How weary, stale, flat—

BLANE: How weary, stale, flat and unprofitable
Seem to me all the uses of this world.

(Music. The lights change for the finale. SAMANTHA *comes forward and says:)*

SAMANTHA: If we shadows have offended,
Think but this, and all is mended,
That you have but slumbered here
While these visions did appear
And this weak and idle theme
No more yielding but a dream.

(The performance ends. The actors bow. The downstage lights go out.)

(The lights come on in the dressing room.)

*(*BLANE *and* SAMANTHA, *exhausted, come back into the dressing room, stunned, utterly spent.)*

BLANE: That was a disaster!

SAMANTHA: A disaster! This damn dress. I kept tripping all over it! Once, I nearly fell flat.

BLANE: You didn't.

SAMANTHA: Only because I caught myself on the proscenium.

BLANE: The floor still wasn't dry! Every time I tried to walk my shoes were rooted to the spot. It was like walking on bubble gum!

SAMANTHA: You went up on your lines five times!

BLANE: Faces! I could see them! A live audience!

SAMANTHA: *I* was supposed to be the one with the bad memory. *You* were supposed to be letter perfect no matter what!

BLANE: Go ahead and gloat! You were letter perfect! But only because you'd plastered post-it notes all over the set! I could hardly speak without my eye catching a blizzard of yellow!

SAMANTHA: Maybe you should have posted some yourself.

BLANE: All right! All right!

SAMANTHA: I can't imagine what my husband will say when he comes back.

BLANE: Was he there?

SAMANTHA: Yes. Though not in the seat I got for him. I wonder why he changed...

BLANE: I think I know what he'll say.

SAMANTHA: He doesn't usually use that kind of language. *(She is fixing herself up, preparing for her husband's visit.)*

BLANE: You have to pretty yourself up for him?

SAMANTHA: I haven't seen him in some time. I'm as nervous as if it were a first date.

BLANE: You weren't bad, you know.

SAMANTHA: Was that a compliment?

BLANE: An observation.

SAMANTHA: You weren't so bad yourself.

BLANE: Thanks for the lie. I was ridiculous. Stumbling about. Forgetting. I could see my hands trembling.

SAMANTHA: You'll get over it.

BLANE: I was lousy. Ask your husband.

SAMANTHA: He always tells me the truth

BLANE: I'm sure he'll tell you the truth about me. Forgive me if I don't wait around to hear.

(SAMANTHA *notices* BLANE *is emptying the contents of his dressing table into his duffel bag.*)

SAMANTHA: What are you doing?

BLANE: Clearing out.

SAMANTHA: What—?!

BLANE: This live theater game is not for me. I'm gonna get out before they ride me out of town on a rail. (*He takes off his costume shirt and throws it down. It lands in the wastebasket.*)

SAMANTHA: You can't—

BLANE: You saw me out there. I was pathetic. Even when I knew my lines—it was as if they were coming out of somebody else.

SAMANTHA: It was only stage fright. We all get it.

BLANE: I didn't realize how much those live faces would throw me. It was horrendous! My brain went numb! I couldn't relax and think, "Oh, well, there'll be another take." All I could think of was "This is it. This is it. It's happening now!" It was like facing a firing squad.

SAMANTHA: You can't walk out the day before the opening!

BLANE: I have an offer to do a film. I'm going to take it.

SAMANTHA: You have a contract—

BLANE: Contract be damned. I'm not going to go out and humiliate myself night after night.

SAMANTHA: You're a coward!

BLANE: True. But I'm not a fool. I'm not going to go out there and get pelted with rotten eggs!

SAMANTHA: There's such a thing as a gentleman's agreement—

BLANE: As you've pointed out so many times, I'm not a gentleman.

SAMANTHA: You'll be sued.

BLANE: I'd rather be sued than slaughtered. At least I will be out of here.

SAMANTHA: What am I going to do?

BLANE: Get another co-star. You've always found me an unworthy match to your talent.

SAMANTHA: That's not true, Blane.

BLANE: Come on, Sam. We've gone beyond lies. You're good. I'm not. Get someone who can truly support you.

SAMANTHA: We won't be able to—

BLANE: You'll find someone.

SAMANTHA: We open tomorrow!

BLANE: He'll come dashing in on his white charger and perform, book in hand.

SAMANTHA: No—

BLANE: The audience will love it. They'll be with you. They love emergencies. It makes them feel they're part of backstage life, the "adventure of theatre".

SAMANTHA: You can't do this!

BLANE: Good luck, babe.

SAMANTHA: For God's sake—!

BLANE: Sorry, Sam. Oddly enough—I really am. *(He takes his bag, picks up his coat and exits.)*

(SAMANTHA stands stunned. At a loss. She doesn't know what to do. Suddenly she knows what she needs. She pulls open the drawers in BLANE's dressing table and, at the back of the bottom one finds what she is looking for—a hidden bottle of Scotch. She smiles and pours a drink into a glass on her dressing table. As she does, her eyes catch a glimpse of her herd of elephants. Furious with them, she cries:)

SAMANTHA: You promised things would be better this time! *(With one gesture she sweeps them onto the floor. Then she raises her glass in a toast to all life's demons and downs its contents in one gulp. Then she calls out to the unseen:)* Would you like to see my Hamlet?

VOICE: *(V O)* Not on your life!

(Blackout)

END ACT ONE

ACT TWO

(At rise:)

(The next day. SAMANTHA *alone, has been napping fitfully on the cot. A half empty bottle of Scotch and a piece of notepaper are on the floor beside her. She stirs uncomfortably, as if from a bad dream. With a start, she wakens. It takes her a moment, then she comes awake to the memory of the night before. The dressing gown she is still wearing. The discomfort of the thin mattress. Her back and shoulders stiff. Her mouth dry. The bottle on the floor. The note. She rises slowly. She is despondent. She stands unsteadily and looks into the mirror. What she sees repels her. Stumbling over something on the floor, she remembers what she did the previous night. She kneels to pick up her elephants, a few broken. As she clears the floor and puts the mascots on her dressing table, she begins to murmur to herself:)*

SAMANTHA: When in disgrace with fortune and men's eyes
I all alone beweep my outcast state,
And trouble deaf heaven with my bootless cries,
And look upon myself and curse my fate,
(She can't remember the next line.)
Curse my fate, curse my fate—
(She hesitates, then continues:)
Wishing me like to one more rich in hope,
Featured like him, like him with friends possessed,
Desiring this man's art, and that man's scope,
With what I most enjoy contented least;
(She knows the rest by heart.)
Yet in these thoughts myself almost despising,
Haply I think on thee; and then my state,
Like to the lark at break of day arising
From sullen earth, sings hymns at heaven's gate;
For thy sweet love remem'bred, such wealth brings
That then I scorn to change my state with kings.
(To herself:)
"Think on thee". That's rich. What "thee" is there to think on? Blane Powers, he of the tiny mind and overdeveloped ego? My husband—? My—dear—

husband—? *(Into the air, she says:)* We're supposed to open tonight. Without my fellow player, what are we going to do?

VOICE: *(O S)* I'm trying to find you a co-star. So far, no one's instantly available.

SAMANTHA: Cowards all! ...Obviously, this Shakespeare hill is much too steep for them to climb. ...We'll have to close.

VOICE: *(O S)* We could postpone the opening for a few days. Then you could go on alone.

SAMANTHA: Carry two hours of this stuff nightly as a solo? I couldn't!

VOICE: *(O S)* Why not?

SAMANTHA: There's the physical endurance, for one thing. For another—the lines. The lines! We were doing mostly scenes. I could remember my lines when I had his to play off of. I'd have to do all monologues! Get them into my brain and perform them alone! I couldn't do it!

VOICE: *(O S)* You could begin on book. The audience would root for you.

SAMANTHA: They wouldn't root for me for long. Beyond the first few days of watching me stumble and flail about they wouldn't buy tickets. ...We have to close.

VOICE: *(O S)* The producers have rented theaters for the next six months!

SAMANTHA: Tell them to plead Act of God.

VOICE: *(O S)* Mister Powers' leaving was not an Act of God. It was an act of will—for which he will definitely pay the consequences. That has nothing to do with you. You have to continue.

SAMANTHA: Oh, no, I don't. Blane walked out, I'm going, too.

VOICE: *(O S)* You have a contract—

SAMANTHA: Sue me! I don't care! I can't be held to a contract that can destroy my life and my reputation.

VOICE: *(O S)* Miss Snow—

SAMANTHA: It's bye-bye for this baby—*(She starts packing up her things. As she does, she says, mostly to herself:)* I don't know why I got involved with this fiasco in the first place. "Revive my career!" It'll bury it ten feet deep! Closing it before we open could be the best thing that ever happened to me!

(SAMANTHA *puts her coat on over her dressing gown and prepares to leave. As she does,* BLANE *enters, wearing street clothes and carrying his stage costume.*)

SAMANTHA: You!

BLANE: Me.

SAMANTHA: What are you doing here? Have you come back to view the wreckage?

BLANE: I came back to play. *(He hangs his costume on the rack.)*

SAMANTHA: To play what? Judas?

BLANE: I've come back to perform. With you.

SAMANTHA: *(Furious)* I see. You can leave whenever you want to, come back whenever you want to and I'm supposed to go up and down this emotional roller-coaster while you —

BLANE: I tell you I've come back permanently.

SAMANTHA: "Permanently" with you could mean five minutes or a day! You put me through hell then come waltzing in expecting me to greet you with relief and adulation. You selfish, self-centered bastard! I've been through a lot of things in this business, but a co-star's leaving the night before the opening, that beats them all.

BLANE: I'm here. I'm back. I'm going to stay.

SAMANTHA: To what do I owe this honor?

BLANE: I realized I was being a total cad.

SAMANTHA: That line wasn't dripping with sincerity.

BLANE: I realized I was being a total shit. Is that better? I'm sorry I gave you a bad night, but now I'm back —

SAMANTHA: You're a little late. I'm leaving.

BLANE: You can't. You have to stay. We owe it to our public.

SAMANTHA: Ha! Our public!

BLANE: If we're going to go out, let's not go out with a whimper.

SAMANTHA: A suicide mission, is that it?

BLANE: It's a roll of the dice isn't it? Always? But we'll never know how the game comes out unless we play.

SAMANTHA: Is that what this torture is called? "Playing?"

BLANE: By some demonic twist of the English language — it is.

SAMANTHA: I don't know why I ever agreed to work with you in the first place.

(SAMANTHA's eyes go to the shattered pieces of elephant on her dressing table. BLANE notes them, too.)

BLANE: I shouldn't have left you in the lurch that way. I humbly beg your pardon. *(He takes a large heavy sack out of his duffel bag and offers it to her.)* A small token of my contrition.

(After some hesitation, SAMANTHA takes it. She opens the sack and takes out a bust of

Shakespeare.)

BLANE: I beg you to forgive me. Willy begs you to forgive me.

SAMANTHA: Willy may forgive you. It's going to take me some time. *(She puts the bust down on her dressing table, then gazes for some time into Shakespeare's face.)*

BLANE: You can't let him down.

SAMANTHA: *(She gazes at Shakespeare again.)* You're right. I can't. ...What is it about this guy—? *(She begins to take off her coat, making the decision to stay.)*

BLANE: I think, God help us, it's his impossible demand for excellence.

SAMANTHA: Daunting.

BLANE: He throws down the gauntlet—

SAMANTHA: And we fools take up the challenge and wade into the fray.

(BLANE indicates the cot.)

BLANE: Did you sleep on that thing all night?

SAMANTHA: If you get sloshed enough, you don't notice. Till morning.

(BLANE notices SAMANTHA is massaging her stiff back.)

BLANE: Would you like me to give you a back rub?

SAMANTHA: No, thank you.

(BLANE starts putting his things back on his dressing table.)

BLANE: What did your husband say about last night's fiasco?

SAMANTHA: ...He never came back.

BLANE: He didn't?

SAMANTHA: He sent in a note.

BLANE: We were that bad?

SAMANTHA: He never mentioned our performances.

BLANE: What did he mention?

SAMANTHA: *(After a long pause:)* ...He's getting married.

BLANE: Ahh...

SAMANTHA: To the blonde who was sitting beside him last night. Did you notice that blonde?

BLANE: I don't know your husband.

SAMANTHA: But you must have noticed the blonde—seventh row, center right.

BLANE: Oh, that one. I must admit I did.

SAMANTHA: I thought she was one of yours.

BLANE: No. More's the pity.

(SAMANTHA *gives a cynical laugh.*)

SAMANTHA: That explains why he exchanged the ticket I left for him. He needed two seats.

BLANE: Did he say anything else?

SAMANTHA: He wishes me the best. His lawyer—he used to be *our* lawyer—will be in touch with me. *(She takes her husband's note from her dressing table, tears it into little pieces and throws them into the wastebasket.)* So. That was that. Little pieces of a marriage.

BLANE: You still love him.

SAMANTHA: Nonsense.

BLANE: You still love him.

SAMANTHA: Whether I do or not is neither here nor there. What I want to do is clear my mind of any extraneous emotions. I don't want to think of anything disturbing or upsetting. All I want to do today is rest and pull my mental and physical energies together.

BLANE: We have to rehearse—

SAMANTHA: Not on the day of the opening—!

BLANE: What we did last night was a disaster!

SAMANTHA: You know what they say—disastrous dress rehearsal, great opening night.

BLANE: That wasn't a dress rehearsal, that was a preview. Our one and only preview.

SAMANTHA: They applauded when we entered.

BLANE: And when we made our final exits, they applauded less.

SAMANTHA: I haven't breathed fresh air in two days. I'm going for a walk.

BLANE: Dressed like that?

SAMANTHA: Who cares? If they pick me up as a vagrant I could get a quiet cell to sleep in.

BLANE: We've got to work—

SAMANTHA: I need to clear my head. *(She goes toward the up right exit. Unseen by us, she tries the door. Then, off-stage, she says:)* The door is stuck. *(She pounds on the door.)* Pops! Pops! The door is stuck. Would you—would someone—come open it?

VOICE: *(O S)* It's not stuck. It's locked.

SAMANTHA: *(O S)* Are you keeping us prisoner?

VOICE: *(O S)* You've got to work.

BLANE: I told you.

(SAMANTHA *pounds and pounds and then stops pounding. She comes back into the dressing room.*)

SAMANTHA: I give up. It's hopeless.

BLANE: We'll rehearse all day.

SAMANTHA: We've been rehearsing for weeks. What makes you think a few more hours will make a difference?

BLANE: Now our lives depend on it.

SAMANTHA: Do they, Blane?

BLANE: You know they do.

(*Defeated,* SAMANTHA *pours herself a glass of water, drinks some, then pulls back her hair, ready to work.*)

BLANE: Oh, by the way. I forgot. This letter was in your box. *(He takes a letter out of his pocket and hands it to her.)*

SAMANTHA: Another nuclear detonation from the outside world? *(She takes it and looks at it.)* No return address. Blurred postmark. Can't tell who it's from.

BLANE: Open it.

SAMANTHA: Oh, no. I've had my quota of bombshells for the moment. When you're appearing at a theatre all kinds of crazies know where they can write you. You've no idea what kind of stuff can come in anonymous letters. I'll save it to amuse or annoy me later. *(She puts it into her mirror and goes behind the screen to change.)* By the way—what did you do last night? Called all your current bimbos, I imagine.

BLANE: I called my—current—girlfriend. Yes.

SAMANTHA: *(Behind the screen)* I suppose she was sympathetic. They always are when their future's not at stake.

BLANE: She told me – *(He looks like he has a lot to say but isn't saying it.)*

SAMANTHA: *(Behind the screen)* Yes?

(He sees the half-empty bottle near her cot.)

BLANE: Could I have a shot of this stuff?

SAMANTHA: *(Looking out at him)* Be your guest.

(BLANE *pours himself a shot and downs it.*)

SAMANTHA: *(Behind the screen)* She told you what?

BLANE: ...She's pregnant.

SAMANTHA: *(Behind the screen)* Ah. What are you going to do about it?

BLANE: Nothing.

SAMANTHA: *(Behind the screen)* Nothing?

BLANE: She knew my rules. She'll have to figure out what to do on her own.

SAMANTHA: *(Behind the screen)* Do you like this woman?

BLANE: More than any I've ever known. But that has nothing to do with it.

SAMANTHA: *(Coming out from behind the screen in rehearsal clothes)* Nothing to do with it! What kind of irresponsible, reckless, inconsiderate—

BLANE: Can we start please? We have work to do—and damn little time. I know it would be diverting to discuss the soap opera my life has suddenly become, but it behooves us to use this time to go over our rough spots.

SAMANTHA: Ah. Our rough spots. And what are they?

BLANE: Usually the parts where you have to seem to be in love with me.

SAMANTHA: When reality is the opposite, "let's pretend" can be impossible.

BLANE: Can we begin? ...Let's start with *As You Like It*.

SAMANTHA: Nothing, at the moment, is as I like it. But what can I do? *(Seeing no alternative, Samantha prepares, getting herself into the character of a girl playing a boy playing a girl. Then she starts:)* Why, how now, Orlando! Where have you been all this while? You a lover!

BLANE: My fair Rosalind, I come within an hour of my promise.

SAMANTHA: Break an hour's promise in love!

BLANE: Pardon me, dear Rosalind.

SAMANTHA: Nay, an you be so tardy, come no more in my sight. *(She turns away.)*

BLANE: Why did you turn away?

SAMANTHA: Because I feel, there, Rosalind would turn away.

BLANE: Yes, but she's Rosalind playing a boy playing Rosalind. As a pretend boy playing a pretend Rosalind, I think she looks directly at him there. "Come no more in my sight." It's a direct command for him to leave her. She would say it to him directly—as a man would.

SAMANTHA: And I say, as a woman, as Rosalind playing a boy playing Rosalind, she would turn away!

BLANE: I don't think so.

SAMANTHA: Are we going to spend the day on this or are we going to move onward?

BLANE: What are you going to do on stage?

SAMANTHA: Whatever I feel at the moment.

BLANE: And what, pray tell, will that be?

SAMANTHA: Wait and see.

(BLANE *turns away, angry.*)

BLANE: *(Under his breath)* Actresses!

SAMANTHA: *(Under her breath)* Actors who have the illusion they're directors!

BLANE: Continue, for god's sake! You're supposed to be deeply in love.

SAMANTHA: Oh, I really earn my pay on this one! ...Come, woo me, woo me; for now I am in a holiday humour and like enough to consent. What would you say to me now, an I were your very very Rosalind?

BLANE: I would kiss before I spoke.

SAMANTHA: Nay, you were better speak first; and when you were gravell'd for lack of matter, you might take occasion to kiss.

BLANE: How if the kiss be deni'd?

SAMANTHA: Then she puts you to entreaty and there begins new matter. Am not I your Rosalind?

BLANE: I take some joy to say you are, because I would be talking of her.

SAMANTHA: Well, in her person, I say I will not have you. *(She turns away.)*

BLANE: That turning away again!

SAMANTHA: I like it, I'm doing it. It's right for the moment!

(BLANE *disagrees but shakes his head, giving up the argument.*)

SAMANTHA: I say I will not have you. *(She turns away.)*

BLANE: Then in mine own person I die.

SAMANTHA: No, faith. Men have died from time to time and worms have eaten them, but not for love.

BLANE: Then love me, Rosalind.

SAMANTHA: Give me your hand, Orlando....

(BLANE *and* SAMANTHA *join hands.*)

SAMANTHA: You must say, "I take thee, Rosalind, for wife".

BLANE: I take thee, Rosalind, for wife.

SAMANTHA: I take thee, Orlando, for my husband. ...*(Then she says:)* Oh that thou didst know how many fathom deep I am in love!

(It is a "moment". BLANE *pulls his hand away.)*

SAMANTHA: Why did you do that?

BLANE: Do what?

SAMANTHA: Pull your hand away like that.

BLANE: The moment became all too real. I suddenly felt strangled by a possible future real "I do". It scared the hell out of me.

SAMANTHA: Singular to the death!

BLANE: And what about you? I suppose as soon as you're out of your present frying pan you'll jump into the fire again with another husband.

SAMANTHA: Never! I'd sooner slit my wrists than get trapped that way again. Ties break, you know. And for the scars to heal can take a lifetime. *(With deep cynicism)* "How many fathom deep I am in love!" If only Rosalind could know what I know!

BLANE: Do you think one has to be in love to marry?

SAMANTHA: Are you asking as Blane or as Orlando?

BLANE: As Blane.

SAMANTHA: Don't tell me you're thinking of it.

BLANE: Just curiosity.

SAMANTHA: I was. I always was in love. I was—three times—betrayed.

BLANE: I suppose one always begins in hope.

SAMANTHA: Yes. Hope. As someone says—it springs eternal. But are you thinking of jumping off the cliff into unholy matrimony?

BLANE: Isn't it time for your tea break?

SAMANTHA: For the first time, *you* thought of it, I didn't. You *must* be discombobulated! *(She goes about making tea.)* Are you thinking of becoming Benedick the married man?

BLANE: ...My friend—my current friend—

SAMANTHA: The one you admire more than you've admired any other—

BLANE: Yes. ...She wants to have the baby.

SAMANTHA: That does complicate matters, doesn't it.

BLANE: You had a child. It doesn't seem to have made you happy. Quite the opposite.

SAMANTHA: We're not talking about me, we're talking about you.

BLANE: Well, what do you think?

SAMANTHA: Some are born to be fathers. Others have fatherhood thrust upon them.

BLANE: But marriage, too? Should marriage, too, be thrust upon them?

SAMANTHA: *(Rubbing the head of Shakespeare)* What thinkest thou, Wise Willy? Should the man take on becoming both husband and father? *(She listens to Shakespeare.)* Willy answers: The man has not mentioned love.

BLANE: No, he hasn't. ...What's Willy's advice about love?

SAMANTHA: *(Holds the sculpture to her ear, then says:)* He is for it and against it. He thinks it's everything, he thinks it's nothing at all. He thinks all are fools who love but that those who never love are the most foolish. He thinks people will not die for love and yet, time after time, they do.

BLANE: But they also live. And, for a time, seemingly happily.

SAMANTHA: If they are lucky.

BLANE: What do you think, Samantha?

SAMANTHA: Only you can answer your own question. Only you can know.

BLANE: But—

VOICE: *(O S)* Are you two going to waste more time talking? Don't you think you should rehearse? Tonight's house is sold out.

SAMANTHA: Oh, God! There are actually people brave enough to come see us!

BLANE: There's always an audience for disasters.

SAMANTHA: Do you think we can fool them?

BLANE: We can make the attempt.

SAMANTHA: Dear God—if it were only eleven o'clock and we had already committed the murder!

BLANE: If it were done when 'tis done, then 'twere well
It were done quickly.

SAMANTHA: Why have you left the chamber?

BLANE: I have no spur
To prick the sides of my intent, but only
Vaulting ambition, which o'erleaps itself
And falls on th' other—
We will proceed no further in this business.

SAMANTHA: Wouldst thou have that
Which thou esteem'st the ornament of life,
And live a coward in thine own esteem,

Letting "I dare not" wait upon "would",
Like the poor cat i' th' adage?

BLANE: Prithee, peace!
I dare do all that may become a man;
Who dares do more is none.

SAMANTHA: What beast was 't, then,
That made you break this enterprise to me?
I have given suck, and know
How tender 'tis to love the babe that milks me;
I would, while it was smiling in my face,
Have pluck'd my nipple from his boneless gums
And dash'd the brains out, had I so sworn as you
Have done to this.

BLANE: If we should fail?

SAMANTHA: We fail!
But screw your courage to the sticking-place,
And we'll not fail. When Duncan is asleep—

(Suddenly she breaks off.)

Are we going to fail? Are we going to fail, Blane?

BLANE: I wish I knew, Sam, I wish I knew.

SAMANTHA: The critics will be there in force.

BLANE: I can't imagine what they'll say.

SAMANTHA: I can. *(She begins, mockingly)* "Last night we were treated to a mishmash of flotsam and jetsam from the works of Shakespeare. ...Ms. Snow's Cleopatra was over-baked. Her Desdemona was desperate, her Rosalind confused. Her Portia couldn't win the case of a fly mangled by a fly-swatter."

BLANE: "And as for her co-star in this folly, several decades as a gumshoe do not equip him to play nobility. His Hamlet wasn't Danish Prince it was cheese Danish!"

SAMANTHA: "As Romeo and Juliet these two relics from the stone age were not just superannuated, they were embalmed!"

BLANE: "And as for Powers' direction: he didn't so much captain the ship as steer it firmly toward the rocks."

SAMANTHA: "Do these two ex-stars think their audience wouldn't notice the entity they claim to be presenting as Shakespeare is, in fact, someone without the grace, humanity, subtlety or splendor of the original?"

BLANE: "So if you can only take your Shakespeare in shreds and patches—"

SAMANTHA: "If you like shards rather than a pot—"

BLANE: "A note or two rather than a symphony—"

SAMANTHA: "Rush down to watch Snow and Powers mutilate the master."

BLANE: "But you'd better hurry. It's hard to see how this load of gibberish will last the week."

SAMANTHA: Listen! If they'll say it's gibberish, let's give 'em gibberish! ...If we're going to be blasted off the face of the earth, let's go out with a bang!

BLANE: Why not? ...Now is the winter of our discontent—

SAMANTHA: Alas, poor Yorick!

BLANE: Me thought I was enamored of an ass.

SAMANTHA: Let me not to the marriage of true minds admit impediments.

BLANE: Sigh no more, lady, sigh no more.

SAMANTHA: The fault, dear Brutus, is not in our stars, but in ourselves.

BLANE: There is a tide in the affairs of men—

SAMANTHA: I met a fool in the forest.

BLANE: Beware the Ides of March!

SAMANTHA: O what a noble mind is here o'er thrown.

BLANE: I am but mad north-northwest—

SAMANTHA: You have no more brain than I have in my elbow!

BLANE: Frailty, thy name is woman!

SAMANTHA: A hit! A very palpable hit!

BLANE: Speak the speech, I pray you.

SAMANTHA: O villain, villain, smiling, damned villain—remorseless, treacherous, lecherous, kindless villain—

BLANE: Brevity is the soul of wit.

SAMANTHA: Oh, how full of briers is this workaday world!

BLANE: Words!

SAMANTHA: Words!

BLANE: Words!

VOICE: *(O S)* What are you doing?

SAMANTHA: Rehearsing!

VOICE: *(O S)* Is this what you plan to present tonight?

SAMANTHA: It most definitely is!

BLANE: This is the great downslide!

SAMANTHA: We're going out in a blaze! A glorious conflagration!

VOICE: *(O S)* You're overstepping your bounds!

SAMANTHA: We have no bounds! We are utterly boundless!

VOICE: *(O S)* You have no right—

BLANE: We're not in your prison any more!

SAMANTHA: When we go on stage, we will say what we want, do what we want—

VOICE: *(O S)* You have left the path—

BLANE: Of righteousness? Of theatrical righteousness?

SAMANTHA: Wherein is it writ that we have to do only what's written?

BLANE: Why can't we do what we want rather than what has been prepared?

VOICE: *(O S)* You're betraying him!

SAMANTHA: Who?

VOICE: *(O S)* Shakespeare!

(BLANE *addresses the bust:*)

BLANE: Darling Willy. Oh most exalted Will. Are we betraying you?

SAMANTHA: He betrayed us. By making it all too hard to do.

VOICE: *(O S)* This is more than I can take. I'm leaving!

BLANE: Ah! Another exit! Go! Go quickly! You know how we all hate farewell scenes.

SAMANTHA: No, don't go! Stay with us! *(Silence)* Speak to us! *(Longer silence)* Pops! Pops!

BLANE: *(More deeply than before)* Lord, what fools these mortals be!

SAMANTHA: There are more things twixt heaven and earth than are dreamt of in your philosophy, Horatio.

BLANE: Tomorrow and tomorrow and tomorrow—

SAMANTHA: Sweet are the uses of adversity.

BLANE: Would that the everlasting had not fixed his canon 'gainst self-slaughter!

SAMANTHA: She sat, like patience on a monument, smiling at grief.

(BLANE *picks up* SAMANTHA's *unopened letter and presents it to her with exaggerated ceremony.*)

BLANE: Ms Snow, I hereby present to you the Never Say Never award for the century's most geriatric Juliet.

(*Bowing graciously,* SAMANTHA *accepts the letter and holds it out to him in return.*)

SAMANTHA: And I bestow upon you the Golden Age Triple Threat Award for the most Horrendous Hamlet, Malodorous Macbeth and Lousy Lear who have ever graced the stages of our time!

(*Bowing graciously in return,* BLANE *takes the letter.*)

BLANE: I humbly thank you. (*He slits open the letter and holds aloft the page which was inside.*) I shall frame this precious document and display it proudly as I sail into the mists of memory with – (*He catches a glimpse of what's on the page. He stops. He becomes suddenly serious. He says:*) ...It's from your daughter.

SAMANTHA: My daughter—! ...What does she say?

BLANE: I—

SAMANTHA: Read it.

BLANE: (*Not wanting the task. Skimming the text*) ...She's getting married.

SAMANTHA: Like daughter, like father.

BLANE: She says—it wouldn't be a wedding if you weren't there.

SAMANTHA: She wants me there?

(SAMANTHA *holds out her hand.* BLANE *gives her the letter. She reads it hungrily, growing more and more joyous.*)

SAMANTHA: Blane! She wants me there. She doesn't know what happened between us but she wants it over. She says she loves—! ...Oh, Blane, you've no idea how many times I've wanted to write her that—but I didn't know where she was.

BLANE: I'm happy for you.

SAMANTHA: You think I've suddenly become a sentimental idiot, don't you.

BLANE: Not exactly.

SAMANTHA: All that we do—succeed or fail—doesn't matter. This is what matters.

BLANE: You're lucky—with us about to face the firing squad—that you have this to inoculate you against the bullets. At least you have something—someone—you can go back to.

SAMANTHA: The firing squad. I nearly forgot! ...She says she's coming to this thing tonight. She's bringing her fiancé. They can't wait to see me in it! (*Terrified*) My God! My God! I can't let them see me go down in flames this way! I'll make up something! Some reason why I can't go on! (*She pounds on the door calling:*) Pops! Pops!

(*Silence*)

BLANE: Guess he's really gone, kid.

SAMANTHA: He couldn't have taken everybody with him! *(She pounds again.)* Hello! Hello! Is anybody there?!

(Silence)

BLANE: Looks like we're all on our own. *(Giving up, he opens the Scotch and starts to drink from the bottle.)*

SAMANTHA: I'm calling the police! They'll get us out! ...Lend me your cell phone—

BLANE: Don't you have one?

SAMANTHA: Don't believe in them. Except in emergencies.

BLANE: Like this one.

(BLANE *hands* SAMANTHA *his cell phone. She tries to make a call. It doesn't seem to work. She slaps it, then hands it to him. He checks it, then says, with a cynical laugh:)*

BLANE: Battery's dead.

SAMANTHA: *(Giving up in despair)* Guess we're really prisoners. *(She paces, as if in a cell.)* ...The place feels so empty.

BLANE: Hope someone comes to feed us.

SAMANTHA: I suppose they'll all flood back and unlock the door minutes before curtain so, like animals, we can only go in one direction—the stage.

BLANE: Where we can face the blood-thirsty, expectant crowd.

SAMANTHA: Blane --I can't do it. ...Elephants smashed to pieces. Pops gone. Luck—gone... My mind's a blank. I don't remember a single word! It's all impossible! *(She indicates Shakespeare.)* He asks too much! I go as far as I can go and still—it isn't good enough.

BLANE: Try it now. For your daughter. Try it.

SAMANTHA: Try what?

BLANE: Your Cleopatra.

SAMANTHA: I tell you, I've forgotten everything! I think I've lost my mind!

BLANE: There's only one road to sanity—the Shakespeare.

SAMANTHA: I can't remember—

BLANE: Try it. Quietly. Right here. I bet you do.

(SAMANTHA *pulls herself together then, knowing what* BLANE's *reaction will be, she says:)*

SAMANTHA: I'd like to do my Juliet.

BLANE: *(Ready to explode)* Always your Juliet—!

SAMANTHA: I've got a bead on her now. Please. Just listen.

BLANE: *(Holding back his tongue)* ...All right.

(SAMANTHA *knowing he hates her doing it, begins:*)

SAMANTHA: Come civil night,
Thou sober-suited matron, all in black,
And learn me how to lose a winning match,
Play'd for a pair of stainless maidenhoods.
Hood my unmann'd blood, bating in my cheeks,
With thy black mantle, till strange love grow bold,
Think true love acted simple modesty.

(SAMANTHA *hesitates. His response a mask,* BLANE *says:*)

BLANE: Go on.

SAMANTHA: Come, night; come, Romeo; come, thou day in night;
For thou wilt lie upon the wings of night,
Whiter than new snow on a raven's back.
Come, gentle night, come, loving, black-brow'd night,
Give me my Romeo; and, when he shall die,
Take him and cut him out in little stars,
And he will make the face of heaven so fine
That all the world will be in love with night
And pay no worship to the garish sun.
O, I have bought the mansion of a love,
But not possess'd it, and, though I am sold,
Not yet enjoy'd. So tedious is this day
As is the night before some festival
To an impatient child that hath new robes
And may not wear them. O, here comes my nurse,
And she brings news; and every tongue that speaks
But Romeo's name speaks heavenly eloquence.
Now, nurse, what news?

(SAMANTHA *ends her speech. For a moment,* BLANE *says nothing. She fears what his response will be. But finally, he says, almost in awe:*)

BLANE: That was—wonderful!

SAMANTHA: "Wonderful"! That's a word I never heard from you before.

BLANE: I never saw you do that kind of work before.

SAMANTHA: I did get through it, didn't I.

BLANE: You more than got through it. You illuminated it. There was—an ageless radiance about you—

SAMANTHA: *(Surprised and touched)* Thank you. ...Thank you very much.

BLANE: I wonder that I've even been allowed to play beside you.

SAMANTHA: What are you talking about? *You're* the one with the television series. The offer of a film.

BLANE: Oh, yes. You want to know about the offer of the film? Last night when I got back to that fleabag they're putting us up in, I found the script had been delivered. I looked at it. My part was one page. One page! A walk-on! A cameo! That's what I've come down to!

SAMANTHA: So you didn't return here out of guilt at leaving me in the lurch.

BLANE: I'm speeding toward a dead end! A minor career in minor roles—!

SAMANTHA: You only came back because you had no place else to go! My God! You said you were a shit. You are. ...I wish I'd never gotten involved in this. I wish I were anyplace in the world but here! *(She calls:)* Pops! Pops! ...You have to let me out! You have to!

(SAMANTHA *starts toward the door. To stop her,* BLANE *says:*)

BLANE: He which hath no stomach to this fight,
Let him depart. His passport shall be made,
And crowns for convoy put into his purse.
We would not die in that man's company
That fears his fellowship to die with us.

(SAMANTHA *turns and begins to truly listen.* BLANE *continues. She listens, impressed by the words and his delivery of them.*)

BLANE: This day is call'd the feast of Crispian.
He that outlives this day and comes safe home
Will stand a tip-toe when this day is named,
And rouse him at the name of Crispian.
He that shall live this day, and see old age,
Will yearly on the vigil feast his neighbours,
And say, "Tomorrow is Saint Crispian."
Then will he strip his sleeve and show his scars,
And say, "These wounds I had on Crispin's day."
Old men forget; yet all shall be forgot,
But he'll remember with advantages
What feats he did that day. Then shall our names,
Familiar in his mouth as household words,
Be in their flowing cups freshly rememb'red.
This story shall the good man teach his son;
And Crispin Crispian shall ne'er go by,
From this day to the ending of the world,
But we in it shall be remembered.

We few, we happy few, we band of brothers.
For he today that sheds his blood with me
Shall be my brother; be he ne'er so vile,
This day shall gentle his condition;
And gentlemen in England now a-bed
Shall think themselves accurs'd they were not here,
And hold their manhoods cheap whiles any speaks
That fought with us upon Saint Crispin's day.

SAMANTHA: *(After a long pause)* ...Now who's being wonderful?

BLANE: Do you mean it?

SAMANTHA: You were splendid.

BLANE: It's the Shakespeare.

SAMANTHA: *(Indicating the bust of Shakespeare)* He does manage to convince one that one can go on—in spite of all, doesn't he?

BLANE: He does that.

SAMANTHA: You think that—whatever comes—we should muddle through?

BLANE: I do.

SAMANTHA: Who knows? Maybe we'll be okay—the two of us.

BLANE: It helps—if you're beside me—fighting the good fight.

SAMANTHA: Comrades in arms.

BLANE: Comrades. Fellow soldiers in the field. That's really why I came back, Sam. Because of you. I didn't want to let you down.

SAMANTHA: I appreciate that, Blane.

BLANE: Whatever I've managed here, I owe to you.

SAMANTHA: It was all there inside you—waiting to be unlocked.

BLANE: Maybe. But before this, no one had the key.

(For a long moment, there is silence. BLANE *and* SAMANTHA *stand looking at each other. Then she says quietly:)*

SAMANTHA: It's almost curtain time. We'd better dress.

BLANE: Yes.

*(*SAMANTHA *starts to go behind the screen.* BLANE *is looking around.)*

BLANE: Where's my shirt—?

SAMANTHA: In the wastebasket.

BLANE: *(He finds it. It's a wrinkled mess.)* Oh... Thanks. *(He puts it on, finds a stain on the sleeve, wets his finger with some spit and tries to get it off.)*

SAMANTHA: Let me— *(She wets a cloth from water in her pitcher and comes to rub his shirt.)*

BLANE: What is it?

SAMANTHA: Mars bar.

(SAMANTHA rubs some more. It is the first time they've personally touched. She's aware of it. He's aware of it. It is a physical "moment". Finally, she finishes rubbing. She pats his shoulder.)

SAMANTHA: There... All gone...

BLANE: *(Looking at her, in a personal way, for the first time)* Thank you...

SAMANTHA: *(Feeling warmly toward him)* You're welcome...

(A "moment". Both pause. With a warm, almost intimate gesture, SAMANTHA picks a piece of lint off BLANE's shirt—then goes behind the screen. In our full view, he continues getting into his costume and putting on his make-up. While doing so, he purses his lips to whistle. Then, looking in her direction, he stops himself. He starts to take a drink, then, looking in her direction once more, stops himself again. He knits his brow. He thinks. Then, suddenly:)

BLANE: Oh, my God! My God!

SAMANTHA: *(From behind the screen, alarmed)* What's the matter?

BLANE: Something awful has happened!

SAMANTHA: *(Behind the screen)* What is it?

BLANE: I'm becoming Benedick!

SAMANTHA: *(Behind the screen)* Benedick?

BLANE: Benedick! The drooling, defeated, delusional, disgusting, love-sick, I-want-to-get-married man!

SAMANTHA: *(Behind the screen)* Not you!

BLANE: Yes! Me!

SAMANTHA: *(Behind the screen)* A turncoat in the battle of love! Let me be the first to wish you well.

BLANE: Wish the both of us well.

SAMANTHA: *(Behind the screen)* Yes. I do. You and your young friend.

BLANE: Not me and my young friend.

SAMANTHA: *(Behind the screen)* Who, then?

BLANE: You! You! Cleopatra! Rosalind! Desdemona! —Juliet! ...You! Samantha!

SAMANTHA: *(Behind the screen)* What are you talking about?

BLANE: Don't you understand? I want to marry you!

SAMANTHA: *(Coming out from behind the screen in her costume)* Blane—!

BLANE: Do you think that I'm ridiculous?

SAMANTHA: *(Aware of her own warm feelings toward him)* Ridiculous? Of course not.

BLANE: I suddenly understand what we've been having—these days together in this hell hole. A merry war. A war like Beatrice and Benedick. A war that has led to love.

SAMANTHA: Oh, Blane—

(A gesture from BLANE*)*

SAMANTHA: All right. Oh, Benedick.

BLANE: Is that all you have to say?

SAMANTHA: *(Deeply, with affection)* You have no idea how lovely it is—at my stage of the game—to get a proposal.

BLANE: Then say yes. Say yes, Samantha! We're good together. We could become a team. An on- and off-stage team. Working together. Sharing a life together. Oh, how many fathom deep I am in love!

SAMANTHA: What has made you suddenly throw all your principles of freedom out the window?

BLANE: You. Who you are and how you make me feel when I'm with you. And then—the joy I saw in you when you read that letter from your daughter. I've never experienced that. It's what I want. A connection. A family.

SAMANTHA: You have a connection pending.

BLANE: With you.

SAMANTHA: *(Regretfully)* No. Not with me.

BLANE: You mean—with the coming baby.

SAMANTHA: Yes.

BLANE: ...You're saying, if I marry, I should marry the mother of my future child...

SAMANTHA: Call me old-fashioned—I do.

BLANE: But you and I—

SAMANTHA: *(Deeply)* I'm tempted. You've no idea how much—

BLANE: Then why don't you—?

SAMANTHA: You don't think we'd kill each other before a week of married life was over?

BLANE: No! I think we'd sail into the sunset on tranquil seas—hand-in-hand.

SAMANTHA: Blane. Dear Blane. I've been down this road before. And if I know nothing else, I recognize a romantic haze when I see one. I don't want to get lost in it again.

BLANE: You won't be lost. You'll be with me.

SAMANTHA: Of course I'll be with you—on the stage.

BLANE: Sam—

SAMANTHA: Thank you, Blane. I'm more touched than I can say. ...But—we have—what we have. And, if this thing runs, we can keep on having it. Side by side. Teammates.

BLANE: We could have so much more! I feel—

SAMANTHA: I know what you feel. I'm not saying I don't feel the same. ...But it always happens, doesn't it? When people are thrown together and have to go into themselves and bring so much out of themselves and accomplish so much, side by side?

BLANE: So it's that? Just the usual?

SAMANTHA: Not for me.

BLANE: Not for me, either—comrade.

SAMANTHA: Comrade...

(BLANE *and* SAMANTHA *clap hands.*)

SAMANTHA: We're a couple of broken down relics.

BLANE: Who says so?

SAMANTHA: *They'll* say so.

BLANE: They might not.

SAMANTHA: They might pelt us with tomatoes and rotten eggs—

BLANE: Or orchids and roses.

SAMANTHA: What a way to live!

BLANE: I wouldn't have it any other way. Would you?

SAMANTHA: No.

(*Over the intercom, suddenly:*)

VOICE: *(O S)* Places, please!

SAMANTHA: He's returned to us! *(She calls out:)* Welcome back, Pops!

VOICE: *(O S)* Are you ready?

BLANE & SAMANTHA: Ready!

(BLANE *and* SAMANTHA *each, for luck, pat the head of Shakespeare. Then* SAMANTHA *says:*)

SAMANTHA: Lead on, MacBlane!

BLANE: Once more unto the breach!

(*Together,* BLANE *and* SAMANTHA *rush forward into the bright stage light.*)

(*Blackout*)

END OF PLAY

HOTEL VICTORY

CHARACTERS & SETTING

Eve Trevelyan
Doctor Baines
Simon Trevelyan
Billy Maitland

Time & Place: Half a dozen years after the end of World War II. A Veterans Hospital. East Coast, USA.

Setting: A common room in a Veterans Hospital.

Upstage rear, a wall of windows. Exits stage right and left. The right leads to reception rooms and the hospital entrance, the left leads to the interior and another hospital wing. Occasionally, as indicated, fragments of two individual patients' rooms—adjacent to the common room stage right and left—appear and disappear.

In the transitions between scenes we hear the sound of military drums.

ACT ONE

(At rise:)

(The common room. EVE TREVELYAN, *an intelligent woman in her mid-thirties, enters from upstage with* DOCTOR BAINES, *a man in his 50s or 60s.)*

EVE: He belongs here, I tell you! He has just as much right to be here as any of the men in your ward.

DOCTOR: We don't have wards.

EVE: What do you have?

DOCTOR: Rooms.

EVE: Rooms...

DOCTOR: Sometimes suites.

EVE: Suites. Like the Plaza Hotel? I suppose you have names for them: The Adolph Hitler Suite. The Mussolini Suite, The Hirohito Suite...

DOCTOR: This is not a prisoner of war camp. It's a Veterans' Administration Hospital.

EVE: Then for God's sake administrate! *I'm* a veteran.

DOCTOR: You? Of what?

EVE: The Women's Army Air Force.

DOCTOR: Very commendable. But, as I understand it, the person you're seeking admission for is your husband.

EVE: He's a veteran, too.

DOCTOR: Of the RAF.

EVE: Last time I looked the RAF was a branch of the armed services.

DOCTOR: Of Great Britain! We don't admit veterans who fought under another flag.

EVE: I told you: We have special dispensation—based on my service. I've given your office a carload of papers—

DOCTOR: Why don't you get your husband treated in England?

EVE: He *was* treated in England. He didn't get better in England. I thought that maybe here—

DOCTOR: If every war bride ends up coming over here and—

EVE: Excuse me, Doctor Baines. I am not a war bride!

DOCTOR: As I understand it, you met in England, you married in England—

EVE: I am not some dewy-eyed chippy who fell for a uniform. I'm an Air Force pilot who met her husband while I was seconded to the RAF!

DOCTOR: You flew planes in the war?

EVE: I ferried planes when I was in the WASPs. It's not my fault that when I transferred to the Air Force they relegated me to a desk job. It wasn't what I wanted. I wanted to fly.

DOCTOR: I wasn't demeaning your service, Mrs. Trevelyan.

EVE: It's on the strength of that service that Simon has been given permission to be treated in this facility. For God's sake, Yanks and Brits cooperated in war, why can't they cooperate in peace!

DOCTOR: *(Giving way just slightly)...* What's your husband's problem?

EVE: Headaches. He gets them all the time. No one seems to be able to cure them.

DOCTOR: He's had medication?

EVE: Yes.

DOCTOR: Hot and cold compresses?

EVE: Yes.

DOCTOR: X-ray?

EVE: Yes.

DOCTOR: Nothing showed up?

EVE: Nothing.

DOCTOR: How often do they come?

EVE: Often. Any time of the day or night. At any provocation—active or not active, calm or tense, happy or unhappy.

DOCTOR: Any sign of tumors or lesions?

EVE: Not that we know of. He can't live with this! I can't either! It's been six years since his plane was hit and he had to bail out over Germany, six years with no visible injuries but with excruciating pain. It causes these terrifying mood swings. One moment he's brimming over with euphoria, the next he's wallowing in the depths of hell. And his ups can be more terrifying than his downs. I don't know from one moment to the next what kind of man I'm married to! In the name of heaven, Doctor, help him! *(She breaks down, stifling sobs.)*

DOCTOR: *(Ill-at-ease with her emotions. He looks at the records.)*... I'll talk with him and see if I think there's anything I can do. *(He goes to the upstage right entrance.)* Flight Commander Trevelyan. Come in, will you?

EVE: Thank you.

DOCTOR: Don't thank me yet. We haven't done anything. And if we do admit him, it would only be probational, you understand.

EVE: I understand. But there's something *you* should understand: ...You're our last hope.

(FLIGHT COMMANDER TREVELYAN *enters. He is in his late 30s, proud, aristocratic, cynical, diffident and every inch the Englishman.)*

EVE: Simon, this is Doctor Baines.

DOCTOR: How do you do?

SIMON: I do fine, thank you. How do *you* do?

DOCTOR: I do fine.

EVE: Doctor Baines thinks he might be able to help you.

DOCTOR: I haven't said—

SIMON: You want to become the bane of my existence. You want to know if I'll be a bane or a boon. You wonder if I'll be a bane in the ass—

EVE: Simon—!

SIMON: She has swum me across the Atlantic, Doctor, seeking a cure I know can never come.

EVE: You don't know that.

SIMON: Actually, the real reason she has swum me across the pond is that, after seven years in jolly England, she got tired of the thousand year old lawns, the lorries driving on the left, the pasties, the steak and kidney pies. She wants a good old American hot dog—

EVE: I want a cure for you—!

SIMON: *Of* me.

EVE: *For* you.

SIMON: We've swum three thousand miles for a cure and a hot dog. Thinkest thou that here we shall find one or both or neither?

EVE: Oh, God, how I hate your antic dispositions!

SIMON: You hate *me*, my dear Eve. You want me to be cured so you can bid me goodbye.

DOCTOR: Please!... Mr. and Mrs. Trevelyan—

EVE: *Flight Commander* and *Captain* Trevelyan—

DOCTOR: Flight Commander and Captain Trevelyan—

EVE: My husband is a hero! A winner of the Victoria Cross! He flew two hundred missions over Germany, spent months as a prisoner of war—

SIMON: Will you stop bringing that up—!

EVE: You deserve *something* for all you did!

SIMON: *(Looking at the space with distaste)* And this is the something?

EVE: This is the best I can—

DOCTOR: I beg you! A truce!... This is a hospital, not a battlefield! *(To* SIMON:*)* I can only admit you here if you wish to be admitted.

SIMON: In that case, I guess I have to wish to be admitted... What I do not wish is to be billeted in this God-forsaken town with the Captain's sister and brother-in-law—whose proximity to your establishment is the major reason we've landed here.

EVE: They have gone out of their way to let us—

SIMON: He reeks of beer. She reeks of laundry soap. Their brats could benefit from a good dose of castor oil—

EVE: *(To the* DOCTOR:*)* Forgive my husband. He makes a point of refusing to have anything to do with the manners which were bred into his family for generations. You have to make allowances—

DOCTOR: Actually, I'm quite used to bad manners in people who are suffering—

SIMON: "Bad manners—!"

EVE: *(To the* DOCTOR:*)* Will you take him?

SIMON: It would be an act of charity, believe me. We, the maimed flotsam of a war we never wanted, come to your shore as penitents.

DOCTOR: Penitent for what?

SIMON: For having survived.

(A pause. BILLY MAITLAND *wheels himself in.* BILLY *is in his late 20s, working-class but highly intelligent, quintessentially American. He seems to be in his own world and, timid and afraid, is muttering to himself:)*

BILLY: "The only thing we have to fear is fear itself..." *(Not seeming to notice the people in the room, he wheels himself to a window and peers out without seeing. He continues, muttering to himself:)* "The only thing we have to fear is fear itself."

DOCTOR: That's Billy Maitland. He's our only patient.

EVE: You only have one patient?

DOCTOR: If your husband is admitted, that would make two.

EVE: I don't understand.

DOCTOR: Before the war, this was a hotel. During the war, they converted it to a Veterans Administration hospital. Gradually, as the service patients got discharged, most of the hospital was converted to take civilian patients. Only this wing is still under the aegis of the VA. They'd be happy to turn it over to civilian patients, but they insist we discharge—as cured—all our veteran patients first... As of last month, we've managed to discharge all but Billy. He's been with us for almost five years now.

SIMON: Can't he be transferred?

DOCTOR: There isn't any other facility in this area. And this, apparently, was his home town. So, in their infinite wisdom, they think he should stay here.

EVE: To be near his family?

DOCTOR: As far as we can tell, he has no family.

EVE: No friends?

DOCTOR: None we've been able to find.

EVE: No girl?

DOCTOR: He was barely eighteen when he was drafted. No time, yet, for a serious girlfriend.

EVE: I should think it would make sense for the VA to move him elsewhere—if only for budgetary reasons.

DOCTOR: Have you ever known a government agency to be governed by what makes sense? So as long as the powers-that-be insist he has a right to be here I'm stuck with this nearly empty wing, manned by a skeleton staff—and a main wing for civilians which is usually overcrowded.

SIMON: What's his problem?

DOCTOR: His spine was shattered—during the invasion of Normandy.

EVE: Poor kid.

BILLY: *(Terrified, calling out:)* "The only thing we have to fear—is fear itself!"

DOCTOR: He's obsessed with FDR. Worships him. Has a personal letter from him which he treasures. He's memorized all Roosevelt's speeches—

BILLY: "I pledge myself to a New Deal for all Americans..."

DOCTOR: Sometimes he likes to pretend he *is* him—and to get the rest of us to join in the pretending. He got a nurse to play Eleanor to his Franklin. He tried to get me to be Harry Hopkins—but I didn't have the flair.

BILLY: "In these unhappy times, let us put our faith once more in the forgotten man."

DOCTOR: Billy never graduated from High School, but he reads everything about FDR he can get his hands on. It's as if fixating on Roosevelt is the only thing that keeps him sane.

EVE: Will he walk again?

DOCTOR: ...No. But in the state he's in I haven't yet dared tell him. *(Clearly conflicted)* I'm a medical doctor, not a psychiatrist. The VA has precious few of those. They don't seem to believe they're necessary. All I'm officially assigned to do is work on rehabilitating Billy physically so he can cope with life outside once he's released from here. I'd like to do more to help his mental state but— *(He calls out to* BILLY, *then introduces:)*... Billy—Corporal Billy Maitland, this is Flight Commander Simon Trevelyan.

SIMON: How do you do, old chap.

BILLY: You're English!

SIMON: Guilty.

BILLY: Do you know Winston Churchill?

DOCTOR: Billy, you can't assume that everyone from England knows Winston Churchill.

SIMON: Actually, I do. Met him quite a few times. His house was not too far from our house—that is, the house we used to have before we became unlanded gentry.

BILLY: What's he like?

SIMON: Short.

BILLY: He and FDR were great friends! There's never been a friendship like it!

SIMON: So they say.

BILLY: FDR's my hero! No one more good. No one more wise. *(With reverence, he quotes:)* "We look forward to a world founded upon four essential human freedoms: Freedom of Speech, Freedom of Religion, Freedom from Want and Freedom from Fear." *(Retreating into his terrified shell)*... Freedom from fear, freedom from fear... *(Terrified)* "The only thing we have to fear is fear itself!" *(He wheels himself away, cowering, repeating his mantra.)*

SIMON: ...He's lucky.

DOCTOR: Lucky?

SIMON: He seems to be living in a world of his own. Without personal memories.

DOCTOR: Actually, he does have memories. Terrible nightmares. Wakes up screaming—sweating—and fighting the war all over again.

EVE: *(Murmuring under her breath)* Sounds familiar...

DOCTOR: Refuses to sleep. Only gets some rest when I manage to get him to take a pill... If only I could find a way to make him less anxious about existence—

SIMON: *(To* BILLY, *very English:)* Take it from me, old chap. All you have to do is find a way to carry on carrying on!

BILLY: You said that just like Winston Churchill! You be him! I'll be FDR! (BILLY *wheels himself to* SIMON *and says, as FDR:)* Congratulations on taking over the leadership of your government, Mr. Churchill!

SIMON: What the—?!

BILLY: *(As FDR)* Prime Minister Chamberlain was an idiot—thinking he could trust a non-aggression pact with Hitler! Now that you're at the helm, you'll deal with the monster more forcefully, won't you!

SIMON: Good God—

BILLY: *(As FDR)* You're the best man England has. You and I must stay in touch with each other personally. Don't go through channels. Contact me directly at the White House by sealed diplomatic pouch.

SIMON: *(Refusing to play)* Oh, no—

DOCTOR: Why can't you—?

SIMON: Play that vain cantankerous runt? That windbag!?

DOCTOR: I gather he's not on your list of favorite people.

SIMON: He's a joke.

DOCTOR: *(Quietly, moving* SIMON *out of* BILLY's *hearing:)* I'm sorry you think so—because the only condition on which I'll agree to admit you to this facility is if you'll agree to assist us in Billy's cure.

SIMON: That's blackmail!

DOCTOR: I don't want another patient, Flight Commander Trevelyan. I want the VA to release this wing for civilian patients and let us move on. Taking on another soul complicates my life considerably. Unless I can see some benefit to—

EVE: *(To* SIMON:) I should think you'd want to help a fellow veteran.

SIMON: I am not going to relive it all all over again—! *(Suddenly overcome with a tremendous headache)* God, oh, God—!

BILLY: *(Crying out as if to comfort* SIMON:*)* "The only thing we have to fear is fear itself!"

DOCTOR: Will you help me—?

SIMON: *(In excruciating pain)* Aspirin! Morphine! A shot—! Please, Doctor—!

DOCTOR: Will you—?

SIMON: Yes! Yes! Only—

DOCTOR: And you'll—

SIMON: Yes! Anything! *(To* BILLY, *in exaggerated imitation of Churchill:)* "We will fight them on the beaches! We will fight them on the fields and in the streets! We will fight them in the hills—!"

BILLY: *(To* SIMON *with great joy:)* That's the spirit, Mr. Churchill!

SIMON: *(What the hell has he agreed to?)* Jeezus—!

(SIMON *breaks off, moaning in pain. The* DOCTOR *says to* EVE:*)*

DOCTOR: Leave him with me. If we're going to begin his cure, we'd better start immediately.

(The DOCTOR *takes* SIMON's *arm to lead him out.* SIMON *pulls his arm away, but, in great pain, accompanies the* DOCTOR. *As they exit up left,* BILLY *shouts after them:)*

BILLY: "The only thing you have to fear is fear itself!"

EVE: That's what you think.

(Blackout)

(Drums. Lights change.)

(Several days later. SIMON *is in his room, stage right off the common room, pacing. The* DOCTOR *enters.)*

DOCTOR: So far, all your tests have come back negative.

SIMON: Negative is positive I take it.

DOCTOR: Any headaches today?

SIMON: Not so far. But the day is young, don't give up hope.

DOCTOR: You have a pessimistic view of life, Flight Commander.

SIMON: That's only because life is such a pessimistic business.

DOCTOR: Is your wife coming to visit today?

SIMON: I hope not.

DOCTOR: Why? She's a lovely woman.

SIMON: Except when exposed to me. I'm not what she thought she was getting when she married me.

DOCTOR: How so?

SIMON: I think she imagined there was a certain amount of romance in marrying into faded nobility. She knew my family had lost everything before the war. But she liked the idea of it—the echoes of once-grand patrician society. She thought she was hitching herself to impeccably mannered British gentility. Instead she's yoked to a cranky invalid. I can curdle people with a glance—or haven't you noticed.

DOCTOR: I've noticed.

SIMON: You have a cure for that?

DOCTOR: Only if someone wants to be cured of it—and I suspect you don't.

SIMON: I like people to stay at a certain distance—and Eve gets too close.

(BILLY *wheels himself across the common room toward him.*)

BILLY *(As FDR): (Calling out)* Mr. Prime Minister—!

SIMON: Bloody hell!

(*The* DOCTOR *makes a gesture for* SIMON *to go into the main space.* SIMON *holds back.*)

DOCTOR: Remember our bargain—. You promised—

(*Reluctantly,* SIMON *goes into the common room. The* DOCTOR *observes from the sidelines.*)

SIMON *(As WSC)*: ...Yes, Mr. President?

BILLY *(As FDR)*: I would like to be able to send you help, Mr. Churchill, but the American people are against it.

SIMON *(As* HIMSELF*): (To the* DOCTOR*:)* He's expecting me to do Churchill's begging bit! When we were deep in the war, desperate for America's assistance, and you wouldn't lift a finger!

BILLY *(As FDR)*: The American people still remember how many men we lost in the last war, Mr. Churchill. They don't want us to get involved in European battles ever again.

(SIMON *is silent. The* DOCTOR *says to him:*)

DOCTOR: Mr. Prime Minister! ...Don't you have a response?

SIMON *(Mockingly, as WSC):* Mr. President, I implore you! Just give us the tools and we will finish the job! *(As himself, aside to the* DOCTOR*:)* Is that Churchillian enough for you, or would you like me to bang a tin cup?

DOCTOR: You're doing fine.

BILLY *(As FDR)*: I am sympathetic to your plight, Mr. Churchill. But any help we give might incite your enemies to act against us.

DOCTOR: *(Prompting)* Mr. Prime Minister...

(The following exchanges as Churchill and FDR:)

SIMON: *(Reluctantly)* Mr. Roosevelt, ...our situation is becoming catastrophic! Hitler has annexed Austria and invaded Czechoslovakia, Poland, Denmark, Norway and the Lowlands. Now he's marching into France! If France falls, we're next. There's only the Channel — twenty miles — between us and the barbarians.

BILLY: He will never take France, Mr. Churchill. The French will fight to the bitter end. So you won't need us to —

(He starts to turn away. SIMON stops him with:)

SIMON: I'm sorry to inform you, Mr. Roosevelt, but France has capitulated.

(BILLY turns back.)

SIMON: Rather than let the Germans bomb their precious monuments, the cowards have given in.

BILLY: I was sure they would resist —

SIMON: *(Warming to the role)* You overestimate the frogs. Some are resisting, but many are collaborating. And now the Huns are attacking Britain nightly from the air! Wave after wave of German bombers! Our people are running out of food. Our fighting men are running out of ammunition. We are just a tiny island! How long can we hold out against the savage hordes?

BILLY: I understand your plight, Mr. Prime Minister. I would like to send assistance, but I have Congress and the American people to answer to.

SIMON: Our cities are burning! Our ships are being sunk by Nazi subs! Our planes are being destroyed on their landing fields! We can't hold out much longer. If we fall, America is next on the monster's list.

BILLY: I want to assist you but my hands are tied.

SIMON: We have no place left to turn! You're the only nation rich enough to help us! *(Dramatically)* In the great history of the world, Mr. President, — this is a thing to do now! ...*(Matter-of-factly)* Besides, you have to help — my mother was American.

BILLY: *(After a pause)*... I tell you what we'll do — we'll *lend* you what you need.

SIMON: *Lend* us —

BILLY: In return for long term leases for American bases on British possessions in the Atlantic.

SIMON: Ninety-nine year leases in return for a handful of leaky buckets and some shiploads of Spam?!

BILLY: Proof of the generosity of the American people!

SIMON: And the delicious satisfaction of our former colonies at seeing us down on our knees! *(Then, as himself, to the* DOCTOR, *breaking from the game:)*... Are you satisfied now? The boy's been distracted for the moment. He's pleased as punch with himself. And I played my part to the hilt—tho' the portrayal would have been helped considerably by a cigar and a glass of Scotch... Now, if you don't mind, I'd like to take a walk around the grounds, if that's permitted.

(SIMON *starts to exit. Still in the game,* BILLY *calls:)*

BILLY: Mr. Prime Minister!

SIMON: What is it now, Mr. President?

BILLY: We've been attacked! Pearl Harbor! The pride of our Pacific fleet up in flames! While the Japs were talking peace, they stabbed us in the back! Oh, this is a day that will live in infamy!

SIMON: Splendid!

BILLY: "Splendid!"

SIMON: Now you'll understand what we've been going through—

BILLY: And Hitler has declared war against us—! A day ago we were at peace, now suddenly we're in a two front war!

SIMON: At last!

BILLY: You like it—!

SIMON: Finally you and I are mixed up in this thing together! Comrades standing shoulder to shoulder!

BILLY: So we are, Mr. Churchill.

SIMON: Call me Winston.

BILLY: So we are, Winston.

SIMON: Now you'll see what it's like to fight for your lives.

BILLY: *(Deeply)* This generation has a rendezvous with destiny...

(BILLY *sits silent, in a contemplative heroic pose, absorbed in being* FDR. SIMON *looks at him for a moment then turns to the* DOCTOR *and asks:)*

SIMON: May I go for my walk now?

DOCTOR: *(Aside to* SIMON:*)* Of course. And thank you. That's the most animated I've seen Billy—ever.

SIMON: *(Aside to* DOCTOR: *)* He doesn't realize his two great heroes are about to send him to war—and when it's over, he'll never walk again.

(Blackout)

(Drums. Lights change.)

(The DOCTOR is in BILLY's room, stage left, talking to BILLY, who is seated in his wheelchair holding his FDR letter.)

DOCTOR: Why don't you let me get that framed for you, Billy?

BILLY: I like to be able to look at it—look at it close... He touched this. President Roosevelt actually touched this piece of paper. And there's my name—"Dear Corporal Maitland..."

DOCTOR: His thanks for your valor and courage.

BILLY: And he signed it, too. His very own hand.

DOCTOR: *(He has seen it a hundred times.)* Yes. Yes, I know.

(BILLY continues to gaze worshipfully at the page.)

DOCTOR: Have you been doing your exercises?

BILLY: Sure, Doc.

DOCTOR: Show me.

(Carefully, BILLY folds the letter, puts it gingerly into its envelope and shows the DOCTOR:)

BILLY: White House stationery—

DOCTOR: Yes. Very nice.

(BILLY puts the envelope into his bedside drawer.)

DOCTOR: Now show me—. *(He hands BILLY some dumbbells.)* Front and side and up—and front and side and up—

BILLY: It's great to have Simon here. Imagine! He actually knows Churchill!

DOCTOR: Keep exercising. You have to do this daily.

(BILLY continues the arm exercises.)

BILLY: His wife's American, isn't she. She seems very nice.

DOCTOR: Keep moving, Billy. You have to build and maintain your upper body strength.

BILLY: But the legs. Why don't we work on the legs?

DOCTOR: We'll get to that. You know I think very soon you'll have enough strength to pull yourself from your chair to the bed and back again—using only your upper body. FDR did lots of upper body exercises.

BILLY: I know he did. But his brain was working all the time. Mine works all the time, too. But sometimes I don't like the way it's working.

DOCTOR: Are you sleeping any better?

BILLY: Sleep scares me.

DOCTOR: Take these right before you go to bed. *(He hands* BILLY *a couple of pills, which* BILLY *puts into his pocket.)* You need to get some rest, Billy. That's what night is for.

BILLY: I have these thoughts—

DOCTOR: What thoughts?

BILLY: It's all so dark. I don't like to think about them.

DOCTOR: Right. Don't think about them.

BILLY: Somehow FDR kept his spirits up. With all the world in flames and him responsible for saving everybody—he didn't get discouraged.

DOCTOR: You shouldn't either.

BILLY: But he could make things happen. I can't—make things happen.

DOCTOR: You can in the world you live in.

BILLY: The little world I live in. He lived in a Big World. A world where you can actually do things. What a guy he was! I wish I were him!

DOCTOR: No, you don't. He's dead.

(Blackout)

(Drums. Lights change.)

(Another day. In the common room, EVE *has come in to visit* SIMON. *She hands him a small wrapped package. He opens it.)*

SIMON: A cigar? What's this—a new kind of torture? You know we're not allowed to smoke here.

EVE: I know you're not allowed to light it but I thought it would give some authenticity to your role as Churchill.

SIMON: When you stuck me in this place I did not expect to have to relive the war all over again! *(He sticks the cigar between his lips.)*

EVE: The spitting image!

SIMON: Say that again and I'll ram this down your throat.

EVE: I see the good doctor hasn't cured you of your distemper.

SIMON: Or the headaches.

EVE: They still come?

SIMON: Worse than ever. And when they do...

EVE: When they do?

SIMON: ...I sink into a despond so deep I don't want to come out. Ever. *(He starts to sink now, retreats, grows more and more mute. A long silence.)*

EVE: Simon... ?

SIMON: *(Suddenly crying out:)* It's unbearable! I'm watching myself sinking deeper and deeper and I'm paralyzed, unable to kick my way up for air! Why did you bring me to this hell hole?

EVE: I know it's not as grand as the gilded halls of your ancestors—

SIMON: What's so wrong in thinking those gilded halls were superior to this?

EVE: Nothing wrong. But they're gone, Simon, gone.

SIMON: Along with my clear bright future. Did I think, when I was at Eton, at Cambridge, that I'd end up here—like this, as this? The difference between my hopes for me then, and what I am now, horrifies me!

EVE: None of us become the person of our dreams, you know, Simon.

SIMON: Except sweet young Billy. He slips himself into the skin of his great hero so easily. I play the game—to divert myself. But my me is always there.

(BILLY wheels into the space from a distance.)

SIMON *(As FDR)*: Look, here he comes—wanting to play—

BILLY: Welcome to the White House, Winston!

SIMON *(As WSC)*: Oh, I'm at the White House now, am I?

BILLY: How was your crossing?

SIMON: *(With a look at* EVE*—"See, I'm playing the game.")* Rough, but we managed to outrun the Narzee U boats.

BILLY: Eleanor and I are pleased as punch to have you visit. If there's anything we can do to make you comfortable—. Anything you want—

SIMON: A long hot bath.

BILLY: Done. And when you're through, we'll talk.

SIMON: Why wait? Come talk to me while I soak. The Prime Minister of England has nothing to hide from the President of the United States!

EVE: *(Interrupting the game)* Mr. President—I have a present for you.

(She hands BILLY *a small package like the one she gave* SIMON*. He opens it and finds in it a cigarette and a cigarette holder. He loves them! He puts the cigarette into the holder, puts the holder into his mouth and tilts his head back in an FDR pose.)*

EVE: You look just like him!

BILLY: *(For the gift)* Thank you! Thank you so much!

SIMON: *(Interrupting)* I haven't crossed the ocean for a smoke! We have serious things to discuss, Franklin!

BILLY: Of course, Winston.

(EVE *moves to the sidelines and observes the FDR and WSC meeting.*)

SIMON: Our goal is the unconditional surrender of the enemy, correct?

BILLY: Absolutely!

SIMON: So we have to come up with a comprehensive strategy—

BILLY: Here's my plan: I'll immediately order as many men as I can spare from our Pacific theatre to staging grounds in England. Your men and mine will cross the Channel, give 'em hell, and have those Heinies surrendering within a month!

SIMON: You think the war in Europe is going to be over in a month?

BILLY: As soon as we Yanks get in it!

SIMON: You're deluded! The Bosche are stronger than you think. If our major thrust is across the Channel—and we fail—that thin barrier between the continent and the British Isles will seem no wider than a stream! The Germans will invade us and that will be the end of jolly England!

BILLY: Then how do you suggest that we proceed?

SIMON: ...Through North Africa.

BILLY: North Africa!

SIMON: Defeat the Axis forces in North Africa, cross the Mediterranean, move north through Sicily, up through Italy, retake France, then attack Germany by land and air—

BILLY: The long way 'round—! It'll take years—! So many men! So many casualties!

SIMON: It's the only way that makes sense! I've studied all the great battles of the past, you haven't. Here's my plan: call it Operation Torch. We crush the Axis forces in North Africa in a pincer movement. We Brits, coming from the west, push Rommel's Afrika Korps back across the Western Desert. You Yanks, coming from the east, engage their rear. That way we secure the Mediterranean, protect Egypt, safeguard British East Africa and regain control of the Suez Canal—the swiftest passage to India and our Far Eastern possessions!

BILLY: We are not in this war to save the British Empire!

SIMON: The British Empire is the nation which spread civilization throughout the world!

BILLY: By subjugating millions of people—!

SIMON: They were savages before we civilized them!

BILLY: They were free people! They were happy, simple, independent people! You had no right—!

SIMON: By God, it's the American Revolution all over again! I have not become the king's first minister to preside over the liquidation of the British Empire!

BILLY: I hate war!

SIMON: Hate it as much as you like. But now that we're in it, we have to stop at nothing to win it! We will burn their cities to bits with incendiaries which will make the bombing of London look like child's play! We will rain destruction from the skies!

BILLY: You frighten me with your cries for blood and death!

SIMON: Fighting a halfway war is fighting a losing war! It's all or nothing, Franklin. Are you with us or are you against us?

BILLY: I am with you, but—

SIMON: But me no buts! This is Armageddon! *(Suddenly he breaks down, holding his head in tremendous pain. Now he isn't Churchill, he is* SIMON.*)* This is Armageddon... Oh, God, God... *(He stifles sobs. He sees* BILLY *looking at him.)* Get out of here!

(He lunges for BILLY, *who wheels himself backward.* SIMON *breaks into tremendous sobs.)*

EVE: Simon! Simon!

(She runs to him. The DOCTOR *enters. He says to* BILLY:*)*

DOCTOR: You'd better go.

*(*BILLY *wheels himself out in the direction of his room. The* DOCTOR *turns to* SIMON *who is weeping uncontrollably.)*

EVE: Using him to cure your other patient is driving him crazy!

DOCTOR: He went too far, that's all. He had to go to the brink before I could pull him back—

EVE: You have to help him!

DOCTOR: Yes. I will. I only had to see this. I know a way.

EVE: What is it?

DOCTOR: ...Shock treatments.

EVE: Shock treatments!

DOCTOR: Mild electric shocks. They clean out all the bad things from the brain.

EVE: But—

DOCTOR: We can cleanse his head from the pain and all the things which are torturing him.

EVE: Are you certain?

DOCTOR: Nothing is certain. But is this how you want him to live, Eve?

(*The* DOCTOR *and* EVE *survey* SIMON *who is cowering in a corner, doubled up with sobs and in great pain.*)

EVE: You should have seen him when I married him. He was the bravest, the most splendid pilot the Royal Air Force had ever seen.

(*Blackout*)

(*Drums. Lights change.*)

(*The common room.* EVE *is alone, pacing.* BILLY *wheels himself in.*)

BILLY: Are they doing it to him now?

EVE: Yes.

BILLY: They wanted to do it to me. I wouldn't let them.

EVE: You don't think shock treatments help?

BILLY: I didn't want to be touched, that's all. I didn't want anything more to happen to me.

EVE: Doctor Baines thinks this will make Simon better.

BILLY: You think that doctor knows what he's doing? You think any of them know what they're doing? What's bothering us can't be removed by a jolt to the brain!

EVE: What's bothering you, Billy?

(*He doesn't answer.*)

EVE: Doctor Baines says you just about never sleep.

BILLY: Why should I sleep? Sleep is when those dreams come—!

EVE: What dreams?

BILLY: I don't want to think about them!... Anyway—I'm not doing so badly. I can hoist myself into bed and back into my chariot again. Of course, if there were a real emergency—. I'm so afraid—

EVE: What are you afraid of?

BILLY: Fire. That's what scares me most. I couldn't escape. If ever I sleep, I wake up in the night and see flames all around me! I try to scream, I open my mouth, but there's no sound! Then I break out in a cold sweat and I realize—I wasn't awake. I was dreaming. And the flames were the flames of Omaha Beach—

EVE: Is that where you were injured?

BILLY: I don't want to talk about it.

EVE: Simon, too, wakes up screaming. He won't talk about it either.

BILLY: You can't imagine the horror—

EVE: Tell me about it—

BILLY: *(Reverting to his mantra)* "The only thing we have to fear is fear itself!"

EVE: Talk to me!

BILLY: If there was anyone I could talk to, it would be you... But I can't—I can't—

(He starts getting really upset.)

EVE: Never mind. It's all right—

BILLY: *You* talk to *me*. Please. Here it's so very lonely.

EVE: What do you want me to talk about?

BILLY: Tell me how you and Simon met.

EVE: All right... It was in 1943. In Portsmouth.

BILLY: Our troopship docked there. For a few days. Before Normandy. Didn't get a chance to see much of it.

EVE: Simon and I were both stationed at a Bomber Command base just outside the city. Before the war, when I was in the WASPs, I ferried planes from one base in the States to another. PT-19s, C-45s, B-24s, the big babies and the small. When the war began, I joined the Air Force hoping to get my licks in. They sent me to England. But they wouldn't let us "ladies" fly.

BILLY: *(Understanding)* "Too dangerous" for women?

EVE: They wouldn't even take us on as co-pilots!... I was chafing at the bit behind a typewriter, watching the guys go out. The Americans—and the boys of the RAF. I knew, each time they headed out, some fliers wouldn't make it back. I was willing to take the risk—but they wouldn't let me.

BILLY: Simon was one of those?

EVE: *(Looking off toward whatever is happening is happening)* Do you think it's going to help? Do you think he's going to be all right?

BILLY: I like Doctor Baines. I'm sure he knows what he's doing... Go on. Tell me about you and Simon—

EVE: He knew how much I wanted to be flying. One night, before one of his bombing runs, he arranged to hide me in his plane. But before we could take off, some snitch reported me. I was reprimanded. Simon was grounded for a week and they revoked our off-base passes for three whole months!

BILLY: That must have been hard.

EVE: Not at all! It was great fun! We were comrades in "shame"! Two hell-cats, grounded! We laughed and drank together! We began to do naughty things together!

BILLY: "Naughty things?"

EVE: I think you know what I'm saying. It was that kind of time, when all you wanted to do was live! Live with every fiber of your being!

BILLY: I know what you mean.

EVE: We lived, all right. Got secretly married. Which got me instantly demoted. If single ladies weren't allowed to fly, married ladies weren't even allowed to type! Any job nobody wanted to do fell to me. The rest of the time I sat in a freezing bed-sitter just outside the base waiting for Simon to come home after his bombing runs... *(She fades off, overcome with bad memories.)*

BILLY: And when the war was over—?

EVE: We stayed on in England—him trying to become again what he had been raised to become—a country gentleman. Though we had very little money. And me trying to become what I was never meant to become—a former country gentleman's wife. But there was something wrong from the beginning. Something terribly wrong—!

(A silence. She looks off to where whatever's happening to SIMON is happening.)

BILLY: ...Lucky Simon.

EVE: *Un*lucky Simon. Unlucky with what's happening to him this minute... Unlucky with what's happened to him since the war... Unlucky to have hitched himself to me.

BILLY: But don't you know? His having you is the biggest luck of all.

(She puts her hand on his shoulder, a gesture of gratitude and compassion. He covers her hand with his.)

(Blackout)

(Drums. Lights change.)

(Rainy day, a few days later. The DOCTOR wheels SIMON into the common room in a wheelchair. SIMON is listless, motionless, an exhausted, empty shell.)

DOCTOR: You could use some air. When the weather's better, I'll let you go outside.

(As SIMON doesn't respond, the DOCTOR continues, awkwardly, to make conversation. He gets no response from SIMON.)

DOCTOR: Your wife said she'd come today. She should be here soon.

(A brief hand gesture from SIMON — *as if to dismiss her, push her away.)*

DOCTOR: Now, now. She's come every day since your—your treatment. She cares for you, you know. It would be nice if, when she came, you responded with a word or two.

*(*SIMON *suddenly turns his chair away from the* DOCTOR.*)*

DOCTOR: We're all here to help you, Simon... You can talk. I know you can talk. I only gave you a fraction of a jolt—

*(*SIMON *raises his fist as if to strike the* DOCTOR *who, in spite of himself, retreats a step or two.)*

DOCTOR: There's no way I can help you unless you cooperate, Flight Commander. I implore you—

(With great ferocity, SIMON *wheels his chair toward the exit—just as* EVE *enters, blocking his way.)*

DOCTOR: There's no escape, Simon. Surely you know that. No escape—either from me, or your wife, or from what's going on in your head—unless you let us know what you're feeling.

(As the DOCTOR *leaves, he passes* EVE *and says to her:)*

DOCTOR: He can talk if he wants to. I know that. Unless he begins to talk, I can't tell if the treatment has succeeded or failed... See what you can do.

(The DOCTOR *exits.* EVE *has brought* SIMON *a book. She puts it in his lap. He pushes it off. She picks it up.)*

EVE: But it's the new volume of your memoirs, Mr. Churchill. *The Grand Alliance.* Excellent reviews! Best-seller! Book-of-the-Month! Clever thing, that,—writing your own life and times before anyone else can take a crack at them. Lets the world know what a splendid fellow you are—at least from your point of view.

*(*SIMON *turns away in ironic disgust. Silence.* EVE *becomes a bit impatient.)*

EVE: Look, Simon. I've come here for five days—smiling, talking endlessly about the weather, bringing you books and candy and telling you every joke I can think of. If you don't want to respond, don't. But you can at least tell me if the wizard has cured you of your headaches.

*(*SIMON *smiles sardonically.)*

EVE: I gather you are not in pain... So what are you punishing us for now? Helping you survive?

(He wheels himself farther away.)

EVE: I promised I'd see you through this, Simon. But if you'd prefer me to start the unhitching process—

(He doesn't respond.)

EVE: No, I can't do that. We're stuck. You're only allowed to be here because of me. If I desert you you'll find yourself on the street. Alone on an American street. Speechless in a wheelchair. Unable to ask in American English where you could find a pot to piss in! So what do you want me to do? What in hell do you want me to—

(BILLY has wheeled himself in, but, hearing the harangue, stops and says:)

BILLY: Sorry. I'll go.

EVE: No. Stay. I came to visit Simon. But since he won't respond, I'll visit with you. How are you, Billy?

BILLY: He still won't talk to you?

EVE: Still in a blue funk and I've no idea how to pull him out of it.

BILLY: Let me try—*(He wheels himself to* SIMON. *As FDR:)* Listen to me, Winston. Operation Torch has succeeded! The German and Italian armies in North Africa have been annihilated! Our combined forces are moving north through Sicily and Italy! Meet me in Casablanca and we'll plan our strategy. Now that the Axis is on the run you and I can—

SIMON: *(Suddenly lashing out)* I do not want to play!

EVE: Hallelujah! I knew you were still in there!

SIMON: I do not want to pretend any more! I do not want to give you or me or the good doctor any scintilla of hope that there's a way out of this dark hole—

EVE: What are you saying?

SIMON: That humiliating treatment you subjected me to—that vaunted treatment you so heartily endorsed—

EVE: I did not—

SIMON: It didn't work!... I was strapped like a dog to a table, I was jolted like a rabbit in a Bugs Bunny cartoon, I was zipped and zapped and brain-fried like a slab of bacon, like a prisoner on execution day. I screamed as I've never screamed before in my life—I confess it to you. And after all that—nothing has changed. Inside this shell, I'm the me that I was before I went in. The ups and downs, the nightmares and pain—all there. Worse than ever. That's why I don't want to speak! You are all out there smiling and simpering, "How are you?" How am I? I wish I were dead!

BILLY: No, no! "Carry on and dread nought. You must not flag or fail, you must never surrender!" You said that. You must tell yourself that! Over and over!

SIMON: You naive, deceived, gullible little fool. You worship the men who made you spend the rest of your life in a chair.

BILLY: No, no! I'm going to walk again—

SIMON: Stick to your illusions!

BILLY: "We must never surrender!"

SIMON: Take comfort from hollow words which were spoken from the protection of marble halls and solid underground bunkers. Wake up and face the truth—!

BILLY: I was only trying to help, only trying to help—

(Crushed, BILLY turns his wheelchair and exits in the direction of his room. EVE turns on SIMON:)

EVE: You've hurt him deeply—

SIMON: *(Throwing off his lap robe and getting up)* He wears me out with his fantasies—

EVE: He's the best friend you have on this earth. He worships and admires you.

SIMON: He admires me as Churchill. Simon Trevelyan has no admirers.

EVE: I used to be one.

SIMON: Thank you for the past tense. I came into this world alone, and that's the way I'll be leaving it.

EVE: It's your own fault if you won't let anyone near you.

SIMON: I haven't got the strength to argue any further. I need to sleep. To sleep—alas, perchance to dream.

(He gets up slowly and walks out toward his room. EVE watches him go. She is still for a moment, thinking, then turns and goes into BILLY's room. She finds BILLY sitting in his chair, disconsolate.)

EVE: You mustn't let him bother you.

BILLY: Is it true—about my never walking?

EVE: You must never say never.

BILLY: FDR never gave up. He always had faith he'd walk again—

EVE: Right! *(Then, only slightly Churchillian:)* You must not flag or fail! You must never surrender!

BILLY: *(Trying to get courage)* No... I mustn't...

EVE: Don't think about it—

BILLY: *(Looking off toward where SIMON exited)*... I thought I could help him.

EVE: I've been thinking that for years. I'm afraid there's nothing any of us can do. He came out of prisoner of war camp as someone completely different...

BILLY: I keep thinking—underneath all that—there's a nice man.

EVE: There was—once. A very nice man.

BILLY: You're nice.

EVE: So are you, Billy. *(She brushes a lock of hair from his forehead. He smiles, grateful.)* Simon won't let me touch him. I used to think that souls could touch each other—help each other—when two people touched.

BILLY: I still think that.

EVE: Do you?

BILLY: I think—sometimes—that kind of comfort can solve everything—at least for a moment. *(He touches her sleeve—wanting her.)*

EVE: ...What else do we have—except moments?

(His eyes beg for what he knows she could give him. He clutches her arm needily. She pulls his head toward her, holding him close. Then, releasing him, she turns out the light, comes to him and gently starts to unbutton his shirt, preparing to make love.)

(Blackout)

(Drums. Lights change.)

(The next day. In the common room, SIMON is in an extremely antic and hyper mood. The DOCTOR, more sober, can only watch as SIMON dances about the space.)

SIMON: What a thrill to be me, what a pleasure!
Who am I? I am me! Don't you know!
Hello me, hello you, I'm delighted—
And delightful, wherever I go!

DOCTOR: I'm sorry the shock treatment didn't work.

SIMON: I'm the electric man! I could light up this light bulb!

DOCTOR: You still have all the symptoms you had before?

SIMON: In even greater measure. *(Exaggerated, telling a secret)* But you and I know, Doctor—there is a cure.

DOCTOR: What is it?

SIMON: "Put out the light—and then, put out the light." *(He pantomimes pulling a string to put out a light then pantomimes collapsing and dying.)*

DOCTOR: No! No, Simon!

SIMON: You don't like losing a patient to the final solution? Do you fear what dreams may come to you should I slip off this mortal coil?

DOCTOR: That's not it, I—

SIMON: Tell me, what did you do in the war, Herr Doktor? Where were you?

DOCTOR: I was here, caring for those who were returning.

SIMON: And you cured them all?

DOCTOR: I tried.

SIMON: Did you succeed?

DOCTOR: I did my best—with the limited tools, the limited staff which I was given.

SIMON: And have you done your best with me?

DOCTOR: Not yet.

SIMON: No?

DOCTOR: ...I have another way to help you—

SIMON: Higher voltage?

DOCTOR: *(A very long pause, then, with deliberate care)*... A lobotomy.

SIMON: Ah! The ice pick cure! What a treat!

DOCTOR: It has worked in many cases. It might work in yours.

SIMON: Drill through the brain? That shouldn't be difficult—since mine is made of Swiss cheese.

DOCTOR: We drill through the eye socket. And it's not drilling. It's done with a sort of hammer. One goes in to the prefrontal lobe and severs it from the rest of the brain.

SIMON: Farewell, brain! It's been nice to know you!

DOCTOR: It's a simple procedure, with local anaesthetic. And—after it—you're well.

SIMON: "Well." As what? As a vegetable? Would I be a potato or an eggplant? Would I be a tomato or a winter squash? If I am to live on as a comestible, I think I'd rather like to be an artichoke. An artichoke has a heart, you know,—while a post-lobotomized Simon would, if I understand correctly, have no emotions whatsoever.

DOCTOR: It's having all these emotions which seems to disturb you.

SIMON: Only the pain disturbs me. The emotions disturb other people. It's a very interesting phenomenon to watch. People overvalue the satin smoothness of social civility, don't you think so, Doctor? Don't you think a little bit of asocial behavior throws life into the mix?

DOCTOR: Live as you wish. If you choose to be asocial then you must bear the consequences. I simply tell you that, to your mental tortures—and your pain, there is a cure available. You and your wife must make the decision. The operation requires the patient's consent—and the mate's as well.

SIMON: Oh, my wife would love to see my emotions in a straightjacket. As for *her* emotions, banked down as they are, as they always have been, they could use a little awakening.

DOCTOR: Perhaps she keeps her emotions under control to keep you from exploding.

SIMON: *(With a glance at BILLY's room)* What are her feelings at the moment, Doctor? Do you know?

(Blackout)

(Drums. Lights change.)

(Another day. EVE enters, wearing a pretty dress and carrying sprays of forsythia. BILLY wheels himself in. There is a warmth between them which is evident but must be hidden because they are in a public space. BILLY worships and adores her. EVE's feelings are much more withdrawn and complex. Between their words, much remains unspoken.)

EVE: Good morning, Billy.

BILLY: Eve—

EVE: How are you?

BILLY: How are *you*?

EVE: Well... Very well... I thought you'd like to have some forsythia from my sister's garden.

(With tenderness, she hands over half of the branches. He takes them and holds them like a gift from the gods.)

BILLY: Thank you... You're kind... So—very—kind.

EVE: It's nothing... I'll get you a vase—*(She starts to leave.)*

BILLY: No. Don't go. I'd rather hold them anyway... I've been thinking about you—

EVE: Billy, I—

(At this moment, SIMON walks in. He instantly picks up on their closeness—on the fact of the flowers in BILLY's arms and in hers.)

SIMON: Ah, it's the flower lady.

EVE: I've brought you some—*(She holds out the remaining spray.)*

SIMON: I see you've brought us *both* some.

EVE: Surely you don't begrudge your fellow guest at this—hotel—a blossom or two.

SIMON: I do not begrudge my fellow guest a blossom... Why should I begrudge my fellow guest anything?

(An awkward silence, then —)

EVE: The weather has turned so much warmer —

SIMON: Have we descended to talking about the weather?

EVE: How are you feeling today?

SIMON: I'm holding on very well — for a potential eggplant.

EVE: Look, Simon, you —

SIMON: *(Suddenly lashing out:)* I don't want to talk about it!

(A beat. EVE changes the subject.)

EVE: How are you coming in the war?

SIMON: Which war?

EVE: That little trifle — the *World* War.

SIMON: Oh, that. It looks as if the tide's beginning to turn in our favor.

BILLY: I want us to go to Tehran — to the first Big Three Conference — but Simon doesn't want to.

SIMON: We have no Stalin.

EVE: I could play him.

SIMON: *(With personal meaning)* You mean, make our duet into a trio? You'd like that, wouldn't you...

EVE: *(Disregarding his remark)* If only I had a big bushy red mustache!

SIMON: Or a whip and a gun and a gulag and a KGB and a thousand armed Cossacks guarding a million political prisoners on the frozen steppes of Siberia —

EVE: You think I can't do cruel?

SIMON: Oh, I know you can do cruel —

EVE: *(Changing the subject)* What does Stalin smoke?

SIMON: A pipe. But his major minor vice is drink!

(EVE fills a drinking glass with water from a pitcher, holds it up as a toast and says, with Russian accent:)

EVE: Vodka!

(She fills two other glasses. As she gives them to the other two she asks:)

EVE: Why did they have to meet in Tehran — the middle of no place?

SIMON: *(Again with personal connotation)* So Stalin could bug every room, of course. Isn't that the best basis for a friendship? To know what others are saying—and doing—behind your back?

EVE: *(Disregarding his intimation, as Stalin:)* Velcome, Comrades! Pleasure to have you as my guests! *(Raising a glass)* To friendship among the three great powers!

BILLY *(As FDR, with special meaning for her)*: To friendship!

SIMON *(As WSC, with a dark look at both of them)*: To friendship.

EVE: From vay Red Army defeat German siege of Stalingrad you know ve Russians more than borscht and blinis!

BILLY: An excellent job, Commissar!

EVE: *(Intimately)* Call me Joe.

SIMON: On a first name basis already, are you?

EVE: *(Another toast) Nazdarovia!*

BILLY: *Nazdarovia!*

SIMON: *(Without enthusiasm) Nazdarovia.*

EVE: Ve not vant much revard—just a bit of Poland, Yugoslavia, the Balkans—

SIMON: See here, Comrade, all of us are full of admiration for your Russian valor, but if you think Roosevelt and I are going to let you grab off most of eastern Europe—

BILLY: *(Interrupting)* If that's your price, Joe, I guess we have to agree.

SIMON: The hell we do, Franklin! We can't let this hungry Bolshevik—

EVE: *(Another toast) Nazdarovia!*

BILLY: *Nazdarovia!*

SIMON: No *Nazdarovia*. I don't agree! *(To* BILLY:) You can't allow Russia to expand its influence over all of eastern Europe and leave Great Britain nothing!

BILLY: You Brits never get tired of gobbling up bits of the world, even if it's nowhere near your little island, do you!

SIMON: We don't have a vast continent to sustain us, like you have.

BILLY: Which doesn't mean you have to have a piece of every continent on the map!

EVE: Vait, Franklin! *(Intimately, to* BILLY:) Let's let him have bit of influence over Greece—

BILLY: Okay. Greece. *Nazdarovia!*

EVE: *Nazdarovia!*

(The two clink glasses. All are quite drunk. SIMON hates their closeness.)

SIMON: *(Sourly)* Nazdarovia. *(To BILLY, aside:)* Franklin, I want to talk with you alone—

BILLY: Sorry, Winston. Anything you want to say to me you must say in front of Joe here.

EVE: You not Big Two any more; ve now Big Three!

SIMON: *(With suspicious thoughts about the two)* Big Three...

EVE: Ven ve take Berlin, ve divide city. You two take Vest—ve take East.

SIMON: Now wait a minute—

BILLY: You don't have much say in the matter, Winston. Your forces aren't the major deciders.

EVE: Franklin's and my forces biggest ones in field now.

SIMON: Damn it, Eve—!

EVE: *Stalin—*

SIMON: Bolshevik!

EVE: Ven Franklin and I agree, it's two to one. You're outvoted, Comrade.

SIMON: Goddam it—! You're practically in FDR's lap!

EVE: That's how it is! British influence at this point is fading. America and Russia are the two great powers.

SIMON: We Brits are still in the fight—

EVE: You may fight, little bulldog. But ze Russian bear can crush you vithin its paws if ve vish!

SIMON: You're making a mockery of this whole thing!

EVE: Isn't it a joke?

SIMON: No. It's deadly serious! What these three men decided between them set the course for the future of the human race—! *(He starts to light his cigar.)*

EVE: Stop it! You know you're not allowed—

SIMON: *(Extinguishing the flame)* I am so bloody tired of hearing what I'm not allowed! I'm not allowed to drink, or swear, or smoke. All I'm allowed is fantasy games and the threat of my head being invaded by a screwdriver!

EVE: *(Reaching for the matches)* Give me those—!

SIMON: Oh, no, Joe! You Russkis and you Yanks may think you have all the power, but I still have something left in my arsenal! *(To EVE, with personal significance:)* Form whatever alliances you wish—jump into bed with Uncle Sammy if you want to. When the time comes, you'll see. We bulldogs still have some bark and some bite to us! *(He strides out in the direction of his room.)*

BILLY: I'm sorry.

EVE: Don't—

BILLY: Do you think he knows—?

EVE: It doesn't matter, does it? It doesn't matter if he knows or if it never happened and he *thinks* he knows. What's real and what's unreal are all mixed up in him... As for what happened, I'm not sure I can even get that straight myself.

BILLY: I can get it straight. I know—

EVE: Don't, Billy. It was a moment... A special moment... but we mustn't...

BILLY: If you knew what I feel—

EVE: I know what you feel. It's not that I don't feel—something. But things are so crazy now. Things are so utterly crazy...

BILLY: I understand.

EVE: I don't see my way clear. Sometimes I think I'm even more lost than Simon.

BILLY: Is he really as lost as he seems?

EVE: For reasons I can't fathom, more than either of us can ever know.

(Blackout)

(Drums. Lights change.)

(Night. Both men are asleep in their separate rooms on opposite sides of the common room. BILLY is sleeping peacefully. SIMON is turning fitfully, having bad dreams. As if hearing what's going on in his imagination, we hear the sound of planes, then of exploding bombs.)

SIMON: *(Still asleep. The sound of a bomber's engine)* Hold course steady... Steady!... No moon tonight. Is that the target? Too dark. Can't pick it out—... Are we over it now?... Oh, what the hell. Bomber command says they don't care what we hit as long as we hit *something*... Bomb bay one! Fire! *(The whistle of a bomb falling and exploding)*... Bomb bay two! Bombs away! *(Again the sound of the descending bomb)*... Look at those flames! Look at that smoke! It's the fires of hell for you Fascist pigs! Burn, you monsters!... Searchlight in my eyes! Can't see! *(Anti-aircraft fire)*... They're shooting at us! Let's get the hell out of there! Bank right! Bank right!... *(Explosion)* Bloody hell! We've been hit! Flames! Left engine!... Bail out!... Bail out!... Damn cord! Where is it? Pull! Chute! Open!... Open, damn you!... Open! Open! *(He wakes up. The battle sounds fade. He tries to shake himself out of the nightmare. He is sweating and trembling.)* The same damn nightmare... Falling... Falling... *(Trembling, he picks up the cigar and chomps on* it. *He gets up, leaves his room and goes into the common room. It seems stifling. He opens the window. He paces. He holds his head. His head hurts worse than ever before.)* God, dear God!... *(Unsteadily, he fumbles in his pajama pocket and finds matches. Trembling, he lights his cigar and inhales deeply.)* So the cure for all this is a chisel through the eye socket. And after it, I won't feel anything, I won't remember anything. The pain will be gone and the nightmares will be gone — and I, my me, will be gone. I'll be there in body, but my mind won't know who I am. *(Shakes his own hand.)* Nice to have known you, old chap. Hero, were you? Did you once know how to fly? Did you get medals, Handsome Flight Commander? Who were you and who are you? *(His eyes light on the forsythia.)* And how does your garden grow? *(He pulls the flowers out of their vase and starts tearing the blossoms from the branches.)* Infidelity, thy name is woman. Simon, dear lost Simon, sleep the sleep of the betrayed. Of those to whom much is given, much is to be expected. What is expected? Nothing less than total victory. *(Smoking his cigar and raising his fingers in the V for Victory sign, he does his best Churchill imitation:)* "Victory at all costs. Victory in spite of all terror. Victory however long and hard the road may be, for without victory there is no survival." *(He becomes himself again. He laughs.)* Chubby leader in your underground bunker, what were your commands? Your commandments? Did you lose sleep over the humanity that you destroyed? But you destroyed nothing. *We* did it all. We did it all in your name, Winston England. We did it all — and there is so much blood on our hands no water, no vodka, no screw into the brain can ever wash us clean!... There is no release! None! From pain or from memory! Damn you, Winston! *(Suddenly the sight of the Churchill cigar disgusts him. He throws it out the window.)* By the waters of Babylon, they wept — because, in destroying, they were destroyed. *(Flames start to rise outside the window.)* Ah! Flames! Beautiful flames! Gorgeous flames! Death by immolation! My final solution.

(Happily, SIMON waits for death among the flames. In bed in his room, BILLY wakens. He smells the smoke. He is terrified. He tries to get himself into his wheelchair. He falls onto the floor. He cries out:)

BILLY: Help! Fire! Help! Help! Fire!

(SIMON hears but doesn't respond.)

SIMON: *(To himself, not loud enough for BILLY to hear:)* Burn with me, friend. The best solution for both of us.

BILLY: Help! For God's sake, help me! *(BILLY, struggling to drag himself forward on his belly, makes it to the space where SIMON is standing.)* Simon—! Simon,—help me!

(For a moment SIMON looks at BILLY and doesn't move. Then he begins to laugh hysterically at the irony of the situation. He knows what he must do.)

SIMON: Damn it! Damn, damn, damn, damn, DAMN!

(He picks BILLY *up, hoists him over his shoulder in a fireman's lift and starts to exit as the flames rise outside the window. The siren of fire engines is heard approaching, their noise becomes overwhelming.)*

(Drumbeat)

(Blackout)

END ACT ONE

ACT TWO

(At rise:)

(SIMON *is pacing the common room in a wildly elevated mood, very hyper.* EVE *and the* DOCTOR *confront him:*)

DOCTOR: What were you trying to do, incinerate us all?

SIMON: What makes you think the fire was my fault?

DOCTOR: A half-smoked Cuban cigar was found in the ruins.

SIMON: Churchill did it!

DOCTOR: Thank heaven the only thing that was destroyed was the laundry shed! You could have burned the entire hospital to the ground!

SIMON: A deliverance devoutly to be wished!

EVE: Simon, be serious!

SIMON: As I understand it, I scored a direct hit on a bundle of cleaning rags. In the war, that would have gotten me a medal!

DOCTOR: Three hundred patients in the other wing had to be evacuated! Your carelessness could have had tragic consequences!

SIMON: All that went up in flames was a bag of rags and a few sheets and pillow cases. Don't worry. I'll pay for them. *(To* EVE:*)* That should warm your cockles.

EVE: Forget my cockles.

DOCTOR: Why did you do it?

SIMON: It was an accident!

DOCTOR: Where did you get the matches?

SIMON: *(With a triumphant smile)* From the bottom of my kit. When I checked in, your minions overlooked them.

DOCTOR: But what suddenly drove you to light up?

SIMON: I don't want to wake up one morning to find I've become a turnip!

DOCTOR: It's my responsibility to let you know your options. If you feel you can live with all that's troubling you—

EVE: The operation can't be done without your consent, Simon. Besides, some relative has to sign off on it—and if that's how you feel, I won't.

SIMON: Swear?

EVE: Swear.

(A moment of understanding between them.)

DOCTOR: But you have to promise to behave. As you are, you're a danger to yourself and everyone around you. I'm not sure it's safe for us to keep you here any more.

SIMON: Give me the boot! I would love to be given the boot!

EVE: To live with Maude and Jocko and the hellions—?

SIMON: *(The horror of that hits SIMON.)* Ah—what a life we lead—when nothing's on offer but lousy options—!

(He begins to pace again. At that moment, BILLY enters. Wheeling himself to SIMON, he says, with immense affection:)

BILLY: You saved my life! Thank you!

SIMON: *(Churlishly)* Don't mention it.

BILLY: Without you, I might have been toast!

SIMON: I said—forget it.

BILLY: But what if you hadn't been there? What if no one had been there?

SIMON: But I was and you're fine so stop talking about it.

BILLY: I only mean—I'm eternally grateful. If there's ever anything I can do—

SIMON: There is: Shut up about it!

BILLY: *(Hurt)* Sorry. Didn't mean to get your dander up. I was only trying to—

(A severe look from SIMON silences him. BILLY, now dejected, wheels himself upstage and sits, head bowed, looking depressed. The DOCTOR goes up to BILLY and tries to soothe him. Downstage, EVE says to SIMON:)

EVE: You really are a bastard!

SIMON: I can't stand maudlin bullshit.

EVE: "Bullshit!" Billy feels he owes his life to you.

SIMON: I don't know what he's grateful for. The poor sod would be better off put out of his misery.

EVE: Now I know why there are times when I can't stand you.

SIMON: You used to say what attracted you to me was my unsentimental way of seeing things.

EVE: Why can't you, every now and then, be human?

SIMON: You think I'm not human because I don't feel like playing buddy-buddy to your lover?

EVE: Billy is not my "lover" and you know it.

SIMON: And what was all that the other evening? A simple tuck-in, lullaby, and "Nighty-night, Billy Boy?"

EVE: What makes you think that he and I—?

SIMON: He never closes his door. That night his door was closed solid. And the next morning I could still smell your scent—

EVE: That's your imagination.

SIMON: Maybe you're tired of me. Maybe the idea of an international romance has lost its thrill. Maybe *he's* your soulmate, this baby American. Two Yanks in a pod.

EVE: Okay! It's true! It happened... But it was just for that once. And it wasn't love—it was an act of compassion.

SIMON: "Compassion!"

EVE: A feeling of which you are incapable... What happened to the man I married? Where's the guy I used to love?

SIMON: ...He died in the war.

EVE: *(With great warmth)* Simon—

SIMON: *(Vulnerably)* You'll leave me for him. You will. I wouldn't blame you—

(The warm moment between them is interrupted by the DOCTOR *who is saying to* BILLY:*)*

DOCTOR: Why didn't I think of this before? I think it's a great idea! I'll put it to Simon!

SIMON: What will you put to me?

DOCTOR: I was saying to Billy—you two should share your Roosevelt/Churchill exchanges with the civilian patients.

SIMON: Are you mad?

DOCTOR: Those two got us through the war. I'm sure everybody'd be interested in seeing your portrayals.

SIMON: Forget it. This is a private thing between Billy and me.

BILLY: I wouldn't mind sharing it with others.

SIMON: I *would* mind.

EVE: For heaven's sake, Simon! It's the least you can do to make amends for what you put those patients through—

SIMON: I don't have to make amends for anything! As far as I'm concerned, this tuppeny establishment with its inedible food and its incompetent quacks, can take itself and—

EVE: *(Cracking at last, she screams:)* Oh, God! Oh, God! I have half a mind to walk out of your life and never come back! I am so bloody tired of staying calm and pretending to "understand" while you rant and rave and behave like an asshole! If only every now and then you could stop wallowing in self-pity and think about other people! If you could cease being so goddam contrary to everyone around you while all of us are tearing ourselves to shreds trying to do everything for your aid and comfort! If you would pull yourself together and stop being this contrary, irascible, insufferable, obnoxious son of a bitch who expects everyone to—!

SIMON: *(To stop her screaming)* All right! All right! *(He turns to the DOCTOR:)* You win, Herr Doktor. Your dog and pony show is on!

(Blackout)

(Drums. Lights change.)

(When the lights come up, the common room has been set up for the performance. A British and an American flag flank the space. The unseen audience of patients sits on the other side of the common room—where the theatre audience sits. The DOCTOR is saying to the audience:)

DOCTOR: As some of you may know—we're fortunate to have two war heroes right here under our roof. Since one's an Englishman and the other an American, they've been passing the time by reviewing the war in the identities of our two great wartime leaders. They've agreed to let us listen in on their exchanges. *(He sets the scene:)* It's December 1943. After meeting with Stalin in Tehran, the President and the Prime Minister have gotten together in Cairo to discuss their plans for the most decisive battle of the war—the cross-channel invasion of Europe by the combined allied forces. Please welcome President Franklin Roosevelt of the United States and Prime Minister Winston Churchill of Great Britain!

(SIMON enters wearing a Churchillian wartime jacket. From the other side, EVE wheels in BILLY who is wearing a Rooseveltian cape. Applause. EVE moves to one side. The DOCTOR retreats to the other, observing.)

SIMON *(As WSC)*: I'm glad we have a chance to meet on our own, Franklin—without the Bolshevik... What'll you have to drink? Your usual?

BILLY *(As FDR)*: You think you can mix it correctly?

SIMON: If I've learned nothing else from this war, I've learned how to make your triple-dry martini. *(He pantomimes making it, very precisely—lots of gin, the tiniest drop of vermouth.)*

BILLY: You should try it. It's far superior to that bilgewater you drink.

SIMON: Scotch. Incomparable, indispensable Scotch. *(He pantomimes pouring a glass and taking a draught with deep appreciation.)* Are you aware there are some who think the fate of the free world is being decided by a couple of drunkards?

BILLY: I don't know about you, Former Naval Person, but where this war is concerned, I have never been more sober in my life.

SIMON: *(Aside to the audience:)* He's gotten greyer since I last saw him. Thinner. And he can hardly hold the glass without trembling—

BILLY: Operation Overlord is going to be the largest sea-air-land invasion ever mounted!

SIMON: Someday, when it's time—

BILLY: Not "someday"! We have to set a date certain! *(To the audience:)* He still doesn't want to commit to the big push when it's from his back yard.

SIMON: We have to make sure the time is right—

BILLY: No more waiting! We have to set a specific schedule and stick to it! I can't get men and materiel over to England at a snap of the fingers! It takes time to manufacture equipment. Time to gather a fleet. Time to transport the men.

SIMON: I see your point but—

BILLY: It should be five months from now. June of '44.

SIMON: I don't know—

BILLY: Screw your courage to the sticking point, Winston.

SIMON: *(A bitter personal aside)* When it comes to screwing, you managed to get your courage up, didn't you, Billy Boy?

BILLY: What—?

EVE: *(From the sidelines, uttering a warning)* Winston—!

SIMON: *(To the audience:)* Oh, excuse me. I was thinking of a skirmish from a different war. *(Returning to the performance)* Back to Cairo... You forget, Franklin. If things go wrong, you'll zip back over the Atlantic. We'll have the Narzeez in our streets, trampling over us with their jackboots.

BILLY: Things are not going to go wrong! The Führer's ability to fight is diminishing daily. We have to strike! It's now or never!

SIMON: *I'm* the strategist. How come *you're* the one coming up with the plan?

BILLY: Because I'm the one who's coming up with the financing.

SIMON: Can't stop rubbing it in, can you! How little cash we Brits have, how we once ruled the waves and now we're your poor cousins—

BILLY: We have to get this war over with! Do the cross-Channel invasion! We can't keep putting it off and putting it off—

SIMON: ...All right! All right. June 1944. Agreed. But if things go wrong—

BILLY: They won't. We'll gather the largest combined air and sea force ever assembled, set forth from Dover and attack the German forces at Calais—

SIMON: No, no! That's exactly what the Huns will be expecting. That we cross the Channel at its narrowest point. We should launch from Portsmouth and Southampton and attack along the beaches of Normandy.

BILLY: But that's the widest part of the Channel!

SIMON: Exactly. We'll take 'em by surprise—

BILLY: Well, you're the warrior. I'm a mere politician.

SIMON: *(Aside to the audience:)* Note the "mere." He looks so innocent. Actually, he's wily as a fox. Do you know what this innocent American can be capable of when you're not looking?

EVE: *(Once again, warning)* Mr. Prime Minister—

SIMON: Sorry. *(Returning to the game)* Back to Operation Overlord! First—we soften up the enemy with bombing attacks over Germany.

BILLY: I'll give the order for our B-17s to start daylight raids on tactical targets—bridges, railroads, factories.

SIMON: And I'll give the order for our Lancasters to start carpet bombing major German cities by night.

BILLY: We'll bring Germany to its knees before you can say "Heil Hitler!"

(A VOICE—*on tape*—*calls out from the audience:*)

FIRST VOICE: I have a question—

DOCTOR: Ah. We have a question from the audience.

SIMON: I didn't agree to answer questions—

FIRST VOICE: Flight Commander, while in the RAF did you fly any missions over Germany?

(SIMON *is silent. The* DOCTOR *prompts:*)

DOCTOR: Flight Commander. Did you hear the question? Did you fly any missions over Germany?

(SIMON *doesn't answer. The* DOCTOR *prompts:*)

DOCTOR: Simon—?

SIMON: *(After a long pause)* ...Yes. I did. I flew missions over Cologne, Hamburg, Dresden—

FIRST VOICE: *(Suddenly, accusatory)* How can you justify the indiscriminate destruction of those cities, the deaths of tens of thousands of innocent civilians—

SIMON: I beg your pardon—?

(EVE steps forward and says to the audience:)

EVE: Please excuse us for a moment—

(She takes the DOCTOR aside and says, in their own light, so none of the others can hear:)

EVE: You're going to allow questions?

DOCTOR: Yes, Eve.

EVE: No matter where they lead?

DOCTOR: Yes. It's time to break a few eggs. They have things in their minds I've got to get them to release—

EVE: This publicly?

DOCTOR: They're servicemen, Eve. They went through hell. And look what happened to them! Forcing them to talk about what they went through might begin to help—

EVE: You said you're not a psychiatrist—

DOCTOR: No. But if the government won't pay for that kind of doctor, I have to do what I can. I want them to get better! I'm not going to fail with my last two veteran patients!... Are you with me?

EVE: *(After a pause)* Yes. Yes. I can see you have to try—

(She returns to her place. The DOCTOR returns to his.)

DOCTOR: *(To the audience:)* Will you repeat the question?

FIRST VOICE: Flight Commander! How can you justify taking part in the indiscriminate destruction of those cities, the deaths of tens of thousands of innocent civilians—?

SIMON: *(To the audience:)* Who asked that question? What are you? A Nazi?... We were giving the Krauts back a bit of their own! Do you have any idea what it was like for us Brits in wartime? London burning nightly in the Blitz! The wail of air raid sirens! Women, children, old folks crowded in the stinking underground listening to Vera Lynn singing *There'll Be Bluebirds Over The White Cliffs Of Dover!* When they emerged, they found the city in ruins! Broken glass everywhere! 40,000 bodies in the charred remains! We were defending you from that! Yes, you! You here on the other side of the wide Atlantic. Did you want us to lose the war and have the Luftwaffe flying over here and bombing the good old US of A? Once they'd laid waste Washington and New York you couldn't wave a white flag and get them to not lay waste your other cities. They wouldn't stop till every inch of America was destroyed! So don't you start throwing your post-war morality at me about the sins of "collateral damage"! The reason you can sit here so safely is because we didn't. You didn't withstand the brunt of their savagery, we did. So we don't have to be judged by you—or by anybody!

(SIMON *strides off into his room.* EVE *crosses after him. The* DOCTOR *says to the audience:*)

DOCTOR: Stay where you are, please. I apologize. Our veterans went through a lot. We have to be patient with them. I hope to convince Flight Commander Trevelyan to return to the performance. If you'll just sit tight for a moment—

(*The* DOCTOR *goes into* SIMON's *room.* BILLY, *not knowing what to do, wheels himself after him.*)

(*Drums. Lights change.*)

(*The lights come up on* SIMON's *room where, in the presence of the* DOCTOR *and* BILLY, EVE *is accusing* SIMON:)

EVE: How could you behave that way? Insult all those people?

SIMON: I'm tired of the holier-than-thou peace-lovers who have no idea what had to be done so they could be at peace.

EVE: You're supposed to be portraying great men!

SIMON: That question was not to Churchill, it was to me! The bomber, not the Prime Minister. And I answered it as the bomber.

DOCTOR: It was a fair question.

SIMON: I don't think so.

DOCTOR: It's what we all want to know.

SIMON: Then ask someone else. Not me. I'm not going back out there.

EVE: You have to.

SIMON: Give me one reason.

DOCTOR: The audience is waiting.

SIMON: Let them fuck themselves!

EVE: You can't treat people that way!

SIMON: Think of how they're treating me!

DOCTOR: They're treating you as if you were a great world leader.

EVE: Someone who's big enough to take criticism.

SIMON: Churchill and Roosevelt had to. I don't have to. Cancel the performance.

BILLY: *(Speaking for the first time)* No! Don't! *(He turns to* SIMON:*)* Stay here if you like. I'm going back out there.

SIMON: Without me?

BILLY: Sure! Let the public see the rest of the war run single-handedly by Franklin Delano Roosevelt!

SIMON: So you've finally developed claws, Billy Boy. I suspected all along you were more than the country bumpkin you pretend to be.

EVE: Simon—!

BILLY: It's fine with me if they think that Winston Churchill sat out the rest of the war sulking in his bunker!

SIMON: Oh, you clever little weasel! I do believe that, with all this pretending, a little FDR has gotten into your blood!

BILLY: *(Turning to wheel himself toward the common room)* See ya—

SIMON: What do you mean, "See ya"?! You think I'm going to let the eagle trump the bulldog?

(SIMON *strides past* BILLY, *goes out of his room and into the common room. Giving a wink and a "V for Victory" sign to* EVE *and the* DOCTOR, BILLY *wheels himself into the common room after him.* EVE *and the* DOCTOR *take their places there as before.*)

(Lights change.)

SIMON: *(Striding center stage and addressing the audience as Churchill:)* It's June 1944. England has been invaded! Tens of thousands of Yanks have arrived on our shores! In the run-up to the invasion, they've launched an invasion! They fill our streets. They swarm all over our hotels and our pubs. They're armed with candy, gum, chocolates, oranges, nylon stockings! Ah, what our English beauties won't do for a pair of nylon stockings! It's a war of seduction! When it comes to seduction by stuff, you Americans win all the way!

BILLY *(As FDR)*: If the New World can't help the Old, what are we for?

SIMON *(As WSC)*: "The Old." Once the sun never set on the British Empire.

BILLY *(As FDR)*: "The old order changeth." It was one of your writers who wrote that.

SIMON: Yes, but when he wrote it, he saw us coming into power. He didn't see it ebbing away. This war is draining our lives and our resources. Once it's over, England will never be the same. We can win the war, but I feel we are entering the twilight of the Empire—

SECOND VOICE FROM THE AUDIENCE: So why did you fight it? Did you really have to defeat Hitler? Couldn't some accommodation have been made?

SIMON: "Accommodation!" With a monster? He was a madman! He wanted to rule the world! He wanted not only to rid the world of Jews, he wanted to exterminate all blacks, browns, yellows and anyone not of what he called the "Aryan" race! He broke every peace treaty he ever signed seconds after he signed it! *(He begins to harangue the audience.)* You're as delusional as he was if you believe that there was any way out for all of us in his path except his death and Germany's total and complete defeat! If you think that appeasement of this monster could in any way have stopped the megalomaniac's appetite for power—

EVE: Calm down, Mr. Prime Minister!

SIMON: What?

EVE: Do calm down, sir.

SIMON: Oh. Yes. *(He takes his seat.)*

THIRD VOICE FROM THE AUDIENCE: You both knew about the concentration camps. Why didn't you bomb them out of existence?

BILLY: And do the Nazi's extermination work for them?

THIRD VOICE : You could have bombed the rail lines bringing people to the camps.

BILLY: They'd just have built new rail lines—or moved the camps elsewhere.

THIRD VOICE : So you were sensitive to the plight of the Jews, Mr. President.

BILLY: I was deeply concerned.

THIRD VOICE : Then why did you refuse entry to a shipload of Jewish refugees who had fled Europe?

BILLY: We had no way of accommodating the hundreds who were seeking asylum on our shores!

SIMON: *(To FDR:)* "Give me your tired, your poor—." Is it only your Statue of Liberty who believes that?

BILLY: How many refugees did *you* take?

SIMON: We are a tight little island! We had problems enough trying to feed our own people! You never faced the deprivations we did! You should have flung open your gates—

BILLY: Accuse all you like! You know as well as I, the only salvation for all who were being oppressed was total victory!

SIMON: Annihilation of the killers.

BILLY: Yes.

SIMON: "Good killing"—as opposed to "Bad killing".

BILLY: Exactly.

FOURTH VOICE FROM THE AUDIENCE: So, Mr. Roosevelt, you approved of dropping the bomb on Hiroshima and Nagasaki?

BILLY: What?

FOURTH VOICE: You approved of dropping the atom bombs on Japan! The bombs which killed and maimed millions!

BILLY *(As himself)*: Roosevelt was dead by then, he had nothing to do with that decision!

SIMON *(As himself, to* BILLY*)*: He gave his blessing to the bomb's development.

BILLY: So did Churchill! FDR never expected that anyone would actually use it!

SIMON: Don't be naive. If you don't expect to use a weapon, what's the use of having it?

BILLY: As a deterrent!

SIMON: There is no such thing as using a weapon of death as a deterrent! The only time it deters anything is if it's used! And FDR would have used it just as his successor did!

BILLY: You don't know that!

SIMON: *You* know it!

BILLY: I am not a killer—!

DOCTOR: Gentlemen! Gentlemen! We've gotten off the track! You are supposed to be *playing* Roosevelt and Churchill, not squabbling about them.

(BILLY *and* SIMON *grow silent.*)

DOCTOR: You were about to tell us about that most glorious day of the war—D-day!

BILLY: ...I was there.

SIMON: Roosevelt was not there!

BILLY: I, Billy Maitland,—I was there.

SIMON: As you've just been reminded, you are not you, you're the President.

DOCTOR: Tell us about it, Billy.

BILLY: I don't like to talk about it—

EVE: *(Warmly)* Tell us...

SIMON: *(To his wife:)* Your hero...

EVE: Tell us...

(It is the personal look she gives BILLY *which encourages him to begin, at first hesitantly, then becoming involved in the telling, which he is doing, mostly, for her.)*

BILLY: I went over in the first wave. We left Portsmouth under cover of darkness. I'd never seen so many ships in the water in my life. We approached the shore of France. Hundreds. Thousands of us. Near the shore, they stuffed us into landing craft. Maybe fifty to a boat. It got us as close to the shore as it could, then the front dropped down and we waded out—waist deep in water, holding our rifles above our heads. *(He stops.)*

EVE: Go on.

BILLY: They were shooting at us from bunkers on the cliffs above the beach.

SIMON: You had air cover.

BILLY: Our own planes were shooting at us! *(To* SIMON:*)* You were supposed to be shooting at the Jerries—but you were hitting our guys in the water!

SIMON: I wasn't there! When D-day came, I was a prisoner—!

BILLY: Some planes, planes on our side, were shooting at us. And the big guns from the German emplacements were shooting at us. We were getting it from both sides. On the beach, my friends were dropping like flies. I walked forward through the wet sand. There were bodies all around me—in pieces. An arm here. A leg there. A head—! ...And where the bodies were whole, they were bleeding, and the boys, kids my age, were crying, "Mama! Mama!". I couldn't help them! ...My orders were to follow the sergeant who was heading my platoon. We were to scale the cliff and somehow put one of the big Bosch guns out of commission.

EVE: You scaled a cliff—?

BILLY: We tried. Our grappling hook broke. But, like a miracle, we found a path. And we started up. But it was a trap! I didn't know it at the time, but one by one the Krauts were picking us off as each of us got near the top. I was working my way up, clinging to the rock. I heard "Pop, pop, pop!" Then a loud bang. And silence. When I peeked over the top, I saw there was no one in front of me! No one who'd gone up before me had survived. All that was left was me and a couple of guys behind me—they were all privates. I—a corporal—was now the senior officer! Their leader! We started crawling forward in tall grass, me in front. We reached a grove of trees. Just as we did, a German soldier jumped out of the bushes about ten feet in front of us. I'd never seen a Hun before—except in pictures. He was as tall as I was. Blond. With bright blue eyes. He stood there for a second, then he raised his gun and aimed it at me. Point blank range. I could see he was trembling. I raised my rifle, like they told us to do in target practice. I pulled the trigger. The boy looked at me with surprise—and a bit of a smile. A trickle of blood began to run from his mouth—and he fell. I'd killed him. The guys behind me were saying, "Thanks, pal." "Good ol' Billy." Stuff like that. But I'd looked him in the eyes, this boy my age, and I'd killed him! ...At that second, one of the big guns from one of our ships off shore lobbed a perfect shot and the bunker right near us exploded. It flew apart in a million pieces. One piece of concrete smashed into my spine. I fell to the ground. When I came to, I was in a triage area on the grass and they were calling me a hero.

DOCTOR: And you were.

EVE: You were.

BILLY: You don't understand! He was a boy my age. We looked into each other's eyes—and I killed him! He looked like someone who could be my friend, and I took his life! And now—if ever I fall asleep, he walks into my room and asks me why did I do that? He keeps asking and asking! And I can't answer!

DOCTOR: You were following orders.

BILLY: That's what the Nazis said when they were tried at Nuremberg. They were "following orders". Why was I following orders? This German boy—

EVE: —could have killed you.

BILLY: I wish he had! But *I* killed *him*! And now he comes to see me every night! *(Vehemently, to the audience:)* I'm not a killer! I am not a killer!

(BILLY *breaks down. He bends forward in his chair, moaning. The* DOCTOR *steps forward and says:*)

DOCTOR: All right, that's enough. *(To the audience:)* Please go back to your rooms. The show is over.

(The lights change. They are still in the common room. It has now once more become their private space. BILLY, *still highly emotional, says:*)

BILLY: I'm sorry. I didn't mean to fall apart that way, in public.

EVE: It's all right, Billy.

BILLY: I've been good. I haven't talked about that day. I've kept it to myself. I'm sorry—

DOCTOR: But now that it's out, don't you see? You will be cured! I don't mean your spine—

BILLY: It's always going to be like this, isn't it.

DOCTOR: *(A long pause, then, compassionately)* ...Yes, Billy.

BILLY: I think I've always known that.

DOCTOR: But now that you've talked about what happened to you, you're cured of your bad dreams. Your ghosts. The things that kept you from sleeping. You've exorcised them. You killed, yes,—but it was war and that boy you shot was the enemy. So you're not guilty—

SIMON: *(Suddenly lashing out, to the* DOCTOR:*)* What do you know about killing? Have you ever killed? Not by a mistake in the operating room. But deliberately! Have you ever set out, night after night, to kill as many living beings as you can? *(To* BILLY:*)* Oh, Billy, Billy—. You spilled the blood of a boy? That's nothing! I spilled the blood of hundreds! Thousands! You saw a trickle of blood! I spilled rivers of it. *(A moment, then:)* Our vaunted leaders said—we must destroy the enemy's cities. Destroy not just their bridges and factories—but where the barbarians lived. That was our assignment: To inflict a savagery on the enemy that even those savages couldn't imagine. And so we set out to smash their cities—and all the people in them—nightly from the skies. That was our assignment—to kill as many as we could, so they would lose their will to fight.

BILLY: You were up in a plane. You didn't see them close. You didn't see their eyes.

SIMON: When they were alive—no. I didn't see them. When they were dead, I saw them then. I was sent to bomb the hell out of the beautiful city of Dresden. I'd visited it once, when I was a kid, with my parents. Even during the war there were no munitions factories, no military installations,—just elegant avenues, elegant buildings, once elegant people. Still, I was assigned to bomb it—so I did. But my Lancaster got hit. I bailed out over the burning town. I was captured, put in prison. And then—

EVE: Then what, Simon—?

SIMON: *(With great reluctance. This is the part he's never said before.)* They set us prisoners to cleaning up the mess we'd made. I got to see, first hand, what my bombs had done to brick and mortar—to the elegant city—and to its people. I had to shovel pieces of charred bodies into wheel-barrows. I had to bury corpses, corpses I had made. And for this I was praised! For this they gave me medals!

(EVE *hides her face in her hands, too moved to speak.)*

DOCTOR: Because of you—of men like you two—the war got to be over!

SIMON: But it's not over. Don't you see that it's not over? It is not possible to live and hate oneself as Billy and I hate ourselves.

BILLY: You understand. You and I understand.

SIMON: ...But did *they*?

BILLY: They?

SIMON: Franklin and Winston... Did they understand what they were sending us into? Did they stay awake at night imagining what we had to do—and did they weep?

EVE: I'm sure they did.

SIMON: I'm not so sure. I think Churchill loved war! While he was waging it, while we were waging it for him, I think he found it the most thrilling time of his life. The destiny he'd been put on earth for.

BILLY: Roosevelt hated war.

SIMON: So he said. But, once in, knowing he was the exalted leader of what had suddenly become the most powerful nation on earth, with the power to command all those forces—he must have looked down from his Presidential perch and revelled in it!

BILLY: You think they didn't think about us? About what we were going through?

SIMON: I think if they thought about us at all, it was like thinking of a swarm of fleas. If the fleas survived or were crushed, it didn't matter. They had bigger things to do than think of the lives and deaths of fleas.

BILLY: But I know FDR felt for us. He sent me a personal letter—thanking me for my service. I have it in my room. It has his signature on it.

SIMON: Are you sure it's his signature?

BILLY: What do you mean?

SIMON: You think the great Commander-in-Chief had time to sign a letter to a flea like you? It was a secretary's hand—or a machine—

BILLY: No, no—! It was from him! From him personally!

SIMON: You gullible little twit! He never thought of you—

BILLY: Stop saying that!

SIMON: Wake up and see the truth!

BILLY: I said shut up!

SIMON: Don't be a goose—

BILLY: Shut up! Shut up or I'll kill you!

(*Overcome with rage,* BILLY *pushes himself up from his wheelchair, trying to attack* SIMON. *But his useless legs crumble and he falls to the floor.* EVE *and the* DOCTOR *rush toward him.* BILLY *cries out:*)

BILLY: Don't touch me!

(*They move away.* SIMON, *suddenly moved by* BILLY's *prostrate form, rushes over to him:*)

SIMON: I'm sorry, old chap! I'm sorry! Forgive me. It just slipped out. You know the kind of thing I say. Of course that was his hand! He wrote you personally—! Why wouldn't he? Look at all you did! Look at what happened to you—!

(He tries to help BILLY up. BILLY cries out:)

BILLY: Go away! ...Go away! *(Then, overcome with guilt and remorse:)*... Didn't you hear? ...I said "I'll kill you". I'm a killer!

SIMON: No, no, kid—

BILLY: I killed for him. He never thought of me. And—for him—I became a killer!

SIMON: *(Full of pity)* You're not, Billy. Neither am I. We got caught in a savage universe. There was no way out except by becoming savages.

BILLY: I don't want to be that!

SIMON: Nor do I... It was the times. Just the times. You can't blame yourself. Whatever you did, the times made you... Let me help you to your room.

(Helpless, BILLY agrees to let SIMON lift him up. As SIMON starts to carry him to his room, EVE says:)

EVE: I'll come in to see you. We won't talk about the past. We'll talk about the future.

BILLY: Is there a future?

(The DOCTOR follows SIMON and BILLY to BILLY's room, saying:)

DOCTOR: I'll give him a couple of pills to help him sleep—

(BILLY's room, adjacent to the common room, becomes visible. SIMON deposits BILLY on his bed. In BILLY's room, the DOCTOR helps BILLY get settled. SIMON returns to EVE in the common room.)

EVE: Poor kid.

SIMON: There's no cure for what he's feeling.

EVE: No cure, perhaps. But, now that he's gotten what was bothering him out in the open, perhaps there's a way of moving on.

SIMON: I hope he can.

(The DOCTOR gives BILLY a couple of pills and a glass of water, waits until he swallows them, then returns to the common room.)

DOCTOR: I'm sorry he got so upset. But I'm sure, once he's slept it off, he'll find talking things out will have made him feel better... I'll look in on him later.

(He exits up left leaving SIMON and EVE alone.)

SIMON: All this talking things out is highly over-rated.

EVE: If it didn't help you, it helped me. Until today I never really realized all you'd been through.

SIMON: I wanted to spare you—

EVE: But don't you know—sharing everything with you, the bad as well as the good, is what I'm here for. Now—and always.

SIMON: Really? Always—?

EVE: *(With a grin)* Guess I'm a glutton for punishment.

SIMON: *(Only slightly Churchillian)* Even if all I have to offer is blood, toil, tears and sweat?

EVE: Even then.

(He looks at her then pulls her to him. They kiss. Then they exit, hand in hand, toward SIMON's room... The lights dim on the common room and come up on BILLY's room. BILLY takes his FDR letter from his nightstand and, overcome with sadness and betrayal, tears it to pieces. Then he reaches under his mattress and takes out a cache of pills. He begins swallowing them by the handful.)

(Slow fade to blackout.)

(Somber, measured drumbeat.)

(Lights change.)

(The lights come up on the common room. In BILLY's room the bed is made and empty. In the common room EVE, wearing her coat, is saying to the DOCTOR:)

EVE: Billy was so sweet! So sweet! What did he have to go and do that for?

DOCTOR: I'm afraid he was on the road to it ever since D-day.

EVE: Simon feels responsible—

DOCTOR: None of us could have saved him. God knows we tried.

EVE: I'm so afraid that Simon, too—

DOCTOR: You mustn't think that! Simon's made of stronger stuff. The mental scars won't go away—but I think, with your support, he'll be able to bear them.

EVE: I hope so.

DOCTOR: You're sure you're both ready for him to be discharged?

EVE: Positive... With Billy dead, Simon doesn't want to stay. One lone patient in this wing? No, Doctor.

DOCTOR: I understand.

EVE: His headaches come less often. And when they do, he says they're bearable.

DOCTOR: What are your plans?

EVE: I've lined up a couple of jobs for us, teaching at a flight school in Colorado.

DOCTOR: Good idea.

(SIMON *enters, wearing a coat and carrying a duffel bag. He looks off toward what was* BILLY's *room.*)

SIMON: Where have you sent him?

DOCTOR: Arlington National Cemetery.

SIMON: ...He deserves that honor.

EVE: Definitely...

SIMON: The only way he could live was with illusions.

EVE: All he wanted was to slip inside the skin of someone great.

DOCTOR: *(To* SIMON:*)* There's something I'm sure he'd want you to have—

(*The* DOCTOR *hands* SIMON BILLY's *cigarette holder.* SIMON *takes it and turns it over in his hand, treasuring it. Then he says:*)

SIMON: "In this man there died the greatest American friend we've ever known."... That's what Churchill said when Roosevelt died.

DOCTOR: Billy'd have liked your saying that in tribute to him.

SIMON: I'll miss him.

DOCTOR: So will I.

EVE: *(To the* DOCTOR *as they begin to take their leave:)* Thank you for everything.

DOCTOR: I wish you both the best—... If ever you need—

SIMON: We won't.

DOCTOR: Excellent.

(They shake hands.)

EVE: With Billy and Simon gone, you'll be able to give this wing over to your civilian patients.

DOCTOR: Yes. Back to normal. After all, now that there's the bomb, the thought of any future war is inconceivable. There won't be need for a place to treat injuries like Simon's and Billy's ever again.

EVE: Thank heaven.

(Drumbeat)

(Blackout)

END OF PLAY

BUFFALOES

CHARACTERS & SETTING

Vicky Fairgrieve
Thelma
Dorothy Fairgrieve
Victoria
Don Jerry

Time & Place: The Present. The living room of a house in a small town.

Setting: The entire action of the play takes place in the living room of a rambling old ark of a house in a small town—a small town which might be anywhere.

The room is high-ceilinged and spacious. Upstage left of center a short flight of steps leads to a landing with a waist-high banister. At the left of the landing a door leads to the mother's bedroom. At the right of the landing is an opening which leads to a second bedroom. On the rear wall of the landing hangs an elaborately framed portrait of a Pilgrim burgher, fat and formidable.

Stage right is the front entrance, half-glazed with frosted glass and crowned with a fanlight. Downstage right is the opening to a small corridor which leads to a subsidiary bedroom. At stage left a pair of tall clear glass terrace doors lead to an off-stage garden whose greenery is slightly visible. Down left is the door to the kitchen.

The immediate effect of the room is one of decorative incongruity. Juxtaposed against a background of worn, nondescript wallpaper and drapes are elements of museum quality. There is a sumptuous Oriental carpet on the floor and an ormolu clock in the bookcase. A Louis XV chair and chaise longue claim center stage. There is a grand piano up right of center and, close beside it, a four foot high mound of something hidden under a cloth. On a side table is a small statuette of a buffalo. On another small table is a telephone.

The room was once extremely ordinary, with worn old objects selected with little or no taste whatsoever. Now, high quality objects of many different provenances and periods sitting beside worn out stuff that could only grace a yard sale proclaim a room in transition. Money is being spent here, and with a taste that is—to say the least—quirky and quixotic.

ACT ONE

Scene One

(At rise:)

(The room is empty. A WOMAN *arrives outside the front door. We can see her through the frosted glass. She rings the bell. There is no answer. She rings it again, more urgently. Again, no response. She searches in her handbag, comes up with a key, turns it in the lock and enters, carrying a small suitcase and an attaché case. She comes into the living room calling:)*

VICKY: Mother!...Mother! *(No answer.* VICKY FAIRGRIEVE, *a woman in her early thirties, dark-haired, energetic, business-like, takes in the period chaise longue and chair and the ancestor portrait with astonishment:)* My God—! *(She opens the door to the kitchen and once more calls:)* Mother! *(Beginning to panic, she runs up the stairs and throws open the door to her mother's bedroom:)* Ma!

(But her mother isn't there. Now wildly upset, VICKY *turns, looking lost, just as* THELMA, *sixtyish,* VICKY's *mother's housekeeper and companion, enters from the kitchen.)*

VICKY: Thelma, what's happened? Where is she? She's always here! I've been calling for days! Always getting that damned tape announcing: "If you want to say something nice, press one. If you want to say something rotten, press two"—and at the end of ten choices, all you get is a goddam dial tone!...When I couldn't get through, I hopped on the shuttle and came as fast as I—. Where is she? Is she in the hospital?

THELMA: No, Vicky—

VICKY: Is she ill—?

THELMA: Not exactly—

VICKY: Oh, God, I knew it! I kept telling her she had to be careful! Tell me the worst, Thelma. Is she—dead?

*(*VICKY's MOTHER, *65, looking hale and hearty and wearing a very original knock-em-dead outfit in fuchsia and pink, enters from the garden. Over her arm is a large basket filled with just-cut zinnias.)*

VICKY: Mother—!

(Vicky's MOTHER says, in an off-hand manner:)

MOTHER: Hello, Vicky. What a surprise to see you. *(She goes over to the answering machine and shuts it off.)*

VICKY: I thought you kicked the bucket!

MOTHER: Sorry to disappoint.

VICKY: That's not what I—

MOTHER: *(Shoving the zinnias at her)* Arrange these for me, will you?

(VICKY takes the flowers and dumps them unceremoniously into a vase.)

VICKY: You haven't answered your phone for days!

MOTHER: So?

VICKY: I left nice messages. I left rotten messages. I left every kind of message there is!

MOTHER: Oh, was that you?

VICKY: You don't recognize the voice of your only child?

MOTHER: *(To THELMA:)* I guess this means defrosting another lamb chop.

THELMA: Wish I'd labelled all those little packages in the freezer...*(She ambles off to the kitchen.)*

VICKY: You know I can't stand lamb.

MOTHER: *I'll* eat it.

VICKY: I can't believe you'd be too busy to return my calls.

MOTHER: You've taken days to get back to me.

VICKY: Once. Once I took two days to get back to you. I was involved round-the-clock with negotiations on a very important case—

MOTHER: And that other time—

VICKY: When Jerry and I were in Barbados—

MOTHER: Without telling your mother.

VICKY: Mother, it may come as a shock to you, but my husband and I do have unlimited overnight permissions!

MOTHER: My dear, you can do anything you like. ...And so can I.

VICKY: Not when you make me sick with worry—

MOTHER: *(Pleased)* Did you worry?

VICKY: And make me leave town in the middle of the week.

MOTHER: Oh, you left the office in the middle of the week.

VICKY: Actually, I—*(She breaks off and, looking at her surroundings, says:)* What the hell has happened to this room? Where's the old sofa? And the Barcalounger? Where's the "original oil painting" of "Sunset on Moonlight Lake"?...All the stuff that's been here since I was a kid, the stuff I couldn't bear the sight of?

MOTHER: Gone with the wind.

VICKY: Everything? Gone? In the three months since I—

MOTHER: It's not my fault you don't come by for dinner every Sunday.

VICKY: Mother, I live in the city now.

MOTHER: I realize this town isn't good enough for you.

VICKY: Here we go again!

MOTHER: *(Changing the subject)* How do you like my ormolu clock?

VICKY: Where's your Bavarian cuckoo?

MOTHER: And my Louis the Fifteenth chaise longue?

VICKY: Not that I adored it, but don't you think the old Castro convertible fit in more with your taste?

MOTHER: My taste has changed.

VICKY: So I see.

MOTHER: *(Indicating a 17th century portrait hanging by the stairs)* How do you like the portrait of your great, great, great, great grandfather?

VICKY: The hell he is.

MOTHER: Well, I may have left off a great or two. He came over on the Mayflower.

VICKY: That's fascinating. Considering that all the time I was growing up you kept telling me our people came over steerage on a considerably more recent cattle boat.

MOTHER: *(Indicating the piano)* How do you like this?

VICKY: Good God! A Steinway!

MOTHER: I bought it for you.

VICKY: What happened to that beat-up upright?

MOTHER: It's been years since you played. Would you like to try it out?

VICKY: No, thank you.

MOTHER: I have all your old music—

VICKY: No. *(Looking around)* This stuff must have cost you a fortune.

MOTHER: I have one.

VICKY: Excuse me?

MOTHER: A fortune. Vicky, I'm rich! Filthy, disgustingly, incredibly rich!

VICKY: What did you do, rob a bank?

MOTHER: Not exactly.

VICKY: Did you win the lottery?

MOTHER: No.

VICKY: Did somebody die and leave you a bundle?

MOTHER: That's it.

VICKY: I didn't know we knew anybody with that much cabbage. Who was it?

MOTHER: A relative of your dear departed father.

VICKY: What relative?

MOTHER: Some bachelor cousin of a second cousin or something. I'm not quite sure.

VICKY: I didn't know my dear departed father had a bachelor cousin.

MOTHER: Neither did I. But one day his representative appeared at my door—and *voilà*!

VICKY: "*Voilà*"?!

MOTHER: I'm taking French. And that's not all. I'm also studying art and music, literature and tennis, Cantonese cooking, Monopoly, yoga, the dance—*(She gives a sample of a Hindu dance, lotus position hands, swiveling neck.)*

VICKY: Excuse me, but who was this cousin and how did he make his pile?

MOTHER: Don't know. Don't care. Why ask questions? Aside from departing early from this vale of tears, this is the only favor your father ever did me.

VICKY: Is there really that much stash?

MOTHER: Vicky, my child, it's a bottomless pit! Suddenly, at my age, after a lifetime of scrimping and saving and trying to make a go of the broken-down beauty products business your father left me, I can have anything I want.

VICKY: *(Gesturing around the room)* And this is what you want?

MOTHER: This is only the tip of the iceberg. I've bought other things. Far more wonderful things—. Like this—

(VICTORIA *enters from the garden. A young woman of* VICKY's *age, she is tall and blonde and attractive.)*

MOTHER: Vicky,—meet Victoria.

VICTORIA: How do you do?

VICKY: "Victoria"?

VICTORIA: I've brought your shawl, Mother.

VICKY: "Mother"?!

VICTORIA: I don't want you to catch cold. *(She drapes it around* MOTHER's *shoulders.)*

VICKY: Who is this?

MOTHER: My Perfect Daughter.

VICKY: The one you always hoped I'd be?

MOTHER: Isn't she grand?

*(*VICTORIA *goes to the vase and starts to arrange the zinnias in artistic fashion.)*

VICKY: But she's skinny—

MOTHER: I always wanted a daughter who was skinny.

VICKY: She's blonde—

MOTHER: I always wanted a daughter who was blonde.

(In a thrice, VICTORIA *has created a splendid floral arrangement.)*

VICKY: She can do ikebana—

MOTHER: I always wanted a daughter who could do ikebana.

VICTORIA: Mother, dear, is there anything I can get you? A cucumber sandwich? A cup of Earl Grey?

VICKY: I may throw up.

VICTORIA: *(To* VICKY:*)* Would you care for some tea?

VICKY: This is *my* mother's house. If I want tea, I can go out and boil water!

*(*MOTHER *extends herself on the chaise.)*

MOTHER: You should hear how she reads to me. I always wanted a daughter who would read me poetry.

VICTORIA: What would you like today, Mother? Longfellow or Keats?

MOTHER: Longfellow today, I think, Victoria, darling.

VICKY: I thought your taste ran more to Barbara Cartland.

VICTORIA: *(Returning with the book and plumping up* MOTHER's *pillows)* Comfy?

MOTHER: Victoria and I are reading the Great Books together. I want to enter heaven in an educated condition.

VICKY: Still the confirmed valetudinarian.

MOTHER: You never know when suddenly I might—. In whatever time I have left, I want to learn all the things that all my life were beyond me. I want to nourish my soul with all the inspiration great literature provides.

(She lies back. VICTORIA *begins to read:)*

VICTORIA: "By the shores of Gitche-gumee,
By the shining big sea water,
Stood the wigwam of Nokomis,
Daughter of the moon Nokomis."

VICKY: If you're doing the Great Books, I wouldn't start with *The Song of Hiawatha.*

MOTHER: Just because you went to college and I didn't—

VICKY: Why do you have to say that every time I come here?

MOTHER: It isn't that I minded selling cold cream and hair color so you could feed the cockles of your brain—

VICKY: A brain doesn't have cockles.

MOTHER: I worked my butt off. Sacrificed everything so you could have a better life than I had—

VICKY: Thank you, Mother. If I haven't said it before, and I believe I have, thank you, thank you very much.

MOTHER: My perfect daughter would never be sarcastic.

VICTORIA: Do you feel a chill? Would you like me to close the terrace doors?

MOTHER: No, dear, just go on reading.

VICTORIA: "Dark behind it rose the forest
Rose the black and gloomy pine trees
Rose the firs with cones upon them
Bright before it beat the water"

(Left out of this inspirational duo, VICKY *says:)*

VICKY: I think I'll put my suitcase in my room. *(She starts up the stairs.)*

MOTHER: Victoria has that room.

VICKY: *I'm* Victoria.

MOTHER: You're Vicky. I named you Victoria, but your friends named you after a cough drop.

VICKY: Where will *I* sleep?

MOTHER: The guest room's vacant.

VICKY: A guest. In my mother's house. I can't believe this!

*(*THELMA, *who has been listening at the kitchen door, now enters and picks up* VICKY's

suitcase.)

THELMA: *(Aside, to* VICKY:*)* Believe it. And it's only the beginning...

(THELMA *exits down right toward the guest room with the suitcase and attaché case.* VICKY *says to* VICTORIA:*)*

VICKY: Excuse me, but is that offer for you to make us Earl Grey still on the table?

VICTORIA: I'd be delighted—*(*VICTORIA *exits to the kitchen.)*

VICKY: *(Sicky sweet)* She'd be delighted—*(*VICKY *turns to her mother.)* Mother, who is she?

MOTHER: I told you. She's my daughter, if my daughter were attentive, solicitous, here. I can have anything I want and that's the thing I want most—a loving daughter.

VICKY: Even if you have to pay for it?

MOTHER: If I can't seem to get it for free.

VICKY: I have a life—a life I'm trying to live to the best of my ability—

MOTHER: How is my son-in-law, the typhoon?

VICKY: I won't listen to your bad-mouthing Jerry.

MOTHER: "Vicky and Jerry". Sounds like a pair of cartoon mice.

VICKY You can't accept that I'm grown, that I married, that I have a career—

MOTHER: How are things at the office? How's your boss and your secretary? How's your phone and your FAX and your frequent flyer? How are your briefs and your torts and your habeas corpuses? How's your water cooler, your industrial strength coffee, your genuine pigskin attaché?

VICKY: What's the matter with you? Have you gone out of your mind?

MOTHER: Oh, no. I've just gone into it! This amazing new sum in my bank account is like manna from heaven.

*(*VICTORIA *enters with tea on a tray.)*

MOTHER: It's brought me a Perfect Daughter! A distinguished Ancestor! Literature! A chaise longue! Music! Art! Drums! *(She whisks the cloth off a shapeless pile near the stairs to reveal a shiny new set of drums.)*

VICTORIA: Mother, dear, calm down! You mustn't get excited or you'll get those palpitations—!

MOTHER: *(Sitting at the drums, she says to* VICKY:*)* You know what I always told you? About money not being everything? That was bullshit! It *is* everything! It's life! It's breath! It's not only being able to have all you've ever wanted to have, but being able to say everything you've ever wanted to say! Like bullshit.

Bullshit, bullshit, bullshit, bullshit, bullshit! I can tell the truth and no one dares contradict me! Isn't that true, Victoria?

VICTORIA: Absolutely, Mother.

MOTHER: I can, for however much time I have left, afford absolutely anything and anyone.

(A key turns in the lock of the outside door. A MAN enters, carrying a large bag of groceries. In his mid-thirties, the MAN is dressed in Western garb—jeans, denim shirt, vest and boots. Handsome and lean, he has deep eyes and a quiet self-contained manner. He strides into the room saying:)

MAN: I got everything on your list, Dorothy—*(Seeing VICKY, he breaks off.)* Oh, hello.

VICKY: Hi.

MAN: *(To MOTHER:)* This her?

MOTHER: Yes, this is her.

MAN: *(To VICKY:)* Don't go anywhere. I'll just drop this stuff then come back to see if the real thing is anything like your mother's description. *(He exits to the kitchen.)*

VICKY: Who the hell is that?

MOTHER: My lover. *(She plays a resounding salvo on the drums.)*

(Blackout)

Scene Two

(Later that afternoon)

(VICKY comes into the living room from the guest room, looks around to see if she's alone, then goes to the phone and dials a long distance number.)

VICKY: Is Jerry there?...Vicky Fairgrieve...Does he know me? I hope so. I'm his wife. ...No, I will not tell you what this is in reference to!...Don't put me on hold—! She is put on hold. She hates it. She waits impatiently.)

(THELMA enters from the kitchen with a vacuum cleaner.)

VICKY: Where is she now?

THELMA: Out in the garden. Doing yoga exercises with Prince Charming.

VICKY: Thelma, who *is* he?

(THELMA shrugs.)

THELMA: He came with the boodle and stayed.

VICKY: You don't have any idea who he is?

THELMA: Honey, if you were brought a check by a messenger like that, wouldn't you keep the messenger?

VICKY: Depends on what else he's peddling.

(THELMA turns on the vacuum. Over it, VICKY shouts:)

VICKY: Jerry?...Jerry—!

(VICKY gestures to THELMA to turn off the vacuum cleaner and give her a moment in private. As THELMA starts out, VICKY covers the mouthpiece of the phone and says to her:)

VICKY: Keep your eyes open.

THELMA: Honey, I've got my eyes open—and my door open, too. Not that it does me much good. *(She exits to the kitchen with the vacuum cleaner.)*

VICKY: Jerry—who was that?...I didn't know you had a new secretary. What happened to the old one?...So she got varicose veins. That doesn't mean she can't still type. ...Listen, things are crazy here. Mother has a stand-in for me living in my bedroom and a gigolo living over the garage. ...I didn't think so either, but it seems she *is* still interested in that sort of thing. ...Her health? No idea. It doesn't seem to be getting in the way of her drum lessons. ...Drum lessons. *(She kicks the bass drum and gives him a sample over the telephone.)* Being here is like being on Mr. Toad's wild ride. ...Mr. Toad. ...From *Wind in the Willows*. ...It's a book! He's a toad! He—oh, never mind. ...And, Jerry, she's come into a fortune. ...I don't know. Some distant relative of my father amassed a bundle, died without issue and it came to her. ...I don't know how much. Asking anybody how much money they have is more personal than asking how often they have sex.

(MOTHER *comes through from the garden wearing exercise clothes. As she passes* VICKY, *she says:*)

MOTHER: Leave the bum. *(She starts up the stairs intoning: "Ohm, Ohm, Ohm..." At the top of the stairs, she turns and says:)* Hurry and get off the phone. I need your advice. I'm adopting a buffalo.

(VICKY *reacts.* MOTHER *exits into her bedroom, leaving the door slightly ajar for eavesdropping.)*

VICKY: *(Into the phone)* You heard her. She said she's adopting a buffalo. ...No, I haven't told her my news yet. No, I am not going to ask her for a loan. ...You would have small change if you weren't so addicted to plastic! Who ever heard of an indigent venture capitalist!...Yes, I know you can't get ahead without taking risks, I only wish you didn't have to take them with other people's money then have to cover with our own. ...I'm sure you'd cover with mine if I had any. ...I like doing pro-bono work! It's what I took up law to go into!...I don't give a damn if it's the one piece of the law that doesn't make money! If you care so much about the green stuff you could—...Look, forget it. We'll talk about this when I get home.

(The mother's door closes. VICKY *hunches more confidentially into the phone:)*

VICKY: I don't know yet. Another day or two, maybe. I have to figure out what's going on here. ...I'll get back as soon as possible. You know how it drives me out of my mind to be here. ...Well, of course I'll call first, don't I always?

(Her mother's LOVER *strides in from the garden with his jacket looped over his shoulder. He is carrying a photograph album.)*

VICKY: Talk to you later. ...No, Jerry, I won't ask her! That subject is closed!

(She hangs up the phone. The LOVER *throws his jacket over the Louis XV chair, opens the album and says:)*

LOVER: Well, now, which of these handsome creatures do you think your mother should adopt?

(VICKY *casts a glance at the photos and is speechless.*)

LOVER: Thunder Cloud... Chief Falling Water... Wild Thing—

VICKY: I'm not really into buffaloes.

LOVER: You ought to be. They're an endangered species.

VICKY: Aren't we all.

LOVER: Your mother's support can feed a buffalo for a year.

VICKY: And how long does she plan to go on feeding *you*?

LOVER: That depends.

VICKY: Thelma says you're part of the inheritance.

LOVER: It wasn't planned. I came with the news. Your mother asked me to stay.

VICKY: What exactly do you do here?

LOVER: Whatever she wants. Teach her drums, tennis, Shakespeare, the tango. Advise her on her investments.

VICKY: Aha—

LOVER: That's a kind of loaded "aha".

VICKY: Is this what you do for a living? Don't you have a profession?

LOVER: I guess you could say I'm a student. A student of human nature.

VICKY: And where do you do your studying?

LOVER: Wherever I am.

VICKY: Are you studying us?

LOVER: I might be.

VICKY: In that case, I'd better be careful.

LOVER: Or not.

(A beat)

VICKY: ...Look, who exactly was this mysterious benefactor?

LOVER: A man I worked with for quite some time.

VICKY: How did he make his bundle?

LOVER: Not from robbing banks, if that's what you mean.

VICKY: Did I say—?

LOVER: I'm trying to set your mind to rest.

VICKY: I hope you'll forgive me, but finding my mother shacking up with a lover half her age has quite the opposite effect.

LOVER: Sorry I disturb you.

VICKY: I didn't say you disturb me—

LOVER: I do, though, and I'm sorry. *(He holds out his hand.)* Why don't we—

VICKY: Please! Please don't say why don't we be friends!

LOVER: I was going to say: Why don't we start over on the right foot.

VICKY: Maybe the right foot would be if you put one foot before the other and got out of here. Or if I did.

(As MOTHER *and* VICTORIA *come out of their separate rooms and descend the steps, arm-in-arm, the* LOVER *says:)*

LOVER: No. Don't go. Stay and defend your territory.

*(*VICKY *looks at him. Could he be on her side?)*

MOTHER: I'm so glad you and Don are getting acquainted.

VICKY: Don. I suppose that stands for Donald.

MOTHER: Actually, it stands for Don Juan.

(She takes VICKY *aside.)*

MOTHER: Aren't I lucky? Isn't he wonderful?

VICKY: I'm reserving judgment. Excuse me for asking, but do you and he actually—? You know.

MOTHER: Do he and I "you know"?

VICKY: You know.

MOTHER: What do you think?

VICKY: Don't know.

MOTHER: Would you, if you were me?

*(*VICKY *doesn't respond.)*

DON: *(Opening the book of buffalo photos)* Well, Dorothy, ready to choose?

MOTHER: Oh, the handsome beasts! Victoria, don't you think they're handsome?

VICTORIA: They are handsome.

MOTHER: Vicky! Which should I adopt as my very own?

*(*VICKY *has been surreptitiously looking for identifying marks inside Don's jacket. Guiltily, she thrusts it aside.)*

VICKY: Are you sure you need a living breathing buffalo? Where's that souvenir one that was always around? *(*VICKY *picks up a carved wooden buffalo from a table.)* Oh, here he is. Isn't he enough?

MOTHER: I want the real thing.

VICKY: How does this "charity" work?

MOTHER: Don knows all about it. He suggested it. You send your check to Injun O'Brien in Wyoming and he makes sure your very own personal buffalo is fed and warm.

VICKY: "Injun O'Brien"?

DON: Indians take names that have personal meaning for them. O'Brien was an Irish trader who befriended the tribe.

VICKY: *(With Irish accent)* Saints preserve us!

MOTHER: It gives me goosebumps to think that I can help save something that is slowly going out of existence, that somewhere out on the Great Plains, there'll be a buffalo who calls me Mom.

VICKY: How do you know these buffaloes exist, "Mom"?

MOTHER: I have their pictures.

VICKY: How do you know Injun O'Brien exists?

MOTHER: I have Don's word. They met.

DON: We did. Honest Injun.

VICKY: How do you know, once you send all this money, that—

VICTORIA: *(Interrupting)* Oh, Mother, please, please, let's adopt a buffalo. I want one. To make up for that time when I was little and I wanted a dog. Remember? You said yes, but Daddy said no.

MOTHER: I remember.

VICKY: I don't.

VICTORIA: One day you brought a puppy home as a surprise. He was wrapped in your big black coat. You said, "Here, Victoria, hold my coat". You put the coat in my arms and out popped this adorable cocker spaniel—

MOTHER: "Cocky".

VICTORIA: Yes. Cocky.

VICKY: *(Under her breath)* Cock and bull, you mean.

VICTORIA: We kept him in the basement, but he cried and cried.

MOTHER: So we took him upstairs and he peed and peed.

VICTORIA: And Daddy ranted and raved—

MOTHER: So we had to give him away...

VICTORIA: I still think of him.

MOTHER: : So do I. It's why, ever since that time—

VICKY: That never happened!

MOTHER: It did, dear.

VICTORIA: I remember it.

MOTHER: I do, too. *(To* VICKY:*)* Funny that you don't, Vicky.

VICTORIA: It's not too late for us to have an animal, is it, Mother?

VICKY: As long as when he pees, he does it on the Great Plains.

MOTHER: *(Perusing the photos)* Which do you like?

VICTORIA: This one. The one with the streak of grey in his mane.

MOTHER: Yes. I like him best, too: Moon Dancer.

VICTORIA: Moon Dancer...

DON: Moon Dancer it is.

(He hands MOTHER *her check book.)*

VICKY: *(As* MOTHER *makes out the check)* As long as you're playing Santa Claus, why stop at Dancer? Why not adopt the whole herd? Prancer and Donner and Blitzen and Spritzen—

MOTHER: *(Thrusting the check into* DON's *hands:)* Ici, mon amour!

*(*VICKY *gets a glimpse of the amount and whistles.)*

VICKY: That's not chicken feed!

MOTHER: Of course not, darling, you can't feed buffaloes on chicken feed. *(She gazes at the photo.)* His picture is going to look so wonderful in my autobiography!

VICKY: You're writing your autobiography?

MOTHER: You think I didn't have a life, don't you? All children think their parents didn't have a life. But you'll see. I'm putting my life on tape. When I'm gone, you can listen to it.

VICKY: I can hardly wait. ...Mother, listen, I'd really like to talk to you—

(She starts to sit on the chaise beside her MOTHER, *but* VICTORIA *slips in before her.* VICKY *goes to sit in the chair, but* DON *sits in that, studying the check.)*

VICKY: It's like musical chairs here! Do you realize this room only seats three people?

MOTHER: There are always the stairs.

VICKY: *(Refusing to sit there)* Tell you what. For dinner, why don't I order in a pizza?

MOTHER: Victoria is making a soufflé.

VICKY: She's making a soufflé. Of course she's making a soufflé.

VICTORIA: *(To* VICKY:*)* Would you like to help?

VICKY: If I made a soufflé, it would come out looking like a pizza.

(VICTORIA *exits to the kitchen.* VICKY *tries to talk to her* MOTHER *alone.*)

VICKY: Mother, seriously, I really think you and I should—

MOTHER: Not now, dear, it's time for my drum lesson.

(DON *goes over to the drums and starts to get things ready.*)

DON: Let's see, where were we? I'd introduced you to the bass and we were just making the acquaintance of the snare.

MOTHER: Oh, yes, the snare...

(VICKY *says, aside, to her* MOTHER:)

VICKY: Listen, Mother, do you realize this Casanova of yours is wearing clothes without any labels?

MOTHER: You want him duded up in outfits from Ralph Lauren?

VICKY: He's deliberately keeping us from knowing who he is!

MOTHER: Look at him. What more do you need to know?

DON: Ready, Dorothy?

MOTHER: Ready and willing.

(MOTHER *sits at the drums. The lesson begins* MOTHER *enjoys* DON's *arms around her as he demonstrates a few beats.* MOTHER *tries it.* DON *shows his approval.*)

DON: Good! Good! We'll have you whacking these things to beat the band in no time.

(*Again, he demonstrates with his arms around* MOTHER.)

VICKY: If you'll excuse me—(VICKY *starts to go to her room.*)

MOTHER: Wait! I forgot my chewing gum! Can't drum without my gum! (*She exits to the kitchen.*)

VICKY: You really know about drums? Is there anything you don't know about?

DON: Mighty little.

VICKY: You're moving ahead pretty presto here, aren't you!

DON: Not at all. Andante moderato is more my style.

VICKY: I'm sorry but I find my mother's pursuit of all this—the drums, the decor, the yoga, the buffalo—ridiculous.

DON: Humor her, Vicky. ...She probably doesn't have much longer to live.
(MOTHER *returns chewing gum, sits at the drums and plays an energetic upbeat riff.*)
MOTHER: Listen, Vicky! I'm a regular Ringo Starr!
(*She continues to beat out a fast bold hard rock rhythm.* VICKY *looks on wordlessly.*)
(*Blackout*)

Scene Three

(One week later)

(VICKY is at the telephone dialing a number. She gets a taped response.)

VICKY: Damn it! The machine! *(She waits impatiently for the tone, then:)* Jerry, where are you? This is the sixth time in six days that I've called home to listen to my own voice on the tape. I know I promised to be back in a day or two, but I just can't leave here. My mother may be in the grip of a couple of fortune-hunters. The one she calls Victoria keeps doing everything I'm supposed to do but doing it right, for Chrissake. And this musical Marlboro Man is so gentlemanly to my mother that he can't possibly be real. *(Looking around to make sure she can't be overheard, she hunches into the phone and says in a low voice:)* Anyway, when you come home and find your mother making out ten thousand dollar checks to feed a buffalo, you can't just abandon the premises. Also, she keeps doing her "Goodbye, forever" number. You know, the one she's been doing ever since her sister dropped dead of heart failure in Filene's basement. So I can't figure out if this is it or not. I called her doctor but he's at a "medical conference"—in Tahiti. I talked to the man who's covering for him, he doesn't know who the hell mother is. So I can't just—

(MOTHER appears at the top of the stairs wearing a snappy white tennis outfit and carrying a tennis racquet.)

MOTHER: Tennis, anyone?

VICKY: *(Into the phone)* Dammit, Jerry, will you get back to me?

MOTHER: *(Starting downstairs)* Divorce the bastard.

(VICKY hangs up the phone.)

VICKY: Mother, what is this costume!

MOTHER: It's for tennis. Haven't you seen it on TV? How do you like my outfit? Victoria made it.

VICKY: She sews. Of course she sews. ...You don't intend to play—?

MOTHER: I signed you up for the tournament, too.

VICKY: Sorry. Didn't bring my whites.

(VICTORIA *appears on the landing looking smashing in her tennis whites.*)

MOTHER: Don't worry, Victoria will lend you something. Won't you, Victoria.

VICTORIA: Gladly, Mother. (*She exits to her room.*)

VICKY: Maybe she could lend me a pair of those legs. ...Mother—

MOTHER: (*Showing some documents*) Look! I've just gotten Moon Dancer's adoption papers. Imagine,—now I have a son.

VICKY: You always wanted a boy, didn't you.

MOTHER: Doesn't everybody?

VICKY: When you didn't hit the jackpot with me, how come you didn't try for more?

MOTHER: How come you didn't try for any?

VICKY: That's my business.

MOTHER: Though I must say bringing into the world a copy of that bum you married would be like cloning the hairy ape.

VICKY: There's no reason to talk that way about Jerry.

MOTHER: He's been out for six nights in a row, hasn't he? He took the opportunity of your absence to exchange varicose veins for a redhead.

VICKY: How do you know she's a redhead?

MOTHER: I called his office and a redhead answered.

VICKY: You called his office—!

MOTHER: The redhead answered. I hung up.

VICKY: I do not like you trying to run my life!

MOTHER: Honey, I'm not trying to run your life, I'm trying to save you from drowning!

VICKY: When I'm drowning, I'll tell you.

MOTHER: (*Sitting down*) All right. Tell me.

VICKY: (*In exasperation*) Mother—!

MOTHER: You know, the thing I most regret is that we never had that little talk—about the things every mother wants to tell her daughter.

VICKY: Like what?

MOTHER: Like—always wear good underwear. You never know when you're going to be hit by a bus.

VICKY: I'll remember that.

MOTHER: Here's Bloomingdale's number. Always keep it handy in case of an emergency.

VICKY: I don't consider fine lingerie top priority—

MOTHER: *(Suggestively)* Fine lingerie can serve a multitude of purposes.

VICKY: That kind of activity, too, can do a person in.

MOTHER: But what a way to go—!

VICKY: Listen, Mother—

MOTHER: You do like my Don Juan, don't you, Vicky? You do think he's handsome and talented?

VICKY: I'll admit he's handsome. As for his talents—

MOTHER: Let me tell you how he's lighting up my sunset minutes—

VICKY: Are you sure I'm old enough to hear this?

MOTHER: What I want to ask you is—do you think he'd make a good husband?

VICKY: Are you serious?

MOTHER: Think about it. I'd really like your opinion.

(VICTORIA *enters from her room carrying a tennis outfit. She tosses it to* VICKY, *who misses the catch and has to pick up the clothes from the floor.*)

MOTHER: Butterfingers!

VICKY: Sorry.

MOTHER: Hurry and change. The game's about to begin.

(VICKY *exits to the guest room.* MOTHER *says to* VICTORIA:)

MOTHER: I'll see if Thelma's ready to play.

(*She starts toward the kitchen.* DON *enters from the garden. As she passes him,* MOTHER *feels his biceps:*)

MOTHER: Mmmm. Lucky this is ladies doubles. With those muscles you could smash a ball into the stratosphere. (*She exits to the kitchen.*)

(VICTORIA *and* DON *are alone.* DON *brings in a pole and stands it downstage center.* VICTORIA *gets the tennis net from a drawer. They start to attach the net across the room from the post at the bottom of the stairs to the post downstage center.*)

VICTORIA: When I applied for this job, I never thought it would go on so long. Did you?

DON: I never applied for any job.

VICTORIA: You mean you didn't answer her ad in Variety, like I did?

DON: No.

VICTORIA: You mean this number you do is the real McCoy?

DON: I wasn't aware I was doing any number.

VICTORIA: You haven't been hired to be nice?

DON: No.

VICTORIA: This is weird!...What game is being played here anyway?

DON: Tennis, Victoria. Tennis is being played here.

(THELMA *enters from the kitchen followed by* MOTHER.)

THELMA: No, no! A thousand times no!

MOTHER: Thelma doesn't want to play.

(VICKY *enters, self-conscious in her tennis costume.*)

VICKY: That makes two of us.

MOTHER: Then *I'll* play Victoria. (*She starts to warm up.*)

(THELMA *says, aside, to* VICKY:)

THELMA: I was saying no so she wouldn't play! We usually only let her referee.

VICKY: *(Catching her meaning)* All right, I'll play! Victoria versus Victoria! And may the best daughter win!

(*As the others take their places,* MOTHER *at the drums,* DON *on the landing and* VICTORIA *on the other side of the net,* VICKY *takes* THELMA *aside and says:*)

VICKY: Listen, Thelma, while we're all here doing this Wimbledon act, you go to Don's room and see if there's anything in there that tells us anything about him. Identification. Clues of any sort. We've got to find out who he is and what he's really doing here.

(MOTHER *cries impatiently:*)

MOTHER: Let the game begin! (*She plays a salvo on the drums.*)

(THELMA *nods to* VICKY *and goes out through the garden.*)

MOTHER: Don, darling, you toss for first serve.

(DON *holds up a coin.*)

VICKY: Heads!

VICTORIA: Tails!

(DON *tosses.*)

DON: Tails it is.

VICKY: I see my luck's holding.

MOTHER: (*A salvo on the drum*) Ready, on your mark, get set—go!

VICKY: Where's the ball?

MOTHER: Ball? With all these heirlooms? *(She stays at the drums and punctuates the action with appropriate drumbeats.)*

(VICTORIA raises her racquet and hits an imaginary ball toward VICKY, who doesn't see it coming.)

MOTHER: Strike one!

VICKY: Wait a minute, I didn't even—

MOTHER: Are you playing or are you talking?

VICKY: I'm playing, but I—

(VICTORIA hits another imaginary ball. At the last second, VICKY swings.)

MOTHER: Foul ball!

VICKY: What do you mean "Foul ball"! That's for baseball!

MOTHER: I refuse to referee any game where "love" means "nothing". ...Play ball!

(VICTORIA serves. VICKY misses again.)

VICKY: Hey! Pitch it over the plate, will you?

(VICTORIA serves again. VICKY swings. VICKY and VICTORIA swat the imaginary ball back and forth. As they do so, the dialogue continues:)

MOTHER: Whoever wins will get her choice of whatever she wants from this room. Vicky, what would you like?

VICKY: Nothing.

MOTHER: The clock, the chaise, the portrait?

VICKY: Nothing.

MOTHER: The piano.

VICKY: I said nothing, I mean nothing.

MOTHER: Strike two!

VICKY: I can't play if you keep on talking.

MOTHER: If you don't take things now, when I'm gone, you'll get it all.

VICKY: I don't want it all. If you want to get rid of the things, why don't you sell them?

MOTHER: All my things! All my wonderful things!

VICKY: Auction them off. Let the highest bidder take all. *(She smashes at the "ball".)*

MOTHER: Strike three!...Victoria wins!

VICKY: I hit that damn ball! It was a home run!

MOTHER: It hit the umpire! *(She rubs her elbow.)* You're out of the game for the season!

(She raises VICTORIA's *arm.)*

MOTHER: The winner!

VICKY: *(Pouting, reduced to babyhood)* The game was fixed. It didn't matter what I did, I was going to lose!

MOTHER: All right. I'll give you a chance to even the score. I'll ask three questions. The one who answers them correctly will win the game. Ready?

VICKY & VICTORIA: Ready.

MOTHER: What time will you be home?

VICKY: Whenever I feel like coming home.

VICTORIA: Whenever you want me home, Mother darling.

MOTHER: Advantage Victoria. ...Question number two: Who are you going out with?

VICKY: Whoever I like.

VICTORIA: Whoever you want.

MOTHER: Advantage Victoria again!...Question number three: Why won't you stop going out with that damn Jerry?

VICKY: I will go out with that damn Jerry if I want to!

VICTORIA: If you don't want me to see him, I won't see him any more.

VICKY: I will not only see him, I will marry him if I want!

VICTORIA: I swear never to see him again.

MOTHER: Advantage Victoria! Victoria's victory! *(To* VICTORIA:*)* Of anything in this room, what would you like?

VICTORIA: *(Thinking first, then choosing carefully)* That locket.

(MOTHER *takes a silver locket from around her neck and puts it on* VICTORIA. VICKY *looks on with jealousy.* MOTHER *notices.)*

MOTHER: *(To* VICKY:*)* You said you didn't want anything in this room.

VICKY: I don't.

VICTORIA: Such a beautiful locket. I love it. But mostly I'll cherish it—because it belonged to you.

(She kisses MOTHER.*)*

VICTORIA: Thank you, Mother.

MOTHER: Dearest daughter. It's so wonderful to have one's precious things appreciated.

(VICKY *reacts. All this makes her nauseous.*)

VICTORIA: *(To* MOTHER:*)* Time for your nap, Mum.

VICKY: *(Aside:)* You'd think she was lady-in-waiting to the Queen of England.

MOTHER: I must record this day for my autobiography: "The Day Victoria Won the Pennant".

VICTORIA: I'll walk you to your room.

(VICTORIA *helps* MOTHER *upstairs and into her room.* DON *and* VICKY *are alone. He starts putting away the net and post.*)

VICKY: If she knew the ringer was going to win, why didn't she just name her champion without our playing? I don't know why she's doing this. Humiliating me at every turn.

DON: Perhaps it's her way of telling you she loves you.

VICKY: Has the world gone mad?

DON: It must be hard for you—coming home and finding your bed slept in, your chair sat in—

VICKY: —and that someone's been eating my porridge.

DON: No one's been eating your porridge. They're just keeping it warm for you.

VICKY: I have no idea what the hell we're talking about!

DON: I'd be happy to talk about anything you like.

VICKY: All right. Let's talk about you. Who are you?

DON: Does it really matter?

VICKY: Suppose I call the police.

DON: On what charge?

VICKY: Suppose I insist you leave.

DON: Suppose you tell me what's bothering you.

VICKY: Isn't it obvious? You and my mother are a very odd Romeo and Juliet.

DON: That's not it. I have the feeling there was something troubling you before you came here. What is it?

VICKY: That's my business.

DON: You might feel better if you talked about it.

VICKY: To a stranger?

DON: Sometimes that's the best ear you can choose. I might be able to help.

VICKY: How? By getting me to sit cross-legged and hold my breath as long as I can, like you're teaching my mother?...Sorry. Don't mean to be rude. This place really gets on my nerves. I thought I could come here, straighten out my mother's problems then get back to my own.

DON: Instead you find you're lost in a hall of mirrors.

VICKY: For God's sake, don't be "understanding"! I can't take it!

DON: All right. I won't be understanding.

VICKY:...If you and Mother hitched up, I guess I'd have to call you Daddy.

DON: Let's wait a bit—before you decide exactly what to call me.

(He takes her tennis racquet and starts to put it away. VICKY gazes at his arms.)

VICKY: Glad I wasn't playing opposite you. With those muscles you could smash a ball into the stratosphere.

DON: That's exactly what your mother said.

VICKY: Good God! If I stick around here too long I'll find myself adopting buffaloes! Before that happens, I think I'd better leave.

DON: Don't go. We're giving your mother a twenty-four-hour surprise party for her birthday, starting tomorrow.

VICKY: Tomorrow's not my mother's birthday.

DON: That's the surprise. She's always saying how she's not going to make it to the next one, so we thought we'd throw a party now, while you're here. Tomorrow night there'll be cake and candles. Next day there'll be a Chinese barbecue in the garden. Stay.

VICKY: Does my presence matter?

DON: Very much,...Victoria.

(There is a "moment" between them. ...THELMA enters from the kitchen.)

DON: If you'll excuse me, I have some last minute arrangements to make for the party. *(He exits toward the garden.)*

VICKY: So? What did you find in his room?

THELMA: I'll tell you what I found: nothing. No credit cards, no license, no social security. Just clean clothes, clean underwear, and a map.

VICKY: A map? Of what?

THELMA: Don't know. Hand drawn. Very suspicious.

VICKY: *(Gazing off in the direction in which DON exited)* Maybe it means he's someone who knows where he's going...

THELMA: You aren't falling for the guy, are you?

VICKY: Me? Like what my mother likes? No way!

(Unthinking, she has picked up a drum stick, and, for emphasis, hits the snare drum with it. Suddenly she realizes what she's doing. She throws the stick away as if it were on fire. It makes an unintentioned clang on the cymbals. THELMA looks at her.)

(Blackout)

Scene Four

(The following evening)

(The room is hung with a few decorations. MOTHER *comes out of her room wearing a dressing gown and, looking around to see that no one is observing, comes downstairs, goes to the telephone and dials a long distance number.)*

MOTHER: Hello, Jerry's tape. This is your mother-in-law again. Did you get my message yesterday? I swear to God it's true! Your wife, my daughter, is having an affair. He's handsome, he's human, he's a hunk — and if I were you I wouldn't put up a fuss, Calamity Jerry. I would abandon ship, beat a retreat, let the bird out of her not-so-gilded-cage —

*(*VICKY *appears from her room wearing a skirt and blouse.* MOTHER *swiftly hangs up.)*

VICKY: You're telling Jerry I'm having an affair?

MOTHER: Isn't it a terrific story?

VICKY: Why are you telling him I'm having an affair when I'm not?

MOTHER: Always helps to put a high value on the merchandise.

VICKY: *(Protesting too much)* I'm not having an affair. I'm not even thinking of having an affair!

MOTHER:*(Examining* VICKY's *face)* Well, if ever you *do* think of it, you should begin using wrinkle cream. In fact, you could use a complete make-over.

VICKY: So you're always saying.

MOTHER: Why don't I —?

VICKY: You already did. You made me over and you came up with the Splendid Victoria!

MOTHER: I wouldn't have to have a Splendid Victoria if I had you.

VICKY: *(Not unkindly)* We've been down this road before, Mother. It doesn't lead anywhere.

MOTHER: When Don and I are settled you can come and live with us.

VICKY: I don't think so.

MOTHER: Now that *I* have someone wonderful, I want *you* to have someone wonderful.

VICKY: I'll keep an eye peeled.

MOTHER: Is that what you're wearing tonight?

VICKY: What's the matter with it?

MOTHER: My perfect daughter would never wear a blouse and skirt to her mother's surprise party! (MOTHER *goes into her room.*).

(VICKY *is disturbed.* THELMA *enters from the kitchen carrying a green frosted cake with candles on it.*)

VICKY: Thelma! What if we give mother a taste of her own medicine? She invented a bogus daughter. What if I invent a bogus mother — you!

THELMA: Oh, I couldn't—!

VICKY: We wouldn't go too far. Just let her see what it's like—

THELMA: No, no. Your mother and I go back so long—

VICKY: Yeah., I forget that. You were friends in high school, weren't you.

THELMA: Not exactly friends. I took secretarial, she took college.

VICKY: I didn't know she took college.

THELMA: Oh, yes. She always thought she would go.

VICKY: But she never—

THELMA: No. She never. There was your Dad, I guess. And the beauty business.

VICKY: Yes. The beauty business.

THELMA: Then, when he was gone, and you were just a little kid, and I was down and out, she took me in. So however she acts, it's little enough to put up with, for what she gives me.

VICKY: But you're bound hand and foot to her.

THELMA: I don't mind.

VICKY: There's the difference between us. I do.

THELMA: Gotta get things ready for the party—

VICKY: Tell me, Thelma, do you think Mother's really serious about this fellow with no last name and no credentials?

THELMA: They've hardly been out of each other's sight since he came here.

VICKY: They do things together, go places together?

THELMA: Whatever they do, they do here, Vicky. Your mother hasn't been away from this house in months.

(DON *enters through the garden, wearing black tie and dinner jacket.*)

DON: Ready for the festivities?

VICKY: As ready as I'll ever be.

DON: You look—

(*At that moment,* VICTORIA, *spectacularly dressed in red, appears on the landing.*)

VICKY: Save your compliments for that.

VICTORIA: Shall I call Mother?

DON: Just a second.

(*He lowers the lights.* THELMA *lights the candles on the cake.*)

DON: Okay. All ready.

(VICTORIA *knocks on* MOTHER's *door.*)

VICTORIA: Mother—. Mother—?

(MOTHER *comes out of her room dressed to the teeth. All but* VICKY *shout:*)

VICTORIA, DON, THELMA: Surprise!

(MOTHER *feigns surprise.*)

MOTHER: Oooh!

(VICTORIA, DON *and* THELMA *start singing "Happy Birthday".* MOTHER *interrupts:*)

MOTHER: Wait! (*She whips out her small tape recorder and turns it on.*) Okay. Now.

(*All except* VICKY *sing:*)

VICTORIA, DON, THELMA: "Happy Birthday to you, Happy Birthday to you" (*etc.*)

(*When they finish singing,* MOTHER *stands on the landing and says into the machine:*)

MOTHER: They're giving me a splendid party for my final birthday. Everyone is here.

(*She looks at* VICKY *and* VICTORIA.) My daughter—(*She looks at* DON.) My lover—

(*She looks at* THELMA.) My friend—

(*All applaud.*)

MOTHER: (*comes downstairs and looks at the cake.*) I'm not as young as that, but, whoever chose that number, thank you for the compliment. (*She blows out the candles.*)

DON: That's the number you look to me.

MOTHER: When I'm with you, I always feel decades younger.

VICKY: Cut the cake. For God's sake, cut the cake!

THELMA: It's your favorite. Chocolate cake with zucchini icing. It's my present to you.

(MOTHER *cuts a slice and samples it.*)

MOTHER: Delicious!...Help yourselves, everybody!

(VICTORIA *cuts a slice of cake and holds it out to* VICKY.)

VICTORIA: Vicky?

VICKY: No thanks. I break out with zucchini.

DON: Moon Dancer has sent you a birthday present. His hoof print. *(He presents the hoof print.)*

(MOTHER *says into her tape recorder:*)

MOTHER: Moon Dancer has given me his hoof print.

VICTORIA: And I have a present for you.

(*She goes into the garden and reappears pulling a six-foot-high flat wooden painted replica of Moon Dancer on wheels. Built like a giant pull-toy, it has a streak of grey in its mane.*)

MOTHER: Oh, how wonderful! *(Into the tape)* Victoria has given me a likeness of Moon Dancer. Full size! *(She puts her arms around the buffalo.)* You handsome creature. You sweetheart. You love.

DON: I have a present for you. *(He hands her an envelope.)* Tickets for a trip around the world. *(Displaying brochures)* London, Paris, Vienna, Istanbul, Bombay, Hong Kong, Tokyo—and any place you want in between. You may take whomever you like.

(MOTHER *looks at* VICKY *whose face betrays such dismay at the thought of accompanying her that* MOTHER *turns to* VICTORIA. VICTORIA *looks eager but* MOTHER *turns to* DON *and says:*)

MOTHER: I want to go with you! When do we leave?

DON: As soon as you like.

MOTHER: *(Into the tape:)* Don has given me the world! *(She says to him:)* How special you are. So fine...*(She turns to* VICKY:*)* And you? What have you gotten your mother for her birthday?

VICKY: Nothing.

MOTHER: *(Into the tape:)* Vicky has brought me absolutely nothing.

VICKY: In the first place, it is not your birthday. In the second place, if you need presents from me to tell you how I feel, there's nothing to be said.

VICTORIA: *(Aside to* DON:*)* Cordelia, *King Lear,* Act One, Scene Two.

VICKY: In the third place, I certainly could not, at the last minute, come up with anything as witty, clever, or expensive as these gifts—

MOTHER: There's one present you could give me.

VICKY: Is there?

MOTHER: You could play the piano for me.

VICKY: I told you: I don't play.

MOTHER: For me. For my birthday.

VICKY: For your non-birthday, a non-present: non-piano-playing.

MOTHER: Victoria would play for me if I asked her.

VICKY: I don't doubt it.

MOTHER: *(Getting the question and* VICTORIA's *response on tape)* Victoria, would you play for me?

VICTORIA: Of course, Mother.

(VICTORIA *sits at the keyboard.*)

VICKY: She plays. Of course she plays. ...But how well does she play?

(VICKY'S *look at* VICTORIA *is a direct challenge.* VICTORIA *raises her hands and attacks the keys. The piece—masterfully played—is Chopin's "Revolutionary Etude", a work of tremendous virtuosity and power.* MOTHER *records it all. As* VICKY *listens, totally bested and shamed, she becomes more and more upset. Finally she can take no more. She slams her hand on the piano top and cries:)*

VICKY: Okay! She plays! She plays like an over-sexed Van Cliburn!

MOTHER: Makes you a little sorry, doesn't it. Makes you sorry you spent your life being a legal beagle when you could have been practicing and coming up with this. Now, instead of Chopin, all you have is your job.

VICKY: Mother, I do not have a job. I am jobless. Did it never occur to you that the only reason I could be away from work this long is that I have no work to be away from?

MOTHER: What happened?

VICKY: I didn't bring enough moola into the firm. They canned me.

MOTHER: Oh, this is wonderful! This is exactly what I want! Dear sweet darling daughter! Welcome! You can have your room back again. We will get you the best teachers. You'll move back here. I'll be as quiet as a mouse. I'll take care of everything. The only thing you'll ever have to do is practice!

(She tries to hug VICKY. VICKY *pulls away.)*

VICKY: Excuse me. I am not going to move in here and practice. I am not going to stay around at all. I am tired of playing games. Tired of pretending you've adopted a non-existent buffalo. Tired of tripping down Memory Lane with you on things that never occurred. Tired of pretending you're about to go around the world when you haven't been away from the house in months. Tired of pretending it's just ducky that you have a younger lover. Tired of pretending I don't really mind much when my place is taken by another me. I promised myself I wouldn't desert the field, that I could take it. But you know—I can't. I don't see why I even try to. Goodbye to all of you! Goodbye to everything! *(She starts toward the guest room.)*

MOTHER: But all this is going to be yours!

VICKY: Auction it off to support your buffalo! *(*VICKY *exits to her room.)*

*(*MOTHER *raises the piano top, rips out the piano roll which is the secret of* VICTORIA's *virtuosity and throws it on the floor.)*

MOTHER: *(Feverishly)* Moon Dancer! Moon Dancer! You are going to graze high on the hog!

(Wildly, she opens a Monopoly set, takes out the play money and distributes handfuls to VICTORIA, DON *and* THELMA.*)*

MOTHER: What am I bid for this ormolu clock?

VICTORIA: Ten dollars!

MOTHER: Sold to the daughter in red!...What am I bid for this chaise?

VICTORIA: Five dollars!

MOTHER: Sold! You are getting a prize!...What am I bid for my ancestor?

VICTORIA: Two dollars!

MOTHER: Sold! You can paint on a mustache.

DON: Dorothy, what are you doing—?

MOTHER: Divesting myself of it all! Setting out on the journey where no baggage is needed! When I go, wrap me in buffalo hide and bury me on the prairie. What am I bid—

*(*VICKY *enters with her suitcase and attaché case, ready to leave.)*

VICKY: Goodbye, goodbye. Parting is such sweet sorrow—

MOTHER: *(Paying no attention to* VICKY:*)* What am I bid for this piano?

VICTORIA: I bid—

MOTHER: Sold! Sold! What else do you want?

(MOTHER *escorts* VICTORIA *around the room saying: "You want this? Take it! Here, this is yours" etc.* DON *takes* VICKY *aside and says:*)

DON: Everything's going to Victoria.

VICKY: Fine. Let her have it.

DON: How can you leave?

VICKY: You're not going to tell me you'll miss me—

DON: I mean how can you go when your mother is dying?

VICKY: You don't understand. She's been dying since I was two. She threatens and threatens, but she never does it!

DON: This time—

VICKY: Has anyone talked to her doctor?

DON: I don't think so—

VICKY: Has *she* talked to her doctor—?

DON: I don't know—

VICKY: Goodbye. As they say: Had we met in another time, another place, in another family—

MOTHER: What am I bid for this attaché case?

VICKY: Give it away. It's not worth anything. ...Happy non-birthday, Mother. If you get to take that trip around the world, drop me a card.

(*She goes toward the front door—but stops suddenly. The outline of a man can be seen through the glass. The doorbell rings.*)

VICKY: Oh, shit! It's Jerry!

(VICKY *retreats into a dark corner of the living room.* MOTHER *goes to the door and opens it.* JERRY, *a sharply dressed Wall Street type, bursts in and, not noticing his wife, says directly to* VICTORIA:)

JERRY: Vicky! What the hell is going on here?!

(*At that,* VICKY *goes furiously into the guest room, slamming the door behind her. Thrusting all the Monopoly money into* VICTORIA's *hands,* MOTHER *snatches back the auctioned objects.*)

MOTHER: Don't mean to be an Indian giver, but I may not be checking out as soon as I thought!

(*Delighted at the turn of events, she goes to the drums and plays a loud triumphant salvo.*)

(*Blackout*)

END ACT ONE

ACT TWO

SCENE ONE

(At rise:)

(Immediately following the previous scene)

(It is night. The remains of the Birthday Party are still strewn around. The impasse continues. VICKY is locked in her room. Even before the curtain rises, we can hear the sound of JERRY pounding on her door. As the lights come up on the scene he is calling:)

JERRY: Vicky, come out of there!

(MOTHER, keyed up and impatient, sits on the chaise. VICTORIA stands behind her, comforting her. DON stands slightly apart, impassively observing the scene. THELMA wheels the life-sized buffalo to the side of the room then starts clearing the dishes.)

THELMA: Hours baking a cake and nobody asks for seconds.

MOTHER: We'll eat it tomorrow, Thelma.

THELMA: For this cake there *is* no tomorrow!

(Loaded with plates, she exits to the kitchen. JERRY pounds on the door again.)

JERRY: Come out, do you hear me! Vicky, this is getting us nowhere!...The light was in my eyes! If I mistook this other woman for you it was only a simple mistake!

(From inside the room, VICKY calls:)

VICKY'S VOICE: Go hang yourself, Jerry.

(JERRY turns for support to his mother-in-law.)

JERRY: You see what I have to put up with? Tantrums. Tantrums all the time. For no reason. I think she's having a nervous breakdown. If she weren't in her thirties I'd say she was going through the change.

MOTHER: *(Under her breath)* Wish *you'd* go through a change.

JERRY: *(Pounding on the door)* Come out or else!

VICKY'S VOICE: I'll take "or else"!

JERRY: *(To the assembled)* I try with her, I really try. *(He comes over to MOTHER.)*

I know you're going through difficult times, Mother. I'm going to help you as much as I can.

MOTHER: *(Sarcastically)* That'll be a major thrill.

(JERRY eyes VICTORIA.)

JERRY: So you're the other Victoria.

VICTORIA: You can call me Vicky.

(JERRY turns to DON.)

JERRY: And you're the guy my wife is having the affair with.

MOTHER: No, no! Don Juan is mine.

JERRY: And where is Vicky's?

MOTHER: That's for us to know and you to find out.

(JERRY pounds on the door again.)

JERRY: Vicky!

(No answer)

MOTHER: She doesn't seem to want to see you.

JERRY: She'll get over it. *(He looks around the room.)* I see you've done some redecorating.

MOTHER: You hate the room?

JERRY: Hell, no. If you like buffaloes, you have buffaloes, Mother dear. Anything you want, you have. *(He pats her shoulder.)*

MOTHER: *(Recoiling from his touch)* How about anything I *don't* want?

JERRY: *(At the door again)* Vicky, goddam it—!

DON: *(Quietly)* Why don't you all go off and let me have a go?

JERRY: How can you—?

MOTHER: Good idea. Come on, Jerry.

VICTORIA: *(Flirtatiously)* Yes. Come on, Jerry.

JERRY: *(To DON:)* You think you can come up with the magic words?

DON: I'd like to give it a try.

(With MOTHER leading and VICTORIA enticing, the WOMEN lead JERRY into the kitchen. When DON is alone in the room he goes to the door and says matter-of-factly:)

DON: Vicky,—your husband is a major asshole.

(VICKY immediately opens the door and comes out.)

VICKY: That is definitely the open sesame.

DON: He's a bully, an opportunist and worse than that, a square.

VICKY: That's Jerry to a J.

DON: Why did you marry him?

VICKY: He got me out of here. Early.

DON: Is that enough?

VICKY: It seemed so at the time.

DON: But it doesn't seem so now.

VICKY: This is not your concern.

DON: Of course it is. Your husband suspects that I'm your lover.

VICKY: He has a limited imagination.

DON: Maybe the one with the limited imagination is you.

VICKY: You think I would get myself involved with a man with no labels on his jeans, no identification in his wallet and a strange map in his bedroom?

DON: So you've been snooping around my bedroom.

VICKY: Thelma has. ...On my say so. You've been stomping around in my life, why shouldn't I sniff around in yours?

DON: Did you discover anything suspicious?

VICKY: The map.

DON: Ah,...the map.

VICKY: What's it of?

DON:...No place.

VICKY: The place where they make your clothes.

DON: A place in my mind. A place I'd like to find, but if it doesn't exist, why then I can invent it.

VICKY: The way you've invented everything about you since you came here!

DON: The landscape of the heart's desire. That's what the map is. You're limiting yourself to what is, Vicky. That's why you're having such a rough time.

VICKY: Oh, yes? And what would I see if I could rise above my limited imagination?

DON: You would see into the future. You would see yourself in a newly-invented landscape. You'd see me in that landscape—not too far away.

VICKY: You belong to my mother!

DON: Actually, I don't belong to anybody.

VICKY: This is getting exceedingly confusing...

DON: You realize that she and I aren't really lovers.

VICKY: I guess I guessed that.

DON: I'm here to ease her way for as long as she needs me. When she doesn't—

VICKY: You mean when she pops off—?

DON: I mean when she's strong enough to go it on her own. Then my responsibility to her is over.

VICKY: So you'll turn around and make a play for me! Are you sure you're talking to the right Victoria? *She's* the one with the legs, the ikebana, the soufflé. I have nothing!

DON: You've got grit.

VICKY: Fat lot of good grit does me!

DON: If I see a filly grazing in a field, I pay no attention. But if I see one neighing and kicking—that's the one I want.

VICKY: So you can break her in! Tame her!

DON: I don't want to tame her—

VICKY: You say so now, but you men are all alike! You want us tamed! I don't want to be tamed! I don't want to be broken! This neighing and kicking—it's all I've got!

(JERRY *enters.*)

JERRY: So you managed to pry her out of there. Okay. I'll take over.

DON: If it's all right with Vicky.

JERRY: Of course it's all right with Vicky. She means the world to me.

VICKY: The hell I do! The one you're lusting after is the doppelganger.

JERRY: What's a doppelganger?

DON: It's a double. It looks like the original, but it isn't. ...Can you distinguish gold from fool's gold, Jerry? I get the feeling you're a man who undervalues the worth of the real thing.

(*He exits to the garden.*)

JERRY: Vicky, what the hell is going on here?

VICKY: Nothing out of the ordinary. (*She gestures in the appropriate directions.*) This is my little brother, Moon Dancer. Don Juan is my mother's lover. That woman in red is me.

JERRY: This is a loony bin. Your mother definitely needs to be given a sanity test.

VICKY: What you mean is: "She's not responsible enough to have her hands on all that cash.'"

JERRY: Exactly.

VICKY: And: "Why don't we take care of it for her?"

JERRY: Right.

VICKY: In fact, since I know nothing of money, why don't you take care of it for her?

JERRY: Now you're showing some sense.

VICKY: *(Lashing out)* You jerk Jerry, you Jerry jerk. Did you come all this way to bilk my mother out of all her money?

(JERRY *is about to respond when* MOTHER *and* VICTORIA *enter from the kitchen.*)

MOTHER: Please don't stop arguing on our account. It just happens to be past my bedtime.

(She starts up the stairs with VICTORIA *following.)*

MOTHER: When you go to sleep, leave on any lights you want to. I have money to burn. *(At her door, she turns.)* Oh, and Jerry, if you're not invited to share a bed anywhere, use the chaise. Louis the Fifteenth used to find it quite comfortable.

JERRY: Thank you very much, Mother.

(MOTHER *starts into her room, then turns.*)

MOTHER: Don has gone to his room at the other end of the garden. Thelma has gone to her room at the other end of the house. You won't be disturbed. Do anything you want. But if it's murder, please don't bleed on the Oriental.

(She goes into her room, shutting the door behind her. VICTORIA *stands peering down from the landing. She and* JERRY *exchange a look.)*

VICTORIA: Goodnight, everybody.

JERRY: *(Attracted)* Goodnight.

VICKY: *(With an edge)* Good Night!

VICTORIA: Sweet dreams. *(She goes off to her room.)*

JERRY: She doesn't look like you.

VICKY: I'll report myself to Elizabeth Arden first thing in the morning.

JERRY: Look, Vicky, what we have to do is have your mother declared incompetent and assume power of attorney.

VICKY: No! Close subject, shred file, burn document!

JERRY: You have to be practical!

VICKY: Money! That's all you think of! I'll bet you're taking this trip off your income tax as a business deduction. I'll bet you got a receipt from the cab driver to show the IRS!

JERRY: *(Guilty)* I—

VICKY: Oh, God—! *(To the full size Moon Dancer:)* Little Brother! Mow the blighter down!

(She shoves the wheeled buffalo toward JERRY. Nearly knocked down, he cries:)

JERRY: Hey—!

(MOTHER opens her door a crack and, unobserved by the two below, stands in her dressing gown, listening.)

JERRY: I'm trying to protect your interests. You're going to be a very wealthy woman and we have to—

VICKY: There's that "we" again. I thought "we" was you and her.

JERRY: Me and who?

VICKY: The redhead.

JERRY: How did you know she's a redhead?

(Throwing open her door, MOTHER steps onto the landing and cries:)

MOTHER: I told you so!

VICKY: Christ!

MOTHER: Don't swear, dear.

VICKY: Shit!

MOTHER: "*Merde.*" It's more polite to say "*Merde*".

VICKY: Go into your room! Shut your door! Go to sleep! And don't do any sleep-walking!

(MOTHER goes back into her room, closing the door firmly. JERRY and VICKY continue their exchange, starting out with voices lowered.)

JERRY: That dame definitely has a screw loose.

VICKY: So you're prowling around bimboland. Again!

JERRY: I don't know where you get off being so high and mighty. I'm not convinced you're not carrying on with that two bit imitation Marlboro Man.

VICKY: I'm not.

JERRY: I bet your mother's saying he's hers is just a cover-up.

VICKY: This is a nightmare—

JERRY: Your infidelity wounds me to the core—

VICKY: I didn't know you had a core.

JERRY: —but I forgive you.

VICKY: Why? Because I finally look like the pot of gold at the end of your rainbow? When are you going to stop praying to the Great God Bottom Line?

JERRY: What's wrong with the bottom line? You think discussing finances is beneath you. You think all life is beneath you. You think *I* am beneath you.

VICKY: That's ridiculous!

JERRY: Believe me, it's no picnic being married to Sister Superior. I come home from the office, take one look at your face, and think: "What have I done wrong now?"

VICKY: What you've done wrong is come home late with lipstick on your collar.

JERRY: That is a recent development. When I realized I never ever on this earth could please you.

VICKY: So everything's my fault—

JERRY: Yes.

VICKY: You're driving me crazy!

JERRY: You always say that, but you never get there!

VICKY: You'd like me to, wouldn't you! You'd like me to go out of my mind.

JERRY: Stop raising your voice.

VICKY: I only raised my voice because you did.

JERRY: You raised your voice first.

VICKY: I did not!

JERRY: I wish to God we had a tape of this! We could play it back, then you'd hear—

VICKY: I turn my life inside out to make you happy!

JERRY: You've got to be kidding!

VICKY: I never do what *I* want to do. I do what *you* want to do! When are we gonna do what *I* want to do!

JERRY: I know what it is: You're upset because you think I'm fooling around.

VICKY: I don't care enough to get upset if you're fooling around!

JERRY: I'm not!

VICKY: Liar!

JERRY: You're in love with the Lone Ranger!

VICKY: I haven't been in love since third grade when I loved a boy named Ben who sat in front of me and lent me his penwiper.

JERRY: What the hell's a penwiper?

VICKY: Ben and I were the only two in our class who insisted on using real ink pens. He had this small felt cloth—

JERRY: Every time you're losing an argument, you start rummaging around in your past. Why don't you bring up how you felt in the womb!

VICKY: I was happy there. That was the last time I was happy.

JERRY: I swear if I have to listen to one more of your dreamy fantasies about life as it could have been I'll—

VICKY: In the name of God, time out! Time out!...Let's leave it here and take up where we left off in the morning.

JERRY: *(With sarcasm)* I'll look forward to it.

(VICKY *goes toward the guest room.*)

VICKY: I'm sure it'll do you good, for once,—to sleep alone.

(She goes into her room closing the door firmly behind her. JERRY *is furious. He stands muttering to himself for a minute.)*

JERRY: Major nut. I married into the nut family. Pecans, almonds, cashews...

(He's hungry. He snacks from the left-overs in dishes here and there. He starts putting out the lights, remembers Mother's words, puts some on again, then, knowing he won't be able to sleep, puts them off again. Then he pulls the Oriental carpet from the floor, covers himself with it and falls asleep on the chaise. He has not been asleep more than a second when MOTHER *and* VICTORIA *tiptoe out of their respective rooms in their dressing gowns. They meet on the landing.)*

MOTHER: *(Whispering)* Did you get it?

(VICTORIA *nods. Quietly she leans down and pulls up a chord on whose end is a tiny microphone which was hidden in the living room. She reels in the mike and takes out the hidden tape recorder to which it is connected. She ejects the tape and holds it up in the air. She and* MOTHER *smile, immensely pleased with themselves.* MOTHER *takes the tape, kisses* VICTORIA *goodnight and, after a conspiratorial glance at* VICTORIA, *goes into her bedroom. When* MOTHER *has closed her door,* VICTORIA *tiptoes downstairs in the darkness and approaches the chaise where* JERRY *is sleeping. She stands there until* JERRY *opens his eyes.)*

JERRY: Who is it?

VICTORIA: It's me.

JERRY: I knew you'd come back.

(He raises the carpet. She gets under it and they caress each other. Silently, VICKY

comes out of her room. She watches the action on the chaise. It becomes so energetic that the couple beneath the carpet tumbles onto the floor. As they do, JERRY *sees that* VICKY *is standing above them. He pulls the carpet around himself, jumps up and declares to her:)*

JERRY: I thought it was *you*!

(Before VICKY *can respond,* MOTHER *bursts from her room, flicks on the switch that lights up the entire room and says:)*

MOTHER: I knew he was going to say that! I bet Victoria that he'd say that! I win! And, Jerry Cheater,—you lose! *(She waves the tape in the air.)* Now we have all the evidence we need to commence legal action!

(Triumphantly she comes downstairs, sits at the drums and raps out a rousing military tattoo.)

(Blackout)

Scene Two

(Late morning of the next day.)

(The room has been straightened up from the night before. MOTHER *enters from her room wearing a black kimono with a long white scarf hanging down on either side—an imitation of a judge's robe. Standing on the landing, she crashes two cymbals together and cries:)*

MOTHER: Hear ye! Hear ye! Divorce court is now in session! The Honorable Judge Mother Dorothy Fairgrieve presiding!

(She crashes the cymbals once more then comes majestically down the stairs. THELMA *enters from the kitchen, perplexed and harried.)*

MOTHER: Where are the multitudes and why don't they assemble? *(She plays a summoning salvo on the drums.)* Multitudes! Hey, there, multitudes!

(The others arrive from all directions. JERRY *enters from the kitchen with a napkin tucked under his chin.* DON *enters from the garden, barbecue fork in hand.* VICTORIA *enters from her room wearing a skimpy exercise outfit—which* JERRY *eyes appreciatively.* VICKY *enters from her room drying her hair.)*

MOTHER: Divorce court is now in session! Will the plaintiffs please approach the bench.

VICKY: What plaintiffs?

MOTHER: You and Jerry. You're the only poor unfortunate marrieds here present.

VICKY: Now look, Mother—

THELMA: I thought we were going to have a barbecue. I spent the whole week marinating strange birds for a Chinese barbecue.

DON: I've already fired up the coals—

MOTHER: That grilling later. This grilling now.

VICKY: I'm not going to stand here while you—

MOTHER: This husband is charged with infidelity, desertion, mental cruelty, failure of character, failure of love, failure of nerve and failure of business.

JERRY: What's the wife charged with?

MOTHER: The same.

JERRY: In that case, we're perfectly suited! I move this case be dismissed.

MOTHER: Not so fast. You're also charged with major hanky-panky.

JERRY: The redhead types. That's all that she was doing for me.

MOTHER: And what about last night's wrestling match on the chaise?

JERRY: I told you—. I thought it was my wife.

VICKY: It's absurd to think you can't tell one lover from another. In the dark we are not all the same.

VICTORIA: I always thought I had some special skills—

JERRY: All right! I knew it was a set-up! *(To* VICKY:*)* I played along to get even with you.

VICKY: You played along to give your thing another diddle. You always think you deserve one more whack at the holy grail.

MOTHER: *(Making notes)* Uncontrollable sex drive—

JERRY: That's one of the major reasons why she married me.

MOTHER: *(To* VICKY:*)* And has your desire cooled?

VICKY: Only toward him.

MOTHER: Then you do want to split up.

VICKY: When I want to split up, I'll deal with it—

MOTHER: I don't have time to wait, Vicky.

VICKY: You want me to spill out all my failures right here on the carpet. Not only my career down the tubes, but my marriage, my life—

MOTHER: I want you to have a clean slate—

JERRY: We're doing fine, Mother.

MOTHER: Oh, yes? Listen to this—*(She gestures to* THELMA *to put on the tape.)* A good marriage is based on good arguing. Yours is pathetic.

(THELMA *starts the tape. We hear* VICKY *and* JERRY'*s recorded voices:)*

VICKY'S VOICE: "Stop raising your voice!"

JERRY'S VOICE: "I only raised my voice because you did!"

VICKY'S VOICE: "You raised your voice first!"

JERRY'S VOICE: "I did not!"

VICKY'S VOICE: "I wish to God we had a tape of this—!"

VICKY: Shut that off!

(The tape continues under.)

MOTHER: All you do is argue about arguing!

VICKY: The way we argue is our own affair!

DON: Dorothy, you are prowling around in a corral where you don't belong.

MOTHER: Anything that happens on my sofa is in my corral. *(To VICKY and JERRY:)* Unless you prove that you're in love, I won't allow this marriage to continue.

VICKY: *You* won't allow—!

DON: Dorothy, you're way out of bounds—

MOTHER: How often do you tell each other you love each other?

VICKY: I smell something burning—

THELMA: Oh, my God—! *(She runs out into the garden.)*

MOTHER: I tell you what smells: This marriage!

DON: Nobody can tell what's really going on inside anybody else's marriage—

MOTHER: You can if you have a tape—*(She starts to turn up the volume on the tape.)*

DON: No! Enough, Dorothy! *(He ejects the tape and tosses it out into the garden.)* You have to let your daughter live her own life!

(THELMA enters holding with tongs a small burnt bird entangled in burnt audio tape.)

THELMA: Do you want this served with mustard or with duk sauce?

MOTHER: *(To DON:)* Do you think, of all the choices my daughter could make for a life, the one she chose is anything worth living?

DON: That's for her to answer.

THELMA: If you don't come out right away, the rest of the birds will be burnt to cinders.

DON: Divorce court adjourned. On to the barbecue!

(THELMA, JERRY, DON and VICKY exit to the garden. MOTHER doesn't move. VICTORIA says to her:)

VICTORIA: Come out—

(MOTHER is unusually silent for some moments, then says, deeply, seriously:)

MOTHER: Why can't I ever make you listen? I thought the whole reason to have a daughter was to save her from making my mistakes. But you won't take my advice.

VICTORIA: I—

MOTHER: My mother didn't tell me anything. She never got beyond ninth grade. Everything was a puzzle to her. She never understood a damn thing I was learning, but she kept telling me I had to learn. ...What I didn't learn was how to choose a husband. I chose badly. I tried to get you not to make the same mistake. But you wouldn't learn! You still won't learn! Why can't I make you see—?

VICTORIA: You should be having this conversation with *her*, Mother. Mrs. Fairgrieve. ...You know I'm not your daughter,—don't you?

(MOTHER *looks at her, searching her face, then says:*)

MOTHER: She could have been a great concert pianist. She didn't have to settle. I wanted everything for her, but she's even more unhappy than I was. It breaks my heart. And I can't tell her—

VICTORIA: You could try—

MOTHER: She and I could never talk. ...At least, to you, I can say anything and you will listen. At least I can say these things, out loud, once in my life.

(*She is silent.* VICTORIA *looks at her with great compassion. Then* VICTORIA *gets up and goes to the entrance to the garden. She calls:*)

VICTORIA: Vicky! Victoria—!

(VICKY *enters.*)

VICTORIA: Your mother wants to talk to you.

VICKY: (*Stiffly, to her* MOTHER) You have something to say?

(MOTHER *suddenly sniffs the air and says:*)

MOTHER: Barbecue! Has to be eaten piping hot! Nothing worse than luke warm barbecue! (*She hurries out into the garden.*)

(VICKY *and* VICTORIA *are alone.*)

VICTORIA: What is it with you two? Why can't you and your mother talk?

VICKY: Maybe it's because she's not my real mother.

VICTORIA: She's not—?

VICKY: I remember the moment I was born. I opened my eyes and cried to the stork: "Wait! There's been a mistake! You've dropped me down the wrong chimney!" When that happens to you, your life's awry from the beginning and there's nothing you can do about it. My mother knows how I feel. And I can't shake it off.

VICTORIA: She cares about you—

VICKY: She cares about *you*! She has always only cared about you, from the beginning!

VICTORIA: What do you mean—from the beginning?

VICKY: You think you just appeared in my life last week? No. You were there beside me in the cradle. Finishing your bottle without burping! Crapping in your diaper, very neatly, only once a day. Learning to read while I just sat there drooling. And then, when we were a little bigger, you were the one who made her bed like the goody-goody girl, while the naughty-naughty girl was out roller-skating. You were the one who put the cap back on the toothpaste, you were the one who remembered to close the refrigerator door. You were the one who did her homework nightly without being nagged to do it. You were the one who did your solfege, never screwing up a note. You were the one who dated only the good little boys, the ones who kissed with their mouths closed. You were the one in college who wrote home daily. You were the one who married the man your mother wanted and called her nightly for a chat. You were the one who not only had six kids but also got herself a career and triumphed in it! I hate you! I hate you! I thought I'd escaped from you—and here you are, in the flesh, in the gorgeous and beautiful flesh! Damn you to hell! Damn you! Damn you!

VICTORIA: *(After a moment)* Wow!...Would you mind if sometime I used that speech in an audition?

(VICKY *bursts out laughing.*)

VICTORIA:...She says you could have been a great concert pianist.

VICKY: Her idea of concert pianist is Liberace playing *Malagueña*! I didn't give it up only because I couldn't stand to hear her nag me to practice. I gave it up because I was no good! No good!

VICTORIA: What happened with your job?

VICKY: I was no good at that either.

VICTORIA: And your marriage?

VICKY: Perfect score. Nothing, nothing, nothing, all around.

VICTORIA: Then why do you stay married?

VICKY: Because she wants me not to.

VICTORIA: I think Don is very interested in you.

VICKY: Oh, yes, wouldn't that be a howl? Go off with my mother's boyfriend!

VICTORIA: Don't you just love the way he talks? Can't tell where he's from.

VICKY: Sounds like Harvard—with just a touch of prairie.

VICTORIA: Those cowboy eyes of his—

VICKY: And his clothes. I want to crawl right into his labeless clothes!

VICTORIA: ...Bet he'd be great in the sack.

VICKY: Don't tell me the goody-goody girl is thinking naughty-naughty.

VICTORIA: Nothing wrong with thinking, is there,—sister?

VICKY: No,..."sister".

(There is a moment of communion between them)

VICKY: You know, you and I could be friends if only—

VICTORIA: —what?

VICKY: If only you would mess up once in a while. Trip. Drop something.

VICTORIA: I'll do my best.

(The telephone rings. VICTORIA goes to get it. She trips and falls, dropping the receiver. VICKY, helping her up, kisses her on the cheek and says:)

VICKY: Perfect! *(Then, into the phone she says:)* Hello? *(As she listens, her face registers incredulity. After a moment, she puts down the receiver and goes to the entrance to the garden calling:)* Don!...Telephone.

(He enters. She says with disbelief:)

VICKY: ...It's Injun O'Brien.

(MOTHER, JERRY and THELMA hear this and come into the living room, JERRY munching on a bird wing. DON takes the phone and says into it:)

DON: Yes?...*(He listens, then says to those in the room:)* Moon Dancer has escaped! He broke through the fence and is heading for the open range!

VICKY: Go, baby, go! *(Then, to DON:)* Is there—?

DON: Yes, Victoria, there *is* a Moon Dancer.

MOTHER: My poor buffalo—*(She picks up the small carved buffalo statuette.)*

DON: They have helicopters following him. ...They've tracked him to the edge of the range. ...He's bounding over the high rocks—...Disappearing among the crags!

JERRY: Excuse me, but do any of us care?

DON: They've lost him!

MOTHER: Gone! Gone!

VICKY: At last he's free! *(Into the phone:)* Keep going, sweetheart! Keep going and going!

(DON hangs up the phone.)

MOTHER: "Keep going, sweetheart. Keep going and going."...Where did I hear that before?

DON: *(Indicating the statuette)*...The day you were given that buffalo.

MOTHER: *(Slowly remembering)* Yes. The day I was given this buffalo.

DON: By a man in a bowler hat—in a small train station in Wyoming.

MOTHER: A man in a bowler hat in a small train station in Wyoming...

VICKY: I didn't know you were ever in Wyoming...

MOTHER: I was. I was. I was running away—. But there was a storm. Snow in the pass. All us travelers had to spend the night in that little station miles from nowhere.

DON: You talked—all that night—to this man.

MOTHER: I never knew his name.

DON: He knew yours. And he vowed—you'd have a life. That's why he sent me to you.

MOTHER: *He* sent you?

DON: I was with him for ten years before the end.

VICKY: Then there is no bachelor cousin?

DON: There is no bachelor cousin.

MOTHER: There is only—a man in a bowler hat who bought me this souvenir.

VICKY: All this—from a man you met, and talked to, a man who never took off his hat?

MOTHER: Actually, he did take off his hat...once. Just once. Then he went on his way.

VICKY:...Why didn't you go with him?

MOTHER:...I had to come home—to you.

*(Silence. ...*DON *ushers* JERRY, VICTORIA *and* THELMA *out into the garden.* MOTHER *and* VICKY *are alone.)*

VICKY: So you had your moment—

MOTHER: Yes, I had my moment.

VICKY: And I was your ball and chain.

MOTHER: I never said that.

VICKY: But it's true. That's why you only had one child. To leave you free—

MOTHER: That's why you never had any. You knew it would tie you forever to a man you didn't love.

VICKY: I never had any because I didn't want to have a daughter. I didn't want it to be with me and her the way it is with you and me.

MOTHER: Why did you marry Jerry?

VICKY: Because you told me not to.

MOTHER: Baby, don't live your life to spite me. Don't feel that whatever I say you have to do the opposite because no matter what I say I have to be wrong.

VICKY: So you know I do that.

MOTHER: Of course, I know you do that. You think I'm a stupid, ignorant woman! It's as if I gave you life so you could grow up and criticize me!

VICKY: Mother—

MOTHER: From the minute you were born it was as if you belonged to some other family.

VICKY: You felt that—?!

MOTHER: We always called you "The Little Stranger". And now look what I've got—The *Big* Stranger! You're my only flesh and blood on this earth and I don't know how to get through to you!

VICKY: I had no idea—*(She sits beside her mother.)* Please. Say what you want to say. I'll listen.

MOTHER: *(After a pause:)* Get rid of the bum. ...I have this wonderful man, I want you to have one. Believe me, there's no greater gift than having the right companion on life's highway.

VICKY: *(Shaking her head, she sings defiantly:)*
"I'll go my way by myself,
All alone in a crowd –"

MOTHER: The solitary life is highly overrated. We come into life alone and go out alone. That's why it means so much to pair off with the right one in the middle.

VICKY: What if the right one belongs to somebody else?

MOTHER: There are no rules in love or war.

VICKY: So you say pursue the man I want. Whoever he is, whose ever he is?

MOTHER: I say go after him.

VICKY: And if that doesn't seem cricket?

MOTHER: Then travel single-o. You'll have my bank account. You'll have your piano. You were a genius at the piano.

VICKY: *(Singing:)* "Me and the night and the music..."

MOTHER: Take it, Vicky. Take whatever you can while you can. Don't wait till it's too late. Like I did. Leave the guy—...What's wrong?

VICKY: I need to come to it myself, don't you understand that? I have to make my own decisions, be my own person, not be told what to do by Jerry or by you. I want to think I can think!

MOTHER: All right, think—as long as you come to the right conclusions.

(DON *enters.*)

DON: You said you wanted to put the finishing touches to the dessert, Dorothy. It's time.

MOTHER: Thank you, darling.

(*Giving him a fond squeeze,* MOTHER *exits to the garden.* DON *and* VICKY *are alone.*)

VICKY: What finishing touches?

DON: She's been practicing how to carve an apple into a swan.

VICKY: You taught her.

DON: Guilty.

VICKY: Wish you could make a swan out of me. Then I could fly away—

DON: Moon Dancer's free, but you haven't cut loose yet.

VICKY: From my mother or from Jerry?

DON: Both.

VICKY: To head out alone down life's highway?

DON: No. To head out with me.

VICKY: I can't take you from her. She needs you!

DON: Not as much as you do.

VICKY: I'll decide what I need and what I don't need!

DON:...People think it's profound, pairing off. But it's really very simple. You and Jerry don't suit. You and I do.

VICKY: Oh, really! You think so!

DON: Let's find out. (*He comes toward her.*)

VICKY: Please don't come so close.

DON: Still confused?

VICKY: More than ever!

DON: Let me make things clear for you.

VICKY: No more philosophy!

DON: I wasn't thinking of philosophy.

(*He takes her strongly by the shoulders, clearly meaning to kiss her if she consents.*)

DON: Do you dare—?

VICKY: You think I don't have the courage?

(Challenged, she kisses him. He kisses her back. It lasts long enough to become very real and very mutual. Half-concealed, VICTORIA *appears and watches from the garden. When* VICKY *and* DON *release each other, they look at each other for a long time.* VICTORIA *enters and says:)*

VICTORIA: Don, Dorothy's waiting for you.

*(*DON *turns and exits to the garden.* VICKY *is frozen in a trance.* VICTORIA *says:)*

VICTORIA: So. Is he as good a kisser as we thought?

VICKY: I think I'd better sit down...

VICTORIA: That good, eh?

VICKY: What should I do?

VICTORIA: Go off with him. I would if I were you. And I am.

VICKY: I can't take my Mother's guy!

VICTORIA: Of course you can.

VICKY: He's all she's got!

VICTORIA: She doesn't love him as much as she pretends.

VICKY: Maybe not. But if he and I got together—

VICTORIA: Don't you see? That's what she's wanted from the beginning.

VICKY: What are you talking about?

VICTORIA: I'm saying there's nothing for you to worry about. Your pairing off with him—that's been her whole plan from the start!

*(*VICTORIA *exits to the garden.* VICKY *cries:)*

VICKY: Merde! *(Agitated,* VICKY *sits down at the piano and, full of rage, starts to play Chopin's "Revolutionary Etude". She starts well, but after a moment her fingers stumble. She tries again but keeps making mistakes. Extremely upset and discouraged, she slams the cover down over the keyboard. She cries:)* Merde! Merde! MERDE! *(She breaks down and weeps.)*

(Blackout)

SCENE THREE

(A short time later)

(Loud music of a tango is blaring from the CD. Dancing with wild determination, MOTHER is alone in the living room doing a tango with occasional flashes of flamenco.)

(VICKY enters from the guest room carrying her suitcase. She shouts over the tango music:)

VICKY: You set me up! It was a trap from the beginning!

(MOTHER continues dancing as if she didn't hear her.)

VICKY: You lured me here for the sole purpose of getting me to ditch my husband and match me up with the man of your choice!

(MOTHER doesn't miss a beat.)

VICKY: You pretended he was out of bounds so I would want him!

(MOTHER stamps her feet to the beat more intently than ever.)

VICKY: For God's sake, don't you know it takes two to tango?!

(VICKY flips off the CD. Silence. For a moment the two women glare at each other)

VICKY: You planned it all, didn't you!

MOTHER: I don't know what you're talking about.

VICKY: You just couldn't keep your hands off my life.

MOTHER: All right! He came to my door. I knew he was right for you. I kept him here—

VICKY: Kept him warm till I arrived. He's not a tuna noodle casserole!

MOTHER: Are you going to stay with the jerk?

VICKY: Jerry and I are going back to the city. We'll talk things out and decide what to do from there.

MOTHER: You'll never get away.

(JERRY *and* VICTORIA *enter from the garden.*)

JERRY: Vicky, are you ready?

MOTHER: This is wrong. All wrong.

VICTORIA: Don't worry, Mother. I'll stay with you.

MOTHER: Oh, stop that nonsense. I paid you to say things like that. Now I'll pay you to stop it.

VICTORIA: You're the boss.

MOTHER: *(To* VICKY:*)* Leave the bum!

JERRY: I'm not what I was, Mother. I'm reformed.

MOTHER: "Reformed!" You'd have to be reconstituted!

JERRY: We're going to make everything turn out all right. You'll see. We'll visit you every weekend.

MOTHER: *(Sarcastically)* That'll be a treat. *(To* VICKY:*)* He only wants your money.

VICKY: I'm disinheriting myself, Jerry.

JERRY: We'll talk about this later. ...There's a plane in half an hour. I'll call a cab.

(*He picks up the phone and dials.*)

MOTHER: Where's Don? Where's my Don?

(DON *enters through the front door.*)

MOTHER: Don, she's leaving!

DON: I see that, Dorothy.

MOTHER: I want you two to get together!

VICKY: Mother, give it up.

DON: *(To* MOTHER:*)* The lady's right.

MOTHER: *(To* DON:*)* Talk her out of it. Tell her you want her.

DON: *(Shaking his head)* I can send smoke signals, but if she insists on looking the other way, there's nothing I can do but quit. ...So long, Vicky.

VICKY: Thank you.

(MOTHER *grabs the phone from* JERRY *and dials a number.*)

MOTHER: Hello, Bloomingdale's? Get me the lingerie department.

VICKY: You're not going to get me this time.

MOTHER: *(Into the phone:)* Hello, lingerie department?

VICKY: You're not going to drag me in.

MOTHER: I want an ivory satin slip, lace panties and a satin underwire bra, size 38 Double D. *(Into the phone:)* What? Five days for delivery! Forget it! *(She hangs up.)* I'll just have to be buried in ancient underwear.

JERRY: Let's get going, Vicky.

VICKY: *(To* DON:*)* She asked you to pursue me.

DON: I'll admit it began that way. Then it turned real.

VICKY: How can I know that?

DON: If you don't know, there's no way I can tell you.

VICKY: Why not? You seem to have the words for everything.

DON: What you and I have to say to each other doesn't need words.

(VICKY *and* DON *look at each other silently.*)

JERRY: Don't come on to my wife!

MOTHER: *(To* VICKY:*)* Leave him. Stay here. I will give you everything.

VICKY: All I want from you—all I've ever wanted—is the freedom to live my own life. ...Goodbye, all. Goodbye.

(*She starts for the door with* JERRY. MOTHER *turns feverishly to* DON *and* VICTORIA.)

MOTHER: Don! Victoria! What were we planning to do today?...Oh, yes—. Henry the Fifth—*(She grabs a large volume and begins to recite:)*
"He which hath no stomach to this fight,
Let him depart. His passport shall be made,
And crowns for convoy put into his purse."

VICKY: What are you doing?

MOTHER: "We would not die in that man's company
That fears his fellowship to die with us."

VICKY: Mother, would you just say goodbye—

MOTHER: "This day is call'd the feast of Crispian.
He that outlives this day and comes safe home –"

(VICKY *calls toward the kitchen door.*)

VICKY: Goodbye, Thelma! Take good care of her!

(THELMA, *who has been eavesdropping, opens the door and says:*)

THELMA: You're making a mistake!

VICKY: Don't *you* start—!

(THELMA *closes the door.* VICKY *once more starts to go.*)

MOTHER: I thought, one day, that we'd talk Shakespeare to each other. I thought I'd listen to you play. I thought we'd stay in an ashram together—

VICKY: Goodbye. Sorry I can't do a farewell speech as well as Shakespeare.

MOTHER: *(Riffling through the Shakespeare)* Wait! I'll find you something—. This man is never at a loss for words.

(The taxi horn beeps outside. VICKY and JERRY start toward the door with their bags. MOTHER cries:)

MOTHER: She can't go! She can't! *(She grabs the buffalo statuette and cries to it hysterically:)* Moon Dancer, do something! Do something!

(The statue doesn't answer. MOTHER shakes it furiously, then raises her arm to throw it across the room. DON shouts:)

DON: Dorothy! No!

(He takes the statuette from her hands and puts it back safely on the table. Then, to calm her, He takes a packet of photos from his jacket pocket and says:)

DON: Look, Dorothy... I've just gotten them back. The photos of the trip we took around the world together.

MOTHER: Vicky, wait! Don't you want to see these pictures?

(At the door, VICKY turns and watches while DON opens the envelope.)

DON: Here's London.

VICTORIA: Where we watched the changing of the guard.

(DON and VICTORIA are on the chaise on either side of MOTHER.)

MOTHER: The changing of the guard. I don't remember...

VICTORIA: Here's Piccadilly Circus.

MOTHER: Piccadilly Circus...

DON: And afterwards we drove to Edinburgh to see the castle.

MOTHER: Edinburgh. The castle.

VICTORIA: Then drove back through the Lake District.

DON: You wandered lonely as a cloud—

VICTORIA: "That floats on high o'er vales and hills."

DON: "When all at once you saw a crowd—
A host of golden daffodils"

VICTORIA: Remember when we ran through the flowers and picked them by the armfuls—

MOTHER: Yes! Yes! I remember!

JERRY: When did this happen?

DON: And here we are in Paris—

JERRY: *(Aside to* VICKY:*)* Your mother's never been to Paris—

MOTHER: The Arch of Triumph—

VICTORIA: The espresso in that little cafe—

JERRY: *(Grabbing the photos)* You're not in any of these pictures.

MOTHER: Of course not, I was behind the camera.

JERRY: *(To* VICKY:*)* This woman has to be put away—

(But VICKY *is mesmerized by the scene on the chaise.)*

VICTORIA: The perfume shops on the Rue de Rivoli—

MOTHER: Chanel Number Five! My Sin! Diorissimo! We tried them all.

(The taxi horn beeps again.)

JERRY: *(To* VICKY:*)* I'll get a court order for us to manage her affairs.

*(*JERRY *starts to pull* VICKY *out with him.)*

DON: Here we are on our first night in Paris, taking a boat ride on the Seine—

JERRY: *(Trying to get* VICKY *to leave:)* It'll take time, of course. Meanwhile, I know this agency. They can get you a job that'll pay Seventy Five thou just for starters. If I can pull off a couple of the deals I'm working on, we can gross a quarter of a mill a year, easy.

VICTORIA: And here we are on our second night—at the Folies Bergère!

JERRY: Then, with the interest on your mother's principle, we can pay off all my debts and—

(Repelled by him, VICKY *suddenly cries:)*

VICKY: We didn't go to the Folies Bergère! We went to the Opera!

MOTHER: The Opera—?

JERRY: You never travelled through Europe with your mother—

VICKY: We saw *Rigoletto*—

DON: *Rigoletto.* Where the daughter is found murdered in a sack.

MOTHER: *(At last!)* I remember—!...We stayed at the Ritz.

*(*VICKY *takes* VICTORIA*'s place on the chaise beside her* MOTHER.*)*

VICKY: We stayed at that little hotel on the Left Bank. I lost the cap off the toothpaste.

MOTHER: You lost the cap off the—?

DON: Dorothy! Who needs a cap on the toothpaste!

MOTHER: Right. Who needs a cap on the toothpaste!

VICKY: I borrowed your panty hose and ran them.

MOTHER: You ran my—? *(Then, collecting herself:)* I like to go around with my legs bare.

VICKY: I lost our passports and all our money.

MOTHER: You lost—?!

DON: Dorothy—

MOTHER: Who needs passports?

(MOTHER and VICKY hug each other.)

JERRY: What's going on here?

DON: Your wife has made her decision.

(Outside, the taxi horn blows again. VICTORIA takes the locket from around her neck and puts it around VICKY's.)

VICTORIA: In my whole life, I've never been happier to lose a part.

(VICTORIA kisses MOTHER warmly on both cheeks and exits.)

JERRY: This is a booby hatch. I'm getting out of here. Vicky, are you coming with me?

VICKY: No, Jerry.

JERRY: Then this is goodbye?

VICKY: It's goodbye.

JERRY: Well, so what! *(He picks up his suitcase.)* Anyway, I prefer you as a blonde. *(He exits through the front door and we can hear him calling:)* Hey! Wait for me—!

(MOTHER smiles.)

MOTHER: And now that they're gone—*(She looks from VICKY to DON with wedding bells in her eyes.)*

VICKY:—I'll say *adios*. *(She goes to the phone.)* There must be more than one taxi in this town.

MOTHER: What are you talking about?

VICKY: Mother, don't be daffy. I'm not going to hitch myself up to the Sundance Kid. *(She turns to DON:)* I think it was absurd of you to say you love me just because she told you to.

DON: I'm not aware I told you that I love you.

VICKY: I would never consider pairing up with a man who can't even say he loves me!

DON: You rely too much on words.

VICKY: You rely too much on mystery!

DON: Why does everything have to be tied down for you? Close your eyes and take the leap—

VICKY: You take a leap!

MOTHER: The perfect match! You two argue beautifully!

DON: *(To* VICKY:*)* Unlike you, I'm willing to admit when your mother is right.

VICKY: Then marry my mother! *(She goes toward her suitcase.)* I'm leaving.

MOTHER: But this—all this—I did it all for you!

VICKY: Mother, I don't want it.

MOTHER: I give up. I can't take this any more. *(She calls out:)* Thelma! Bring me some tea. I'm going to the garden to do my meditations.

VICKY: Then I'll say goodbye.

MOTHER: I'm not up to any more farewell scenes. *(She walks slowly out into the garden murmuring:)* Ohm..., Ohm...

(When she has gone, VICKY *says:)*

VICKY: It's nothing against you, I just can't see myself living out the rest of my life on a path my mother laid out for me.

DON: I understand completely.

VICKY: For God's sake, don't understand completely!

DON: All right. I don't understand at all.

VICKY: But you do, goddam it. You do. You understand everything. *(She looks at the statuette.)* Is there a Moon Dancer?

DON: There is if you think there is.

VICKY: I'm getting out of here!

DON: Where are you going?

VICKY: The first plane to the farthest destination! You have some perfect landscape. Well, I have mine—

DON: Where is it?

VICKY: I'll find out when I get there!

*(*THELMA *comes into the room from the garden. She is in shock.)*

THELMA: I can't wake her! I tried to get her to take her tea. She doesn't move!

DON: Dorothy—!

(He and VICKY *run out to the garden.* THELMA *goes to the telephone, picks it up, but doesn't know the number she's calling. She searches for a phone index, muttering:)*

THELMA: Doctor..., doctor...*(Finding no number, she rushes to a cabinet, finds a phone book and begins to riffle through it, saying in panic:)* Oh, God—what's his name—? *(Lost and confused, she throws the book aside, and rushes to the phone muttering:)*

THELMA: Police—! Operator—!

(She starts to dial but at that moment, VICKY *and* DON *return.)*

DON: Well, that's it. We can't revive her.

VICKY: Don tried. I couldn't go near...

(Stunned, THELMA *puts down the phone, bursts into sobs and runs into the kitchen.* VICKY *is in a daze. Slowly, she says:)*

VICKY: So she's actually done it. After years of crying wolf, she's finally popped off. *(Then, suddenly:)* It's all my fault! Why couldn't I have given her more of what she needed? Why couldn't I have tried harder to be the Perfect Other Me?

DON: Don't blame yourself.

*(*VICKY *covers the drums with a cloth, then gets the statuette of the buffalo and sits holding it.)*

VICKY:...It's very quiet here all of a sudden. ...She must have been expecting this. That's why she was doing the tapes. At some point, I guess I'll have to listen to them...

DON: She was quite a dame, your mother.

VICKY: I'm glad toward the end she had someone who appreciated her for what she was—whatever that was.

DON: You'll be a very rich woman.

VICKY: I don't want her money.

DON: I'm sorry, but, in the event of your mother's demise, my instructions are that it go directly to you.

VICKY: I'll give it away! I'll give power over it to you, to do with as you think best.

DON: To whom do you want it to go?

VICKY:...To people who've lost their way.

(She takes out a fountain pen, gets a notepad from the telephone table and starts to write.)

DON: Wouldn't you like to make the gifts yourself?

VICKY: No. You're the wisest among us, you'll know what to do. You always know what to do. *(Her fountain pen leaks.)* Damn! I've made a huge splotch!

DON:...Want to borrow my penwiper? *(He takes a penwiper from his pocket and holds it out to her.)*

VICKY:...Ben?

(He nods)

VICKY: *Ben!*...

(She runs over to him)

VICKY: You're the only one I ever loved!

DON: The feeling is mutual.

VICKY: I chose you from the beginning! Of my own free will!

DON: And I chose you.

VICKY: What a pair we will make!

(She comes to him and kisses him with abandon. MOTHER *strides in from the garden and cries:)*

MOTHER: At last!

VICKY: Oh, My God! Your popping off—it was fake! I should have known! You two cooked it up!

MOTHER: No. I did it all on my own.

DON: Congratulations, Dorothy! You actually achieved suspended animation!

MOTHER: *(To* VICKY*:)* I knew I'd have to die for you to come to your senses.

VICKY: I can't stand this!

MOTHER: You love Don.

VICKY: He's not Don, he's Ben.

MOTHER: Little Ben? The one you had a crush on since Miss Turkington's class?

VICKY: Yes.

MOTHER: The one who gave you your first boy-bought ice cream?

DON: Yes.

MOTHER: The one with the scar on his right arm from where you bit him when he pulled your braids?

*(*VICKY *inspects his arm, near his biceps. Then, stunned by the revelation:)*

VICKY: Yes.

MOTHER: I always said you were meant for each other!

VICKY: Oh, my God—!

MOTHER: Don't the Indians have a saying: "Once you take a bite out of somebody, you're paired for life?" Outside of that bite, he's as perfect as they get!

VICKY: But you chose him for me!

MOTHER: Yes! And you agree with my choice!...At last I can die happy!

VICKY: All right. Go ahead. Die if you like, but don't try to threaten, manipulate or control me. I'm my own self now, not an adjunct of you, not a slave to some man. If you think you can't stand to live on the same planet as this woman, croak again. I'll miss you. But if you think you can stand this dame—on her own two feet, with her own mind—stick around and watch me fly!

(There is a long, stunned pause. Then at last MOTHER *says:)*

MOTHER: My God! It's Victoria!

*(*MOTHER *hugs an astonished* VICKY, *then she says:)*

MOTHER: Call a cab! We're all going out to lunch! To celebrate your coming wedding!

VICKY: Excuse me, I am not getting married at the moment! I am not hitching myself forever to a man I only got reacquainted with this week. I am going to think out my life, and marry when and whom I want, if and when I'm ready!

(But MOTHER *isn't listening. Putting on an orange coat and wild straw hat, she is loudly humming an upbeat version of "Here Comes the Bride". Raising her voice to be heard over her mother's singing,* VICKY *confronts* DON:*)*

VICKY: Do you understand?

DON: Yes, I understand completely.

VICKY: I have to have room to breathe! I have to have a life!

DON: So do I!

VICKY: If we're going to live together, I need two things: Total freedom and total commitment!

DON: That's exactly what *I* need!

*(*MOTHER's *singing has risen in volume.* VICKY *makes a violent "cut" sign. Miraculously,* MOTHER *shuts up. Suddenly there is total silence.* VICKY *turns to* DON *and asks, quietly and seriously:)*

VICKY:...Do you think it's possible?

DON:...I think we can give it one hell of a try.

*(*VICKY *looks at him for a moment. Then, abandoning all restraint, she rushes to him and throws herself into his arms. They kiss.* MOTHER *watches for a moment, then taps*

VICKY *on the shoulder and says in a small voice:)*

MOTHER: Excuse me. May I play the *Wedding March* now?

VICKY: *(Joyously)* Mother, darling, I don't give a damn what you play!

(She enthusiastically returns to kissing DON. MOTHER *presses the start button on the CD. A jazzed-up version of the Mendelssohn Wedding March floods the room. Triumphant,* MOTHER *grabs the drumsticks and beats out a loud rhythmic tattoo in time to the music. Hearing the noise,* THELMA *enters from the kitchen, her eyes red from crying. Shocked at seeing* MOTHER *resurrected and whacking away on the drums, she collapses in a dead faint. The music rises.* MOTHER *plays one last brilliant salvo.* VICKY *and* DON *continue to embrace.)*

(Blackout)

END OF PLAY

THE SKY POOL

CHARACTERS & SETTING

Joan Oliver
Tiffany Manning
Robert
Abby Delacourt
Alexis Manning
Claire Palmer
Jennifer Palmer

Time & Place: The Present. The glass-enclosed solarium adjoining a rooftop pool atop a high-rise apartment building in New York City.

Setting: An oasis in the city. Under a dome of glass, a sense of air and space.

Upstage is a head-high frosted glass barrier that separates the solarium from the pool area. Before it are several low-frond palm trees in large pots. On either end of this barrier are openings that lead to the pool area.

Before the barrier is a row of three or four reclining lounge chaises. At stage right is an umbrella-shaded table around which are several chairs.

At stage left, steps lead up to a raised platform on which are the entrance doors from the building into the solarium and, downstage of these, an opening to the corridor that leads to the men's lavatory and sauna and the equipment room. The pool guard's desk is downstage at the bottom of the steps.

Stage right is the opening leading to the women's lavatory, exercise room and sauna.

The entire space, covered by a retractable glass roof, suggests an atmosphere of light and air. Through the glass roof can be seen sky and clouds, the changing light indicating time of day and change of seasons. On the glass and on the walls, the light reflects the activity in the pool—sometimes active, sometimes still.

Music: The breaks between scenes are defined both by lighting (usually blackouts) and by music, the music of Vivaldi's "The Four Seasons". The musical phrases should not be chosen to match the seasons assigned to the Vivaldi work with the seasons of the play, but to match the thematic and emotional meanings of the music with the thematic and dramatic meanings of each specific moment in the play.

ACT ONE

(At rise:)

(Darkness. JOAN OLIVER, *a vibrant intelligent woman one side or the other of 70, is revealed in her own light. She says to us:)*

JOAN: What do you know about the people in the house—or the apartment—next door to you? Do you have any idea who they really are or what they're really thinking? What turmoil they might be suffering as they pass you with a nod or a smile in the corridor or on the street? ...Oh, the civil surfaces of social situations! *(She stops and repeats the phrase, emphasizing the "s" sounds.)* Civil surfaces of social situations. *(She smiles.)* ...Lovely alliteration! Lousy fact!

Except for my sister, I knew next to nothing about the other members of the rooftop pool in the apartment building where we lived. Shrouded in anonymity, we hid behind our impenetrable enameled faces. The opaqueness of our social intercourse was very comforting. It was our safety.

When did things begin to change? ...I think it was about the same time as the arrival of our new pool guard. He was in no way responsible for all that happened. But it was about the time he came to us that the enamel began to crack, the civilized surfaces began to chip away—and things began, irrevocably, to change...

What I wouldn't give to turn back the clock to two years ago! When the surface of the waters seemed so untroubled—and we didn't know about each other—more than I wished to know...

(Blackout on JOAN. *She exits.)*

(The lights come up full on the solarium. It is a bright late summer day. TIFFANY MANNING *enters. She is sixteen, energetic, edgy, sassy. She goes over to the sign-in page on the desk. No pen. She can't sign in. She hears a male voice humming in the pool area. She goes upstage and looks into the pool area. What she sees delights her. She turns and says to us:)*

TIFFANY: He's gorgeous! Absolutely gorgeous! Usually they hire pool guards who are glum, dumb and skinny. The last one was so scrawny I don't think he could have saved a drowning sardine! But this one—he is handsome! Tall—with dark eyes. Greek God muscles. And a smile that makes you melt like a grilled cheese sandwich. ...I caught a glimpse of him in the lobby when he came in today. He looks like one of those magnet people. You know—the kind who all they have to do is look at you and they start reeling you in. I was hell on the guys before. But this one—with him, I won't be a hellion. But at the same time, I won't exactly be a saint!

(ROBERT *comes into the solarium area carrying the long-handled net used for cleaning the pool. He is a young man in his early 20s. He looks quite like her description and has a self-contained polite straight-forward manner.*)

ROBERT: Good afternoon.

TIFFANY: Hi.

ROBERT: Did you sign in?

TIFFANY: There's no pen.

ROBERT: Oh. Sorry. *(He starts to look for one on the desk.)*

TIFFANY: Top right hand drawer.

ROBERT: Thanks.

(He finds it and hands it to her. She signs in.)

ROBERT: First day. Takes a bit of getting used to.

TIFFANY: Ask me anything.

ROBERT: Thanks. I will, Miss—*(He looks at the sign-in sheet.)*—Manning.

TIFFANY: Tiffany.

ROBERT: Tiffany.

TIFFANY: How's the water?

ROBERT: Excellent.

TIFFANY: I mean—what's the temperature?

ROBERT: 84 degrees.

TIFFANY: Ugh.

ROBERT: You don't like 84?

TIFFANY: I like it colder. My mother likes it warmer.

ROBERT: 84 is what it's officially supposed to be. So it's perfect.

TIFFANY: *(Admiring him)* Perfect. ... *(Then, after a pause:)* What's your name?

ROBERT: Robert.

TIFFANY: Robert! Great! ...But extremely unusual!

ROBERT: Why unusual?

TIFFANY: We've had a Diego, a Pedro, an Eduardo. Once we even had a José!

It's nice—at long last—to have a "Robert".

ROBERT: *(Not reacting to this obviously racist remark)* Are you going to swim?

TIFFANY: *(As she starts toward a chaise)* Actually, I thought I'd relax for a while. Soak in the last days of summer.

ROBERT: Make yourself comfortable. I have to familiarize myself with where things are here.

TIFFANY: Anything you want to know—

ROBERT: Umm... The control button to open the roof?

TIFFANY: In that corner.

ROBERT: See it. Thank you.

TIFFANY: Have you worked for Sun Leisure for long?

ROBERT: First time. Before this, I worked at city pools. Lots of kids. Lots of roughhouse.

TIFFANY: You'll find this very different.

ROBERT: I'm looking forward to it. *(Looking out)* You have a terrific view. Both ways. River and city.

TIFFANY: There aren't many apartment buildings with private rooftop pools in this city. We're the highest building around. I think we have a more spectacular view than anybody.

ROBERT: I think you're right.

TIFFANY: You'll like it here.

ROBERT: I'm sure I will.

TIFFANY: I hope you manage to stay longer than our last guard.

ROBERT: Was there a problem?

TIFFANY: Some people said he wasn't friendly enough with the members.

ROBERT: I won't make that mistake.

TIFFANY: *(Flirtatiously)* I'm glad. ...We all like it when the guards are friendly.

(She goes to lie on a chaise in the sun. JOAN and her sister ABBY enter. They resemble each other somewhat. ABBY is slightly older and thinner. They are both intelligent and in good health. But their bodies look the way women's bodies look one side or the other of 70.)

ROBERT: *(To JOAN and ABBY:)* Good afternoon.

JOAN: Good afternoon.

(JOAN and ABBY sign in.)

ABBY: You must be the new pool guard.

JOAN: *(Aside to her sister:)* That's obvious, isn't it?

ABBY: Your name is—?

ROBERT: Robert.

ABBY: We're pleased to meet you, Robert.

ROBERT: Pleased to meet you,—*(He looks at the sign-in sheet.)*—Miss Delacourt.

ABBY: Mrs.

ROBERT: *Mrs.* Delacourt. ...

ABBY: You look exactly like my son!

JOAN: Abby—

(JOAN *gives* ABBY *a look.* ABBY *looks away.*)

ROBERT: Pleased to meet you— *(Again checking the sign-in sheet)*—Mrs. Oliver.

JOAN: Miss. Or Ms., if you prefer.

ROBERT: *Miss* Oliver. I'll get things straight eventually.

JOAN: Behind our backs people call us the Olive Sisters. You're free to do that. I'm Joan. She's Abby. And, yes, we're not so old that you can't call us by our first names.

ROBERT: Oh, I couldn't. I—*(He looks at the sign-in sheet.)* You don't live in the same apartment?

JOAN: It's because we don't live together that we're still talking to each other!

ROBERT: Didn't mean to pry. I—

JOAN: Think nothing of it. Welcome to The Beach in the Sky—and all the denizens thereof.

ABBY: We're a good lot—most of us—most of the time.

JOAN: But when some of us aren't—well, that's what makes your job interesting!

(JOAN *and* ABBY *go to sit at the umbrellaed table.*)

(ALEXIS MANNING, TIFFANY'S *mother, in her mid-40s, enters, wearing street clothes. She is a tall angular woman who takes great care of her clothes and her person. As she enters,* ABBY *says, aside, to her sister:*)

ABBY: Oh, my God, it's the Shark!

ALEXIS: Tiffany, what are you doing here? You know you're supposed to—

(She starts to cross to TIFFANY. ROBERT *stops her in her tracks, calling out:)*

ROBERT: Please don't walk in the pool area with street shoes!

ALEXIS: *(Offended)* I beg your pardon—

ROBERT: I'm sorry. They track in dirt and stones from outside. That's dangerous. People go barefoot here.

ALEXIS: I'm aware that people go barefoot here. I am a long time member of this pool.

ROBERT: Then you know that—

ALEXIS: No guard has ever stopped me before.

ROBERT: They should have.

ALEXIS: *(Aside to her daughter, who has come over to her at the entrance:)* Who is this fellow?

TIFFANY: Robert. New pool guard. He's kind of nice.

ALEXIS: A little too authoritative for my taste. ...It's time for you to leave for your piano lesson.

TIFFANY: Oh, Mum! Do I have to?

ALEXIS: I told you you are taking lessons till you graduate from high school.

TIFFANY: Two more years of this will kill me!

ALEXIS: At least you'll die being able to play the piano. You need some accomplishments to put on your college applications.

TIFFANY: Tell them I can swim like a fish!

ALEXIS: But you can't.

TIFFANY: So what? You can *say* it! *(She pulls off her robe and starts for the pool area.)*

ALEXIS: Tiffany—!

ROBERT: *(Hurrying after* TIFFANY*)* If you're going to swim, always make sure I'm in the pool area! And you ought to be wearing a cap—!

(Rushing out after TIFFANY, *he passes* ALEXIS, *who says:)*

ALEXIS: You really are a stickler for the rules, aren't you!

ROBERT: Yes, Ma'am. I'm going to see that you have the best-run pool in town!

(We hear a splash. He exits to the pool. ALEXIS *exhales in frustration, turns and exits into the building. The* SISTERS *exchange a smile.)*

JOAN: The Shark has lost today's skirmish!

ABBY: She still doesn't say hello to us.

JOAN: To women of her age, we are invisible.

ABBY: Invisible...

(The lights begin to change. ABBY *goes to a chaise, lies back and falls asleep.* JOAN, *in her own light, comes forward and says to us:)*

JOAN: The Shark doesn't want to know that, if she lives long enough, we are what she will become. The lined faces, the grey hair, the sagging breasts. She thinks, if she doesn't look at us, it won't happen to her. And who are we to tell her otherwise?

My sister and I have lived in this building since it was built, over thirty years ago. She with her husband, me with the man I never married, but who, for decades until his death, was the center and the sharer of my life. My—friend—and I were too devoted to freedom to ever want the bonds of marriage. Abby was different. She wanted marriage—and children. But an accident took her only child, her son. And several years ago death took her husband. So both of us are saddled with that awful label—"widows".

Abby and I are both retired academics. I taught English, she taught "SocRel". The science of social relations. I don't think it's really a science, but that's another story. This pool is certainly a rich mine for research in SocRel. At this hour of the afternoon, when the men are all busy at the office, the place is a study in the Ages of Woman. The young who talk only of the future. The midlife women who are totally obsessed with the present day. And we—elders—I hate the word—who don't want to find ourselves dwelling on the past but so often find ourselves talking about it—or comparing things to it.

Now that Abby and I are no longer teaching, we amuse ourselves endlessly, watching everyone's behavior at the pool. We know nothing of their home lives. But we speculate.

And now, with this new pool guard, Robert, there's a new dynamic, a new atmosphere. He's not like any that we've had before. Brighter, I would say. With a good deal more intellectual curiosity. He's brought a new sense of life to the mix. It will be very interesting to see how things change!

(Blackout. Music.)

(Early September. ALEXIS *emerges from the pool area, drying herself off after a swim.* ROBERT *follows her into the solarium.* ABBY *is reclining on a chaise, reading—but also silently observing.)*

ALEXIS: The water is freezing! Raise the temperature!

ROBERT: I'm not allowed to, Mrs. Manning. Germs thrive in water that's—

ALEXIS: For God's sake, who's swimming in that water—humans or germs!

ROBERT: It's my job to see that it isn't both. The Rules of the Pool say—

ALEXIS: I am tired of your quoting the rules of the pool to me, Robert! If you don't do something about the temperature of the water, I will speak to your supervisor.

ROBERT: You're free to do so. I think you'll find that he'll agree with me.

ALEXIS: I'm going to warm up in the sauna. When Tiffany comes, tell her where I am.

ROBERT: I will, Mrs. Manning. Enjoy your sauna.

(She gives him a look and exits off right. ABBY *says to him:)*

ABBY: She's a Complainer. Pay no attention.

ROBERT: I try, but I can't please everybody.

ABBY: My son was like you. Always wanted to please. That's why it was so very hard when—when I lost him.

ROBERT: I'm sorry.

ABBY: It was a bright day in September, just like today, when he—. ...It happened so suddenly—

ROBERT: That must be very hard. *(His brow knitting with his own concerns)* Harder even than when someone is very ill and you know it's inevitable that—

(A woman enters with her daughter. They are CLAIRE PALMER *and her daughter,* JENNIFER. CLAIRE *is pleasant and composed with a quality that is slightly recessive.* JENNIFER, *16 or 17, is unassuming and steady, but behind her quietness is clearly someone very intelligent.* CLAIRE *says to* ROBERT:)

CLAIRE: I'm Mrs. Palmer, apartment 9C. This is my daughter Jennifer.

ROBERT: Oh, yes, Mrs. Palmer. We received your application and check. All's in order. Welcome to the pool.

CLAIRE: We just moved here from San Diego. So warm there. We felt it would be nice to be able to swim in a climate where it can sometimes get so cool. Anything else you need from us?

ROBERT: Just sign in, please. Name, apartment number and time. The rules for the pool are posted outside on the bulletin board. But I see you already know the few things you're supposed to do. *(Both are in sandals and have bathing caps.)* I'm Robert.

CLAIRE: Pleased to meet you.

JENNIFER: Hi.

ROBERT: Hi. Let me know if you have any questions. Glad to have you with us.

*(*CLAIRE *and* JENNIFER *cross to find a place to put their bath towels. As they pass* ABBY, CLAIRE *says:)*

CLAIRE: Hello.

ABBY: Hello! *(Aside, to herself:)* She spoke to me! She actually spoke to me! *(To* CLAIRE:*)* You don't seem to know that I'm invisible

CLAIRE: I beg your pardon?

ABBY: Nothing. ...You're new to the building?

CLAIRE: Just moved in three days ago. Joining the pool is a bit of an indulgence for us. But we thought it would help us adjust to the northern climate.

ABBY: You'll like the building. Clean, well-run, friendly—for the most part.

CLAIRE: That's good to hear. Frankly, the rents seem—astronomical.

ABBY: At least it's rent controlled. My sister and I have lived here so long that for us it's quite a bargain. Though I know that for new tenants—

CLAIRE: It'll be all right. My husband assures me it's the way things are in this city. Anyway, we wanted a place near Jennifer's school. She'll be starting—

(At that moment, ALEXIS comes out of the sauna area like a whirlwind and confronts ROBERT:)

ALEXIS: The sauna isn't working!

ROBERT: It takes time to heat up.

ALEXIS: I waited and waited.

ROBERT: Did you turn the dial past the click point?

ALEXIS: Of course I did. It's cold. Ice cold. Everything about this entire place is like an icebox.

ROBERT: I'll see what I can do about it.

(He starts to exit toward the sauna. Seeing that JENNIFER is about to head for the pool, he says to her politely:)

ROBERT: Please don't go into the pool until I return.

JENNIFER: I won't.

(As he heads toward the sauna, ALEXIS throws after him:)

ALEXIS: I don't know what things are coming to in this building!

(ROBERT goes out. CLAIRE has been studying ALEXIS intently. Now she says to her:)

CLAIRE: Excuse me.

ALEXIS: *(Annoyed)* Yes?

CLAIRE: Aren't you Alexis Hall?

ALEXIS: I was. I'm now Alexis Manning.

CLAIRE: I think we were at Wellesley together. I'm Claire Palmer. Was Claire Griffin. We were in the same class.

ALEXIS: Were we?

CLAIRE: Yes. I majored in art. You majored in—

ALEXIS: Government. Thought it would be a snap. It was not. *(Looks at her)* Now I remember you. Didn't you do cartoons for the newspaper?

CLAIRE: Guilty.

ALEXIS: You did a vicious one of me once.

CLAIRE: I'm sure I didn't mean it to be vicious. It must have just been inept. I apologize.

ALEXIS: Apology accepted.

CLAIRE: We've just moved in. It's nice to know I know someone here already.

ALEXIS: What floor are you on?

CLAIRE: Ninth.

ALEXIS: Ah. ...We're on the thirty-third. Do you look out on the river or the city?

CLAIRE: The city.

ALEXIS: That's a shame. River view, on a high floor, that's the best. On the lower floors you're so boxed in by surrounding buildings, it's not like living in the same place at all!

CLAIRE: This apartment was available. Affordable. And we're near Spence.

ALEXIS: Oh, is your daughter going to Spence? So's mine. *(To* JENNIFER:*)* What grade are you in?

JENNIFER: Eleventh.

ALEXIS: Why so is Tiffany! Spence is so hard to get into. I'm surprised they'd accept a transfer into the eleventh grade.

CLAIRE: *(Modestly)* I guess Jennifer managed to impress them.

JENNIFER: *(Embarrassed)* Mom—!

CLAIRE: I wasn't boasting, love. But I am glad you managed it. *(To* ALEXIS:*)* I think it would be lovely if we could get our two girls together.

ALEXIS: *(Cool)* We'll have to arrange it sometime.

CLAIRE: And perhaps you and—and your—husband—? *(She isn't sure* ALEXIS *has one.)*

ALEXIS: Yes. I have a husband.

CLAIRE: Perhaps the three of you would like to come down and join the three of us for dinner one night.

ALEXIS: *(Fending it off)* How kind. But Darren usually works late. Venture capitalism is a twenty-four hour a day business. What does your husband do?

CLAIRE: He's—he's an idea man. Loves to think up things. Invent things. Goes in many directions seeking many different types of opportunities. That's why we moved here. City of opportunity, he said—at least we hope it is.

ALEXIS: *(Puzzled and unimpressed)* I see—well—that sounds—extremely interesting.

(ROBERT *returns.*)

ROBERT: Sauna's heated up now. You can go in. You hadn't, actually, turned the dial past the click point.

ALEXIS: I'm sure I did. It just didn't work.

(She exits to the sauna in a huff. JENNIFER *puts on her bathing cap and goes into the pool area.* ROBERT *follows. As* CLAIRE *is about to go toward the pool,* ABBY *says to her:)*

ABBY: Interesting that you and Mrs. Manning knew each other.

CLAIRE: I wouldn't exactly say "knew each other". Everybody knew *her*, but she didn't know everybody. She stood out from the crowd—if you know what I mean. *(*CLAIRE *goes toward the pool and exits.)*

ABBY: *(To herself:)* Oh, I do. I most certainly do.

(Blackout. Music.)

(Another autumn day. ABBY *and* JOAN *are standing, doing aerobic exercises. As they stretch, they say:)*

ABBY: And the Shark turned to her and gave her this look of "Oh, do I know you?", and this lovely woman either didn't clue in to the fact she was being lorded over, or chose not to recognize the fact. She went on sweet as honey while the Shark mowed her down with "You live on the ninth floor? I live on the thirty-third. You look at bricks? I look at water. Your daughter got into Spence? Mine has gone there since she was teething! You invite us to dinner? My dear, I wouldn't take a bite of your cooking unless it was prepared personally by Escoffier himself!"

JOAN: I assume Madame Shark did not invite the new arrival to dinner at her place—which I think would be socially correct in the circumstances.

ABBY: Are you kidding? I don't think she would allow this sweet thing—who obviously is nowhere near as well-heeled—the other side of her firmly closed apartment door. Besides, there's a bit of a mystery there.

JOAN: What mystery?

ABBY: The Shark's husband seems always to be among the absent. The Accumulator, name of Darren, by the way, not only works days—he works nights. Are his absent nights spent alone, that's what I'd like to know.

JOAN: Oh, you're impossible. Always inventing life stories for people.

ABBY: Social relations. It's what I'm trained in. I am going to make a list of the Shark's Complaints and Competitions. Complaints, Competitions and Confrontations. The three C's. She's a mine of material. You should write a novel about her.

JOAN: I have quite enough to do thinking about the hidden meanings which link the works of Hawthorne and Melville.

ABBY: Believe me, Sis, the hidden meanings in the lives in this building could outdo Nathaniel and Herman any day!

JOAN: *(Upset. Stopping exercising.)* Thanks. Thanks very much.

ABBY: What's the matter?

JOAN: You've done this all our lives.

ABBY: What?

JOAN: This. Belittling what I do. You know I've been involved with this work for the better part of three decades. You know I'm close to being ready for publication. And you say, with great ease, that these authors are not worth looking at, that I should look, instead, at what *you're* looking at—the people in this building!

ABBY: I didn't mean—

JOAN: You never mean. You just don't think, that's all. And people wonder why, now that we're both "widowed"—alone—whatever—we don't share one apartment! I couldn't stand to live with you if we had an apartment the size of Versailles!

ABBY: Joan! I'm sorry! Believe me, I—

JOAN: Oh, God, Abby. I'm sorry, too. Funny, it's you who usually flakes, this time it's me. It's just that—I'm coming down to writing the final chapters. The conclusions. There's a raft of academics out there waiting to jump on any original insights and say they have no basis in fact. I have an editor screaming for the pages and a publisher adamant about setting a publication date. And here I am, doing aerobics, devoting myself to gossip and quarreling with the one person in this world I truly care about.

ABBY: You're exhausted. Why don't I try to make dinner for both of us tonight? Something really simple. Omelettes. Only—unfortunately, last week, I broke my spittoon.

JOAN: Your spittoon?

ABBY: What?

JOAN: You said "spittoon". You said you broke your spittoon.

ABBY: Did I say that? I didn't mean to. I mean—what do they call that thing? That turning thing.

JOAN: Spatula.

ABBY: Spatula. Yes. I'll have to borrow your spatula. Of course.

JOAN: *(Worried)* Of course.

(Blackout. Music.)

(When the lights come up, we hear TIFFANY'S *and* JENNIFER'S *voices from the pool area.)*

TIFFANY: *(O.S.)* Hey, Jennifer! Race you to the deep end!

JENNIFER: *(O.S.)* Gotta leave. Gotta study.

TIFFANY: *(O.S.)* Come on! Just once!

JENNIFER: *(O.S.)* All right.

(We hear major splashing as they race. Then:)

TIFFANY: *(O.S.)* Okay. You won that one. I got off course. Race you one out of three.

JENNIFER: *(O.S.)* Next time, Tiffany. I've gotta go.

*(*TIFFANY *and* JENNIFER *come out of the pool area toweling themselves off.)*

TIFFANY: I wish Robert hadn't been watching. ...You've got speed. I don't. I could use swimming lessons. ...Lessons! That's it! I'll hire him to give me lessons!

JENNIFER: Is he allowed to do that?

TIFFANY: I don't see why not. I bet he wouldn't mind making a few extra bucks. I thought of pretending to drown so he could save me. But he'd probably bar me from the pool. No, I'll hire him to give me lessons!

*(*JENNIFER *takes off her swim cap.* TIFFANY, *who wasn't wearing one, begins to dry her hair on a towel.* ROBERT *comes into the solarium area from the pool.)*

ROBERT: I keep telling you, Miss Manning—

TIFFANY: Tiffany.

ROBERT: —that you always have to wear a cap.

TIFFANY: *(Flirtatiously)* Yes, Robert.

ROBERT: This is the last time I can allow you to go in without one. Please remember.

TIFFANY: Yes, Robert. I will. Thing is—mine tore.

ROBERT: Get another.

(He starts to go to his desk. She wants to continue some communication so she says:)

TIFFANY: Is there any particular kind of cap you think is best?

ROBERT: One that keeps your hair dry—and keeps strands from falling into the pool and clogging the drains.

TIFFANY: You wouldn't know where to get one, would you?

ROBERT: In your neighborhood, I have no idea. Ask your friend.

TIFFANY: She got hers in San Diego. Have you no suggestions?

ROBERT: Look on the web under "bathing caps".

TIFFANY: But a store. Can't you think of a place where I could see and touch them? If your sister needed a bathing cap, where would you tell her to go?

ROBERT: If I had a sister, I'd tell her to use her own initiative. *(He takes the broom and goes back into the pool area.)*

TIFFANY: He's so rough. I love it! But he's so impersonal! Tells us nothing about himself or where he lives.

JENNIFER: What do you want to know for?

TIFFANY: I don't know. I just do. I like him better than I like anybody. Before this, all our guards were Latino. Really lower class. But Robert, he's a possibility, if you know what I mean.

JENNIFER: You mean you're thinking of dating him?

TIFFANY: Why not? He's distant and severe—but that makes him all the more exciting! Whatever you do, don't let on to my Mother! She'd have a fit!

(Blackout. Music.)

(December. It's very snowy outside. ROBERT opens the corridor door with a key and comes in. He takes off his winter jacket. He is carrying a small sack tied with ribbon. He says to us:)

ROBERT: Someone's been leaving me cookies. Not store bought. Home made! Sometimes they're at the door when I come to unlock it. Other times, I might leave the solarium to be at the pool—and when I get back, these little offerings are on my desk. At Halloween there were bats and ghosts and jack-o'-lanterns. At Thanksgiving there were turkeys and pumpkins and pilgrims in tall hats. *(He unties the ribbon, opens the package and looks in.)* Ah. A snowman. A frosted star. A Christmas tree. A little early, but welcome. They're always very tasty. And they're always wrapped. Someone actually recognizes that no food is allowed in the pool area. *(His cell phone rings. He answers it.)* Hello? Yes. I made it safely. A little delay on the subway because of the snow, but it was fine. ...Guess what? More cookies! I'll bring them home to you. ...No, I still have no idea who they're from. ...Secret admirer? I don't think so. Put it this way: They're good. But not as good as yours. ...How are you feeling? ...Don't bother to wait up. The pool closes at nine tonight. I'll be home as soon after that as I can. Angela said she was going to drop in to see you. Now don't start treating her like a future daughter-in-law. She's just a friend! If she does come by, tell her I'll see her tomorrow. *Te amo, madre. Buenas noches. Adiós.*

(Blackout. Music.)

(Another winter day. ALEXIS *is confronting* ROBERT:*)*

ALEXIS: About these swimming lessons. Tiffany says she's getting nowhere!

ROBERT: She's perfectly free to stop them if she thinks so.

ALEXIS: Are you saying she's not a good student? Maybe it's that you're not a good teacher.

ROBERT: She doesn't like criticism.

ALEXIS: Who does.

ROBERT: I tell her things, she hardly listens. Or, if she hears and understands me once, the next time she comes, she just—forgets.

ALEXIS: What would you say is her basic problem?

ROBERT: Insubordination.

ALEXIS: I mean with her swimming!

ROBERT: She doesn't breathe correctly. She doesn't like to put her face in the water. You can't swim well if you don't put your face in the water.

ALEXIS: Show me what she should be doing.

ROBERT: *(Demonstrating the breast stroke)* The right arm should go straight up, the face should be turned to the left and out of the water and she should be breathing. Every time the right arm pulls down and the left takes a stroke, the face should turn to the right and go into the water.

ALEXIS: Show me how to do it. Maybe I can show Tiffany.

(She puts her arm up indicating he should demonstrate on her. He takes her arms, then head, showing her how to breathe and do the strokes.)

ROBERT: One ...two. One ...two. It's very simple.

ALEXIS: Yes. I see. It *is* simple. *(She is attracted to him.)* Maybe *I* should take lessons.

ROBERT: If you wish, I'd be happy to teach you.

ALEXIS: I'd like to learn. *(A pause, then:)* By the way, Tiffany said you didn't tell her how much the lessons would cost. How much do I owe you?

ROBERT: I don't like taking money. She hasn't learned anything.

ALEXIS: I insist. How much do you want? And to whom should I make out the check?

(He says nothing.)

ALEXIS: Your full name, Robert.

(He doesn't answer.)

ALEXIS: You'd prefer cash?

ROBERT: If you don't mind.

ALEXIS: I don't mind at all. And if you don't mind, maybe *I'll* be the one to decide how much the lessons are worth—when we see how we get along.

(Blackout. Music.)

(February. JOAN *is sitting in a chair, reading.* JENNIFER *arrives and signs in. As she does, something in the sign-up sheet catches her eye. As she crosses the space, she greets* JOAN:*)*

JENNIFER: Good afternoon.

JOAN: *(Looking up from her book)* Oh. Good afternoon.

JENNIFER: How's the water?

JOAN: Haven't gone in yet. There was some cold air seeping through the cracks between two of the windows. Robert's taking care of it. I'm surprised to see you here at this hour.

JENNIFER: It's study period. Thought I'd take a break for a few minutes before I have to go back to the books. Mid-terms loom.

JOAN: Yes. I remember.

JENNIFER: I have to do well. It's all going to count on our college applications.

JOAN: That's right. You're a Junior. Things get rather serious now, don't they?

JENNIFER: Very. I'm trying for scholarships, so I have to get good grades.

JOAN: I understand.

JENNIFER: *(After a pause)* Excuse me—

JOAN: Yes?

JENNIFER: I wondered—I saw the name Oliver on the sign-up sheet. Might you be the Joan Oliver who wrote an essay in this book I have—on American Literature?

JOAN: *(Surprised to be recognized)* Why—yes, I am.

JENNIFER: That's really interesting! I used your essay as a reference for a paper I wrote last month.

JOAN: You study Hawthorne and Melville in High School now?

JENNIFER: We could choose whatever books we wanted. I chose *The Scarlet Letter* and *Billy Budd*.

JOAN: Did you! Why did you choose those?

JENNIFER: I thought it would be really interesting to compare the two. Do you have to succeed to be heroic? And what is the meaning of justice when someone's deeds seem to be bad but the people themselves seem essentially good.

JOAN: Interesting point. Billy Budd dies for mutiny and murder but seems innocent. And Hester Prynne, although she has a baby out of wedlock, also seems to be unjustly condemned.

JENNIFER: I was thinking—if Billy Budd met Hester Prynne on the street, would they think each other heroic? Would she think him ridiculously naive? Would he think of her as nothing but a bad girl and not even deign to say hello? I mean, would each have tolerance for the other? I mean, as readers, we have compassion for each of them, but if they came in contact with each other, would they feel the same?

JOAN: That's a very original approach. I never thought about those two that way.

JENNIFER: It's tricky, isn't it—to somehow "live" according to your own lights without having society destroy you in the process.

JOAN: Yes, it is tricky. But living any other way makes one's whole life a lie.

JENNIFER: *(After a moment's thought)* Yes. It does, doesn't it. And who would want to live a whole life not being who you really want to be or acting how you really want to act. ...I liked your essay. It's—a privilege—to know you.

(She goes off to swim. At that moment, ABBY enters, sits beside JOAN and takes out her knitting.)

JOAN: Can you believe it? I've just been having a talk about Hawthorne and Melville with that young Jennifer. She's read them both and has some truly original ideas.

ABBY: At her age? Miraculous.

JOAN: She has promise, that girl.

(ALEXIS and CLAIRE enter.)

ABBY: Oh, dear! Here comes the Shark—followed closely by the Minnow.

(As the WOMEN sign in—)

ABBY: What'll we be subjected to today? Complaints, Competitions or Confrontations?

(As they pass JOAN and ABBY, CLAIRE says "Hello". ALEXIS walks by without looking at them. As CLAIRE and ALEXIS walk to the far side of the solarium and sit in chairs, ALEXIS says:)

ALEXIS: Can you imagine, my limo pulled into the driveway to pick me up and the doorman didn't even come out to open the door to help me in!

ABBY: *(Aside to* JOAN:*)* Complaints.

CLAIRE: Perhaps he was busy.

ALEXIS: He was not. He was completely absorbed behind his desk. Never looked up.

CLAIRE: Which doorman was it?

ALEXIS: Oh, I don't know. I don't know their names. There are supposed to be two on duty at all times anyway. Where was the other?

CLAIRE: They do get bathroom breaks—

ALEXIS: Oh, you're always making excuses. Do they help you into your car?

CLAIRE: I usually walk out and get a cab at the corner—when I get a cab. Actually, I'm getting quite good at the bus system. I'm planning to tackle the subways next.

ALEXIS: Good Lord, don't. Let me give you the name of the limo service I use.

CLAIRE: Alexis, really, I—

ALEXIS: Did you ever call my cleaning lady to see if she had some time free?

CLAIRE: We only have three rooms. We don't need a cleaning lady.

ALEXIS: And what about my nail salon? Did you ask for Kim? I told her you'd be coming in.

CLAIRE: I only have ten fingers. I can do my nails myself.

(As their talk continues and fades under, ABBY, *mocking* ALEXIS, *mutters, unheard by them:)*

ABBY: Do you live on a high floor or a low floor? Do you have a view of the river or are you stuck with city views? ...Do you take a limo or taxi? ...Do you have a Mercedes or a Honda? Do you park it in a garage or on the street? ...Do you have a place in the country—what country?— or do you spend your weekends imprisoned in town? ...Do you shop at Bergdorf's or JC Penney? ...Do you collect first editions or do you buy used paperbacks off a cart in the street? ...Do you go to the Met or the movies? Do you sit in the orchestra or the last row of the stalls? ...Do you—

JOAN: Abby! You're talking to yourself again.

ABBY: *(Becoming more and more agitated)* Do you have a regular table at the Four Seasons or stand in line at Kentucky Fried Chicken? Did you sprain your ankle or did you merely have the gout? Do you have a wall-sized plasma TV or a black-and-white portable? Do you have cable, inter-planetary internet access or a stupid old typewriter? Do you have an Ipod, Blackberry, Blueberry,

Strawberry or merely a telephone? Do you have video telephonic display with instant redial to every corner of the universe or do you—

JOAN: Abby! Please ! Calm down!

(ABBY *quiets down. She and* JOAN *are able to overhear* ALEXIS *and* CLAIRE.)

ALEXIS: I'm so bored! I don't know what to order in for dinner.

CLAIRE: I was thinking of broiling some sea bass—

ALEXIS: When I was in Chile we had the most splendid sea bass.

CLAIRE: And I'll steam some carrots, maybe, and make some rice—

ALEXIS: Now the Japanese really know how to do rice. When I was in Kyoto—

(ABBY *erupts again with:*)

ABBY: Are you just back from Zanzibar, Siam and the Himalayas or did you spend the year watching reality TV? Are you planning to climb the Matterhorn or take a stroll through the park? Are you about to cruise down the Nile or walk to the cleaners? Are you—

JOAN: Abby—

CLAIRE: And perhaps some fresh figs for dessert—

ALEXIS: Figs! Let me tell you! The absolute best come from North Africa. Last year, when I was in Morocco—

ABBY: (*To* JOAN, *in a fierce whisper:*) If I hear "when I was in—blah-blah" one more time—I will scream!

JOAN: (*Agreeing with humor, but warning*) Hush! The Shark will hear you!

CLAIRE: If I'm going to make those things, I really should get started—

ALEXIS: I hate eating early. Why, when I was in Spain—

(ABBY *screams—long and loud.* ALEXIS *and* CLAIRE *break off and stare at her.* ALEXIS *asks* JOAN:)

ALEXIS: Is there something wrong with your sister?

JOAN: No, nothing. She just stabbed her finger.

(ALEXIS *and* CLAIRE *continue their conversation.* ABBY *turns to* JOAN:)

ABBY: How can the Minnow stand her?

JOAN: Those exchanges. That's what's called being friends.

(*Blackout. Music*).

(*March.* ROBERT *is doing endless push-ups on the solarium floor. He is counting and is very serious about it. After a few moments,* TIFFANY *comes in quietly, wearing street clothes, and stands at the entrance. She watches him, admiring what he can do. But then, feeling a presence watching him,* ROBERT *stops and jumps up.)*

TIFFANY: Sorry! Didn't mean to make you lose count. How many was that?

ROBERT: *(Embarrassed at being seen)* I don't know. Fifty maybe.

TIFFANY: Wow.

ROBERT: I have to do them. I'm in training.

TIFFANY: For what?

ROBERT: For the triathlon.

TIFFANY: You mean in the Olympics?

ROBERT: Not exactly. It's a competition run by the state.

TIFFANY: What do you compete in?

ROBERT: Swimming. Biking. Running.

TIFFANY: When's it happening?

ROBERT: In May. ...Did you want something?

TIFFANY: *(Making it up)* Oh, umm... I thought I might have lost my bracelet up here. It was a Valentine's present. It has hearts on it. Did you find it?

ROBERT: *(He knows she's making it up.)* No. I didn't find a bracelet.

TIFFANY: Do you mind if I look for it?

ROBERT: No, but—*(He looks at her feet.)*

TIFFANY: Don't worry. I'll look in bare feet.

(He laughs.)

ROBERT: Would you excuse me for a minute? The water level is low. I have to go down to the control room to turn on the taps. I assume, while I'm gone, you won't go in swimming in your street clothes.

TIFFANY: Don't worry.

ROBERT: I'll be back in a second.

(He goes out. She takes off her shoes. Then, with one eye on the door, she pretends to be looking for her bracelet. But as soon as she's sure he's gone, she goes over to his desk. She looks through his things, his papers. An envelope catches her eye. The name on the envelope puzzles her. She opens the letter. She looks at the page inside. Her mouth and eyes open wide in surprise—and then understanding. This explains everything! Hearing someone approaching from outside, she slips the page back into the envelope. JENNIFER *enters, in street clothes.)*

TIFFANY: Jennifer—!

JENNIFER: There you are. I got your message. What is it?

TIFFANY: I was wondering if you'd cracked the math assignment.

JENNIFER: Yes. Did you want me to go over it with—

TIFFANY: Never mind. I have something to tell you. I should have guessed before—but now I know. His name isn't Robert. It's Roberto!

JENNIFER: How do you know that?

TIFFANY: Look yourself! There's an envelope on his desk—with his application for the triathlon inside.

JENNIFER: You opened his mail—?!

TIFFANY: Oh, come on, Jennifer. I had to find out if the person the envelope was addressed to was him. "Roberto Rodriguez!" ...Wouldn't you just know? If you're going to be a "Roberto", you should definitely be a "Rodriguez!"

JENNIFER: What has this got to do with anything?

TIFFANY: He's been passing! I wondered how come every other pool guard we've ever had was Hispanic, while he—. And he turns out to be one of them after all!

JENNIFER: So what?

TIFFANY: So that's why he didn't want my mother to pay for her and my swimming lessons with a check! We'd have to know his name, his real name!

JENNIFER: And now that you know it—?

TIFFANY: Suddenly it makes him all the more fascinating. "Roberto Rodriguez". A man with a secret! Don't you just love people who have secrets?

JENNIFER: Most people have. And I think the thing to do is to let them have them.

TIFFANY: Oh, I'll let him have his secret, all right. Till I think he should know that I know.

JENNIFER: I'm going down. ...SAT's in a week. Are you ready?

TIFFANY: If I'm not ready now, I'll never be. Cramming doesn't help.

JENNIFER: I think we should try to know as much as we can know.

TIFFANY: I think we can never know enough—so why try?

(JENNIFER *starts to leave. As she does,* ALEXIS *arrives, prepared for swimming.* JENNIFER *and* ALEXIS *nod to each other as they pass.* JENNIFER *goes out. When* ALEXIS *and her daughter are alone:*)

TIFFANY: Robert has gone down to turn on the tap. The pool needs more water.

ALEXIS: Oh, I hate to go into the pool when he's just done that! It's always cold water.

TIFFANY: You could have your lesson on dry land. Or you could just sit and talk. You wouldn't mind that at all, would you.

ALEXIS: What do you mean by that?

TIFFANY: Does Dad know you're taking swimming lessons with a hunk?

ALEXIS: I mentioned it. I wasn't certain he was paying attention.

TIFFANY: When does he ever pay attention?

ALEXIS: What are you doing up here? You'd better go study.

TIFFANY: *(Jealous)* I leave him to you, then. Just remember...

ALEXIS: What?

TIFFANY: Robert's less than half your age.

ALEXIS: He's too old for you.

TIFFANY: And too young for you.

ALEXIS: We'll just have to make the best of things, won't we.

TIFFANY: What are you planning—?

ALEXIS: What are you?

TIFFANY: Nothing.

ALEXIS: Likewise. Nothing.

TIFFANY: In that case—

ALEXIS: Yes. In that case. You'd better go hit the books, Tiffany.

TIFFANY: And leave him alone with you, is that it?

ALEXIS: I am taking a swimming lesson!

TIFFANY: Just make sure, that in that cold, cold water, you don't find an excuse to go mouth-to-mouth by pretending to drown!

(ROBERT *reappears. Passing him without speaking,* TIFFANY *goes.* ALEXIS *starts to remove her robe.*)

(*Blackout. Music.*)

(*Early Spring. At the table,* CLAIRE *is doing a crossword puzzle.* JENNIFER *is reading a school book.*)

CLAIRE: This crossword puzzle is impossible! ...What's a twelve letter word for obstinate?

JENNIFER: *(After a moment's thought)* ...Recalcitrant.

CLAIRE: Excellent! ...What's a four letter word for a curly-headed green vegetable?

JENNIFER: ...Kale.

CLAIRE: I don't know why I'm doing this. It should be you. ...What's a thirteen letter word for the director of a choir? Starts with a K.

JENNIFER: *(After longer thought)* ...Kapellmeister.

CLAIRE: I give up, love! No wonder you passed your SAT's with flying colors! "Kapellmeister!" He should sing your praises!

JENNIFER: I don't think a kapellmeister actually sings.

CLAIRE: *(Looking at her daughter fondly)* About you, he should.

(Suddenly ABBY enters, disturbed, wearing bedroom slippers.)

ABBY: Have you seen my sister?

CLAIRE: No. Sorry.

ABBY: I called her apartment. I even knocked on her door. She isn't there.

CLAIRE: I'm sure she's fine. Did you need something? Can we help?

ABBY: No. I just—. Have you heard—?

CLAIRE: Have we heard what?

ABBY: The building's going co-op!

CLAIRE: *(Stunned)* No. We didn't hear that.

ABBY: They're going to send a notice around. I just happened to be passing the manager's office and I overheard—. It's going to happen soon!

CLAIRE: What does this mean?

ABBY: I don't exactly know. I think it means we'll all be forced to buy our apartments.

CLAIRE: *Buy* them!

JENNIFER: When is this supposed to happen?

ABBY: Soon, I think.

CLAIRE: What do you mean by "soon"?

ABBY: I don't know. I don't know. It's so pre—, pre—

CLAIRE: Preposterous?

ABBY: Pre—precipitate. So sudden. We've been living here—almost—almost—

CLAIRE: Thirty-three years, I think your sister said.

ABBY: Yes. Thirty-three years. And suddenly—. Is she here? Is my sister here?

CLAIRE: No, Mrs. Delacourt. You look tired. Perhaps you should go down and rest. It may be just rumor. Let's not get ourselves upset until we get a printed notice.

ABBY: I left a message on Joan's phone telling her I was coming up here. I hope she—

(JOAN, *wearing street clothes, enters and stands on the steps.*)

ABBY: Joan! Where have you been? Did you get my message?

JOAN: It was extremely garbled. You said something about—

ABBY: The building's going co-op! Oh, Joan. What are we going to do? You know neither of us has enough money to buy our apartments!

JOAN: Abby, I hardly think this is the time or the place to discuss—

CLAIRE: *(To* JOAN:*)* I was telling your sister: So far it's all rumor. Let's not get upset about it before we know for certain.

ABBY: *(To* CLAIRE:*)* Could you afford to buy your apartment?

JOAN: *(Chastising her sister for this personal question)* Abby—!

CLAIRE: I don't mind answering. The answer is: Definitely not.

(JENNIFER *picks up her books.*)

JENNIFER: I think I'll go study downstairs.

CLAIRE: Don't think about all this, sweetheart. It may have nothing to do with us.

JENNIFER: I won't, Mum. ...I'm sure everything will work out just fine.

(*Kissing her mother lightly on the cheek,* JENNIFER *goes. When she has gone,* CLAIRE *says:*)

CLAIRE: I don't know what to tell her. If they don't allow renters to stay, we'll have to move.

JOAN: ...We will, too.

(*Blackout. Music.*)

(*Early Spring.* ALEXIS, *in exercise clothes and with a towel around her neck, enters from the exercise room. She says to us:*)

ALEXIS: This is what I've always wanted—to own a piece of the sky! Or at least a piece of this urban universe. Property! Owning something! It's what life is all about! My husband invests in companies. He says that's the way to profit. And he's certainly made a pile from it. But I want something I can touch and hold. Only if you own something solid—the roof over your head, the floor under your feet—are you really safe. ...I pray that this thing goes through and I can convince my husband that this is a great opportunity. The space we live in can be ours. We can do whatever we want with it! Redo the kitchen. Build in some cabinets. Break down a couple of walls. Sell the place at a handsome profit if we ever want to get rid of it. Yes. That's the way to convince him. Mention, down the line, if we sell, there could be a handsome profit. He'd understand that, my husband, my dearly beloved who so dearly beloves the bottom line. This is like hidden treasure falling into our laps! Who knew, when this day began, that the future would open up this way! I look ahead and I see—pure gold!

(Blackout. Music.)

(Late Spring. JENNIFER *is alone at the table, her head down, weeping quietly.* JOAN *arrives for a swim. She sees* JENNIFER *before* JENNIFER *sees her and immediately goes over to her.)*

JOAN: What is it, Jennifer? What's wrong?

JENNIFER: Oh. I'm sorry. I didn't mean—

JOAN: Is there something I can do?

JENNIFER: Thank you. Nothing. I'm sorry. I—*(Then, after a long pause:)* ...We have to move.

JOAN: *(Compassionate. She knew this was what it was.)* Oh...

JENNIFER: We've just moved here. I just made new friends. I just started at this school. And now—

JOAN: I know. I know.

JENNIFER: My father says—we can't afford to buy. Even at the "insider price" everybody talks about. People standing around grinning, with dollar signs in their eyes. A "bargain" they say! We can't afford it.

JOAN: Neither can we.

JENNIFER: Do you have to move, too?

JOAN: No. As it happens, they've finally told us my sister and I are "grandmothered" in. We've lived here so long we have some kind of seniority. Apparently the law says you can't throw old ladies out on the street.

JENNIFER: You're lucky.

JOAN: There are some advantages to ageing. *(She hands* JENNIFER *a Kleenex from the pack in her pocket.)* Where will you go?

JENNIFER: I don't know. My Dad says maybe we can find some place in the outer boroughs. If we do find some place we can afford, I might still be able to commute in to school here.

JOAN: So it might not be so hard after all...

JENNIFER: We've moved so often in my life. I've hardly been able to stay in any school two years in a row. My father—he's a wonderful man. A dreamer, really. Has an idea for this and an idea for that. Tries to get someone to back it.

But it never works out, for some reason. Bad luck sometimes. Or people take advantage of him and skip out with what should have been his.

JOAN: You're very fortunate.

JENNIFER: "Fortunate!"

JOAN: Because you love your father. I sense your mother loves him, too. And he must love you both.

JENNIFER: I think he does. But we're never secure—!

JOAN: Years from now, that will seem less important.

JENNIFER: It doesn't seem important to my mother.

JOAN: When you marry, you take your mate with all of his flaws—and he takes you with yours. If the love is great, the flaws don't matter. If it's not, the flaw is all there is.

JENNIFER: That may be true, but still—

JOAN: I think, no matter what, that you and your mother are secure in love. Eventually you'll discover—it's all that matters.

JENNIFER: You never married—?

JOAN: I "lived with someone"—before the time when that was common. I may not look it now—but my friend and I were rebels. We refused to bow to "bourgeois morality". We wanted freedom! Of course everybody lives that way now. It's an ideal that has become quite debased.

JENNIFER: What was he like—this man you didn't marry?

JOAN: My lover was, perhaps in my eyes alone, a very great man. But greatest of all was our love for each other. We both found that a bond stronger than any official attachment.

JENNIFER: You never thought of having children?

JOAN: That unconventional, we were not. "Single Mom" is such a common phrase nowadays. It has a courageous—even a beatific sound to it. That wasn't so when I was in my 20s and 30s. I regret the decision now. I would have liked to have had someone in my life—*(Quietly, after a moment:)*—someone like you.

JENNIFER: *(Touched. After a pause:)* May I stay in touch with you? After we've moved?

JOAN: I would like that. And don't worry. Life has these curves sometimes. It can be a damn twisty roller-coaster. But I have an instinct you are going to be able to hang on for the entire ride just fine.

(Blackout. Music).

(Early Summer. A great storm. Thunder and lightning. TIFFANY *and* JENNIFER *are*

playing catch with an inflatable ball. They throw it back and forth. JENNIFER *never misses.* TIFFANY *sometimes drops the ball.*)

TIFFANY: I'm going to try out for the soccer team.

JENNIFER: Really? Do you think you can make the cut?

TIFFANY: I'm sure I will. Mom's going to talk to the coach. We're big contributors to the school. The least they can do is let me play on the team! (TIFFANY *misses the ball and has to run after it.*) Are you going to try out?

JENNIFER: If I do get to stay at the school for senior year—and I have to commute—I don't think I would have the time.

TIFFANY: Too bad.

(ROBERT *enters from the pool area.*)

ROBERT: The roof's leaking. I'll have to climb up there. Have to go get a ladder.

TIFFANY: *(Flirtatiously)* We'll assist. Help steady it for you.

ROBERT: Thanks, but I think I'll be able to manage.

(TIFFANY *says, aside, to* JENNIFER:)

TIFFANY: Say you forgot your goggles.

JENNIFER: What?

TIFFANY: Pretend you forgot your goggles in the shower room. You have to go get them.

JENNIFER: *(Catching on that* TIFFANY *wants to be alone with* ROBERT:) Oh. Okay. *(Aloud)* I forgot my goggles. Be back in a minute.

(*She exits. When she has gone,* ROBERT *says:*)

ROBERT: I'm glad we have a minute alone.

TIFFANY: *(Romantically)* Are you?

ROBERT: I've wanted to talk to you—

TIFFANY: I'm very interested in hearing anything you might want to say.

(*He doesn't speak.*)

TIFFANY: What is it you want to talk to me about?

ROBERT: ...The cookies.

TIFFANY: The cookies? What cookies?

ROBERT: The ones you've been leaving on my desk.

TIFFANY: I haven't—

ROBERT: Come on. Own up. I appreciate your thoughtfulness, but—

TIFFANY: I haven't left you cookies. But if you want me to, I will—Roberto.

ROBERT: *(Taken aback)* Why did you call me Roberto?

TIFFANY: I just felt like it. "Roberto." I like the sound of it. Don't you?

ROBERT: No. Not particularly.

TIFFANY: Why not?

ROBERT: I just don't. You don't like to be called anything but your real name, do you?

TIFFANY: You can call me Tiffano if you want to.

ROBERT: I don't want to.

TIFFANY: What do you want to call me?

ROBERT: Tiffany, I—

TIFFANY: Yes, Roberto—?

ROBERT: I told you—!

TIFFANY: Why are you so angry about it? Why don't you just be who I know you are!

(JENNIFER *returns with her goggles.* TIFFANY *and* ROBERT *are silent. There is a great crash of thunder, then lightning. There is the sound of rain pelting down on the glass roof.* ROBERT *says:*)

ROBERT: I have to go downstairs to see if they have a ladder tall enough to reach the leak. Don't go in while I'm gone.

(Thunder crashes, lightning flashes.)

ROBERT: I don't want anyone in the pool while there's lightning. It's dangerous.

TIFFANY: No it's not. The building's completely grounded.

ROBERT: Let's not test it, all right? I don't want you to get electrocuted.

TIFFANY: Nice of you to care.

ROBERT: It's just common sense.

TIFFANY: The other guards allowed it.

ROBERT: Well, I don't. So don't do it. *(He goes out.)*

TIFFANY: What a meanie!

JENNIFER: He's right about the lightning. I wouldn't feel right going into the water in such a big storm.

TIFFANY: I don't care. Who is he to tell me what to do?   *(She strips down to her bathing suit.)*

JENNIFER: You're not going in!

TIFFANY: I have soccer tryout practice in an hour. I can't wait till the storm passes over.

JENNIFER: You're not supposed to go in when the pool guard's not here anyway.

TIFFANY: He wouldn't do anything to me.

JENNIFER: Tiffany, don't—

TIFFANY: Who's going to stop me!

JENNIFER: Tiffany, please—

TIFFANY: I'm not going to get electrocuted!

(She dashes into the pool area. We hear a great splash!)

(Blackout. Music.)

(The next day. The sun is shining. Wearing day clothes, ALEXIS *is confronting* ROBERT:*)*

ALEXIS: How dare you tell Tiffany she can't use the pool for two weeks!

ROBERT: I told her not to go into the pool when I wasn't here. She disobeyed me.

ALEXIS: She used her own judgement.

ROBERT: Her judgement has nothing to do with it. Those are the rules.

ALEXIS: The rules! The rules!

ROBERT: It was a lightning storm—

ALEXIS: Did she get electrocuted?

ROBERT: No, but I told her—

ALEXIS: You have no right—

ROBERT: I have every right.

ALEXIS: I'll report you to your supervisor.

ROBERT: He'll back me up. If something had happened—

ALEXIS: Nothing did.

ROBERT: Your daughter has to know that I'm in charge here and what I say goes.

ALEXIS: You are a paid employee.

ROBERT: Paid to keep your daughter safe, Mrs. Manning. My word is law here.

ALEXIS: We are paying for the privilege of this club. You can't dock her—

ROBERT: I do have that power.

ALEXIS: I, too, have some power here. I want you to know that I'm running for President of the Board of the Owners Corporation of this building. As soon as the building goes co-op, I expect to be elected.

ROBERT: Good luck to you.

ALEXIS: I can report you to the management. You could lose your job.

ROBERT: I'd rather lose my job than not do it correctly.

ALEXIS: You don't seem to have any idea of your position here,—Roberto.

(He is silent.)

ALEXIS: Yes. Tiffany told me. Is there some reason why you don't want us to know who you really are?

ROBERT: You know who I am. I'm the person who runs your pool. And does it quite well, I believe. What my name is or is not has nothing to do with it.

ALEXIS: That's a matter for us to decide, isn't it? ...You are brash, rude and insubordinate. You have exercised your authority beyond all reasonable bounds. On top of this, by disguising your true identity you have shown yourself to be an imposter, a double-dealer, and a brazen-faced liar! Who knows what other deceptions you have foisted on us or are about to foist upon us!. ...You are in real trouble, "Roberto".

ROBERT: *(Protesting)* Mrs. Manning—

ALEXIS: *(Coming close to him suggestively)* On the other hand—there is a way for you to extricate yourself from your difficulties...

(She touches him seductively. He doesn't move.)

(Blackout. Music.)

END ACT ONE

ACT TWO

(At rise:)

(The following September. ROBERT *is straightening the chairs.* JOAN *and* ABBY *enter and sign in.* ROBERT *says:)*

ROBERT: Ah, Mrs. Delacourt. Ms. Oliver. Good to see you! How was your summer?

JOAN: Beautiful, Robert. We spent it in a small town high up in the Rockies. The air there is so cool and crisp.

ABBY: Joan was keynote speaker at a symposium on the American novel. I tagged along.

JOAN: Afterwards, we rented a cabin in the mountains. A wonderful place to clear the soul. Clear the mind... *(Something is worrying her as she looks at* ABBY.*)*

ROBERT: It's good to have you back.

JOAN: Any—developments—since we were here?

ROBERT: Only that it's harder working under a board of owners than it was when the building was run by an impersonal corporation. Everybody thinks they're your boss. Especially—

(He breaks off as ALEXIS *sweeps in. She signs in, then looks down and says:)*

ALEXIS: This floor is filthy!

ROBERT: I washed the floor last night before I left.

ALEXIS: Try washing it by day—when you can see the dirt! When Tiffany and I were in Singapore this summer we saw how pools should be run! You could use a lesson!

(As they go to relax on chaises, ABBY *turns to* JOAN *and says, aside:)*

ABBY: Complaints.

ALEXIS: There's a leaf on the floor!

ROBERT: Leaves fall—

ALEXIS: This one has been there for three days!

ROBERT: Are you sure it's the same leaf? It may be another.

ALEXIS: Don't be a smart aleck! If leaves are falling, it means the plants need watering.

ROBERT: I'm sure they've been watered enough, but if you think—

ALEXIS: Take care of it immediately! I reported you to your supervisor for insubordination once before. If you don't shape up, I am going to report you again. If I were you, I'd change my attitude. If you don't, you could find yourself out of a job!

(On her way to a chair beside the umbrellaed table she passes JOAN and ABBY without speaking to them. ABBY sticks her tongue out at her. ALEXIS stops in her tracks.)

ALEXIS: Did I see what I think I saw?

JOAN: I don't think so.

ALEXIS: See that I didn't.

(She sits and immediately takes out her cell phone. JOAN confronts her sister:)

JOAN: Why did you do that?

ABBY: You said we were invisible!

JOAN: We're not *that* invisible.

ABBY: I don't like the way she treats Robert. As if he were a servant. Ever since she got to be president of the owner's association, the Shark thinks she's the boss of the universe!

JOAN: I think she's tougher on him since she found out he's Latino.

ABBY: One of the doormen told me that, last Spring, she tried to chat Robert up and he turned a cold shoulder.

JOAN: I'd like to have been a fly on the wall for that confrontation.

ABBY: I'm glad he refused her. I'd hate to have the Shark as a daughter-in-law.

(JOAN looks at her sister, troubled at the remark but letting it pass. ALEXIS dials and says into her cell phone:)

ALEXIS: Mr. Barrett, there are marks on the wall of elevator three. Please have them washed off immediately. ...This is a luxury building, not a pig sty.

ABBY: *(To JOAN:)* She's in great form today! I must start taking notes! *(She takes pen and paper out of her sack and begins to take notes, her words a counterpoint to ALEXIS'S continuous flow.)* Dirty floor...Marks in elevator...

ALEXIS: *(Into the phone)* I'm not the building manager, *you* are. Why do all these grievances keep coming to me? The couple in 29F are still arguing at the tops of their lungs. You were told to speak to them!

ABBY: *(Writing)* Couple arguing—

ALEXIS: Some public areas are a disgrace to civilization. Sneakers, carriages, umbrellas, bikes in the hall. Those are strictly against the rules!

ABBY: *(Writing)* Sneakers, carriages, umbrellas, bikes in the hall...

ALEXIS: On the 18th floor, someone's cat is scratching the hall wallpaper!

ABBY: Cat scratching wallpaper...

ALEXIS: 16B insists on hanging their children's' drawings on their apartment door! That is not allowed!

ABBY: Children's' drawings on door. A hanging crime.

ALEXIS: I went from garbage room to garbage room yesterday and no one was sorting glass and paper and putting them into the receptacles!

ABBY: Glass, paper, glass, paper, glass, paper...

ALEXIS: But it *is* your responsibility! ...For heaven's sake, post signs! Do I have to do everything around here? ...In a building of this calibre you would think that neighbors would have consideration for one another! This is not a slum tenement! It's a first class, high class, exclusive, luxury accommodation which—

ABBY: *(Loudly)* The entire world has become one big phone booth!

(ALEXIS *breaks from her call and says:*)

ALEXIS: I am having a private conversation!

ABBY: Why don't you have it in private?

ALEXIS: *(To* JOAN:*)* Are you going to allow your sister to talk to me that way?

JOAN: She's a grown woman. If you wish to speak to her, speak to her yourself.

ABBY: *(To* ALEXIS:*)* You're very rude and very noisy.

ALEXIS: *(Furious)* You—RENTERS! I'll have you know that—*(She breaks off and turns to* ROBERT *who has been sitting at his desk inwardly enjoying listening to their exchanges.)* Are you going to deal with this?

ROBERT: I'm a pool guard, not a referee. This is outside my area of responsibility.

ABBY: *(To* ALEXIS:*)* You have no consideration for others. You have no compassion, no humanity, and your hair dye color is ridiculous for a woman your age!

ALEXIS: *(To* JOAN:*)* Is your sister out of her mind?

JOAN: My sister is suffering from a rare form of dementia: She says exactly what she's thinking!

ALEXIS: Madness!

(ALEXIS *leaves the area in a huff. Troubled and confused,* ABBY *quietly makes a note.*)

ABBY: Sister out of her mind...

(*Blackout. Music.*)

(*Autumn.* CLAIRE, *in her terry cloth robe, is reading. We can hear activity from the pool area and see its reflections on the walls.*)

CLAIRE: (*To us:*) It's so odd, coming to the pool when we no longer live here. The people at Sun Leisure said : "You paid for a two year's membership, so, as far as we're concerned, whether you're living in the building or not, you still belong to the health club." I could have asked for a refund instead. With Peter's latest ideas not quite catching on and my earning only a pittance drawing bits for a local paper we certainly could use the money. But with Jennifer commuting daily from our apartment in Queens to Spence, which is right in this neighborhood, I thought she'd like to be able to exercise in the pool —and see her friends. Not that Tiffany's a real friend. But Jennifer might just as well experience that kind of friend—the kind who doesn't want a comrade as much as they want an attendant, an audience. Learning to realize you're actually superior to the ones who think they're superior to you—it's a good life lesson. I think Jennifer's beginning to get the hang of it—quietly managing to go *mano-a-mano* with Tiffany—as I go *mano-a-mano* with Alexis—and not come away feeling wounded. It takes a lot of practice. To tell you the truth, I'm just beginning to get the hang of it myself.

(TIFFANY *and* JENNIFER *come out of the pool area after a swim.*)

JENNIFER: You ought to go in, Mom! The water's just the way you like it!

CLAIRE: Warm?

JENNIFER: So warm, Robert's threatening to lower the temperature. So hurry!

CLAIRE: Guess I could use the exercise. Okay. Here goes.

(*She takes off her robe and heads for the pool.* TIFFANY *turns to* JENNIFER, *as if continuing a conversation she doesn't want anyone at the pool to hear.*)

TIFFANY: You've got to come with me!

JENNIFER: No, Tiffany. How did you get his address?

TIFFANY: It was on that envelope I looked at last Spring.

JENNIFER: And you remembered it? Why?

TIFFANY: It helps us find out who he really is! Where he lives. That tells us a lot.

JENNIFER: Where does he live?

TIFFANY: In Spanish Harlem.

JENNIFER: So?

TIFFANY: So one day, when we know he's here on duty, I want you to take the bus with me and go up there and see exactly what kind of place he lives in and what his neighborhood looks like.

JENNIFER: I don't think we should—

TIFFANY: Come on, Jennifer. You like him, don't you?

JENNIFER: Yes, but—

TIFFANY: I think, if we want to really know him, we have to know what his life is like away from the pool.

JENNIFER: What does it matter? He's who he is—we can see that—I don't have to know any more about him.

TIFFANY: You're scared, that's all.

JENNIFER: I don't get to come up here often. When I come, I like to swim. It's nice to see Robert but—

TIFFANY: Roberto.

JENNIFER: —but I don't have time for running around. I have to study.

TIFFANY: Study! Study! You're as dull as you were when you lived here!

JENNIFER: Mid-terms are only a few weeks from now. And colleges count our senior grades. Aren't you concerned?

TIFFANY: Not much.

JENNIFER: I thought you said you were going to take the SAT's again.

TIFFANY: I won't do any better than I did the first time. Why kid myself. My Mom and Dad went to good colleges. They can always get me in.

JENNIFER: The only way *I'll* get in is by getting good marks.

TIFFANY: Oh, you're such a stick-in-the-mud. Are you up for this adventure, or aren't you?

JENNIFER: Go yourself, Tiffany. Let me know what you find out.

(*Blackout. Music.*)

(*Early Winter.* ROBERT *opens the pool area with a key and comes in somberly. He has a black armband around the sleeve of his jacket. He takes his jacket off and puts it over the back of his chair. Then he exits toward the equipment room with his duffel bag.*)

(ABBY *enters. She looks around. Seeing that* ROBERT *isn't there, she takes a small paper sack out of her bag and puts it on his desk. As she does, a pencil from his desk falls to the floor. Hearing the sound,* ROBERT *returns and sees her. He says:*)

ROBERT: So it was you!

ABBY: *(Taken aback at being discovered)* Oh, dear! ...Do you mind?

ROBERT: Not at all. *(He opens the sack and takes out a cookie.)* Why did you think you had to leave these anonymously?

ABBY: I thought you might prefer them to come from—someone younger.

ROBERT: No. I'm happy they're from you. They've been a lovely surprise. And all delicious. Wish I could eat them here. These look particularly tasty.

ABBY: They were always your favorites. I used to make them for you—every year on your birthday. Don't you remember?

ROBERT: *(Extremely puzzled)* I—

ABBY: I've missed you so. Why did you move so far away?

ROBERT: Mrs. Delacourt—

ABBY: There's not a moment since you were born that my thoughts haven't been with you. Don't you know that? I wanted to be in your life, be in it every day. I wanted to watch you grow. To keep you safe. To keep from your path anything that might harm you.

ROBERT: It's good of you but—

ABBY: I'm here to protect you and to love you. Every son, no matter how old he gets to be, must want that. Now that you've come back to me, a full-grown young man, bringing you sweet treats is the least I can do. You've no idea how happy it makes me—just to see you!

ROBERT: Mrs. Delacourt—

ABBY: Please—call me Mother.

ROBERT: I—

ABBY: Please. It's been so many years. I want—I need—to hear it. It's just a little word. Two syllables. ...Please...

ROBERT: *(After a very long pause)* ...Mother.

ABBY: Thank you. ...Thank you.

(Happy and content, she leaves. When she has gone, ROBERT touches the black band around the sleeve of his jacket, then murmurs:)

ROBERT: Madre...

(Blackout. Music.)

(Winter. ALEXIS, dressed from a session in the exercise room, is saying to CLAIRE:)

ALEXIS: You mean Jennifer applied only to Harvard?

CLAIRE: With her grades and test scores and a report on how her interview went, her adviser at Spence thought she'd have a very good chance. What about Tiffany?

ALEXIS: Taking tests has never been her strong suit. But my husband's on the boards of several institutions. And a big contributor. I'm not worried.

CLAIRE: I see. ...How are things in the building?

ALEXIS: I had no idea being president of the board would be a twenty-four hour a day job! If someone plays a piano too loudly, that's my responsibility. If someone's maid shakes out their mop onto the balcony below, that has to be settled by me. A psychiatrist was using his apartment as an office—with streams of patients coming for appointments! A woman on a low floor was running a catering service out of her kitchen. Oh, the oders! Another woman was entertaining too many male guests. I think she was running a bordello! I had no idea that people do the kinds of things they do! They behave as if they were royalty and it's a building full of nobodies!

CLAIRE: I'm not so sure about that.

ALEXIS: Don't tell me there are some somebodies here—and they're keeping it a secret!

CLAIRE: There's Joan Oliver.

ALEXIS: Oliver? You mean one of those old biddies who come so often to the pool you'd think they'd taken up residence?

CLAIRE: That's the one. Joan. You haven't seen the articles on her book?

ALEXIS: Her book?

CLAIRE: On Hawthorne and Melville. It's been very well reviewed. The critics say: "Most searching and original work ever done on these two writers in a decade."

ALEXIS: Really.

CLAIRE: I heard her interviewed on the radio yesterday. She's quite the celebrity.

ALEXIS: I didn't know.

CLAIRE: We never do know much about the people in our buildings, do we? What goes on behind those totally alike closed doors.

ALEXIS: No. We never know. ...Although, with what I've found out these months, because of my position, you're lucky you don't live here any more.

CLAIRE: Actually, we may be moving back in.

(ALEXIS *reacts as if receiving a blow.*)

(*Blackout. Music.*)

(February. ABBY and JOAN are doing a puzzle at the table.)

ABBY: He didn't send me a valentine.

JOAN: Why should he send you a valentine?

ABBY: A son should send his mother a valentine.

JOAN: Abby, Robert is not your son!

ABBY: The least he could do is—

JOAN: Please, dear. Don't go on this way.

ABBY: You mean—don't embarrass him by pointing out that he's neglected me?

JOAN: Yes. Exactly.

ABBY: Perhaps he thinks—she must know I love her—she doesn't need a store bought card.

JOAN: I'm sure that's it. ...Now try to find a place for this piece.

ABBY: All right. ...Getting a card from him would have been nice, though.

JOAN: Abby. Forget it!

ABBY: Didn't he grow up to be handsome?

JOAN: Think no more about it! Solve the puzzle, Abby.

ABBY: Right. Solving the puzzle.

(ABBY picks up a piece but is actually daydreaming. JOAN looks very worried. ALEXIS enters and signs in. She comes over to the women and says:)

ALEXIS: Good morning.

ABBY: *(To JOAN:)* She said good morning!

(ABBY said this loud enough for ALEXIS to hear, but ALEXIS decides to pretend not to have noticed.)

JOAN: Good morning.

ALEXIS: Nice weather today.

ABBY: *(To JOAN:)* She's talking to us! Maybe we're not invisible after all!

ALEXIS: *(Ignoring the remark. To JOAN:)* How are you? How are you—both?

JOAN: We're fine, thank you.

ALEXIS: Nice weather for February.

JOAN: Yes. Nice weather for February.

ALEXIS: *(To JOAN:)* ...I wanted to congratulate you.

JOAN: Congratulate me?

ALEXIS: On your reviews.

JOAN: Ah. The reviews.

ALEXIS: Claire Palmer told me about them. I didn't know you were somebody.

(JOAN *smiles.*)

ALEXIS: You know what I mean.

JOAN: Yes. I know what you mean.

ALEXIS: Nobody knows anything about anybody, do they?

JOAN: Well, we can know a great deal, but what you say is true. It's not much.

ABBY: *(Aside to* JOAN *but loud enough for* ALEXIS *to hear:)* She wants something.

JOAN: Abby,—

ALEXIS: *(To* JOAN:*)* Your sister's quite right. I have to admire her directness.

JOAN: Is there something I can do for you?

ALEXIS: As a matter of fact—it's about Tiffany. I'm afraid she won't get into any of the schools she applied to.

JOAN: I see.

ALEXIS: She's very smart. She just doesn't test well.

ABBY: You have money. Money talks. Couldn't you just buy—

JOAN: Hush, Abby. There are some things money can buy—and some things it can't.

ALEXIS: *(To* JOAN:*)* I thought—with your name—perhaps you could write a recommendation—

JOAN: *(The epitome of social grace)* I don't really know your daughter, Mrs. Manning.

ALEXIS: You've seen her for years here at the pool. You've watched her grow up.

JOAN: True. But in all that time, I don't remember her—or you—ever even saying hello to me.

ALEXIS: We like to grant people their privacy.

ABBY: Ha! "Privacy!"

ALEXIS: It's a sign of respect—not of neglect, I assure you.

JOAN: *(The soul of courtesy)* I hear what you're saying. I'll be happy to write. But you understand, I'd write exactly what I experienced. I'd have to say that I don't know your daughter very well, that for years we've seen each other at the pool, but that we've never actually talked to each other. I could say that she swims moderately well—if you think that would be some recommendation.

ALEXIS: What you're saying is—what you'd write wouldn't be helpful.

JOAN: You wouldn't want me to lie, would you?

ALEXIS: *(Icily)* Now I know why we've never talked in all these years. You're a cold heartless old woman!

JOAN: Old, in your eyes, perhaps. Yes. But as for the other adjectives, I think you're describing yourself.

ALEXIS: You harpy!

(ALEXIS *turns and starts to exit the area.* ABBY *says, loudly, to* JOAN:)

ABBY: You think *I'm* cracking up. *She's* cracking, too!

(ALEXIS, *furious, exits without turning.*)

(*Blackout. Music.*)

(*March. Early evening.* ROBERT *is alone at his desk, reading.* TIFFANY *enters in street clothes and pool clogs.*)

TIFFANY: Hello.

ROBERT: Oh, hello.

TIFFANY: You look surprised to see me.

ROBERT: This isn't your usual hour.

TIFFANY: My parents are both out. Not together. My father's at one of his interminable business meetings. My mother's out God-knows-where. I thought I'd come up and visit for a while.

ROBERT: They leave you alone?

TIFFANY: I'm a big girl now. Or didn't you notice?

ROBERT: I notice.

TIFFANY: I notice you, too.

ROBERT; *(Uncomfortable with her suggestiveness)* Are you going to swim?

TIFFANY: No. I just came up to talk. I was lonely.

ROBERT: Oh, come now. With your cell phone, your internet and a host of friends, I can't believe you're ever lonely.

TIFFANY: Everybody bores me. ...Except you.

ROBERT: I have to check the pool—

(*He tries to move toward the pool area, she blocks his path.*)

TIFFANY: I saw where you live.

ROBERT: What?

TIFFANY: I saw where you live. ...I took the bus up there and saw the building.

ROBERT: Whatever for?

TIFFANY: To know a little more about you.

ROBERT: I'm sure that's nice of you, but—

TIFFANY: I saw the little bodega downstairs from your apartment. Do you shop there?

ROBERT: Tiffany—. Miss Manning—.

TIFFANY: I saw the restaurant up the block where you must go with your girlfriend. Do you have a girlfriend?

ROBERT: Miss Manning, I—. I can't imagine why you'd—

TIFFANY: Can't you? I want to know all there is to know about you. I want to know what your life is when you're not playing pool guard. I want to know why you call yourself Robert when your name is Roberto.

ROBERT: My private life is my private life. It has nothing to do with what I do here.

TIFFANY: Why don't you use your real name here?

ROBERT: I can be Robert if I want. This is America. We can all be whoever we want.

TIFFANY: You're hiding something.

ROBERT: I'm just being who I want to be.

TIFFANY: What does your mother call you?

ROBERT: My mother is dead.

TIFFANY: She must have called you Roberto. I will call you Roberto.

ROBERT: Miss Manning, please—

TIFFANY: Would you take me out tonight after you get through here, Roberto?

ROBERT: No. I wouldn't.

TIFFANY: When the pool closes, will you come down to my apartment?

ROBERT: No. I absolutely will not.

TIFFANY: Why not?

ROBERT: You know why not.

TIFFANY: You think you're too good for me.

ROBERT: No.

TIFFANY: Too old for me.

ROBERT: No.

TIFFANY: Too what, then?

ROBERT: I think I'm too pool guard and you're too pool member. That's all it is. It's very simple.

TIFFANY: But—

ROBERT: Let's leave it at that, shall we?

TIFFANY: But I like you!

ROBERT: And I like you, too. But it's important that we keep our distance.

TIFFANY: You're a snob, Robert-Roberto.

ROBERT: And you're supposed to be home. Studying.

TIFFANY: You know where I live. When you close the pool tonight, I'll be waiting for you.

ROBERT: You can wait—but I won't come.

TIFFANY: Why not?

ROBERT: Because after hours, when the health club is closed, I swim. I'm in training.

TIFFANY: For the triathlon?

ROBERT: Yes.

TIFFANY: I thought that was last year.

ROBERT: Last year I came in second. This year I intend to come in first.

TIFFANY: I'll stay and time your laps.

ROBERT: No! Go home! Go to bed!

TIFFANY: With you—

ROBERT: Miss Manning, you are out of line here!

TIFFANY: *(Rejected, she suddenly becomes superior and authoritarian, like her mother.)* You're the one who's out of line, Roberto. I'm sure you know that when the health club is closed no one is allowed to swim in the pool. I could tell my mother on you. And you know how much power she has in this building!

(She goes.)

(ROBERT stands looking after her. These people, they're really too much.)

(Blackout. Music.)

(Spring. JOAN is sitting reading. CLAIRE enters, ready to swim.)

JOAN: Mrs. Palmer! I heard you moved back in!

CLAIRE: Yes. It's good to be back here.

JOAN: It's good to have you. ...I don't mean to pry, but—you must have been blessed with a reversal of fortune.

CLAIRE: My husband came up with an idea that really works. Someone has paid him ever so much—! ...Sorry. I don't mean to talk about money. But—I think—I hope—the security will be permanent this time.

JOAN: I hope so.

CLAIRE: I knew one of his ideas would work one day.

JOAN: I hope, for your sake, this is the beginning of untroubled times.

CLAIRE: *(After a pause)* If you don't mind my asking, how is your sister? I passed her in the lobby yesterday. We had a brief conversation. She—forgive me—she didn't seem to be making much sense.

JOAN: That happens a lot of the time now. Her mind wanders. She starts a thought—but then can't quite grab it out of the air.

CLAIRE: That must worry you.

JOAN: *(Hesitant, but needing to talk)* Last week she left a gas burner on in her apartment. If I hadn't happened to come down to visit, she could have—! ...I don't know what to do. She can't be left alone.

CLAIRE: I'm sorry to hear it.

JOAN: She had a cracker-jack mind. Crystal-clear diamond-hard insight.

CLAIRE: I thought that both of you—

JOAN: No. I was the dreamer. She was the one with the precise analytical mind.

CLAIRE: Perhaps she used it all up—and it deserves a rest.

JOAN: She seems happy—

CLAIRE: That's a blessing.

JOAN: Still. I don't know what it's going to be like for her—down the line.

CLAIRE: Time will tell.

JOAN: Time. The one irrefutable fact—as I think every time I put on my bathing suit.

(Seeing ALEXIS *enter,* JOAN *exits to the sauna.* ALEXIS *says to* CLAIRE*:)*

ALEXIS: Well! You're one of us again.

CLAIRE: Yes. There was only one vote on the board against us. Can't imagine who cast it. *(She knows.)* Apparently he—or she—voiced doubts about our financial stability. But the others approved us enthusiastically and—here we are.

ALEXIS: Yes. Here you are. ...What apartment did you finally buy?

CLAIRE: 44A.

ALEXIS: But that's two apartments together! Eight rooms!

CLAIRE: Yes. But don't worry. It's already paid for.

ALEXIS: Good heavens, do I seem worried?

CLAIRE: You must come up to dinner sometime soon. You and Tiffany and your husband. Somehow we didn't manage that when I lived here before.

ALEXIS: Kind of you. I accept. ...As for my husband—. Well. ...These things happen. Nights in business turned out to be nights with his secretary. It's the old, not very original, story.

CLAIRE: I'm sorry. We'll arrange for you and Tiffany to come to dinner very soon.

ALEXIS: If it's one of the alternate weekends on which I have her. Tiffany has chosen to live with her father. She didn't get into any of the colleges she applied to. I assume Jennifer did?

CLAIRE: Yes. She'll be going to Harvard.

ALEXIS: I wash my hands of responsibility for Tiffany's education. Maybe her father can make her understand what life is all about. I can't! You have to push to make the grade! It's competition every step of the way! But I can't tell her. She never listens to a single word I say!

(JOAN *reappears from the sauna.* ALEXIS *turns to her:*)

ALEXIS: Ah, Ms. Oliver, I've been wanting to talk with you. ...I've received many complaints about your sister. Her behavior—

JOAN: Her behavior?

ALEXIS: She wanders down to the lobby in her nightgown. ...She roams the corridors at night—singing at the top of her lungs! ...In the laundry room, she took everybody's clothes out of the dryers and folded them!

JOAN: She's an extremely neat person.

ALEXIS: She put everybody's underwear and towels in with everybody else's!

JOAN: I'm thinking of having her move in with me.

ALEXIS: Unless you can supervise her night and day, that might not be enough to curb her inappropriate behavior. I'm sure you're as aware as I that the best solution—for her, for you, for all of us—is for her to be institutionalized. As soon as possible.

(*Blackout. Music.*)

(*Late Spring.* ABBY, *wearing disheveled street clothes and slippers, is reclining on a* chaise. ROBERT *is sitting at his desk. As* ABBY *comes forward to talk to us, the light irises in on her.* ROBERT *disappears into shadow, not hearing her.*)

ABBY: I'm moving! Someplace very nice. With a room of my own. And lots of lawn. They'll cook for me. I do not like cooking. Cookies are all I know and all I wish to know. Perhaps they'll let me into the kitchen to make a few of those.

It's my brain, you see. I can't depend on it any more. It clears and clouds, clears and clouds. It goes out of focus. I cross the room to get something and can't remember what I came for. Entire years are gone from my memory. People in them, their names, their faces, have faded and disappeared—or merged. (*She looks over toward* ROBERT.) My mind has empty spaces in it. And I know it. That's the worst part. Knowing. I watch myself from the outside—watch my brain falling apart. And it was my good sturdy friend for all of my life. But now, everything and its opposite seems true—and not true. That should frighten me—but it doesn't.

As I move toward the end of my existence, I am obsessed by the wonder of life! Even in a tiny flea. The tiniest creature—a bug the size of a speck—has that inexplicable thing—that spark—that mysterious gift of life surging through it. ...But even the tiniest creature knows danger when it threatens. It scampers away as quickly as it can. To speed away from any force which might exterminate its spark.

But my little boy, my sweet little boy, with the spark of life running through him, did not know danger. He peddled peacefully on—on his little red tricycle—wheeling along the sidewalk as a great car backed out of a driveway. My little boy peddled peacefully, happily, into its path—and his spark was snuffed out—in the blink of an eye.

(JOAN *appears.*)

JOAN: That was long ago.

ABBY: (*To* JOAN:) Everything that ever was—is. All the awful things. All the triumphs. If once they were, they still are now. For I know this secret, little sister: Time does not exist. It's an illusion. All the pain that ever was exists forever. And all the joy that ever was—that's still here, too. In my cracking brain, in my dissolving mind, in my new little room, even if I forget it all, it will exist, forever. Even you, when you're not with me, will always be there.

JOAN: God keep you, Abby.

ABBY: You remember, when we were young, and one of us couldn't figure something out, we'd ask each other, "Which of us is using the brain?"

JOAN: I remember.

ABBY: You can have it now. It's all yours.

(ABBY *goes out.*)

(The lights dim. Music under. Time passes.)

(When the lights come up again, ROBERT *is still motionless in the shadows,* JOAN, *in her own light, says to us:)*

JOAN: It all goes so quickly! We were little girls together. Abby two years older than I. We were friends and rivals simultaneously. She did things. I was expected to do them as well as she—just two years later. Two years from today, will I be in the state that she is now?

How terrifying the speed of her descent! From word mistakes, to "senior moments", to a splendid world of seeing truth and speaking truth, she became the oracle who voiced what we in our infinite wisdom keep tacitly unspoken. She had risen to a plane where she knew, instinctively, it was too late for lies. But because of that she was forced to go live where what she had become would seem more "normal". She herself made the decision to move—away from all she knew. Away from me.

She's in a place we can afford. Cleaning out her apartment, I found the diary in which, over the years, she spoke of her love for everyone around her. For our mother and father—from whom she seemed so distant. And for me. ...Love. We never said that to each other. And now—we'll never say that to each other. ...Yesterday, when I went to see her, she didn't know who I was.

(A pause.)

And yet, in this strange world of truth-speaking, which the doctors tell me will devolve eventually into total non-communication, I have come to know her as I never knew her. She is my sister. She is the only flesh of my flesh. When she is gone, there will be—on this lonely island—only me.

(Blackout. Music.)

(Late Spring. Night. After hours. The door to the area is locked. The solarium is empty. Vigorous reflections animate the walls and ceiling—evidence that someone is swimming energetically. After a few moments, the key turns in the lock of the solarium door. ALEXIS *enters. She is dressed in going-out-for-the-evening clothes. It is evident that she has been drinking. She comes into the area, smiles when she sees the reflections and starts to descend the stairs. Then she remembers the prohibition against wearing street shoes. She falls into a sitting position on the stairs and, fuzzily, takes off her high-heeled shoes. In stocking feet, she weaves her way to the entrance of the pool area and stands there, observing the swimmer admiringly. The water stops churning.* ALEXIS *retreats farther into the solarium. Unaware that anyone is present,* ROBERT *comes out of the pool into the solarium, dripping wet, toweling himself off. After drying his face, he sees her and reacts with surprise.)*

ROBERT: You are not allowed to be here!

ALEXIS: You are not allowed to swim after hours!

ROBERT: How did you get in?

ALEXIS: I have a key. Till tomorrow, at least, I am still President of the Board.

ROBERT: What do you want?

ALEXIS: What were you doing?

ROBERT: You know what I was doing. Training. I'm at the pool every day, from early till late. Water, water everywhere but never a chance for me to swim!

ALEXIS: When's the big event?

ROBERT: Tomorrow.

ALEXIS: So you stole this time—

ROBERT: Was there something you wanted?

ALEXIS: Was there something you wanted me to want?

ROBERT: Only that you go and let me get dressed.

ALEXIS: *(Suggestively)* Do you have to get dressed?

ROBERT: I think you should leave, Mrs. Manning.

ALEXIS: I was voted out of the presidency. Did you know that?

ROBERT: No. I didn't.

ALEXIS: They thought I was very efficient—but lacked people skills. "Lacked people skills!" In this rag-tag tower of rich bitch flotsam and jetsam—I lacked people skills!. Wait till they see how things fall apart when some poor sod with people skills but no organizational abilities gets to head the board!

ROBERT: You certainly were a stickler for the rules.

ALEXIS: But so are you! We're alike, you and I, Robert-Roberto.

ROBERT: I have to get dressed, get some dinner—

ALEXIS: At Macdonald's? Or is it La Cubana del Sol?

ROBERT: This suit is wet—

ALEXIS: Change here. I won't look—if you're modest. ...But, if you like we could skip the getting dressed part and I could pare myself down to where you are. *(She starts undressing.)*

ROBERT: Mrs. Manning, what are you doing!

ALEXIS: Oh, Roberto. Roberto—

ROBERT: Don't call me Roberto!

ALEXIS: Why are you in disguise here?

ROBERT: In this building, everyone's in disguise in one way or another.

ALEXIS: But you, you only have to be yourself. Why pretend to be what you're not?

ROBERT: I can remake myself if I choose.

ALEXIS: You're ashamed of your heritage!

ROBERT: No! I'm proud of my heritage! But I refuse to be held back by it. I would be happy to be Roberto if the world would then not see me through Roberto eyes. But as soon as I label who I am, they think that's all I am.

ALEXIS: Not true!

ROBERT: It is! As soon as I become "Roberto" I'm the person who lives where none of you live—in Spanish Harlem. I am lumped in with Puerto Ricans, Cubans, Mexicans, Dominicans and all the others.

ALEXIS: Well, what are you?

ROBERT: You really want to know?

ALEXIS: I do.

ROBERT: I'm from Colombia! My parents, educated beyond what you may think, decided to leave Bogota when I was young to make sure I never got involved with the drug trade. ...Back home my father was an important minister in the government. But he could never quite make his way in this country. He died not long after we got here. And recently my mother—

ALEXIS: I didn't know.

ROBERT: You don't want to know. You want to know your image of "Roberto"—not the one who's trying to earn enough to quit this job, go to college and return to help those less fortunate in my country, but the one who plays the guitar, dances the flamenco and dines every night on *Arroz con Pollo*.

ALEXIS: *Arroz con Pollo*. I've always wanted to know how to make—

ROBERT: Go on! Go on! Ask me for the recipe!

ALEXIS: Actually, I—

ROBERT: I've never made *Arroz con Pollo* in my life! Don't you see? I need to be free of all of it!

ALEXIS: I need to be free, too. In fact, I am. Free. Supremely free. Free of husband, of daughter, of presidency—

ROBERT: Of pool membership.

ALEXIS: What?

ROBERT: Your husband didn't renew your membership—didn't you know that?

ALEXIS: The bastard!

ROBERT: I was going to have to talk to you about it. You have to make out a check—

ALEXIS: A check! That slimebag closed all my accounts!

ROBERT: You could pay in cash—

ALEXIS: I hardly have a penny to my name!

ROBERT: I'm sorry—

ALEXIS: Oh, you who exist on your weekly stipend—and I, who existed on the scattered crumbs of my husband's wealth. Don't think I didn't have to beg for them! Don't think I didn't have to keep myself thin, and have eye-tucks, and tummy-tucks and face-lifts. And still he ran off with his secretary!

ROBERT: You don't want me to hear this—

ALEXIS: Comfort, Robert. Give me comfort, Robert, please, please, please—

(She comes to him, begins to caress him. He grabs her by the arms trying to fend her off.)

ROBERT: Don't! Don't!

ALEXIS: Why not? Am I too old? Too poor? Too what? What is it about me that repels you?

ROBERT: I'm not repelled.

ALEXIS: Then please—please. There's an exercise mat in the women's sauna. It's private there. And dark. And this door is locked. We won't be disturbed.

ROBERT: I am sorry for what's happened to you, Mrs. Manning, but—

ALEXIS: Is this another one of your rules? No love-making at the pool! Where is that written?

ROBERT: You think you can just walk in and command me to sleep with you! You live an unreal life. All of you. You in your rooms with heat and hot water whenever you want it. Apartments with no roaches crawling across the floor, no mice making holes in your walls and in your bread.

ALEXIS: You can tell me about all that.

ROBERT: You wouldn't understand. You wouldn't even listen! You in your protected caul, so coddled, so secure!

ALEXIS: *(With irony)* "Secure—!"

ROBERT: You have everything you want and still you go crazy wanting something other!

ALEXIS: You have no idea what wanting is! You in your ghetto world—and I in mine.

ROBERT: We have two worlds and let's keep it that way! I am not going to service you because, at the bottom of a glass or three or four, you feel unwanted! What you're after isn't going to happen. It isn't going to happen, do you hear me? ...You have to leave, Mrs. Manning. You have to leave.

ALEXIS: *(Finally giving up)* ...I'll leave. ...But what a time we could have had together.

ROBERT: You'll think better of it when you wake up in the morning.

ALEXIS: "When I wake up in the morning." What a simple sentence.

ROBERT: *(With a certain amount of pity for her)* Things always look better in the morning if one hasn't done what one shouldn't do the night before.

ALEXIS: How do you know? Have you ever done what you shouldn't do?

ROBERT: Where I live, there's temptation every minute to do what I shouldn't do. I try to do what I should. It's the major thing that holds me together.

(She doesn't respond. After a silence:)

ROBERT: I'm going to get dressed. That'll give you some time to pull yourself together. When I come back, I want to find that you're gone.

(He takes his clothes and exits to the men's lavatory. ALEXIS *says, partly to herself, partly to us:)*

ALEXIS: I don't even know why I want him. Because he's there, I guess. Because he's there. What a strange thing it is—other people. There—and then not there. And each of us—there—and then not there. The world of loss and the world of wanting. Wanting. It's what keeps us alive. Wanting this—and wanting that. Something just beyond—just beyond one's grasp. Like little lights on a distant path. But how does one find one's way when there are no more lights—and no more wanting—

(She takes out her cell phone and begins to type in some text messages. After some moments, she hears ROBERT *returning. She exits swiftly to the women's sauna.)*

*(*ROBERT *returns, fully clothed. He is relieved to find her gone. He puts on his jacket, picks up his duffel bag, and puts out the lights.* ROBERT *exits, locking the door. The space is illuminated only by the moonlight.)*

(Moments later, ALEXIS *re-enters. She says to us, hardly conscious that we're there:)*

ALEXIS: I was thinking—about my honeymoon with the man I chose to marry. The world seemed so full of promise then. I had so many hopes! I knew my life was going to be splendid! Everything seemed to be opening up, opening up wide. And now—it has all closed in—a giant NO, from every direction. *(Slowly, turning her head with each syllable)* No. ...No. ...No. ...No... *(She turns to us:)* I say NO to NO! *(She turns and exits to the pool. We hear a tremendous splash and see the reflection of that splash. Then the waters become still. Silence.)*

(Blackout. Music.)

(Next day. At the entrance to the solarium is a sign saying "Pool Closed Today". The opening which leads from the solarium to the pool is blocked by ropes. When the lights come up, ROBERT, *wearing street clothes, is saying to* JOAN:*)*

ROBERT: The police think I killed her!

JOAN: No, Robert—!

ROBERT: I could tell by the way they were questioning me. They were looking at me with suspicion in their eyes.

JOAN: No, no—

ROBERT: They say I was the last one to see her alive. And then, this morning, for the first time ever, I came in late—

JOAN: Surely you told them it was the day of the triathlon—

ROBERT: They kept harping on the fact that I call myself Robert when my real name is Roberto. Just the fact that I used a slightly different name here makes me a criminal! Oh, I should have known my place. I never should have crossed the divide between Spanish Harlem and this unreal world.

JOAN: Don't say things like that. Somehow you'll be cleared. They can't possibly—

ROBERT: *(Looking over the rope)* The pool looks so unhappy—drained and empty. ...Who found her?

JOAN: One of the handymen.

ROBERT: If it had been a regular day, it would have been me. ...Last night, late, she came up here. She'd been drinking. She was in a state. And she wanted. She wanted—

JOAN: She wanted—you.

ROBERT: What should I have done! I had no idea she was on the brink of—! It never occurred to me that she could—! I thought when I locked up that she had left here! ...They think I killed her!

*(*TIFFANY, *looking somber and restrained, has appeared at the entrance in time to hear this. Drained, emotionless, in an almost shell-shocked state, she says:)*

TIFFANY: No, they don't. She had enough pills and liquor in her to do her in without going near the water. And—last night—she sent me and my father messages. We didn't realize what they were till we got the news this morning. ...They were goodbye.

JOAN: Tiffany—

ROBERT: Miss Manning—

JOAN: We're very, very sorry—

TIFFANY: *(In a cold tight voice)* I came over to get a dress to bury her in. You can't be buried in the dress you drowned in.

JOAN: Is there anything we can do—?

TIFFANY: I hope you—both—will come to the funeral. Jennifer and her mother say they'll come. As far as I can tell, you four were her only—friends.

(She starts to leave. JOAN says:)

JOAN: Come see us every now and then.

TIFFANY: Thanks. I don't think so. I couldn't bear to remember—

JOAN: We understand.

TIFFANY: *(A pause. Then, like ice:)* Hating her was the one thing that kept me going. ...I wonder what's going to keep me going now.

(TIFFANY goes. After a long pause, JOAN says:)

JOAN: I can't imagine what's in that girl's future.

ROBERT: Whatever it is, she'll have created it on her own.

JOAN: I think you're right. *(After a very long pause)* ...Tell me, Robert, what happened at the triathlon?

ROBERT: *(With quiet modesty)* ...I won.

JOAN: *(Seriously, warmly)* Congratulations.

ROBERT: What about you? Yesterday, when I came through the lobby, I saw that a florist was delivering a huge bouquet of roses to your apartment.

JOAN: *(As modest as he)* Oh. That. ...They've named a chair after me—at my alma mater.

ROBERT: *(Warmly, quietly)* Congratulations to you. *(He glances toward the pool.)* ...Funny how often good things and bad things happen at the same time.

JOAN: It's a little trick Fate has—to make us appreciate the good things all the more.

ROBERT: We'll have to celebrate.

JOAN: As a matter of fact, along with that bouquet came a split of champagne. With Abby not here, I thought I'd give it to you.

(She takes it out of her bag and hands it to him.)

ROBERT: Let's you and I split it.

JOAN: Delighted.

(He prepares to open it.)

JOAN: You'll let us drink it here?

ROBERT: Just for once, to hell with the rules of the pool!

JOAN: I'll drink to that!

(He pops the cork and pours the champagne into two plastic glasses. They raise their glasses. Then, smiling, but with their pleasure tempered by an understanding of the transient nature of human life and achievement.)

JOAN: *Skol.*

ROBERT: *Skol.*

JOAN: To those who, in spite of everything, manage to keep their heads above water.

(They touch their glasses together and drink.)

(Blackout. Music.)

END OF PLAY

THE ARDENT PHILANTHROPIST

CHARACTERS & SETTING

JULIA
DEVON
WILLOW
BETH
DAMIEN LUCEREAU
MRS. ALDEN STANHOPE

Time & Place: The Present. A house in the country outside Washington, D.C.

Setting: The living room. Spacious and imposing, centuries old with classic lines and furnishings collected and added to by generation after generation, the room exudes an informality within formality that reflects breeding and self-confidence. From a prominent location, a portrait of a distinguished man surveys the scene. Upstage is a foyer revealing a portion of a staircase leading to an upper floor with the main entrance off left and access to the rest of the house off right. Stage left we get a glimpse into a wintergarden with a profusion of plants. In the living room there is an easel with a canvas on it — a canvas facing away from us.

ACT ONE

(At rise:)

(JULIA -- in her mid-thirties, an artist, loose, full of wild energy, given to verbal extravagances—is pacing back and forth. DEVON—her brother, about 40, a capitalist type whose controlled buttoned-up personality only shows cracks when he's drinking—enters from outside and deposits a suitcase in the hall. JULIA starts to say something to him but he goes out again. She paces impatiently. DEVON returns and drops another large suitcase. JULIA can be silent no longer. She blurts out:)

JULIA: Devon! You're four hours late and lunch was at its peak two hours ago! *(She throws a pizza box into a wastebasket, saying to it:)* Arrivederci!

DEVON: *(From the hall)* Willow couldn't decide which dress to wear to the dinner.

JULIA: *(Mockingly)* Major dilemma.

DEVON: What are you wearing?

JULIA: Me? I'm planning to go in the nude.

DEVON: I bet you would!! *(He enters the living room and air-kisses her briefly on both cheeks.)* Hello, Julia. How are you?

JULIA: As you see. Fit as a fiddle and still holding down the fort.

(DEVON looks at the canvas.)

DEVON: That your latest?

JULIA: It's been there for years. You know that. It's practically grimy with age.

DEVON: Aren't you—?

JULIA: No. I aren't—! And let's forget about it.

(WILLOW enters carrying an evening dress in a transparent garment bag. WILLOW'S name once suited her. Now, in her late thirties, she compensates for her fading beauty by too much make-up and too-bright clothes. JULIA and DEVON speak with accents which indicate centuries of good breeding. WILLOW does not.)

WILLOW: *(To JULIA:)* Your brother drives like a madman! The way he speeds down these country roads—! And I like to get a look at the mansions—!

JULIA: Hello, Willow.

WILLOW: *(To* DEVON—*about the gown in her hands:)* I found this smashed between the spare tire and your heaviest suitcase! I'll never get out the wrinkles!

DEVON: You can iron them out.

WILLOW: *(Is he an idiot?)* You can't iron raw silk!

(DEVON—*who has lost many of these woman's-things arguments before*—*rolls his eyes and leaves to get more luggage.*)

JULIA: You can steam them out in the bathroom.

WILLOW: I don't know, Julia. I don't think I chose the right dress anyway. And I do so want to look my best for your father.

JULIA: Being dead, I'm sure he'll appreciate your efforts.

WILLOW: I liked him.

JULIA: So did we all.

WILLOW: I think he liked me. It still bothers me that he died alone.

JULIA: Well, dying is a lonely business.

WILLOW: I always feel so weird coming to your folks' house now that your father's not in it.

JULIA: Why?

WILLOW: I don't know, Julia. It's just not the same without him.

JULIA: Look, Willow, why don't you go upstairs and—

WILLOW: Do we have the room we always have?

JULIA: Devon's old room? Yes.

WILLOW: I just keep hoping some visit I wouldn't have to keep tripping over his old toys!

JULIA: You could pick them up.

WILLOW: What?

JULIA: Nothing. Go do what you have to do. And don't worry. You'll figure out your costume. The testimonial's not till Saturday. You have a whole two days.

(WILLOW *takes her dress and starts toward the stairs just as* DEVON *enters with more luggage.* WILLOW *passes her luggage but doesn't take any of it with her.*)

DEVON: Couldn't you—?

WILLOW: Couldn't I what—?

DEVON: Nothing. I'll lug everything up later.

(WILLOW *exits upstairs.* DEVON *turns to* JULIA.)

DEVON: Is Beth here yet?

JULIA: No. Her plane should have gotten into Dulles half an hour ago. She said she didn't want me to pick her up, she'd get a taxi.

DEVON: That's Beth ! ...Where's she coming from this time?

JULIA: Somalia.

DEVON: What was she there for? Famine? Flood? Earthquake?

JULIA: Who knows. I think some dread disease.

DEVON: Some day she's going to catch one of those things.

JULIA: She's always careful.

DEVON: You summoned her back from Africa. You summoned me here from Philadelphia. I assume Mother'll be barging in from New York any minute—

JULIA: No. Not till late tomorrow, the night of the testimonial.

DEVON: Damn it, Julia! What the hell did you have to get Beth and me here for—and two days early? You and Mother usually handle these tributes to Dad by yourself. Couldn't you two have just gone to the dinner and e-mailed Beth and me about it later?

JULIA: Not this time.

DEVON: What in heaven's name is going on?

JULIA: A crisis, Dev. A real crisis.

(*She starts to speak. He holds up his hand.*)

DEVON: Wait! Wait—! I'm not going to listen to crisis news on an empty stomach. *(He looks around.)* What happened to the drink table?

JULIA: I put the stuff in the cabinet. I couldn't stand those bottles staring at me all the time.

(*Devon opens the cabinet, takes out a bottle of Scotch, starts to pour himself a drink but pauses to ask:*)

DEVON: You—?

JULIA: No, thanks. Not yet.

(DEVON *takes a long draught, sits down and asks:*)

DEVON: Okay, Julia. What is it?

JULIA: ...Damien Lucereau is planning to make a documentary about dad's life.

DEVON: That's it? That's the crisis?

JULIA: You know Lucereau. He always hated father for some reason. Anything rotten he could say about him he would. If you heard the words "Philanthropist Alden Stanhope" come out of Lucereau's mouth on any of his broadcasts you knew something malicious was going to follow.

DEVON: Aren't you used to this by now? You know there are legions of critics out there whose sole reason for existence is to throw stones at anyone in public life. It's a hazard of the game. Why should you care so much this time?

JULIA: Because Lucereau is a malevolent louse. A louse with a very large television audience. He was a thorn in Dad's side all of Dad's life, and now, when Dad's no longer around, he's out to ruin his reputation forever!

DEVON: Ah, the bubble reputation!

JULIA: Dad can't defend himself—we have to do it for him.

DEVON: Oh, God! Don't tell me we have *two* Joan of Arcs in the family!

JULIA: I'm not trying to save the world like Beth is. I just think we owe it to Dad to try to save his good name—not to mention what damaging his image will do to the philanthropies named after him.

DEVON: We spent our lives being good to protect his good name while he was with us, we don't have to continue doing that forever and ever now that he's gone!

JULIA: But—

(WILLOW *appears at the top of the stairs.* JULIA *says to* DEVON:)

JULIA: We'll talk about this later.

(DEVON *goes to the cabinet and pours himself another, very large, drink.* WILLOW *calls down:*)

WILLOW: Our bathroom is a mess!

JULIA: It's exactly the way you left it after your last visit.

WILLOW: Can't we get someone in to—

JULIA: No, Willow. I let 'em all go. I want to live the way I want to live, without anyone looking on. If you want a clean bathroom, I'm afraid you'll have to clean it yourself.

(WILLOW *disappears back upstairs.* JULIA *says to* DEVON:)

JULIA: You had to marry a beauty queen!

DEVON: Willow wasn't a beauty queen, she was a model.

JULIA: Same thing.

DEVON: When are you going to give her a chance?

JULIA: When are you going to divorce her?

DEVON: How's your love-life going?

JULIA: How's your venture capitalism going?

DEVON: When are you going to start painting again?

JULIA: When are you going to stop hitting the bottle?

DEVON: When are you going to stop playing Playgirl of the Western World?

JULIA: When I've smashed my last tennis ball, skied my last slope, raced my last stallion—!

DEVON: You're into more sports than Peter and Jonathan!

JULIA: *(Calling a truce, a sincere query)* ...How are those two nephews of mine?

DEVON: Fine. They love Choate. It's tough. But it's good for them.

JULIA: Anyplace would be good—away from mommy.

DEVON: Lay off her, Julia.

JULIA: Oh, Willow's not a bad sort. She's just not right for you, Devon. Or, frankly, for the kids.

(WILLOW *comes downstairs asking:*)

WILLOW: Are there some rubber gloves somewhere?

JULIA: In the kitchen.

(*Crossing toward it,* WILLOW *sees* DEVON *with a full glass in his hand.*)

WILLOW: I thought you—?

DEVON: Don't worry. I'm on the wagon.

WILLOW: It's a rather rickety wagon!

(*She exits to the kitchen.* DEVON *takes a long, deep draught.* JULIA *goes over and pours herself a Scotch.*)

DEVON: Aha!

JULIA: Why is it, ten minutes with family and I'm desperate for a pain-killer? (*She, too, takes a long deep draught.*)

DEVON: What's for dinner?

JULIA: Since I did Italian for lunch—(*She pulls a collection of take-out menus out of a drawer.*) How about Thai,—Chinese,—Lebanese—?

DEVON: Remember the days when Dad was alive and we had all those servants swarming about us?

JULIA: Ring a bell and there was milk and cookies.

DEVON: Cough and a hankie appeared under your nose.

JULIA: Lie back and wait for dinner to be served—a dinner I didn't have to think about in advance, didn't have to prepare and didn't have to clean up from afterward.

DEVON: Here's to the days of yore! *(He drains his glass and goes to pour himself a drink.)*

JULIA: I make that number three.

DEVON: This place always gets to me. Dad staring at us from over the mantle. Him standing beside the world's notables in silver frames. How can you bear having these around all the time?

JULIA: To tell the truth, I took them out of a drawer because Mother's coming.

DEVON: How is she?

JULIA: Still deeply devoted to the animal kingdom. I think she went to a polar bear convention last week.

DEVON: I can just see Mom—drifting off on an ice floe to the North Pole.

JULIA: Don't I wish!

DEVON: Are you two still constantly at each other's throats?

JULIA: You wouldn't want either of us to give up the fight, would you?

DEVON: What's the latest bone of contention?

JULIA: The usual. My men. She thinks that, since she's so kind as to let me live in this house while she's not in it, she should know what's going on in the bedrooms.

DEVON: What *is* going on the bedrooms?

JULIA: What is this, the third degree?

DEVON: Are you still seeing that rock star?

JULIA: He rocked out of here.

DEVON: What about the yachtsman?

JULIA: He sailed away.

DEVON: So who've you got on a leash at the moment?

JULIA: It's a state secret!

DEVON: Don't tell me Miss Man-on-Each-Arm-and-Half-a-Dozen-in-the-Bushes is without her usual convoy of escorts!

JULIA: I tell you, Devon, I'm bored out of my mind! I'm in danger of becoming my virgin sister. If I don't find someone or something to divert me soon, she and I will be battling for twin sainthoods!

DEVON: Say not so!

(The bell rings. JULIA goes to the door. While she's out, DEVON pours himself another drink. JULIA returns with BETH—the youngest of the three. She's in her early-thirties, thin and pale with short hair and an open face untouched by make-up. She wears slacks, shirt and flat shoes, and is carrying only a duffel bag.)

BETH: Dev!

DEVON: Beth.

(They hug, genuinely glad to see each other. But JULIA and DEVON exchange a look. BETH doesn't look well.)

JULIA: How many pounds have you lost since we saw you last?

DEVON: Willow will want to know your diet.

BETH: She wouldn't like it. Is she here?

DEVON: She—

(WILLOW enters from the kitchen with cleaning equipment.)

WILLOW: Beth!

BETH: Willow—

(They hug. BETH notes the rubber gloves.)

BETH: What are you up to?

WILLOW: I'm cleaning our bathroom!

BETH: Oh, Willow, that's not a task for you. I'll come up and help you in a bit. You shouldn't—

JULIA: No, Beth—

BETH: Go on, Willow. Rest. I'll come up soon. Your hair looks very nice, by the way.

WILLOW: You think? I'm going to a new guy. He really understands my face, knows how to style my hair to suit my personality.

BETH: He's caught you perfectly. Don't you get mussed. I'll come up shortly.

(Grateful, WILLOW goes upstairs.)

JULIA: You shouldn't offer to—

BETH: She's not used to that kind of—

DEVON: You look like hell.

BETH: I'm fine. How's Mother?

JULIA: She's fine. She'll be getting here on Saturday—for the dinner.

DEVON: You look like you haven't eaten in a month.

BETH: *They're* the ones who are starving. I'm not starving.

JULIA: Now that you're back, we're going to fatten you up.

BETH: I'm not "back". I'm just—here. For Dad's night. Then I have to—

JULIA: We'll talk about that later.

BETH: Do you know any more about the film? Your e-mails sounded so upset about it.

DEVON: You e-mailed Beth all about it and didn't e-mail me?

JULIA: If I'd told you about this in advance, you'd have said forget about it and you wouldn't have come.

DEVON: You're absolutely right. And that's exactly what I say now. Forget about it. Father was a public person. He lived a public life. There are hours and hours of footage on him, miles and miles of documents and public records— over none of which we have any control. If someone wants to take a negative view of his accomplishments, there's nothing we can do.

JULIA: I think there is.

BETH: Dad told us never to respond to criticism.

DEVON: Beth is right. The family's position has always been: "Let the arrows fall where they may. We'll show you they don't wound."

JULIA: I know. Dad always said—"Let it be and just move on." But this film is going to be seen by millions. It'll become the definitive view of Dad that people will remember for decades.

DEVON: What makes you think it's going to be a hatchet job?

JULIA: Because of who's making it.

BETH: It always astonished me that anyone could find anything bad to say about father. Unlike lots of people who were born to what Dad was born to, he spent his life giving money away. Whatever cause, whatever art, whatever creatures were needy or suffering, he was always there to write a check and offer his good offices. I can't believe Lucereau is intent on finding negative things to say about all that he did.

JULIA: It seems to be an obsession.

BETH: What do you think we should do? Say he'll have to get our approval?

JULIA: He'd only laugh at us.

DEVON: We could sue.

JULIA: We couldn't do that until we'd seen the film. By then it'd be too late.

DEVON: That's the problem—we don't know what he's about to say. The thing could be full of matters of opinion—to which he's entitled. Or matters of fact—

JULIA: —to every one of which he'll give a negative spin. We have to somehow have our say on the project.

DEVON: Censor it, you mean. Do you know how that would look? Grown children trying to censor a film that might say bad things about their Daddy! We'd look ridiculous!

BETH: There's no way we can influence the man.

JULIA: Actually, I believe there is.

DEVON: How, may I ask?

JULIA: Cooperate.

BETH: "Cooperate!"

JULIA: Try to change his point of view. We can't stop the film from being made, but we can influence it to get Lucereau to see Dad as we see him. If we give him a glimpse of Dad through our eyes he might begin to appreciate how wonderful Dad really was.

BETH: It might work—

DEVON: You're romantics, both of you! In the first place, participating in the guy's project in any way would make it look as if we're vetting anything he has to say—and we aren't. In the second place, I don't think he'd accept an offer of our participation. In the third place, Mother would never allow it.

JULIA: We won't tell her.

BETH: I don't like going behind Mother's back—

JULIA: She'd never let us have anything to do with Lucereau if she knew. She always thinks it's best to keep ourselves above the fray. I disagree. I think the best defense is a good offense.

BETH: That may be true. But what if Lucereau won't listen to what we have to say?

JULIA: We'll find out tomorrow. ...I invited him for tea.

BETH: You didn't!

JULIA: I did. I told him I understood he was doing a film on Dad's life and I thought perhaps he might like to see the house in which, all his life, Dad lived.

DEVON: Why in hell did you do that?

JULIA: Why not? You two have causes. *(To* DEVON:*)* You're out to make as much money as possible.*(To* BETH:*)* You're out to save the world. ...I want to have a cause, too. And my cause is saving Dad from the jaws of his enemy!

DEVON: Miss Impetuous!

JULIA: Lucereau will be here at four tomorrow and I expect you two to be here and say everything wonderful about Father that you can think of.

DEVON: Oh, God—!

BETH: I wish you'd consulted us beforehand.

JULIA: I know, Beth. You don't like boasting—about yourself or about Dad. But this time you have to get over your innate modesty and brag about Father in a voice that's loud and clear. (JULIA *looks at her father's portrait and says:*) Don't worry, Dad. We'll defend you. Keep an eye on us tomorrow, when we entertain the viper! ...Welcome, Mr. Lucereau. ..."Won't you come into our parlor, said the spider to the fly."

(*Blackout*)

(*In the darkness we hear a melody played on a solo flute. It is a happy sound full of promise and excitement. Soldiers marching happily off to battle. People in power! People making plans!*)

(*When the lights come up it is the next day.* BETH *is straightening up the room.* DEVON *is straightening his tie. The front door bell rings.* JULIA *crosses the hallway from the interior of the house and goes to answer the front door. A moment later she ushers in* DAMIEN LUCEREAU. *He is the embodiment of the television personality. Even in a living room he looks camera-ready and speaks very much as if he were on the air. He is slick and incisive, with an ingratiating manner which he uses to disarm his on-air guests and get them off their guard. The family's tone is overly-friendly, wary.* LUCEREAU *looks around the room and says:*)

LUCEREAU: It's very kind of you to invite me over.

JULIA: We're honored to have you. We thought, since you were doing a film on Father's life, you might like to see the house which was his home from the day he was born to the day he died.

LUCEREAU: I haven't been in this house in more than twenty years.

JULIA: You were here before?

LUCEREAU: When I was a green reporter. There was a reception here when your father had given millions for relief to some benighted country or other. I was assigned to cover it. I was so busy scribbling in my notebook I never got any hors d'oeuvres.

BETH: Let us make up for that now. ...Won't you have tea?

LUCEREAU: Perhaps in a while. (*He takes a small digital camera out of his pocket.*) Would you mind if I snap some pictures?

BETH: I don't know—

JULIA: Please. ...Go ahead.

LUCEREAU: Thank you.

(He snaps a general picture of the room. Throughout his visit he continues to do this every time something catches his eye. Each time he does it the three are slightly uneasy. But now he holds out his hand to shake theirs.)

LUCEREAU: You're Beth, I believe. And you're Julia And you, of course, are Devon. Where is your beautiful wife? Maple...? Magnolia...?

DEVON: Willow.

LUCEREAU: An actress, isn't she?

DEVON: A former model. She's upstairs. Polishing her nails.

LUCEREAU: I hope we'll get a chance to meet.

DEVON: *(Who hopes not)* Mmm.

LUCEREAU: And is your lovely mother in residence?

JULIA: Not at the moment.

LUCEREAU: Pity. *(Snidely)* I wanted to congratulate her for her recent efforts to preserve the life of the Russian sturgeon. I love caviar. How noble it is that there's someone out there working to preserve its future!

JULIA: Someone has to.

LUCEREAU: Of course! It must be wonderful to have a mother who's devoting her life to the preservation of so many fast-disappearing species. *(Even more deeply mocking)* The red-cockaded woodpecker, I understand, will soon no longer be with us. And as for the Patagonian toothfish—

JULIA: *(Changing the subject)* Do tell us about the film you're planning, Mr. Lucereau.

LUCEREAU: Your father's life. That's it. In a nutshell. Your father's life—from beginning to end. ...The end came early.

BETH: Far too early.

DEVON: He supported many causes which were deeply heart-felt. Perhaps his heart just couldn't stand it.

LUCEREAU: Possibly.

BETH: It's been seven years—but we're all still in shock.

JULIA: Tell us, how did you come to choose our father as a subject?

LUCEREAU: I knew him slightly.

DEVON: Did you?

LUCEREAU: Oh, yes. We were at Princeton together. You didn't know that?

JULIA: He never mentioned it.

LUCEREAU: I don't know why he would. We were in the same class—but we weren't in the same class, if you know what I mean. He was a brilliant scholar; I was a scholarship boy. We lived in the same dorm, took many of the same courses. But—naturally—we didn't belong to the same clubs. He was born to the purple, while I—*(He gives a cynical shrug. His lowly beginnings still bother him.)*

DEVON: Were you friends?

LUCEREAU: I wouldn't say that, no. We knew each other in passing. Then he became a doer on the world stage—and I became a commentator. So later it was only in those separate capacities that we would get to meet. *(Changing the subject)* I appreciate your giving me this view of the Stanhope mansion.

BETH: We don't think of it as a mansion. We just think of it as home.

LUCEREAU: I understand it's been in the family for centuries.

DEVON: Since Jefferson.

LUCEREAU: Yes. It does seem a bit Monticello.

(He snaps a photo. They react.)

BETH: Of course a lot has been changed over the decades.

(LUCEREAU looks toward the wintergarden.)

LUCEREAU: I don't remember a wintergarden.

BETH: Father had it added about fifteen years ago.

LUCEREAU: It seems to be flourishing.

JULIA: Not due to us. Dad's will provided for a gardener on a lifetime retainer. Whether we're here or away, he comes in twice a week to clip and prune. Of course, when Dad was here, he insisted on doing all of that himself.

LUCEREAU: I didn't know he'd taken up gardening. I thought his hobby was playing the flute.

JULIA: That, too.

LUCEREAU: Why on earth did he choose that particular instrument?

BETH: It was easy to pack when he went on trips. It gave him solace, he said, at those times when he had to view so much human suffering and knew, in spite of all he could give, he could never alleviate all of it.

LUCEREAU: What a privilege it must have been, to live with a man whose main purpose in life was to make people happy. ... Were you happy in this house?

(They answer almost simultaneously.)

DEVON: Terrifically!

JULIA: Ecstatically!

BETH: No one could have had a happier childhood.

LUCEREAU: In spite of the fact that you must so often have had to be on your best behavior? When your father was in residence I imagine there were distinguished visitors daily. And lavish parties nearly every night.

BETH: We used to sit at the top of the stairs in our pajamas and peer through the banisters.

JULIA: It was marvelously exciting!

LUCEREAU: But this place is decorated so formally! What was it like when the family was home alone? You must have constantly been warned not to touch.

BETH: Oh, we each had our own rooms which we could keep as messy as we wished.

DEVON: And in which we could keep any pet we wanted.

JULIA: Dad got me a gorgeous white cat I called Kilimanjaro!

BETH: He got me a beautiful parakeet—Jenny Lind—who sang all day long!

DEVON: I had a pet ferret. Ratso.

(WILLOW *appears, nails still wet, from upstairs.*)

WILLOW: I don't know why you had to have Ratso stuffed—and why I have to see him every morning when I wake up here!

DEVON: Willow—

LUCEREAU: Do introduce us.

DEVON: Sweetheart, this is Damien Lucereau—

WILLOW: I know! I've seen you often on TV! You do those terrific exposés!

LUCEREAU: Ah, you've watched my program. I hope that you—

JULIA: *(Interrupting)* Willow, how would you like to make us all some tea?

WILLOW: *(Not wanting to)* I—

DEVON: In the kitchen.

(*Taking* WILLOW *aside:*)

DEVON: Make sure you boil the water. ...For many minutes.

(*He ushers her out.*)

LUCEREAU: Attractive woman.

DEVON: Yes.

LUCEREAU: Could still model.

DEVON: She gave it up so she can care for our two wonderful sons.

LUCEREAU: How old are they?

DEVON: Fourteen and sixteen. At boarding school. ...I thought you wanted to hear about our father.

LUCEREAU: Sorry. Forgive me for asking so many questions. It's what I do.

JULIA: Yes. We know it's what you do.

LUCEREAU: This room has so many things of interest in it. *(He goes over to a wall.)* This painting—

(He snaps a photo of the painting. Each time he takes a photo the three react with unease.)

DEVON: A Claude Lorrain. From our great-great-grandfather. He was something of a collector.

LUCEREAU: How lucky you are to have had a great-great-grandfather with a good eye and the wherewithal to be a collector! ...This mask—*(He snaps a photo of the mask.)*

JULIA: A gift. From Nigeria. There'd been famine. Our father had carloads of grain brought in. He saved many lives.

LUCEREAU: This hanging? *(He snaps a photo of the hanging.)*

BETH: From the Amazon. Father contributed heavily to eradicating the diseases brought in by foreign oil workers, diseases which were decimating the primitive tribes.

LUCEREAU: How far they spread, these Stanhope Philanthropies!

DEVON: Father devoted his life to promoting peace and justice—

BETH: —to guaranteeing human rights for the world's vulnerable and insecure.

(He comes to JULIA's *painting.)*

LUCEREAU: This? Do I know the artist?

JULIA: *(Swiftly taking it off the easel and hiding it behind a chair.)* It's a new acquisition. I'm thinking of buying it.

LUCEREAU: Don't.

JULIA: Thanks for your advice.

LUCEREAU: *(Looking around)* I don't see any of the plaques, awards, citations, medals I know your father received in his lifetime.

BETH: He wouldn't allow them to be put on display.

JULIA: He was immensely modest.

LUCEREAU: Was he.

JULIA: Modest. Intelligent.

DEVON: A straight shooter.

BETH: Kind. Compassionate.

JULIA: With a wonderful sense of humor.

LUCEREAU: A paragon, it seems. With all the deadly virtues.

BETH: He was a very fine man, Mr. Lucereau.

LUCEREAU: And who would know him better than his children?

DEVON: Our father was our hero.

JULIA: Our god.

BETH: Our guardian angel.

LUCEREAU: How splendid it is—to find three children who worship their dad. I'd like to interview you each—on camera—in this room—for my film.

BETH: Oh, no—. We couldn't—!

LUCEREAU: You could say whatever you wanted to say. You loved the man— you would let that be seen. And if we could show how he lived—it would tell my audience who he really was.

DEVON: I don't know—. Our father always shunned publicity—

JULIA: Would you leave in exactly what we say? Without fancy cutting?

LUCEREAU: Perhaps not all of it—there are time restraints, you understand. But everything would appear exactly as you said it.

JULIA: It would give us a chance to show him as we knew him to be.

BETH: We'd have to discuss it.

LUCEREAU: Please. Go ahead. I can wait.

(*They hadn't meant discussing it while he was here, but he moves downstage to give them privacy. They move upstage to talk where he can't hear. As they confer,* LUCEREAU *turns to the father's portrait and says:*)

LUCERAU: What do you think, Alden, will they agree to do it? You don't want them to, do you? You want your image to remain what it always was— mysterious, aloof. You always seemed just a bit above everything that was merely human. Your children, of course, are mere flesh and blood—so their thoughts aren't quite so elevated. ...The money man is thinking: "It might bring in some hefty clients." The hedonist is thinking: "What a lark this would be! I'm so bored." The saint is thinking: "How wonderful Daddy will seem to the world when we show his generosity, his integrity, his wisdom." They seem to have been completely taken in by you. I wonder if they know who you really were. ...I bet not. I bet they are all convinced of your unblemished sainthood. And I will bet you, Alden, that they will accept my proposal. It's irresistible—

the desire to have one's face projected to millions on the tube.

(The three break from their huddle.)

JULIA: Very well, Mr. Lucereau. We agree.

LUCEREAU: Ah, splendid! *(He gives an "I told you so" look to the portrait.)* I'd like to interview each of you separately, if you don't mind. Is that all right?

(The three look at each other and exchange nods.)

JULIA: It is. But we have one condition.

LUCEREAU: I seldom agree to conditions.

JULIA: Mother mustn't know.

LUCEREAU: She's still the one who oversees the Stanhope Philanthropies, isn't she?

DEVON: Yes.

LUCEREAU: I was hoping she'd participate.

BETH: She wouldn't. She's a very private person.

JULIA: To be honest—she doesn't trust the media.

LUCEREAU: Well, I'm honored that you three do. …All right. I agree. Mum's the word when it comes to Mum. We'll just let your words stand—in ringing testament to your father's greatness.

BETH: It will give us a chance to show our father as the exemplary human being we knew him to be.

LUCEREAU: I'm touched by your devotion. There are so few children of prominent men who, if they're honest, truly admire their fathers.

(WILLOW enters, not with a tray, but with a pot of tea in one hand and a few mugs held by their handles in another.)

WILLOW: I'd like to be in your film too! I have lots of good things to say about my father-in-law.

LUCEREAU: The film wouldn't be complete without your contribution, Willow.

DEVON: *(Uneasy about Willow's participation)* I don't think she'll have time. We're not going to be in town long. We leave the day after tomorrow night's testimonial—

LUCEREAU: In that case, if you agree, we can do all the interviews tomorrow. During the day. Not a large crew. Just a cameraman, a sound man and me. We'll be careful of all your knick-knacks.

BETH: "Knick-knacks!"

LUCEREAU: Sorry. *Mementoes*. What's left of a man when the man's life is ended.

BETH: These—things—are not what's most important of what remains of our father, Mr. Lucereau.

LUCEREAU: Of course not. I was being callous. You'll tell me, won't you, all of you—about all the wonderful things your father accomplished in his life, and how important his foundation continues to be to the future of humanity.

(He starts out. WILLOW *comes over with the teapot.)*

WILLOW: But your tea—

LUCEREAU: Keep it hot till I return.

*(*LUCEREAU *exits. When the others are alone—)*

WILLOW: Can you keep tea hot for twenty-four hours?

DEVON: Dump it.

BETH: What have we just done? There's not one thing Lucereau said that didn't have some insidious implication to it! We should never have agreed—

JULIA: Don't back down. It's the only thing that gives us a fighting chance to counteract his negative view.

BETH: Maybe. ...I suppose, no matter what Lucereau says, if we appear and talk about Father, his specialness will show through.

DEVON: I hope so. Lucereau's a slimy bastard. You never know how he could twist things.

WILLOW: He's even better-looking in person than he is on the screen. I like him.

DEVON: You'd like anybody who might put you on camera. ...I can't imagine what Mother will say when she finds out.

JULIA: We have the right to defend—

DEVON: Perhaps. But maybe we should have talked to her first before agreeing—

JULIA: Still her precious little fellow, aren't you!

DEVON: I am not her precious little fellow!

JULIA: Always gotta do what Mommy says to do. Scared Mommy might spank!

DEVON: And you—always gotta always do what Mommy says *not* to do, scared you might compromise your precious independence!

BETH: Stop it, you two! *(Then, fading:)* ...If you'll excuse me, I think I'll go upstairs—

JULIA: You don't look well.

BETH: I'm okay.

WILLOW: I think you have a fever. *(She touches* BETH's *forehead.)* You do!

BETH: It's nothing. I'll be fine. *(She goes upstairs.)*

JULIA: Even as a kid she would never admit she was sick. Little Miss Martyr.

WILLOW: I'll go up and get her an aspirin.

DEVON: Don't catch anything. You know how you hate it when your face gets all puffy.

(WILLOW *goes upstairs.*)

DEVON: All Willow has to do is get a cold and she acts like she's dying.

JULIA: When are you going to admit you made a mistake?

DEVON: Get off my back! There's never been a divorce in this family and I'm not going to start carving out new territory!

JULIA: What's the matter with you, Devon? Wake up! Live your life! Why don't you look this relationship in the eye and—

DEVON: Who are you to talk about relationships? In your whole life, you haven't had a single one that's lasted more than a couple of weeks!

JULIA: I have to have variety—!

DEVON: And I have to have the relationship side of my life on an even keel so I can do the work I have to do to keep my business afloat! If you think it's easy to be Dad's son and constantly have to try to—

(They hear a key in the lock. They stop. DEVON *goes to the archway to see who could be coming in. Before we glimpse her, he calls back to* JULIA:*)*

DEVON: My God! It's Mother!

(MRS. ALDEN STANHOPE *enters with a large suitcase. She is a woman in her mid-sixties, vital, alive, capable, supremely intelligent.*)

JULIA: Mother! What are you doing here?

MRS. STANHOPE: I live here sometimes.

JULIA: You said you were coming for the dinner. It isn't till tomorrow night.

MRS. STANHOPE: I suddenly realized there's a symposium on saving the whale taking place in DC tomorrow. I want to be there.

JULIA: You should have phoned—

MRS. STANHOPE: Do I have to telephone to come to my own house?

JULIA: No, of course not. ...But—there's a leak in the roof. Your room—.

MRS. STANHOPE: Oh, I know about that leak. We'll fix it sometime. I'm planning to sleep downstairs, in the maid's room.

DEVON: Off the kitchen—?

MRS. STANHOPE: Why not? The better to get a midnight snack. ...Has Beth arrived?

JULIA: She's upstairs. Resting.

MRS. STANHOPE: I'll drop my things and then go up to see her.

(She turns to DEVON.)

MRS. STANHOPE: And your doxy? Is she on the premises?

DEVON: Would everyone please get off my back about Willow! *(Then, instantly contrite)* Sorry.

MRS. STANHOPE: It's all right. You had a perfect opening to say "I love her, Mother." I take it that doesn't enter the equation. *(She turns to JULIA:)* What about you? Any permanent suitor on the near or far horizon?

JULIA: You really cut to the chase, don't you!

MRS. STANHOPE: Your father taught me never to pussyfoot around the most important topics. Well?

JULIA: I told you—my love life is private.

MRS. STANHOPE: And I told you it's going to get worn out from over-use. I suspect it already has.

JULIA: Your analysis is deeply appreciated, but I'm a big girl now and—

MRS. STANHOPE: —and your Mother's advice is not appreciated. The older and wiser we get the less our children can bear to listen. ... Have you each rehearsed your speeches for the dinner?

DEVON: We're working on it.

MRS. STANHOPE: In other words, you haven't. You know, your father would never have assented to this testimonial. I only agreed to it because there are certain donors who might be reminded of all he did, think again of his major causes and write large checks for the Fund. I hope you can come up with suitable tributes. Your father's counting on you. *(Turning to the portrait:)* Aren't you, Alden? *(She seems to hear an answer. She says to JULIA and DEVON:)* He is. So I know you'll come through. *(She starts to go toward her room.)* ...Excuse me, won't you?

JULIA: I don't mean this question the way it'll sound but—how long do you intend to stay here?

MRS. STANHOPE: Till all the whales of all the oceans are saved forever! *(She exits toward the kitchen.)*

JULIA: Oh, my God!

DEVON: She was joking!

JULIA: Why the hell didn't we keep the in-town apartment? It would have been so much more convenient for her to stay in town!

DEVON: Maybe, since Dad died there, it held bad memories.

JULIA: So she has to come and make more bad memories here?

DEVON: Tough break.

JULIA: What are we going to do, Dev? We told Lucifer he could shoot here tomorrow.

DEVON: We'll have to wait till she's out of the house—

JULIA: We'd never know when she might walk back in!

DEVON: We'll have to chance it.

JULIA: No. Much as Lucereau might like to have family knick-knacks in the background, we'll just have to shoot in his studio. I think it's somewhere in Alexandria. Not far from here.

DEVON: I'm beginning to wish we'd never agreed to be part of this enterprise.

JULIA: Don't chicken out now. It's for Dad. We have to do it—and Mother mustn't find out.

(Blackout)

(In the darkness we hear a melody on the flute. It's a hesitant sound, a sound of doubt. "What's going to happen next?")

(The living room disappears in darkness. The lights come up on the center and downstage areas, which become Lucereau's studio. It is the next day. As the scene begins, DEVON is seated in an armchair, isolated in bright light. LUCEREAU moves around in the shadows, just outside the spotlight's rays. The "camera" LUCEREAU indicates is unseen, somewhere out in the audience. DEVON nervously arranges his tie and collar and clears his throat.)

LUCEREAU: You're fine, Devon. Just relax. We're checking the camera angle. Can you hear me?

DEVON: Yes. But I can't see you. These lights—

LUCEREAU: You'll adjust to them after a while. Say a few words, please.

DEVON: My name is Devon Stanhope and I don't know why the hell I agreed to do this.

LUCEREAU: Perfect. The mike is picking you up loud and clear.

DEVON: Aren't you going to be sitting near me?

LUCEREAU: Oh, no. This is *your* interview. I'll throw questions at you from out here.

(DEVON *fidgets.*)

LUCEREAU: It won't be as hard as you think. Just look directly at the camera as if you were speaking to a friend.

DEVON: I wish I were in Siberia.

LUCEREAU: Didn't you go there with your father?

DEVON: Once.

LUCEREAU: Did he often take his children with him on his philanthropic forays?

DEVON: Oh, yes. Each of us. Separately. To show us the world.

LUCEREAU: Did he take you often?

DEVON: Oh no! I was always getting into scrapes.

LUCEREAU: Like what?

DEVON: Like that time in Morocco when this dancer and I ran off to the desert for two nights and three days. My God, he was furious!

LUCEREAU: I didn't know Alden Stanhope was capable of fury.

DEVON: Oh, yes. You should have seen him that other time, in Rio! I met this incredible beauty on the beach and brought her back to my room. Father happened to barge in when we—. But that's another story. ... When are you going to begin filming?

LUCEREAU: Oh, we've been filming for quite some time now.

DEVON: I didn't realize you—. You'll erase all that, won't you?

LUCEREAU: *(Lying)* Naturally.

(DEVON *composes himself and inwardly vows to be more cautious.*)

LUCEREAU: Tell me, Devon, what did you admire most about your father?

DEVON: *(Still a bit off his pins)* Er—I guess—his intelligence. He had this uncanny way of grasping every angle of a problem—and seeing a way out.

LUCEREAU: Was he a good father?

DEVON: Terrific.

LUCEREAU: In spite of his frequent absences?

DEVON: When he came back, he always brought us gifts. He brought me this great set of toy soldiers from India. A wonderful fur hat from Nepal. A glass snow globe from Vienna with a ferris wheel that went round and round inside it. I still have all these things.

LUCEREAU: So you loved to have him home.

DEVON: Of course we did.

LUCEREAU: Why?

DEVON: "Why?"

LUCEREAU: When he was home did he play ball with you?

DEVON: No. He was too busy.

LUCEREAU: Take you to the movies?

DEVON: No.

LUCEREAU: Read you to sleep at night?

DEVON: No, never.

LUCEREAU: Then what makes you say he was a good father?

DEVON: Look here—

LUCEREAU: I mean—what exactly did he do to make you feel he cared?

DEVON: I just felt it! It wasn't the things he did, it wasn't how often he was with us, it was that in those brief times it was—

LUCEREAU: *(Cynically)* "Quality time."

DEVON: Yes. Quality time.

LUCEREAU: Which one of you children did he like best?

DEVON: What kind of a question is that?

LUCEREAU: Parents seem to favor one child over another. Perhaps you had a sense of that with you and your sisters.

DEVON: *(After thinking:)* ...I'd say—Beth. ...She's shy and reserved. But even as a kid she was able to put grown-ups at ease. And, oddly enough, for someone who never touches the sauce, she could fix their drinks better than any of us.

LUCEREAU: I understand you have a talent for it. Perhaps a too good a talent...

DEVON: That's in the past! I haven't had too much to drink in—! *(He stops himself.)* You'll edit that, of course.

LUCEREAU: *(Not meaning it)* Of course. ...Tell me, what is it like to be the son of a prominent father? Is it an advantage or a disadvantage?

DEVON: I don't know what you mean.

LUCEREAU: Oh, I'm sure you do. Does being your father's son grease the wheels or does it set up expectations you can never fulfill?

DEVON: I think I'm like any son of any father.

LUCEREAU: So you don't suffer from Son-of-the-Great-Man syndrome?

DEVON: Not at all.

LUCEREAU: You don't feel you're a failure? That no matter how much you achieve you can never measure up?

DEVON: This interview is not about me, it's about my father!

LUCEREAU: Sorry. didn't realize the question would distress you. We'll drop the subject. ...Let me ask you something that I know my viewers are curious about: Where did your father get the money that he gave away with such an open hand? I mean, as I understand it, your forebears arrived on this shore penniless. How did they amass the fortune that your father managed to inherit and increase exponentially—the fortune on which you, your mother and your sisters all now base your lives?

DEVON: As I think most people know, the family fortune began generations ago, when our ancestors first came to this country. They were very good at trade and then at banking and investments. And every generation managed to enlarge the original holdings.

LUCEREAU: So there's nothing in the rumors that your family's fortune is based on illegal enterprise?

DEVON: I don't know what you're talking about.

LUCEREAU: Come on. You know that people say the original Stanhopes acquired their fortune from profits made in the slave trade!

DEVON: That's not true!

LUCEREAU: So they didn't import human cargo from Africa and sell them to the—

DEVON: They acquired their fortune by legitimate means! By cleverness and hard work and luck and perseverance!

LUCEREAU: *(Cynically)* The American dream to the nth power!

DEVON: You've seen our place. Does that look like the home of brigands and cutthroats?

LUCEREAU: Everyone knows that profiteers surround themselves with the finer things of life in order to disguise their wealth's less-than-respectable origins.

DEVON: I resent your accusations!

LUCEREAU: I make no accusations. I merely repeat some rumors so you can clear things up and lay the rumors to rest—if you can.

DEVON: These allegations have no basis in fact! My father and his ancestors were noble—

LUCEREAU: Haughty—

DEVON: Forthright—

LUCEREAU: Wily—

DEVON: Intelligent—

LUCEREAU: Cunning—

DEVON: I have nothing more to say! *(He gets up.)*

LUCEREAU: Your father wouldn't desert the field of battle—

DEVON: When it was a worthy battle. But this is not. You said you wanted to interview me about my father. What you're actually doing, is putting him—and all our family—on trial!

(Blackout)

(The lights go out on Lucereau's studio. The armchair there disappears. In the transition we hear the sound of a flute, confused, disturbed.)

(The lights come up on the living room. As DEVON *walks upstage into it,* JULIA *and* WILLOW *are there, waiting for his return.)*

DEVON: The man's a danger to society! He ought to be drawn and quartered! Drummed off the airwaves! *(He goes to pour himself a drink.)*

WILLOW: Devon! You promised—!

DEVON: Leave me alone, for Chrissake! I'm sick and tired of everybody counting every sip I take!

JULIA: Lucifer is that tough, is he?

DEVON: Julia, don't go. It's a trap! He made me say things about Dad—about us—I didn't even feel. He's out to do us in!

JULIA: But we knew that! You were supposed to counter—!

DEVON: He's cleverer at the game than we are. He can invent a lie, get me to deny it, and, in the very act of denying it, it somehow takes on the aura of fact!

WILLOW: He's terrific on the tube. He can always get people to break down. I love to watch him when he does that!

DEVON: Great. If you ever get to talk to him—which I sincerely hope you won't—you can break down in front of all America and tell us how you feel about it afterwards. *(To* JULIA:*)* Where's Mother?

JULIA: Still in the city, waltzing with whales. ...Beth's resting. I don't think she's up to doing an interview today. I want her to save her energy for tonight's dinner.

DEVON: She mustn't be exposed to that monster.

JULIA: *(Looking at her watch)* Time for me to leave.

DEVON: Julia. I'm serious. Don't do this!

JULIA: Dad wouldn't run from a fight. I won't either.

DEVON: I advise you not to—

JULIA: If I didn't have to go before, I have to go now—to pick up the pieces after you.

DEVON: You'll be sorry.

JULIA: He caught you off guard. I'll be prepared.

DEVON: You think.

JULIA: I have things to say about Father and I'm going to say them. Lucereau will have to use *some* of them.

DEVON: Be careful. Be very careful.

JULIA: Don't worry about me, Dev. I'm walking into the fray with eyes wide open and pistols loaded.

DEVON: I'm warning you—when you get into the arena—watch your back—and don't get mauled.

(Blackout)

(The music of the flute is heard. An undercurrent of threat. The tiger lying in wait, ready to spring his trap.)

(When the lights come up downstage, on the "studio", JULIA is just arriving. LUCEREAU says:)

LUCEREAU: Miss Julia! I'm glad you've come. After your brother broke off our little conversation so precipitously, I thought perhaps you and Miss Beth would decline to be interviewed.

JULIA: There are so many positive things to say about Father. I can't resist the opportunity to say them.

LUCEREAU: I'll be interested in hearing them.

JULIA: I hope you'll not only hear them, Mr. Lucereau, but use some of them in your film.

LUCEREAU: Of course I will—if they're the truth. ...Do sit down.

(JULIA sits in the armchair he places for her. The light irises down so she is illuminated, as in a spotlight.)

LUCEREAU: Are you comfortable?

(JULIA nods. LUCEREAU begins. As before, he walks here and there in the shadows.)

LUCEREAU: ...Tell me something about yourself. You're the middle child, aren't you.

JULIA: Yes. Devon was born first, then me, then Beth.

LUCEREAU: It's the youngest who often turns out to be the most rebellious. But in this family, that role seems to have fallen to you.

JULIA: We each have our separate natures.

LUCEREAU: And it fell to you to be the one to devote yourself to pleasure.

JULIA: It was a natural gravitation.

LUCEREAU: You're an anomaly in this day and age, you know. An intelligent woman with inherited wealth who doesn't even pretend to devote herself to good works.

JULIA: They bore me. The charity balls. The dressing up. The surface chatter. The pretense that one's life is devoted to the unfortunates of the world when it's really all about one's own enjoyment. I write the odd check or two without talking about it. And when I enjoy myself it's not in the guise of doing something for the world.

LUCEREAU: You make unabashed hedonism sound like the worthiest of callings.

JULIA: You should try it.

LUCEREAU: Few of us can afford it, Miss Julia. ...Have you no ambition to do something more ambitious?

JULIA: None, Mr. Lucereau. I was put on earth to have a good time.

LUCEREAU: What did your father think about your tabloid life?

JULIA: If there weren't people like you describing it that way I wouldn't seem to be living one.

LUCEREAU: I wonder if your insistence on doing nothing is a reaction against your father's doing so much.

JULIA: Not at all.

LUCEREAU: You're sure?

JULIA: Positive!

LUCEREAU: Tell me—what lucky swain is showering attendance on you at the moment?

JULIA: Whoever he may be, he has nothing to do with the life of my father.

LUCEREAU: Thank you for getting me back on track. ...Your mother and father. What was their relationship?

JULIA: Totally devoted.

LUCEREAU: Do you think it was to compensate for his absences that she started devoting herself to the preservation of the wildlife of the world?

JULIA: If he'd needed her on his trips she'd have been there for him. She arranged all his receptions at our home—and did it beautifully. She is a brilliant conversationalist, an elegant hostess, and was the perfect wife.

LUCEREAU: All that on top of saving gray bats, cockatoos, and other vanishing species?

JULIA: She has her own life, yes. That's an admirable thing in this day and age—or haven't you heard?

LUCEREAU: And their affection endured—in spite of his frequent absences?

JULIA: I've never seen as loving a couple. They adored being together, talking together, laughing together. Even when my father travelled they talked constantly. He called her several times a day.

LUCEREAU: Forgive me—could she trust him, handsome as he was, and so often away?

JULIA: Of course she could. He worshipped my mother. She was his one and only—and he was hers.

LUCEREAU: And you children never suffered from your parents being totally involved with their own occupations?

JULIA: Life with those two was an absolute dream.

LUCEREAU: What an exemplary family you come from!

JULIA: You make having fine character traits sound positively criminal!

LUCEREAU: Oh, was I doing that? Sorry. We'll drop the subject. ...Tell me, which of you was your father's favorite?

JULIA: Beth. Definitely Beth. Dad liked her best. Mother favored Devon.

LUCEREAU: That rather leaves you out.

JULIA: I never felt deprived. I'm independent. I couldn't stand the responsibility of being one parent's favorite. You have to be too goody-good.

LUCEREAU: So you cast yourself as the wicked sister?

JULIA: Absolutely. Don't cross me or you're liable to find molasses between your sheets.

LUCEREAU: I'll be on my guard. ...I take it Beth is the vulnerable one.

JULIA: Beth loves everything in the world. Unreservedly. She's so unaware of the existence of negative forces, she's completely untouched by any that might come her way.

LUCEREAU: Let me ask you what I asked your brother: Has being your father's daughter helped or hindered you in life?

JULIA: Oh, helped. Immeasurably.

LUCEREAU: In what way?

JULIA: Money gives me freedom.

LUCEREAU: So you don't see a certain purposelessness to your existence? A sense of aimless drifting?

JULIA: I am not aimlessly drifting!

LUCEREAU: You don't have a sense of being worthless?

JULIA: Now see here, Lucereau—! *(She starts getting furious, then, with effort, controls herself.)* Oh, you're good. You're very good. I'm sorry I rose to the bait that time. Chalk up one for your side.

LUCEREAU: Don't mention it. Let's return to the subject at hand. Tell me this: What one adjective most describes your father?

JULIA: Charming.

LUCEREAU: Charm is a glut on the market.

JULIA: On the contrary, I find there's a great lack of it in this world.

LUCEREAU: Did it never occur to you that charm is a mask? That those who practice it are usually hiding more than they're revealing?

JULIA: Not with my father. It's what made him so immensely appealing.

LUCEREAU: Charmers often use their charm to deceive.

JULIA: My father was incapable of that kind of guile.

LUCEREAU: You don't think your father used charm to keep you and everyone he met from knowing who he really was?

JULIA: We knew him well. And we knew him to be perfect.

LUCEREAU: Perfectly charming. The charm being the cover which kept all of you from knowing his secrets.

JULIA: He had no secrets!

LUCEREAU: I think he had many. And I think he hid them all with his infinite charm.

JULIA: His charm was as natural to him as breathing.

LUCEREAU: And so were his deceptions.

JULIA: I tell you my father deceived nobody!

LUCEREAU: And I tell you you have no idea who your father really was. ... He was proud—

JULIA: He had reason to be.

LUCEREAU: He was arrogant—

JULIA: He didn't suffer fools gladly, if that's what you mean.

LUCEREAU: He had a great sense of his own superiority—

JULIA: Mr. Lucereau, my father *was* superior!

LUCEREAU: Miss Julia, you don't really know your father.

JULIA: One thing I know, he had no admiration for you—and now I completely understand why! *(She gets up to leave.)*

LUCEREAU: Another Stanhope deserts the field! My, my. I suppose I won't get the opportunity to interview offspring number three.

JULIA: If Beth chooses to submit to your questioning, which I sincerely hope she doesn't, you would never get through her armor—because it is the armor of innocence. There is nothing you could say that would convince her that her father was anything but perfection incarnate.

LUCEREAU: Well, then, I sincerely hope to get the opportunity to immortalize her father-worship on film.

JULIA: And I sincerely hope that she will refuse to submit to your interrogations! As soon as I get home I'm going to warn her not to—

(At that moment, BETH *enters, looking weak and ill.)*

JULIA: Beth—!

BETH: I've come to do my interview.

JULIA: I don't think you're well enough to—

BETH: I'm fine.

LUCEREAU: I'm very pleased you've consented to—

JULIA: There's no reason for you to submit to this man's bullying—

LUCEREAU: Surely I'm not as frightening as all that.

JULIA: *(To* BETH:*)* I beg you not to—

BETH: You can go. I'll be all right.

JULIA: I'm staying.

LUCEREAU: We agreed I was to interview each of you separately.

JULIA: You set traps, Lucereau. I don't want my little sister to fall into them.

BETH: I'll be fine. You can go, Julia.

JULIA: Not on your life.

(JULIA *touches* BETH's *cheek. She doesn't like what she feels.)*

JULIA: I wish you wouldn't—

LUCEREAU: Shall we begin?

(LUCEREAU *gestures toward the armchair.* BETH *sits down. The light irises in to illuminate only her.* JULIA *retreats to the shadows on one side of her,* LUCEREAU *moves through the shadows on the other side.)*

JULIA: *(To* BETH:*)* I'll be right here. Call on me if you need me.

BETH: Don't worry.

(LUCEREAU *begins.)*

LUCEREAU: Miss Beth—tell me something of your work for humanitarian causes.

BETH: What I do is very little compared to what my father managed.

LUCEREAU: You admired him.

BETH: Very much.

LUCEREAU: Which is why you've devoted your life to following in his footsteps.

BETH: His was a fine example, very much worth following.

LUCEREAU: What was it like to be your father's favorite?

BETH: I wasn't his favorite.

LUCEREAU: That isn't your brother and sister's perception.

BETH: I never saw the slightest bit of favoritism—from him or from my mother. They loved us all equally.

LUCEREAU: Even though, as I hear it, you never crossed them, and your brother and sister frequently did? Did their rebelliousness disturb you?

JULIA: *(Breaking in)* That's unfair. If you want to interview Beth, interview Beth. Don't try to start a feud between us.

LUCEREAU: I wasn't aware that that's what I was doing. However, you do understand, Julia, that when you interrupt, your interruptions will be caught on film.

(JULIA *retreats, muttering to herself.* LUCEREAU *continues:)*

LUCEREAU: But you'll agree, Beth, that you're the angel of the trio and your siblings are the devils?

BETH: No. I do not agree. They're more spirited than I. That's the difference. I only see the straight and narrow. They always see other—more adventurous—paths. That's not a fault, it's something I admire in them. In fact, it's something that I sometimes envy.

LUCEREAU: What you're saying is: your limited nature keeps you in a kind of cloister while the other two lack the moral constrictions which keep you on a straighter path. Perhaps you took up your humanitarian calling to counterbalance their more uninhibited behavior—

(Furious, JULIA *interrupts:)*

JULIA: Why are you trying to make trouble between us? Ask what you want to ask about my father. Leave our relationships with each other alone!

LUCEREAU: Sorry these truly innocent questions seem to distress you. ...Beth, let me ask you the same question I asked your brother and sister: What one adjective most describes your father?

BETH: *(With no hesitation)* Loving.

LUCEREAU: "Loving." That's interesting. Your siblings didn't come up with that.

BETH: It's how I see him.

LUCEREAU: Of course it would be. ...I find, when people answer questions about someone else it's often actually a litmus test of themselves. Perhaps, as you're a loving creature, that's what you saw in your father.

BETH: It's what he was.

LUCEREAU: A man of great power and wealth who was also loving.

BETH: He loved the causes for which he was fighting.

LUCEREAU: Or perhaps you're talking about his being loving in quite another sense.

BETH: What do you mean?

LUCEREAU: I mean—perhaps you knew him as a man who loved.

BETH: He was.

LUCEREAU: It was you, wasn't it, the night he died, who discovered his body?

BETH: Yes.

LUCEREAU: Tell me about that night.

BETH: I don't like talking about—

LUCEREAU: It was after midnight. You let yourself into the Georgetown apartment your family maintained for the nights when it was too late to drive back to the house in the country. You let yourself in and you found his body.

BETH: Yes. Yes, I did.

JULIA: *(Interrupting:)* There's no reason to put her through all this again—

LUCEREAU: You happened to be in town that night and decided—at the last minute—to stay at the apartment. You walked in and were unlucky enough to be the one who discovered he was dead.

BETH: It was a great shock.

LUCEREAU: A shock that he was dead? ...Or a shock your father had died in the arms of his mistress?

JULIA: That's a lie! My father never had a—

LUCEREAU: I put it to you, Miss Beth Stanhope, that you are the only one who knows the true facts of your father's demise and that you have hidden this little detail.

JULIA: That's enough, Lucereau!

LUCEREAU: I put it to you that you knew your father had had a mistress, for decades, that you knew who that mistress was, that you assisted her to leave after his death and then pretended it was you who, by accident, arrived and discovered his body.

JULIA: That's enough, Lucereau! We don't have to subject ourselves to this inquisition!

LUCEREAU: I knew you Stanhopes would abandon ship as soon as the winds of truth began to blow!

JULIA: You're a liar and a bastard, Lucereau!

LUCEREAU: Remember, everything you say is being recorded.

JULIA: Fine! Record it! Broadcast it to the world! And also broadcast this: I was under the illusion that by talking with you we could give the world a fair representation of who my father really was. But it's clear you intended all along to soil his reputation by any means—fair or foul—that you can manage! ...Beth, let's go!

LUCEREAU: I'm sorry you retreat just as the trumpet of truth is being sounded.

JULIA: I warn you, Lucereau, if you persist in perpetrating these lies, we'll sue you for slander! Practice your gutter journalism as much as you like. We will prosecute you to the full extent of the law!

(Blackout)

(The flute sounds, highly upset, urgent, a passionate wail. The studio disappears.)

(As the lights come up on the living room, JULIA *and* BETH *have just entered after* BETH's *interview. The telephone is ringing. Neither of them moves to get it.)*

*(*DEVON *comes downstairs in a tuxedo. He picks up the phone.)*

DEVON: Hello? ...Yes. Thank you. We'll be ready. *(To* BETH *and* JULIA *he says:)* What's the matter with you two? Didn't you hear the phone? ...They're sending a limo to take us all to the dinner. It'll be here shortly. You have to hurry up and dress.

(Neither woman moves.)

JULIA: Is Mother back?

DEVON: Yes.

JULIA: Where is she?

DEVON: In her room, dressing. ...Hurry up! We have to leave!

(The women don't move.)

DEVON: You two look like you've been hit by a train. What happened? Did the beast do his usual number?

JULIA: More than his usual number. This time what he said about father was so patently false we walked out.

DEVON: Was that wise?

JULIA: Perhaps not wise. But necessary.

DEVON: He made ridiculous accusations about Dad when he confronted each of us.

JULIA: Yes. But he saved his worst accusation for our weakest link.

DEVON: What accusation?

JULIA: That Father had a mistress.

DEVON: Father had a—?

JULIA: That Father had a mistress. And she was with him when he died. *(To* BETH:*)* What was wrong with you? I know you hate to fight, but in this case it would have behooved you to come to father's defense. Why didn't you say anything? Your silence seemed like corroboration! Why couldn't you, for once, have opened your mouth and screamed and denied everything that scum of the earth was saying?

BETH: *(After a pause)* Because—what he said—was true.

JULIA: What are you talking about?

BETH: It sounded melodramatic and sordid the way Lucereau said it. But it's true—Father did die in the arms of his mistress.

JULIA: *(To* BETH:*)* How could you possibly know that?

BETH: *(After a long pause)* ...Because I'm the one who arranged for her to be there.

(Blackout)

(In the darkness we hear the sound of the flute—disturbed, urgent, climaxing with an air of foreboding, the promise of troubles to come.)

END ACT ONE

ACT TWO

(At rise:)

(Immediately after the preceding scene.)

(JULIA and DEVON are still in a state of astonishment. BETH, feeling weak, has taken a seat. Now DEVON says:)

DEVON: For God's sake, will you tell me what you two are talking about!

JULIA: Lucereau said Father had another woman in his life. For many years, apparently. I don't know how long. Ask Beth. She seems to have known all about it. The little saint actually seems to have arranged many of their trysts!

DEVON: Beth?

BETH: We don't have time for this now. We have to leave for the dinner.

JULIA: I don't want to go.

BETH: Julia, please—. We have to dress.

JULIA: Oh, no. This is more important. What the hell do you mean? Father died in the arms of his mistress—and you arranged for her to be there? You're going to drop a little bombshell like that and go off and get into your fancy dress? I think you owe us—

DEVON: Hold on, Julia. I'm sure Beth wants to tell us what she knows.

JULIA: I always knew you were great at keeping secrets. This is a doozy.

DEVON: Beth, as clearly—and as quickly as you can—tell us what this is all about.

(BETH hesitates.)

JULIA: Come on, Beth. Give.

BETH: Where's Mother?

DEVON: I told you—in her room. Getting dressed.

(BETH glances in that direction then, after a long pause, begins:)

BETH: I only found out about the relationship by accident. I recognized this woman—in the back row at several speeches that Dad gave in this country. And then, on a couple of trips I took with him abroad, I noticed her again. I wondered how come this woman often happened to be in the same city at the same time as Father. She just seemed to—show up—particularly when Mother wasn't around.

JULIA: How convenient!

BETH: Not thinking she had any personal connection with Dad, I asked if he'd noticed her also. I guess he thought he could confide in me. He told me—he and this woman were—very close.

DEVON: Who was she?

BETH: Someone who'd been at a conference he'd attended quite some time ago. She was working for one of the groups his foundations support. She was pleasant. Uncomplicated. A creature to unwind with. He enjoyed her company. He could relax with her—in a way that he could never quite relax with Mother. He respected Mother greatly—but she wasn't easy to be with. And this woman—

JULIA: Oh, yes. We know the type.

BETH: No, you don't. She wasn't a floozy, someone just for sex, she was—a sweet diversion. She had a way of putting people at ease rather than, like Mother, challenging them. She made no demands, but was always available, attentive to his needs. She seemed utterly devoted to Dad. I could see that when we met.

JULIA: You met?

BETH: On one trip, he introduced me to her. I liked her.

DEVON: Did Dad support her?

BETH: In some measure or other, I assume he did. There was a husband somewhere loosely in the picture for a few years. But eventually Dad seemed to be her whole life. I suspect she was the only one he knew with whom he could find total repose—and who asked nothing of him.

JULIA: Unlike the rest of us.

BETH: I was disturbed about the relationship at first. Then I realized—she wasn't really taking anything that belonged to Mother—or even to us. It was something quite outside the marriage. She was reserved and gentle and had a splendid sense of humor. After that first introduction, Father would sometimes ask me to arrange their meetings.

JULIA: Be a go-between.

BETH: Yes.

DEVON: His alibi.

BETH: Sometimes. I wasn't comfortable doing it. But there was no one else he could trust!

JULIA: And you did that? You pimped for your Dad?

BETH: He needed—something. He so often seemed to have the weight of the world on his shoulders.

JULIA: You betrayed your Mother?

BETH: I suffered the tortures of the damned about that! But Dad needed—he deserved—this kind of special friend.

JULIA: So it turns out Miss See No Evil, Hear No Evil, Speak No Evil actually had the biggest evil to hide of all of us!

DEVON: That's unfair, Julia!

JULIA: What do you want me to say? "Thank you for helping Dad to rendezvous with his whore?"

BETH: She wasn't at all like that—

JULIA: I suppose you did all this out of your famous compassion!

DEVON: Lay off, Julia! Why have you become so puritanical all of a sudden?

JULIA: I knew Beth and Dad had secrets together. I thought the secrets were as petty as their sharing comments about us behind our backs—but it turns out there was quite a bit more depth to their collusion.

BETH: You have to understand—

JULIA: It didn't bother you one bit—what you were facilitating in the middle of your father's marriage?

BETH: It tore me apart! But if you could have seen how happy those two were together—!

JULIA: "How happy." I thought you were the one who believed happiness wasn't everything. I thought you believed self-sacrifice was the highest ideal of all.

DEVON: *(To* JULIA:*)* And I thought you were the one who believed in the free life, no chains, no bows to bourgeois morality. Obviously, you mean it only for yourself—not for anybody else, not for your father!

JULIA: This little revelation doesn't matter to you?

DEVON: Oh, yes. It matters. It matters a lot! It means the man I could never equal, the man beside whom I could never measure up, was actually just a tin god, a womanizer, an adulterer!

BETH: Devon—

DEVON: *(To the portrait:)* Great work, Dad! I love it! You know what it does? It lets me off the hook! *(He gets himself a drink.)*

JULIA: That's you all over! Blaming your father for your own inadequacies!

DEVON: Yeah? And who do you blame for yours?

BETH: Devon! Julia!

JULIA: Look, we have to go to this dinner now. We each have to say our little piece about how wonderful Dad was—and sound sincere as we're saying it. We also have to seem like one big happy family—a happy loving family—where sibling rivalry is not the name of the game. *(To* BETH:*)* You've won, you know. You've achieved the highest level of betrayal. I wouldn't have wanted that— even if it meant becoming the first and only favorite of Dear Old Dad.

BETH: Dad loved each of us the same. It's just that, by accident, I happened to discover—

JULIA: Little traitor—

BETH: Can either of you ever forgive me?

DEVON: It's Mother who's going to have to forgive you.

BETH: God willing, all of this is something she'll never know.

JULIA: She'll definitely know it when Lucereau's interview with you hits the airwaves.

(The doorbell rings. DEVON *looks out:)*

DEVON: The limo's here. *(He goes toward the kitchen entrance and calls:)* Mother! The car's here! *(Calling upstairs:)* Willow! Hurry up! We have to leave! Now!

BETH: I don't want to go. I can't—

DEVON: You have to. We all have to.

BETH: I won't get up in front of all those people. I wouldn't be able to get out a word!

DEVON: Neither would I. With any luck, by the time it comes for us to speak, I'll be under the table. So it's over to you, Julia!

JULIA: Oh, marvelous! I have to get up in front of a ballroom full of worshipful people and praise our father to the skies!

(Blackout)

(The sound of a flute—agitated, disturbed.)

(The living room disappears into darkness. We hear the sound of applause. A spotlight picks out JULIA, *downstage center, holding a champagne glass. She addresses us as if we were the banquet audience at the testimonial dinner. She is the slightest bit the worse for the wine. Everything she says is tinged with irony.)*

JULIA: Thank you. My sister and brother are too moved by the splendor of this evening to trust themselves to speak. My mother, as she did in my father's life, prefers to stay in the background. So the task of speaking for all of us has fallen on my all-too-unworthy shoulders. ...If my father were here I know he'd say "I don't deserve this. Please—take your money and your time and give them to the sick and starving." But I would say—in some way—we all are the sick and starving, sick with his loss, and starving for someone of his calibre to come again into this world.

...He was unique, my father. He didn't live for himself. He lived for everybody. Wherever there was a country, an institution or a single person who needed something or who had a problem, he was ready in an instant to see that their problem was solved. A magic man. A good man. A man who lived—not for his own pleasure—but to bring some pleasure, some relief, to those less fortunate in this difficult world. ...But you know all that. Perhaps, from a member of the family, what you want to know is—what was he like at home? He was wonderful! With the same instinct he used to bring comfort and ease to the needy, the underprivileged, he brought comfort and ease to the three of us, understanding us, soothing us, being the ideal father everyone should have. We knew this even while he was living. We appreciate it more and more every day now that he is gone.

...Of course the one who misses him most is my mother. He was that rare thing—a husband of impeccable fidelity. His love for our mother was palpable in everything he did, everything he said. I remember those lines from Hamlet—"So loving to my mother that he might not beteem the winds of heaven visit her face too roughly." That was my father's love. Strong. Steady. Utterly faithful. As a married couple, both at home and abroad, they were the nonpareil of pairs. ...Selfless philanthropist. Exemplary father. Kind and faithful husband. None of us are worthy to follow in his footsteps. However, with the light of his inspiration to guide us—we can all try.

(Applause)

(Blackout)

(The sound of a flute—on a note of admiration and triumph, with sadness beneath.)

(When the lights come up on the living room it is later that night. MRS. STANHOPE, BETH, JULIA, DEVON *and* WILLOW *enter, returning from the testimonial dinner. They are all tired—*BETH *more than anyone. They spent the evening keeping up a facade and now are ready to unwind. As they take off wraps and scarves they say:)*

DEVON: I'm glad that's behind us!

WILLOW: I wanted to speak! I had things to say! Why didn't you let me say a few words?

DEVON: Because, by the time of the after dinner speeches, you'd had a glass or two of every wine that was on offer! Red, white, and several colors in between!

WILLOW: I didn't notice *you* refusing any.

MRS. STANHOPE: Children! Children!

(DEVON *goes over to the drink table and starts pouring himself a drink.*)

MRS. STANHOPE: Child.

(*He gives his mother a look, pours, then defiantly begins to drink.*)

JULIA: I'll have one, too. (*Deliberately challenging her mother's disapproval,* JULIA *goes over and gets herself a drink, too.*)

MRS. STANHOPE: I thought the evening went very well, as those things go. I'm sure your father would have appreciated every sentence.

JULIA: Heaven—if that's where he is—would be the only place that could tolerate such drivel. As for our earthly audience—

MRS. STANHOPE: They're used to this kind of evening. They don't go to a testimonial dinner to listen to people stab the honoree in the back. I think your father would have been proud.

JULIA: I think he'd have gotten a laugh out of the endless fabrications. What do you think Beth?

BETH: I think he'd have been embarrassed at all the money wasted on truffles and trifles.

MRS. STANHOPE: Personally, I was appalled at the number of mink stoles that seem suddenly again to be in fashion. If things keep going in this direction, minks will soon be extinct!

JULIA: It's *we* who are becoming extinct! A dying breed—those who still attempt to preserve for the world a surface of civility!

DEVON: (*Warningly to* JULIA:) Julia—

JULIA: (*Wild*) Some must lie and some must cheat and some must hold their tongues!

MRS. STANHOPE: (*Trying to defuse the growing tension*) I'm sure you're all tired—

WILLOW: *I* am. This strapless bra is killing me. I've got to get it off. (*She starts toward the stairs, then turns and asks* DEVON:) You coming up?

DEVON: (*At the drink table*) Just one for the road.

WILLOW: I wish to hell you'd get off that road! (*She goes angrily upstairs.*)

JULIA: (*Sarcastically*) One big happy family. It's a wonder they don't give us the Family of the Year award!

DEVON: Will you shut up! I'm tired of your sarcastic remarks!

BETH: And I'm tired of listening to the squabbling of both of you!

MRS. STANHOPE: What's the matter with you three? You've been at each other's throats all evening. I've never seen such a display of familial disharmony in my life! I'm utterly stunned at this behavior. Especially, Beth, from you!

BETH: I'm sorry, Mother, I—

(BETH *starts to speak but cannot. She collapses and crumples to the floor.*)

(Blackout)

(*The sound of the flute. Fever. Nightmare. A sense of confusion and bad dreams.*)

(*When the lights come up it is the next morning.* DEVON *is sprawled on a chair, his shirt unbuttoned, still wearing the tuxedo he wore the night before.* WILLOW, *freshly dressed, is saying:*)

WILLOW: Malaria—?!

DEVON: You didn't hear the doctor come? He was here till three in the morning.

WILLOW: You don't die of this thing, do you?

DEVON: Not if you take your pills, which apparently she didn't. Seems she's had it before and this was a recurrence.

WILLOW: I've got to see her!

DEVON: Let her sleep.

WILLOW: Is there coffee?

DEVON: If you make it, there's coffee. (*He gets up and goes to the drink table.*)

WILLOW: My God, can't you stop for one minute!

DEVON: I'd be happy to have coffee instead.

WILLOW: Make it yourself.

DEVON: You're cute, you know. You drive me to drink then get upset when I get there!

(*The telephone rings.* DEVON *doesn't move to answer it.* WILLOW *picks it up.*)

WILLOW: Hello? ...No. This is Willow. ...Oh! Hello! ...Well, yes, I'd love to. ...Whenever you say. ...No, I'm sorry. Beth can't come to the phone. She has malaria—

DEVON: Who is that?

WILLOW: Damien Lucereau. He wants to interview me!

DEVON: Hang up!

WILLOW: (*Into the phone*) Yes, I'm free this after—

DEVON: Hang up, I say!

(*He pulls the phone from her hand and smashes it down on the receiver.*)

DEVON: What the hell are you doing?

WILLOW: He asked—

DEVON: You agree to talk to him?! You just blurt out that Beth has malaria?! Jesus Christ!

WILLOW: So what? So someone's sick, so we say what it is. So what?

DEVON: You've been in this family for all these years and you don't know when to keep your mouth shut?

WILLOW: I don't know why it's such a secret! Malaria isn't a sin! It's a disease!

DEVON: If you were married to the son of Joe Doakes you could announce that someone in the family has leprosy, gonorrhea and St. Vitus dance, it wouldn't be news. But with us—. You know damn well we don't talk about our problems publicly.

WILLOW: It's not publicly—

DEVON: Once you've blabbed to Lucereau, it is! He'll find some way to give it a negative twist. You'll see! My God, haven't you learned by now that in this family—

WILLOW: This family! This family! I have to turn myself into a pretzel to figure out what's okay with you guys and what isn't!

DEVON: You don't understand. You've never understood from the beginning.

WILLOW: Why can't all of us just be who we are!

DEVON: Because we're—

WILLOW: No! Don't say it! "Because we're Stanhopes!" I wish I'd never become a Stanhope!

DEVON: I wish so, too!

(Sudden silence. A beat.)

WILLOW: *(Somberly, after a long time:)* ...Well—that's that, then.

DEVON: That's what, then?

WILLOW: The Big Goodbye...

DEVON: *(Slowly)* ...Is it?

WILLOW: It's what you want, it's what I want. Why make a big deal out of it?

DEVON: The children—

WILLOW: I like them. They don't much care for me. They've been educated just enough to begin to be ashamed of me. ...You keep 'em. ... I'd like to visit.

DEVON: Let's think about it—

WILLOW: I know what you're thinking: How will the first ever Stanhope divorce play in the press?

DEVON: Willow—

WILLOW: When other people say my name, I sound tall and willowy. When you say it, I sound like a weed.

DEVON: Are you sure you—?

(JULIA *enters from upstairs.*)

JULIA: I overslept.

WILLOW: How's Beth?

JULIA: Still sleeping. I looked in. Didn't touch her forehead. But she seems to be breathing normally. I think her fever has abated. Or at least it's less.

WILLOW: Good. Good.

JULIA: Mother's asleep on the couch in Beth's room. She stayed up with her the whole night. ...I need coffee.

WILLOW: I'll get it.

DEVON: Ah. For her you'll get it. For me—

(WILLOW *gives him a look and goes out to the kitchen.*)

JULIA: What was that all about?

DEVON: Nothing. You may get your wish.

JULIA: What wish?

DEVON: To see her surgically removed from the family.

JULIA: *(Hopefully)* Really—! What happened?

DEVON: I don't want to go into it. It doesn't feel as splendid as I thought it would.

JULIA: Poor baby.

DEVON: She fielded a call from Lucereau. He said he wants to interview her. She told him Beth has malaria.

JULIA: Oh, shit.

DEVON: Julia—what are we going to do about that bastard and his blasted film?

JULIA: I can't think before I've had my coffee. What's keeping that girl?

(JULIA *exits to the kitchen.* DEVON *goes to the drink table. He pours a drink, but can't bring himself to drink it. He puts it down on the table. He looks up at his father's portrait and says:*)

DEVON: You really started something, Dad, you know it? You pop off and leave us with a mess for the rest of our lives. Everything we do, everything we say, every move we make has you, you, you written all over it. Some people disappear when they're gone. You're more with us now than you ever were when you were alive! Now, thanks to Damien Lucereau, you're about to be made infamous! And you know what? It's exactly what you deserve!

(Blackout)

(The sound of a flute—mournful, troubled.)

(A short time later, JULIA is sitting drinking her coffee. BETH comes downstairs wearing a robe.)

JULIA: You should be in bed—sleeping!

BETH: The phone kept ringing.

JULIA: Lucifer calling! I have no idea how we're going to get that bloodsucker out of our lives! ...How do you feel?

BETH: Better. Much better. Fainting. That was silly of me.

JULIA: It was silly of you not to be taking your pills.

BETH: Mother's still asleep on my couch. She didn't have to stay up all night and nurse me—

JULIA: Of course she did. ...Beth, I want to apologize.

BETH: For what?

JULIA: For the rotten things I said to you. I shouldn't have. And I'm sorry.

BETH: Forget it. ...The house is so quiet. Where are Devon and Willow?

JULIA: They went out for a walk. Not together. Devon went north and Willow went south. By the way, that might be the general direction of their marriage.

BETH: Split?

JULIA: So it seems.

BETH: It's probably the best thing. They weren't happy.

JULIA: Are *you* happy, Beth?

BETH: Why do you ask?

JULIA: You were restless last night. In the midst of your fever you kept muttering something.

BETH: Something incriminating?

JULIA: Who's Jack?

BETH: Ah...

JULIA: So? Who is he?

BETH: A friend.

JULIA: A friend who's so much on your mind you call his name when you're unconscious?

BETH: He's someone I work with. A doctor.

JULIA: Go on.

BETH: We met in the Sudan four years ago. We seemed to think alike on everything. We were comrades in an instant.

JULIA: And so—?

BETH: We let our lives take us where they would—and often—as if by chance—they took us to the same place at the same time. Those days and nights were very precious to us.

JULIA: Days—and nights, too?

BETH: Yes. Nights, too.

JULIA: Why didn't you tell us?

BETH: The old Stanhope habit of keeping things secret. When things become public property, they get spoiled somehow.

JULIA: I know what you mean.

BETH: I'll give you his name—and how to contact him. If anything ever happens to me,—I'd like him to know I was buried with his ring. *(She opens her collar to show a ring she is wearing on a chain around her neck.)*

JULIA: You're being morbid!

BETH: Will you do it?

JULIA: Of course I will, but—. ...Beth—?

BETH: Yes?

JULIA: ...I'm glad you have a life. ...I envy you.

BETH: *(With compassion)* Julia, talk to me. Tell me what's happening in your life. What you're doing, what you're feeling. All this rushing about you claim to be doing. It's not the real you, it's not—

(The phone rings.)

JULIA: Don't answer!

BETH: It might be someone who needs one of us.

JULIA: *You* maybe. Never me. ...I bet it's that blasted vulture again. *(She picks up the phone.)* Hello? *(She listens a second then slams the phone back down on the receiver.)* I win the bet.

BETH: We're like some prey he's got clenched in his teeth and he won't let go.

JULIA: How in the name of God are we going to shake free of him?!

(DEVON *enters from outside* JULIA *says to him:*)

JULIA: Lucereau called again.

DEVON: What did he want?

JULIA: I don't know. I hung up on him. ...What are we going to do? If Dad's affair becomes known, what he'll be remembered for most won't be the great things he did in this life, it'll be the way he died. "Alden Stanhope? Oh, yes. Isn't he the one who died in the arms of his mistress?"

BETH: I should have talked to Dad. I should, somehow, have gotten him to stop. I thought it was a private thing, that it was over when he died, that the whole thing was dead and buried. Now I realize—it's going to come out eventually, why not let it come out now and let the bombs fall where they may?

JULIA: If Lucereau knows this much, he may know about your years of collusion. He'll expose you as the facilitator—

BETH: So what? Let it happen! I have it coming!

DEVON: Do you really want to see the family name dragged through the mud?

JULIA: I thought you didn't care—

DEVON: I changed my mind. I realize my investors might desert if they catch a whiff of scandal.

JULIA: So—this is where we stand: *(To* BETH:*)* You're willing to have the story come out because you think you should be punished. *(To* DEVON:*)* You don't want the story to come out because it might hurt your bottom line.

DEVON: *(To* JULIA:*)* And you? I think you'd like the story to come out—just for the excitement.

JULIA: I wouldn't! I want it kept secret! I'm not thinking of me, I'm thinking of Dad.

DEVON: *(Cynically)* Oh, yes.

JULIA: I am!

DEVON: I know you are! I believe you think of him so much that no other man will ever satisfy you.

BETH: That's an awful thing to say!

DEVON: Really? Isn't it true that you throw yourself into dangerous work to expiate your guilt over collaborating in his betrayals?

JULIA: *(To* DEVON:*)* What about you? Aren't you always comparing yourself to him and coming up wanting?

DEVON: Being the son of this father ruined my life!

BETH: And also made it very special.

DEVON: We were cursed—all of us—from the moment we saw the light of day! *(To the portrait:)* We'll never be free of you, Dad. Never!

(WILLOW enters from outdoors, having heard this last.)

WILLOW: Will you, for God's sake, all stop obsessing about your father! Why can't you just let him go and live your own lives!

DEVON: You married me for his name!

WILLOW: And you married me because my face was on magazine covers!

DEVON: You're leaving me because he's gone now, don't think I don't know it!

WILLOW: When he was alive there was something special about all of you! Now that he's gone, you're running around like chickens with your heads cut off! *(She rushes upstairs.)*

JULIA: She has a way with an image, that girl. But she's right. The loss of Dad decapitated all of us. ...Oh, I wish I'd been left at birth on a doorstep. Free to create my own world—without preconceptions, without forebears, without strings!

DEVON: Do it now! Walk away from the past! From this oh-so-grand house! Change your name, give up the monthly checks that come with it and start over! Ms. Anonymous!

JULIA: It's too late!

DEVON: It was always too late. For you, for me, for all of us. From the moment we were born, it was already too late.

(The telephone rings.)

JULIA: Don't answer! It'll be Damien Lucereau. It's the umpteenth time this morning!

(After two rings, the phone stops ringing.)

JULIA: Mother must have picked it up upstairs!

DEVON: Good lord! What is he saying to her?!

BETH: He promised not to tell her we were talking with him—

JULIA: Do you think a man like that would keep his word?

BETH: How are we going to explain to her why we agreed to get involved—?

JULIA: Maybe she hung up on him. Maybe they're not still talking—*(Stealthily, she picks up the phone, listens for a moment, then says:)* They're not! Maybe she cut him off before he had a chance to—

(MRS. STANHOPE appears on the staircase.)

MRS. STANHOPE: All right, you three. Why didn't you tell me you were giving interviews to Damien Lucereau?

BETH: He swore he wouldn't tell you!

MRS. STANHOPE: Don't you know that, with Lucereau, his word is not his bond?

DEVON: What did he say?

MRS. STANHOPE: He called to ask if I'd confirm the fact that your father died in the arms of his mistress.

DEVON: Oh, my God—!

MRS. STANHOPE: It has a ring to it, doesn't it? "Died in the arms of his mistress?" The woman could have been in the living room with him playing Parcheesi, she could have been making an omelet, they could both have been asleep on their separate sides of the bed—but it comes out "died in the arms of his mistress".

BETH: We didn't want you to know—

MRS. STANHOPE: Until when? Until I saw the broadcast?

JULIA: We told him it's a lie. We denied it vehemently. On camera.

MRS. STANHOPE: You said that? ...Even though it's the truth?

BETH: You know that?

MRS. STANHOPE: Of course.

JULIA: How long have you known?

MRS. STANHOPE: I knew about the affair—almost since the beginning. I've known about her being there at the end—since the night he died.

BETH: How could you possibly have known that?

MRS. STANHOPE: Her scent.

(They look at her. She continues.)

MRS. STANHOPE: I remember the first time I became aware of it. It was in the tenth year of our marriage. Your father came home—and there was this scent about him. This most distinctive—feminine—scent. Jasmine. Lavender. Quite lovely. I teased him about it. He said he'd been at a dinner. A lot of women had been there. Quite a number of them had kissed him on the cheek—leaving evidence of their presences. We laughed about it together. ...From then on, when, at the end of a day, he came home looking brushed and polished and freshly showered—I knew he'd been with her. The night he died—and you called me, Beth—and I hurried to the apartment—I smelled that scent on his body. I knew that she had been there. I knew, had he lived, he'd have showered before coming home that evening. *If* he came home that evening. But, as it was, he had the bad luck to die before he could shower and make the evidence of her disappear.

BETH: Then—all these years—you've known—this woman was in his life?

MRS. STANHOPE: Yes.

JULIA: When you confronted him about it, what did he say?

MRS. STANHOPE: I never confronted him about it.

JULIA: You must have argued—

MRS. STANHOPE: We never mentioned it.

DEVON: Mother—!

MRS. STANHOPE: What good would it have done? It would only have driven a wedge between us.

JULIA: Did he suspect you knew?

MRS. STANHOPE: I think he must have.

DEVON: You tolerated his being constantly unfaithful?

BETH: Didn't it hurt?

MRS. STANHOPE: Of course it hurt. Do you think I have no feelings? At first I felt it all—anger, inadequacy, betrayal. Then I realized—it would hurt more to go through life without him.

JULIA: It's so goddam nineteenth century! How could you have stuck with him and said nothing!

MRS. STANHOPE: Children never see their parents' marriage clearly. They say children sense things—but perhaps you didn't sense how much I loved your father. I loved and admired him more than anyone I've ever known in this life. He was, quite simply, the most extraordinary being I've ever known. His vision, his understanding, his grace—and, yes, his love, were all beyond anything I could have known with any other.

BETH: And he loved you—in spite of the other woman.

MRS. STANHOPE: Yes. I know. That's why, in spite of her, I stayed. A bit more independent, perhaps. A bit busier with my own life. But I stayed.

JULIA: Then the whole marriage was a sham!

MRS. STANHOPE: No. It was an excellent marriage. Everything you said at the dinner—

JULIA: Was fake! Was lies!

MRS. STANHOPE: No. It was absolutely true. As far as it went. So it didn't tell all. We don't owe the public everything.

JULIA: I still can't understand how you could have stayed!

MRS. STANHOPE: Every marriage has its secrets, known to only the two. How they make their way through the days of their lives is their business, nobody else's. It's when the world outside insists on knowing their secrets that what to the couple might seem beautiful may appear ugly.

DEVON: So there was another woman in our parents' marriage—and my mother stayed, although she knew.

MRS. STANHOPE: Yes. I knew. *(She turns to* BETH:*)* What I didn't know—until Lucereau just now enlightened me—was that you, Beth, had facilitated his meetings with her.

BETH: I didn't know what to do! Every time he asked me to arrange a meeting it would kill me! But—he needed her.

MRS. STANHOPE: Yes. Actually, I know that.

BETH: I didn't know how to refuse him.

MRS. STANHOPE: No. He had that way about him. People wanted to do what he wanted them to do.

BETH: I hated betraying you! As soon as I could find work that would send me to the ends of the earth, I fled. To escape from having to assist him in betraying you!

MRS. STANHOPE: Poor Beth. You needn't have gone that far for my sake.

BETH: There were days when he'd call and ask me to set up a rendezvous for him—and I wanted to die! All the covering-up! All the lying—! ...Please forgive—

MRS. STANHOPE: Beth, dear, there's nothing to forgive. I understand completely. I'm only sorry that you had so many hours being troubled. We could have comforted each other.

BETH: Oh, Mother—!

(She goes to her mother. They embrace warmly.)

BETH: If only I had known—!

MRS. STANHOPE: Those are the saddest words in the English language...

(She kisses BETH *gently. A tender moment.)*

JULIA: *(After a pause)* Well, we can understand—but that doesn't mean the world will. When it all comes out—

MRS. STANHOPE: Perhaps it won't.

DEVON: But Lucereau knows all. And there's no way to stop him!

MRS. STANHOPE: Isn't there? ...Pull yourselves together. I've invited Lucereau over.

DEVON: He'll eat you alive!

MRS. STANHOPE: I think you children underestimate me. ...Hurry now. He'll be here very shortly. He seems to enjoy confrontations. Let's see how he survives a confrontation with me.

(Blackout)

(The sound of the flute. Girding for action.)

(When the lights come up JULIA, BETH *and* DEVON *are just finishing rearranging some furniture in preparation for* LUCEREAU's *visit.)*

BETH: What makes Mother think she can handle Lucereau *mano a mano*?

JULIA: I have no idea.

DEVON: I hope he doesn't turn the tables on her—as he did with us. He could—

(He breaks off as WILLOW *comes downstairs in her coat, carrying a suitcase.)*

DEVON: What's this—?

WILLOW: I'm leaving.

DEVON: Right now?

WILLOW: I've got a taxi coming.

DEVON: Where are you going?

WILLOW: *(She shrugs.)* Leaving is leaving, Dev. You can send things on to me when I figure out where I'm going to be.

DEVON: Willow—

WILLOW: It's the right thing. I'm not a good fit with you all. You know it. I know it. Best just to hit the road.

DEVON: What road?

WILLOW: London first, maybe. Then Paris. Then Rome. Then—who knows. ...Will you pay my credit card bills till we can make some arrangements?

DEVON: If you don't stay at the most expensive—.

BETH: *(Chiding him)* Devon—

DEVON: Yes, of course.

WILLOW: And you'll see there's enough in my account so I can use my bank card—

(A look to DEVON *from* BETH.*)*

DEVON: Certainly. ...What'll I tell the boys?

WILLOW: I'll send them postcards. Tell them we broke up friendly. ...Tell them I'll see them. ...I love them...

(A horn toots outside.)

WILLOW: My cab's here. ...Julia,—goodbye.

JULIA: Goodbye, kid. Have happy journeys. I mean it.

WILLOW: Thank you. ...Beth—Beth—

(Very fond of Beth, she can hardly speak. They hug.)

BETH: You take care of yourself.

WILLOW: You take care of *your* self.

BETH: Get in touch if you need anything.

WILLOW: Who knows. I might drop by sometime—to wherever you are. *(She turns to* DEVON:*)* 'Bye, Dev. It was good while it lasted.

DEVON: Willow, are you sure—?

WILLOW: Surer than I've ever been of anything.

(The horn toots again. WILLOW *starts to leave.* MRS. STANHOPE *enters from the kitchen.)*

MRS. STANHOPE: What's all that noise—?

WILLOW: 'Bye, Mrs. Stanhope. Give Damien Lucereau hell.

*(*DEVON *sees her out and returns immediately.)*

JULIA: So. A classy exit from the girl who had no class.

DEVON: I suppose there'll be problems in the future.

BETH: I don't think so.

MRS. STANHOPE: Has she actually left you?

DEVON: I prefer to say we came to a mutual agreement.

JULIA: "We'll always be good friends" as they say in the tabloids. It seems—if people aren't tied together, they can actually be friendly.

MRS. STANHOPE: *(To* DEVON:*)* That kicked-in-the-stomach feeling will disappear, Devon—after a while.

JULIA: The inquisition chamber is ready. I hope you know what you're doing.

MRS. STANHOPE: When Lucereau arrives, I want you three to leave me alone with him.

JULIA: Not on your life!

DEVON: We're staying!

MRS. STANHOPE: If you're going to stay, let me handle things.

BETH: But—

MRS. STANHOPE: What's the matter? Don't you think I have the intelligence to go head-to-head with the monster?

DEVON: We want to spare you—

JULIA: Father would never have let you—

MRS. STANHOPE: I know your father better than you knew him. I know his methods. I know how he worked. I know what he used to do to face an opponent down.

(The doorbell rings.)

MRS. STANHOPE: Bring the gentleman into our parlor. ...And don't look so green around the gills. I may look to you like Methuselah's aunt, but I still have a few arrows left in my quiver!

(JULIA goes to answer the door.)

(She re-enters with LUCEREAU, who stands at the entryway and says:)

LUCEREAU: Ah! The gathering of the clan. Miss Julia. Mr. Devon. And Miss Beth. I'm glad to see you're better. Malaria—if that's what it was—is obviously no match for you. And the Grande Dame herself. In person. I'm honored.

MRS. STANHOPE: Please come in, Mr. Lucereau.

LUCEREAU: And where is the willowy Willow? I was looking forward to—

DEVON: She's go—

MRS. STANHOPE: *(Interrupting)* She's out for the moment.

LUCEREAU: Perhaps I'll get to see her on her return.

MRS. STANHOPE: Perhaps you will.

LUCEREAU: May I express my sincere congratulations at the honors which were bestowed last night upon your husband and your father.

JULIA: Oh, come now, Lucereau. It's hard for you to express your sincere anything.

MRS. STANHOPE: Julia, my dear! The man is a guest in our house. However he may have treated any of you in the studio, here we treat him with courtesy and grace.

LUCEREAU: I always felt you were even better at diplomacy than your husband, Mrs. Stanhope. I see the talent hasn't deserted you.

MRS. STANHOPE: Would you care for a drink?

LUCEREAU: A Scotch, please. Neat.

(DEVON *goes to pour it.*)

DEVON: My father always drank Scotch. Neat.

LUCEREAU: I know he did. That's why I asked for it. Drinking his Scotch—or at least his *brand* of Scotch—*(Pointedly, to* DEVON:*)* I assume the carafe has been drained more than once since his death—might bring me closer to him.

JULIA: You could stand in the same room, locked eye-to-eye, clasped hand-to-hand, you could never be close to him.

LUCEREAU: I admire your loyalty.

JULIA: There are giants who stride the earth—and there are pygmies who make a career of throwing spitballs at them. My father was the former, while you—

MRS. STANHOPE: *(Who had let Julia's speech continue on purpose)* Julia! Enough! We haven't brought this gentleman here to insult him. We've invited him here to have a private conversation.

LUCEREAU: By that, do you mean that anything said here must remain confidential?

MRS. STANHOPE: Not at all. I'd be happy to see everything we say here broadcast to the world at large.

LUCEREAU: Excellent.

MRS. STANHOPE: I've asked you here, mainly, to clear the air between us.

LUCEREAU: A remark worthy of your husband.

(She gestures him to a chair. He sits.)

LUCEREAU: Do proceed.

MRS. STANHOPE: What I propose is an exchange of information. There are some things *you* can tell *us*—and some things *we* can tell *you*.

LUCEREAU: What can I possibly tell *you*, Mrs. Stanhope?

MRS. STANHOPE: How you discovered that my husband died—as you so poetically put it—in the arms of his mistress.

LUCEREAU: You don't deny it.

MRS. STANHOPE: No. I don't deny it. Tell us how you came upon this information.

LUCEREAU: Very simple. It began with the dog that didn't bark.

(All look at him questioningly)

LUCEREAU: Or, to put it more directly, the phone call that wasn't mentioned.

MRS. STANHOPE: Please continue.

LUCEREAU: Some months ago I was at a dinner party. People there were talking about the night your husband died. One person mentioned that, on that night, he happened to be at a gathering where Beth also was in attendance.

BETH: A benefit for the African AIDS mission.

LUCEREAU: I believe that's what it was. Yes. *(To* BETH*:)* He said—your cell phone rang and you left the gathering instantly.

BETH: I was at that event. My cell phone rang. That indicates nothing.

LUCEREAU: It indicates something if you never mentioned that call—to the police—to anyone.

BETH: It slipped my mind!

LUCEREAU: Oh, no, Miss Beth. I think that call was from your father's apartment. From his mistress. I think she called you in a panic saying your father had had a heart attack and died. You rushed to the apartment and arranged for his mistress to leave. As soon as she was safely gone you called the police, and, pretending you'd just arrived, announced you just happened to come home and found your father's body.

BETH: That is pure invention!

LUCEREAU: No, Miss Beth. I think it's truth. If there was a call to you from the apartment it meant that there was someone at the apartment when your father died.

JULIA: If there *was* such a call, why jump to the conclusion that it was from a mistress?

LUCEREAU: Quite simple. I talked your father's doorman. Doormen observe a good deal more than you think they do. This old doorman—Eric—knew a lot about the comings and goings on that night. And on many a night before that.

BETH: Eric.

LUCEREAU: He was very well aware of the comings and goings of that woman. He knew—that night—what time you came. He knew what time the woman left. Should we ask the police to check the phone records? Should we check the time that phone call was made against the time you arrived at the apartment and the time when you reported the death?

BETH: No! No. ...It's true. ...Everything occurred just as you say it did. She called. I hurried over. She left. I reported the death.

LUCEREAU: I knew my Sherlockian instincts wouldn't fail me!

MRS. STANHOPE: And now that you have this information, what do you intend to do with it?

LUCEREAU: As you know, I am addicted to truth—and its dissemination.

MRS. STANHOPE: So you intend to make all these details public?

LUCEREAU: Of course. The public has a right to know.

MRS. STANHOPE: You mean a right to gossip about, chew up and spit out the life of another human being. I'll fight to my last breath their right to devour my husband.

LUCEREAU: Your husband was a man of many passions.

MRS. STANHOPE: He had a passion for civility, for justice, for the end of hunger and disease, and, yes, for a woman not his wife. But that last counts very little against his passion for more public concerns.

LUCEREAU: You can't protect him from the unblinking light of history, Mrs. Stanhope.

MRS. STANHOPE: Oh, those high-sounding words! All you're really devoted to is getting a larger audience for your exposé! To do it you will feed the public's appetite for the lurid, the sickening need, in those who live off gossip, to throw garbage at those they've put on pedestals, to have the thrill of bringing them down.

LUCEREAU: May I point out—you don't own your husband's life. And if I, or anybody else, want to say or show anything about him, we have a perfect right to do so. I not only have the right, but the obligation, to broadcast everything I know.

MRS. STANHOPE: *(With great intensity)* Does everything have to be known about everybody? Is there no such thing as privacy any more?

LUCEREAU: For a public person—no.

MRS. STANHOPE: Why not? What makes them so different? I venture to say there's not one person on earth who doesn't have some secret they'd prefer to keep hidden.

LUCEREAU: In prominent figures, knowing everything about them matters.

MRS. STANHOPE: Why? Why should achieving celebrity make them fair game for wagging tongues?

LUCEREAU: People like to feel the rich and famous are just like they are. Flawed. Imperfect.

MRS. STANHOPE: Does all history come down to "Was Lincoln happy with his wife? Was Elizabeth the First really a Virgin? Did Jefferson have black children by his black mistress?" Why should any of these things need to be dwelt on, considering these people's achievements? At some level, even public people have the right to keep some things to themselves.

LUCEREAU: I don't agree.

MRS. STANHOPE: So you believe that, in this arena, everyone should know everything about everybody.

LUCEREAU: Absolutely.

MRS. STANHOPE: Would you say that the everyone we should know everything about would include you?

LUCEREAU: I would. Being open and above board about myself is one of my greatest talents.

MRS. STANHOPE: You are modest.

LUCEREAU: Not *too* modest, I hope.

MRS. STANHOPE: There is one talent you have about which you've never boasted.

LUCEREAU: Tell me, so I can rectify the omission.

MRS. STANHOPE: ...Your ability to write my husband's signature.

(LUCEREAU *says nothing.*)

MRS. STANHOPE: You don't reply. Perhaps you don't want to boast about this particular proficiency.

LUCEREAU: As you say, in some things I am quite modest.

MRS. STANHOPE: But you should be proud of this. It's a talent which you developed over a long, long time.

LUCEREAU: Go on.

MRS. STANHOPE: You were at college with Alden.

LUCEREAU: *(With an edge of bitterness)* I've always treasured those memories.

MRS. STANHOPE: You also treasured a few slips of paper on which he had written his name. Starting then, you began to forge his signature. Not too often. Just when you needed something and your qualifications weren't sufficient for you to get it on your own. His recommendation in a letter could achieve it for you.

LUCEREAU: He is—was—a powerful man, your husband.

MRS. STANHOPE: He built a reputation for integrity. A word from him could help you greatly on your climb. He became, in these letters you wrote, your greatest promoter. It was a forged letter, seemingly from him, which got you your first fellowship. It was a forged letter, seemingly from him, which got you your first job at the network where you work now.

LUCEREAU: Why shouldn't they have? I had a brain as good as his brain. A wit as quick as his. I had equal intelligence. Equal charm—if I cared to exert it. The only thing I didn't have was lineage—the accident of a distinguished birth. I gained that by having his name attached to a letter vouching for me.

MRS. STANHOPE: And you think your forging those letters was a perfectly legitimate action?

LUCEREAU: We hold this truth to be self-evident: that all men are *not* created equal. But by associating my name with his, I achieved a measure of equality with him. You might say I was his evil twin. But if one circumstance had been different, *he'd* have been the evil one.

MRS. STANHOPE: Never.

LUCEREAU: How did you discover—?

MRS. STANHOPE: Did you think that those to whom you'd written wouldn't ever mention to Alden the glowing letter of recommendation, supposedly from him, which they'd received?

LUCEREAU: And did your husband reveal—?

MRS. STANHOPE: No. Never. He said nothing. And he said nothing when other references you wrote, supposedly from him, on your behalf came to his attention over the years. A letter of introduction which got you an interview with a world leader. A letter of recommendation to a reclusive star. Perhaps a few went unreported to him. But year after year Alden knew what you were doing and when you were doing it.

LUCEREAU: And he did nothing?

MRS. STANHOPE: He was sorry for you.

LUCEREAU: Sorry—!

MRS. STANHOPE: He understood your envy. He realized exposing you might mean the end of your career. His not exposing you was his way of giving you a leg up. His discretion was—a gift to you—a kind of charity.

LUCEREAU: Charity! My God!

MRS. STANHOPE: Alden's philanthropy was expressed in a love of mankind in all its manifestations. It didn't limit itself to the obviously helpless and deserving. It was wide enough to encompass all aspects of human frailty and enmity. Including yours—which he well understood.

LUCEREAU: *(Bitterly)* Alden Stanhope my benefactor—?

MRS. STANHOPE: My husband was a quiet benevolent presence watching over you all your life, Lucereau,—since college.

LUCEREAU: And I never knew—?

MRS. STANHOPE: Of course not. That's the measure of his generosity—to give without the recipient's knowledge. To give without expecting gratitude or thanks.

LUCEREAU: He just looked on from a distance with that self-satisfied smirk and let me get away with this for years—?

MRS. STANHOPE: He was able to assist you and forgive you in one noble gesture.

LUCEREAU: I didn't want to be on the receiving end of his noble gestures! I still don't!

MRS. STANHOPE: Why do you hate us all so much?

LUCEREAU: Because of your infinitely smug do-goodism! This outpost of rampant altruism makes me sick! All so committed to saving humankind! So selfless and self-sacrificing. You can do it because you have the wherewithal to be above the struggle the rest of us have to be consumed with all of our lives!

MRS. STANHOPE: It's not poverty of pocketbook, it's poverty of spirit that keeps you where you are, Lucereau.

LUCEREAU: You snobs! You set yourself up above everybody!

MRS. STANHOPE: On the contrary, it's you with your microphone and camera and ability to communicate with millions who think yourself smugly above all rules of propriety and mutual respect.

LUCEREAU: I speak for the people.

MRS. STANHOPE: Lucereau, if the people were as rude and crude as you, this country would be in a very bad state indeed. Fortunately, there are people like my husband who—

LUCEREAU: No matter what I do, he wins! Even in death he reaches out to ruin me!

MRS. STANHOPE: Alden never destroys, he nourishes.

LUCEREAU: His cursed green thumb—leaving its filthy imprint all over my life!

MRS. STANHOPE: He pitied you.

LUCEREAU: I didn't want his pity! Or his charity!

MRS. STANHOPE: Of course not. Actually, I understand. And I understand why you've taken on the making of this film. While he was alive you hated him and needed him in equal measure. His name opened doors for you. Which is why, in spite of your overwhelming jealousy, you criticized but never attacked him with full force. But now that he's gone, and your talent at writing his name is useless, you can attempt to do what you have always wanted to do—destroy his good name.

LUCEREAU: You have no proof of any of my supposed transgressions—!

MRS. STANHOPE: Oh, but I do, Lucereau. Everything Alden knew, *I* know. Quite a few times, when he was away, and another incident happened, he wrote me about it. "Do you know who Lucereau wrote to this time—praising himself to the skies and signing my name?" I have all his letters. It would be extremely satisfying, now, to bring forth this little cache of evidence. Shall we get in touch with those who received your self-composed letters of reference and see if they have your forged letters still in their files? It would be so interesting, now, to check the signatures and reveal their true provenance.

LUCEREAU: You mean—you'd make all this information about me public?

MRS. STANHOPE: Make it radiantly public. *(Then, the coup de grace:)* After all—the public has a right to know.

LUCEREAU: You bastards! You always triumph! You always have the method and the means! No matter how hard the rest of us try, we can never win against you! You start at the top and you end at the top—and, no matter how the rest of us struggle, at the end you always stand victorious, holding the winning hand in your smug superior way!

MRS. STANHOPE: You have a choice—

LUCEREAU: You know damn well, if this comes out, my credibility, my work, my life—is over! *(He paces, furious. The others say nothing. After a long silence, he speaks.)* ...What do you want?

MRS. STANHOPE: Your silence. We want no film about my husband to come out under your auspices. We want your promise that you will not publish anything about the circumstances surrounding my husband's death. We want to be assured that copies of the interviews you trapped my children into making will be destroyed.

LUCEREAU: That's blackmail!

MRS. STANHOPE: Yes. It is. And I can't tell you how much I enjoy it.

LUCEREAU: Whether or not I reveal the truth about the circumstances surrounding your husband's death, you realize it will all come out eventually.

MRS. STANHOPE: I know that.

LUCEREAU: You can't censor the whole world.

MRS. STANHOPE: I wouldn't even try. But when the truth comes out I hope it will be revealed by a compassionate voice, a voice of moderation and balance, the voice of someone with a breadth of understanding of the full range of human achievements and human frailties.

LUCEREAU: The truth—

MRS. STANHOPE: —is colored by the voice which speaks it. The truth about my husband is: His qualities far outweigh his flaws.

LUCEREAU: That is your opinion.

MRS. STANHOPE: No, Lucereau. That is truth. ...So? Do you assent to what we ask?

LUCEREAU: Silence.

MRS. STANHOPE: Silence.

LUCEREAU: *(After a very long pause)* ...Agreed. *(Then, caught—)* God damn you!

MRS. STANHOPE: Should you ever break your promise, I will make public not only my collection of letters, but our tape of this meeting.

LUCEREAU: You've taped this meeting?!

MRS. STANHOPE: Come now, Lucereau. If you can make tapes of interviews, so can I.

LUCEREAU: *(Preparing to go)* I think we've said all that's necessary.

MRS. STANHOPE: Yes, I think we have.

LUCEREAU: Goodbye. I wish I could say it's been a pleasure.

MRS. STANHOPE: But it was!

(LUCEREAU *exits. Mrs. Stanhope's offspring erupt with joy.*)

JULIA: Fantastic!

DEVON: Incredible!

BETH: Amazing!

MRS. STANHOPE: Extremely satisfying.

JULIA: Where's the tape—?

MRS. STANHOPE: Oh, ...I don't have one.

DEVON: You lied?

MRS. STANHOPE: It just occurred to me.

DEVON: It was a great touch.

BETH: An inspiration.

JULIA: What a performance!

BETH: I'm sure Father's very proud of you.

JULIA: So are we all.

(MRS. STANHOPE *opens her arms. All three grown children come to be enfolded into them. As they share this ungainly once-in-a-lifetime simultaneously moving and comic embrace,* MRS. STANHOPE *looks at the portrait of her husband and says:*)

MRS. STANHOPE: I'm embracing your brood—but you're embracing us all, Alden. And your arms are longer!

(*She releases the children from her grasp, then:*)

MRS. STANHOPE: I have to finish packing. Devon, will you drop me at the airport?

DEVON: Of course, Mother. Glad to.

(MRS. STANHOPE *exits to her room.*)

DEVON: I'll just get my stuff. Be down in a jif. *(He exits upstairs.)*

BETH: I'm leaving, too. My duffel bag's in the hall.

JULIA: You shouldn't go so soon! You need pills, you need shots, there are mosquitoes everywhere!

BETH: Do you know, as you said that you sounded just like Mother.

JULIA: God help me. Look, kid, you're not ready to go back to the jungle—

BETH: I'm not going to the jungle—I'm going to the desert.

JULIA: Is he there?

BETH: Who?

JULIA: Your friend.

BETH: Perhaps. But that's not what I'm going back for. They need me.

JULIA: I wish someone needed *me*. Life without purpose is beginning to get me down.

BETH: Come with me. We could use you.

JULIA: I'd be useless!

BETH: You could sketch what you see—

JULIA: Not good enough.

BETH: You're good for *something*. Hands. A mind. We need 'em, you've got them both. Or don't you want to leave your fellas?

JULIA: There are no fellas.

BETH: Come with me.

(JULIA *thinks a minute. Then—*)

JULIA: ...Why not? I'll do it!

BETH: Just throw a couple of things in a bag. You won't need much.

(JULIA *dashes upstairs just as* DEVON *comes down with his luggage.*)

DEVON: Where's she going in such a hurry?

BETH: She's coming with me.

DEVON: That's great!

BETH: Where are you off to?

DEVON: After I drop you and Mom—and Julia—at the airport. Home. Alone.

BETH: Best thing.

DEVON: *(Knowing it but not yet at ease with it)* Yes. Best thing.

(MRS. STANHOPE *enters with her suitcase.*)

MRS. STANHOPE: Ready.

DEVON: Just one more. Julia's going with Beth.

MRS. STANHOPE: Excellent! *(To* BETH:*)* You two can look after each other.

BETH: And who'll be looking after you?

MRS. STANHOPE: Your father.

DEVON: Oh, Mother, please—!

MRS. STANHOPE: I know you children—yes, children—have to break free from his grip. But one day you'll find his wisdom and courage will be needed and they'll be there for you. Then—as I am—you'll be grateful for his constant presence, wherever you are, as long as you live.

(JULIA *reappears, coming downstairs with a small bag.*)

JULIA: Ready! ...On the road of life it is sometimes best to have no idea what the hell you're headed for in your next adventure! *(She turns to the portrait. A delighted-to-be-leaving farewell:)* 'Bye, Dad! *(She exits.)*

BETH: *(A serious leave-taking, remembering and forgiving all)* 'Bye, Dad. (BETH *exits.)*

DEVON: *(A mature, man-to-man parting valediction and reconciliation:)* 'Bye, Dad. *(He exits.)*

MRS. STANHOPE: *(With independence and immense love:)* Goodbye, Alden. Guard the house and, wherever they may be, guard your children. ... What a hell of a rascal you were! ...I wouldn't have had it any other way.

(*She starts to exit. There comes the sound of the flute, alive, triumphant.* MRS. STANHOPE *pauses for a moment. She seems to hear the music. She smiles, turns, salutes her husband's portrait and continues out. The lights begin to fade. For a moment they illuminate only his portrait and the green of the wintergarden, then—*)

(Blackout)

END OF PLAY

STILL LIFE WITH APPLES

CHARACTERS & SETTING

A Man
A Woman
A Girl
Two Servants *(non-speaking)*

Time & Place: The Present. An attic.

Setting: The attic of a substantial town house. Empty. Upstage is a large window. On stage right is a large door.

ACT ONE

(At rise:)

(Midday. THE MAN *is alone in the empty room. He is looking out of the window, meditating. A* WOMAN'S *voice is heard calling to him from far away.)*

WOMAN: *(O.S.)* Charles! ...Charles! ...Charles, where are you?

(He makes no move to answer. The voice comes nearer.)

WOMAN: Charles! I'm looking for you! ...Charles, can you hear me? ...Are you anywhere in the house? ...Charles?

(The voice is very near now. THE MAN *moves to the wall near the doorway and flattens himself against it. The door opens.* THE WOMAN *enters. She doesn't see him.)*

WOMAN: Charles? *(She sees that the window is open. She goes over and closes it. As she is turning to exit, she sees* THE MAN.*)*. Charles! So there you are! I've been calling you and calling you. Didn't you hear me calling you?

MAN: No.

WOMAN: You must be going deaf.

MAN: I'm trying.

WOMAN: I didn't know there was a room up here.

MAN: I know you didn't.

WOMAN: So this is where you've been disappearing to! Well, that explains it.

MAN: Explains what?

WOMAN: Your dirty elbows. I've been noticing for weeks that everything you put on mysteriously gets dirty elbows.

MAN: Is that why you climbed four flights? To gloat about my dirty elbows?

WOMAN: Of course not, Charles. Don't be silly. I came to tell you about the telegram. I found it just a minute ago when I came back from the shops. By the way, guess what I found this morning.

MAN: Don't tell me...

WOMAN: A marvelous length of heirloom chiffon—

MAN: I knew you'd have to tell.

WOMAN: I couldn't resist it. It was a toss-up between this exquisite cloth and a seventeenth century pewter decanter, and finally—

MAN: What was in the telegram?

WOMAN: The telegram? Oh, yes. Charles, brace yourself for marvelous and overwhelming news.

MAN: I'm braced. Tell me.

WOMAN: Charles...we're going to have a guest.

MAN: A guest! Who?

WOMAN: Cousin Joanna.

MAN: Why?

WOMAN: Because she wired she was coming.

MAN: Do we have to take in everybody who wires us?

WOMAN: We've never had a guest. Not one. Ever.

MAN: Let's not change course now, shall we? So far in midstream? Wire her not to come.

WOMAN: Don't be absurd.

MAN: I'm not in the mood for guests!

WOMAN: You're not in the mood for anything!

MAN: What did the wire say?

WOMAN: "I'm coming. Cousin Joanna."

MAN: Short and to the point. Like a poison dart.

WOMAN: You're becoming positively misanthropic! A recluse and a misanthrope!

MAN: Are there any other compliments you want to pay me? Because if not, you might as well climb back downstairs. *(He walks toward the window.)*

WOMAN: Oh, Charles. Charles. There isn't any need to argue. You know yourself you've been strange as a hermit for months now. Never going out. Keeping to yourself for hours and hours. Never showing up when our crowd gathers. Do you know what they're beginning to say about you?

MAN: I can guess—and it doesn't matter.

WOMAN: They don't understand you.

MAN: They would if they could hear themselves.

WOMAN: They're a delightful group of people who—

MAN: I just can't listen to them any longer!

WOMAN: Just who would you prefer to listen to?

MAN: Fresh air.

WOMAN: I don't know what's come over you. Ever since we got back from that vacation in the country you've been repelled by any conversation above the level of a moo!

MAN: A moo, at least, is genuine

WOMAN: Here we go again!

MAN: Not at all. I'm not going to discuss it.

WOMAN: I'll bet you are. I'll bet it will be the only thing you'll discuss at tonight's party.

MAN: I'm not going.

WOMAN: Again, Charles?

(He walks away from her.)

WOMAN: Oh, I hope you get over this anti-social phase before Cousin Joanna comes. You'll be a terrible host.

MAN: I'm in no mood to play host to your arthritic relatives!

WOMAN: You aren't...

MAN: No.

WOMAN: Then you don't have to.

MAN: Thank you.

WOMAN: Because she doesn't happen to be *my* arthritic relative—she's *yours*.

MAN: What?!

WOMAN: She's *your* relative and you certainly can manage to be polite to her.

MAN: I would if she were, but she isn't. I have no Cousin Joanna.

WOMAN: Don't joke, Charles.

MAN: I'm not joking. I have no Cousin Joanna. I never did have.

WOMAN: Well, *I* certainly don't have any.

MAN: Maybe you forgot her.

WOMAN: That's more like you than me. I don't go around misplacing relatives.

MAN: To which of us was the telegram addressed? That'll settle it.

WOMAN: I didn't notice.

MAN: So you've been reading my mail again—!

WOMAN: Was it your mail? Then it must be your relative.

MAN: It isn't!

WOMAN: You knew she was arthritic—

MAN: I don't know whether she's male or female, yours or mine, indigent or in the first pink blush of puberty—I'm not going to shepherd her around anywhere and that is that!

WOMAN: You're exasperating! Truly exasperating!

MAN: I'm going to lock myself in this room for the entire length of her visit. If she hears noises, tell her you've got large bats.

WOMAN: That's an interesting explanation. She might or might not have believed it. I'd have been very happy to try it except for one thing, Charles—

MAN: What?

WOMAN: I've decided to give her this room.

MAN: No—!

WOMAN: Yes. I've been looking at it since I found you in your little corner—and I think it has hidden possibilities.

MAN: You've already brought out the hidden possibilities in twelve rooms downstairs—

WOMAN: And this is the greatest challenge of them all. I'll have tapestried walls, I think, and ivory woodwork. I'll have the window draped in plum and hung with that chiffon I bought this morning—

MAN: You won't touch this room—

WOMAN: Why, Charles! What will I do with Cousin Joanna?

MAN: I don't care what you do with Cousin Joanna. Give her my room, my bed, if you like. But leave me this.

WOMAN: You'd actually give up your bed for this? That magnificent antique bed I just bought for you?

MAN: Put her in my bed—beneath the three-hundred-and-twenty-six overwrought virgins—

WOMAN: You didn't count them—

MAN: I count them every night, while I'm waiting for the canopy to fall on me.

WOMAN: Oh, Charles, you're such a child! Now stand back while I try to visualize this room once I get off the dust and—

MAN: This is *my* room! *My* dust! You will not drape it in plum or drag in one single gilt-assed Cupid!

WOMAN: If you want to live *au naturel*, go do it in the yard, Charles. Meanwhile, I intend to make this room as comfortable as possible for your cousin—

MAN: Yours!

(A MANSERVANT enters.)

WOMAN: Yes? What is it?

(THE SERVANT hands THE WOMAN a card.)

WOMAN: Cousin Joanna! She's here! Already!

MAN: See her downstairs—

WOMAN: *(To THE SERVANT:)* Send her up.

(THE SERVANT bows and exits.)

WOMAN: I hope you recognize her.

MAN: See her downstairs.

WOMAN: So selfish of you—to want to keep this place all to yourself.

MAN: See her downstairs. Please.

WOMAN: Impossible.

MAN: Why?

WOMAN: She must have reached the second floor already.

MAN: See her on the second floor—

WOMAN: She must have reached the third.

MAN: See her on the third floor—

WOMAN: I can hear her steps. She must have reached the fourth—

MAN: See her on the fourth floor!

WOMAN: Dust off your elbows, Charles. And try to be polite.

(THE GIRL comes into the room. She is about eighteen, and very supple. Her long blonde hair flows unconfined, past her shoulders, down the small of her back. She is wrapped in a cloak. She comes fluidly, soundlessly, a few steps into the room. She stands silently, her face registering no emotion. After a moment of looking at her, the MAN turns away, regarding her as an intruder. THE WOMAN continues to look at her. For a long time no one says anything. Then, at last, and rather hesitantly, the THE WOMAN asks:)

WOMAN: ...Cousin Joanna?

(THE GIRL turns her gaze upon THE WOMAN and regards her in that still, silent

way she has. Then, after what seems a long time to leave such a question hanging, THE GIRL's *lips curve upward in a gentle, affirmative smile.* THE WOMAN *waits for a spoken answer, but, getting none, she continues in off-hand social prose:)*

WOMAN: I had no idea you were coming so quickly, dear. Your telegram was just delivered, barely minutes ago. So I hope you won't mind if you find us just the slightest bit unorganized. We do so want to make you comfortable and figure out just the perfect place for you to stay.

(THE GIRL's *lips curve into a soft smile.* THE WOMAN *waits for some word, but when none is forthcoming, she continues, feeling rather awkward:)*

WOMAN: Did you have a nice trip?

(That smile again, warm and gentle, saying nothing)

WOMAN: I hope you didn't have far to come.

(That smile, no different from before. THE WOMAN, *now getting slightly desperate:)*

WOMAN: You didn't have much trouble finding us, did you?

(That smile again!)

MAN: *(To* THE WOMAN:*)* By God, she's dumb!

WOMAN: *(Aside to* THE MAN:*)* Do you recognize her yet?

MAN: *(Shaking his head)* She's yours, all yours.

WOMAN: If it was years ago that you last saw her, she'd be very much changed by now. She seems to be at the height of the—developing age.

MAN: All my cousins are male. I don't think they'd develop in quite this direction.

WOMAN: Think, Charles.

MAN: *You* think.

WOMAN: I'll try her again. If you get any clues, please tell me.

(THE WOMAN *approaches* THE GIRL *once more.)*

WOMAN: Is this your first trip?

(THE GIRL *smiles again.* THE MAN *gestures annoyance.* THE WOMAN *refuses to give up.)*

WOMAN: Did it take you long to get here?

(That smile again!)

MAN: This is getting us nowhere—

WOMAN: *(Specifically, to* THE GIRL, *giving the words some weight:)* How are your father and mother?

(The only response is the smile.)

MAN: *(Aside to* THE WOMAN:*)* Never mind how are her father and mother. *Who are her father and mother!*

WOMAN: Charles—

MAN: For heaven's sake, ask her straight out. She ought to be able to answer a simple question.

WOMAN: Ask her what?

MAN: Ask her who she is, damn it!

WOMAN: You can't—

MAN: *(Bursting out and addressing* THE GIRL *himself:)* Look, Cousin. Point, if you can. To which of us do you belong? *(Clearly and insistently:)* Whose cousin are you?!

*(*THE GIRL *smiles again.* THE MAN *is about to give up all hope when* THE GIRL's *mouth moves and a word comes gently out of her:)*

GIRL: ...Yes. ...

MAN: *(To* THE WOMAN:*)* Good lord, she's not dumb, she's deaf!

WOMAN: It runs in your family—

MAN: She's not in my—*(Confronting* THE GIRL:*)* Where did you come from?

GIRL: *(After a pause, quietly)* ...Yes. ...

MAN : *(Pursuing it bluntly)* How long do you intend to stay?

GIRL: *(After a pause, quietly)* ...Yes. ...

MAN : How did you get the idea to pick yourself up and come here?

GIRL: *(After a pause, quietly)* ...Yes. ...

MAN : *(To* THE WOMAN:*)* What on earth have we got here?!

WOMAN: *(Aside to* THE MAN:*)* Will you please keep your voice down?

MAN: She's not related to us. She's related to a Ouija board!

WOMAN: Hush, Charles!

MAN: What fascinating company! A girl who only says yes!

WOMAN: Charles, I won't have you insulting her!

MAN: How can you insult a cipher? We don't know who she is, what she is, or what she's doing here.

WOMAN: She's related to you somehow—

MAN: She isn't! And I think, if you can find any way of conveying it to her clearly, you ought to ask her to go.

(TWO MANSERVANTS *enter with a large trunk. They put it down and go out.*)

WOMAN: I won't do any such thing.

MAN: You must ask her to go—and take her baggage with her.

WOMAN: We can't just throw her out into the street, Charles—

MAN: Then throw her out into a luxury hotel.

WOMAN: She came to us—

MAN: What are we running—a waystation for feminine enigmas?

WOMAN: Do you mean she's not worth bothering with because she's a woman?

MAN: Oh, take her downstairs and leave me in peace, will you? (*He goes to the window and stands looking out.*)

WOMAN: (*Stubbornly*) Vice versa, darling. *You* go downstairs and leave the peace to us.

MAN: I need this place where I can—

WOMAN: What if she's ill or something? She ought to stay here, high up, above the noises of the city. I'll stay with her till we find out just what's troubling her. (*She turns to* THE GIRL.) This is my room, Cousin Joanna. I'll be glad to have you share it with me.

(THE GIRL *smiles and nods in quiet acceptance.*)

MAN: (*Equaling* THE WOMAN's *stubbornness*) This is *my* room, Cousin Joanna. I'll be glad to have you share it with *me*.

(THE GIRL *turns to the* MAN *and gives him the exact same look of quiet acceptance.* THE MAN *turns away in annoyance.*)

MAN: Good lord—!

WOMAN: (*To* THE MAN:) Now let's not have this nonsense any longer. She's staying. Here. And that's the end of that.

(*He gestures a protest.*)

WOMAN: You're not going to make a scene, are you? Are you?

(THE MAN *looks at* THE WOMAN *angrily but says nothing.*)

WOMAN: Now go downstairs and have some things sent up to make this room habitable. The velvet couch for Cousin Joanna, my bed for me, my nightstand, my lamp—. Do you hear me, Charles?

MAN: (*Rebelliously*) I hear you.

WOMAN: (*Sarcastically*) Do you think you can handle the assignment?

MAN: (*Bitingly*) I'll do my level best.

(He goes. THE WOMAN *and* THE GIRL *are alone.)*

WOMAN: There! Well, that takes care of that! He's such a goose—and oh so moody lately! It's really because of that I insisted you and I stay up here. To push him out. Push him back into the world again. A minute to one's self now and then can be refreshing. But hour after hour of solitude—. Why, it's positively seditious!

(She looks at THE GIRL *who is standing nearby, not moving.)*

WOMAN: Relax, my dear. You don't have to be afraid of me. And you certainly don't have to be afraid of Charles. He's quite, quite harmless. Perhaps more harmless than he'd like to be! ...Come, relax. ...Why don't you sit on your trunk?

*(*THE GIRL *makes no move to do so.)*

WOMAN: Do you mind if I do?

*(*THE GIRL *gives a small smile.* THE WOMAN *sits.)*

WOMAN: I must say, I'm awfully glad you're here. Very glad. What a bore life's been here lately. One large yawn from morning till night. What with Charles spreading gloom in every corner, and absolutely refusing to go out—! ...Well, never mind. You and I will enjoy ourselves. There's so much to be seen. So much I can show you. Is there anything special you want to do? Any sights you want to see? Any places you particularly want to visit?

(There is no response from THE GIRL.*)*

WOMAN: Oh, well. I'm sure we can fit everything in.

*(*THE WOMAN *looks at* THE GIRL. THE GIRL'S *silence is beginning to unnerve her.)*

WOMAN: Are you sure you wouldn't like to sit?

*(*THE WOMAN *rises to give the seat to* THE GIRL, *but* THE GIRL *makes no move to take it.* THE WOMAN *continues, rather nervously:)*

WOMAN: You're going to adore your stay I know it! Our life here's such a whirl! In the shops all day, and parties every evening. A splendid one tonight. And who knows where tomorrow and tomorrow. There's something doing every minute. I hope you came prepared for anything. You must have,—with a trunk that size.

(She starts over to the trunk as if to open it.)

WOMAN: Let's see if you have a suitable outfit for—

GIRL: *(Flat, expressionless)* Tic... Toc...

(Surprised, THE WOMAN *turns and takes her hand off the trunk.)*

WOMAN: I beg your pardon. Did you say something? ...I thought I heard you say something. ...I didn't quite hear what you...

(She fades off. THE GIRL *is standing, expressionless.* THE WOMAN *isn't sure* THE GIRL *said anything. She continues:)*

WOMAN: Anyway, whatever you wear, we'll have enormous fun! Though you'll have to understand if Charles doesn't join us, he—

GIRL: *(Slowly, without expression)* Butter soup...

(THE GIRL *speaks slowly and deliberately, always in the same expressionless way, looking straight ahead and giving equal weight to each syllable. Her manner is serious, nearly unearthly.* THE WOMAN *stops. She is sure* THE GIRL *spoke this time, but can't believe she heard correctly. She shrugs and goes on:)*

WOMAN: As I was saying,—what was I saying?—oh, yes, as I was saying—. You and I will go on our own, most likely, and Charles will stay at home. Because lately I—

GIRL: *(Slowly, without expression)* Chicken... pox...

WOMAN: *(Beginning to become rather disconcerted)* Darling, I rather thought you just said "chicken pox". ...Did you say "chicken pox"? Was it "chicken pox" you said or—...

GIRL: *(Slowly, without expression)* Drain... spout...

WOMAN: "Drainspout". ...I see... Well... (THE WOMAN *stops, rather shaken. How is she to cope with this? She doesn't know. She plunges on disconcertedly:)* As I was saying,—let's see,—what was I saying?—oh yes: Not that it isn't embarrassing to go to these places on one's own—while Charles keeps to himself, giving the most ridiculous reasons for it. It's an insult to our friends, but no one can get near him. It's as if he were a—

GIRL: *(Slowly, without expression)* Porcupine...

WOMAN: As if he were a porcupine who—

(She breaks off. She had picked up the word without even thinking. Now she looks at THE GIRL. *Is it possible* THE GIRL *has been making sense?* TWO MANSERVANTS *enter with a couch.* THE WOMAN *directs them to put it near the wall, stage left. While they are doing it,* THE WOMAN *looks at* THE GIRL *with awakening interest.* THE WOMAN *repeats to herself: "Porcupine, porcupine."* THE GIRL *remains, as ever, enigmatic and detached.* THE MANSERVANTS *finish their work and go out.)*

WOMAN: Yes, he is like a porcupine. Exactly like a porcupine! He's put out his quills and—

GIRL: *(Slowly, without expression)* Blue...

WOMAN: Blue? ...Blue... *(She considers. What could be* THE GIRL's *meaning? ...Then it strikes her:)* And the rest of us can talk to him till we're *blue* in the face—there's no way to approach him! ...Is that it, Cousin Joanna? Is that what you were trying to tell me?

GIRL: *(Slowly, without expression)* Horse...

WOMAN: He gets on his high horse and refuses to socialize, even though, months ago, when he did consent to see people—

GIRL: *(Slowly, without expression)* Salt...

WOMAN: —I always had to smooth the way for him. Always had to *pepper* the conversation with the few topics he shines on. Why, I actually had to steer the talk so he could join in!

GIRL : *(Slowly, without expression)* Mud...

WOMAN: Yes, yes. He's clay—and *I* make the mold. He thinks I call him Samson for his strength, but it's only because he's vulnerable. He thinks I call him Samson for his muscle,—but I call him that because a woman can cut him down.

GIRL: *(Slowly, without expression)* Noodle...

WOMAN: *(Understanding completely!)* Noodle! Yes, noodle!—

(The TWO MANSERVANTS *bring in an ornate canopied bed and assemble it near the center of the room. While they are doing this,* THE WOMAN *paces about repeating "Noodle, noodle!" as if she were bursting to discuss this with* THE GIRL *and can't wait till* THE MANSERVANTS *go.* THE MANSERVANTS *leave.* THE WOMAN *bursts out:)*

WOMAN: Noodle! Noodle! Yes!—Why have men no more backbone than old macaroni? Why don't they show us sometimes that they have a spine? ...I bought us new beds. This is mine. His is twice as grand. I love mine—but I know he can't stand his at all. It's been three weeks—and what has he done? He's slept in it! I bought it so he'd throw it out the window! I bought it so he could show me he's a man.

GIRL: *(Slowly, without expression)* Knees...

WOMAN: Oh, yes, *knees*. You understand me, don't you! I'd worship him if he'd show one ounce of real rebellion! If he tore that bed apart, instead of sleeping in it, I'd go to him on my knees!

GIRL: *(Slowly, without expression)* Chit... Chat...

WOMAN: Instead he does nothing but talk, talk, talk—about how he'd rather sleep in a haystack, or on a pallet of straw—

GIRL: *(Slowly, without expression)* Woof... Woof...

WOMAN: It's nothing but bark without bite! Noise without meaning! Sound without substance! ...Oh, my dear, how you know him! Three minutes here and you see right through him! ...You're an absolute genius! ...

(A MANSERVANT *comes in with a folding screen. He puts it down near* THE GIRL'S *couch and exits)*

WOMAN: ...But you ought to rest. You must be tired.

(*She leads* THE GIRL *to the couch.*)

WOMAN: ...Rest now. Rest. I won't let a thing disturb you.

(*She has* THE GIRL *lie down on the couch, then she puts the screen around it, hiding* THE GIRL *from view. To herself,* THE WOMAN *says excitedly:*)

WOMAN: What an amazing girl! She'll be the event of the season! I can't wait to spring her on the crowd!

(THE MAN *re-enters.*)

WOMAN: Charles! Charles! There's something I must tell you about your cousin!

MAN: *Your* cousin—

WOMAN: I don't care *whose* cousin she is any more. Charles—she is superb.

MAN: *(Flatly)* Is she?

WOMAN: A true find! A real triumph!

MAN: *(More flatly)* So very glad to hear it.

WOMAN: Oh, Charles, you're not sulking because we have the room, are you?

MAN: *(Stiffly)* Of course not.

WOMAN: Then turn to me. Look at me—and listen. ...Cousin Joanna isn't deaf—or dumb—or anything like that. You know what she is, Charles?

MAN: *(Sarcastically)* I can hardly wait to hear it.

WOMAN: Charles—she is *profound*!

MAN: *(Mockingly)* "Profound!"

WOMAN: As deep as the sea—or even deeper. With a mind as swift as lightning, and a quality—most incredible—of hitting instantly on *le mot juste*. The right word. The right word only. As if sentences were a waste of time, and all one should do is utter the heart of them. The sum. The answer. The one word...telling all.

MAN: That is incredible—for a female.

WOMAN: You don't believe me, do you. But soon you'll see it's true. She knows you inside out, Charles. After seeing you for only minutes, she called you a porcupine.

MAN: *(Toward the screen, mockingly)* Oh, thank you, Cousin!

WOMAN: Which you may not find flattering, but it's absolutely true.

MAN: What else did she say?

WOMAN: She said "woof-woof" and "chicken pox"—

MAN: Oh, deafeningly profound!

WOMAN: You ought to listen, you would learn something—

MAN: Or catch something!

WOMAN: If you would make your mind receptive—

(He runs toward the door and runs back. He seems to be expecting something.)

WOMAN: What's the matter with you?

MAN: Nothing's the matter with me.

WOMAN: What are you grinning about?

MAN: I'm not—

WOMAN: What's that noise in the corridor?

MAN: Just the woof-woof of an old porcupine!

WOMAN: I insist on knowing what that noise is!

MAN: You don't have long to wait now—

(The door flings open—and in comes a stupendously ornate and canopied bed.)

WOMAN: Your bed!

(THE MANSERVANTS work to assemble it.)

MAN: *(Self-satisfied)* So it is.

WOMAN: What's it doing here?

MAN: It happened to be passing by—

WOMAN: So *that's* the little game you're planning—

MAN: This room is mine and I intend to keep it. If you and the colossus of wisdom want to stay, you're very welcome. If you want to leave—go ahead.

(Having finished their work, THE MANSERVANTS depart.)

WOMAN: We will not move!

MAN: Well, fine. We'll have some jolly times together.

WOMAN: You're making me angry, Charles.

MAN: Yes. I know it.

WOMAN: You know when I'm angry you lose in the end.

MAN: Not this time.

WOMAN: You're really prepared to go on with this boyish stubbornness?

MAN: I'm not budging.

WOMAN: Very well, Charles. If that's a challenge, I accept. You'll see how far your little gesture of defiance gets you. If you want to play war games, sonny,—count me in.

(She slams out the door. When the THE MAN is alone, he loses a little of his bravado. He mutters to himself:)

MAN: Do I want to play war games...! Who does she think she is? Here's the one room in the house that hasn't got museum stench. Why can't I have it? Why can't they live downstairs?

(THE GIRL comes out from behind her screen. THE MAN doesn't see her. She has taken off her outer wrap. Her simple dress covers her body but leaves her arms bare. The dress fits in an awkward but revealing way. THE GIRL stands quietly listening as THE MAN talks to himself.)

MAN: She thinks I'll lose my nerve on this. She thinks, when they start to undress and climb under their sheets at night, that I'll run out. Well, I won't! ... I'm here to stay, and nothing's going to move me.

(He turns and sees THE GIRL. He shouts at her:)

MAN: I want this room, can you understand that?! Do you know *why* I want it?

GIRL: *(After a long pause:)* ...Sky.

(THE GIRL's attitude with THE MAN is a little less detached than it was with THE WOMAN. She still has the same detached ethereal quality, but her voice is warmer and, after a while, she looks at him when she speaks.)

MAN: Yes, *sky!* *(He looks at THE GIRL Is it possible she has understood him?)* ...Sky.— And to get away from her things. *Things*!

(There are noises in the corridor. A MANSERVANT comes in carrying a table and a lamp. He is followed by the other MANSERVANT who carries a vase containing paper flowers.)

MAN: Here they come now! Do you see what her game is? She thinks if she moves in enough of these infernal objects, that Charlie will run. Well, I'm not going to run. I'm not going to notice them!

(As THE MANSERVANT walks by with the vase, THE MAN grabs the paper flowers and shouts:)

MAN: There are places in the world where flowers *grow*! I've been there!

(THE MANSERVANTS, unmoved, put their objects in place and leave.)

MAN: Do you know what I think of her things?

GIRL: *(After a long pause)* ...Tuba.

MAN: Tuba!... *(He looks at her strangely and repeats)* Tuba!... *(He tries the low razzing sound of the tuba and is amazed).* That's it! That's exactly it! I think her junk is—*(He repeats the razzing sound and laughs heartily.)* I think her junk is tuba! It's as tuba as can be! *(He laughs again.)* As a matter of fact, our whole relationship is tuba!...Do you know her whole purpose in life is to make a fool of me? She's got very subtle ways. You almost have to admire her. Public ways and private ways. The public ways are something to behold!

(More objects—furniture and bric-a-brac—are brought in by THE MANSERVANTS. THE MAN *watches in defiance until they leave.)*

MAN: When we go out with our crowd, she lavishes me with attention, puts the spotlight on me, is always saying: "What do you think about that, Charles?" or "Charles and I were just talking about that yesterday. Charles what was that brilliant thing you said?"—and I have to speak... *(Angrily)* Is anything brilliant that's called brilliant?! And she knows what she's doing. Oh, God, does she know! It's public assassination, that's what it is! In front of all those fakes! Fakes! They're fake!—Like this ship of state here. *(He points to his bed.)* But I don't let her do it to me any more. I'm showing her. ... I don't go out.

*(*THE MANSERVANTS *come in with more things to furnish the room. He stands watching them, getting more and more agitated. When they leave, he continues:)*

MAN: Her private ways of humiliating me are even better. Her private ways involve this bed. She bought it for me—as a surprise—three weeks ago. She spirited off my old one behind my back. ...She thinks I don't know why she bought this. But I do know. She bought this nightmare with one hope and one hope only: she has the fervent desire to see me throw it out. She wants me to tear it apart with my bare hands and smash it through the window—so she can shout to the roof tops: "Charles is a beast! Charles is an animal!" ...She thinks, because I hate these "things"—that I'm an animal. But I outfox her. I don't tear it apart and smash it out the window. I leave it in one piece. I even lie on it. ...But, as I said, I do outfox her. I lie on it—but I don't sleep. ...So what do you think of that?

GIRL: Vermillion!

*(*THE GIRL *still retains her strangeness, but she seems to be coming to life now. Her responses are almost opinions. She acquires some expression in her face and voice.)*

MAN: I should have been allowed to have this room to myself—uncluttered— shouldn't I? She shouldn't be making it like downstairs, where every time you want to see daylight, you've got to see it through acres of organza, and when you go to sleep you're hung about with miles and miles of tulle!

GIRL : ...Noose...

MAN: I'd give my soul for a yard of burlap. I'm smothering to death in this rococo!

GIRL: *(After a long pause)* ...Nose...

MAN: So you think it stinks, too, do you, Cousin! Smells to high heaven, doesn't it! Let's throw open the windows and get some air!

(He throws open the window. THE GIRL walks to the window and breathes the air. There is a pungency hovering about the words she says here. There is a silence before each, during which THE MAN waits with expectation while the meaning sinks in.)

GIRL: ...Nutmeg...

MAN: It *is* a gorgeous day, isn't it?

GIRL: ...Porcelain...

MAN: I come up here very often. I think, from here, there's a special color to the sky.

GIRL: ...Tickle...

MAN: That's how it hits me, too! So good you want to laugh with it. ... Feel the breeze—

GIRL : ...Peppermint...

MAN: Touch the glass—

GIRL: ...Waltz...

MAN: Breathe in—

GIRL: ...Flutes...

MAN: Touch my hand—

GIRL: *(Taking his hand)* ...Sunlight...

MAN: *(In a soft, warm mood, overwhelmed by the touch on his hand)* ... Where did you come from? ...Who are you? ...What wonderful kind of a creature are you? ...There's nothing like you anywhere around here. Not a soul here who can breathe or feel or see—

(THE GIRL moves softly away from him.)

MAN: There must be something I can do for you. ...Anything you ask me. There must be something I can get for you. Is there something you want?

(She turns toward the MAN. She looks at him It is a long time before she answers, then, finally, she says softly:)

GIRL: ...Shrimp...

MAN: Shrimp?...Is that what you want?

(THE GIRL smiles.)

MAN: If that's what you want then—*(He shrugs, then goes to the door and shouts downstairs:)* Shrimp for the lady! *(He turns back to* THE GIRL.*)* Anything else?

GIRL: *(Softly and seriously)* More shrimp...

(THE MAN is surprised at this, but then he goes to the doorway and shouts down:)

MAN: More! *(Then, to* THE GIRL:*)* You must need more than that to make you happy.

(THE GIRL is silent.)

MAN: Come on now. Don't be shy. Mention anything you want—

GIRL: *(After a time, quietly)* ...Feathers.

MAN: Feathers! ...I'm not sure we have feathers—

GIRL: Feathers...

MAN: Well—if what you want is feathers—*(He shouts downstairs:)* Feathers!

GIRL: *(Softly)* More...

MAN: *(Shouting downstairs)* Lots of feathers! *(To* THE GIRL:*)* Anything else?

(She raises her arms, inhaling deeply and luxuriously. As she lowers them slowly, she says:)

GIRL: Air...

MAN: Oh, god, Joanna, but you're welcome here!

(A MANSERVANT *enters with a large china pitcher and basin.* THE MAN *says to him:)*

MAN: What's this?

(THE GIRL pours some water from the pitcher into the basin, then scoops up a great wave of water and splashes it into the air.)

GIRL: Birds!

MAN: Ah!

GIRL: *(Splashing water high into the air again, she says softly:)* More!

(THE MANSERVANT exits to get it. THE GIRL scoops up water into the air and lets it flow down.)

GIRL: More! More!

MAN: I've never seen anything like you!

(THE GIRL splashes over and over. There is a quality of intense exhilaration about her which delights the MAN.*)*

GIRL: More!

MAN: Go on! Go on! Keep doing it!

GIRL: *(Softly, as she lets the water flow down)* More... More...

(THE MAN watches, enchanted. THE WOMAN *returns, carrying a long length of white chiffon. At first she sees only the* MAN.*)*

WOMAN: So you haven't backed down! You're really still here, Charles!

MAN: I am. Oh, am I! I wouldn't leave now for anything in the world!

(THE MAN *stands aside and suddenly the* WOMAN *sees* THE GIRL.)

WOMAN: What's happening? What is this? (*She rushes to* THE GIRL.) My dear, you're getting water all over the furniture. Cousin Joanna, my dear—

(THE GIRL *takes the cloth from the* WOMAN's *hands and waves it in the air like a pennant, enjoying watching it float.*)

WOMAN: No, no! That's heirloom chiffon! For the windows! Oh, don't catch it on anything! It will snag! Oh, my dear—

(*But* THE GIRL *doesn't stop.* THE WOMAN *can't stop her.* THE GIRL *continues to wave the chiffon in the air.* THE WOMAN *approaches the* MAN.)

WOMAN: What's happened to her?

MAN : (*Explaining*) Water—! Air—!

(*A* MANSERVANT *enters with a great basket of shrimp in their shells.* THE GIRL *drops the chiffon and takes the basket saying:*)

GIRL: More—

MAN: (*To* THE MANSERVANT *just before he exits:*) More shrimp for the girl! Keep it coming!

(THE GIRL *sits cross-legged on her bed, back to the audience, eating the shrimp and tossing away the shells.*)

WOMAN: (*Picking up the chiffon and attempting to straighten it*) What's happened to her? I left you with her for five minutes and she's falling apart!

MAN: Not apart. Together!

WOMAN: Look at her eating!

MAN: Beautiful!

WOMAN: The shells are going all over!

MAN: Beautiful!

WOMAN: (*To* THE GIRL:) Don't get the shells on the coverlet!

(THE GIRL *pays no attention. She keeps tossing the shells over her head. Many fall on* THE WOMAN's *bed.* THE WOMAN *says to* THE MAN:)

WOMAN: What have you done to her?

MAN: Nothing. Just stood back and let her come to life!

WOMAN: All over my bed!

MAN: You see, she's not profound, she's simple. Absolutely simple.

WOMAN: *(Scrubbing at her bed)* I'll never get the sea smell out!

MAN: As natural as earth, air, fire and water —

(Shells fall upon the WOMAN's bed.)

WOMAN: This has got to stop —

MAN: As natural as birds, rain, sun and wind —

(A MANSERVANT enters with a large basket of feathers. He puts them down near THE GIRL.)

WOMAN: What's this? What's this? Where did you find those feathers?

(THE MANSERVANT exits without answering. THE GIRL comes to take them.)

WOMAN: No, no! I won't let you have them!

(THE WOMAN tugs at the basket.)

MAN: Why can't she have them? Are they yours?

(THE WOMAN gives him a sharp, almost guilty, look. She relinquishes the basket.)

WOMAN: Charles, I really must insist that you leave us. I don't know how I'll ever get her cleaned up in time to take her to the party tonight, but —

(A MANSERVANT enters with a larger basked of shrimp.)

WOMAN: Don't bring her any more of those!

MAN: *(Taking the basket)* Keep them coming —

(THE MANSERVANT exits. THE MAN puts the basket down by THE GIRL.)

GIRL: More! *(THE GIRL starts in avidly on the new supply.)*

MAN: *(Watching her in admiration)* Ah, that's something, isn't it?!

WOMAN: Something perfectly repelling! *(She throws the screen around THE GIRL, hiding her from view.)*

MAN: The way she sinks her teeth in! The way she bites and chews!

WOMAN: You always were intrigued by anything the least bit vulgar. If it bordered on the barbaric — all to the good.

MAN: She has a way of gnawing at that food —

WOMAN: I know, I know. Like the apple girls we came across last summer, the ones who seemed to wait for you behind every tree in every orchard, beckoning and beckoning. You loved the way *they* chewed, too!

MAN: *(Ecstatically)* The way their teeth would pierce the apple flesh! The way the apple juices trickled down their chins onto their breasts...

WOMAN: *(Derisively)* The way, when they came to the pits, they'd spit them out all over the place.

MAN: ...They knew things when they ate those apples...

WOMAN: They were awfully willing to share what they knew, it seemed to me. Always beckoning you from behind the bushes—

MAN: Wanting me to take one quick bite. You could have let me join them!

WOMAN: For one quick bite'? Ha, ha. It would have been one, two, three and down the hatch with you, if I hadn't held you back, dearie.

MAN: Oh, do you think so? Well, let me tell you, you are wrong I can hold my own with any little apple girl.

WOMAN: You ran from one—

MAN: You wouldn't let me to them! If you had let me to them for one fast minute—

WOMAN: You'd be dry bones in dry earth now, a carcass, eaten clean.

(From behind the screen THE GIRL *calls:)*

GIRL *(O.S.)*: More shrimp!

WOMAN: Good lord, where is she putting all of it?!

*(*THE GIRL *comes out from behind the screen.)*

GIRL: More. More water. *(She scoops up water and lets it flow down upon herself in a slow and languorous way.)*

MAN: *(Slowly, entranced)* ...I think I'll take her to the party...

WOMAN: This puddle?

MAN: I'll take her on the town...

WOMAN: You haven't been out of the house in months and you'll appear with that?

GIRL: More. More water.

(She scoops up some water, and then, in a slow and languorous way, she lets it flow gently down—upon THE MAN.*)*

MAN: *(In a warm delicious spell)* I want...to show those fakes...the genuine article...

*(*THE GIRL *bathes* THE MAN *again.* THE GIRL *and* MAN *are in some private world. Their togetherness threatens* THE WOMAN. *She tries to break in.)*

WOMAN: The genuine article! You can't know what you're saying! She hasn't proven to my satisfaction that she's a cousin to either of us—

GIRL: *(Offering the bowl of water smilingly to* THE MAN*)* Wash...

WOMAN: Has she, Charles? Charles, are you listening to me? You were absolutely right before, Charles. We don't know who she is. Why should we keep her?

(THE MAN *scoops up water and lets it flow down upon himself.*)

WOMAN: Charles, I think she ought to go as soon as possible—

GIRL: *(To* THE MAN, *smiling:)* Breathe...

(THE GIRL *inhales luxuriously.* THE MAN *copies her.*)

WOMAN: I think she ought to take her trunk and go. Don't you, Charles?

GIRL: *(Softly, to* THE MAN:*)* Wash...

MAN: Wash...

(THE MAN *and* GIRL *let water fall upon themselves, one after the other.*)

WOMAN: Help me get her trunk out, Charles. Take the other side. *(She tries to push it. It is very heavy.)* What's in here? ...Charles, will you help me move this?

GIRL: Run—

(She runs freely across the room. THE MAN *follows, trying to copy her movements.)*

WOMAN: Charles, you look absurd—

MAN: Don't look then—

GIRL: Laugh!

(She breaks into laughter and the MAN *copies her.)*

GIRL: Shout!

(She shouts and the MAN *does, too.)*

GIRL: Run!

(She runs around the room, trailing the chiffon behind her. Faster now, with more abandon. THE MAN *follows her, becoming flushed and breathless and falling more deeply under her spell.)*

WOMAN: My cloth! Don't snag it!

GIRL: Turn!

(She pivots, waving the chiffon in the air. THE MAN *pivots also.* THE GIRL'S *commands are coming more quickly now.)*

GIRL: Blow!

(THE GIRL *drops the cloth and dips her hands into the feathers. She throws them into the air and blows on them to keep them aloft.* THE MAN *follows her example.*)

WOMAN: Stop! It's a mess! My lamp! Be careful!

(The action gets wilder, more impassioned. THE MAN *is panting and almost feverish.* THE WOMAN *looks on in growing horror.* THE GIRL'S *commands quicken and intensify.)*

GIRL: Turn!

(THE GIRL *turns, the* MAN *turns.*)

GIRL: Blow!

(*They blow the feathers into the air.*)

GIRL: Jump!

(*They jump.*)

GIRL: Eat!

(THE GIRL *and the* MAN *set upon the basket of shrimp, tearing at the shells, eating and laughing.*)

WOMAN: Oh, Charles! Come to! You don't know what you're doing!

(THE MAN, *in defiance, begins to lead the game himself.*)

MAN: *(Panting and going faster, ever faster)* Blow!

(THE GIRL *and the* MAN *blow feathers into the air.*)

GIRL: Fly!

(*They jump onto the* WOMAN's *bed and fly off of it.*)

WOMAN: My bed!

MAN: Eat!

(*At the shrimp again. Hardly time to stuff in a mouthful*)

MAN: Wash!

(THE GIRL *and the* MAN *go at the water wildly.*)

WOMAN: Push the girl out, Charles!

(*Instead, he splashes water on the* WOMAN.)

WOMAN: No! Oh, stop!

(THE GIRL *and the* MAN *are beyond reach now, trading commands and getting wilder, ever wilder.*)

GIRL: Hop!

(*They hop.*)

MAN: Turn!

(*They turn.*)

GIRL: Eat!

(*They eat.*)

MAN: Fly!

(They fly.)

GIRL: Slide!

(They slide.)

GIRL: Bump!

(They bump. THE MAN likes this. He repeats:)

MAN: Bump!

(They bump.)

GIRL: Sing!

(She lets her voice out on a high sustained note. THE MAN takes up a note in dissonance. THE WOMAN can bear it no longer. Over the terrible sounds she shouts:)

WOMAN: Charles! Charles! Can't you see what's happening? Shake yourself out of this! Charles, Charles, Charles—!

(THE MAN and GIRL take up another two dissonant notes and sustain them as they run about the room doing the actions they have done—but wilder and without words now.)

WOMAN: The girl is insane! Oh, Charles, can't you see that? Mad! A lunatic! Charles, quiet down! She's mad, can't you see?

MAN: She isn't!

WOMAN: She is, Charles!

MAN: *(Turning on THE WOMAN as THE GIRL continues to play:)* I'd rather have a mad woman than a clever one. I'd rather have a mindless woman than one who was doing me in!

WOMAN: What? What's that?

MAN: Didn't you switch beds on me when I wasn't looking? Aren't you stuffing more feathers into my mattress every day?

WOMAN: What?

MAN: It's getting softer and softer, softer and softer. Each night I sink deeper and deeper. Don't you think I can tell? And one night soon—how soon are you planning it?—I'll sink so deep it will close over me altogether!

WOMAN: No! You're mad!

(THE GIRL is into the basket of feathers, scattering them into the air.)

GIRL: *(To the feathers:)* Blow! Fly!

WOMAN: You can't sleep at night! I'm making the bed softer—!

MAN: Till one night it covers me—

WOMAN: No! It's not that soft! I swear to you, it's nowhere near that soft, Charles!

MAN: I don't believe you.

WOMAN: Don't believe me. Ask the girl!

MAN: Girl! Girl! Come over, Girl...

(THE GIRL *stops what she was doing. Stillness. Silence.*)

MAN: Come over to the bed, girl...

(*They are at the* MAN's *bed. Obediently,* THE GIRL *approaches.* THE MAN *speaks quietly.*)

MAN: Take your hand and lay it flat. On the center.

(THE GIRL *does so.*)

MAN: Now press. Press hard. ... What does it feel like?

(*A long silence.* THE GIRL's *hand remains on the center of he bed.* THE MAN *and* THE WOMAN *look at her expectantly.*)

MAN: What does it feel like? Speak now. Tell us. What does it feel like?

(*A long pause. Then, finally,* THE GIRL *breathes and speaks.*)

GIRL: ...Marble...

WOMAN: (*Triumphantly*) You see? There you are! No one's trying to hurt you!

(THE MAN *looks at* THE WOMAN. *Silence.* THE MAN *looks puzzled, his brow knits.* THE GIRL *breaks from the group. She moves toward the shrimp basket and sets upon it avidly, chanting abstractly.*)

GIRL: Eat now. Eat, eat, eat now.

MAN: (*Echoing her. Being drawn back to her by the sound of her voice*) Eat now.

WOMAN: Oh, God, Charles—

MAN: Eat now!

WOMAN: Oh, God, Charles—! I beg you—! Those shrimp are *alive*!

MAN: (*To* THE WOMAN:) Eat now! Eat now! Come on and eat now! Come to the table now. Join us in our shrimp.

WOMAN: No!

GIRL: (*To no one:*) Eat... Eat...

MAN: Come tear the shells off—

GIRL: Eat...

WOMAN: No!

MAN: Come on now. It's the Feast of the Ages! Come on and join us.

WOMAN: No!

MAN: Share my shrimp.

(He approaches THE WOMAN *with a shrimp half out of his mouth.)*

WOMAN: No!

GIRL: Eat! Eat!

MAN: *(Pursuing* THE WOMAN, *inviting her to bite off the other half of his shrimp:)* Share my shrimp! Oh, share my shrimp!

(He pants, waiting, with the shrimp dangling from his mouth and his face thrust forward to THE WOMAN.*)*

GIRL: Eat! Eat!

WOMAN: *(Turning on* THE MAN *and screaming:)* AN-I-MAL!

(She looks at him for an instant, her face contorted with disgust. Then she runs from the room, slamming the door behind her. THE MAN *stands still, breathing hard, looking after her.* THE GIRL *comes lightly to him and bites off the shrimp with a snap. He swallows his half, relieved, relaxing.* THE GIRL *runs lightly to the door, locks it and throws away the key.* THE MAN *murmurs:)*

MAN: Safe... Safe...

*(*THE GIRL *comes smiling toward him, humming a waltz. She swings the chiffon and dances with it, wafting it into the air as she hums.* THE MAN *begins to dance, too, and she drapes the cloth around him. They move in rhythm, connected by the cloth. He says, with his voice expressing infinite peace:)*

MAN: She's gone... She's gone... I hate those clever women... They try to own you. They don't let you move... They stuff your bed and they want the Power... But we scared her off, you and I, didn't we... She won't come back now... We can stay here and be absolutely at peace...

(They dance. She hums, and drapes him playfully with the cloth.)

MAN: We can dance on and on... We can dance and dance and dance...

(They dance. She winds the cloth playfully around him.)

MAN: It doesn't even matter if we don't speak a word...

(They dance. She continues to wind the cloth playfully around him).

MAN: That's a little tight...

(They dance.)

MAN: Say, that's tight...

(She dances and winds the cloth around him.)

MAN: Girl? ...Girl, I can't move my hands... My feet... I—

(She dances away from him, still humming happily. He is wound in cloth from shoulder to feet.)

MAN: Listen here. Can you hear me? What's happening?

(She dances.)

MAN: Girl! Come and untie me! Free me! I can hardly breathe!

(She dances away.)

MAN: What's the matter with you? I said come and untie me! ...Girl! Girl! I said come—!

(She dances away from him, humming gaily. Bound to the feet, he pursues. He crashes into the trunk and it bursts wide open. Bushels of apples tumble from it all over the floor.)

MAN: What's this? ...What's this? ...Why—it's nothing but apples!

(THE GIRL, in a firm, new self-possessed voice says:)

GIRL: Of course. What did you expect?

(She takes out a knife and spears an apple.)

MAN: I didn't know—. But I thought—

GIRL: Never think.

(She turns to him, her manner bold, voluptuous and smiling. Afraid, he tries to move away.)

GIRL: And never run from an apple girl. She'll catch you—every time.

(She laughs and starts coming toward him. He tries to hop away. Bound helplessly, he falls back onto the bed. She bends over him with the speared apple. Laughing, she force feeds him.)

(Blackout)

END OF PLAY

THE FALL OF ATHENS

CHARACTERS & SETTING

Haemon
Eurydice
Creon
Ismene
Antigone
Thaletas

Time & Place: Any Golden Age—Now or Then. Any Golden Place—Athens or Here.

Setting: An open terrace outside the palace of the king, high on a hill overlooking the city.

Upstage, capping a raised platform reached by several steps, is the facade of the palace. Three doors punctuate the facade. The central, most prominent, door leads to Creon's rooms of state; the two flanking doors lead to lesser rooms of the palace.

Downstage, suggested by fragments of low wall left and right, is the overlook to the city. Access to and from the city is downstage right. Access to and from the garden is downstage left.

The lines of the architecture are both classic and contemporary. All the visual elements express timelessness, having those classic proportions, simplicity and confidence of style which typify any golden age.

The costumes, too, have a purity and timelessness, the way people dressed then—and will undoubtedly dress in some space-age future.

"Antigone" and "Athens" and "Greece" and all the other proper names are metaphors. The stories one knows of them are not told here. These characters and these places are used to tell a story that is new.

ACT ONE

(At rise:)

(HAEMON, son of Creon, and a Prince, is practicing magic tricks with a scarf. A serious young man in his mid-twenties, he tries a trick—it fails. He tries it again—it fails again. He tries a third time. This time the trick works. Feeling self-confident, he calls out:)

HAEMON: Mother! Come see my magic trick!

(EURYDICE, the Queen—a typical society matron—enters from the upstage left door.)

EURYDICE: Well, Haemon—let me see.

(He tries it again. He fails.)

HAEMON: Sorry—

EURYDICE: Never mind, dear. I'll come back when you—

(She starts to exit. He stops her.)

HAEMON: No, wait! Wait! I'll show you the trick I do with knives—! *(He puts the scarves into a cubby in the wall and takes out some knives and a target. He throws the knives toward the target. None of them hit their mark.)*

EURYDICE: *(Still trying to leave)* It doesn't matter, I—

HAEMON: Wait! I do this trick with potions. I mix two vials of colorless liquid and, by magic, they turn bright red and explode! *(He puts away the knives and takes out two vials. He tries the trick. Nothing happens. The potions spill onto the floor.)* I don't know what I did wrong, I—

EURYDICE: Keep trying, dear. *(Obviously impatient, she looks over the parapet.)* Only a few more hours till the Apollo contest. I wonder who'll win this year? Who'll rule the games and have his form carved into stone.

HAEMON: Have you seen the candidates?

EURYDICE: I've seen their measurements. They're overwhelming! Apollo himself will be thrilled with us this year—how closely the men of Greece resemble gods. Haemon, dear, I wish you'd enter.

HAEMON: Magic's what I do best—and I don't even do that passably.

EURYDICE: Still. Your father would be so proud—

HAEMON: I'm sure he would. But one doesn't enter to please a father. One enters, I imagine, to please a girl.

EURYDICE: Oh, darling, is there someone? You've no idea how long I've waited to hear that! I've wanted for oh so long to make a wedding—!

HAEMON: My girl—is far away.

EURYDICE: But you can't mean—! You can't still love—! Why, Haemon, it's eleven years since she left Athens!

HAEMON: Eleven years, five months, three days.

EURYDICE: You can't adore a girl you haven't seen since she was—that high. It's biologically impossible!

HAEMON: It's possible.

EURYDICE: If only you could fall for her sister. Someone you see around the palace every day. But to waste your lovely manhood pining for Antigone—

HAEMON: *(Interrupting)* Tell me, Mother—are you all prepared for your banquet in honor of the new Apollo?

EURYDICE: Oh, yes. And it's going to be splendid! I'm serving specialities from all the different states of Greece! Fried anchovies the way they make them in Ionia. The stewed fig pudding that the Thracians so adore. Those boiled rabbit pies I hear they positively live on in Macedonia. Of course, I don't think I could actually eat any of it—but I do think it's a nice gesture to have these things on the menu, don't you?

HAEMON: I suppose...

EURYDICE: Oh, Haemon! What a lovely time of year this is! The games! The great Athenian games! *(She looks out toward the audience.)* Look at them all, swarming into Athens from all directions. The Miletians with their funny wooden carts, the Cretans in those prickly woollen capes of theirs, the Dorians with their mouths moving—they always bounce along singing their funny native songs. See them all come, the athletes—bringing their wives and mothers, their fathers and sisters, their hopes, their dreams, their muscles—and filling the city—

(CREON *enters from the upstage center door.*)

CREON: —with the most tremendous stink that has ever assailed a royal nostril!

EURYDICE: Creon—

(CREON, *the king, has a cultivated, urbane, impeccable smoothness. He endures all the failings of the world with a civilized half-smile.*)

CREON: Why do you think we have the games only once a year now? As an act of mercy to the Athenian nose. Have you ever been introduced to a Spartan armpit? Have you ever met a laughing Corinthian who blessed you with a "Hah, hah, hah!" right in your face? Holy Zeus, what we won't put up with for international brotherhood! The barbarians don't even know how to defecate! That is, the know *how*, but not *where*. *(He sees the remains of the potions on the floor.)* Is this the triumph of the magician's art?

HAEMON: Sorry, father. *(He kneels and starts to clean it up with the scarves.)*

CREON: How refreshing it would be someday—to have success from you, instead of apologies. Must I have distressing elements under my own roof? I am trying to survive this week in the sanctuary of the palace!

EURYDICE: But it's a wonderful week, husband—

CREON: "Wonderful." ...This is the week that Athens invites in the hordes. We open our gates to all our friends and neighbors. They do vile things by daylight, and even worse things—mostly horizontal—by dark. But still we welcome them. They dress like baboons, eat like pigs, and speak in the accents of heat-crazed donkeys. But still we welcome them. They are noisy, wild, illiterate, drunken, stupid, diseased, and unspeakably dirty. But still we welcome them. Love today—and fumigate tomorrow.

HAEMON: Why do you have the games then, father?

CREON: Why?...To win.

(From downstage right, ISMENE runs in. She is in her early 20s. Bright-eyed, she seems much younger.)

ISMENE: Oh, Aunt! Uncle! Haemon—!

EURYDICE: Ismene, dear, what is it?

ISMENE: Oh, Aunt—I heard—I heard—. I was walking in the city and everywhere I went I heard—

EURYDICE: What, dear?

ISMENE: My sister's name!

HAEMON: Antigone!

ISMENE: They say she's coming back!

HAEMON: Could it be possible—?

ISMENE: Some say that she's coming from the east, by chariot. Some say it's from the north, by horse. I even heard it said that she was flying in on the back of Zeus's eagle! But everyone is saying that she's coming home. Could it be true?

EURYDICE: So *that's* what it meant! Apollo's oracle. When I was down at Delphi last week, that's all the sibyl in the cave kept shouting: "A-a-a-a!...A-a-a-a!" He must have meant "A-a-a-Antigone!"

CREON: He could have meant A-a-apples, A-a-apricots, or A-a-aspidistras! What makes you think your oracle meant A-a-Antigone?

EURYDICE: We don't expect her, so she must be coming home. Expect the unexpected with Antigone. I learned long ago never to guess at what she'll do. *(To* ISMENE:*)* Now after that dreadful incest business, when your father plucked his eyes out in that appalling way, and had to leave town because of all that bleeding, who do you say would have been the perfect nurse for him? You, Ismene. And who was it that went? Antigone, of course,—though she never before had shown the slightest humanitarian impulse, had refused, even at the age of eight, to sell cookies at our hospital bazaar. ...And more, when your dear father died at last, and was mercifully out of all his misery, wouldn't you have expected Antigone to come back to us then? If only to be with you, Ismene, the only surviving member of her immediate family? But no. She stayed on in Colonus, in the farthest corner of our state, putting flowers on his grave, refusing all our offers of professional mourners. It would make me so depressed—pitching camp in a graveyard. But that's Antigone. Where others shudder, she thrives.

ISMENE: She used to play with snakes—and dare me to touch them.

HAEMON: She used to balance on that parapet—and dare me to do so, too.

ISMENE: But is she coming?

CREON: Why not ask *me*? Kings may be assumed to possess *some* information.

HAEMON: Father, is she coming? Is she? Is she?

CREON: Why don't you save your palpitations till you see her?

HAEMON: Then she is!

CREON: ...Yes. She is.

ISMENE: Oh—!

EURYDICE: I knew it! Always believe Apollo's oracle!

HAEMON: But how do you know she's coming, father?

CREON: My spotters saw her on the western road.

HAEMON: When?

CREON: Yesterday.

HAEMON: And you didn't tell us?

CREON: I didn't think you could contain yourself till she arrived.

HAEMON: I would have run out on the road to meet her—

CREON: Exactly.

HAEMON: But, Father, aren't you in the least excited?

CREON: Oh, I can take her coming in my stride. As her uncle, I will make her welcome. As her host, I'll make sure there are no bedbugs in her bed. But as for jumping up and down with glee—I'll wait till I see *why* she's decided to return to us.

HAEMON: What difference does it make—why?

CREON: That's what I like: a man who never asks essential questions.

ISMENE: I wonder what she'll look like. And will she be the same. Can she stay with me in my room, Aunt?

EURYDICE: If she wants to. *(To* CREON:*)* How long will it be till she's here?

CREON: Not long. They should arrive any minute.

HAEMON: "They?"

CREON: Antigone and friend.

HAEMON: What friend? A nurse? A handmaiden? A companion?

CREON: Who knows who only sees at a distance? All I know of her nurse, handmaiden and companion is—it's male.

HAEMON: What man? Where from? Who is he?

CREON: Father knows much—but not all, Haemon. If you want to know everything, ask Antigone herself.

(ANTIGONE *runs in joyously from downstage right. Alone. A shining young woman in her mid-twenties, wearing all white. Suddenly, very much moved, she stops. She greets each member of her family slowly gazing at each deeply, with emotion:)*

ANTIGONE: Uncle. ...Aunt. ...Cousin. ...Sister. ...*(Then, suddenly exuberant)* Oh, Athens, Athens, Athens, Athens, Athens!

CREON: *(Dryly)* I think she likes us.

ANTIGONE: Athens! Athens! How good it is to be home! If I were as blind as my father was, I'd know that this was Athens. I could sense the presence of those indestructible olive trees. I could feel the ground—it's more alive here. And I would know the air. The air of Athens! Nowhere else in all the universe is air so fresh and pure.

CREON: Joy must have clogged your nose.

ISMENE: *(Near tears)* I can't believe you're here! I can't believe it!

HAEMON: *I* can. ...And now that I see you again, it's as if you never were away. You grew up in my mind, Antigone. Does that sound strange to you? I drew the passing years in my imagination. And all that I imagined—was not wrong.

I dreamed —

EURYDICE: *(Aside to* CREON:*)* Aren't they charming together!

CREON: Embarrassing! *(To* HAEMON:*)* Could you save this dualogue till you're alone?

HAEMON: *(Continuing, to* ANTIGONE:*)* But I never thought that when you came, you'd bring somebody with you —

CREON: Haemon! I thought you had the gift of tact. *(Turning from him)* How is your father's grave, Antigone?

ANTIGONE: Quiet.

EURYDICE: Thank goodness!

CREON: The Furies that pursued him have been laid to rest?

ANTIGONE: I've made them my best friends.

CREON: But all is well in that remote corner of the world where you chose to raise yourself?

ANTIGONE: All is well there.

CREON: Then you won't mind my asking to what — after an absence of eleven years — we owe this windfall of your presence?

HAEMON: Antigone! Please! Who did you bring with you?

CREON: I'd be obliged if you'd answer first things first. Antigone, — why have you come?

ANTIGONE: For love.

(HAEMON *draws his breath in sharply.*)

ANTIGONE: ...For love of Athens.

HAEMON: Antigone —?

ANTIGONE: I fell back in love with Athens — and I had to come. For years the injuries we suffered here were much too painful. My father, my mother, and all my brothers gone. I couldn't bear the wounds. ...But time has healed them. And over all the hurts was the vision of the perfect city in its greatest moments. I thought of Athens — and I had to come.

HAEMON: With whom —?!

ANTIGONE: Do you know that the birds bring messages about this city? The peasants who return from market here wear a permanent sparkle Athens gives them for their eyes. The waves of the Aegean, as they pass Colonus on their way to Athens, pick up speed — so anxious are they to wash these shores and no others. ...This time, this place, this wonder —!

CREON: I should hire you out to our chamber of commerce.

ANTIGONE: I hardly think that I'd be needed. Look at them all, swarming through the gates from all directions.

EURYDICE: For the games, Antigone. Have you forgotten the games?

ANTIGONE: Oh, no. This was my favorite time of year when I was small. I used to think: "When I grow up, I'll be a javelin thrower!"

CREON: You are not a javelin thrower! You are not prepared to face the hazards of the road! You should have let me know you wished to come. I would have sent the royal carriage.

ANTIGONE: And made me see the city through your purple drapes? Oh, no. I wanted to see it clear and unencumbered.

CREON: And did you?

ANTIGONE: I did.

CREON: And what you've seen—?

ANTIGONE: Has thrilled me. Moved me to the bone. The hill..., the sea below..., the—(*She is looking skyward—out toward the audience. She breaks off suddenly. Her tone changes.*)—that cloud—

EURYDICE: We have the most delicious clouds here, don't we?

ANTIGONE: There's something strange about that cloud...

CREON: (*Teasing*) A flaw in Athens?

ANTIGONE: It gives me a feeling of—. I don't know. There's something strange...

CREON: Love us, love our clouds, Antigone.

HAEMON: Never mind the clouds. Who did you bring with you?

ANTIGONE: I brought with me—

CREON: Oh, spare the boy his misery!

ANTIGONE: —a charioteer.

HAEMON: A charioteer! A friend of yours from Colonus?

ANTIGONE: Oh, no. I met him on the road. He was on his way to compete in the games.

HAEMON: He forced his company upon you?

ANTIGONE: No. I was walking along alone, staring upward, eager to catch my first glimpse of the Acropolis rock—and I fell into a gully. He pulled me out.

HAEMON: He touched you with his hands?

ANTIGONE: Just one.

EURYDICE: Just one! He must be strong as Hercules!

ANTIGONE: He well may be.

ISMENE: He saved your life.

ANTIGONE: No. Just my dignity.

HAEMON: But he touched you!

ANTIGONE: Yes. I hardly felt it.

ISMENE: He sounds extremely gentle—for an athlete.

ANTIGONE: He is. Both Herculean strong and extremely gentle. You'll meet him. He has to tether his horses. But then I asked him to take a minute to come in.

EURYDICE: Is that the man? That one coming toward us up the path?

ANTIGONE: Yes. It is.

HAEMON: He's a bloody beauty!

EURYDICE: A beauty...

ANTIGONE: I could have told you that he was. But don't expect him to talk a lot. He doesn't. We'd walk for hours on the road and he'd say nothing. Yet, he seemed to make more sense than a dozen chattering philosophers.

CREON: I think you've brought us someone very special, Antigone.

ANTIGONE: I think I have, Uncle.

CREON: We can always use a man like that.

ANTIGONE: Yes, I thought perhaps you could.

(THALETAS *enters. He is heroic and quiet.*)

ANTIGONE: Family... This is Thaletas.

CREON: *(Shaking hands)* Welcome to the royal family, young man. I understand you rescued my niece.

THALETAS: I happened to be there...

CREON: We owe you our thanks.

THALETAS: Not at all, Sir.

EURYDICE: A young girl has no business tramping along the road throwing herself on the mercy of handsome heroes. Don't you agree?

THALETAS: I agree when a Queen asks me, Ma'am.

CREON: *(To* ANTIGONE:*)* He's wise, this friend of yours.

HAEMON: "Wise!" He's hardly said one sentence!

CREON: Would you like to sit in the royal box for the games tomorrow?

THALETAS: Thank you very much, Sir. But I came to win, not watch.

CREON: A noble thought. I wish you well. Are you a good charioteer, Thaletas?

ANTIGONE: Tell them of the trick you do.

THALETAS: I don't know why I described it to you. The telling is nothing. The doing is all.

CREON: Modest, too. You *have* brought us a paragon!

HAEMON: Can he balance a knife on his tongue? Can he make a flaming arrow disappear?

CREON: *(Aside to* HAEMON:*)* Can you?

(HAEMON *shrinks and moves aside.*)

ANTIGONE: I'll tell you what he does, since he's so modest. ...After he's won a race, while the horses are still running, he climbs out of the chariot onto the two forward horses. He unhitches the horses from the chariot and from each other and, with one foot on each, races them onward, together, apart, together, apart, still going like the wind. Then, after a moment, he shouts, "Hey!", drops the reins and jumps to the ground. The horses break apart and speed away in opposite directions. Each makes a perfect circle then returns to the place where Thaletas stands. He jumps up on their backs again and rides, one foot on each, to the judge's box to collect his laurel crown. Now what do you think of that?

CREON: I think he risks ripping his privates. But if that doesn't bother him, I'd say it takes great courage and skill.

HAEMON: My magic takes great courage and skill! I am this country's champion in magic!

CREON: And I am this country's champion in chess. But we hardly risk our lives—

HAEMON: I risk my tongue, I risk my hands, I risk my eyes! I do a trick with puncture needles that's as dangerous as anything soldiers do in war. *(To* THALETAS:*)* Would you like to see it?

THALETAS: I'd like to very much. But just this moment I must go see that my horses are settled. I thought I caught a glimpse of some very good stables in that direction.

CREON: By the western wall? Why that's where the Spartans have chosen to camp. If I were you, I'd avoid it. The savages have no idea about sanitation or hygiene. Their cooking odors alone could turn your stallions into geldings. The Spartans consume so much lard they leave fatty footprints on the sidewalks. And if one of them should shake your hand, you'd bear the grease for weeks.

EURYDICE: Besides, I'm not sure it's at all safe to camp near the Spartans. Last week I asked a friend who'd travelled there to tell me what they eat—I wanted to add a favorite Spartan dish for my bazaar. You know what I was told? Their favorite dish? Their grandmothers!

(THALETAS *looks at her in surprise.*)

EURYDICE: It's true! They eat their grandmothers! And not only that, they—

ANTIGONE: I'm afraid you'll have to save your tales for later, Aunt. Thaletas really has to go.

THALETAS: *(Amused)* Oh, yes. I want to get to camp in time for lunch. After all, I wouldn't want to miss the tastiest bits of grandma.

(THALETAS *winks at* ANTIGONE, *smiles, and goes out downstage right.*)

EURYDICE: I didn't know! He didn't look—! Oh, my! I must be pink all over!

CREON: Dear wife. Surely you have something left to do for the Apollo celebration.

EURYDICE: Why, yes. I guess I do. *(She starts to go.)* Imagine! I've talked to a man who has eaten ancestors! I must tell—

CREON: You'll tell no one!

EURYDICE: All right, dear. But how utterly exciting! ...It gives me chills all up and down my spine!

(EURYDICE *exits into the palace.* CREON *turns to* ANTIGONE:)

CREON: So. He's a Spartan. *(He is staring at his right hand.)*

ANTIGONE: Greasy, Uncle?

CREON: Tell me, dear prodigal niece. Why did you bring him here?

ANTIGONE: Because he's wise, strong, noble, and a bloody beauty.

CREON: He's a Spartan!

ANTIGONE: So he is.

CREON: You didn't know?

ANTIGONE: I didn't.

CREON: Why not?

ANTIGONE: I never asked him.

CREON: I should have known he was! Those perfect manners. That oh-so-correct pronunciation! They're always so on guard in civilized society. Must be careful that the inner beast doesn't pop out!

ANTIGONE: I never saw the beast, and I spent two days on the road with him.

CREON: Perhaps the things you did required no conversation.

ANTIGONE: You love to shock for effect, Uncle. You always did.

CREON: And you love to rebel for effect. When you were young, you'd sneak wild skunks into the palace. Now you're grown up, it's Spartans.

ANTIGONE: Are we at war with Sparta?

CREON: Not at the moment.

ANTIGONE: I thought there was some talk of uniting with them, and with all the states of Greece.

CREON: Of course there's talk. Much talk. The more we talk, the less we have to do it.

ANTIGONE: But why not do it really?

CREON: Us? Unite with them? Us share our temples, ships and souls, while they share—what? Their fatty grandmas?

ANTIGONE: I'm sure they have much to offer.

CREON: Like what?

ANTIGONE: Find out for yourself—this afternoon—at tea.

CREON: You invited the Spartan to have tea with us?

ANTIGONE: I did.

CREON: In the name of Zeus, why?

ANTIGONE: For lemon tarts. He loves lemon tarts.

CREON: You invited him in order to defy me.

ANTIGONE: I invited him to thank him for pulling me out of a hole in the road.

CREON: I put up with this assorted rabble for the games, for the city. I don't have to undermine my digestive system by entertaining them privately at tea!

ANTIGONE: But, Uncle, he might say something interesting.

CREON: On what subject? Music? Philosophy? Maybe architecture. I understand the Spartans are nearly on the verge of inventing the cave.

ANTIGONE: Uncle—

CREON: I won't have one of them to tea!

ANTIGONE: Why not?

CREON: Because they scratch when they itch.

ANTIGONE: And what do *you* do when you itch, Uncle?

CREON: I wait till I'm in private.

ANTIGONE: Then what?

CREON: *Then* I scratch.

ANTIGONE: I cast my vote for the public itcher-scratchers! They're much more honest!

CREON: I order you to disinvite him!

ANTIGONE: But how can I, Uncle? In etiquette there is no form—

CREON: A girl as clever as you can surely invent one—

ANTIGONE: Sorry, Uncle...

CREON: He will not come to tea, Antigone,—because I say so!

ANTIGONE: *(Pleasantly)* Don't be silly. I'm going to set a place for him. ... See you all at four. (ANTIGONE *goes inside, upstage right.*)

CREON: *(To* ISMENE:*)* Whatever she sets,—unset it.

ISMENE: *(Timid, conflicted)* I'll try, Uncle. (ISMENE *goes inside, upstage right.*)

CREON: There it goes—the Oedipus blood. The Oedipus self-assurance. Five minutes of Antigone in the palace and the columns begin to shake.

HAEMON: I'm sure she didn't realize—

CREON: That up-tilt of the chin. Her father used to hold his head that way. Do you remember?

HAEMON: No, father.

CREON: A consciousness of near-divinity, of heaven's special blessings on their lives. They always seem to be shouting: "I sprang full-blown from Zeus's pinky!" ...While the rest of us, not being descended from Zeus's pinky, are always something a little other, a little less. ...This is not, any longer, her father's palace! If she wants to partake of my hospitality, she will go out of her way to do what pleases me!

HAEMON: She has a will—

CREON: I know about her will. I'm counting on you to tame it.

HAEMON: How, father?

CREON: With love. Steady applications of love—the great softener.

HAEMON: There's nothing in the world I want more than to walk beside her in the moonlight, to hold her hand, to whisper in her ear the—

CREON: Oh, for heaven's sake! It's the *lady* who's supposed to go all limp and misty!

HAEMON: Yes, father.

CREON: Well, see that she does. And visibly! The people adore a little romance in the palace. It makes them think we all have milky centers like their own. And they like to think we're like them—it keeps them manageable.

HAEMON: Yes, father.

CREON: So go on in. Get her mind out of the teapot and into the nuptial chamber. Make her so warm with unreasoning emotions that she forgets all about having her guest in for tea.

HAEMON: Father?

CREON: Yes?

HAEMON: I know it's not my place—. I mean, I'm not fond of the man, but—

CREON: Well? What is it?

HAEMON: Does it matter so much if a Spartan comes to tea?

CREON: You blasted innocent! Does it matter? In a country throbbing with Democracy? Where the king now rules by the people's consent? ...I don't give a damn who Antigone befriends. Let her entertain the barnyard if she wants to! But next week are the elections. What do you think the people want? A king whose palace is throbbing with young love? Or a king who breaks bread with barbarians? ...I'll tell you what they want. They want a king who's civilized, who associates himself only with the best that civilization has. I intend to be that king, now and for many years into the future. It's not that I care so much about my teacups. But I am very much attached to the crown. ...Ensure it for me. Go, with all your youthful ardor. And when I come in in a few minutes, I want to discover there are only five of us to tea.

(HAEMON *exits upstage into the palace.* CREON *watches him exit—then follows him out.*)

(*Lights change.*)

(*A table appears, set for tea.* ISMENE *enters. She counts the places. There are six! She removes one. It is still in her hand when* ANTIGONE *appears.*)

ANTIGONE: Sister! Sister! You are not bold!

ISMENE: Antigone—!

ANTIGONE: I'll have to be daring enough for the two of us.

ISMENE: You always were. (*She puts the teacup down, not on the table, and says:*) ...Oh, how I've missed you!

ANTIGONE: And I missed you. How lovely you have gotten.

ISMENE: Sometimes it seemed as though I was only holding my breath these years—sleepwalking—till you came back.

ANTIGONE: And now that I'm here—?

ISMENE: We'll do everything we do—together. Pick flowers. Sing. Weave on the same loom.

ANTIGONE: We'll sleep in the same chamber—and share our dreams.

ISMENE: We'll whisper secrets.

ANTIGONE: And ride. And swim.

ISMENE: What did you do most in Colonus?

ANTIGONE: Read. And think.

ISMENE: You'll tell me all you thought?

ANTIGONE: I will. We'll find a plane tree in a quiet place, and I will tell you all I thought, Ismene.

(*As she talks,* ANTIGONE *picks up the sixth cup and starts to put it back on the table.*)

ISMENE: Antigone!

ANTIGONE: Yes?

ISMENE: Please don't defy our uncle.

ANTIGONE: (*Holding the cup*) I absolutely swear I won't defy him. I'm only planning to have a friend to tea.

ISMENE: You'll cause such trouble!

ANTIGONE: You can't cause trouble by a little thing like that!

ISMENE: With him you can.

ANTIGONE: Oh, Creon and his little tyrannies! ...(*Putting the cup on the parapet, she looks around.*) Where are the goldfish that you used to keep here?

ISMENE: Creon doesn't like them.

ANTIGONE: And you allow him to command your life? Even in the tiny corners? You let him dictate whether or not you can keep fish? And who you'll share a lemon tart with?

ISMENE: Antigone. Don't set yourself against the King—

ANTIGONE: You're just the same now as you were when we were infants. Whatever is is acceptable to Ismene. If the wet nurse doesn't come—that is acceptable to Ismene. If her diapers aren't changed for twenty hours—Ismene never cries.

ISMENE: Antigone would scream—

ANTIGONE: Enough for two! And you should still be grateful for it. ...When a mother dies, and a father tears his handsome face to shreds—for fate, for nothing human!—that is acceptable to Ismene.

ISMENE: No! But what was there to be done?

ANTIGONE: I don't yet know. But when I know, I'm certain I will do it. (*She gazes upward and outward, puzzled.*) That cloud... That cloud...

ISMENE: A lovely cloud. Why do you keep remarking on it?

ANTIGONE: I know what's wrong with it, Ismene!—It doesn't move!

ISMENE: Why should it move? It's perfect as it is.

ANTIGONE: But clouds are meant to move and change—

ISMENE: You're new to Athens.

ANTIGONE: Are things so terrifying here?

ISMENE: Terrifying? No! Everything's beautiful! You said yourself it was a special time.

ANTIGONE: But—

ISMENE: Here, clouds that reach perfection never change. It's as if they were hammered out of stone by dear Praxiteles. The cypress trees all grow to just the perfect height—and stay—all just the same, all without clipping. Hot food always stays hot, and cold stays cold. Men always fall in love in May. In June, they marry. The women's tides all run the same. The babies are all born one day each month. And that makes one day every month the perfect birthday! We celebrate and sing and dance! The birthday boys are all the perfect height, the birthday girls are all the same amount of pretty. Why everything's the grandest it can be! And never changes!

(ANTIGONE *has been staring at her, her eyes growing wider and wider.*)

ANTIGONE: You haven't heard a word I said!

(ANTIGONE *picks up the sixth cup and plants it firmly on the table.*)

ANTIGONE: Ismene—you must go out right away and get some goldfish!

ISMENE: Oh, no, Antigone! I wouldn't dare!

(HAEMON *enters. Knowing the two must want to be alone,* ISMENE *discretely exits.*)

HAEMON: I performed magic tricks—tricks of sorcery—to call you back to Athens. They worked!

ANTIGONE: So it would seem, Haemon.

HAEMON: We each grew up apart from each other.

ANTIGONE: Yes. Quite separately.

HAEMON: And yet, I always felt—that the final growing up which we must do—we have to do—together.

ANTIGONE: Perhaps that's so...

HAEMON: How did you remember me?

ANTIGONE: Through the eyes of a girl of ten.

HAEMON: And what did she see?

ANTIGONE: A young man three heads taller than she was.

HAEMON: And now?

ANTIGONE: Now, we face each other eye-to-eye.

HAEMON: You're talking in metaphors!

ANTIGONE: Oh, no. A wife-to-be should never talk in metaphors.

HAEMON: A wife-to-be?!

ANTIGONE: Didn't we dip our fingers into the blood of that terrible day and swear to each other that one day we would marry?

HAEMON: I thought you had forgotten—

ANTIGONE: Forgotten—! That—?

HAEMON: You have feelings for me! You had dreams far away in which you loved me! You spent days staring into space and remembering—

ANTIGONE: I swore in the life blood of my father that I would marry you. Such an oath is sacred. It is one that I will keep.

HAEMON: Then why did you bring in the Spartan?

ANTIGONE: Haemon—

HAEMON: And why did you ask him to tea?

ANTIGONE: Please don't begin—

HAEMON: If I'm to be your mate, aren't I enough for company? Why did you ask him?

ANTIGONE: ...Because he tells me stories.

HAEMON: I can tell you stories.

ANTIGONE: Thaletas tells me stories whose endings I do not know.

HAEMON: I can do that! I can do anything that he can!

ANTIGONE: Can you?

HAEMON: If I tell you a story with an ending you can't guess, will you disinvite the Spartan?

(ANTIGONE *takes the sixth cup from the table and sets it between them, as if it were now up for judgement.*)

ANTIGONE: There, Haemon. ...You may try.

(*Then, as* HAEMON *hesitates:*)

ANTIGONE: Well? ...Begin...

HAEMON: (*Nervously*) I'll tell you—I'll tell you the story of a man who fought a giant minotaur within a labyrinth—

ANTIGONE: You mean the one where he kills the minotaur and finds his way back out with a string?

HAEMON: Yes, that's the one! You told the end!

ANTIGONE: Well, Haemon. You may have three chances. Try another.

HAEMON: All right. ...Let's see. ...Yes. This one. ...There was once a girl who said she'd only marry a man who could beat her in a foot race. The man she ran against was very clever—

ANTIGONE: He won by dropping golden apples in her path. She paused to pick them up and—

HAEMON: Antigone! You know that story, too!

ANTIGONE: I'm afraid I do. But you have one other chance. Surely you know a story where I don't know the ending.

HAEMON: Of course I do. Yes, yes. It's this. ...Once upon a time there was a man who loved his wife so much that when she died he pleaded with the powers of Hades to let him have her back alive again—

ANTIGONE: *(Dully, as if by rote)* They said he could if, till he got her back to earth, he didn't look at her.

HAEMON: You don't know whether he looked at her or not!

ANTIGONE: *(Dully)* He did. And as he did she turned to stone.

HAEMON: Forget it all! Forget about the tea! Which Wednesday will you marry me?

ANTIGONE: Is Wednesday now the wedding day in Athens?

HAEMON: Why, yes, of course.

ANTIGONE: And no one marries any other day?

HAEMON: On which one will we—?

ANTIGONE: *(Wildly)* The first Tuesday Wednesday. Any Sunday Friday that you like. In June October, or April March—!

HAEMON: Of course you do not know his stories! He comes from another place!

ANTIGONE: I do not know his stories because he *invents* them! Thaletas makes up his stories as he goes along!

HAEMON: You're trying to humiliate me! So he can sit beside you, nibble at your cakes, drink from your cup—

ANTIGONE: Haemon, you don't understand! I don't want to know the endings of your stories. I am afraid to find myself in a city where the clouds stand still, where everything is known and regulated. The air is beginning to solidify! Soon we will be motionless, like statues—the best of statues,—but utterly frozen and still. Invent for me! Create! Invent new stories!

HAEMON: I would if I could, Antigone. ...Oh, gods! If only I could!

(ANTIGONE *takes the sixth cup and sets it firmly on the table. As she does so,* CREON *and* EURYDICE *enter, followed meekly by* ISMENE.)

CREON: Here she is—the female prodigal. *(He looks at the table and notes the number of cups.)* The woman who knows her own mind. ...A welcoming committee from the citizens of Athens has asked to meet with you tomorrow, Antigone. Smile at them—if you can manage it. They vote a week from Tuesday.

ANTIGONE: Tuesdays vote, Wednesdays marry. And what do you do on Thursdays, Uncle?

EURYDICE: Why, on Thursdays we have our charity teas! ...You simply must join us, Antigone. We've collected so much for unfortunates everywhere. ...But your clothes, my dear, your clothes. No one wears styles like that any more in daylight. I have this marvelous little dressmaker. I simply must take you in hand!

HAEMON: You can help her, Mother, to choose a wedding dress.

EURYDICE: A wedding dress! Oh, is it settled? My dear boy—! *(She hugs her son.)*

CREON: I think he will be getting more than he bargained for. *(He removes and sets aside the sixth cup.)*

ISMENE: *(Concerned, aside, to* ANTIGONE:*)* Is it true?

ANTIGONE: You know me. I always keep my promises.

ISMENE: Then I wish you every happiness. At least it will keep you here—and in my life. *(She hugs* ANTIGONE.*)*

EURYDICE: Creon, we must announce it this very afternoon—at the Apollo contest.

ANTIGONE: The Apollo contest—

ISMENE: You remember—where the handsomest, the bravest, the most glorious specimen of manhood is chosen from all the city-states to do honor to Apollo.

ANTIGONE: I remember. ...Anyone can enter, is that still true?

CREON: Of course it's true. Even a Miletian. Even a Libyan. Even a Spa—tan! *(Pronouncing the last like a dirty word)*

ANTIGONE: But can they win?

EURYDICE: Of course they can win! If they can make it to the finals! The trouble is—they never do! The Libyans have such spindly legs! The Miletians are all so hairy! And as for the Spartans, since they're always training for war with endless gymnastics, you can hardly tell their bodies from the chimpanzees!

CREON: Anyone from the barbarian hordes can enter. We are nothing if not democratic in Athens. The problem is—they always rule themselves out in one way or another!

EURYDICE: So—fairly and squarely—it's always an Athenian who wins!

(THALETAS *enters. Seeing him,* ANTIGONE *says suddenly:*)

ANTIGONE: Ladies and gentlemen—I would like you to meet my candidate for the Apollo contest!

CREON: Antigone—

ANTIGONE: Here he is, like a god incarnate! See the thrust of his shoulders, see his noble stance—

THALETAS: *(Aside)* Antigone, what's this all about?

ANTIGONE: Don't you want to wear the laurel crown and rule the games, Thaletas?

THALETAS: I want to race my chariot—

ANTIGONE: Why, you can win at both. You can have more glory than a king tomorrow! Winner of the Apollo crown this afternoon. Winner of the chariot races tomorrow! You can crown yourself champion of the games!

EURYDICE: *(Admiring)* He certainly is a raving beauty—

ANTIGONE: But first, Thaletas, I invite you to join us now—for tea.

(*She sets the sixth cup.* CREON *pounds his hand on the table.*)

CREON: There will be no tea!

(ANTIGONE *speaks calmly.*)

ANTIGONE: Of course there will be no tea. It's getting much too close to the time for choosing our new Apollo. *(She looks over the parapet.)* Look. I can already see the contestants readying themselves and standing tall. They're straightening their costumes. They're being given their masks. *(To* THALETAS:*)* Off you go, my champion! This afternoon you might find yourself the second king in Athens, the ruler of the games, the symbol of all that's beautiful and true.

(THALETAS *goes out downstage right.* CREON *turns to* EURYDICE, HAEMON *and* ISMENE:*)*

CREON: Leave us. All of you. I wish to talk to Antigone alone.

(EURYDICE, HAEMON *and* ISMENE *go into the palace.* CREON *turns to* ANTIGONE:*)*

CREON: Troublemaker!

ANTIGONE: "The Miletians are hairy! The Spartans are all like chimpanzees!"

CREON: So you've found yourself a cause. How like your father!

ANTIGONE: When Thaletas first came in you all said he was a bloody beauty! Apollo should be a bloody beauty, shouldn't he, my king and uncle? As radiant as the sun!

(Riffling in the cubby where Haemon keeps his magic things, she takes out cards, black ink and a brush. She draws a SUN on a card and puts it up against a column.)

CREON: There she goes, the country-raised romantic, off on her crusade to save the world!

ANTIGONE: And gentle, too, you said. Apollo should be gentle. *(She draws a FEATHER on a card and props that up, too.)*

CREON: I'll bet in Colonus you used to gambol on the grass with every shepherd, slave and herring-seller!

ANTIGONE: And noble. It was you who called him noble. *(She draws a CROWN and puts it on display.)*

CREON: No doubt you used to sit beneath the plane trees on that green peninsula and listen to your ancient blind and bearded father tell you of "Equality" and "Love of Every Man".

ANTIGONE: You called Thaletas wise— *(She draws an open EYE on a card.)*

CREON: You never heard the subtler, more important lesson your father was teaching you. The lesson? "How to Choose." How to tell which plum will be sweeter than another, which sheep will give more wool, which oil flask has a shape that is more pleasing, which wandering minstrel sings the better tunes. Discriminate and choose, choose and discriminate—

ANTIGONE: *You* chose! You called Thaletas strong— *(She draws a LIGHTNING BOLT.)*

CREON: It's why you're wearing white instead of puce, why you are swathed in linen and not muslin, why you let your hair fall free instead of plaiting it with wax and wires. It's why you're you, the excellence of your choices. A thousand times a day, Antigone, more often than the most fastidious Athenian,—you choose.

ANTIGONE: If I choose, I do it with my eyes wide open. I consider every element, each time, in itself.

CREON: Do you, indeed? You get up each morning and deliberate which side of the bed you will get out on? Once you discover mackerel doesn't agree with you, you taste it every time you find it on your plate?

ANTIGONE: Thaletas is no fish—

CREON: Some questions are closed, Antigone. Otherwise we would go mad!

ANTIGONE: Perhaps it's worth the risk. ...You said my friend was modest— *(She draws a CLOSED EYE.)*

CREON: A member of a race of savages.

ANTIGONE: Because they speak with a different accent?

CREON: Because they speak with a *lesser* accent! ...Yes, I, Creon, dare to choose. I dare to say Athenian pronunciation is superior. Just as I dare say that health is better than illness, and wealth is better than poverty. And just as my dear prodigal niece this morning dared to find superior the great Athenian air. Inequality is nature's way, Antigone.

ANTIGONE: I certainly agree. I found Thaletas—who, by the way, pronounces Athenian speech quite correctly—

CREON: Too correctly—

ANTIGONE: I found Thaletas highly unequal.

CREON: His people are barbarians! Uncivilized. Stupid! They opt for war at every provocation! I'm not inventing this!

ANTIGONE: If so, you could be tolerant—

CREON: Why not? We of them and they of us. We'll tolerate their eating their grandmothers—

ANTIGONE: You know they don't –

CREON: —and they'll tolerate our building the Parthenon. Did the Spartans design the Parthenon?

ANTIGONE: Did you?

CREON: I object to mediocrity and barbarism!

ANTIGONE: *I* object to mediocrity and barbarism! And I put forth the best Apollo of them all!

CREON: It hasn't sunken in. Not a single syllable.

ANTIGONE: I heard your syllables, Uncle. Not one of them describes my friend.

CREON: He is an exception!

ANTIGONE: Heroes always are.

CREON: He may not be as exceptional as he seems on the surface. In a pile of rotten apples, seldom does one single one escape the blight. Beneath his shiny skin, your apple may be wormy.

ANTIGONE: So may we all.

CREON: His qualities may last no longer than those cards you've drawn. I hate to be the one to tell you,—for you have a great deal of artistic talent, but you've gone to all that trouble in disappearing ink. All one has to do is—(*He takes one of her cards, dips a cloth into water, and rubs the drawing.*) You simply, with a drop of moisture, go—(*He tries again. Still, the drawing remains.*)

ANTIGONE: Thaletas, too, may surprise you.

CREON: *(Becoming very serious)* Then I am forced to tell you the truth behind the truth. The reality you didn't need to know beneath the plane trees of Colonus. ...Apollo is the symbol of what's best in Greece. And for that symbol one does not choose an exception. One chooses what represents the truth. The self-evident and blazing truth is this: that Athens is the best of Greece. Apollo, then, should be Athenian. Anything else would be sheer mockery.

ANTIGONE: And would also lose you votes next Tuesday.

CREON: I suppose, dear niece, I shouldn't be concerned with that! Can you really still be that naive?! ...But selfishness is not the only reason. I preserve the vision of Athens-the-Great—even by illusion if I have to—to discourage others—particularly the Spartans—from attempting war. As long as they're convinced we're unassailable, they won't attack us. We have peace. We've had it for some years now. But should one of those Others ascend these steps on my arm, the honored universal hero,—heaven knows what they'll get into their heads to try.

ANTIGONE: The greatness of Athens can't be safe if it's based on illusions.

CREON: You believe all this—is an illusion?!

ANTIGONE: Oh, no, Uncle! I believe it's beautiful and great and glorious! I believe it is strong enough to bear honesty and truth! I believe it is not so weak as to collapse if a Spartan wins the Apollo crown. I believe, in fact, it needs some waking up, something to get the clouds to move again! For the love that I bear Athens, three cheers for my Spartan Apollo!

CREON: Cheer if you like, your candidate won't win, Antigone.

ANTIGONE: Why not?

CREON: Because I'm the judge and I won't choose him.

ANTIGONE: You won't know who he is; they'll all be masked.

CREON: I'll know. You see, all Spartans, the moment they are born, are chained to a mountaintop, to test their hardiness against the elements. They only want the sturdiest to survive. Those who do, bear, for life, the scars of iron chains around their ankles. So I will know your Spartan, Antigone. That little bit of savagery—is true.

(CREON *goes into the palace.* ANTIGONE *calls in the direction* ISMENE *exited:*)

ANTIGONE: Sister! Come to me! And bring your rouge!

(ANTIGONE *collects the cards and puts them away.* ISMENE *enters carrying a small pot of rouge.*)

ISMENE: Antigone—what are you going to do?

ANTIGONE: I'm going to shove the clouds a bit—by making all Apollo contestants equal. One, you see, is better than the rest. One of them, when he was just a few days old, triumphed over trials the rest have yet to imagine. Fastened to a mountain-top, he tamed the gods by the perfection of his naked infant body. With his fragile baby fingertips, he charmed the hungry wolves. And when the circling vultures heard the beauty of his cries, they brought him food instead of feeding on him. He bears the scars of this tremendous triumph. Each ankle has a slight red mark. If this were seen, it would give him too great an advantage over all the others. So—I am going to make all of the Apollos equal to the best—by art—lent me by my sister.

(ANTIGONE *exits downstage right, followed by* ISMENE, *who is protesting all the way.*)

(*Lights change.*)

(*The tea table has been removed. When the lights come up,* CREON *is discovered, downstage, overlooking the city, addressing the unseen crowd below.*)

CREON: My people—each year, on the eve of the great games, we meet to choose a stand-in for the god Apollo. This year the choosing has particularly great significance, for we are honored by the return of the wandering daughter of Oedipus to our ranks. For her benefit, she who has been so far removed for so long from the glories of Athens, we wish to choose especially wisely. For she is a girl with an uncommon appreciation of excellence. In fact, if any of us can fit her idea of perfection, we will be fortunate indeed. (*He raises up the laurel crown.*) Here is the crown of laurel leaves. Laurel, sacred to the god Apollo. He who wins shall wear this crown and, tomorrow, shall be honored at the banquet and preside over the opening of the games. He shall have his name engraved on the pediments of temples, and he shall have his form immortalized in perfect stone. He who wins shall represent the best of all Greek manhood. And, being the best of all the Greeks, shall represent the best in all the world. (*He holds out the laurel crown.*) In the name of the god Apollo, son of Zeus, I consecrate this crown to the enduring glory of the spirit of Greece and of the god Apollo, supple of mind and beautiful of body. God Apollo—giver of the light. May the gods give us the wisdom to choose wisely. ...On to the choice!

(*As* CREON *exits downstage right he passes* ANTIGONE, *just entering, carrying her pot of rouge, which she hides from him.* HAEMON *enters from the palace.*)

HAEMON: Aren't you going to watch the Apollo contest?

ANTIGONE: I don't need to.

HAEMON: You're rooting for the Spartan, aren't you.

ANTIGONE: I'm rooting for the best there is.

HAEMON: You think he'll win.

ANTIGONE: I'm sure.

HAEMON: But they're all masked.

ANTIGONE: His qualities will shine through. They will be unmistakable.

HAEMON: My father has devised a host of tests—

ANTIGONE: I'm not worried. Thaletas will pass. How many contestants are there?

(HAEMON, *looking over the parapet, answers:*)

HAEMON: Twelve.

ANTIGONE: *(Not looking)* What is he testing now?

HAEMON: Muscle.

ANTIGONE: Thaletas is built to absolute perfection.

HAEMON: Three have been eliminated.

ANTIGONE: What is he testing now?

HAEMON: Balance. Each one must stand, without wobbling, on one foot, arms extended.

ANTIGONE: Thaletas will manage that just fine.

HAEMON: Four fell down! They're out!

ANTIGONE: And now?

HAEMON: Father is testing the way they walk.

ANTIGONE: Thaletas walks as nobly as a god.

HAEMON: Three stumbled! Only two are left.

ANTIGONE: Only two. ...I'm sure my candidate is one of them.

HAEMON: You don't know—!

ANTIGONE: I know.

HAEMON: *(Surprised and puzzled)* Good heavens! You know what he's testing now?

ANTIGONE: Yes. Ankles.

HAEMON: They've never tested that before! ...My father has asked that a basin of water be brought.

ANTIGONE: *(Seeing it in her mind's eye.)* Yes. Yes.

HAEMON: He—he himself!—is washing their ankles! Red paint is coming off the ankles of one of the contestants! ...Underneath, his ankle is unscarred! ...My father calls for another cloth. ...He washes the ankles of the last Apollo. ...The paint comes off. ...But there's a scar! ...The one with the scar is eliminated. My father raises the arm of the one whose ankles are unblemished! ...The crowd is shouting for Creon to remove the mask of their new Apollo. He is wearing a bright smile. He knows the Athenians wonder which of their brothers, sons, nephews, cousins has been chosen. Prolonging their suspense, he lifts the mask and peeks beneath. ...What! His smile has faded! He looks as angry as thunder! ...He is refusing to unmask the winner! The crowd is becoming impatient! They are calling for him to crown the victor! He plants the laurel crown on the winner's head. But he's not unmasking him! Instead, he is pushing the Apollo before him up the path to the palace! The crowd is still calling out to know the identity of the winner! Why wouldn't my father show them who it is?

ANTIGONE: Don't you know?

(HAEMON *looks at her.*)

ANTIGONE: The ankle scar. The Miletian had one! And—in spite of your father's preconception—Thaletas did not! *(Ecstatic, she cries:)* The Spartan has won the contest! ...On his own, chosen by the great king—the Spartan has been declared the best!

HAEMON: *(After a silence)* ...His place—is mine!

ANTIGONE: Haemon, what is it? You look so pale!

HAEMON: That place—beside the king—the hero youth—the handsomest and strongest in the kingdom—. That place—belongs to me!

ANTIGONE: But, Haemon, if you wanted it, you should have stood in line, all masked, with the other Apollos.

HAEMON: To lose? I can lose without ever entering—and keep all of my humiliation to myself.

ANTIGONE: Haemon... Cousin...

HAEMON: There was a time when sons of kings rose to the kingship. You saw the crown on your father's head when you were little—and when you grew to his height, that crown was yours. ...But now it's changed. Nothing is natural. All is at the will of the people. You can get as tall as your father and find your head completely bare. The promises I lived on as a child and boy—have come to nothing! I ought now to fulfill them by myself. But I am not equipped! Look at these hands, they're not prepared to fight their way to the front rank, and hold me there—as hero.

ANTIGONE: There is no need to fight—

HAEMON: See the terror of the idiot sons! The ones who are shorter and weaker and less wise—and who cannot seem to earn a woman's love—

ANTIGONE: *(Compassionately)* Dear friend and future husband—

HAEMON: I don't want you to be with me only because you promised years ago! I want you to want me now!

(She looks away.)

HAEMON: Can I create a manhood with my magic set? Achieve it through potions? Carve away impotence with knives? What incantations, tricks and sleight-of-hand can make a man of me?

ANTIGONE: To create a manhood, Haemon—all that is needed—is love.

HAEMON: I don't dare ask—

ANTIGONE: You do not need to ask. ...A girl, or woman, at my time, thinks very often about love. Since you and I were sworn to each other as children, I came back here curious to see what my life was sworn to.

HAEMON: And what you see—?

ANTIGONE: Is a beginning.

HAEMON: Antigone, I am afraid.

ANTIGONE: I'll hold you.

HAEMON: Take me to any dark place. I do not know what I am doing. I know no magic which will bind us one to the other. I can't—. I can't—.

ANTIGONE: Come, child, infant,—husband. Let us find a corner—where we can grow up. ...There is time for us to be together—now that, in Athens, all is well.

(She takes his hand and they exit downstage left, into the garden.)

(Lights change.)

(It is evening. Drums sound. Two chairs and a table have been set out. On the table is something covered with a cloth.)

(The center doors open. CREON *enters with the* APOLLO, *wearing his mask and the laurel crown.)*

CREON: Welcome to my humble home, Apollo. ...Please don't compare it with Olympus. We try, of course, for heavenly splendor, but all we can achieve, I am afraid—is this.

(The APOLLO *lifts his hands to his face to remove the mask.)*

CREON: No, don't unmask! It is said no mortal eyes can bear to gaze upon the true face of a god's beauty. And although my eyes are a good deal hardier than most, I don't think I should risk it. ...How excellent you were in all your tests, Apollo! So excellent I must compete against you myself. You will accept another challenge, won't you? Surely one fears nothing—when one not only is the god of beauty, but the god of intellect. So you won't mind one more challenge. Let us see, my deity, which of us can win—at chess.

*(*CREON *whisks the cloth away to reveal a chess board.)*

CREON: You play, of course?

(The APOLLO nods.)

CREON: Do you prefer the ivory or the jade?

(The APOLLO indicates no preference.)

CREON: The jade has been quite lucky for me. Here, you can have them. ...Be seated. Do be seated.

(The APOLLO sits.)

CREON: You wonder, don't you, how I dare to play against a god? Because I'm good, extremely good. I could win against Zeus. Or isn't that considered politic. ...But you and I needn't hold back, need we, Apollo? We'll give each other fair game. Hard and honest. For truth is hard, is it not, god of Truth and Beauty? It's a wonder your knowledge of the truth hasn't etched itself into your face.

(The APOLLO reaches up to remove his mask but CREON stops him with:)

CREON: Begin. Please do begin, Apollo.

(The APOLLO makes the first move.)

CREON: Excellent! I can tell this game will be very fine. You don't mind conversation while we play, do you? One seldom has a chance for a tête-à-tête with a deity. And there are questions I have yearned, for years, to ask—.

(The APOLLO again moves to remove his mask.)

CREON: Oh, you needn't speak. I know the sound of Apollo's voice would strike deaf the ears of ordinary mortals. Just let me voice what I have guessed of certain large eternal truths. And you deny or affirm by gestures—as you do for the priests at your shrines.

(The APOLLO makes a frustrated gesture.)

CREON: Yes. Exactly like that. ...Oh, I'm so excited I can hardly keep my mind on my game. ...Your move, Apollo. ...There's so much I want to know...

(A pause. Then, as they begin to play, CREON begins:)

CREON: Were you there at the creation of the world, when the dark was separated from the light, when Order was created out of Chaos, when it was decided what would go above and what beneath, when the borders of the lands were set, and the oceans brought up to them? Were you there when Man was put upon the earth?

(The APOLLO's hands move up in reply, but CREON interrupts with:)

CREON: Oh, look! I've missed my turn. It's being this near to truth. It quite unnerves me. Being this near to someone able to reveal all.

(CREON *makes his move.*)

CREON: I have wondered how it was, in the Beginning, when Man was first put on earth, as he multiplied and his descendants wandered between the rocky promontories and began to separate themselves, tribe from tribe. As each went each their separate ways you must have watched them. How soon after our lands were formed did you decide that Athens deserved your special care? What promise did you see in us that made you bless us above all others?

(*The* APOLLO *makes a gesture of protest.* CREON *pretends not to notice.*)

CREON: ...For I have guessed correctly, have I not, Apollo, that Athens is especially beloved of the gods? That here you did ignite that special flame whose lights will illuminate the world forever? That in a world of night and dim imaginings, Athens is the center and the sun?

(*The* APOLLO, *by the gestures of his hands, reveals a rising emotion.*)

CREON: Do make your move while I continue. For I've spent many hours wondering why we were singled out. And I have come to think that in those first dim moments there were some new humans who shone above the rest by the beauty of their thoughts and actions. But there were others who sinned against the principles of life. Perhaps these last committed nameless horrors, fornicating with the writhing devils or piercing the air with endless screams of primeval hate. For ever since, they have been spat upon by the gods.

(*The* APOLLO *reveals high agitation.*)

CREON: Aha! I have hit on the truth! The gestures of your hands reveal it! You needn't speak. I see with all the vision of a man possessed. To you, the god of Truth, I can speak freely. What I have guessed is so. This concept of a difference burned into man soon after his creation. So that even though, somehow, the simpering notion has seeped into the world that all men are the same and equal—never was it so, nor meant to be, above the clouds or anywhere beneath.

(*The* APOLLO *rises precipitously from his chair.*)

CREON: Come, make your move! Keep playing! I've guessed it, have I not, Apollo! The secret of preserving human life in years to come. It is for those of us beloved by the gods to keep our full lights surging upwards, to guard against the wild, dark forces which every moment try to pull mankind back into the slime. For there are those today, descendants of the wilder creatures, who roam the earth in civilized disguises, clothed for all the world like the greater breed. But they are not the greater breed, are they, Divine Apollo! ...They masquerade in good behavior, but the savage foams, deep, deep beneath. And though they wash, purge, disguise, and cover as they will—the sins are in them, flesh and bone, from generation unto generation. And one day, inescapably,—the beast will out! If we are not on guard, it will destroy the human race forever!

(Shaking with emotion, the APOLLO *tears off his mask and crown.* THALETAS *stands before* CREON, *speechless with fury.)*

CREON: Did you enjoy my little joke, Spartan?

*(*THALETAS *reaches out threateningly.)*

CREON: Touch me, and you prove my point!

*(*THALETAS *pulls back, wounded and enraged, controlling his confused emotions with great effort.)*

CREON: Oh, god of prophecy, would you like me to see into the future for you? Would you like me to tell you what it would be like if you, the Spartan, were to rule the games? ...You'd sit beside me on the throne, and the heady altitude of glory would begin to bubble through you. Then everything within you of civilized pretense would suddenly dissolve. Before the day was out, you would betray the falseness of your godhood. ...Distasteful as my words have been to you,—they're true. Within yourself, you carry your destruction. Before too many hours had passed, the Apollonian disguise would melt, the beast would out. You would disqualify yourself by some demeaning act that would blast that laurel crown from off your brow and leave you what you truly are:—a Spa—tan. ...If I were you, I'd give the glory up. I'd leave—before the beast emerges.

*(*THALETAS *is silent.)*

CREON: Well, open your mouth! Speak up! Is there nothing you can say?

THALETAS: *(After a long silence, making one last move then shouting out in anguish:)* Check—mate—!

*(*CREON *looks down. To his astonishment, it's true. Momentarily, he's staggered.* THALETAS *cries out again:)*

THALETAS: Checkmate! Checkmate!

*(*CREON *stares at the board for a moment. Then he sweeps the chess pieces onto the ground and strides into the palace, leaving* THALETAS *alone.)*

(Blackout)

END ACT ONE

ACT TWO

(At rise:)

(On the terrace. Early dawn. THALETAS *is standing alone staring at the laurel crown. Like a thing which puzzles him, which has caused him too many problems, he puts it down on the parapet.* EURYDICE *enters carrying an earthen flask.)*

EURYDICE: So *you're* the one who won! My husband told me!

THALETAS: Is he furious?

EURYDICE: Of course he is! Imagine! You not only won the Apollo contest, you won over him at chess!

THALETAS: I didn't mean to make him angry.

EURYDICE: Can you blame him? He thinks himself the world's chess champion! And as for you winning as Apollo, I *told* him you Spartans have a special something. It sticks out all over you — a certain ripple to the muscle — a certain rhythm to the walk.

THALETAS: Now that he knows who I am, he thinks I should give up the crown, not preside over the opening of the games —

EURYDICE: What do you care? It's just a ceremony.

THALETAS: You're right. What I came to do is race. I was only waiting for the dawn, hoping to see Antigone before I —

EURYDICE: Forget Antigone. I've brought you something. A flask of very special wine. The liquid in here has been aged over centuries. I bought it last week when I visited the cave of the oracle at Delphi. The one who sold it to me said it has special powers — to fortify the body and enhance — certain skills.

THALETAS: *(Accepting it)* Thank you.

EURYDICE: Well — open it and drink!

THALETAS: I prefer to keep my head clear — on the course, that's necessary.

EURYDICE: I can understand that. Do you mind if I take just a taste? I'd like to try —

THALETAS: *(Handing the flask to her)* Please. Be my guest.

(EURYDICE *uncorks the flask and takes a sip.*)

EURYDICE: Exquisite! It is said all mysteries are answered at the bottom of this bottle. It is said that, with each sip, knowledge enters one as if one were possessed. ...Oh, do try it.

THALETAS: As I said—I never drink on the morning of a race.

EURYDICE: Well, *I'm* not racing! And this is the nectar of the gods. Would you mind if I take another sip?

(He gestures that she may. She drinks—more than a sip.)

THALETAS: Do you think Antigone will wake soon?

EURYDICE: Let her sleep. We're enjoying ourselves together, aren't we? *(She continues drinking.)* Tell me, Thaletas, how do you celebrate, you Spartans, when the games are over? Do you sing?

THALETAS: Sometimes.

EURYDICE: Do you dance? I heard you Spartans love to dance.

THALETAS: Some do.

EURYDICE: Come dance with me.

THALETAS: You must excuse me, Queen Eurydice. It's time for me to go and groom my horses. *(He tries to leave.)*

EURYDICE: No, don't go. Not yet. It's early. *(She takes another draught.)* Oh, this magic brew! It's moving all throughout my body. All my senses are aflame! ...Come and dance—*(She does a few turns then moves toward him seductively.)*

THALETAS: I'm sorry, but I truly should—*(He tries to escape but she confronts him straight on.)*

EURYDICE: I've wanted you, Spartan, from the moment that I saw you.

THALETAS: *(Pulling back)* Please—

EURYDICE: I never thought I'd see the day that I'd envy Antigone. But when I saw you two together, I felt—. How was she, Thaletas? Did you two—enjoy—each other on the road?

THALETAS: We were—we are—companions! Friends!

EURYDICE Well, you needn't confide in me. But I'll confide in you: The men in this city are so weak! So boring! But you Spartans! I've dreamt of knowing one of you ever since I was a girl—and now you're here!

THALETAS: Please let me go—

EURYDICE: Athenians are so reserved, so "cultured". But you—you're so primitive! With you people animal desire is always just below the surface, isn't it! Into the bushes and out again! A dozen times a day, I've heard! It must be so! *(The wine is taking possession of her. She weaves and sways as if she were hearing music.)* Come dance with me! Come dance! And then you and I will lie together.

THALETAS: *(Resisting)* Queen Eurydice, I beg you—

EURYDICE: What's the matter? Is it my royal rank? Forget that!

THALETAS: It isn't that—

EURYDICE: What is it, then? Am I not beautiful enough for you? Am I too old?

THALETAS: I am a guest in your husband's house! Among my people what you suggest is totally forbidden!

EURYDICE: Nothing is forbidden to the rulers in the palace! If I declare it, it is not forbidden here!

THALETAS: Excuse me, I—

EURYDICE: *(Swaying under the influence of the wine)* You're a warrior! You have the hot Spartan blood! Come! Ravish me! ...If you do, I won't tell my husband; if you don't, I'll tell him that you did.

THALETAS: Queen Eurydice—

EURYDICE: No, I didn't mean that, Thaletas. It will always be our secret. *(Drunkenly, she throws her arms around his neck.)*

THALETAS: Stop, please—!

EURYDICE: What's the matter with you? You're a Spartan, aren't you! Act like one! Take me by force! Be the savage beast I know you are—*(She pulls him forcefully to her.)*

THALETAS: Please let me be!

(He pulls her arms away from his neck and thrusts her away from him. Stumbling backward, intoxicated with drink, she falls on the steps. She lies still. THALETAS *runs over and tries to revive her.)*

THALETAS: Queen—! Eurydice—! *(He cannot rouse her.)* Help! ...Help!

*(*ANTIGONE *runs in followed by* ISMENE.*)*

ANTIGONE: What happened?

THALETAS: I don't know—

ISMENE: Is she alive?

THALETAS: She breathes. Her eyes are closed.

ISMENE: Aunt! Aunt!

(CREON *and* HAEMON *enter and see* EURYDICE, *unconscious.*)

CREON: What happened here?

THALETAS: She fell—

ANTIGONE: She is still breathing. I see no wound—

CREON: *(To* THALETAS:*)* What were you doing with the Queen?

THALETAS: Nothing. We were doing nothing. She had some wine—

CREON: That cheap wine she bought from a peddlar outside the temple of Apollo—?

THALETAS: She said so.

CREON: And you forced her to drink—

THALETAS: Not at all, I—

CREON: This is what happens when we let barbarians into our country! *(To* ISMENE:*)* Summon the physician!

(ISMENE *runs into the palace.* CREON *turns to* HAEMON:*)*

CREON: Help me move her inside.

(HAEMON *tries to lift her but has difficulty.* THALETAS *tries to assist but* CREON *gestures him off.)*

CREON: Do not touch her!

(HAEMON *manages to lift* EURYDICE. CREON *says to* THALETAS:*)*

CREON: Wait here! Do not leave till I return! *(To* ANTIGONE:*)* You see what happens when we let the animals out of the barnyard?

(HAEMON *carries* EURYDICE *inside,* CREON *follows.* ANTIGONE *and* THALETAS *are alone.)*

THALETAS: She wanted—

ANTIGONE: I know what she wanted.

THALETAS: I tried to get her to stop, but she kept on.

ANTIGONE: She is used to having her way.

THALETAS: She said I was a beast—and I became one!

ANTIGONE: She incited you—!

THALETAS: When we were playing chess, Creon said that's what all Spartans are,—perhaps he's right!

ANTIGONE: No, no!

THALETAS: I see myself through their eyes—and the sight repels me!

ANTIGONE: We have to make them see you as I see you!

THALETAS: I see myself—and now I wonder—if everything they said is true.

ANTIGONE: Don't say that! If you do, they win. You mustn't let them win! You're the hero! You're the victor! You're Apollo!

THALETAS: I am no one!

(CREON *re-enters.*)

CREON: The Queen will live. But her brain is muddled. She's muttering things. Things no one would want to hear. The physicians say—her body will repair itself, but they fear for her mind.

THALETAS: I'm sorry! I didn't mean—!

CREON: *(To* ANTIGONE:*)* You thought I was making it all up, didn't you! You thought it was some rabid conceit of mine that these beasts bring ruin. Now look! This is what you get when you open your doors to the savage hordes!

ANTIGONE: It was an accident, Uncle. This is a terrible thing that's happened, but you must try to understand—

CREON: Understand! My wife near dying and I must understand! It's an age when all transgressions are forgivable. We are to be struck at in our own houses and have the magnanimity to forgive! At what point shall we stop forgiving? When we are all slaughtered?

ANTIGONE: No one has been slaughtered. An accident has happened and—

CREON: I've decided to be generous with you, Spartan. I'm going to let you leave Athens—unpunished.

ANTIGONE: You'll "let him leave"—?!

CREON: I've already sent the people a substitute Apollo to preside over the opening celebrations.

ANTIGONE: A substitute! You think Apollo's nothing but a costume?!

CREON: I'm doing this for your friend's benefit! *(To* THALETAS:*)* You will, of course, not compete in the games. Give me the laurel crown and get beyond the gates—or I will not answer for your safety.

(THALETAS *starts to hand* CREON *the crown.*)

ANTIGONE: *(Stopping him)* No, no—. You mustn't give it up! You earned it!

CREON: I can't keep his secret for long, you know. The people will want to know how the Queen came to be injured. And I will have to implicate the Spartan. The people aren't as charitable as I am. *(To* THALETAS:*)* If I were you, I'd go.

ANTIGONE: How wonderful that would be for you, dear Uncle! If only Thaletas and his people would disappear! If only they did not exist! If only they had never come—with their odd, strange manners, and their troublesome propensity for winning contests.

CREON: I'm giving him a chance, Antigone. I advise him to take it.

ANTIGONE: I admire your generosity, Uncle. But I suspect it.

CREON: Of what?

ANTIGONE: Of being born of guilt. *Your* guilt. What was it that you said to him over chess which drove him nearly wild?

CREON: If your hero doesn't go at once, I won't answer for the consequences. He is subject to great punishment under the law—the law which says one unworthy of the crown must forfeit it!

ANTIGONE: You invent a law so you can punish him under it!

CREON: How dare you—!

ANTIGONE: I'll tell you how I dare: It's because I see in your face something so appalling I can hardly believe it. Yet I look again, and it's still there.

CREON: What is it?

ANTIGONE: It is—joy. Joy! Relief, delight that this has happened! And joy is the wrong emotion for this moment, Uncle.

CREON: I hear people coming. If he doesn't go now, I can't take any responsibility. There's already an Apollo out there. I'll say this one is an imposter—

ANTIGONE: Thaletas came to Athens to compete in the races—and he will do so. You may strip him of the Apollo crown but it is not in your power to forbid his competing in the games. Come in, Thaletas. No charioteer can win a race on an empty stomach.

THALETAS: If I'm to race, I must go get ready—

ANTIGONE: There is time. Come in while I prepare nourishment for you. It is our custom. I will serve it here—for all to see.

CREON: I'm warning you, Antigone. Be careful of what you're doing. You'll bring disaster down on everyone!

ANTIGONE: Disaster! Oh, how you misread the heavens! ...Haven't you noticed, Uncle? The clouds have begun to move!

(*Making sure he takes the Apollo crown with him,* ANTIGONE *leads* THALETAS *into the palace through the upstage right door.*)

(HAEMON *enters from the palace and says to* CREON:)

HAEMON: Father! Your substitute Apollo fainted!

CREON: What?!

HAEMON: A delegation from the people is waiting for you in your audience chamber. They are complaining that at the ceremonial feast Apollo acted very strangely. ...Who was he?

CREON: A servant from the palace.

HAEMON: No wonder he behaved the way he did! Apparently, instead of toasting the god, he drank the wine set out for the libations. And when he saw the ceremonial roast boar, instead of blessing it, he ripped off his mask and began to gorge himself as if he'd never eaten before in his life! The people were appalled. What's more, they realized none of them knew him. And Apollo is always related to at least one of them! They feel—this cannot be the genuine winner! And they keep asking—why are there great celebratory bonfires blazing in the Spartan camp? Could the God of Truth and Beauty be a Spartan?

CREON: What did you tell them?

HAEMON: I tried to defend you. I said—the one you picked for Apollo turned out to be a Spartan and unworthy. So you chose another.

CREON: And how did they respond?

HAEMON: They're offended that you lied to them. They asked me: Did you think they couldn't be trusted to know the truth?

CREON: Easy enough to say! But how they'd have screamed if they knew at the start that one from the inferior race had been chosen as the best among them!

HAEMON: They say they don't want a king who keeps secrets from his people.

CREON: They have no idea how much I spare them.

HAEMON: They asked me what other secrets have you kept—are you now keeping?

(At that moment, a strange unearthly sound is heard—half moan, half wail—coming from inside the palace.)

EURYDICE'S VOICE: A-a-a-a—-

CREON: What is it? What's that sound?

EURYDICE'S VOICE: A-a-a-—-

CREON: It's terrifying! Barely human!

HAEMON: It's Mother.

CREON: Eurydice—?!

(EURYDICE comes rushing in from the upstage left door moaning prophecies. Her mouth is a slash of red. She moans in a hypnotic trance-like voice:)

EURYDICE: No weddings...! There will be no weddings...! Take off your clothes for weddings...! *(She tears at her clothing.)*

CREON: In the name of mercy—! Eurydice—

EURYDICE: The rock on which the palace stands will shatter! ...The gods will weep and their tears will rain from the skies!

HAEMON: She claims that she's been visited by the god Apollo. She says that she is speaking in his voice!

EURYDICE: Flames will rise! Night will be turned to day with funeral pyres!

CREON: Her face—

HAEMON: She ordered me to paint her mouth. But as I did, the prophecies kept gushing—

EURYDICE: Burn offerings! Tear your flesh! Put out your eyes! ...Still it will come! ...The end. ...The end of Athens!

CREON: The pain must have unhinged her mind! Get her handmaidens to control her!

(EURYDICE begins to exit, crying:)

EURYDICE: Athens is dying!...

(She exits into the palace, still crying out. CREON calls after her to unseen servants:)

CREON: Take her to a room in the palace from which she cannot be heard!

(The cries disappear into the distance and stop.)

CREON: The Spartan's to blame! Antigone's Spartan.

HAEMON: It's not Antigone's fault—!

CREON: He must leave this city immediately! As for Antigone—

HAEMON: What about her?

CREON: She's the one who brought him into the palace. She'll have to suffer the consequences.

HAEMON: You can't pronounce a judgment against Antigone—

CREON: Oh, *I* won't make the decision. The people of Athens will be her judge.

(ANTIGONE enters carrying a tray on which are a basin and a variety of fruit and pastries. CREON gives her a haughty stare and exits upstage center. HAEMON follows, saying:)

HAEMON: I beg you, Father—

(THALETAS, the laurel crown over his arm, enters carrying a pitcher.)

ANTIGONE: Come, come, Thaletas.

(She puts the tray down on the top step.)

THALETAS: *(Distraught)* I can still see the eyes of the Queen as she was falling! Did you see her face as she lay on the ground? I didn't mean to hurt her! She insisted on drinking the wine, insisted on dancing—. I couldn't stop her—

ANTIGONE: I know, Thaletas. Now come and eat—

THALETAS: I should have locked myself inside the stable with my horses and never come into the palace. How are they, I wonder, my beautiful horses? Do you think they know this is the morning of the race?

ANTIGONE: Come sit. I have chosen for you the best fruit from Athens' best hillsides—

(ISMENE *enters, running.*)

ISMENE: Antigone! What are you doing?

ANTIGONE: I'm about to serve Thaletas breakfast. Will you join us?

ISMENE: The people are very angry. They've seen Aunt Eurydice—. She screams wild prophecies she claims come from the mouth of Apollo—

ANTIGONE: Then she's an impostor. Apollo and his prophecies are here.

ISMENE: They're horrified at what the Spartan did to her!

ANTIGONE: He is not responsible—!

ISMENE: They're coming to take his crown and send him out of Athens.

ANTIGONE: I won't let them!

ISMENE: Antigone, if you're seen protecting him, they'll banish you from Athens, too!

THALETAS: I must go! I can't let you—!

ANTIGONE: Do not move, Thaletas! Where's your courage? *(She turns to her sister:)* You used to love sweet rolls dripping down their sides with honey. Do you still, Ismene? I used to wipe the honey from your infant chin.

ISMENE: Antigone, I'm lonely. The hallways of the palace moan at night. You've just come back to me. Don't get yourself sent away—

ANTIGONE: They haven't looked at him.

ISMENE: You're all the close family I have. We have to stay here, you and I. Survive and make a future. We have to marry and bear children. So something will be left of our great family—

ANTIGONE: I want them all to look at him. To see him as he is. To know him as I know him.

ISMENE: In a family so often visited by death—

ANTIGONE: Death, too, has its uses—

ISMENE: Antigone! You frighten me! Don't let them find you both together here. It's best for both of you—

ANTIGONE: I must—I don't know why—must give him breakfast. Must give him bread—in succor, benediction,—and apology... *(She fills the basin with water.)* The daughter of the royal house must wash the feet of her guest.

ISMENE: Antigone—I think the king is coming.

ANTIGONE: Come help me to remove his sandals...

ISMENE: Antigone, I beg you—

ANTIGONE: If you won't help me, then I—*(She kneels at* THALETAS' *feet.)*

ISMENE: He's almost here!

THALETAS: Antigone, I can't put you in danger—

ANTIGONE: Let me have your sandals, my friend and my companion of the road!

ISMENE: Creon is approaching—!

THALETAS: I can't put you in danger! Not for my sake!

(THALETAS *hides himself around the side of the building just as* CREON *enters.*)

CREON: Antigone, the citizens of Athens have delegated me to talk with you. They are disturbed that the Apollo crown was bestowed on one who is not worthy of the honor.

ANTIGONE: I think he is supremely worthy.

CREON: It distresses them that the one who introduced him into Athens was you.

ANTIGONE: Of course I introduced him—and I'm proud to do so. Come, Uncle, I invite you to have breakfast with a gentle man, a strong man– *(As she lists his qualities she displays each of the signs she drew earlier.)*—a handsome man, a modest man, a man of wisdom and nobility—

CREON: There's something you left out.

ANTIGONE: Oh?

CREON: The man is Spartan.

(She marks a card with "S" and adds it to the others.)

ANTIGONE: Add Spartan and you change nothing. Take away gentle, you have a cruel man. Take away strong, you have a weakling. Subtract his beauty, you have an ugly man. Subtract his wisdom, you have a stupid man. Take away his modesty and nobility—you have a common braggart. But take away Spartan—and you lose nothing. *(She removes the Spartan sign.)*

CREON: What do you get if you put up "criminal"?

ANTIGONE: What happened to the Queen was an accident!

(CREON *gives a cynical laugh.*)

ANTIGONE: An accident incited by herself!

CREON: Now you claim her wounds are self-inflicted!

ANTIGONE: You're lucky Aunt's injury isn't just a broken fingernail, aren't you? A broken fingernail is nothing. But a broken mind, a broken soul—for these, all punishments are justified. And you can indulge your hatreds, protected by the great banners of Justice and the Law.

CREON: We don't let criminals wear the Apollo crown!

ANTIGONE: Oh? Are criminals now declared in Athens? Is there now no such thing as a trial?

CREON: It is clear—

ANTIGONE: Not to me.

CREON: Isn't it clear to you that Spartans are different? That evil infects them? That it catches from one to another, like a disease?

ANTIGONE: Like pride is catching? Like arrogance is catching?

CREON: Accidents always happen where Spartans gather. Wherever they go, they always cause trouble and disaster!

ANTIGONE: How odd that you should know what all Spartans do always. Do you know all Spartans?

CREON: You don't have to know them all to know that they—

ANTIGONE: I only know one—and what he is is this... (*She gestures toward the signs.*)

CREON: Sham virtues!

ANTIGONE: I see. If one of them is a criminal, you assume they all are. But if one of them has aspects like a god, it's obvious it's a sham.

CREON: Give me the Apollo crown, Antigone.

ANTIGONE: Certainly. Here it is. (*She holds it out in her hands.*) If you can justly be called by all these names, come and claim it.

(CREON *doesn't move.*)

CREON: The crown isn't yours to bestow or withhold—!

ANTIGONE: The crown is a laurel that's earned! ...If there is one man in Athens who can be called by all the words of praise the Spartan can be called by, let him take it.

CREON: I don't have to debate with you!

ANTIGONE: I'll tell you why you hate the Spartans. It's because they win! They win at chess. They win Apollo's crown. Today they may trounce Athens in the games. So why not get the best ones out? That way you'll be assured of Athens' victory!

CREON: Antigone, you are on the brink of treason!

ANTIGONE: So truth is treason, is it? Then what is patriotism? Belief in your own superiority—whether or not it's true?

CREON: Produce your friend or—

ISMENE: Antigone, don't taunt him any more—

CREON: I am here to administer the people's justice.

ANTIGONE: "Justice!" No. It isn't anything as pure as justice. It isn't even as pure as the hate for an enemy in war. This feeling that you have—whose name I do not even know—is dirty. It isn't a matter of evil or high tragedy—but of vomit and disgust.

CREON: You use words like that to me? Who do you think I am?

ANTIGONE: Something so vile that the gods cry out in pain to see it!

CREON: The gods cried out in pain before—years ago, when famine and disease were ravaging our city. They cried out that it was the sin of one man that was bringing this curse down on all of us. That was your father. Could it be that you, his daughter, have brought the curse back within our gates?

ANTIGONE: You'll judge me as if I were my father. Just as you'll judge the Spartan as if he were all Spartans who went before.

CREON: There is a cancer in Athens that must be cut out!

ANTIGONE: You want to know what must be cut out of Athens to avoid disaster? I can show you. Come look into this basin. *(She holds out the basin of water.)* The identity of the guilty party is here.

(CREON holds back.)

ANTIGONE: What is it, Uncle? Can't you bear to look upon the image of what you have become?

CREON: I am not the one who must be cut out of Athens!

ANTIGONE: No, not you. Something inside you—some awful thing which has invaded each of the citizens of this once-wondrous city. Some disease—blind hatred of everything which signifies The Other. Blind pride which makes every Athenian believe that only that which is Athenian can be the best.

CREON: Every word you utter is an outrage! If you pursue this course, you will be banished!

ISMENE: You cannot banish her for words! She has done nothing wrong!

ANTIGONE: Thaletas! Come here! It is time to let me bathe your feet!

(THALETAS *does not appear.* CREON *looks on coldly as* ANTIGONE *goes to the corner of the building, brings* THALETAS *out and says to him:*)

ANTIGONE: It is the custom in Athens for the daughter of the house to bathe the feet of her guests. Sit down. Let me take off your shoes. We cannot go against time-honored custom... (*She sits him down and begins to bathe his feet.*) Thaletas, what shall I do? I am afraid for my country. It has become a place where all that holds the people together is their hates. Where they speak in one voice, think the same thoughts, where they cling to each other because, alone, they are afraid. If you put one down on the road, alone, naked, without his label "Athenian", he would perish, because, without the label, he is nothing. They each know this, that's why they wrap the label tighter. Without that label, they do not exist.

CREON: You wanted me to put my image in that basin so you could wash his feet in it!

ANTIGONE: Your other foot, Thaletas. Your other, unscarred, perfect foot—

CREON: (*To* ANTIGONE:) *You* are the cancer of the prophecy! If this state is threatened with disaster, it's because of *you*! Are you so debased you despise your people and revel in the company of savages!

ANTIGONE: Oh, open your eyes and look at this man! See him as he is! This one, single being! See the intelligence of his eyes and the gentleness of his fingers. See how he walks, with a stride that would do proud any hero. Try him, if you like, for any crime of which you think him guilty. But try *him*. See *him*. This is what he is—(*She gestures toward the cards.*) You need these things in Athens!

CREON: (*Sweeping the cards to the floor and stomping on them*) If you love barbarians so much, go live with them!

ANTIGONE: You're trampling on the best of Greek manhood!

CREON: (*Crying out*) The—best—is—us!

ANTIGONE: (*Quietly*) I am afraid for you...

CREON: Even if I, with all my familial compassion, would spare you, the people of Athens would insist. And I will not be so foolhardy as to lose the throne on your account.

ANTIGONE: I wouldn't expect you to.

CREON: Antigone, it is the will of the people of Athens—

ISMENE: Oh, no! No, please—!

THALETAS: Antigone, don't suffer this for my sake—!

ANTIGONE: Hush, my hero—

CREON: The unanimous will of the people of Athens—

ISMENE: No—!

CREON: —that you be banished from this land.

ISMENE: Let me be banished, too! I want to be with her!

ANTIGONE: No, no, little sister. One wanderer per generation is enough.

CREON: From now on, and for the rest of your life, the city of Athens and all its territories are barred to you, Antigone. Your feet may not enter here while you live, your bones may not be buried here when you die. And if, for any reason, you disobey this ban, and re-enter this city, you will pay for your disobedience with your life.

ISMENE: Antigone, please beg him to let you stay! You couldn't be in love with Athens if you—

ANTIGONE: I love Athens—with all my heart and all my soul. I'm not sure I shall live very long outside it. But so long as this is a place where only Athenians can breakfast with Athenians, Athens is not free, it is falling.

CREON: Take your counterfeit hero and go, before we show you the strength of a people you say are "falling".

ANTIGONE: In the midst of all its beauties and revelations, Athens is dying of self-love.

CREON: You have been corrupted. Somehow these savage people have poisoned your mind! If they can so corrupt a princess of Athens, are any of our citizens safe? What comes next? Assault, murder, war, total destruction? No! We will not tolerate their kind anywhere within our borders!

ANTIGONE: And all one of them did was win this wreath of parsley...

CREON: In the name of the citizens of Athens I decree—all Spartans must be out of this city by sundown!

(*Silence.*)

CREON: Now give us back the laurel crown, Antigone.

ANTIGONE: Come. Take it.

(*She holds it out.* CREON *comes and takes it from her. It crumbles in his hands.*)

CREON: It fell apart! We'll have to make another!

ANTIGONE: You may search the countryside from one sea to the other. Not a single laurel leaf will consent to be a crown for you. Each one you touch will wither in your hands.

CREON: I won't waste time listening to false prophecies. ...It is a wonderful feeling—to have done justice—and to have set a country back on its triumphant path...

(*A trumpet sounds in the distance.*)

CREON: The games! It is time to go to the arena! Now begins the day of victories! ...Antigone, by the close of this day's games, you will be gone.

(CREON *goes to look at the city over the parapet.* ISMENE *runs to* ANTIGONE, *weeping.*)

ISMENE: Oh, Antigone—

ANTIGONE: There, there, little sister. You will have the husband, you will bear the children. You will not be lonely for long.

ISMENE: We'll never see each other.

ANTIGONE: Yes, we will. We can wave to each other over the hills of Attica. You can travel to the distant borders of the state. I can stand outside them and you within, and we can exchange our news and watch each other grow old at a distance.

(ISMENE *sobs.*)

ANTIGONE: Will you go pack my things, sister? I'll come in to help you very soon.

(ISMENE *exits into the palace, weeping.* ANTIGONE *goes to* THALETAS. CREON *watches them from a distance.*)

ANTIGONE: My poor unhorsed charioteer. I'm sorriest for that mostly. I was so eager to see you today, on the course, surging out in front of all the others. ...Oh, well, I know you would have won. That's all that matters. ...You are so silent. Banishment from Athens. To you, all it can mean is—going home. Don't be afraid I'll throw myself for life on your protection. We'll walk together to the city limits of Athens, and then we'll go our separate ways. Thaletas? Do you hear?

THALETAS; (*After a long silence, deeply*) ...What did my people do? ...When did we do it? ...It must be true. We must be guilty. But when? And how?

ANTIGONE: Thaletas... please... What are you saying?

THALETAS: Sometime...in the ancient past...it must have happened. ...My people...committing acts of such unmentionable horror...that ever since, we have been damned. But what did we do? ...And when did we do it?

ANTIGONE: Thaletas,—pull yourself together. Go get your things. I'll meet you at the western gate within the hour.

THALETAS: We're guilty, I say! If we weren't, the whole world wouldn't be so sure of it! ...But what did we do? What awful act was it? That from that time on, forever and ever and ever, no matter what we do, no matter how we try—

(EURYDICE's *voice is heard in the distance shouting terrible, incomprehensible prophecies.*)

THALETAS: —we are fated forever to leave a trail of terror and destruction—

ANTIGONE: Oh, that my city should do this to you!

THALETAS: —a trail of terror and destruction forever, in payment for our awful guilt.

ANTIGONE: Your guilt! I know your guilt! Your guilt is that you acquiesced too soon to unjust accusations. You accepted the judgments of people no better than yourself. You began to look as they said you would and act as they predicted. ...You were not proud...

THALETAS: "Proud!" Of being the stinking dregs of humanity?! Proud of having the passions of a foaming, raging beast—?

ANTIGONE: *(Searching in the remnants of the cards)* The cards! The cards! Where are they?

THALETAS: Damn the cards, Antigone! Look at me! I am—a—a Spar—tan! *(He spits out the word with all possible self-hatred and disgust. Then he runs out downstage right.)*

ANTIGONE: *(To* CREON:*)* There's your victory. You've done it now. Destroyed another being because you could not see him as himself. He came to Athens glorious—and your eyes broke him down.

CREON: Antigone, repent. I have no desire to see you wandering the mountains with that person. Tell the people you were mistaken, misguided. Plead youth and innocence. They will let you stay.

ANTIGONE: Stay, Uncle? In this nightmare place? Where people can only see what is already written on the insides of their eyelids? ...How odd it is to touch my Athens. In all my years of wanderings, Athens, in the distance, shining on her hill, was like the fire of life to me. I molded my life by that vision. Now, close up, I see it is a place where justice and the love of every person are a mockery—and where all those new ideas it burst, like sunshine, upon the world, it now has given the lie.

(She goes inside, upstage right.)

*(*CREON *is alone for a moment.* EURYDICE's *voice is heard, shouting unintelligibly in the distance.)*

*(*HAEMON *enters alone, shouting behind him:)*

HAEMON: Keep her in control! Hold onto her! *(He turns to* CREON:*)* You're sending Antigone away?

CREON: It is the will of the people.

HAEMON: And what great crime has she committed?

CREON: She loves our enemies more than ourselves.

HAEMON: The Spartans were not our enemies yesterday morning.

CREON: They became so over the shattered spirit of your mother.

HAEMON: Father, take back the banishment decree—

CREON: And find myself deposed tomorrow? How long do you think a king survives when he doesn't rule by the will of the people?

HAEMON: The collective will of idiots!

CREON; It's easy for you to call names. You're not the one in power.

HAEMON: If I were, I'd spit into their smirking faces! Father, I beg you, don't send Antigone away—

CREON: You think her presence is worth losing the throne for?

HAEMON: Of course it is!

CREON: By god, you've got a heart where your mind should be! You'll find someone else to simper over when she's gone.

HAEMON: Do you think Antigone is just another girl? How little you know her. Last night we found a dark corner where we would have performed the marriage act without the rite of marriage. But no. It could not be done. She has a force of life so pure it would have been sacrilege to take her that way.

CREON: Or is it that your force of life's so weak you couldn't manage it?

HAEMON: How can you talk to me that way—!

CREON: I've had enough of your sensual nonsense! Antigone's a breaker of the law. The very embodiment of disobedience and deliberate defiance. I don't give a damn what selfish titillating thrills you feel by moonlight. Her presence here is bad for the people of Athens.

HAEMON: Why? Because they might suddenly wake up and see everything the way it truly is? Including their beloved ruler?

CREON: How dare you—!

HAEMON: Everything Antigone has said is true! Is this the place where speaking truth is a cause for banishment?

CREON: Antigone is being exiled from the city because she insists on associating herself with enemies of the state!

HAEMON: "Enemies of the state!" Tell me, Father, how does it feel to know that your people have to invent foul names and nonexistent crimes for others, just to preserve the illusion they are the greatest of all peoples? Doesn't it make you afraid?

CREON: I'm afraid of nothing!

HAEMON: Not even of the gods? Of heaven's retribution as they watch you send Antigone off down the road?

CREON: The gods must be able to understand when humans are caught in impossible circumstances!

HAEMON: Then I must warn you—Antigone is going to be my wife. If she goes, I go with her.

CREON: That's blatant melodrama! I should like to see the day when you take to the road with your little magic set! Why, you've hardly ventured out of the palace since the day you were born!

HAEMON: Nevertheless, if you cut her off, you cut off me.

CREON: But why do you think I'm grasping to the crown with all this obstinacy? For you! For when it's time for you to rule!

HAEMON: I thank you, Father. But it seems more than likely that, when that time comes, I will not be here.

CREON: You're out of your mind!

HAEMON: No. *You're* the one who's lost his senses. How long do you think you can go on running a country at the command of those you know to be blind? You see them rushing toward the future with their eyes shut tight and you run along beside them, eager for their approval. But they're rushing, all unknowing, to land's end! They'll fall into the sea and drag the country with them! You see the danger. Why can't you shout out "Stop! Stop now! Before the ultimate disaster!"

I know you are afraid. They may think you're a negative Cassandra and depose you. But perhaps—oh, just perhaps—there may be some who have begun to sense that they are lost, who, even while they scream out in hate and prejudice, are yearning for some strong voice to recall them from the edge of madness, back to love.

Father—you know that compassion and forgiveness are better than revenge. That courage is better than fear, intelligence better than stupidity, vision better than blindness, love better than hate. And they, the people, know it also. They only need a strong voice to speak out.

Father, I want to stay. I will if she does. Think, for once, only of what you know to be the higher justice. And don't be afraid for your crown. Couldn't there still be, in Athens, a memory of true justice? Couldn't an act of pity and understanding from you strike some chord in the hearts of the people, recalling them to their former glories, and setting us once again on the higher paths?

But even if not—even if the eyelids of the people are so sealed they can never be opened, their hearts are so frozen they can never be warmed—even then, wouldn't you have a victory? Wouldn't the gods be watching you, Father? And wouldn't they cheer?

CREON: *(Moved, but hesitant)* The cheering of the gods is cold comfort to a man who strips himself of his country for one symbolic gesture toward an old ideal.

HAEMON: Then take some human comfort. No, not from the mobs, I can't predict them. But from me.

CREON: From you?

HAEMON: I always loved you. You always seemed the best to me. Not Oedipus the King, but Creon, the human being. Not Oedipus, the half-god, but Creon, the man. Creon—not the hero, but my father. Oh, Father, this is what we need—this love, one man to another, not crowds and thrones and universes, but the love, one son for his father, given—for the sparing of a girl.

(HAEMON *touches his father's arm.*)

CREON: ...You and I—have not touched—have not come close—since you were small enough to want to kiss—

(HAEMON *impulsively kisses his father's hand.*)

HAEMON: Please, father...

CREON: *(Slowly)* Antigone—will stay...

HAEMON: Oh, love—!

CREON: She has a boldness that we mustn't lose from Athens.

HAEMON: Thank you!

CREON: You're right. I never loved the mob. Why should I let them lead me? I'll do what should be done—and damn the consequences!

HAEMON: With me behind you we're an army!

CREON: Yes, quite enough for any siege. But just in case—go get yourself a legionful of sons. Seed that girl, and have her give you children with all the courage, strength and vision that are in her!

HAEMON: I love you, Father!

(ISMENE *enters.*)

ISMENE: Antigone is almost prepared to go. Uncle, I've come to plead with you—

HAEMON: It isn't necessary. Your sister will stay!

ISMENE: Oh, Uncle! Is it true?

CREON: Tonight will be her wedding.

ISMENE: I'll dress her! I will comb her hair! I've sewn a gown for her, a wedding gown, she's never seen yet.

HAEMON: And may we have a wedding present, Father?

CREON: Anything.

HAEMON: Let Thaletas be Apollo. He won the crown fairly. Let him compete in the race. Withdraw your banishment decree and let all the Spartans stay. Let them and us win or lose fairly on the field.

CREON: Well, I've gone this far, why not go all the way? I'll have a new crown of laurel made. I'll make it myself,—then, by the gods, it'll stay together. And as for the Spartans, let them compete in the games! I'll judge—and fairly, too. I'll be the wonder of Olympus!

(*Suddenly* EURYDICE *runs in shouting wildly.*)

EURYDICE: There are two Apollos! ...There are no Apollos! ...He has doubled himself! ...He does not exist! ...He is everywhere, he is nowhere—

CREON: Is there no one taking care of her?

HAEMON: The servants keep running away. She frightens them.

EURYDICE: Great stones falling! ...Giant vultures circling! ...Oh Athens! ...Antigone! ...Apollo-o-o!

CREON: Can't anyone keep her still?

ISMENE: Aunt? Dear Aunt—

EURYDICE: Goodbye, you sweet Apollo! ...Handsome Apollo! ...Order dates and honey!

CREON: (*To* HAEMON:) Go find the Spartan and tell him he's no longer sentenced. Tell him he can prepare himself for the games.

EURYDICE: Start the funeral games!

CREON: Her mind is gone. Go on. I'll start the preparations for the wedding.

EURYDICE: There will be no weddings!

CREON: (*To* HAEMON:) For heaven's sake, get going! Your mother is *insane*! Go on!

(HAEMON *exits, downstage right, running.*)

(EURYDICE *circles the space crying:*)

EURYDICE: Blood! Deaths! Dying!

CREON: Keep her in control! Take care of her!

ISMENE: But who will tell Antigone—?

CREON: I will tell Antigone.

ISMENE: *(Impulsively)* I love you, Uncle.

EURYDICE: Blood! Deaths! Dying!

CREON: Take her where she can't be heard!

(ISMENE *ushers* EURYDICE *off, still shouting.*)

(CREON *turns to find that* ANTIGONE *has entered and is slowly walking toward him. A silence, then:*)

ANTIGONE: *(Quietly)* Thaletas—is dead. ...From my window, I saw it. ... You barred him from the competition. But before the games, when the arena was deserted, he led his stallions onto the course to put them through their special trick. He lined them up side by side, then mounted and stood, one foot on the back of each. He gave the signal and they began to race in perfect precision. Near, apart, near, apart—until they reached the speed of the wind. Then he gave the signal and apart they streamed, each stallion in his own direction, each outward in his perfect circle, each in stride... How could they know their master had tied one of his ankles to each of them? How could they know that their perfection meant his death? ...He tore himself in two—and his steeds went on to make their perfect circles. He tore himself in two before my eyes!

CREON: I was sending word that I forgave him! I was sending word that he could race his chariot and would rule the games!

ANTIGONE: So...a Spartan is dead. Will anyone notice?

CREON: Antigone, you must believe me, I—

ANTIGONE: Look, Uncle, look! ...The clouds are gone! The sky is absolutely open! There is a clear view from here to heaven, and from heaven down to us. The gods must now be watching. In moments such as this the things we do are seared into the gods' memories—and into the souls they bring to life in all the years to come. ...What shall we do? What could we do that would be worth eternal preservation?

CREON: Antigone, is there nothing I can say that—

ANTIGONE: *(Slowly, as in a trance)* A Spartan is dead. Is that any reason to drain a cup of poison? *(She puts* HAEMON'*s magic goblet to her lips.)* A Spartan is dead. Is that any reason to slit one's veins? *(She takes a knife from* HAEMON'*s magic kit and presses it against her wrist.)* A Spartan is dead. Is that a reason for anyone to protest? To die to protest—just because a Spartan is dead? *(She collapses slowly on the steps and is still.)*

CREON: *(Fearful. Not certain whether or not she has really killed herself)* Get up, you fool! No cause, no human in the world, is worth one's life! Get up!

(But ANTIGONE *is motionless.*)

(EURYDICE *runs in like a whirlwind followed by* ISMENE, *who is desperately trying to control her.* EURYDICE *whirls in circles, tearing her hair.*)

CREON: The world is going mad—!

ISMENE: Uncle, she's wild! I can't control her!

(CREON *grabs* EURYDICE *and holds her fast as she keeps struggling.* ISMENE, *involved with* EURYDICE, *doesn't notice* ANTIGONE *on the steps.*)

CREON: Eurydice! Give me a prophecy! ...What is going to happen? To us? To the kingdom? ...Are we on our way to oblivion? ...Eurydice! ...Are we too blind? Too proud? Too corrupt? ...Answer me!

(She struggles, but doesn't respond.)

CREON: Speak! I promise I will listen! ... See into the future for me. ... Wife, dear wife, a prophecy!

(She shakes once, violently, then falls limp in his arms.)

ISMENE: What's wrong with her?

CREON: I think she's sleeping.

ISMENE: Her eyes are open.

CREON: But still I think she's sleeping.

ISMENE: Sleeping without breathing.

CREON: *(Suddenly crying out)* Eurydice! *(Stunned)* She is dead...

ISMENE: Dead? ...Oh, help! Help! Antigone!

(Terrified, she runs into the palace, seeking her sister. CREON *lowers* EURYDICE *to the ground and stands staring at her. Her eyes are open.* HAEMON *runs in.)*

HAEMON: Father, the Spartan is dead—

CREON: I know.

HAEMON: *(Noticing* EURYDICE*)* She isn't shouting...

CREON: No. She isn't shouting.

(HAEMON *looks closer and cries:*)

HAEMON: Mother—!

CREON: Well, you didn't expect her to live forever, did you?!

(HAEMON *closes her eyes.*)

CREON: Thank the gods for their mercy to her!

(For the first time HAEMON *notices* ANTIGONE *lying on the steps.)*

HAEMON: Is that Antigone? What's happened to her?

CREON: Oh, that's her joke. No. Don't go near. Don't go closer—

HAEMON: That long red stain—

CREON: It's only her joke!

HAEMON: ... Her father—left Athens—with that long, thin stain upon his robe... *(He bends and kisses her mouth. When he rises there is a strange look in his eyes.)* That is—a very cold kiss—for a wedding morning. *(He raises her in his arms and gives a cry of grief loud enough to reach her in the afterworld:)* AN-TI-GO-NE! *(But there is no response. He lowers her to the ground, picks up the knife which is lying near her and turns it toward himself.)*

CREON: No! No more! Haven't we already an overabundance of death?

HAEMON: *(Slowly putting aside the knife and speaking with a cold, stunned, icy irony)* It doesn't matter. Others will perform the office for us. Why should we dispatch ourselves when the Spartans will be only too happy to save us the trouble?

CREON: What are you saying?

HAEMON: *(Looking over the parapet)* Come and look, Father. ...The Spartans are refusing your kind invitation to them to go home. The death of their charioteer has moved them, for some reason. And they seem to be pursuing our people in the streets with fists and clubs and knives.

CREON: That's murder! Outright murder!

HAEMON: *(Laughing)* A few less votes, eh, Father? Well, maybe you could get the Spartans to elect you.

CREON: Go talk to them—

HAEMON: Only Antigone spoke their language.

CREON: Get them to stop! Ask them to be friends! Tell them I invite them all to breakfast!

HAEMON: I doubt they would like our bread. ...*(Noticing the remains of the breakfast that* ANTIGONE *had earlier prepared for* THALETAS, *he turns to* CREON *and says:)* Come sit. ...Come eat. ... I invite you to watch the fall of Athens... Shall we eat, just us two, this lovely breakfast? ...Don't get indigestion, Father,—when Athens goes boom! *(He laughs and laughs and serves the breakfast. The sun shines brightly.)*

(Blackout)

END OF PLAY

www.ingramcontent.com/pod-product-compliance
Lightning Source LLC
Chambersburg PA
CBHW071055230426
43666CB00009B/1718